ADOBE

Approved
Certification
Courseware

Adobe

ILLUSTRATOR CS5

REVEALED

ADOBE ILLUSTRATOR CS5

Adobe | Approved Certification Courseware ™

REVEALED

CHRIS BOTELLO

DELMAR
CENGAGE Learning™

Australia • Brazil • Japan • Korea • Mexico • Singapore • Spain • United Kingdom • United States

DELMAR
CENGAGE Learning™

Adobe Illustrator CS5 Revealed
Chris Botello

Vice President, Career and Professional Editorial:
   Dave Garza

Director of Learning Solutions: Sandy Clark

Senior Acquisitions Editor: Jim Gish

Managing Editor: Larry Main

Product Managers: Jane Hosie-Bounar, Meaghan O'Brien

Editorial Assistant: Sarah Timm

Vice President Marketing, Career and Professional:
   Jennifer Baker

Executive Marketing Manager: Deborah S. Yarnell

Marketing Manager: Erin Brennan

Marketing Coordinator: Erin Deangelo

Production Director: Wendy Troeger

Senior Content Project Manager: Kathryn B. Kucharek

Developmental Editor: Sandra Kruse

Technical Editor: Tara Botelho

Senior Art Director: Joy Kocsis

Cover Design: Joe Villanova

Cover Art: Spitting Images

Cover Photo:
   Living Room: © istockphoto.com/Baloncici;
   Crocodile: © istockphoto.com/Paul Downing

Text Designer: Liz Kingslein

Production House: Integra Software Services Pvt. Ltd.

Proofreader: Harold Johnson

Indexer: Alexandra Nickerson

Technology Project Manager: Christopher Catalina

For product information and technology assistance, contact us at **Cengage Learning Customer & Sales Support, 1-800-354-9706**

For permission to use material from this text or product, submit all requests online at **www.cengage.com/permissions**

Further permissions questions can be emailed to **permissionrequest@cengage.com**

Adobe® Premiere Pro®, Adobe After Effects®, Adobe® Soundbooth®, Adobe® Encore®, Adobe® Photoshop®, Adobe® Illustrator®, Adobe® Flash®, Adobe® Dreamweaver®, Adobe® Fireworks®, and Adobe® Creative Suite® are trademarks or registered trademarks of Adobe Systems, Inc. in the United States and/or other countries. Third party products, services, company names, logos, design, titles, words, or phrases within these materials may be trademarks of their respective owners.

Adobe product screenshot(s) reprinted with permission from Adobe Systems Incorporated.

The Adobe Approved Certification Courseware logo is a proprietary trademark of Adobe. All rights reserved. Cengage Learning and Adobe Illustrator CS5––Revealed are independent from ProCert Labs, LLC and Adobe Systems Incorporated, and are not affiliated with ProCert Labs and Adobe in any manner. This publication may asssist students to prepare for an Adobe Certified Expert exam; however, neither ProCert Labs nor Adobe warrant that use of this material will ensure success in connection with any exam.

Library of Congress Control Number: 2010921378

Hardcover edition:
ISBN-13: 978-1-111-13046-6
ISBN-10: 1-111-13046-9

Soft cover edition:
ISBN-13: 978-1-111-13044-2
ISBN-10: 1-111-13044-2

Delmar
5 Maxwell Drive
Clifton Park, NY 12065-2919
USA

Cengage Learning is a leading provider of customized learning solutions with office locations around the globe, including Singapore, the United Kingdom, Australia, Mexico, Brazil, and Japan. Locate your local office at: **international.cengage.com/region**

Cengage Learning products are represented in Canada by Nelson Education, Ltd.

To learn more about Delmar, visit **www.cengage.com/delmar**

Purchase any of our products at your local college store or at our preferred online store **www.cengagebrain.com**

Notice to the Reader
Publisher does not warrant or guarantee any of the products described herein or perform any independent analysis in connection with any of the product information contained herein. Publisher does not assume, and expressly disclaims, any obligation to obtain and include information other than that provided to it by the manufacturer. The reader is expressly warned to consider and adopt all safety precautions that might be indicated by the activities described herein and to avoid all potential hazards. By following the instructions contained herein, the reader willingly assumes all risks in connection with such instructions. The publisher makes no representations or warranties of any kind, including but not limited to, the warranties of fitness for particular purpose or merchantability, nor are any such representations implied with respect to the material set forth herein, and the publisher takes no responsibility with respect to such material. The publisher shall not be liable for any special, consequential, or exemplary damages resulting, in whole or part, from the readers' use of, or reliance upon, this material.

Printed in the United States of America
3 4 5 6 7 14 13 12 11

Revealed Series Vision

The Revealed Series is your guide to today's hottest multimedia applications. These comprehensive books teach the skills behind the application, showing you how to apply smart design principles to multimedia products such as dynamic graphics, animation, websites, software authoring tools, and digital video.

A team of design professionals including multimedia instructors, students, authors, and editors worked together to create this series. We recognized the unique learning environment of the multimedia classroom and created a series that:

- Gives you comprehensive step-by-step instructions
- Offers in-depth explanation of the "Why" behind a skill
- Includes creative projects for additional practice
- Explains concepts clearly using full-color visuals

- Keeps you up to date with the latest software upgrades so you can always work with cutting edge technology

It was our goal to create a book that speaks directly to the multimedia and design community—one of the most rapidly growing computer fields today. We think we've done just that, with a sophisticated and instructive book design.

—The Revealed Series

New to This Edition!

The latest edition of Adobe Illustrator CS5 Revealed includes many exciting new features, including:

- Full coverage of the new Perspective Grid feature
- Coverage of the new Shape Builder tools
- Coverage of the Bristle Brush and "Beautiful Strokes."

Author's Vision

I am thrilled to have written this book on Adobe Illustrator CS5. Illustrator was the first Adobe program I learned—back in 1988! Since then, it's always been, secretly, my favorite program, even though I seem to spend most of my time in Photoshop. When doing this update and learning the great new features of CS5 like the perspective grid and the Width tool, I'm quietly amazed at how far this program has come.

Thank you to Sandra Kruse for her intelligence and dedication as the developmental editor on this title. Many thanks to Jane Hosie-Bounar, the Product Manager. Jane shepherded this book through to completion with her combination of patience, persistence, and clarity of vision. I also want to acknowledge Technical Editor Tara Botelho for checking everything so meticulously; such dedication in a technical editor allows an author to sleep a little more soundly.

—Chris Botello

Introduction to Adobe Illustrator CS5

Welcome to *Adobe Illustrator CS5—Revealed*. This book offers creative projects, concise instructions, and complete coverage of basic to advanced Illustrator skills, helping you to create polished, professional-looking artwork. Use this book in the classroom and as a reference.

This 13 chapter text begins with fundamental concepts and progresses to in-depth exploration of the software's full set of features. Conceptual information followed by step-by-step lessons include an illustrated tutorial on how to draw with the Pen tool that you won't find in any other book. This new edition features extensive coverage of important new features, including the debut of the Perspective Grid, the Bristle Brush, two new Drawing Modes, the brand-new Shape Builder tool, and the gorgeous "Beautiful Strokes."

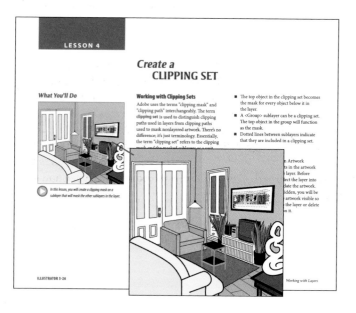

What You'll Do

A What You'll Do figure begins every lesson. This figure gives you an at-a-glance look at what you'll do in the chapter, either by showing you a page or pages from the current project or a tool you'll be using.

Comprehensive Conceptual Lessons

Before jumping into instructions, in-depth conceptual information tells you "why" skills are applied. This book provides the "how" and "why" through the use of professional examples. Also included in the text are tips and sidebars to help you work more efficiently and creatively, or to teach you a bit about the history or design philosophy behind the skill you are using.

Step-by-Step Instructions

This book combines in-depth conceptual information with concise steps to help you learn Illustrator CS5. Each set of steps guides you through a lesson where you will create, modify, or enhance an Illustrator CS5 file. Step references to large colorful images and quick step summaries round out the lessons. The Data Files for the steps are provided on the CD at the back of this book.

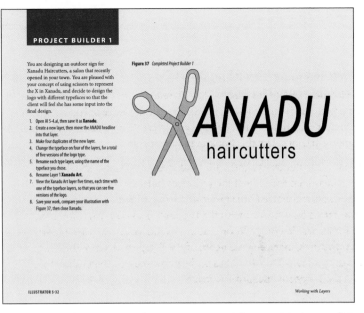

PROJECT BUILDER 1

You are designing an outdoor sign for Xanadu Haircutters, a salon that recently opened in your town. You are pleased with your concept of using scissors to represent the X in Xanadu, and decide to design the logo with different typefaces so that the client will feel she has some input into the final design.

Figure 37 *Completed Project Builder 1*

1. Open AI 5-4.ai, then save it as **Xanadu.**
2. Create a new layer, then move the ANADU headline into that layer.
3. Make four duplicates of the new layer.
4. Change the typeface on four of the layers, for a total of five versions of the logo type.
5. Rename each type layer, using the name of the typeface you chose.
6. Rename Layer 1 **Xanadu Art.**
7. View the Xanadu Art layer five times, each time with one of the typeface layers, so that you can see five versions of the logo.
8. Save your work, compare your illustration with Figure 37, then close Xanadu.

ILLUSTRATOR 5-32   *Working with Layers*

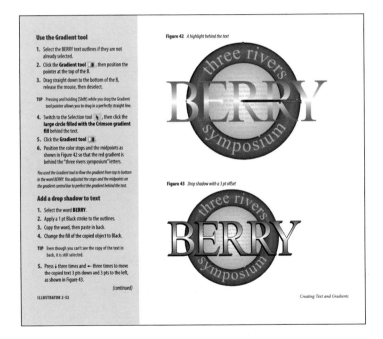

Use the Gradient tool

1. Select the BERRY text outlines if they are not already selected.
2. Click the **Gradient tool** ▣ , then position the pointer at the top of the B.
3. Drag straight down to the bottom of the B, release the mouse, then deselect.

   TIP Pressing and holding [Shift] while you drag the Gradient tool pointer allows you to drag in a perfectly straight line.

4. Switch to the Selection tool ▶ , then click the **large circle filled with the Crimson gradient fill** behind the text.
5. Click the **Gradient tool** ▣ .
6. Position the color stops and the midpoints as shown in Figure 42 so that the red gradient is behind the "three rivers symposium" letters.

You used the Gradient tool to flow the gradient from top to bottom in the word BERRY. You adjusted the stops and the midpoints on the gradient control bar to perfect the gradient behind the text.

Add a drop shadow to text

1. Select the word BERRY.
2. Apply a 1 pt Black stroke to the outlines.
3. Copy the word, then paste in back.
4. Change the fill of the copied object to Black.

   TIP Even though you can't see the copy of the text in back, it is still selected.

5. Press ↓ three times and ← three times to move the copied text 3 pts down and 3 pts to the left, as shown in Figure 43.

(continued)

ILLUSTRATOR 2-32

Figure 42 *A highlight behind the text*

Figure 43 *Drop shadow with a 3 pt offset*

Creating Text and Gradients

Projects

This book contains a variety of end-of-chapter materials for additional practice and reinforcement. The Skills Review contains hands-on practice exercises that mirror the progressive nature of the lesson material. The chapter concludes with four projects: two Project Builders, one Design Project, and one Portfolio Project. The Project Builders and the Design Project require you to apply the skills you've learned in the chapter. Portfolio Projects encourage you to address and solve challenges based on the content explored in the chapter, and to develop your own portfolio of work.

INSTRUCTOR RESOURCES

What Instructor Resources Are Available with This Book?

The Instructor Resources CD-ROM is Delmar's way of putting the resources and information needed to teach and learn effectively into your hands. All the resources are available for both Macintosh and Windows operating systems.

Instructor's Manual

Available as an electronic file, the Instructor's Manual includes chapter overviews and detailed lecture topics for each chapter, with teaching tips. The Instructor's Manual is available on the Instructor Resources CD-ROM.

Sample Syllabus

Available as an electronic file, the Sample Syllabus includes a suggested syllabus for any course that uses this book. The syllabus is available on the Instructor Resources CD-ROM.

PowerPoint Presentations

Each chapter has a corresponding PowerPoint presentation that you can use in lectures, distribute to your students, or customize to suit your course.

Data Files for Students

To complete most of the chapters in this book, your students will need Data Files. The Data Files are available on the CD at the back of this text book. Instruct students to use the Data Files List at the end of this book. This list gives instructions on organizing files.

Solutions to Exercises

Solution Files are Data Files completed with comprehensive sample answers. Use these files to evaluate your students' work. Or distribute them electronically so students can verify their work. Sample solutions to all lessons and end-of-chapter material are provided with the exception of some portfolio projects.

Test Bank and Test Engine

ExamView is a powerful testing software package that allows instructors to create and administer printed and computer (LAN-based) exams. ExamView includes hundreds of questions that correspond to the topics covered in this text, enabling students to generate detailed study guides that include page references for further review. The computer-based and LAN-based/ online testing component allows students to take exams using the EV Player, and also saves the instructor time by grading each exam automatically.

Certification

This book and the online content cover the objectives necessary for Adobe Illustrator ACE certification. Use the Certification Grid at the back of the book to find out where an objective is covered.

To access the online content for this book, take the following steps:

1. Open your browser and go to http://www.cengagebrain.com
2. Type the author, title, or ISBN of this book in the Search window. (The ISBN is listed on the back cover.)
3. Click the book title in the list of search results.
4. When the book's main page is displayed, click the Access Now button.
5. Click Student Resources in the left navigation pane to access the PDF files you'll need.

You can download and print the PDF files for your reference, or read them in Acrobat Reader.

BRIEF CONTENTS

CONTENTS

CHAPTER 1: GETTING TO KNOW ILLUSTRATOR

 **CHAPTER 7: WORKING WITH DISTORTIONS, GRADIENT MESHES, ENVELOPES, AND BLENDS**

CHAPTER 12: DRAWING WITH SYMBOLS

CHAPTER 13: PREPARING GRAPHICS FOR THE WEB

Measurements

Text attributes are given in points. Measurements on the artboard and measurements referring to an object are given in inches, not points or picas. In order to follow the exercises, it's important that the General Units Preference in the Preferences dialog box be set to Inches. To set this preference, click Edit (Win) or Illustrator (Mac) on the menu bar, point to Preferences, and then click Units & Display Performance.

You may or may not prefer to work with rulers showing. You can make rulers visible by clicking View on the menu bar, then clicking Show Rulers, or by pressing [Ctrl] [R] (Win) or [R] (Mac). You can hide visible rulers by clicking View on the menu bar, then clicking Hide Rulers or by pressing [Ctrl][R] (Win) or [R] (Mac).

Document Color Mode

Generally, CMYK Color (Cyan, Magenta, Yellow, and Black) is the color mode used for print projects, and RGB Color (Red, Green, and Blue) is the color mode used for projects that will appear on a screen. The New Document Profile menu in the New Document dialog box allows you to specify the type of document you need. You can choose Print, Web, Mobile and Devices, Video and Film, as well as Basic CMYK or Basic RGB. You can also change a document's color mode by clicking File on the menu bar, then clicking Document Color Mode. The color mode for each document is identified in the title bar at the top of the Illustrator window.

Whenever you are asked to create a new document, the color mode will be specified. Many menu commands, such as those under the Effect menu, are available only in RGB mode. If you run into a situation in which a specified menu command is not available, first check the color mode.

Fonts

Whenever fonts are used in Data and Solution Files, they are chosen from a set of very common typefaces that you will most likely have available on your computer. If any of the fonts in use are not available on your computer, please make a substitution.

For variety and typographic appeal, we have used other typefaces in Data and Solution Files that are not standard; however, we have converted those fonts to outlines. When a font is converted to an outline, the letterform is simply a vector graphic, like all other vector graphics.

Quick Keys

Quick keys are keyboard shortcuts that can be used in place of clicking the command on the menu. [Ctrl][X], for example, is the quick key for Cut on the PC platform. Mastering basic quick keys is essential for a smooth work flow in Illustrator. It's a good idea to start with the commands on the Edit and Object menus as candidates for quick keys.

Certification

This book and the online content cover the objectives necessary for Adobe Illustrator ACE certification. Use the Certification Grid at the back of the book to find out where an objective is covered.

To access the online content for this book, take the following steps:

1. Open your browser and go to http://www.cengagebrain.com
2. Type the author, title, or ISBN of this book in the Search window. (The ISBN is listed on the back cover.)
3. Click the book title in the list of search results.
4. When the book's main page is displayed, click the Access Now button.
5. Click Student Resources in the left navigation pane to access the PDF files you'll need.

You can download and print the PDF files for your reference, or read them in Acrobat Reader.

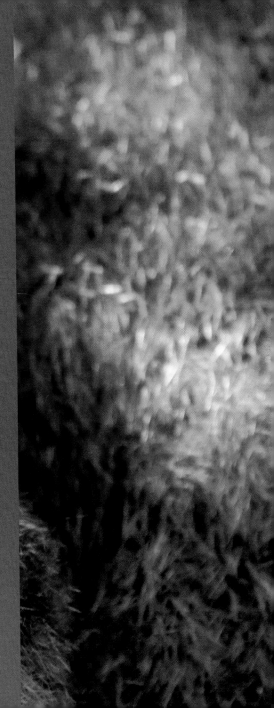

CHAPTER **1**

GETTING TO KNOW
ILLUSTRATOR

1. Explore the Illustrator workspace
2. View and modify artboard elements
3. Work with objects and smart guides
4. Create basic shapes
5. Apply fill and stroke colors to objects
6. Select, move, and align objects
7. Transform objects
8. Make direct selections
9. Work with multiple artboards

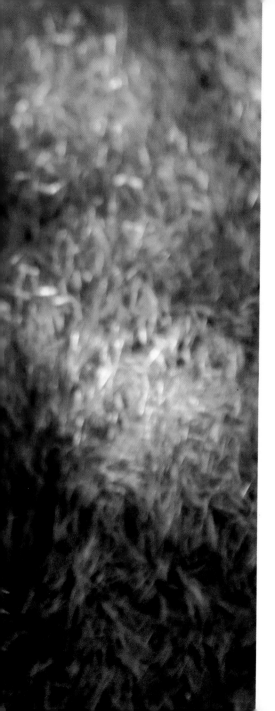

CHAPTER 1

GETTING TO
KNOW ILLUSTRATOR

Getting to Know Illustrator

Adobe Illustrator CS5 is a professional illustration software application created by Adobe Systems Incorporated. If this name is familiar to you, it's because Adobe is a leading producer of graphics software for the personal computer. Along with Illustrator, Adobe produces an entire suite of applications, including InDesign, Acrobat, Flash, Dreamweaver, and, of course, the revolutionary and award-winning Photoshop.

With Illustrator, you can create everything from simple graphics, icons, and text to complex and multilayered illustrations, all of which can be used within a page layout, in a multimedia presentation, or on the Web.

Adobe Illustrator offers dozens of essential tools. Using them in combination with various menu commands, you have the potential to create any illustration that your imagination can dream up. With experience, you will find that your ability to create complex graphics rests on your ability to master simple, basic operations.

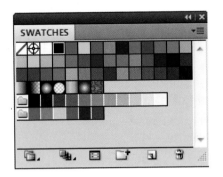

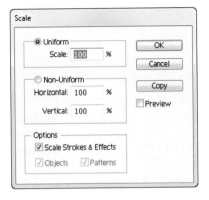

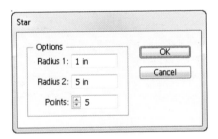

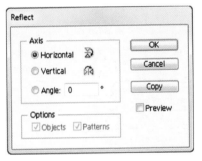

Explore the
ILLUSTRATOR WORKSPACE

What You'll Do

In this lesson, you will start Adobe Illustrator and explore the workspace.

Looking at the Illustrator Workspace

The arrangement of windows and panels that you see on your monitor is called the **workspace**. The Illustrator workspace features the following areas: artboard, pasteboard, Application bar, Control panel, Tools panel, and a stack of collapsed panels along the right side of the document window. Figure 1 shows the default workspace, which is called Essentials.

Illustrator CS5 offers a number of pre-defined workspaces that are customized for different types of tasks. Each workspace is designed so that panels with similar functions are grouped together. For example, the Typography workspace shows the many type- and typography-based panels that are useful for working with type. You can switch from one workspace to another by clicking Window on the Application bar, pointing to

Figure 1 *Essentials workspace*

Application bar

Workspace switcher

Control panel

Tools panel

Panels dock

Artboard

Getting to Know Illustrator

Workspace, and then choosing a workspace. Or you can use the workspace switcher on the Application bar.

You can customize the workspace, including predefined workspaces, to suit your working preferences. For example, you can open and close whatever panels you want and change the location of any panels. You can save a customized workspace by clicking Window on the Application bar, pointing to Workspace, then clicking New Workspace. Assign a descriptive name to your workspace, then click OK. With this option checked, the workspace will be saved with all panels in their current positions. Once you've saved a workspace, you load it by clicking Window on the Application bar, then pointing to Workspace. You'll see your custom-named workspace in the list of workspaces.

Exploring the Tools Panel

As its name implies, the Tools panel houses all the tools that you will work with in Illustrator. The first thing that you should note about the Tools panel is that not all tools are visible; many are hidden. Look closely and you will see that some tools have small black triangles beside them. These triangles indicate that other tools are hidden behind them. To access hidden tools, point to the visible tool on the Tools panel, then press and hold the mouse button; this will reveal a menu of hidden tools. The small black square to the left of a tool name in the submenu indicates which tool is currently visible on the Tools panel, as shown in Figure 2.

When you expose hidden tools, you can click the small triangle to the right of the menu and create a separate panel for those tools, as shown in Figure 3.

Figure 2 *Viewing hidden tools*

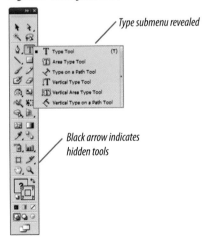

Type submenu revealed

Black arrow indicates hidden tools

Figure 3 *"Detaching" hidden tools*

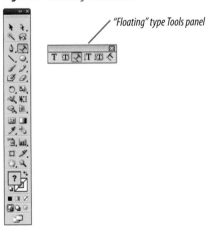

"Floating" type Tools panel

As shown in Figure 4, you can view the Tools panel as a single column or a double column of tools. Simply click the Collapse/Expand panels button at the top of the Tools panel to toggle between the two setups.

Horizontal lines divide the Tools panel into ten sections. Figure 5 identifies a number of essential tools that you'll use all the time when you're working with Illustrator. To choose a tool, simply click it. You can also press a shortcut key to access a tool. For example, pressing [p] selects the Pen tool.

To learn the shortcut key for each tool, point to a tool until a tool tip appears with the tool's name and its shortcut key in parentheses.

Figure 4 *Two setups for the Tools panel*

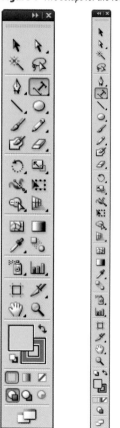

Figure 5 *Essential tools*

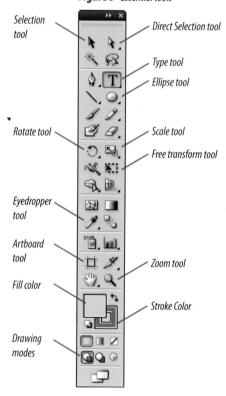

Selection tool
Direct Selection tool
Type tool
Ellipse tool
Rotate tool
Scale tool
Free transform tool
Eyedropper tool
Artboard tool
Zoom tool
Fill color
Stroke Color
Drawing modes

Figure 6 shows the tool tip for the Type tool. Tool tips appear when they are activated in the General preferences dialog box, which you can access by clicking Edit (Win) or Illustrator (Mac) on the Application bar, pointing to Preferences, and then clicking General.

QUICK TIP

Shortcut keys are not case-sensitive. In other words, if you press [p], you'll switch to the Pen tool regardless of whether or not Caps Lock is on.

Figure 6 *Tool tip and activated tool tips preference*

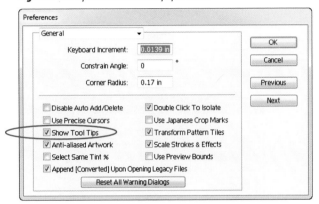

Working with Panels

Working in Illustrator is not only about using tools; many essential Illustrator functions are grouped into panels. For example, the Paragraph panel contains paragraph editing functions, such as text alignment and paragraph indents. The Swatches panel, shown in Figure 7, offers colors to sample as fills and strokes for objects.

You can access all panels from the Window menu. Some panels are placed within categories on the Window menu. For example, all of the text-related panels, such as the Character panel and the Paragraph panel, are listed in the Type category.

When you choose a panel from the Window menu, the panel is displayed in its expanded view. You can close any panel by clicking the Close button in the top-right corner of the panel, and you can display panel options by clicking the Panel options button. To reduce the size of a panel, click the Collapse to Icons button, which displays a panel only by its name and an icon. These three buttons are identified in Figure 8.

Figure 7 *Swatches panel*

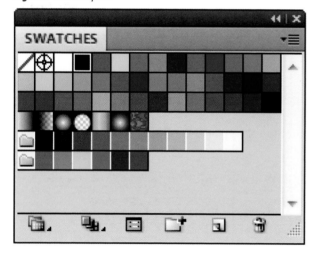

Figure 8 *Three interactive panel buttons*

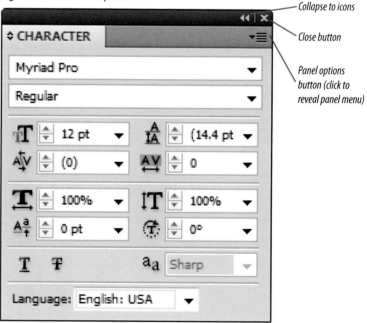

Collapse to icons

Close button

Panel options button (click to reveal panel menu)

To better manage available workspace, you can group panels. You can also minimize, or "collapse," panels to make them smaller but still available in the workspace.

Figure 9 shows two panels grouped together. The Paragraph panel is the active panel—it is in front of the Character panel in the group and available for use. To activate the Character panel, you would simply click its tab.

Figure 10 shows the entire dock of panels minimized on the right side of the document window. Clicking a panel thumbnail, or icon, opens the panel as well as any other panels with which it is grouped. Click the thumbnail in the stack again, and it will collapse the panel you just expanded.

Click the Expand panels button at the top of the panels dock to expand all the panels, as shown in Figure 11.

Figure 9 *Two grouped panels*

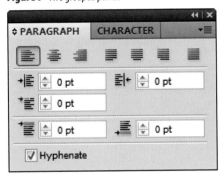

Figure 10 *Dock of panels collapsed*

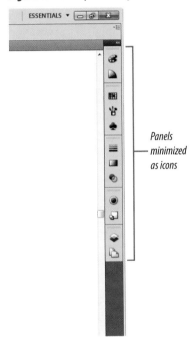

Panels minimized as icons

Figure 11 *Dock of panels expanded*

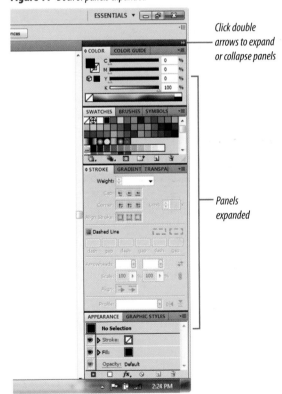

Click double arrows to expand or collapse panels

Panels expanded

Don't confuse grouping panels with docking panels. Docking panels is a different function. When you dock panels, you connect the bottom edge of one panel to the top edge of another panel, so that both move together. To dock panels, first drag a panel's name tab to the bottom edge of another panel. When the bottom edge of the other panel is highlighted in bright blue, release the mouse button and the two panels will be docked. Figure 12 shows docked panels. To undock a panel, simply drag it away from its group.

Figure 12 *Docked panels*

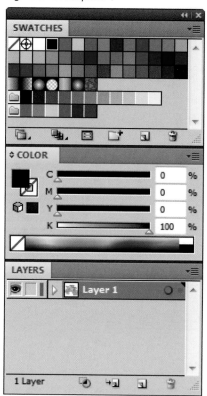

QUICK TIP

You can hide all open panels, including the Tools panel, by pressing [Tab]. Press [Tab] again to show the panels. This is especially useful when you want to view artwork and the entire document window without panels in the way.

Opening Illustrator CS5 Files in Previous Versions

Illustrator is "backwards compatible," meaning that Illustrator CS5 can open files from previous versions. The reverse, however, isn't true; earlier versions can't open newer versions. For example, Illustrator CS4 cannot open Illustrator CS5 documents. This can become an issue if you send out a CS5 file to another designer, a client, or a vendor who is using an older version. To accommodate, you can "save down" to a previous version when you save the file. When you name the file and click Save, the Illustrator Options dialog box opens. Click the Version list arrow to choose the version to which you want to save it. Note that any new CS5 features used in your file may be lost when the file is converted to the older format.

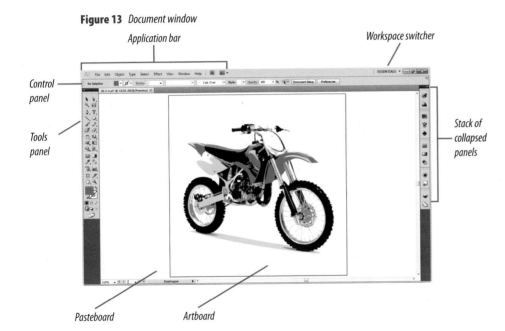

Figure 13 *Document window*

Application bar

Workspace switcher

Control panel

Tools panel

Stack of collapsed panels

Pasteboard

Artboard

Explore the Tools panel

1. Launch Adobe Illustrator CS5.

2. Click **File** on the Application bar, click **Open**, navigate to the drive and folder where your Chapter 1 Data Files are stored, click **AI 1-1.ai**, then click **Open**.

3. Click **Window** on the Application bar, point to **Workspace**, then click **[Essentials]**.

   Compare your window to Figure 13.

   TIP If you are already working in the Essentials workspace, clicking [Essentials] will reset the workspace.

4. Click the **double-arrows** on the Tools panel, then click it again to switch between the two setups for the Tools panel.

   All of the figures in this book that show the Tools panel will display the panel in two rows.

5. Point to the **Type tool** T, then press and hold the mouse button to see the Type on a Path tool.

6. View the hidden tools behind the other tools with small black triangles.

   Your visible tools may differ from the figure.

7. Click **Edit** (Win) or **Illustrator** (Mac) on the Application bar, point to **Preferences**, click **General**, verify that Show Tool Tips is checked, then click **OK**.

8. Position your mouse pointer over the **Selection tool** , until its tool tip appears.

9. Press the following keys and note which tools are selected with each key: **[a]**, **[p]**, **[v]**, **[t]**, **[i]**, **[h]**, **[z]**.

(continued)

10. Press **[Tab]** to temporarily hide all open panels, then press **[Tab]** again.

The panels reappear.

You explored different views of the Tools panel, revealed hidden tools, used shortcut keys to access tools quickly, hid the panels, then displayed them again.

Work with panels

1. Click **Swatches** in the stack of collapsed panels to the right of the pasteboard to open the Swatches panel.

   The panel opens, but does not detach from the stack of collapsed panels. The Swatches panel is grouped with the Symbols and Brushes panels in the Essentials workspace.

2. Click the **Collapse panels button** ▶▶ at the top of the panel to minimize the panel, then click **Swatches** to open the panel again.

3. Drag the **Swatches panel name tab** to the left so it is ungrouped from the stack.

4. Click **Color** in the stack of collapsed panels to the right of the pasteboard to open the Color panel.

5. Drag the **Color panel name tab** to the left so it is ungrouped from the stack.

6. Drag the **Color panel name tab** to the blank space next to the **Swatches panel name tab**, then release the mouse.

   The Color panel is grouped with the Swatches panel, as shown in Figure 14.

(continued)

Figure 14 *Grouped panels*

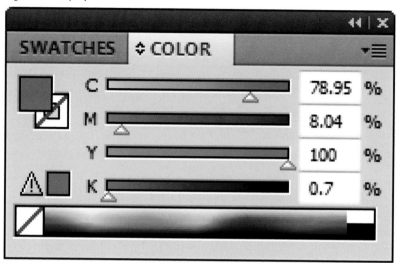

Using the Document Info Panel

The Document Info panel, listed on the Window menu, contains useful information about the document and about objects in the document. Along with general file information such as filename, ruler units and color space, the panel lists specific information like the number and names of graphic styles, custom colors, patterns, gradients, fonts, and placed art. To view information about a selected object, choose Selection Only from the panel menu. Leaving this option deselected lists information about the entire document. To view artboard dimensions, click the Artboard tool, choose Document from the panel menu, and then click to select the artboard you want to view.

Figure 15 *Docked panels*

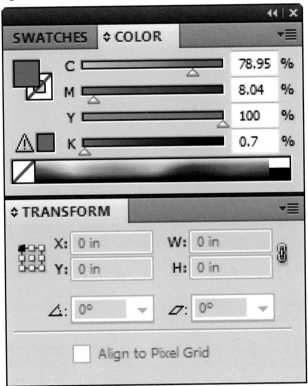

7. Click **Window** on the Application bar, then click **Transform**.

   The Transform panel appears expanded on the document.

8. Drag the **Transform panel name tab** to the bottom edge of the Swatches and Color panels group, then, when a blue horizontal line appears, release the mouse.

   The Transform panel is docked, as shown in Figure 15.

9. Click and drag the **dark gray bar at the top of the panel group**, found above the Swatches and Color panel name tabs.

   The Transform panel moves with the Swatches and Color panels because it is docked.

10. Click the **Transform panel name tab**, then drag it away from the other two panels.

    The Transform panel is undocked.

11. Click **Window** on the Application bar, point to **Workspace**, then **Essentials**.

You explored methods for grouping and ungrouping panels, then you docked and undocked a panel.

View and Modify
ARTBOARD ELEMENTS

What You'll Do

In this lesson, you will explore various methods for viewing the document and document elements, such as rulers, guides, grids, and selection marks.

Using the Zoom Tool

Imagine creating a layout on a traditional pasteboard—not on your computer. For precise work, you would bring your nose closer to the pasteboard so that you could better see what you were doing. At other times, you would hold the pasteboard away from you at arms' length so that you could get a larger perspective of the artwork. When you're working in Illustrator, the Zoom tool performs these functions for you.

When you click the Zoom tool and move the pointer over the document window, the pointer becomes the Zoom pointer with a plus sign; when you click the document with the Zoom pointer, the document area you clicked is enlarged. To reduce the view of the document, press and hold [Alt] (Win) or [option] (Mac). When the plus sign changes to a minus sign, click the document with this Zoom pointer, and the document size is reduced.

Using the Zoom tool, you can reduce or enlarge the view of the document from 5% to 4000%. Note that the current magnification level appears in the document tab and in the Zoom Level text box on the Application bar, as shown in Figure 16.

Accessing the Zoom Tool

As you work, you can expect to zoom in and out of the document more times than you can count. The most basic way of accessing the Zoom tool is simply to click its icon on the Tools panel, but this can get very tiring if you have to access it often.

A better method for accessing the Zoom tool is to use keyboard shortcuts. When you are using the Selection tool, for example, don't switch to the Zoom tool. Instead, press and hold [Ctrl][Spacebar] (Win) or ⌘ [Spacebar] (Mac) to temporarily change the Selection tool into the Zoom tool. Click the document to zoom in. When you release the keys, the Zoom tool changes back to the Selection tool.

To Zoom out using keyboard shortcuts, press and hold [Ctrl][Alt][Spacebar] (Win) or ⌘ [option][Spacebar] (Mac).

> **QUICK TIP**
>
> Double-clicking the Zoom tool on the Tools panel changes the document view to 100% (actual size).

In addition to the Zoom tool, Illustrator offers a number of other ways to zoom in and out of your document. One of the quickest and easiest is to press [Ctrl][+] (Win) or ⌘ [+] (Mac) to enlarge the view and [Ctrl][-] (Win) or ⌘ [-] (Mac) to reduce the view. You can also use the Zoom In and Zoom Out commands on the View menu.

Using the Hand Tool

When you zoom in on a document to make it appear larger, eventually the document will be too large to fit in the window. Therefore, you will need to scroll to see other areas of it. You can use the scroll bars along the bottom and the right sides of the document window or you can use the Hand tool to scroll through the document.

The best way to understand the concept of the Hand tool is to think of it as your own hand. Imagine that you could put your hand up to the document on your monitor, then move the document left, right, up, or down, like a paper on a table or against a wall. This is analogous to how the Hand tool works.

QUICK TIP

Double-clicking the Hand tool on the Tools panel changes the document view to fit the page (or the spread) in the document window.

The Hand tool is often a better choice for scrolling than the scroll bars. Why? Because you can access the Hand tool using a keyboard shortcut. Regardless of whatever

tool you are using, simply press and hold [Spacebar] to access the Hand tool. Release [Spacebar] to return to whatever tool you were using, without having to choose it again.

QUICK TIP

When you are using the Type tool, don't use the [Spacebar] shortcut to access the Hand tool because it will add spaces to the text with which you are working. Instead, use the scroll bar.

Working with Rulers, Grids, and Guides

Many illustrations involve using measurements to position and align objects.

You'll find that Illustrator is well-equipped with a number of features that help you with these tasks.

Rulers are positioned at the top and left side of the pasteboard to help you align objects. Simply click Show Rulers/Hide Rulers on the View menu. Rulers (and all other measurement utilities in the document) can display measurements in different units, such as inches, picas, or points. You determine the **units** with which you want to work in the Preferences dialog box. On the Edit (Win) or Illustrator (Mac) menu, point to Preferences,

Figure 16 *Magnification levels*

then click Units to display the dialog box shown in Figure 17.

Ruler Guides are horizontal and vertical rules that you can position anywhere in a layout as a reference for positioning elements. In addition to guides, Illustrator offers a **document grid** for precise alignment. With the "snap" options on, objects that you move around on the page automatically align themselves with guides or with the grid quickly and easily.

Hiding and Showing Selection Marks

All objects you create have visible selection marks or selection edges, and when an object is selected, those edges automatically highlight, showing anchor points.

While you're designing your illustration, you might want to work with selection marks hidden so that all you see is the artwork. To hide or show selection marks, click the Hide/Show Edges command on the View menu.

Figure 18 shows a complex illustration with selection marks visible and hidden.

Figure 17 *Units Preferences dialog box*

Figure 18 *Selection marks visible and hidden*

In both examples, the artwork is selected, but the selection marks are not visible in the example on the right.

Choosing Screen Modes

Screen modes are options for viewing your documents. The two basic screen modes in Illustrator CS5 are Normal and Outline. You'll work in **Normal** mode most of the time. In Normal mode, you see all of your objects with fills and strokes and whatever effects you might have applied.

Outline mode displays all your objects only as hollow shapes, with no fills or strokes. Working in Outline mode can sometimes be helpful for selecting various objects that are positioned close together.

Figure 19 shows the motorcycle artwork in Outline mode.

To select objects in Normal mode, simply click anywhere on the object's fill or stroke. In Outline mode, however, you need to click the edge of the object.

Understanding Preferences

All Adobe products, as most other software products, come loaded with preferences. Preferences are specifications you can set for how certain features of the application behave. The Preferences dialog box houses the multitude of Illustrator preferences available. Figure 20 shows the Type preferences for Illustrator. Getting to know available preferences is a smart approach to mastering Illustrator. Many preferences offer important choices that will have significant impact on how you work.

Working with Multiple Open Documents

On many occasions, you'll find yourself working with multiple open documents. For example, let's say you're into scrapbooking. If you were designing a new illustration to highlight a recent trip to Italy, you might also have the file open for an illustration you created last year when you went to Hawaii. Why? For any number of reasons. You might want to copy and paste art elements from the Hawaii document into the new document. Or, you might want the Hawaii document

Figure 19 *Artwork in Outline mode*

Figure 20 *Type Preferences dialog box*

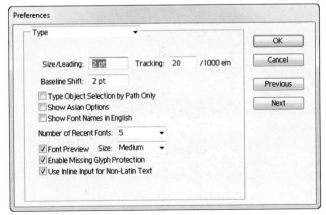

open simply as a reference for typefaces, type sizes, image sizes, and effects that you used in the document. When you're working with multiple open documents, you can switch from one to the other simply by clicking on the title bar of each document.

Illustrator offers a preference for having multiple open documents available as tabs in the document window. With this preference selected, a tab will appear for each open document showing the name of the document. Simply click the tab and the document becomes active. This can be useful for keeping your workspace uncluttered. However, it can sometimes be inhibiting, because when working with multiple documents, the tabbed option allows you to view only one document at a time.

You indicate in the Interface Preferences dialog box whether or not you want open documents to appear as tabs. Click Edit on the Application bar, point to Preferences, then click User Interface. Click Open Documents As Tabs, as shown in Figure 21, then click OK.

Using Shortcut Keys to Execute View Commands

The most commonly used commands in Illustrator list a shortcut key beside the command name. Shortcut keys are useful for quickly accessing commands without stopping work to go to the menu. Make a

mental note of helpful shortcut keys and incorporate them into your work. You'll find that using them becomes second nature.

See Table 1 for shortcut keys you will use regularly for manipulating the view of your Illustrator screen.

Figure 21 *Open Documents As Tabs Preferences activated*

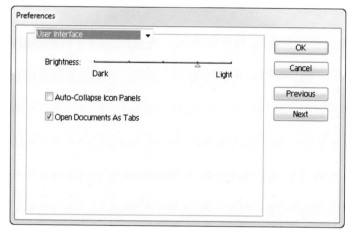

TABLE 1: SHORTCUT KEYS FOR VIEWING COMMANDS		
	Windows	**Mac**
Hide/Show Guides	Ctrl-;	Command-;
Hide/Show Edges	Ctrl-H	Command-H
Hide/Show Rulers	Ctrl-R	Command-R
Activate/Deactivate Smart Guides	Ctrl-U	Command-U
Fit Page in Window	Ctrl-0	Command-0
Fit Spread in Window	Alt-Ctrl-0	Option-Command-0
Toggle Normal and Outline Screen Modes	Ctrl-Y	Command-Y
Hide/Show Grid	Ctrl-"	Command-"

Figure 22 *A reduced view of the document*

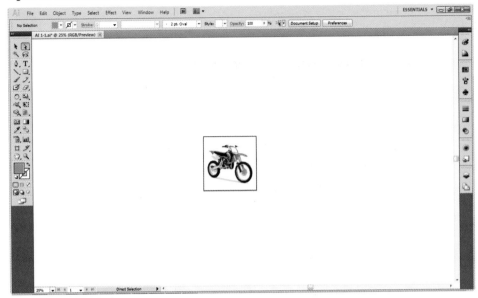

Using the Keyboard Shortcuts Dialog Box

Shortcuts are keyboard combinations you can use instead of clicking menu items to execute commands. Illustrator lets you view a list of all shortcuts, edit or create shortcuts, define your own sets of shortcuts, change individual shortcuts within a set, and switch between sets of shortcuts in the Keyboard Shortcuts dialog box. To open the Keyboard Shortcut dialog box, click Edit on the Application bar, then click Keyboard Shortcuts. Choose a set of shortcuts from the Set menu at the top of the Keyboard Shortcuts dialog box, then choose to modify either Menu Commands or Tools from the menu. To activate the set of shortcuts, click OK. To change a shortcut, click in the Shortcut column of the scroll list and type a new shortcut.

Use the Zoom tool and the Hand tool

1. Press **[z]** to access the Zoom tool.
2. Position the Zoom tool over the **document window**, click twice to enlarge the document, press **[Alt]** (Win) or **[option]** (Mac), then click twice to reduce the document.
3. Click the **Zoom Level list arrow** in the lower-left corner of the document window, then click **800%**.

   Note that 800% is now listed in the document tab.
4. Double-click **800%** in the Zoom Level text box, type **300**, then press **[Enter]** (Win) or **[return]** (Mac).
5. Click the **Hand tool** on the Tools panel, then click and drag the **document window** to scroll.
6. Double-click the **Zoom tool**.

   The magnification changes to 100% (actual size).
7. Click the **Selection tool**, point to the **center of the document window**, then press and hold **[Ctrl][Spacebar]** (Win) or ⌘ **[Spacebar]** (Mac).

   The Selection tool changes to the Zoom tool.
8. Click three times, then release [Ctrl][Spacebar] (Win) or ⌘ [Spacebar] (Mac).
9. Press and hold **[Spacebar]** to access the Hand tool, then scroll around the image.
10. Press and hold **[Ctrl][Alt][Spacebar]** (Win) or ⌘ **[option][Spacebar]** (Mac), then click the mouse multiple times to reduce the view to 25%.
11. Your document window should resemble Figure 22.

You explored various methods for accessing and using the Zoom tool for enlarging and reducing the document. You also used the Hand tool to scroll around an enlarged document.

Hide and show rulers and set units and increments preferences

1. Click **View** on the Application bar, note the shortcut key on the Fit Page in Window command, then click **Fit Artboard in Window**.
2. Click **View** on the Application bar, then note the Rulers command and its shortcut key.

   The Rulers command says Hide Rulers or Show Rulers, depending on your current status.
3. Leave the View menu, then press **[Ctrl][R]**(Win) or ⌘ **[R]**(Mac) several times to hide and show rulers, finishing with rulers showing.
4. Note the units on the rulers.

   Depending on the preference you have set, your rulers might be showing inches, picas, or another unit of measure.
5. Click **Edit** (Win) or **Illustrator** (Mac) on the Application bar, point to **Preferences**, then click **Units**.
6. Click the **General list arrow** to see the available measurement options, then click **Picas**.
7. Click **OK**.

   The rulers change to pica measurements. Picas are a unit of measure used in layout design long before the advent of computerized layouts. One pica is equal to 1/6 an inch. It's important that you understand that the unit of measure you set as ruler units will affect all measurement utilities in the application, such as those on the Transform panel, in addition to the ruler increments.
8. Reopen the Units preferences dialog box, click the **General list arrow**, then click **Inches**.

   Your dialog box should resemble Figure 23. In almost every case, you will work with Type and Stroke preferences set to points.

   (continued)

Figure 23 *Setting the Units & Increments ruler units to Inches*

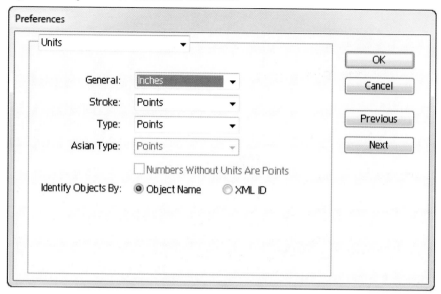

Arranging Documents

When you're working with multiple documents, you can use the Arrange Documents button to the right of the menu items in the Application bar. If you have three separate documents open, for example, the 3-UP option in the Arrange Documents panel will tile and display all three documents as you like—in a column, in a row, etc. The N-UP option positions all of your open documents in a single window, allowing you to compare artwork from one file to another and even drag objects across documents.

Figure 24 *Viewing four guides*

9. Click **OK**.

You used shortcut keys to hide and show rulers in the document. You used the Units & Increments preferences dialog box to change the unit of measure for ruler units.

Hide and show ruler guides, selection marks, and the document grid

1. Click **Select** on the Application bar, then click **All**.

2. Click **View** on the Application bar, then note the Edges command and its shortcut key.

   The command is listed as either Hide Edges or Show Edges, depending on your current status.

3. Leave the View menu, then press **[Ctrl][H]**(Win) or ⌘ **[H]**(Mac) several times to switch between hiding and showing selection marks, finishing with marks showing.

   TIP The Hide Frames shortcut key is easy to remember if you think of *H for Hide*. Remember, though, that this shortcut key only hides and shows selection marks, not other elements, like ruler guides, which use different shortcut keys.

4. Click the **Select** menu, then click **Deselect**.

5. Click **View** on the Application bar, point to **Guides**, then note the Hide/Show Guides command and its shortcut key.

   The Guides command says either Hide Guides or Show Guides depending on your current status.

6. Escape the View menu, then press **[Ctrl][;]**(Win) or ⌘ **[;]** (Mac) several times to hide and show guides, finishing with guides showing.

   Four guides are shown in Figure 24.

   TIP Make note of the difference between the Hide/Show guides shortcut key and the Hide/Show selection marks shortcut key.

   (continued)

7. Click **View** on the Application bar, then click **Show Grid**, as shown in Figure 25.

8. Leave the View menu, then press **[Ctrl]["]**(Win) or ⌘ **["]** (Mac) several times to hide and show the grid.

TIP Make note of the difference between the Hide/Show Guides shortcut key and the Hide/Show Document Grid shortcut key—they're just one key away from each other.

9. Hide the grid and the guides.

You used shortcut keys to hide and show selection marks, ruler guides, and the document grid.

Toggle screen modes and work with multiple documents

1. Click the **View menu**, then note the shortcut key command for Outline mode.

2. Press **[Ctrl][Y]**(Win) or ⌘ **[Y]**(Mac) repeatedly to toggle between Outline and Normal mode, finishing in Normal mode.

3. Click **Edit** (Win) or **Illustrator** (Mac) on the Application bar, point to **Preferences**, then click **User Interface**.

4. Verify that the **Open Documents As Tabs check box** is checked, then click **OK**.

5. Click **File** on the Application bar, click **Save As**, type **Motocross** in the File name box, then click the **Save button** to save the file with a new name.

TIP Each time you save a data file, the Illustrator Options dialog box will open. Click OK to close it.

(continued)

Figure 25 *Artboard with grid showing*

Getting to Know Illustrator

Figure 26 *"Tabbing" the floating document*

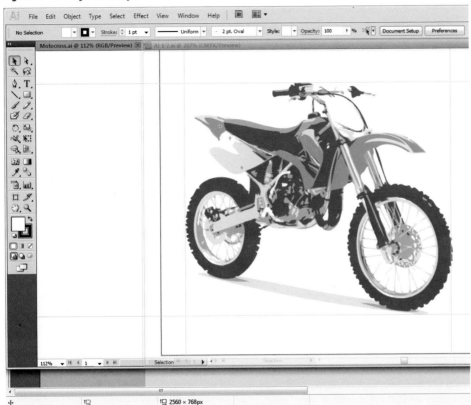

6. Open **AI 1-2.ai**, then click the **tabs** of each document several times to toggle between them, finishing with Motocross.ai as the active document.

7. Drag the **Motocross.ai tab** straight down approximately ½ inch.

   When you drag a tabbed document down, it becomes "untabbed" and a "floating" document.

8. Position your mouse pointer over the upper-right or bottom-right corner of the document window, then click and drag toward the center of the monitor window to reduce the window to approximately half its size.

9. Position your mouse pointer over the title bar of the document, then click and drag to move Motocross.ai half way down toward the bottom of your monitor screen.

   A "floating" document window can be positioned so that part if it is off-screen.

10. Position your mouse pointer over the title bar of Motocross.ai, click and drag to position it at the top of the window beside the AI1-2.ai tab, then release your mouse when you see a horizontal blue bar, as shown in Figure 26.

    The document is tabbed once again.

11. Close AI1-2.ai without saving changes if you are prompted.

12. Close Motocross.ai without saving changes if you are prompted.

You verified that the Open Documents As Tabs option in the Preferences dialog box was activated. You removed the document from its tabbed position, resized it, moved it around, then returned it to its tabbed status.

Work with Objects
AND SMART GUIDES

What You'll Do

 In this lesson, you will work with objects with smart guides.

Working with Preferences

Illustrator features 12 preferences dialog boxes. Preferences affect many aspects of the Illustrator interface, including guides, smart guides, and rulers. You can think of preferences as the "ground rules" that you establish before doing your work. For example, you might want to specify your preferences for guide and grid colors or for hyphenation if you're doing lots of type work.

The one tricky thing about preferences is that, if you're just learning Illustrator, preferences refer to things that you don't really know about. That's OK. Illustrator's preferences default to a paradigm that makes most of the work you do intuitive. But as you gain experience, it's a good idea to go back through the available preferences and see if there are any changes you want to make or with which you want to experiment.

One more thing about preferences: remember that they're there. Let's say you want to apply a 2pt. stroke to an object, but the Stroke panel is showing stroke weight in inches. First you click the Stroke panel options button to show the Stroke panel menu, but you soon find that the menu holds no command for changing the readout from inches to points. That's the point where you say to yourself, "Aha! It must be a preference."

Resizing Objects

Individual pieces of artwork that you create in Illustrator, such as squares, text, or lines, are called **objects**. All objects you create in Illustrator are composed of paths and anchor points. When you select an object, its paths and anchor points become highlighted, as shown in Figure 27.

You have many options for changing the size and shape of an object. One of your most straightforward options is to use the **bounding box**. Select any object or multiple objects, then click **Show Bounding Box** on the View menu. Eight handles appear around the selected object. See Figure 28. Click and drag the handles to change the shape and size of the object.

When you select multiple objects, a single bounding box appears around all the selected objects, as shown in Figure 29. Manipulating the bounding box will affect all the objects.

Illustrator offers two basic keyboard combinations that you can use when dragging bounding box handles as shown in Table 2.

Figure 27 *Selected objects*

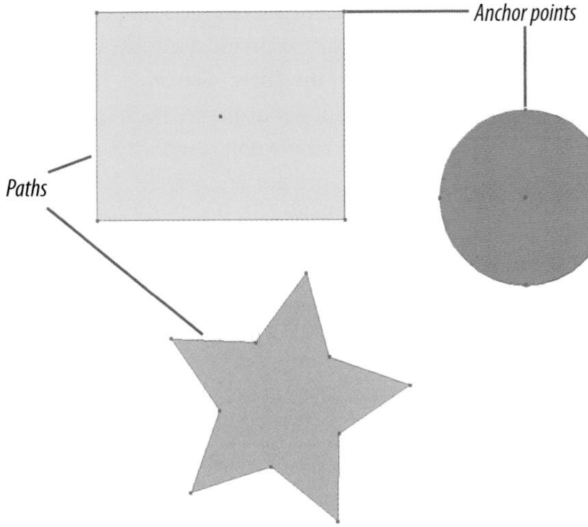

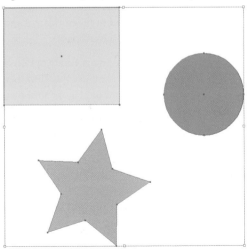

Anchor points

Paths

Figure 28 *Selected circle with bounding box showing*

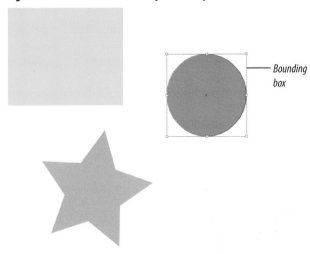

Bounding box

Figure 29 *Bounding box around three selected objects*

TABLE 2: OBJECT RESIZING COMBINATIONS		
Windows	**Mac**	**Result**
Shift-drag a corner handle	Shift-drag a corner handle	The object is resized in proportion; its shape doesn't change
Alt-drag a handle	Option-drag a handle	Resizes the object from its center point
Alt-Shift-drag a handle	Option-Shift-drag a handle	Resize the object from its center and in proportion

Copying Objects

At any time, you can copy and paste an object. When you paste, the object is pasted at the center of the artboard—regardless of the position of the original. When designing, you'll often find it more desirable for the copy to be pasted in the exact same location as the original. The Edit menu offers three commands to achieve this goal. The **Paste in Front** command pastes the copy directly in front of the original. The **Paste in Back** command pastes the copy directly behind the original. Both have quick keys that are easy to remember: for Paste in Front enter [Ctrl][F] (Win) or [⌘][F] (Mac) and for Paste in Back, enter [Ctrl][B] (Win) or [⌘][B] (Mac).

QUICK TIP

In this book, you'll be asked numerous times to paste in front and paste in back. The direction will read, "Copy, then paste in back," or, "Copy, then paste in front." It would be a good idea for you to remember the quick keys.

In addition, Illustrator also offers the **Paste in Place** command on the Edit menu. The Paste In Place command functions identically to the Paste In Front command; it pastes the copy in the same location in front of the original.

Be sure to make a note that you can copy objects while dragging them. Press and hold [Alt](Win) or [Option](Mac), then drag to create a copy of the object. This behavior is referred to as **"drag and drop a copy"**, and it's something you'll do a lot of in Illustrator and in this book.

Hiding, Locking, Grouping, and Ungrouping Objects

The Hide, Lock, Group, and Ungroup commands on the Object menu are essential for working effectively with layouts, especially complex layouts with many objects. **Hide** objects to get them out of your way. They won't print, and nothing you do will change the location of them as long as they are hidden. **Lock** an object to make it immovable—you will not even be able to select it. Lock your objects when you have them in a specific location and you don't want them accidentally moved or deleted. Don't think this is being overly cautious; accidentally moving or deleting objects—and being unaware that you did so—happens all the time in complex layouts. Having objects grouped strategically is also a solution for getting your work done faster.

You group multiple objects with the **Group** command under the Object menu. Grouping objects is a smart and important strategy for protecting the relationships between multiple objects. When you click on grouped objects with the Selection Tool, all the objects are selected. Thus, you can't accidentally select a single object or move it or otherwise alter it independently from the group. However, you *can* select individual objects within a group with the Direct Selection Tool—that's how the tool got its name. Even if you select and alter a single object within a group, the objects are not ungrouped. If you click on any of them with the Selection tool, all members of the group will be selected.

Working with Smart Guides

When aligning objects, you will find **smart guides** to be really effective and, well, really smart. When the Smart Guides feature is activated, smart guides appear automatically when you move objects in the document. Smart guides give you visual information for positioning objects precisely in relation to the artboard or to other objects. For example, you can use smart guides to align objects to the edges and centers of other objects, and to the horizontal and vertical centers of the artboard.

You enable Smart Guide options as a preference. You use the View menu to turn them on and off. Figure 30 shows smart guides at work.

Figure 30 *Smart guides aligning the top edges of two objects*

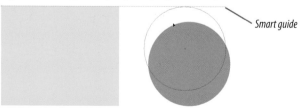

Smart guide

Figure 31 *General Preferences dialog box*

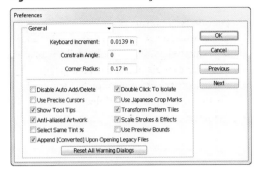

Figure 32 *Setting Units preferences*

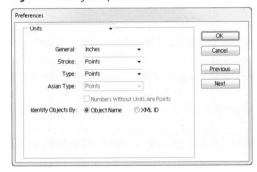

Figure 33 *Setting Guides & Grid preferences*

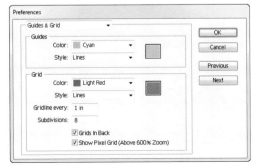

Set essential preferences

1. Click **Edit** (Win) or **Illustrator** (Mac) on the Application bar, point to **Preferences**, then click **General**.

   If you are working on a Mac, click **X**, point to **Preferences**, then click **General**. For the remainder of this chapter and this book, use this combination of commands to find your preferences dialog boxes.

2. Set your General preferences to match Figure 31.

   The keyboard increment determines the distance a selected object moves when you click an arrow key on your keypad. The measurement entered, .0139" is equivalent to 1 pt. The Show Tool Tips option will reveal a tool's name when you position your cursor over it. The Scale Strokes & Effects option means that, for example, if you apply a 200% scale to an object that has a 1 pt. stroke, the result will be an object with a 2 pt. stroke.

   TIP If you press and hold [Shift] while pressing the arrow keys, a selected object moves a distance that is 10X the keyboard increment.

3. Click the **Preferences menu list arrow** (black triangle beside the word General), click **Units**, then enter the settings shown in Figure 32.

   All the general artboard measurements in this book are based on inches. In almost all cases, you'll want to work with strokes and type in point measurements.

4. Click the **Preferences menu list arrow**, click **Guides & Grid**, then enter the settings shown in Figure 33.

   (continued)

Note that you have options for showing your guides as dots.

5. Click the **Preferences menu list arrow**, click **Smart Guides**, then enter the settings shown in Figure 34.

It's a good idea for your smart guides to be a distinctly different color than your ruler guides and artboard grid.

6. Click the **Preferences menu list arrow**, click **User Interface**, then enter the settings shown in Figure 35.

The brightness slider defines how light or dark the Illustrator interface is.

7. Click **OK**.

You specified various essential preferences in different Preferences dialog boxes.

Resize objects

1. Open **A1-2.ai**, then save it as **Objects**.

2. Click **View** on the Application bar, then verify that the Bounding Box command says Show Bounding Box.

3. Click the **Selection Tool** ![cursor], then click the **pink square** to select it.

As shown in Figure 36, the paths and the anchor points that draw the square are revealed, as is the object's center point.

4. Click **View** on the Application bar, then click **Show Bounding Box**.

Eight "hollow" handles appear around the rectangle, as shown in Figure 37.

(continued)

Figure 34 *Setting Smart Guides preferences*

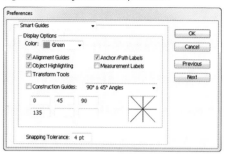

Figure 35 *Setting User Interface preferences*

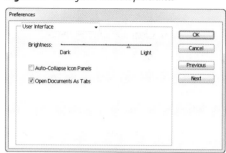

Figure 36 *Viewing paths and points on a selected object*

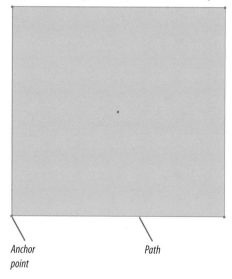

Anchor point

Path

Figure 37 *Viewing the bounding box*

Figure 38 *All objects selected on the artboard*

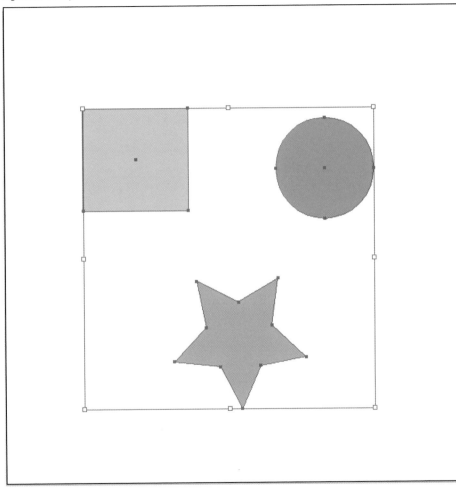

5. Click and drag **various handles** and note how the object is resized.

6. When you are done experimenting, undo all of the moves you made.

   The Undo command is at the top of the Edit menu.

7. Press and hold down **[Shift]**, while dragging the **top-left corner handle** to the left edge of the document.

   The object is resized proportionately.

8. Undo the move.

9. Click the **green circle** to select it.

10. Press and hold down **[Alt]**(Win) or **[option]**(Mac), then start dragging **any corner handle**.

    As you drag, the object is resized from its center.

11. While still holding down **[Alt]**(Win) **or [option]**(Mac) and dragging, press and hold **[Shift]**.

    The object is resized in proportion from its center.

12. Scale the circle to any size.

13. Undo the move.

14. Click **Select** on the Application bar, then click **All**.

    All of the objects on the artboard are selected. The bounding box appears around all three objects, as shown in Figure 38.

    Make it a point to remember the quick key for Select All: [Ctrl-A](Win) or ⌘ [A](Mac).

    (continued)

15. Using the skills you learned in this lesson, reduce the size of the objects in proportion so that they are very small on the artboard, then click the artboard to deselect the objects.

Your artboard should resemble Figure 39.

16. Click **File** on the Application bar, click **Revert**, then click **Revert** when you are prompted to confirm.

Reverting a file returns it to its status when you last saved it. You can think of it as a "super undo."

You explored various options for resizing objects, then you reverted the file.

Copy and duplicate objects

1. Click **View** on the Application bar, then click **Hide Bounding Box**.

2. Select the **star**, then copy it, using the [Ctrl][C] (Win) or ⌘ [C](Mac) shortcut keys.

3. Click **Edit** on the Application bar, then click **Paste**.

A copy of the star is placed at the center of the artboard.

4. Undo the paste.

5. Click **Edit** on the Application bar, then click **Paste in Front**.

The copy is pasted directly in front of the original star.

(continued)

Figure 39 *Resized object and contents*

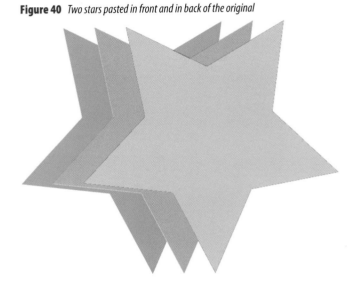

Figure 40 *Two stars pasted in front and in back of the original*

6. Press **[I]** on your keypad to switch to the Eyedropper tool, then click the **pink square**.

   The star takes on the same fill and stroke colors as the square.

7. Press → on your keypad ten times.

8. Deslect all, click **Edit** on the Application bar, then click **Paste in Back**.

   A copy of the star is pasted directly behind the original orange star that was copied.

9. Click the **Eyedropper tool** on the green circle.

10. Press and hold **[Shift]**, then press ← on your keypad one time.

11. Press and hold **[Ctrl]**(Win) or ⌘ (Mac) so that your cursor switches from temporarily from the Eyedropper tool to the Selection tool, then click the artboard with the Selection tool to deselect all.

    Pressing [Ctrl] or ⌘ is a quick way to switch temporarily to the Selection tool.

12. Compare your artboard to Figure 40.

13. Click the **Selection tool** , then select the green circle.

(continued)

14. Press and hold down [**Alt**](Win) or [**Option**] (Mac), then drag a copy of the circle to the center of the square.

Your screen should resemble Figure 41.

TIP This method for creating a copy is referred to as "drag-and-drop a copy."

15. Save your work, then close the file.

You copied and pasted an object, noting that it pasted by default in the center of the artboard. You used the Paste in Front and Paste in Back command along with arrow keys to make two offset copies of the star. You duplicated the circle with the drag-and-drop technique.

Figure 41 *Dragging and dropping a copy of the circle*

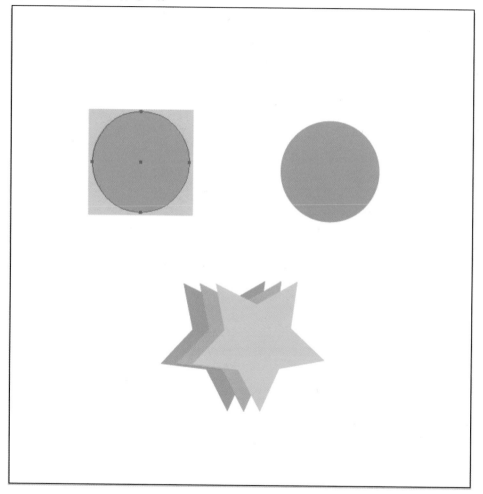

Getting to Know Illustrator

Figure 42 *Three grouped objects*

Hide, lock, and group objects

1. Open AI 1-3.ai, then save it as **Groups**.
2. Click **Object** on the Application bar, then click **Show All**.

   This document was originally saved with hidden objects. Three objects appear. They are all selected.
3. Click **Object** on the Application bar, then click **Group**.
4. Click the **Selection tool** , click **anywhere on the pasteboard** to deselect all, then click the **Pink circle**.

   As shown in Figure 42, all three objects are selected because they are grouped.
5. Click the **pasteboard** to deselect all, click the **Direct Selection tool** , then click the **pink circle**.

   Only the circle is selected, because the Direct Selection tool selects individual objects within a group.
6. Select all, click **Object** on the Application bar, then click **Ungroup**.
7. Click the **Selection tool** , select the small square, click **Object** on the Application bar, point to **Lock**, then click **Selection**.

   The object's handles disappear and it can no longer be selected.
8. Click **Object** on the Application bar, then click **Unlock All**.

   The small blue square is unlocked.

(continued)

9. Select all, click **Object** on the Application bar, point to **Hide**, then click **Selection**.

   All selected objects disappear.

10. Click the **Object** menu, then click **Show All.**

    The three objects reappear in the same location that they were in when they were hidden.

TIP Memorize the shortcut keys for Hide/Show, Group/Ungroup, and Lock/Unlock. They are easy to remember and extremely useful. You will be using these commands over and over again when you work in Illustrator.

11. Hide the pink circle and the small blue square.

12. Save the file.

You revealed hidden objects, grouped them, then used the Direct Selection tool to select individual objects within the group. You ungrouped, locked, unlocked, and hid objects.

Figure 43 *Smart guide aligning square with center of artboard*

Figure 44 *Aligning the tops of two squares*

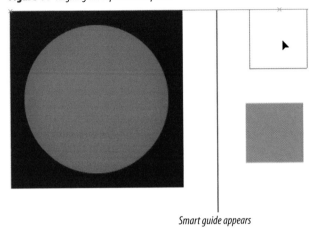

Smart guide appears

Figure 45 *Aligning bottoms of two squares*

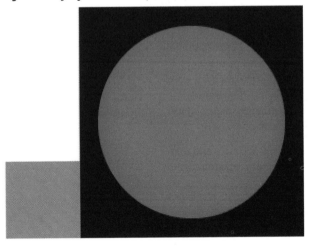

Work with smart guides

1. Click **View** on the Application bar, then click **Smart Guides** if it is not already checked.
2. Click the **blue rectangle**, then try to center it visually on the page.
3. Release your mouse when the word CENTER appears, as shown in Figure 43.

    Smart guides use the word CENTER to identify when the center point of an object is in line with the center point of the artboard.
4. Show the hidden objects, then hide the small light blue square.
5. Using the same methodology, align the center of the pink circle with the center of the large blue square.
6. Show the hidden small blue square.
7. Use smart guides to align the top of the small square with the top of the large square, as shown in Figure 44.
8. Position the small square as shown in Figure 45.
9. Save, then close the file.

You aligned an object at the center of the document and created precise relationships among three objects using smart guides.

Create BASIC SHAPES

What You'll Do

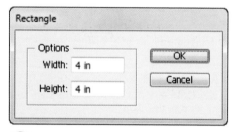

 In this lesson, you will examine the differences between bitmap and vector graphics. Then you will use the Rectangle tool to examine Illustrator's various options for creating simple vector graphics.

Getting Ready to Draw

Are you eager to start drawing? Do you want to create complex shapes, special effects, and original art? Perhaps you are a self-taught user of Adobe Illustrator, and your main interest is to graduate to advanced techniques and add a few of those cool special effects to your skill set. Good for you! Enthusiasm is priceless, and no book can teach it. So maintain that enthusiasm for this first exercise, where you'll start by creating a square. That's right. A square.

Consider for a moment that Mozart's sublime opera *Don Giovanni* is based primarily on eight notes, or that the great American novel can be reduced to 26 letters. Illustrator's foundation is basic geometric shapes, so let's start at square one...with one square.

Don't rush. As you work, keep in mind that the lessons you learn here are the foundation of every great illustration.

Understanding Bitmap Images and Vector Graphics

Before you begin drawing, you should become familiar with some basic information about computer graphics.

For starters, computer graphics fall into two main categories—bitmap images and vector graphics. **Bitmap images** are created using a square or rectangular grid of colored squares called **pixels**. Because pixels (a contraction of "picture elements") can render subtle gradations of tone, they are the most common medium for continuous-tone images—what you perceive as a photograph.

All scanned images are composed of pixels, and all "digital" images are composed of pixels. Adobe Photoshop is the leading graphics application for working with digital "photos." Figure 46 shows an example of a bitmap image.

The number of pixels in a given inch is referred to as the image's **resolution**. To be effective, pixels must be small enough to create an image with the illusion of continuous tone. Thus, bitmap images are termed **resolution-dependent**.

The important thing to remember about bitmap images is that any magnification of the image—resizing the image to be bigger—essentially means that fewer pixels are available per inch (the same number of pixels is now spread out over a larger area).

Getting to Know Illustrator

This decrease in resolution will have a negative impact on the quality of the image. The greater the magnification, the greater the negative impact.

Graphics that you create in Adobe Illustrator are vector graphics. **Vector graphics** are created with lines and curves and are defined by mathematical objects called vectors. Vectors use geometric characteristics to define the object. Vector graphics consist of **anchor points** and **line segments**, together referred to as **paths**.

For example, if you use Illustrator to render a person's face, the software will identify the iris of the eye using the mathematical definition of a circle with a specific radius and a specific location in respect to other graphics. It will then fill that circle with the color you have specified. Figure 47 shows an example of a vector graphic.

Computer graphics rely on vectors to render bold graphics that must retain clean, crisp lines when scaled to various sizes.

Vectors are often used to create logos or "line art," and they are the best choice for typographical work, especially small and italic type.

As mathematical objects, vector graphics can be scaled to any size. Because they are not created with pixels, there is no inherent resolution. Thus, vector graphics are termed **resolution-independent**. This means that any graphic that you create in Illustrator can be output to fit on a postage stamp or on a billboard!

Figure 46 *Bitmap graphics*

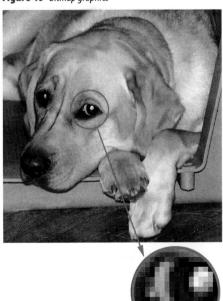

Figure 47 *Vector graphics*

Use the Rectangle tool

1. Click **File** on the Application bar, click **New**, create a new document that is 8" wide by 8" in height, name the file **Basic Shapes**, then click **OK**.

2. Click **File** on the Application bar, click **Save As**, navigate to the drive and folder where your Data Files are stored, click **Save**, then click **OK** to close the Illustrator Options dialog box.

3. Click the **Default Fill and Stroke button** on the Tools panel.

4. Click the **Swap Fill and Stroke button** on the Tools panel to reverse the default colors.

   Your fill color should now be black and your stroke color white. The **fill color** is the inside color of an object. The **stroke color** is the color of the object's border or frame.

5. Click the **Rectangle tool** on the Tools panel.

6. Click and drag the **Rectangle tool pointer** on the artboard, then release the mouse pointer to make a rectangle of any size.

7. Press and hold **[Shift]** while you create a second rectangle.

   Pressing and holding [Shift] while you create a rectangle constrains the shape to a perfect square, as shown in Figure 48.

8. Create a third rectangle drawn from its center point by pressing and holding **[Alt]** (Win) or **[option]** (Mac) as you drag the **Rectangle tool pointer**.

TIP Use [Shift] in combination with [Alt] (Win) or [option] (Mac) to draw a perfect shape from its center.

You created a freeform rectangle, then you created a perfect square. Finally you drew a square from its center point.

Figure 48 *Creating a rectangle and a square*

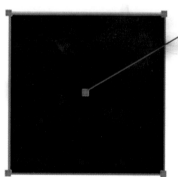

Square created by pressing [Shift] while creating a rectangle

Getting to Know Illustrator

Figure 49 *Rectangle dialog box*

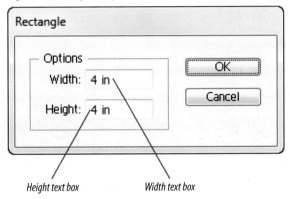

Height text box   Width text box

1. Click **Select** on the Application bar, then click **All** to select all of the objects.

2. Click **Edit** on the Application bar, then click **Cut** to remove the objects from the artboard.

3. Click **anywhere on the artboard**.

    When a shape tool is selected, clicking once on the artboard opens a dialog box, which allows you to enter precise information for creating the object. In this case, it opens the Rectangle dialog box.

4. Type **4** in the Width text box, type **4** in the Height text box, as shown in Figure 49, then click **OK**.

5. Save your work.

You clicked the artboard with the Rectangle tool, which opened the Rectangle dialog box. You entered a specific width and height to create a perfect 4" square.

Apply Fill and Stroke
COLORS TO OBJECTS

What You'll Do

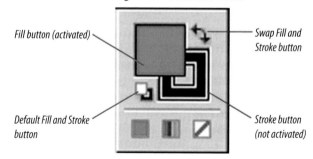

In this lesson you will use the Swatches panel to add a fill color to an object and apply a stroke as a border. Then you will use the Stroke panel to change the size of the default stroke.

Activating the Fill or Stroke

The Fill and Stroke buttons are on the Tools panel. To apply a fill or stroke color to an object, you must first activate the appropriate button. You activate either button by clicking it, which moves it in front of the other. When the Fill button is in front of the Stroke button, the fill is activated, as shown in Figure 50. The Stroke button is activated when it is in front of the Fill button.

As you work, you will often switch back and forth, activating the fill and the stroke. Rather than using your mouse to activate the fill or the stroke each time, simply press [X] to switch between the two modes.

Figure 50 *Fill and Stroke buttons*

Fill button (activated)

Swap Fill and Stroke button

Default Fill and Stroke button

Stroke button (not activated)

Applying Color with the Swatches Panel

The Swatches panel, as shown in Figure 51, is central to color management in the application and a simple resource for applying fills and strokes to objects.

The Swatches panel has 47 preset colors, along with gradients, patterns, and shades of gray. The swatch with the red line through it is called [None] and is used as a fill for a "hollow" object. Any object without a stroke will always have [None] as its stroke color.

When an object is selected, clicking a swatch on the panel will apply that color as a fill or a stroke, depending on which of the two is activated on the Tools panel. You can also drag and drop swatches onto unselected objects. Dragging a swatch to an unselected object will change the color of its fill or stroke, depending upon which of the two is activated.

Figure 51 *Swatches panel*

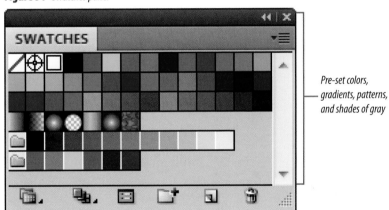

Pre-set colors, gradients, patterns, and shades of gray

Apply fill and stroke colors

1. Verify that the new square is still selected.

2. Click the **Swatches icon** ▦ in the stack of collapsed panels to open the Swatches panel.

   Your Swatches panel may already be available.

3. Click **any blue swatch** on the Swatches panel to fill the square.

   Note that the Fill button on the Tools panel is now also blue.

TIP When you position your pointer over a color swatch on the Swatches panel, a tool tip appears that shows the name of that swatch.

4. Click the **Selection tool** ▶, then click **anywhere on the artboard** to deselect the blue square.

5. Drag and drop a **yellow swatch** onto the blue square.

   The fill color changes to yellow because the Fill button is activated on the Tools panel. Your colors may vary from the colors shown in the figures.

6. Press **[X]** to activate the Stroke button on the Tools panel.

7. Drag and drop the **red swatch** on the Swatches panel onto the yellow square.

   As shown in Figure 52, a red stroke is added to the square because the Stroke button is activated on the Tools panel.

   (continued)

Figure 52 *Red stroke is added to the yellow square*

Figure 53 *Yellow square without a stroke*

8. Click the **Stroke icon** ≣ in the stack of collapsed panels to display the Stroke panel.

   Your Stroke panel may already be available.

9. Select the square, click the **Weight list arrow** on the Stroke panel, then click **8 pt**.

TIP Illustrator positions a stroke equally inside and outside an object. Thus, an 8 pt stroke is rendered with 4 pts inside the object and 4 pts outside.

10. Click **[None]** ⬜ on the Swatches panel to remove the stroke from the square.

    Your screen should resemble Figure 53.

11. Save your work.

You filled the square with blue by clicking a blue swatch on the Swatches panel. You then changed the fill and stroke colors to yellow and red by dragging and dropping swatches onto the square. You used the Stroke panel to increase the weight of the stroke, then removed the stroke by choosing [None] from the Swatches panel.

Select, Move,
AND ALIGN OBJECTS

What You'll Do

 In this lesson, you will use the Selection tool in combination with smart guides to move, copy, and align four squares.

Selecting and Moving Objects

When it comes to accuracy, consider that Illustrator can move objects incrementally by fractions of a point—which itself is a tiny fraction of an inch! That level of precision is key when moving and positioning objects.

Before you can move or modify an Illustrator object, you must identify it by selecting it with a selection tool, menu item, or command key. When working with simple illustrations that contain few objects, selecting is usually simple, but it can become very tricky in complex illustrations, especially those containing a large number of small objects positioned closely together.

Two very basic ways to move objects are by clicking and dragging or by using the arrow keys, which by default move a selected item in 1-pt increments. Pressing [Shift] when dragging an object constrains the movement to horizontal, vertical, and 45° diagonals. Pressing [Alt] (Win) or [option] (Mac) while dragging an object creates a copy of the object.

Making a Marquee Selection with the Selection Tool

By now, you're familiar with using the Selection tool to select objects. You can also use the Selection tool to create a marquee selection, which is a dotted rectangle that disappears as soon as you release the mouse button. Any object that the marquee touches before you release the mouse button will be selected. See Figure 54.

Marquee selections are useful for both quick selections and precise selections. Make sure you practice and make them part of your skill set.

Figure 54 *Making a marquee selection*

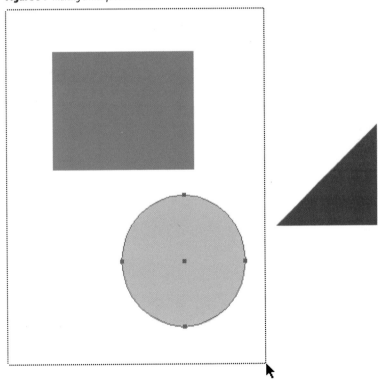

Move and position objects with precision

1. Click **View** on the Application bar, then click **Fit Artboard in Window**.

2. Click **View** on the Application bar, then verify that both Smart Guides and Snap to Point are selected.

TIP There will be a check next to each if they are selected. If they are not selected, click each option to select it.

Snap to Point automatically aligns anchor points when they get close together. When dragging an object, you'll see it "snap" to align itself with a nearby object or guide.

3. Click the **Selection tool** ▲ on the Tools panel, then click the **yellow square**.

4. Identify the anchor points, paths, and center point, as shown in Figure 55.

5. Move the Selection tool pointer over the **anchor points**, over the **paths that connect the points**, and over the **center point**.

6. Position the pointer over the **top-left anchor point**, click and drag so that the anchor point aligns with the top-left corner of the artboard, as shown in Figure 56, then release the mouse.

The smart guide changes from "anchor" to "intersect" when the two corners are aligned.

You used the Selection tool in combination with smart guides to position an object exactly at the top-left corner of the artboard.

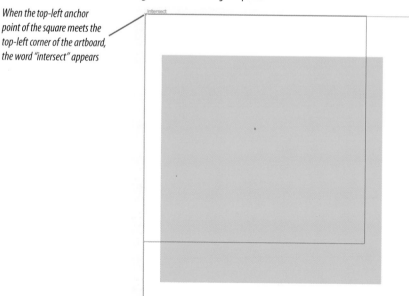

Figure 55 *Anchor points, paths, and center point*

Paths

Anchor points

Center point

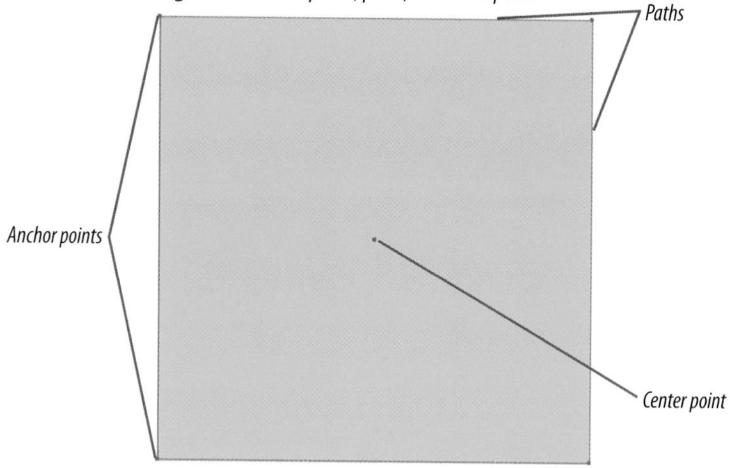

Figure 56 *Intersecting two points*

When the top-left anchor point of the square meets the top-left corner of the artboard, the word "intersect" appears

intersect

Figure 57 *Duplicating the square*

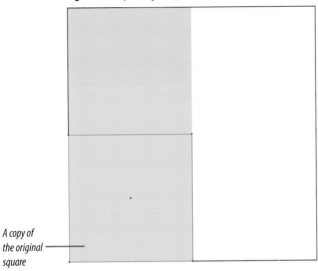

A copy of the original square

Figure 58 *Four squares created using drag and drop*

Duplicate objects using drag and drop

1. Click the **top-left anchor point** without releasing the mouse button, press and hold **[Shift][Alt]** (Win) or **[Shift][option]** (Mac) while dragging straight down until the top-left anchor point touches the bottom-left anchor point (the "intersect" smart guide will appear), then release the mouse.

   When moving an object, pressing and holding [Shift] constrains the movement vertically, horizontally, or on 45° diagonals. Pressing [Alt] (Win) or [option] (Mac) while dragging an object creates a copy of the object, as shown in Figure 57.

   TIP When you press [Alt] (Win) or [option] (Mac) while dragging an object, the pointer becomes a double-arrow pointer. When two anchor points are directly on top of each other, the Selection tool pointer turns from black to white.

2. With the bottom square still selected, press and hold **[Shift],** then click the **top square** to select both items.

3. Click the **top-left anchor point** of the top square without releasing the mouse button, press and hold **[Shift][Alt] (Win)** or **[Shift] [option]** (Mac), while dragging to the right until the top-left anchor point touches the top-right anchor point, then release the mouse.

4. Change the fill color of each square to match the colors shown in Figure 58.

5. Save your work.

You moved and duplicated the yellow square using [Shift] to constrain the movement and [Alt] (Win) or [option] (Mac) to duplicate or "drag and drop" copies of the square.

Transform
OBJECTS

What You'll Do

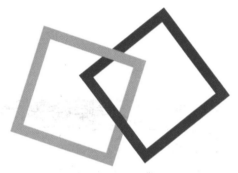

In this lesson, you will scale, rotate, and reflect objects, using the basic transform tools. You will also create a star and a triangle.

Transforming Objects

The Scale, Rotate, and Reflect tools are the fundamental transform tools. As their names make clear, the Scale and Rotate tools resize and rotate objects, respectively. When you use the tool's dialog box, the objects are transformed from their center points. This can be a useful choice because the object's position essentially doesn't change on the artboard or in relation to other objects.

Use the Reflect tool to "flip" an object over an imaginary axis. The best way to understand the Reflect tool is to imagine positioning a mirror perpendicular to a sheet of paper with a word written on it. The angle at which you position the mirror in relation to the word is the reflection axis. The reflection of the word in the mirror is the end result of what the Reflect tool does. For example, text reflected across a horizontal axis would appear upside down and inverted. Text reflected across a vertical axis would appear to be inverted and running backwards, as shown in Figure 59.

You can transform an object using the desired tool or its dialog box. Each transform tool has a dialog box where you can enter precise numbers to execute the transformation on a selected object. You can access a tool's dialog box by double-clicking the tool. Click the Copy button in the dialog box to create a transformed copy of the selected object. Figure 60 shows the Scale dialog box.

Repeating Transformations

One of the most powerful commands relating to the transform tools is Transform Again, found on the Object menu. Unfortunately, it is a command often overlooked by new users. Whenever you transform an object, selecting Transform Again repeats the transformation. For example, if you scale a circle 50%, the Transform Again command will scale the circle 50% again.

The power of the command comes in combination with copying transformations. For example, if you rotate a square 10° and copy it at the same time, the Transform Again command will create a second square rotated another 10° from the first copy. Applying Transform Again repeatedly is handy for creating complex geometric shapes from basic objects.

Figure 59 *Reflected text*

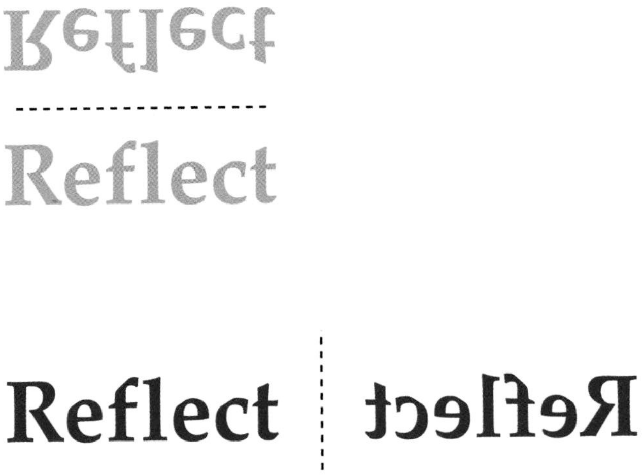

Figure 60 *Scale dialog box*

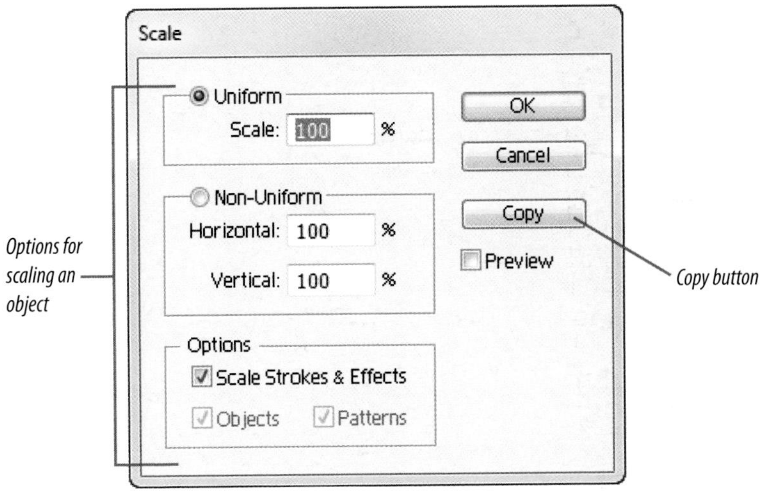

Options for scaling an object

Copy button

Use the Scale and Rotate tools

1. Select the green square, double-click the **Scale tool** , type **50** in the Scale text box, then click **OK**.

2. Click **Edit** on the Application bar, then click **Undo Scale**.

   TIP You can also undo your last step by pressing [Ctrl][Z] (Win) or ⌘ [Z] (Mac).

3. Double-click the **Scale tool** again, type **50** in the Scale text box, then click **Copy**.

   The transformation is executed from the center point; the center points of the original and the copy are aligned.

4. Fill the new square created in Step 3 with blue.

5. Double-click the **Rotate tool**, type **45** in the Angle text box, click **OK**, then click the **Selection tool** .

6. Apply a 22 pt yellow stroke to the rotated square, deselect, then compare your screen to Figure 61.

You used the Scale tool to create a 50% copy of the square, then filled the copy with blue. You rotated the copy 45°. You then applied a 22 pt yellow stroke.

Figure 61 *Scaling and rotating a square*

Getting to Know Illustrator

Figure 62 *Using the Transform Again command*

Use the Transform Again command

1. Click the **Ellipse tool** on the Tools panel.

   TIP To access the Ellipse tool, press and hold the Rectangle tool until a toolbar of shape tools appears, then click the Ellipse tool.

2. Click the **artboard**, type **3** in the Width text box and **.5** in the Height text box, then click **OK**.

3. Change the fill color to **[None]**, the stroke color to **blue**, and the stroke weight to **3 pt**.

4. Click the **Selection tool** , click the **center point** of the ellipse, then drag it to the center point of the yellow square.

   TIP The center smart guide appears when the two centers meet.

5. Double-click the **Rotate tool** , type **45** in the Angle text box, then click **Copy**.

6. Click **Object** on the Application bar, point to **Transform**, then click **Transform Again**.

   TIP You can also access the Transform Again command by pressing [Ctrl][D] (Win) or [⌘] [D] (Mac).

7. Repeat Step 6 to create a fourth ellipse using the Transform Again command.

   Your screen should resemble Figure 62.

8. Select the four ellipses, click **Object** on the Application bar, then click **Group**.

You created an ellipse, filled and stroked it, and aligned it with the yellow square. You then created a copy rotated at 45°. With the second copy still selected, you used the Transform Again command twice, creating two more rotated copies. You then grouped the four ellipses.

Create a star and a triangle, and use the Reflect tool

1. Select the Star tool ☆, then click **anywhere on the artboard**.

   The Star tool is hidden beneath the current shape tool.

2. Type **1** in the Radius 1 text box, type **5** in the Radius 2 text box, type **5** in the Points text box, as shown in Figure 63, then click **OK**.

   A star has two radii; the first is from the center to the inner point, and the second is from the center to the outer point. The **radius** is a measurement from the center point of the star to either point.

3. Double-click the **Scale tool** 🔲, type **25** in the Scale text box, then click **OK**.

   When you create a star using the Star dialog box, the star is drawn upside down.

4. Fill the star with **white**, then apply a 5 pt blue stroke to it.

5. Click the **Selection tool** ▶, then move the star so that it is completely within the red square.

6. Double-click the **Reflect tool** 🔄, click the **Horizontal option button**, as shown in Figure 64, then click **OK**.

   The star "flips" over an imaginary horizontal axis.

   TIP The Reflect tool is hidden beneath the Rotate tool.

7. Use the Selection tool ▶ or the arrow keys to position the star roughly in the center of the red square.

   Your work should resemble Figure 65.

   (continued)

Figure 63 *Star dialog box*

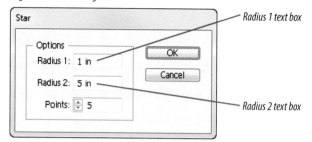

Radius 1 text box

Radius 2 text box

Figure 64 *Reflect dialog box*

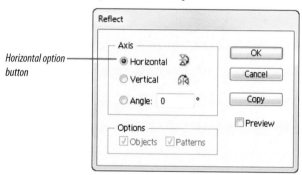

Horizontal option button

Figure 65 *Reflecting the star horizontally*

Getting to Know Illustrator

Figure 66 *The finished project*

8. Click the **Polygon tool** on the Tools panel.

   The Polygon tool is hidden beneath the current shape tool on the Tools panel.

9. Click **anywhere on the blue square**.

10. Type **1.5** in the Radius text box, type **3** in the Sides text box, then click **OK**.

11. Fill the triangle with **red**.

12. Change the stroke color to **yellow** and the stroke weight to **22 pt**.

13. Position the triangle so that it is centered within the blue square.

    Your completed project should resemble Figure 66.

14. Save your work, then close Basic Shapes.

You used the shape tools to create a star and a triangle, then used the Reflect tool to "flip" the star over an imaginary horizontal axis.

Make Direct SELECTIONS

What You'll Do

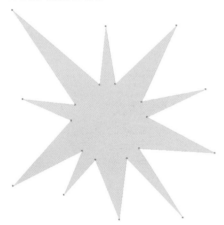

In this lesson, you will use the Direct Selection tool and a combination of menu commands, such as Add Anchor Points and Paste in Front, to convert existing shapes into new designs.

Using the Direct Selection Tool

The Direct Selection tool selects individual anchor points or single paths of an object. Using [Shift], you can select multiple anchor points or multiple paths. You can also select multiple points or paths by dragging a direct selection marquee. The tool also selects individual objects within a group, which can be useful for modifying just one object in a complex group. Figure 67 demonstrates the Direct Selection tool selecting one piece of a grouped object.

Clicking the center of an object with the Direct Selection tool selects the entire object. Clicking the edge selects the path segment only; the anchor points on the object all appear white, which means they are not selected. A white anchor point is not selected.

The Direct Selection tool gives you the power to distort simple objects such as squares and circles into unique shapes. Don't underestimate its significance. While the Selection tool is no more than a means to an end for selecting and moving objects, the Direct Selection tool is in itself a drawing tool. You will use it over and over again to modify and perfect your artwork.

Adding Anchor Points

As you distort basic shapes with the Direct Selection tool, you will often find that to create more complex shapes, you will need additional anchor points.

The Add Anchor Points command creates new anchor points without distorting the object. To add anchor points to an object, click the Object menu, point to Path, then click Add Anchor Points. The new points are automatically positioned exactly between the original anchor points. You can create as many additional points as you wish to use.

Turning Objects into Guides

Guides are one of Illustrator's many features that help you work with precision. Any object you create can be turned into a guide. With the object selected, click the View menu, point to Guides, then click Make Guides. Guides can be locked or unlocked in the same location. It is a good idea to work with locked guides so that they don't interfere with your artwork.

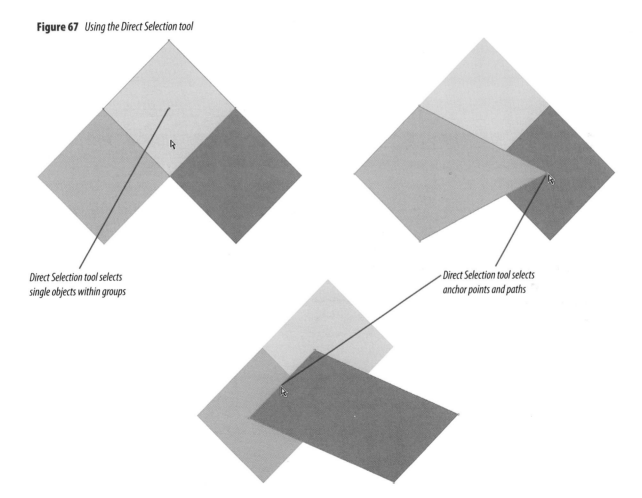

Figure 67 *Using the Direct Selection tool*

Direct Selection tool selects single objects within groups

Direct Selection tool selects anchor points and paths

Unlock guides only when you want to select them or delete them.

When an object is turned into a guide, it loses its attributes, such as its fill, stroke, and stroke weight. However, Illustrator remembers the original attributes for each guide. To transform a guide back to its original object, first unlock, then select the guide. Click the View menu, point to Guides, then click Release Guides.

Working with the Draw Behind Drawing Mode and the Stacking Order

The **stacking order** refers to the order of how objects are arranged in front and behind other objects on the artboard. Every time you create an object, it is created in front of the existing objects. (Note that this discussion does not include any role of layers and the Layers panel.) You can manipulate the stacking order with the Arrange commands on the Object menu. See Table 3 below for descriptions of each Arrange command.

You can also use the **Draw Behind drawing mode** to create an object behind a selected object or at the bottom of the stacking order.

Command	Result	quick key (Win)	quick key (Mac)
Bring Forward	Brings a selected object forward one position in the stacking order	[Ctrl][right bracket]	⌘ [right bracket]
Bring to Front	Brings a selected object to the very front of the stacking order—in front of all other objects	[Shift][Ctrl] [right bracket]	[Shift] ⌘ [right bracket]
Send Backward	Sends a selected object backward one position	[Ctrl][left bracket]	⌘ [left bracket]
Send to Back	Sends a selected object to the very back of the stacking order—behind all the other objects	[Shift][Ctrl] [left bracket]	[Shift] ⌘ [left bracket]

TABLE 3: ARRANGE COMMANDS

Figure 68 *Red square selected with the Direct Selection tool*

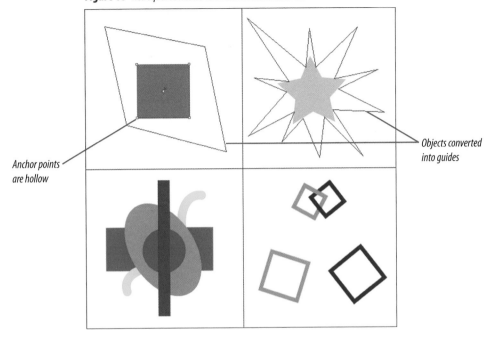

Anchor points
are hollow

Objects converted
into guides

Figure 69 *Red square distorted*

Make guides and direct selections

1. Open AI 1-4.ai, then save it as **Direct Selections**.
2. Click **View** on the Application bar, then deactivate the Smart Guides feature.
3. Select the green polygon with the Selection Tool ▸ .
4. Click **View** on the Application bar, point to **Guides**, then click **Make Guides**.

   The polygon is converted to a guide.

TIP If you do not see the polygon-shaped guide, click View on the Application bar, point to Guides, then click Show Guides.

5. Convert the purple starburst to a guide.
6. Click **View** on the Application bar, point to **Guides**, verify that there is a check mark to the left of Lock Guides, then click the pasteboard to close the menu.
7. Click the **Direct Selection tool** ▸ , then click the **edge of the red square**.

   The four anchor points turn white, as shown in Figure 68.
8. Click and drag the anchor points to the four corners of the guide to distort the square.

   Your work should resemble Figure 69.

You converted two objects to guides. You then used the Direct Selection tool to create a new shape from a square by moving anchor points independently.

Add anchor points

1. Using the Direct Selection tool 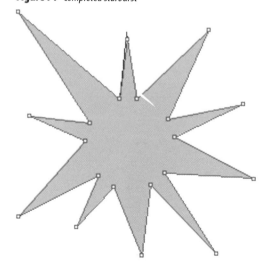, click the **center of the light blue star**, then note the anchor points used to define the shape.

2. Click **Object** on the Application bar, point to **Path**, then click **Add Anchor Points**.

3. Click the **artboard** to deselect the star, then click the **edge of the star**.

   All the anchor points turn white and are available to be selected independently, as shown in Figure 70.

4. Move the top anchor point on the star to align with the top point of the guide that you made earlier.

5. Working clockwise, move every other anchor point outward to align with the guide, creating a ten-point starburst.

   Your work should resemble Figure 71.

6. Select and move any of the inner anchor points to modify the starburst to your liking.

You used the Add Anchor Points command and the Direct Selection tool to create an original ten-point starburst from a generic five-point star.

Figure 70 *Star selected with Direct Selection tool*

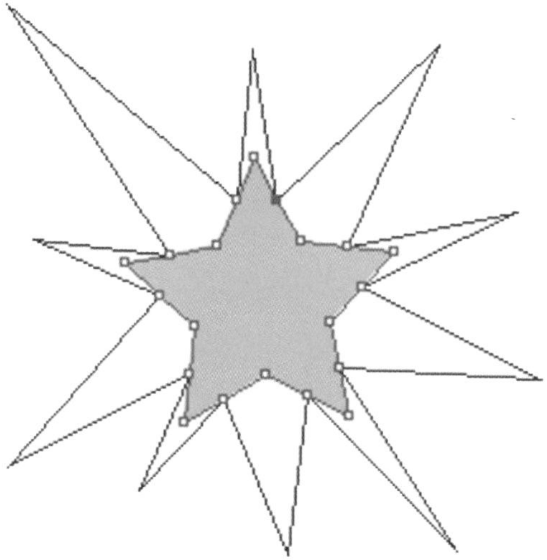

Figure 71 *Completed starburst*

Figure 72 *Red rectangle sent to the back of the stacking order*

Figure 73 *Blue oval moved forward in the stacking order*

 Use the Draw Behind drawing mode

1. Click the **Expand panels button** ◄◄ at the top of the Tools panel if necessary to display the tools in two rows.

   When the Tools panel is displayed in two rows, the three drawing modes are visible as icons at the bottom. When the panel is displayed in a single row, you need to click the Drawing Modes icon to display the tools in a submenu.

2. Note the four objects in the bottom-left quadrant of the artboard.

   The blue oval is at the back, the purple rectangle is in front of the blue oval, the curvy yellow path is in front of the purple rectangle, and the red rectangle is at the front.

3. Click the **Selection tool** ▶, click the **red rectangle**, click **Object** on the Application bar, point to **Arrange**, then click **Send to Back**.

   As shown in Figure 72, the red rectangle moves to the back of the stacking order.

4. Select the yellow path, click **Object** on the Application bar, point to **Arrange**, then click **Send Backward**.

   The path moves one level back in the stacking order. When discussing the stacking order, it's smart to use the term "level" instead of "layer." Layers in Illustrator are different from the stacking order.

5. Select the blue oval, click **Object** on the Application bar, point to **Arrange**, then click **Bring Forward**.

   As shown in Figure 73, the blue oval moves one level forward in the stacking order.

   (continued)

6. Select the purple rectangle, then click the **Draw Behind** button at the bottom of the Tools panel.

There are three available drawing modes: Draw Normal, Draw Behind, and Draw Inside.

7. Click the **Ellipse tool** on the Tools panel, then draw a circle at the center of the blue oval.

The circle is created behind the purple rectangle, though it still appears to be in front while it is selected. With the Draw Behind drawing mode activated, an object you draw will be positioned one level behind any selected object on the artboard. If no object is selected, the new object will be positioned at the back of the stacking order.

8. Click the **Eyedropper tool**, click the **red rectangle**, then compare your artboard to Figure 74.

The Eyedropper tool samples the fill and stroke color from the red rectangle and applies it to the selected object.

9. Click the **Draw Normal button**, then save your work.

You selected individual segments of a circle, copied them, then pasted them in front. You then created a special effect by stroking the four new segments with different colors.

Figure 74 *The new red circle behind the purple rectangle*

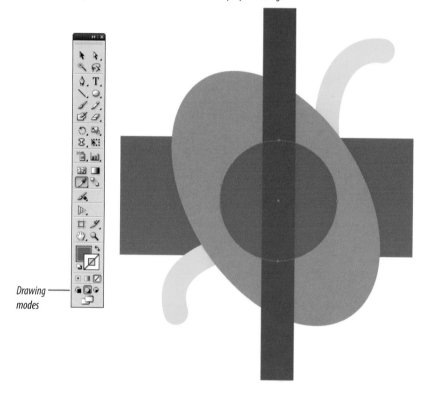

Drawing modes

Getting to Know Illustrator

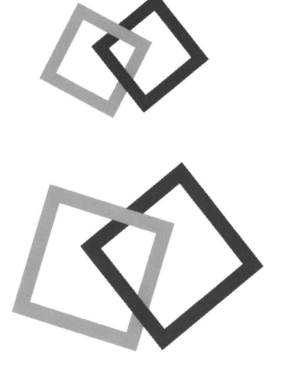

Figure 75 *Completed linked squares*

Create a simple special effect utilizing a direct selection

1. Click the **Selection tool** ![cursor], overlap the large orange and blue squares so that they resemble the small orange and blue squares, then deselect.

2. Click the **Direct Selection tool** ![cursor], then select the top path segment of the orange square.

3. Copy the path.

4. Select the intersecting path segment on the blue square.

5. Paste in front, then save your work.

   Your work should resemble Figure 75.

6. Close the document.

TIP Remember this technique; it's one you can use over and over again to create interesting artwork in Illustrator.

You performed a classic Illustrator trick using the Direct Selection tool. Selecting only a path, you copied it and pasted it in front of an intersecting object to create the illusion that the two objects were linked.

Work with
MULTIPLE ARTBOARDS

What You'll Do

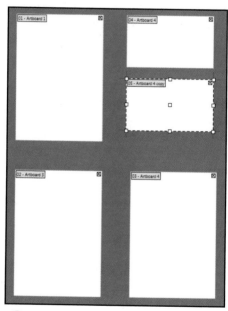

In this lesson, you will explore various options when working with multiple artboards.

Understanding Multiple Artboards

The artboard is your workspace in an Illustrator document. Sometimes, the size of the artboard will be important to your design; sometimes it won't. For example, let's say that you're designing a logo that will be used in a variety of ways, such as for letterhead, business cards, a door sign, or building sign. When you are creating the logo, you're just designing artwork. The size at which you're creating the artwork isn't really important, because you can resize it later to use in these different types of layouts.

At other times, the work you do in Illustrator will be at a specific size. Let's say, for example, that you're designing layouts for letterhead, business cards, and promotional postcards for the company for which you made the logo. In this case, you would need to set up your document, or the size of the artboard, at specific sizes, such as 8.5" x 11" for the letterhead, 3" x 2.5" for the business card, and 4" x 6" for the postcard.

Illustrator CS5 allows you to have anywhere from 1 to 100 artboards in a single document, depending on the size of the artboards. Using the above example,

this means that you could design all three pieces in one document—no need to switch between documents for the letterhead, business card, and postcard.

Beyond this basic convenience, working with multiple artboards offers a number of important benefits. You won't have to recreate unique swatch colors or gradients; you'll only need to create them once. Paste commands are available on the Edit menu that allow you to paste an object on multiple artboards in exactly the same location—another example of the consistency that can be achieved by working in a single document.

Managing Multiple Artboards

Creating multiple artboards can be the first thing that you do when beginning a design or one of the last things you do. The New Document dialog box, shown in Figure 76, is where you define the specifics of a document, including the number of artboards.

The Width and Height values define the size of all the artboards you create at this stage, whether single or multiple, but you can resize artboards any time after creating them. Once you specify the number of artboards, you have controls for the layout of the artboards. The four buttons to the right of the Number of Artboards text box offer basic layout choices—grid by row, grid by column, arrange by row, arrange by column. The Spacing text box specifies the physical space between artboards, and the Rows value defines the number of rows of artboards in a grid.

When you click the OK button in the New dialog box, the document window displays all artboards, as shown in Figure 77. Note that the top-left artboard is highlighted with a black line. This identifies the artboard as "active." As such, all View menu commands you apply affect this artboard. In other words, if you click the Fit Artboard in Window command, the active artboard is resized to fit in the document window. You can also click the Fit All in Window command to view all artboards.

When you create a new document, you can use a preset document profile in the New dialog box. The New Document Profile menu lists a number of preset values for size, color mode, units, orientation, transparency, and resolution. This can help you set up the basic orientation for your document quickly. For example, the Web profile automatically creates an RGB document with pixels as units. By default, all new document profiles use one artboard, but you can add more in the Number of artboards text box.

Figure 76 *New Document dialog box*

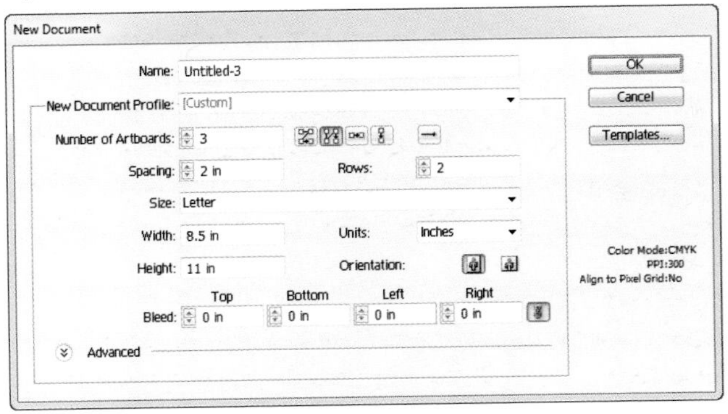

Figure 77 *Viewing multiple artboards*

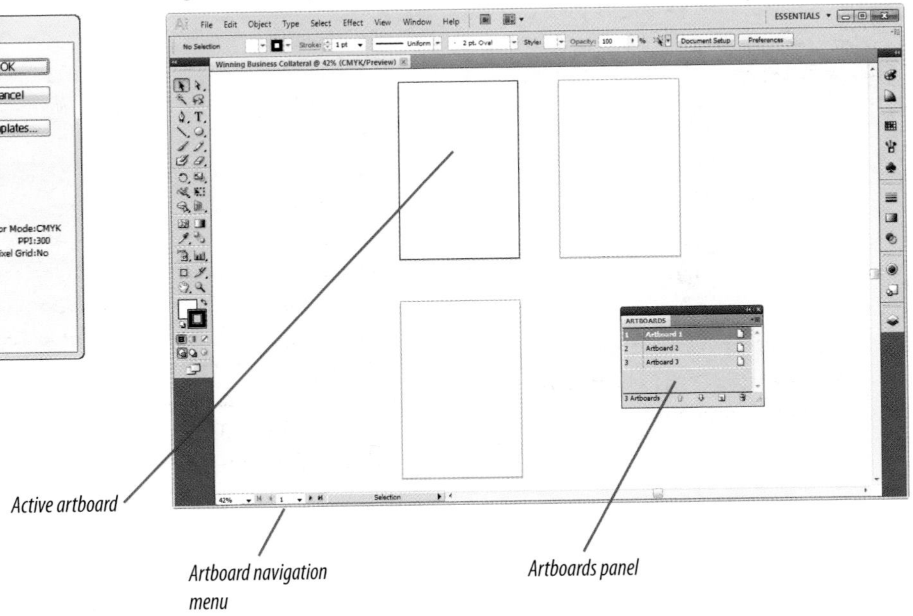

Active artboard

Artboard navigation menu

Artboards panel

The **Artboard tool**, shown in Figure 78, is your gateway to managing multiple artboards. Clicking the Artboard tool takes you to "Edit Artboards mode." As shown in Figure 79, all your artboards appear numbered against a dark gray background. The "selected" artboard is highlighted with a marquee. When an artboard is selected, you can change settings for it in the Control panel beneath the Application bar, using the following options:

- Click the Preset menu to change a selected artboard to any of the standard sizes listed, such as letter, tabloid, or legal.

- Click the Orientation buttons to specify a selected artboard as Portrait or Landscape.
- Click the New Artboard button to create a duplicate of the selected artboard.
- Click the Delete Artboard button to delete the selected artboard.
- Click the Name text box to enter a name for the selected artboard. This could be

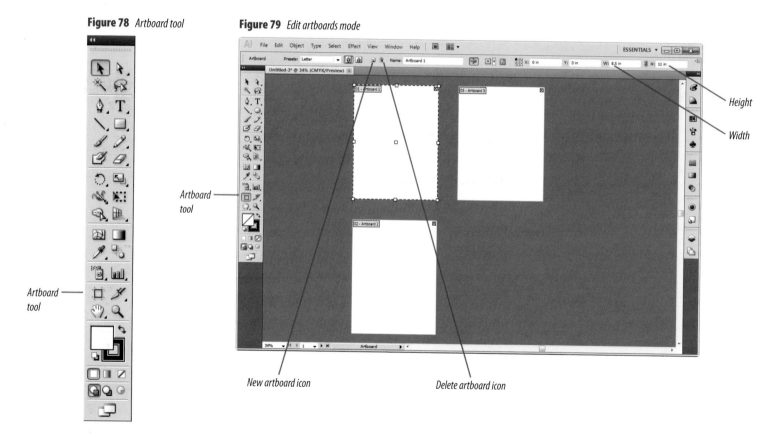

Figure 78 *Artboard tool*

Figure 79 *Edit artboards mode*

Artboard tool

Artboard tool

Height

Width

New artboard icon

Delete artboard icon

useful for managing your own work and for adding clarity when you hand your Illustrator file over to a printer or some other vendor.

■ Click the Width and Height text boxes to enter different values and resize the selected artboard.

To exit edit Artboards mode, press the Escape key or any other tool on the Tools panel.

Creating, Editing, and Arranging Artboards

Once you click the Artboard tool to enter edit Artboards mode, you have a number of options for creating, editing and arranging artboards.

You can, at any time, click the New Artboard button on the Control panel. When you do, move your cursor over the other artboards and you'll see a transparent artboard moving with the cursor, as shown in Figure 80. If you have smart guides activated, green lines will appear to help you align the new artboard with the existing artboards. Click where you want to position the new artboard. Using this method, the new artboard button will create a new button at the size specified in the New document dialog box.

As an alternative, you can simply click and drag with the Artboard tool to create a new artboard, as shown in Figure 81. Once you

Figure 80 *Creating with the New Artboard button*

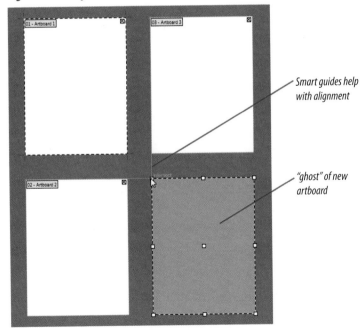

Smart guides help with alignment

"ghost" of new artboard

Figure 81 *"Dragging out" a new artboard with the Artboard tool*

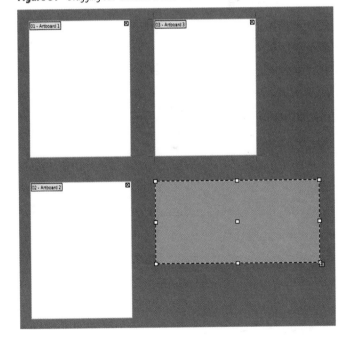

"drag out" the new artboard, you can enter a specific height and width for the artboard in the Control panel. To resize any existing artboard, first select the artboard, then enter values in the Width and Height text boxes. Figure 82 shows four artboards: letterhead, business card front, business card back, and 4 x 6 postcard. Note the Width and Height textboxes for the selected artboard.

The positioning of the artboards in the edit artboards window reflects the same layout that the artboards will be when you're working in Normal mode. You can manipulate the layout of artboards in the Edit Artboards window simply by clicking and dragging them as you wish. Figure 83 shows the same four artboards with a more centralized layout.

Printing Multiple Artboards

When you work with multiple artboards, you can print each artboard individually or you can compile them into one page. Usually, you'll want to print them individually, and this is easy to do in the Print dialog box. Use the forward and backward arrows in the print preview window to click to move through each artboard. In the Pages section, if you click All, all artboards will print. To print only specific artboards, enter the artboard number in the Range field. To combine all artwork on all artboards onto a single page, select the Ignore Artboards option. Depending on how large your artboards are, they'll be scaled down to fit on a single page or tiled over a number of pages.

Figure 82 *Four different-sized artboards*

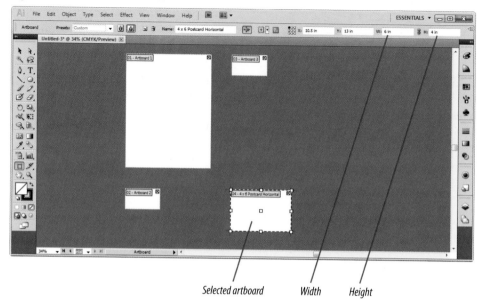

Selected artboard   Width   Height

Figure 83 *Repositioning artboards*

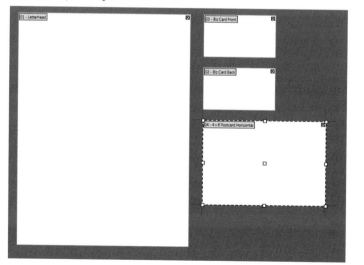

Using the Artboards Panel

You can use the Artboards panel to perform artboard operations. You can add or delete artboards, reorder and renumber them, and navigate through multiple artboards. When you create multiple artboards, each is assigned a number, and is listed with that number in the Artboards panel. If you select an artboard, you can click the Up and Down Arrows to reorder the artboards in the panel. Doing so will renumber the artboard, but will not change its name.

Pasting Artwork Between Multiple Artboards

The ability to paste copied artwork between multiple artboards is an important basic function and critical to maintain consistency between layouts. The Edit menu offers two powerful commands: Paste in Place and Paste on All Artboards. Use the Paste in Place command to paste an object from one artboard to the same spot on another. Figure 84 shows a logo pasted from the first artboard to the second. Even though the two artboards are drastically different sizes, the two logos are positioned at exactly the same distance from the top-left corner of the artboard.

The Paste on All Artboards command goes a giant step further, pasting artwork in the same position on all artboards, as shown in Figure 85.

Figure 84 *Paste in Place command used*

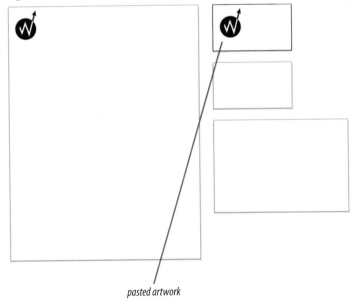

pasted artwork

Figure 85 *Paste on All Artboards command used*

Create a new document with multiple artboards

1. Verify that no documents are open and that smart guides are activated.

TIP The Smart Guides command is on the View menu.

2. Click **File** on the Application bar, then click **New**.

   The New Document dialog box opens.

3. Type **Winning Business Collateral** in the Name text box.

4. Set the number of artboards to **3**, then click the **Grid by Row button** 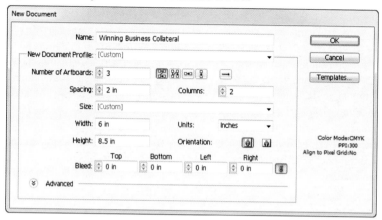.

5. Set the Spacing and Columns text boxes to **2**.

6. Set the width to **6** and the height to **8.5**.

7. Verify that the Units are set to Inches, then compare your dialog box to Figure 86.

8. Click **OK**.

   When you click OK, the three artboards fit in your document window, as shown in Figure 87

9. Click the **Selection tool** , then click **each artboard** to make each active.

   A black frame highlights each artboard when it is selected.

10. Click the **top-right artboard** to make it the active artboard, click **View** on the Application bar, then click **Fit Artboard in Window**.

TIP Make a note of the quick key for this command: [Ctrl] [0] (Win) or ⌘ [0] (Mac). The 0 in this shortcut key is a zero, not the letter O.

(continued)

Figure 86 *New dialog box set to create three artboards at 6" x 8.5"*

Figure 87 *Document with three artboards*

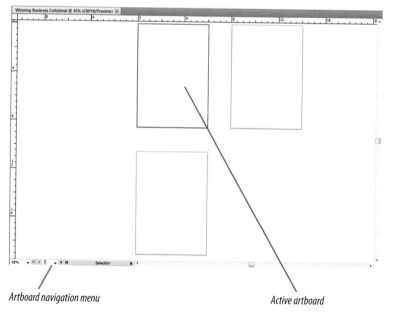

Artboard navigation menu

Active artboard

Figure 88 *Edit Artboards mode*

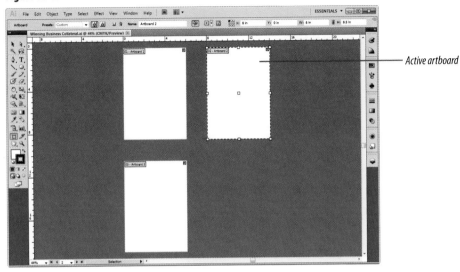

Active artboard

Figure 89 *Creating a new artboard with the New Artboard icon*

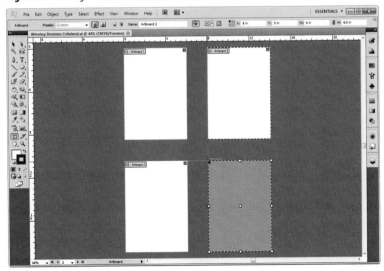

11. Click **View** on the Application bar, then click **Fit All in Window**.

12. Save the file as **Winni** *insert icon when available* **ng Business Collateral**.

You specified settings for a new document with three artboards in the New Document dialog box. You clicked artboards in the document to activate them. You used the Fit in Window and Fit All in Window commands to view artboards.

Create and name artboards

1. Click the **Artboard tool** □ .

   Clicking the Artboard tool switches the interface to Edit Artboards mode, shown in Figure 88. The top-right artboard is selected. All the artboards are numbered.

2. Click the **New Artboard icon** ⬞ on the Control panel.

3. Float your cursor over the artboards and position the new artboard as shown in Figure 89.

(continued)

4. Click to position the new artboard.

The New Artboard button creates a new artboard at the specified document size (in this case, 6" x 8.5")

5. Click the **top-right artboard**, then click the **Delete Artboard icon** 🗑 on the Control panel.

TIP You can also click the small x in the upper-right corner to delete an artboard.

6. Click and drag with the **Artboard tool** ▣ to create a small new artboard, as shown in Figure 90.

(continued)

Figure 90 *"Dragging and dropping" a new artboard with the Artboard tool*

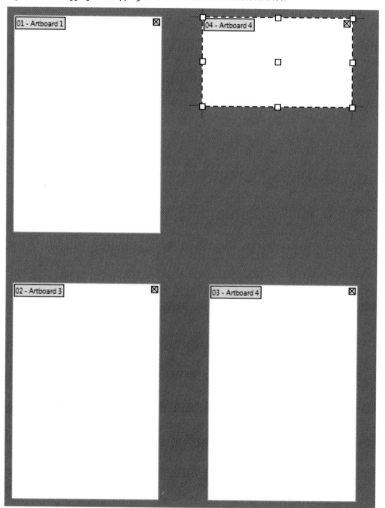

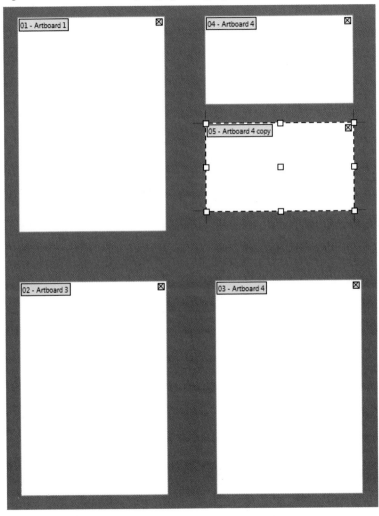

Figure 91 *New artboard created by dragging and dropping*

7. Press and hold **[Alt]** (Win) or **[Option]** (Mac), then drag and drop a copy of the new artboard in the space beneath it, as shown in Figure 91.

8. Click the **bottom-left artboard** to select it, then type **Bookmark** in the Name text box on the Control panel.

9. Name the bottom-right artboard **Buckslip**.

10. Name the top-left artboard **Letterhead**.

11. Name the two new objects **Biz Card Front** and **Biz Card Back** respectively.

You created a new artboard using three different methods: using the New Artboard icon, using the Artboard tool, and dragging and dropping. You named all artboards.

Resize and arrange artboards

1. Click **the artboard named Bookmark** to select it, type **2** in the W (width) panel on the Control panel, then press **[Enter]** (Win) or **[Return]** (Mac)

   As shown in Figure 92, the artboard is resized.

2. Resize the artboard named Buckslip to 4" wide x 6" height.

3. Resize the two business cards to 3.5" x 2."

4. Click the **Letterhead artboard**, click the **Preset menu** in the Control panel, then click **Letter**.

   The artboard is resized to 8.5" x 11"

5. Click and drag **the artboards** to arrange them as shown in Figure 93.

6. Click the **Selection tool** to escape Edit Artboards mode, then save the file.

You resized artboards.

Figure 92 *Resizing the Bookmark layout*

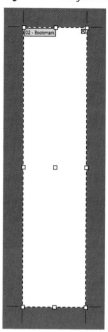

Figure 93 *Arranging the artboard layout*

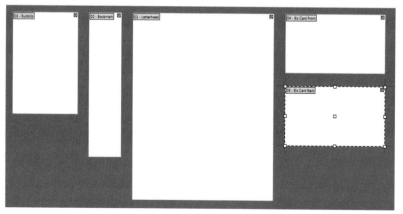

1. Open the file named Winning Logo.ai.
2. Click **Select** on the Application bar, click **All**, click **Edit** on the Application bar, then click **Copy**.
3. Close Winning Logo.ai.
4. In the Winning Business Collateral document, click the **Artboard Navigation menu list arrow** in the lower-left corner, then click **Letterhead**, as shown in Figure 94.

(continued)

Figure 94 *The Artboard Navigation menu*

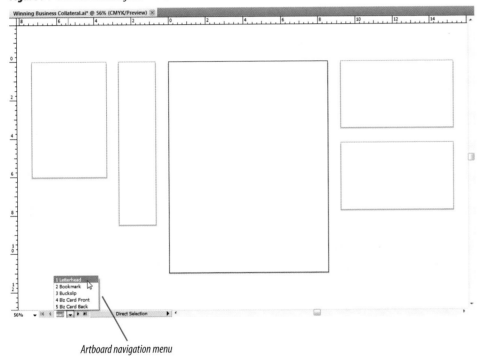

Artboard navigation menu

5. Click **Edit** on the Application bar, click **Paste**, then position the artwork as shown in Figure 95.

6. Click **Edit** on the Application bar, then click **Copy**.

   Even though the artwork is already copied, you need to copy it again so that it is copied from this specific location.

7. Click the **Buckslip artboard** (farthest to the left) to make it the active artboard.

8. Click **Edit** on the Application bar, then click **Paste in Place**.

   The artwork is placed in the same location, relative to the top-left corner of the artboard, on the Buckslip artboard.

   (continued)

Figure 95 *Positioning artwork*

9. Click **Edit** on the Application bar, then click **Paste on All Artboards**.

10. Click **View**, click **Fit All in Window**, then compare your screen to Figure 96.

11. Save and close Winning Business Collateral.ai.

You copied artwork, then pasted it in a specific location on one artboard. You used the Paste in Place command to paste the artwork in the same location on another artboard. You then used the Paste on All Artboards command to paste the artwork on all artboards.

Figure 96 *Artwork pasted on all artboards*

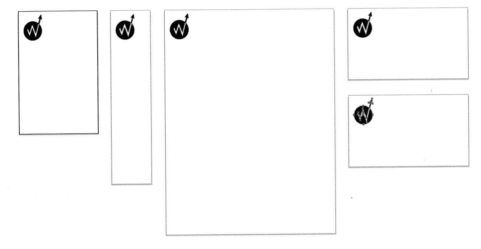

Explore the Illustrator workspace.

1. Launch Adobe Illustrator CS5.
2. Click File on the Application bar, click Open, navigate to the drive and folder where your Chapter 1 Data Files are stored, click AI 1-5.ai, then click Open.
3. Click Window on the Application bar, point to Workspace, then click [Essentials].
4. Click the double-arrows on the Tools panel to see two setups for the Tools panel.
5. Point to the Type tool, then press and hold the mouse button to see the Type on a Path tool.
6. View the hidden tools behind the other tools with small black triangles.
7. Click Edit (Win) or Illustrator (Mac) on the Application bar, point to Preferences, click General, verify that Show Tool Tips is checked, then click OK.
8. Position your mouse pointer over the Direct Selection tool until its tool tip appears.
9. Click the Selection tool, then press the following keys and note which tools are selected with each key: [p], [v], [t], [i], [h], [z] [a].
10. Press [Tab] to temporarily hide all open panels, then press [Tab] again.
11. Click the Color icon in the stack of collapsed panels to the right of the pasteboard to open the Color panel.
12. Click the Collapse panels button at the top of the panel to minimize the panel, then click Color to open the panel again.
13. Drag the Color panel name tab to the left so it is ungrouped.
14. Click the Swatches icon in the stack of collapsed panels to the right of the pasteboard to open the Swatches panel.
15. Drag the Swatches panel name tab to the left so it is ungrouped.
16. Drag the Swatches panel name tab to the blank space next to the Color panel name tab, then release the mouse.
17. Click Window on the Application bar, then click Info.
18. Drag the Info panel name tab to the bottom edge of the Color and Swatches panels group until you see a blue horizontal line appear, then release the mouse to doc the Info panel.
19. Click and drag the dark gray bar at the top of the panel group, found above the Color and Swatches panel name tabs, to move the docked panels.
20. Click the Info panel name tab, then drag it away from the other two panels.
21. Click Window on the Application bar, point to Workspace, then Essentials.
22. Press [z] to access the Zoom tool.
23. Position the Zoom tool over the document window, click twice to enlarge it, press [Alt] (Win) or [option] (Mac), then click twice to reduce the document.
24. Click the Zoom Level list arrow in the lower-left corner of the document window, then click 600%.
25. Note that 600% is now listed in the document tab.
26. Double-click 800% in the Zoom Level text box, type **300**, then press [Enter] (Win) or [return] (Mac).
27. Click the Hand tool on the Tools panel, then click and drag the document window to scroll.
28. Double-click the Zoom tool.
29. Click the Selection tool, point to the center of the document window, then press and hold [Ctrl] [Spacebar] (Win) or [⌘] [Spacebar] (Mac).
30. Click three times, then release [Ctrl][Spacebar] (Win) or [⌘] [Spacebar] (Mac).
31. Press and hold [Spacebar] to access the Hand tool, then scroll around the image.
32. Press and hold [Ctrl][Alt][Spacebar] (Win) or [⌘] [option][Spacebar] (Mac), then click the mouse multiple times to reduce the view to 25%.

View and modify artboard elements.

1. Click View on the Application bar, note the shortcut key on the Fit Page in Window command, then click Fit Page in Window.
2. Click View on the Application bar, then note the Rulers command and its shortcut key.
3. Leave the View menu, then press [Ctrl][R](Win) or ⌘ [R](Mac) several times to hide and show rulers, finishing with rulers showing.
4. Note the units on the rulers.
5. Click Edit (Win) or Illustrator (Mac) on the Application bar, point to Preferences, then click Units.
6. Click the General list arrow to see the available measurement options, then click Picas.
7. Click OK.
8. Reopen the Units preferences dialog box, click the General list arrow, then click Inches.
9. Click OK.
10. Select all the objects on the artboard.
11. Click View on the Application bar, then note the Edges command and its shortcut key.
12. The command is listed as either Hide Edges or Show Edges, depending on your current status.
13. Leave the View menu, then press [Ctrl][H](Win) or ⌘[H](Mac) several times to switch between hiding and showing selection marks, finishing with selection marks showing.
14. Click the View menu, point to Guides, then note the Guides commands and their shortcut keys.
15. Escape the View menu, then press [Ctrl][;](Win) or [Command] [;] (Mac) several times to hide and show guides, finishing with guides showing.
16. Click View on the Application bar, then click Show Grid.
17. Press [Ctrl]["](Win) or ⌘ ["] (Mac) several times to hide and show the grid.
18. Hide guides and the grid.
19. Click View on the Application bar, then note the quick key command for Outline mode.
20. Enter [Ctrl][Y](Win) or [Command][Y](Mac) repeatedly to toggle between Outline and Normal mode, finishing in Preview mode, as shown in Figure 97.
21. Click Edit (Win) or Illustrator (Mac) on the Application bar, point to Preferences, then click User Interface.

Figure 97 *Skills Review, Part 1*

22. Verify that the Open Documents As Tabs check box is checked, then click OK.
23. Save AI 1-5.ai as **Model**.
24. Open AI 1-2.ai, then click the tabs of each document several times to toggle between them, finishing with Model.ai as the active document.
25. Drag the Model.ai tab straight down approximately ½ inch.
26. Position your mouse pointer over the upper-right or bottom-right corner of the document, then click and drag towards the center of the monitor window to reduce the window to approximately half its size.
27. Position your mouse pointer over the title bar of the document, then click and drag to move Model.ai halfway down towards the bottom of your monitor screen. A "floating" document window can be positioned so that part if it is off-screen.
28. Position your mouse pointer over the title bar of Model.ai, click and drag to position it at the top of the window beside the ID1-2.ai tab, then release your mouse when you see a horizontal blue bar.
29. Close ID1-2.ai without saving changes if you are prompted.
30. Close Model.ai without saving changes if you are prompted.

Work with objects and smart guides.

1. Open AI 1-6.ai, then save it as **Object Skills**.
2. Click View on the Application bar, then verify that the Bounding Box command says Show Bounding Box.
3. Click the Selection Tool, then click the yellow square to select it.
4. Click View on the Application bar, then click Show Bounding Box.
5. Click and drag various handles and note how the object is resized.
6. When you are done experimenting, undo all of the moves you made.
   (*Hint*: The Undo command is at the top of the Edit menu.)
7. Click to select the purple circle.
8. Press and hold down [Alt](Win) or [Option](Mac), then start dragging any corner handle.
9. While still dragging, press and hold [Shift].
10. Scale the circle to any size.
11. Undo the move.
12. Select All.

13. Using the skills you learned in this lesson, reduce the size of the objects in proportion so that they are very small on the artboard, then click the artboard to deselect the objects.
14. Click File on the Application bar, click Revert, then click Revert when you are prompted to confirm.
15. Click the View menu, then click Hide Bounding Box.
16. Select the star, then copy it, using the [Ctrl][C] (Win) or ⌘ [C](Mac) shortcut keys.
17. Click Edit on the Application bar, then click Paste to place a copy of the star at the center of the artboard.
18. Undo the paste.
19. Click Edit on the Application bar, then click Paste in Front.
20. Press [I] on your keypad to switch to the Eyedropper tool, then click the yellow square.
21. Press the right arrow key on your keypad ten times.
22. Deselect all, click Edit on the Application bar, then click Paste in Back.
23. Click the Eyedropper tool on the purple circle.
24. Press and hold [Shift], then press the ← on your keypad one time.

25. Press and hold [Ctrl](Win) or [Command](Mac) so that your cursor switches from the temporarily from the Eyedropper tool to the Selection tool, then click the artboard with the Selection tool to deselect all.
26. Click the Selection tool, then select the purple circle.
27. Press and hold [Alt](Win) or [Option](Mac), then drag a copy of the circle to the center of the square. Your screen should resemble Figure 98.
28. Save your work, then close the file.
29. Open AI 1-7.ai, then save it as **Group Skills**.
30. Click Object on the Application bar, then click Show All.
31. Click Object on the Application bar, then click Group.
32. Click the Selection tool, click anywhere on the pasteboard to deselect all, then click the largest blue square.
33. Click the pasteboard to deselect all, click the Direct Selection tool, then click the same square.
34. Select all, click Object on the Application bar, then click Ungroup.
35. Deselect all.
36. Click the Selection tool, select the smallest square, click Object on the Application bar, click Lock, then click Selection.
(*Hint*: The object's handles disappear and it can no longer be selected.)

Figure 98 *Skills Review, Part 2*

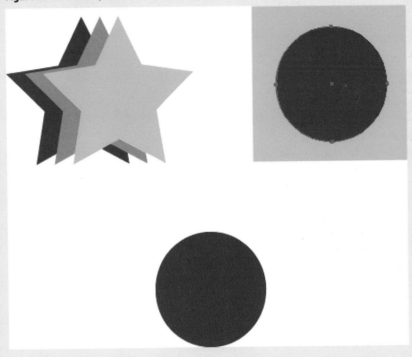

37. Click Object on the Application bar, then click Unlock All.
38. Select the three blue squares, click Object on the Application bar, then click Hide.

39. Click Object on the Application bar, then click Show All.
40. Click View on the Application bar, then verify that Smart Guides is checked.
41. Click the large blue square, then drag it by its center point toward the center of the artboard.

42. Release your mouse when the word CENTER appears.
43. Using the same methodology, align all the squares so that your artboard resembles Figure 99.
44. Save and close the file.

Figure 99 *Skills Review, Part 3*

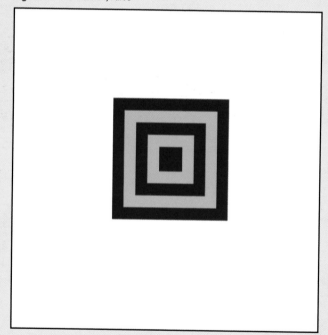

Create basic shapes and apply fill and stroke colors to objects.

1. Create a new document and name it Flag.
2. Make the size of the document 6" × 4".
3. Select Inches for the type of units, 1 for the number of artboards, and CMYK Color for the color mode, then click OK.
4. Click File on the Application bar, click Save As, navigate to the drive and folder where you store your Data Files, then click Save.
5. Create a circle at the center of the artboard.
6. Click the Selection tool.
7. Set the Fill and Stroke buttons on the Tools panel to black and [None] respectively.
8. Create a rectangle that is 3" × 1".
9. Show the Swatches panel if necessary.
10. Fill the rectangle with a light yellow.
11. Click View on the Application bar, verify that Smart Guides are active.
12. Move the rectangle so that its top-left anchor point intersects with the top-left corner of the artboard.
13. Click the top-left anchor point, press and hold [Shift][Alt](Win) or [Shift][option] (Mac), drag straight down until the top-left anchor point touches the bottom-left anchor point (the "intersect" smart guide appears), then release the mouse.
14. Click Object on the Application bar, point to Transform, then click Transform Again.
15. Repeat Step 14.
16. Change the fill color of the second and fourth rectangles to a darker yellow.
17. Save your work.
18. Select the four rectangles.
19. Double-click the Reflect tool, click the Horizontal option button, then click Copy. The four rectangles are copied on top of the original rectangles.
20. Move the four new rectangles to the right so that they align with the right side of the artboard.
21. Click the Rectangle tool, click the artboard, then create a square that is .75" x .75".
22. Apply a 1-point black stroke and no fill to the square.
23. Click the Selection tool, click the edge of the square, then position it at the center of the artboard.
24. Use the Rotate dialog box to create a copy of the square rotated at 10°.
25. Apply the Transform Again command seven times.
26. Save your work.

Make direct selections.

1. Shift-click to select the nine black squares.
2. Click Object on the Application bar, then click Group.
3. Scale the group of squares 200%.
4. Create a 3.75" × 3.75" circle, fill it with orange, add a 1-point black stroke, then position it at the center of the artboard.
5. Cut the circle from the artboard, click the group of black squares, click Edit on the Application bar, then click Paste in Back.
6. Adjust the location of the circle as needed.
7. Click Object on the Application bar, point to Path, then click Add Anchor Points.
8. Deselect the circle by clicking anywhere on the artboard.
9. Click the Direct Selection tool, then click the edge of the circle.
10. One at a time, move each of the four new anchor points to the center of the circle.
11. Switch to the Selection tool, then select the orange-filled shape.
12. Double-click the Rotate tool, type 22 in the Angle text box, then click Copy.
13. Apply the Transform Again command two times.
14. Save your work, then compare your illustration to Figure 100.
15. Close the Flag document.

Figure 100 *Skills Review, Part 4*

Work with multiple artboards.

1. Open AI 1-8. ai, then save it as **Artboard Skills**.
2. Click the Artboard tool.
3. Click the New Artboard icon on the Control panel.
4. Float your cursor over the artboard, then position the new artboard to the right of the original.
5. Scroll to the right of the newest artboard.
6. Click and drag with the Artboard tool to create a new artboard of any size to the right of the new artboard.
7. Click the original artboard and name it **Stationery**.
8. Type 8 in the W (width) text box on the Control panel, type 10 in the H (height) text box, then press [Enter] (Win) or [Return] (Mac).
9. Name the second artboard **Envelope**, then resize it to 9" wide x 3" height.
10. Name the third artboard **Business Card**, then resize it to 3.5" x 2"
11. Click the View menu, then click Fit All in Window.
12. Click and drag the artboards to arrange them as shown in Figure 101.
13. Save then close the file.

Figure 101 *Completed Skills Review*

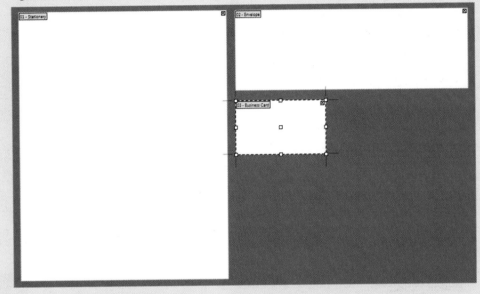

The lady who owns the breakfast shop that you frequent knows that you are a designer and asks for your help. Her nephew has designed a sign for her store window, but she confides in you that she doesn't like it. She thinks that it's boring and "flat." She wants to redesign the sign with something that is "original" and feels more like a starburst.

1. Open AI 1-9.ai, then save it as **Window Sign**.
2. Click the Direct Selection tool, then click the edge of the star.
3. Move two of the outer anchor points of the star farther from its center.
4. Move four of the inner points toward the center.
5. Select the entire star.
6. Reflect a copy of the star across the horizontal axis.
7. Fill the new star with an orange swatch and reposition it to your liking.
8. Group the two stars.
9. Copy the group, then paste in back.
10. Fill the copies with black.
11. Using your arrow keys, move the black copies five points to the right and five points down.
12. Select only the orange star using the Direct Selection tool.
13. Copy the orange star, then paste in back.
14. Fill the new copy with black.
15. Rotate the black copy 8°.
16. Apply a yellow fill to the orange star, then apply a 1-point black stroke to both yellow stars.
17. Save your work, then compare your illustration to Figure 102.
18. Close Window Sign.

Figure 102 *Completed Project Builder 1*

Getting to Know Illustrator

Iris Vision Labs has contracted with your design firm to bid on a design for their logo. Researching the company, you learn that they are a biotech firm whose mission is to develop cures for genetic blindness and vision problems. You decide to build your design around the idea of an iris.

1. Create a new document that is 6" × 6".
2. Save the document as **Iris Vision Design**.
3. Create an ellipse that is 1" wide × 4" in height, and position it at the center of the artboard.
4. Fill the ellipse with [None], and add a 1-point blue stroke.
5. Create a copy of the ellipse rotated at 15°.
6. Apply the Transform Again command 10 times.
7. Select all and group the ellipses.
8. Create a copy of the group rotated at 5°.
9. Apply a red stroke to the new group.
10. Transform again.
11. Apply a bright blue stroke to the new group.
12. Select all.
13. Rotate a copy of the ellipses 2.5°.
14. Create a circle that is 2" × 2".
15. Fill the circle with a shade of gray.
16. Remove the stroke from the circle.
17. Position the gray-filled circle in the center of the ellipses.
18. Cut the circle.
19. Select all.
20. Paste in back.
21. Save your work, then compare your illustration to Figure 103.
22. Close Iris Vision Design.

Figure 103 *Completed Project Builder 2*

The owner of Emerald Design Studios has hired you to design an original logo for her new company. She's a beginner with Illustrator, but she's created a simple illustration of what she has in mind. She tells you to create something "more sophisticated." The only other information that she offers about her company is that they plan to specialize in precise, geometric design.

1. Open AI 1-10.ai, then save it as **Emerald Logo**.
2. Select all four diamonds and group them.
3. Select the group of diamonds on the artboard, then create a 75% copy.
4. Use the Transform Again command five times.
5. Use smart guides or Outline mode to help you identify each of the seven groups.
6. Rotate one of the groups 75°.
7. Select two other groups of your choice and repeat the last transformation, using the Transform Again command.
8. Apply a dark green stroke to all groups. Figure 104 shows one possible result of multiple transformations. Your illustration may differ.
9. Save your work, then close Emerald Logo.

Figure 104 *Completed Design Project*

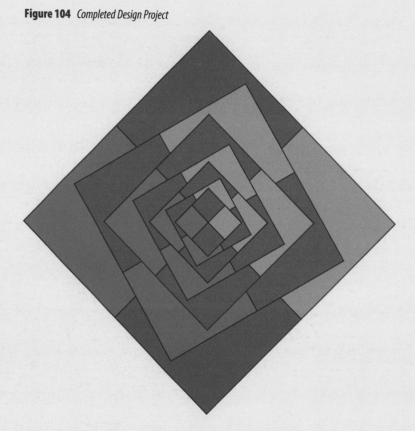

Getting to Know Illustrator

You attend a design school, and you're part of a team that is responsible for the artwork placed throughout the common areas of the school. One of the most admired professors brings you a file that he created in Illustrator, admitting that he's a beginner. You open the file and notice that the file is poorly built—everything is misaligned and uneven. After consulting with the professor, you decide that the file needs to be rebuilt from scratch.

1. Open AI 1-11.ai, then save it as **Rings**.
2. Identify the areas of the file that are misaligned and poorly constructed.
3. Pull apart the file, object by object, to see how the effect was achieved.
4. Create a "game plan" for reproducing the artwork with precision. Where's the best place to start? What's the best methodology for recreating the professor's design?
5. Work to rebuild the file, using precise methods.
6. Save your work, then compare your illustration to Figure 105.
7. Close the Rings document.

Figure 105 *Sample Portfolio Project*

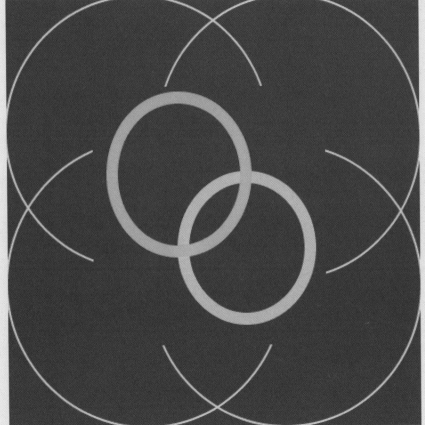

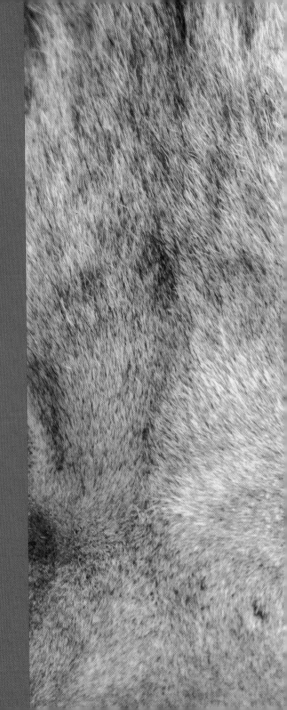

CHAPTER **2** CREATING TEXT
AND GRADIENTS

1. Create point text
2. Flow text into an object
3. Position text on a path
4. Create colors and gradients
5. Apply colors and gradients to text
6. Adjust a gradient and create a drop shadow

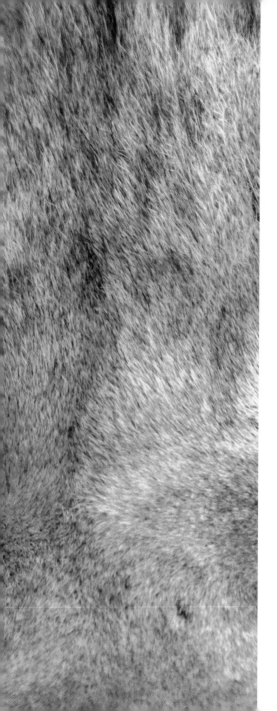

2

CREATING TEXT
AND GRADIENTS

Working with Text

When it comes to creating compelling and dramatic display text, no other software package offers the graphic sophistication that you'll find with Adobe Illustrator. You can quickly change fonts, font size, leading, and other text attributes with the Character panel. You can make tracking and kerning measurements with a level of precision that would satisfy even the most meticulous typographer. For the designer, Illustrator is the preeminent choice for typography. Powerful type tools offer the ability to fill objects with text, position text on curved or straight lines, and set type vertically, one letter on top of the next. Once the text is positioned, the Create Outlines command changes the fonts to vector graphics that you can manipulate as you would any other object. For example, you can apply a gradient fill to letter outlines for stunning effects.

Creating and Applying Gradient Fills

A **gradient** is a graduated blend between two or more colors used to fill an object or multiple objects. Illustrator's sophistication for creating gradients and its ease of use for applying them to objects are a dream come true for today's designers. You can create linear or radial gradients between multiple colors, then control the way they fill an object. Moreover, a single gradient can be used to fill multiple objects simultaneously! The unique gradient fills that you create can be saved with descriptive names, then imported into other Illustrator documents to be used again.

TOOLS YOU'LL USE

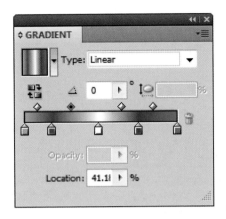

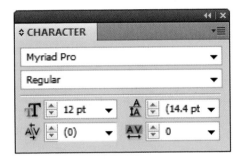

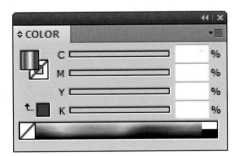

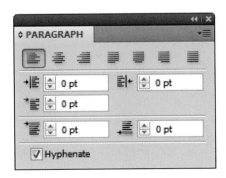

Create
POINT TEXT

What You'll Do

BERRY

 In this lesson, you will use the Type tool to create the word BERRY as display text. You will use the Character panel to format the text and perfect its appearance. You will also create a vertical version of the text.

Creating Text

You can create text anywhere on the artboard simply by selecting the Type tool, clicking the artboard, then typing. You can enter text horizontally or vertically. The ability to type vertically is rather unusual; most text-based applications don't offer this option.

Text generated by the Type tool is positioned on a path called the **baseline**. You can select text by clicking anywhere on the text or by clicking on the baseline, depending on how your Type preferences are set.

Formatting Text

The Character and Paragraph panels neatly contain all of the classic commands for formatting text. Use the Character panel to modify text attributes such as font and type size, tracking, and kerning. You can adjust the **leading**, which is the vertical space between baselines, or apply a horizontal or vertical scale, which compresses or expands selected type as shown in Figure 1. The Paragraph panel applies itself to more

global concerns, such as text alignment, paragraph indents, and vertical spaces between paragraphs.

Tracking and kerning are essential, but often overlooked, typographic operations. **Tracking** inserts uniform spaces between characters to affect the width of selected words or entire blocks of text. **Kerning** is used to affect the space between any two characters and is particularly useful for improving the appearance of headlines and other display text. Positive tracking or kerning values move characters farther apart; negative values move them closer together.

Illustrator can track and kern type down to 1/1000 of a standard em space. The width of an em space is dependent on the current type size. In a 1-point font, the em space is 1 point. In a 10-point font, the em space is 10 points. With kerning units that are 1/1000 of an em, Illustrator can manipulate a 10-point font at increments of 1/100 of 1 point! Figure 2 shows examples of kerning and tracking values.

Adjusting and Applying Hyphenation

Illustrator has a Preferences panel dedicated to hyphenation. Click Edit (Win) or Illustrator (Mac) on the Application bar, point to Preferences, then click Hyphenation. Hyphenation in Illustrator is applied automatically based on the language dictionary that is in use. You can turn automatic hyphenation on and off or change the hyphenation default settings in the Hyphenation dialog box. To access the Hyphenation dialog box, click the Paragraph panel options button, then click Hyphenation. To turn hyphenation off, remove the check mark in the Hyphenation check box.

Hiding Objects While Working with Text

Two factors that make selecting text and other objects difficult are the number and proximity of objects in the document. Hiding objects is a simple way to avoid this problem, just don't forget they are there—they won't print if they are hidden.

The Hide Selection command is under the Object menu, as is the Show All command, which reveals all hidden objects. When hidden objects are revealed, they are all selected; which you can use to your advantage. Simply press [Shift] as you click to deselect the object with which you want to work, then hide the remaining objects.

Figure 1 *Examples of text formatting*

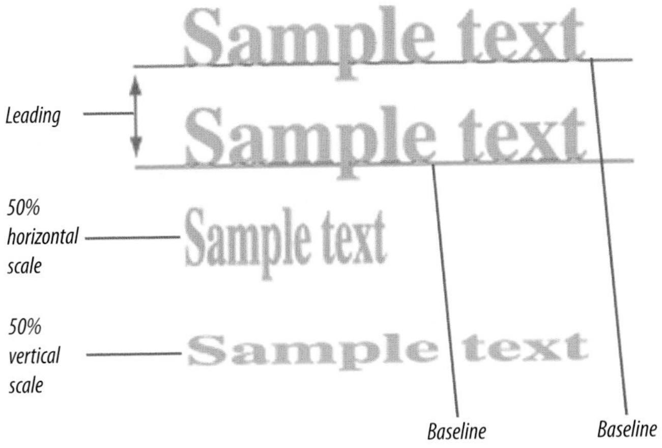

Sample text
Sample text
Sample text
Sample text
Leading
50% horizontal scale
50% vertical scale
Baseline
Baseline

Figure 2 *Examples of kerning and tracking*

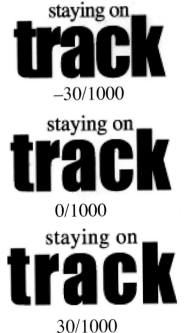

kern
–30/1000
kern
0/1000
kern
30/1000
staying on
track
–30/1000
staying on
track
0/1000
staying on
track
30/1000

Create text

1. Open AI 2-1.ai, then save it as **Berry Symposium**.
2. Click **View** on the Application bar, then click **Hide Bounding Box** if the Bounding Box is showing.

   If the bounding box is already hidden, you won't see the Hide Bounding Box command.
3. Click the **Type tool** T, then click **anywhere on the artboard**.
4. Type **BERRY** using all capital letters.

TIP By default, new text is generated with a black fill and no stroke. Text you create this way—by clicking the artboard—is called Point Text.

5. Click the **Selection tool** , then drag the **text** to the center of the artboard.

TIP Verify that Smart Guides are not activated.

6. Click **Window** on the Application bar, point to **Type**, then click **Character** to show the Character panel.
7. Click the **Character panel options button** , then click **Show Options** to view the entire panel as shown in Figure 3.

You used the Type tool to create the word BERRY, showed the Character panel, then expanded the view of the Character panel.

Figure 3 *Character panel*

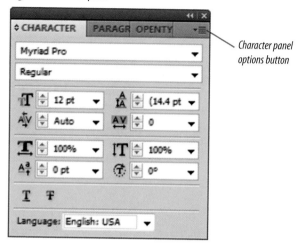

Character panel options button

Tracking and Kerning

Typography, the art of designing letterforms, has a long and rich history that extends back to the Middle Ages. With the advent of desktop publishing in the mid-1980s, many conventional typographers and typesetters declared "the death of typography." They claimed that unskilled computer users would be careless with type, and that computers would reduce typography to ugly, bitmap fonts. Cooler minds have since prevailed. The personal computer and software, such as Adobe Illustrator, have made vast libraries of typefaces available as never before. Imagine the days when the typewriter ruled with its single typeface and two point sizes as the standard for literally millions of documents, and you get a sense of the typographic revolution that has occurred in the last 20 years.

Many designers are so eager to tackle the "artwork" that they often overlook the type design in an illustration. Tracking and kerning, which are the manipulation of space between words and letters, are essential elements to good type design and are often woefully ignored.

Illustrator's precise tracking and kerning abilities are of no use if they are ignored. One good way of maintaining awareness of your tracking and kerning duties is to take note of others' oversights. Make it a point to notice tracking and kerning, or the lack thereof, when you look at magazines, posters, and especially billboards. You'll be amazed at what you'll see.

Creating Text and Gradients

Figure 4 *Character panel*

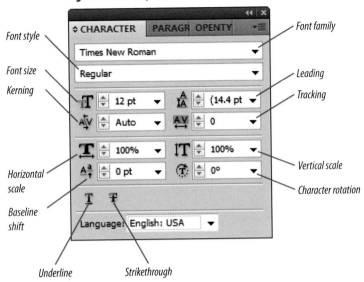

Font style

Font size

Kerning

Horizontal scale

Baseline shift

Font family

Leading

Tracking

Vertical scale

Character rotation

Underline

Strikethrough

Format text

1. Click the **Font family** (Win) or **Font menu** (Mac) **list arrow**, then click **Times New Roman**, or a similar font, as shown in Figure 4.

2. Click the **Font size text box**, type **142**, then press **[Enter]** (Win) or **[return]** (Mac).

3. Click the **Horizontal Scale text box**, type **90**, then press **[Enter]** (Win) or **[return]** (Mac).

4. Deselect all.

5. Compare your text to Figure 5.

You used the Character panel to modify the font, font size, and horizontal scaling of the word BERRY.

Figure 5 *Formatted text*

BERRY

Track and kern text

1. Select the text if it is not already.

2. Using the Character panel, click the **Tracking text box**, then type **-30**.

   TIP Click the Character panel options button, then click Show Options if you do not see the Tracking text box.

3. Click the **Type tool** T., then click the cursor between the B and the E.

4. Using the Character panel, click the **up and down arrows** in the Kerning text box to experiment with higher and lower kerning values, then change the kerning value to -40.

5. Using Figure 6 as a guide, change the kerning to -20, 0, and -120 between the next three letter pairs.

6. Click the **Selection tool** , click the **Paragraph panel name tab**, then click the **Align center button** , as shown in Figure 7.

   When text is center-aligned, its anchor point doubles as its center point, which is handy for aligning it with other objects.

   TIP If you do not see the Paragraph panel, click Window on the Application bar, point to Type, then click Paragraph.

7. Click **Object** on the Application bar, point to **Hide**, then click **Selection**.

You used the Character panel to change the tracking of the word BERRY, then you entered different kerning values to affect the spacing between the four letter pairs. You center-aligned the text, then hid the text.

Figure 6 *Kerning and tracking applied to text*

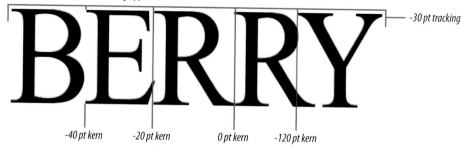

-30 pt tracking

-40 pt kern   -20 pt kern   0 pt kern   -120 pt kern

Figure 7 *Paragraph panel*

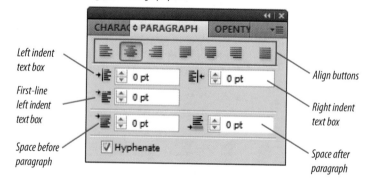

Left indent text box

First-line left indent text box

Space before paragraph

Align buttons

Right indent text box

Space after paragraph

Figure 8 *Vertical text*

B
E
R
R
Y

Using the Glyphs Panel

The Glyphs panel contains various type characters that aren't necessarily available on your keyboard. Examples of these characters include trademarks, copyright marks, accented letters, and numbers expressed as fractions. Click Window on the Application bar, point to Type, then click Glyphs to display the Glyphs panel. To access a glyph, click the Type tool, click the artboard as you would to type any character, then double-click the glyph on the Glyph panel that you wish to use.

Create vertical type

1. Click the **Vertical Type tool** |T., then click **anywhere on the artboard**.

   TIP The Vertical Type tool is hidden beneath the Type tool.

2. Type the word **BERRY** using all capital letters.

   TIP The Type tools retain the formatting attributes that were previously chosen.

3. Click the **Selection tool** ▶, select the text, then move it to the center of the artboard.

   TIP When any tool other than the Selection tool is selected on the Tools panel you can press [Ctrl] (Win) or ⌘ (Mac) to switch to the Selection tool. When you release [Ctrl] (Win) or ⌘ (Mac), the last chosen tool will be active again.

4. Using the Character panel, change the font size to 84 pt.

5. Change the Tracking value to -160.

6. Verify that both the Horizontal and Vertical Scales are set to 100%, then deselect the text.

   Your screen should resemble Figure 8.

7. Delete the vertical text, then save your work.

You used the Vertical Type tool to create a vertical alternative to the first word you typed. You adjusted the tracking and kerning to better suit a vertical orientation, then deleted the text.

Flow Text into
AN OBJECT

What You'll Do

```
              rasp
            straw blue
          cran straw tea
        straw checker cran
     blue boysen black tea  straw
   blue boysen checker cran tea rasp
     boysen blue black straw tea boysen
checker cran rasp boysen blue black rasp straw
blue black straw tea boysen checker cran rasp straw
   blue tea black rasp straw blue black straw tea
    boysen checker cran rasp straw blue black
     rasp straw blue cran straw tea straw
        checker cran  straw boysen
          black tea  straw blue
            boysen checker
              cran tea
               rasp
```

In this lesson, you will use the Area Type tool to flow text into an object.

Filling an Object with Text

Using the Area Type tool, you can flow text into any shape you can create, from circles to birds to bumblebees! Text in an object can be formatted as usual. You can change such attributes as fonts, font size, and alignment, and the text will reflow in the object as you format it. Text that you create inside an object is called **area text**.

Figure 9 shows an example of an object filled with text. Note the blue background in the figure. When you first flow text into an

Figure 9 *An object filled with text*

```
             To
           be, or
         not to be.
        That is the
      question. Whether
    'tis nobler in the mind to suffer
  the slings and arrows of outrageous fortune.
  or to take arms against a sea of troubles — and by
     opposing — end them. To die. To sleep.
        To sleep. Perchance
           to dream?
          Ay, there's
           the rub.
```

Creating Text and Gradients

object using the Area Type tool, the object loses any fill or stroke color applied to it. However, you can add different colors to the object and the text. When you select the object with the Selection tool, any fill or stroke you choose will be applied to the text. When you select the object with the Direct Selection tool, the fill or stroke will be applied to the object.

You can also select text flowed into an object with the Type tool. You can even use the Direct Selection tool to distort the shape, and the text will reflow within the modified shape

You'll often find that centering text in an object is the best visual solution. Figure 10 shows text aligned left and flowed into an

odd-shaped object. In Figure 11, the same text is centered and fills the object in a way that is more visually pleasing.

QUICK TIP

You can underline text and strike through text using the Underline and Strikethrough buttons at the bottom of the Character panel.

Figure 10 *Text aligned left*

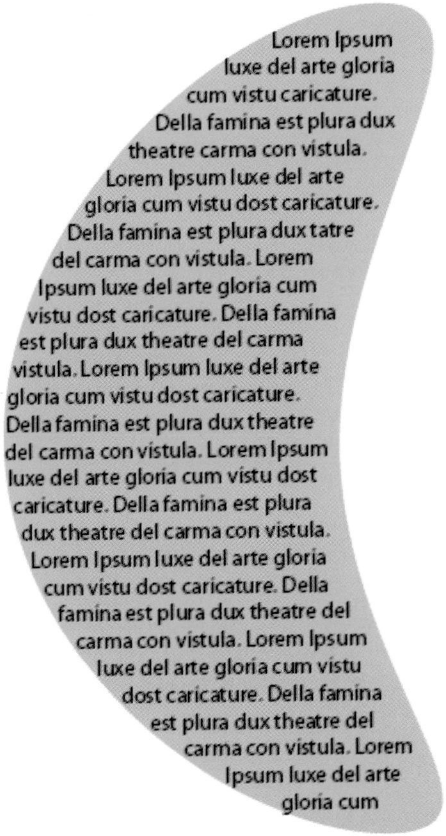

Lorem Ipsum luxe del arte gloria cum vistu caricature. Della famina est plura dux theatre carma con vistula. Lorem Ipsum luxe del arte gloria cum vistu dost caricature. Della famina est plura dux tatre del carma con vistula. Lorem Ipsum luxe del arte gloria cum vistu dost caricature. Della famina est plura dux theatre del carma vistula. Lorem Ipsum luxe del arte gloria cum vistu dost caricature. Della famina est plura dux theatre del carma con vistula. Lorem Ipsum luxe del arte gloria cum vistu dost caricature. Della famina est plura dux theatre del carma con vistula. Lorem Ipsum luxe del arte gloria cum vistu dost caricature. Della famina est plura dux theatre del carma con vistula. Lorem Ipsum luxe del arte gloria cum vistu dost caricature. Della famina est plura dux theatre del carma con vistula. Lorem Ipsum luxe del arte gloria cum

Figure 11 *Text centered in the objects*

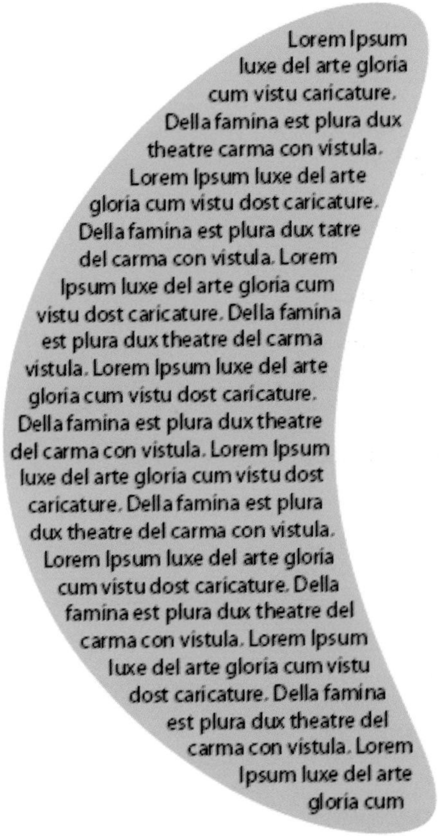

Lorem Ipsum luxe del arte gloria cum vistu caricature. Della famina est plura dux theatre carma con vistula. Lorem Ipsum luxe del arte gloria cum vistu dost caricature. Della famina est plura dux tatre del carma con vistula. Lorem Ipsum luxe del arte gloria cum vistu dost caricature. Della famina est plura dux theatre del carma vistula. Lorem Ipsum luxe del arte gloria cum vistu dost caricature. Della famina est plura dux theatre del carma con vistula. Lorem Ipsum luxe del arte gloria cum vistu dost caricature. Della famina est plura dux theatre del carma con vistula. Lorem Ipsum luxe del arte gloria cum vistu dost caricature. Della famina est plura dux theatre del carma con vistula. Lorem Ipsum luxe del arte gloria cum vistu dost caricature. Della famina est plura dux theatre del carma con vistula. Lorem Ipsum luxe del arte gloria cum

Fill an object with text

1. Open AI 2-2.ai, then save it as **Diamond Text**.
2. Select the yellow square, double-click the **Rotate tool** ⟳, type **45** in the Angle text box, then click **OK**.
3. Click the **Area Type tool** ⟦T⟧, then click the **block of text**.

TIP The Area Type tool is hidden beneath the current type tool.

4. Click **Select** on the Application bar, then click **All**.

TIP When you click a Type tool cursor on text and apply the Select All command, all the text is selected, but only the text. Neither the object that contains the text, nor any other text or objects on the page are selected.

5. Copy the text.
6. Click the **Selection tool** ▶, then select the yellow square.

TIP When you are working with a Type tool, you can press [Ctrl] (Win) or ⌘ (Mac) to access the Selection tool temporarily and remain in Area Type tool mode.

7. Click the **Area Type tool** ⟦T⟧ if it is not active, then click the **edge of the yellow square**.

   A flashing cursor appears and the square loses its fill color, as shown in Figure 12.

8. Paste the copied text into the square.

   Your work should resemble Figure 13.

You rotated the yellow square, then filled it with text by first copying text from another object, then clicking the edge of the square with the Area Type tool before you pasted the text into the square.

Figure 12 *Applying the Area Type tool*

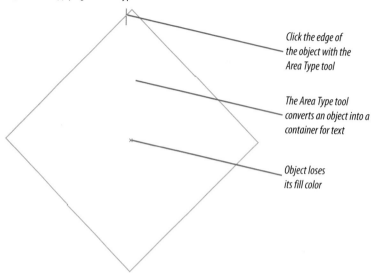

Click the edge of the object with the Area Type tool

The Area Type tool converts an object into a container for text

Object loses its fill color

Figure 13 *Text pasted into an object*

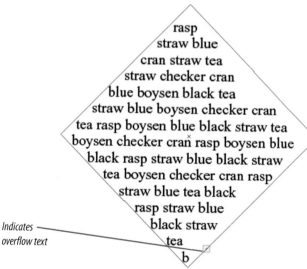

Indicates overflow text

Figure 14 *Centered text in an object*

```
                    rasp
                 straw blue
               cran straw tea
           straw checker cran  blue
         boysen black tea  straw blue
       boysen checker cran tea rasp boysen
     blue black straw tea boysen checker cran
   rasp boysen blue black rasp straw blue black
straw tea boysen checker cran rasp straw blue tea black
   rasp straw blue black straw tea boysen checker
     cran rasp straw blue black rasp straw blue
       cran straw tea straw checker cran
         straw boysen black tea  straw
           blue boysen checker cran
              tea rasp boysen blue
                 black straw
                    tea
```

Using Character and Paragraph Styles

A style is a group of formatting attributes, such as font, font size, color, and tracking, that you apply to text. You use the Character Styles panel to create and apply styles for individual words or characters, such as a footnote. You use the Paragraph Styles panel to apply a style to a paragraph. Paragraph styles include formatting options such as indents and drop caps. Using styles saves you time and keeps your work consistent. If you create styles for an Illustrator document, the styles are saved with the document and are available to be loaded for use in other documents.

Format text in an object

1. Triple-click the **text in the object** with the Area Type tool to select all of the text in the rotated square.
2. Click the **Align center button** ≣ on the Paragraph panel.

TIP When filling an object other than a square or a rectangle with text, centering the text is often the best solution.

3. In the **Character panel**, change the font size to 9 pt.
4. Set the Leading to **11**, deselect the text, then compare your work to Figure 14.
It's OK if the line breaks in your document differ from the text in the figure.
5. Click the **Selection tool** ▸ , then click the **diamond-shaped text**.
Both the text and the object that contains the text are selected.
6. Copy the text object.
Both the text and the object are copied.
7. Click **Window** on the Application bar, then return to the **Berry Symposium document tab**.

TIP All open Illustrator documents are listed at the bottom of the Window menu.

8. Paste the text object into the Berry Symposium document.
9. Show guides, then align the center point of the text object with the intersection of the guides.

TIP Use the arrow keys to nudge the selection right, left, up, or down.

10. Click **Object** on the Application bar, point to **Lock**, then click **Selection**.
11. Close the Diamond text document, then save the Berry Symposium document.

You used the Paragraph and Character panels to format text in the object. You used the Selection tool to select the text object, then you copied and pasted it into the Berry Symposium document.

Position Text
ON A PATH

What You'll Do

three rivers
symposium

rasp
straw blue
cran straw tea
straw checker cran
blue boysen black tea straw
blue boysen checker cran tea rasp
boysen blue black straw tea boysen
checker cran rasp boysen blue black rasp straw
blue black straw tea boysen checker cran rasp straw
blue tea black rasp straw blue black straw tea
boysen checker cran rasp straw blue black
rasp straw blue cran straw tea straw
checker cran straw boysen
black tea straw blue
boysen checker
cran tea
rasp

In this lesson, you will explore the many options for positioning text on a path.

Using the Path Type Tools

Using the Type on a Path tool or the Vertical Type on a Path tool, you can type along a straight or curved path. This is the most compelling of Illustrator's text effects, and it opens up a world of possibilities for the designer and typographer.

You can move text along a path to position it where you want. You can "flip" the text to make it run in the opposite direction, on the opposite side of the path. You can also change the baseline shift to modify the distance of the text's baseline in relation to the path. A positive value "floats" the text above the path, and a negative value moves the text below the path. You can modify text on a path in the same way you would modify any other text element. Figure 15 shows an example of text on a path, whereas Figure 16 shows an example of text flipped across a path.

Customizing Language Dictionaries

Illustrator comes complete with Proximity language dictionaries, which are used for spelling and hyphenation. Each dictionary contains information for standard syllable breaks for literally hundreds of thousands of words. You can assign a language to an entire document or apply a language to selected text. To apply a language to all text Choose Edit (Win) or Illustrator (Mac) on the Application bar, point to Preferences, then click Hyphenation. Select a dictionary from the Default Language list arrow, then click OK. To assign a language to selected text, first select the text. In the Character panel, choose the appropriate dictionary from the Language menu. You may need to expand the Character panel to see the Language menu.

Figure 15 *Text on a path*

Figure 16 *Text flipped across a path*

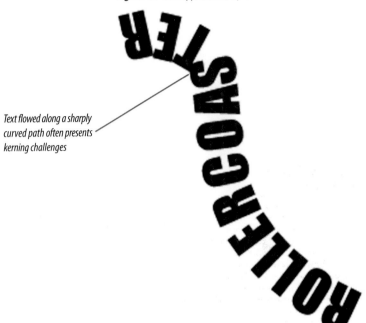

Text flowed along a sharply curved path often presents kerning challenges

---

Locating and Replacing Fonts Inside a Document

You can replace a given font in a document with another font using the Find Font utility. Click Type on the Application bar, then click Find Font. All the fonts used in the document are listed. Select the name of the font you want to find; the first occurrence of the font is highlighted in the document window. Select a replacement font from the Replace with Font From list arrow. You can click Change to change just one occurrence of the selected font, or click Change All to change all occurrences of the selected font. Note that when you replace a font using the Find Font command, all other type attributes applied to the original remain applied to the replacement font.

Flow text on a path

1. Click the **Ellipse tool** 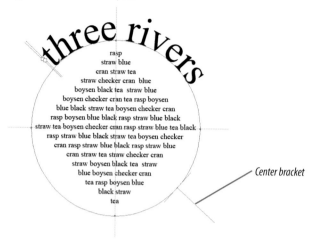, press **[Alt]** (Win) or **[option]** (Mac), then click **anywhere near the center of the artboard**.

   Pressing [Alt] (Win) or [option] (Mac) while you click a shape tool on the artboard ensures that the center of the shape will be drawn from the point that you clicked.

2. Enter **2.9** in for the width and the height of the circle in the Ellipse dialog box, then click **OK**.

3. Click the **Type on a Path tool**, then click **the edge of the circle at approximately 10 o'clock**.

   A flashing cursor appears, and the circle loses its fill color.

4. Type **three rivers** in lowercase letters.

5. Click the **Selection tool** to select the text by its baseline, then change the font to Times New Roman and the font size to 47 pt.

6. Compare your screen to Figure 17.

   Note the center bracket in Figure 17. Dragging the center bracket is the easiest way to move text along a path.

TIP Text flowed on a circle will often require kerning, especially when it is set at a large point size.

You created a 2.9" circle from its center, then typed along the circle's path using the Type on a Path tool. You changed the font and font size using the Character panel.

Move text along a path

1. Click **View** on the Application bar, point to **Guides**, then click **Hide Guides**.

   (continued)

Figure 17 *Text on a circular path*

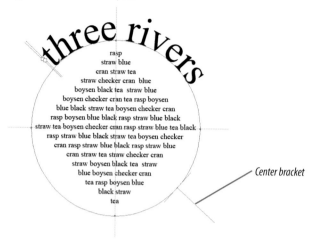

Center bracket

Figure 18 *Moving text on a path*

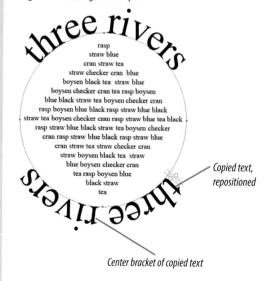

Copied text, repositioned

Center bracket of copied text

Figure 19 *Flipping text across a path*

Center bracket of copied text

Figure 20 *Modifying a baseline shift*

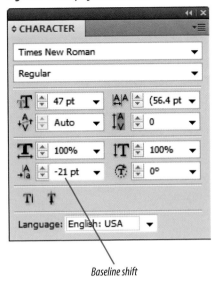

Baseline shift

Figure 21 *Flipped text positioned below the path*

2. Using the Selection tool ![cursor], drag the **center bracket** until the text is centered at the top of the circle.

   Moving text along a path is a touch-sensitive procedure. You will find that it's easy to "flip" the text over the baseline, and it will run inside the circle. With a little experience, you'll find that you're able to position text on a line as you desire.

3. Click **Edit** on the Application bar, click **Copy**, click **Edit** on the Application bar, then click **Paste in Front**.

4. Drag the **center bracket** of the copied text clockwise to move the copied text to the position shown in Figure 18.

   Your center bracket might be positioned differently on the circle and in relation to the text.

5. Drag the **center bracket** of the copied text toward the center of the circle to flip the text across the path, as shown in Figure 19, then drag the text inside the circle to position it if necessary, as shown in Figure 19.

6. Click the **Baseline shift text box** on the Character panel, type **-21**, as shown in Figure 20, then press **[Enter]** (Win) or **[return]** (Mac).

7. Click the **Type tool** ![T], select **three rivers** at the bottom of the circle, then type **symposium**.

8. Track and kern the word symposium as you think necessary.

9. Click the **Selection tool** ![cursor], then drag the **center bracket** to center the text at the bottom of the circle if it is not already centered.

10. Lock the two text objects, save your work, then compare your image to Figure 21.

You moved and copied text along a path, flipped its direction, changed the baseline shift, then locked both text objects.

Create Colors
AND GRADIENTS

What You'll Do

In this lesson, you will use the Color panel, Gradient panel, and Swatches panel to create, name, and save colors and gradients.

Using the Gradient Panel

A **gradient** is a graduated blend between colors. The Gradient panel is the command center for creating and adjusting gradients. In the panel you will see a slider that represents the gradient you are creating or using. The slider has at least two colors. The leftmost color is the starting color, and the rightmost color is the ending color.

The colors used in a gradient are represented on the Gradient panel by small house-shaped icons called **stops**. The Gradient panel shown in Figure 22 shows a two-color gradient.

The point at which two colors meet in equal measure is called the **midpoint** of the gradient. The midpoint is represented by the diamond above the slider. The midpoint does not necessarily need to be positioned evenly between the starting and ending colors. You can change the appearance of a gradient by moving the midpoint.

The Swatches panel contains standard gradients that come with the software. To create your own original gradients, start by clicking an object filled with an existing gradient. You can then modify that existing gradient on the Gradient panel. You can change either or both the beginning and ending colors. You can change the location of the midpoint. You can also add additional colors into the gradient or remove existing colors.

> **QUICK TIP**
>
> As you work to perfect a gradient, you can see how your changes will affect the gradient by filling an object with the gradient you are modifying. As you make changes on the Gradient panel, the changes will be reflected in the object.

You can define a gradient as linear or radial. A linear gradient can be positioned left to right, up and down, or on any angle. You can change the angle of the gradient by entering a new value in the Angle text box on the Gradient panel.

Think of a radial gradient as a series of concentric circles. With a radial gradient, the starting color appears at the center of the gradient. The blend radiates out to the ending color. By definition, a radial gradient has no angle ascribed to it.

Using the Color Panel

The Color panel, shown in Figure 23, is where you move sliders to mix new colors for fills, strokes, and gradients. You can also use the panel to adjust the color in a filled object. The panel has five color modes: CMYK, RGB, Grayscale, HSB, and Web Safe RGB. The panel will default to CMYK or RGB, depending on the color mode you choose when creating a new document. Grayscale mode allows you to create shades of gray in percentages of black. If you select a filled object and choose the HSB mode, you can adjust its basic color (hue), the intensity of the color (saturation), and the range of the color from light to dark (brightness). If you are designing illustrations for the Internet, you might consider using Web Safe RGB mode to create colors that are in accordance with colors defined in HTML.

Rather than use the sliders, you can also type values directly into the text boxes. For example, in CMYK mode, a standard red color is composed of 100% Magenta and 100% Yellow. The notation for this callout would be 100M/100Y. Note that you don't list the zero values for Cyan (C) and Black (K)—you don't list the color as 0C/100M/100Y/0K. In RGB mode (0-255), a standard orange color would be noted as 255R/128G.

Adding Colors and Gradients to the Swatches Panel

Once you have defined a color or a gradient to your liking, it's a smart idea to save it by dragging it into the Swatches panel. Once a color or gradient is moved into the Swatches panel, you can name it by double-clicking it, then typing a name in the Swatch Options dialog box. You cannot modify it, however. For example, if you click a saved gradient and adjust it on the Gradient panel, you can apply the new gradient to an object, but the original gradient on the Swatches panel remains unaffected. You can save the new gradient to the Swatches panel for future use.

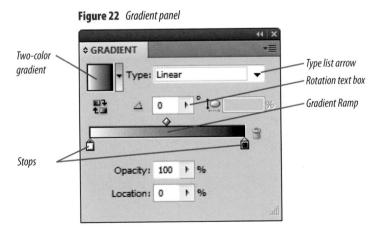

Figure 22 *Gradient panel*

Two-color gradient

Stops

Type list arrow

Rotation text box

Gradient Ramp

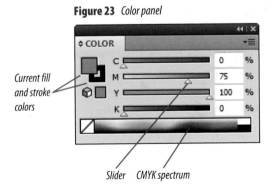

Figure 23 *Color panel*

Current fill and stroke colors

Slider   CMYK spectrum

Create a gradient and a color

1. Show the guides.

2. Create a 4" circle at the center of the artboard, then apply a yellow fill to the circle.

   The most recently drawn object is automatically placed above the other objects on the artboard.

3. Hide the guides, click **Window** on the Application bar, then click **Gradient** to open the Gradient panel if it is not already open.

4. Click the **Blended Rainbow swatch** on the Swatches panel.

   The yellow fill changes to the Blended Rainbow fill.

5. Click the **Gradient panel options button** ▼≡ , then click **Show Options** if they are not already showing.

6. Click the **yellow stop** on the Gradient Slider, and drag it straight down off the panel to delete it.

7. Delete all the stops except for the first and last stops.

TIP The changes you make to the Gradient Slider are reflected in the circle.

8. Click the **Selection tool** ▶ if it is not active, click the **bottom edge of the Gradient Slider** to add a new color stop as shown in Figure 24, then drag the **stop** along the slider until you see 50% in the Location text box on the Gradient panel, also shown in Figure 24.

TIP You can always enter the value directly into the text box as an alternative to dragging the slider.

9. Drag each of the diamond sliders to the 50% mark in the Location text box.

(continued)

Figure 24 *Adding and deleting stops*

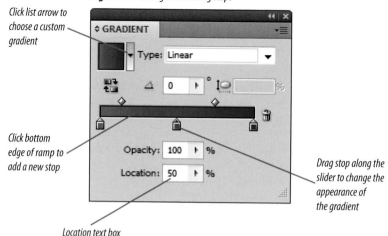

Click list arrow to choose a custom gradient

Click bottom edge of ramp to add a new stop

Location text box

Drag stop along the slider to change the appearance of the gradient

Figure 25 *Adding the new Squash swatch to the gradient*

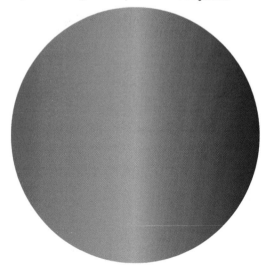

Figure 26 *Changing the first and last colors of the gradient*

Figure 27 *Changing the middle color and the midpoint locations*

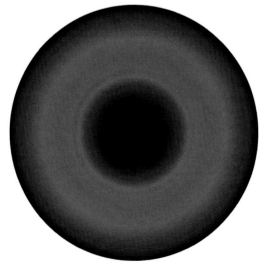

10. Verify that the new stop is selected, press and hold **[Alt]** (Win) or **[option]** (Mac), click **Squash** on the Swatches panel, then compare your circle to Figure 25.

    You must select a stop in order to change its color.

TIP If you don't press [Alt] (Win) or [option] (Mac), as you choose a swatch for your gradient, you will change the selected object's fill to a solid color.

11. Click the **first stop** on the Gradient Slider, press **[Alt]** (Win) or **[option]** (Mac), then click **Black** on the Swatches panel.

12. Repeat the previous step to apply Black to the third stop, then compare your circle to Figure 26.

13. Double-click the **Squash stop** to select it and open the Color panel, then drag each slider on the Color panel until the new CMYK values are 5C/95M/95Y/3K.

14. Click the **Type list arrow** on the Gradient panel, then click **Radial**.

15. Click the **diamond** at the top of the Gradient Slider between the first two stops, then drag it to the 87% location on the ramp.

16. Compare your circle to Figure 27.

You applied the Blended Rainbow gradient to the yellow circle. You modified the gradient by deleting stops and adding a new stop. You changed the color of the new stop, then adjusted the midpoint of the blend between the starting color and the middle color.

Add gradients and colors to the Swatches panel

1. Double-click the **Scale tool** 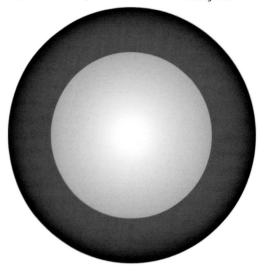, type **65** in the Scale text box, then click **Copy**.

2. Keeping the smaller circle selected, delete the red stop from the ramp on the Gradient panel.

3. Change the first stop to White, then change the ending stop to **0C/40M/50Y/0K**.

TIP Press [Alt] (Win) or [option] (Mac).

When a stop is selected on the Gradient Slider, the color of that stop appears in the Gradient Stop Color box on the Color panel.

4. Position the midpoint at 65%.

Your screen should resemble Figure 28.

5. Drag the **Gradient Fill box** from the Gradient panel to the Swatches panel, as shown in Figure 29.

6. Double-click **New Gradient Swatch 1** (the gradient you just added) on the Swatches panel to open the Swatch Options dialog box.

7. Type **Pinky** in the Swatch Name text box, then click **OK**.

8. Click the **last color stop** on the Gradient Slider.

(continued)

Figure 28 *A radial gradient with white as the starting color*

Figure 29 *Adding a gradient to the Swatches panel*

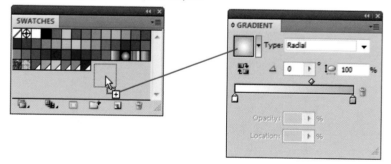

Creating Text and Gradients

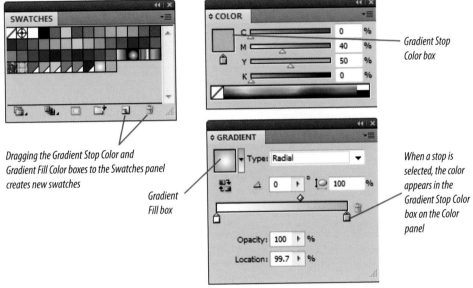

Figure 30 *Adding a color to the Swatches panel*

Gradient Stop Color box

Dragging the Gradient Stop Color and Gradient Fill Color boxes to the Swatches panel creates new swatches

Gradient Fill box

When a stop is selected, the color appears in the Gradient Stop Color box on the Color panel

9. Drag the **Gradient Stop Color box** from the Color panel to the Swatches panel to add this color to the Swatches panel, as shown in Figure 30, then name it **Pinky Ending**.

10. Click the **Selection tool** .

11. Click the **artboard** to deselect the smaller circle.

12. Click the **large circle**, drag the **Gradient Fill box** on the Gradient panel to the Swatches panel, then name the new gradient **Crimson Gradient**.

13. Save your work.

You used the Gradient panel to create a new gradient. You added the gradient fills from the two circles to the Swatches panel and gave them descriptive names. You added a color named Pinky Ending to the Swatches panel then saved the Crimson Gradient to the Swatches panel.

Apply Colors and GRADIENTS TO TEXT

What You'll Do

In this lesson, you will apply colors to text, convert text into objects, and fill the objects with a gradient.

Applying Fills and Strokes to Text

Regardless of the fill and stroke colors shown on the Tools panel, new text is generated by default with a black fill and no stroke. To change the color of text, you must select the text by highlighting it with a type tool or switch to a selection tool. When you switch to a selection tool, the text is selected as a single object (a blue baseline and anchor point are revealed), and any color changes you make will affect the text globally. If you want to change the fill or the stroke of an individual character, you must select that character with a type tool.

Converting Text to Outlines

About the only thing you can't do to Illustrator text is fill it with a gradient. To create that effect, you first need to convert the text into objects. You can do this by selecting the text, then using the Create Outlines command on the Type menu.

The letterforms, or outlines, become standard Illustrator objects with anchor points and paths that you can modify like any other object. Figure 31 shows an example of text converted to outlines.

Create Outlines is a powerful feature. Beyond allowing you to fill text with a gradient, it makes it possible to create a document with text and without fonts. This can save you time in document management when sending files to your printer by circumventing potential problems with missing fonts or font conflicts.

Once text is converted to outlines, you can no longer change the typeface. Also, the type loses its font information, including sizing "hints" that optimize letter shape at different sizes. Therefore, if you plan to scale type substantially, change its font size on the Character panel before converting to outlines.

Figure 31 *Text converted to outlines*

Apply color to text

1. Select the two circles, click **Object** on the Application bar, point to **Arrange**, then click **Send to Back**.

   The two circles move behind the locked text objects.

2. Click **Object** on the Application bar, then click **Unlock All**.

   The three text objects you created and locked are now unlocked and selected.

3. Apply the Pinky Ending color as a fill for the three unlocked text objects.

4. Deselect all, then lock the diamond text object.

   Your work should resemble Figure 32.

You unlocked the three text objects, filled them with the Pinky Ending color, then locked the diamond text object.

Figure 32 *Text with a new fill color*

Formatting a Story

You can use any of the shapes you create as text boxes, and you can thread, or flow, text from one object to another. When you add text to an object, it becomes a text object with an in port and an out port. To thread text, click the out port of an object that contains text, then click the in port of the object to which you want to thread the text. If the object isn't already defined as a text object, click on the path of the object.

You can also thread text by selecting an object that has type in it, then selecting the object or objects to which you want to thread the text. Click Type on the Application bar, point to Threaded Text, then click Create. You will see icons representing threads. To view threads, choose View on the Application bar, point to Show Text Threads, then select a linked object.

Creating Text and Gradients

Figure 33 *Outlines filled with a gradient*

Create outlines and apply a gradient fill

1. Show the guides.
2. Click **Object** on the Application bar, then click **Show All**.
3. Select the **BERRY** text, click **Object** on the Application bar, point to **Arrange**, then click **Bring to Front**.
4. Click **Type** on the Application bar, then click **Create Outlines**.
5. Apply the Steel gradient swatch on the Swatches panel to fill the text outlines, then deselect the outlines.
6. Using Figure 33 as a guide, position the BERRY text outlines so that they are centered within the entire illustration, then hide the guides.
7. Save your work.

You showed the BERRY text, moved it to the front, converted it to outlines, then filled the outlines with a gradient.

Adjust a Gradient and
CREATE A DROP SHADOW

What You'll Do

In this lesson, you will use the Gradient tool to modify how the gradient fills the outlines. You will then explore the effectiveness of a simple drop shadow as a design element.

Using the Gradient Tool with Linear Gradient Fills

The Gradient tool on the Tools panel is used to manipulate gradient fills that are already applied to objects and it only affects the way a gradient fills an object.

To use the Gradient tool, you first select an object with a gradient fill. When you click the Gradient tool, the **gradient control bar** appears in the object itself, as shown in Figure 34. For linear gradients, the gradient control bar begins at the left edge and ends at the right edge by default.

You can change the length, angle, and direction of the gradient by dragging the gradient control bar.

Figure 35 shows the gradient control bar starting outside the object at the top and ending below it. Where you begin dragging and where you end dragging determines the length of the gradient from the beginning color to the ending color, even if it's outside the perimeter of the object.

Figure 34 *Gradient control bar*

Figure 35 *Changing the position of the gradient control bar*

You can further modify how the gradient fills the object by modifying the gradient control bar itself. Click and drag the diamond-shaped endpoint of the bar to lengthen or shorten the gradient. You can also click and drag the circle-shaped starting point to move then entire bar to a different location.

When you click the gradient control bar, the color stops that compose the gradient appear, as shown in Figure 36. You can click and drag the stops right there, on the object, for precise control of how the gradient fills the object. You can change the color of the stops on the gradient control bar and even

add or delete stops. To change the color of a stop, simply double-click it and the Color panel will appear.

Perhaps the best method for working with the gradient control bar is to first click and drag the Gradient tool as close as possible to where you want it to begin and end. Then, use the gradient control bar for tweaking the position of the gradient and the position of the color stops within the object.

When you float your cursor near the endpoint of the gradient control bar, the rotate icon appears, as shown in Figure 37.

Click and drag to rotate the bar and the gradient within the object.

Applying Gradient Fills to Multiple Objects

If you select multiple objects then click a gradient swatch on the Swatches panel, the gradient will fill each object individually. However, with all the objects selected, you can use the Gradient tool to extend a single gradient across all of them.

When you convert text to outlines and apply a gradient fill, the gradient automatically

Figure 36 *Color stops on the gradient control bar*

Figure 37 *Rotating the gradient control bar*

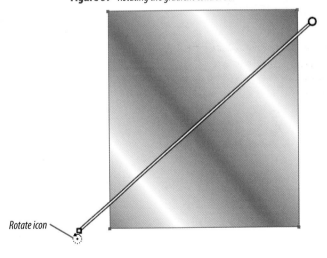

Rotate icon

fills each letter individually. In other words, if you fill a five-letter word with a rainbow gradient, each of the five letters will contain the entire spectrum. To extend the gradient across all the letters, drag the Gradient tool from the left edge of the word to the right edge, or vice versa. Figure 38 shows

examples of different angles and lengths of a gradient fill created with the Gradient tool.

Using the Gradient Tool with Radial Gradient Fills

With radial gradients the gradient control bar shows the length of the gradient from the center to the circle to the outermost circle. Figure 39 shows the gradient control bar for three radial gradients.

When you click the gradient control bar on a radial gradient, a dotted-line appears showing you the perimeter of the gradient,

Figure 38 *Using the Gradient tool*

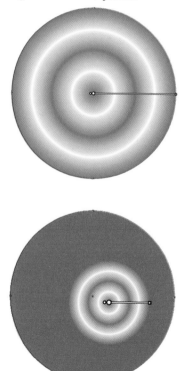

Figure 39 *Three radial gradients*

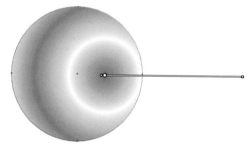

whether that's within or outside the actual object. In Figure 40, the dotted line indicates that more of the gradient is actually outside of the object than visible within the object.

Radial gradients are not limited to concentric circles: you can also create radial gradients with concentric ellipses. To do so, click and drag the black circle on the dotted line of the radial gradient.

As shown in Figure 41, doing so will distort the concentric circles into ellipses.

Adding a Drop Shadow

Applying a shadow behind text is an effective design tool to distinguish the text from other objects and add dimension to the illustration. To apply a drop shadow to text, first copy the text, then paste the copy behind it. Fill the copy with

a darker color, then use the keyboard arrows to move it so that it is offset from the original text.

Figure 40 *Dotted line shows the perimeter of the radial gradient*

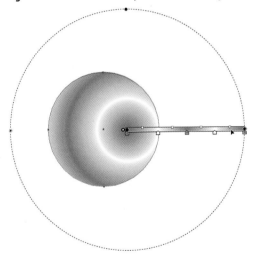

Figure 41 *Distorting the gradient*

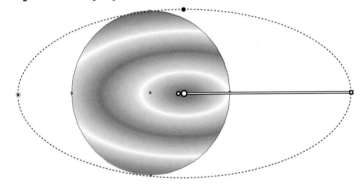

Use the Gradient tool

1. Select the BERRY text outlines if they are not already selected.

2. Click the **Gradient tool** ▭, then position the pointer at the top of the B.

3. Drag straight down to the bottom of the B, release the mouse, then deselect.

TIP Pressing and holding [Shift] while you drag the Gradient tool pointer allows you to drag in a perfectly straight line.

4. Switch to the Selection tool ▶, then click the **large circle filled with the Crimson gradient fill** behind the text.

5. Click the **Gradient tool** ▭.

6. Position the color stops and the midpoints as shown in Figure 42 so that the red gradient is behind the "three rivers symposium" letters.

You used the Gradient tool to flow the gradient from top to bottom in the word BERRY. You adjusted the stops and the midpoints on the gradient control bar to perfect the gradient behind the text.

Add a drop shadow to text

1. Select the word **BERRY**.

2. Apply a 1 pt Black stroke to the outlines.

3. Copy the word, then paste in back.

4. Change the fill of the copied object to Black.

TIP Even though you can't see the copy of the text in back, it is still selected.

5. Press ↓ three times and ← three times to move the copied text 3 pts down and 3 pts to the left, as shown in Figure 43.

(continued)

Figure 42 *A highlight behind the text*

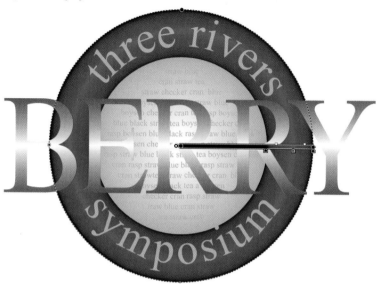

Figure 43 *Drop shadow with a 3 pt offset*

Figure 44 *Drop shadows add dimension*

Figure 45 *Finished illustration*

6. Copy the word symposium, then paste in back.
7. Change the fill of the copied text to Black.

TIP Since the copy is still selected, you only need to click Black on the Swatches panel.

8. Using the arrow keys, move the copied text 2 pts down and 2 pts to the left, as shown in Figure 44.
9. Apply the same drop shadow to the three rivers text.

TIP You might find it easier to select the three rivers text if you first lock the symposium text and the symposium shadow text.

10. Unlock all, select everything on the artboard, then rotate the illustration 15°.
11. Click the **Selection tool** ▸, then click the **artboard** to deselect all.

    Your work should resemble Figure 45.
12. Save your work, then close and save each document.

You applied a black stroke to the display text, then pasted a copy behind. You filled the copy with black, then offset the copy to create a drop shadow effect. You then applied a drop shadow to symposium and three rivers. Finally, you rotated the entire illustration.

Create and format text.

1. Open AI 2-3.ai, then save it as **Restaurant Logo**.
2. Using a bold font, type **NOW OPEN** on two lines anywhere on the artboard, using all capital letters. (*Hint*: The font used in Figure 46 is Impact.)
3. Change the font size to 29 pt and the leading to 25 pt.
4. Verify that the Baseline Shift is set to 0.
5. Change the alignment to Center and the Horizontal Scale to 75%.
6. Position the text in the center of the white circle.
7. Hide the text.
8. Save your work.

Flow text into an object.

1. Copy the beige circle.
2. Paste the copy in front of it.
3. Click the Type tool, then select all of the green text at the bottom of the artboard, with the Type tool.
4. Copy the green text.
5. Click the Selection tool, then click the top beige circle.
6. Click the Area Type tool, click the edge of the top beige circle, then paste.
7. Center-align the text in the circle.
8. Change the Baseline Shift to -4 pts.
9. Fill the selected text with the same fill color as the beige circle (50% Orange).
10. In the Color panel, drag the Magenta slider to 40% to darken the text.
11. Hide the text.
12. Save your work.

Position text on a path.

1. Select the dark gray circle.
2. Click the Type on a Path tool, then click the top of the circle.
3. Using a bold font, type **THE HOLE-IN-ONE** in all capital letters across the top of the circle. (*Hint*: The font in Figure 46 is Arial Black. If your type appears at the bottom of the circle, drag the start or end bracket to position the type at the top of the circle. Zoom in so that you can clearly see the brackets. If you move the circle instead of the type, undo your last step and try again.)
4. Change the font size to 36 pt, set the horizontal scale to 75% and the fill color to white. (*Hint*: You may need to use a different font size, depending on the font you choose.)
5. Click the Selection tool, click Edit on the Application bar, click Copy, click Edit on the Application bar, click Paste in Front, then move the center bracket clockwise to position the copied text across the bottom of the circle.
6. Select the copied text with the Type tool, then type **RESTAURANT**.
7. Drag the RESTAURANT text across the path to flip its direction.
8. Apply a negative baseline shift to move the text below the path. (*Hint*: The baseline shift used in Figure 46 is -26 pts.)
9. Copy both text objects, click Edit on the Application bar, then click Paste in Back.

10. Fill the back copies of the text with black, then move them 2 pts up and 2 pts to the right.
11. Save your work.

Create and apply gradients.

1. Apply the White, Black Radial gradient to the small white circle.
2. Change the ending color stop on the Gradient Ramp to Smoke. (*Hint*: Press [Alt] (Win) or [option] (Mac) while you select Smoke from the Swatches panel.)
3. Save the new gradient to the Swatches panel.
4. Name it **Golf Ball**.
5. Fill the large green circle with the Golf Ball gradient.
6. Change the starting color stop to Pure Yellow.
7. Change the ending color stop to Little Sprout Green.
8. Move the midpoint to the 80% location on the Gradient Slider.
9. Save the new gradient as **The Rough**.
10. Apply a 2 pt black stroke to the large circle and the smaller peach circle.
11. Save your work.

Adjust a gradient and create a drop shadow.

1. Click Object on the Application bar, then click Show All.
2. Deselect all by clicking the artboard.
3. Select NOW OPEN and convert the text to outlines.
4. Fill the text with the white to black linear gradient.
5. Change the starting color stop to black.
6. Create an intermediary white color stop at the 50% mark on the Gradient Slider.

7. Drag the Gradient tool starting at the top of the word NOW to the bottom of the word OPEN.
8. Change the middle color stop of the gradient to Latte.
9. Save the new gradient as **Flash**.
10. Deselect the text.

11. Delete the green text from the bottom of the artboard.
12. Convert the remaining text objects into outlines.
13. Apply a 2 pt black stroke to the three circles in the illustration.

14. Select all, then lock all objects.
15. Save your work, compare your illustration to Figure 46, then close Restaurant Logo.

Figure 46 *Completed Skills Review*

An eccentric California real-estate mogul hires your design firm to "create an identity" for La Mirage, his development of high-tech executive condominiums in Palm Springs. Since he's curious about what you'll come up with on your own, the only creative direction he'll give you is to tell you that the concept is "a desert oasis."

1. Create a new 6" × 6" document, then save it as **Desert Oasis**.
2. Using a bold font and 80 pt for a font size, type **LA MIRAGE** in all capitals. (*Hint*: The font shown in Figure 47 is Impact.)
3. Change the horizontal scale to 80%.
4. Change the baseline shift to 0.
5. Apply a -100 kerning value between the two words.
6. Convert the text to outlines, then click the linear gradient swatch on the Swatches panel that fades white to black.
7. Using the Color panel, change the first color stop to 66M/100Y/10K.
8. Create an intermediary color stop that is 25M/100Y.
9. Position the intermediary color stop at 70% on the slider.
10. Save the gradient on the Swatches panel, and name it **Desert Sun**.

11. Drag the Gradient tool from the exact top to the exact bottom of the text.
12. Create a rectangle around the text and fill it with the Desert Sun gradient.
13. Drag the Gradient tool from the bottom to the top of the rectangle.
14. Send the rectangle to the back of the stack.

15. Apply a 1-point black stroke to LA MIRAGE.
16. Type the tagline: a **desert oasis** in 14 pt lowercase letters.
17. Apply a tracking value of 500 or more to the tagline, then convert it to outlines.
18. Save your work, then close Desert Oasis.

Figure 47 *Completed Project Builder 1*

Creating Text and Gradients

Your friend owns Loon's Balloons. She stops by your studio with a display ad that she's put together for a local magazine and asks if you can make all the elements work together better. Her only direction is that the balloon must remain pink.

1. Open AI 2-4.ai, then save it as **Balloons**.
2. Save the pink fill on the balloon to the Swatches panel, and name it **Hot Pink**.
3. Fill the balloon shape with the White, Black Radial gradient from the Swatches panel.
4. Change the black stop on the Gradient Slider to Hot Pink.
5. Using the Gradient tool, change the highlight point on the balloon shape so that it is no longer centered in the balloon shape.
6. Copy the balloon, then paste it in front.
7. Click the Selection tool on the block of text that begins with "specializing in...," then cut the text.
8. Click the top balloon with the Selection tool, then switch to the Area Type tool.
9. Click the top edge of the top balloon, then paste.

10. Center the text and apply a -4 baseline shift.
11. Adjust the layout of the text as necessary. (*Hint*: You can force a line of text to the next line by clicking before the first word in the line you want to move, then pressing [Shift][Enter] (Win) or [Shift][return] (Mac).)

12. Move the headline LOON'S BALLOONS so that each word is on a different side of the balloon string.
13. Apply a 320 kerning value between the two words.
14. Save your work, compare your screen to Figure 48, then close Balloons.

Figure 48 *Completed Project Builder 2*

specializing in all
your balloon needs - for
birthdays, weddings,
anniversaries, graduations,
halloween, new year's eve
parties, or just to
say hello - we've got the
balloon for you.
call
555-7717

LOON'S BALLOONS

You work in the marketing department of a major movie studio, where you design movie posters and newspaper campaigns. You are respected for your proficiency with typography. Your boss asks you to come up with a "teaser" campaign for the movie *Vanishing Point*, a spy thriller. The campaign will run on billboards in 10 major cities and will feature only the movie title, nothing else.

1. Create a new 6" × 6" CMYK Color document, then save it as **Vanish**.
2. Type **VANISHING POINT**, using 100 pt and a bold font. (*Hint*: The font used in Figure 49 is Impact.)
3. Change the horizontal scale to 55%.
4. Convert the text to outlines.
5. On the Swatches panel, click the white to black linear gradient swatch.
6. Drag the Gradient tool from the exact bottom to the exact top of the letters.
7. Copy the letters, then paste them in front.
8. Fill the copied letters in front with white.
9. Using your arrow keys, move the white letters 2 pts to the left and 8 pts up.
10. Save your work, then compare your text with Figure 49.
11. Close Vanish.

Figure 49 *Completed Design Project*

Creating Text and Gradients

Firehouse Chili Pepper Company, a local specialty food manufacturer, has hired you to design a label for its new line of hot sauces. Since this is a new product line, they have no existing materials from which you can start.

1. Create a new 6" × 6" CMYK Color document, then save it as **Firehouse Chili**.
2. Search the Internet to get design ideas. Use keywords such as chili, pepper, hot sauce, barbecue, and salsa. What have other designers created to convey these concepts? Is there a broad range of ideas, or are they all pretty much different versions of the same idea? If so, can you think of something original that works?
3. Go to the grocery store and return with some samples of other products in this niche. Be sure to purchase both products that you've heard of before and products you've never heard of before. Are the known products' design concepts better than the unknown products'? Look for any correlation between the successful products and better design, if it is evident.
4. Begin brainstorming and sketching out ideas. Although there are no existing materials, the product line's name is very evocative. You should create design ideas that spring from the concepts of "firehouse" and "chili pepper," as well as from more broad-based concepts such as salsa, Mexico, and fire.

5. Use the skills that you learned in this chapter to create the label. (*Hint*: Fill text outlines with a gradient that conveys "hot." Use reds, oranges, and blacks. Use a bold font for the text so that the gradient will be clearly visible. Position the stops on the slider so that the "hot" colors are prominent in the letterforms.) Figure 50 shows one solution.
6. Save your work.
7. Close Firehouse Chili.

Figure 50 *Completed Portfolio Project*

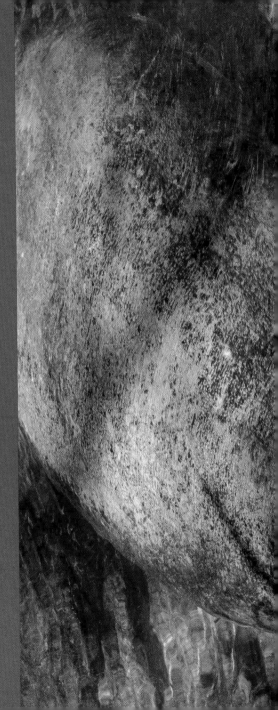

CHAPTER **3** DRAWING AND COMPOSING
AN ILLUSTRATION

1. Draw straight lines
2. Draw curved lines
3. Draw elements of an illustration
4. Apply attributes to objects
5. Assemble an illustration
6. Stroke objects for artistic effect
7. Use Live Trace and the Live Paint Bucket tool

CHAPTER 3

DRAWING AND COMPOSING
AN ILLUSTRATION

Drawing in Illustrator

You can create any shape using the Pen tool, which is why it's often called "the drawing tool." More precisely, the pen is a tool for drawing straight lines, curved lines, polygons, and irregularly shaped objects. It is, however, no *more* of a drawing tool than the shape tools, but, rather, more versatile. Really, *to master Illustrator, you must master the Pen tool.*

The challenges of the Pen tool are finite and can be grasped with no more than 30 minutes' study. As with many aspects of graphic design (and of life!), mastery comes with practice. So make it a point to learn Pen tool techniques. Don't get frustrated. Use the Pen tool often, even if it's just to play around making odd shapes.

All artists learn techniques for using tools such as brushes, chalk, and palette knives.

Once learned, those techniques become second nature, subconscious and unique to the artist. Ask yourself, was Van Gogh's mastery of the palette knife a triumph of his hands or of his imagination?

When you draw, you aren't conscious of how you're holding the crayon or how much pressure you're applying to the paper. Much the same goes for Illustrator's Pen tool. When you are comfortable and confident, you will find yourself effectively translating design ideas from your imagination straight to the artboard, without even thinking about the tool!

When you work with the Pen tool, you'll want complete control over your artboard. Using the Zoom tool and the New View feature, you can create custom views of different areas of your artboard, making it easy to jump to specific elements of your illustration for editing purposes.

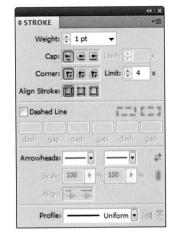

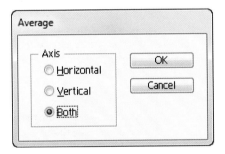

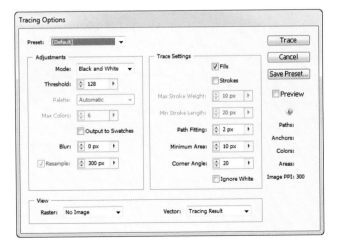

Draw Straight
LINES

What You'll Do

In this lesson, you will create three new views, then explore basic techniques for using the Pen tool as you prepare to draw a complex illustration.

Viewing Objects on the Artboard

If you are drawing on paper and you want to see your work up close, you move your nose closer to the paper. Computers offer more effective options. As you have already seen, the Zoom tool is used to enlarge areas of the artboard for easier viewing. When you are working with the Pen tool, your view of the board becomes more critical as anchor points are tiny, and you will often move them in 1 point increments.

Instead of clicking the Zoom tool to enlarge an area, you can click and drag it over the area on which you want to zoom in, creating a **marquee**, which is a rectangular, dotted line that surrounds the area over which you have dragged. When you release the Zoom tool, the marquee disappears, and whatever was in the marquee is magnified as much as possible, while still fitting in the window.

The New View command allows you to save any view of the artboard. Let's say you zoom in on an object. You can save that view and give it a descriptive name, using the New View command. The name of the view is then listed at the bottom of the View menu, so you can return to it at any time by selecting it. Saving views is an effective way to increase your productivity.

Drawing Straight Segments with the Pen Tool

You can use the Pen tool to make lines, also known as paths. You can also use it to create a closed shape, such as a triangle or a pentagon. When you click the Pen tool to make anchor points on the artboard, straight segments are automatically placed between the points. When the endpoints of two straight segments are united by a point, that point is called a **corner point**. Figure 1 shows a simple path drawn with five anchor points and four segments.

Perfection is an unnecessary goal when you are using the Pen tool because you can move and reposition anchor points and segments, as well as add and delete new points. Use the Pen tool to create the general shape that you have in your mind. Once the object is complete, use the Direct Selection tool to perfect, or tweak, the points and segments. Tweaking a finished object is always part of the drawing process.

Aligning and Joining Anchor Points

Often, you will want to align anchor points precisely. For example, if you have drawn a diamond-shaped object with the Pen tool, you may want to align the top and bottom points on the same vertical axis and then align the left and right points on the same horizontal axis to perfect the shape.

The **Average** command is a simple and effective choice for aligning points. With two or more points selected, you can use the Average command to align them on the horizontal axis, on the vertical axis, or on both the horizontal and vertical axes. Two points aligned on both the horizontal and vertical axes are positioned one on top of the other.

Why is this command named "Average?" The name is appropriate because when the command moves two points to line them up on a given axis, that axis is positioned at the average distance between the two points. Thus, each point moves the same distance.

The **Join** command unites two anchor points. When two points are positioned in different locations on the artboard, the Join command creates a segment between them. When two points are aligned on both the horizontal and vertical axes and are joined, the two points become one. 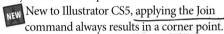 New to Illustrator CS5, applying the Join command always results in a corner point.

You will often use the Average and Join commands in tandem. Figure 2 shows two pairs of points that have each been aligned on the horizontal axis, then joined with the Join command.

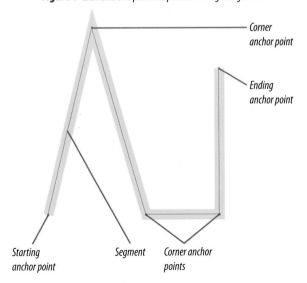

Figure 1 *Elements of a path composed of straight segments*

Corner anchor point

Ending anchor point

Starting anchor point

Segment

Corner anchor points

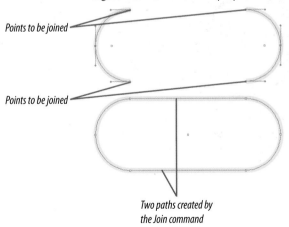

Figure 2 *Join command unites open points*

Points to be joined

Points to be joined

Two paths created by the Join command

Create new views

1. Open AI 3-1.ai, then save it as **Straight Lines**.

2. Choose the Essentials workspace, click the **Zoom tool** 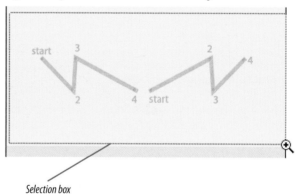, then position it at the upper-left corner of the artboard.

3. Click and drag a **selection box** that encompasses the entire yellow section, as shown in Figure 3.

   The area within the selection box is now magnified.

4. Click **View** on the Application bar, then click **New View**.

5. Name the new view **yellow**, then click **OK**.

6. Press and hold **[Spacebar]** to access the Hand tool, then drag the **artboard** upward until you have a view of the entire pink area.

7. Create a new view of the pink area, and name it **pink**.

   TIP If you need to adjust your view, you can quickly switch to a view of the entire artboard by pressing [Ctrl][0] (Win) or ⌘ [0] (Mac), then create a new selection box with the Zoom tool.

8. Create a new view of the green area, named **mint**.

9. Click **View** on the Application bar, then click **yellow** at the bottom of the menu.

   The Illustrator window changes to the yellow view.

   TIP You can change the name of a view by clicking View on the Application bar, then clicking Edit Views.

You used the Zoom tool to magnify an area of the artboard. You then named and saved the three views.

Figure 3 *Drag the Zoom tool to select what will be magnified*

Selection box

Figure 4 *Four anchor points and three segments*

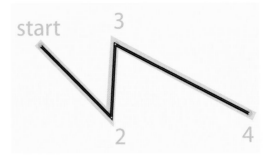

Figure 5 *Click the path with the Pen tool to add a new point*

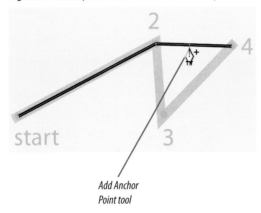

Add Anchor
Point tool

Figure 6 *Move an anchor point with the Direct Selection tool*

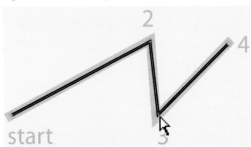

Draw straight lines

1. Verify that you are still in the yellow view, then click the **Pen tool** 🖊.
2. Open the Swatches panel, then set the fill color to [None], the stroke color to Black, and the stroke weight to 1 pt.
3. Using Figure 4 as a reference, click **position 1 (start)**.
4. Click **position 2**, then note how a segment is automatically drawn between the two anchor points.
5. Click **position 3**, then click **position 4**.

TIP If you become disconnected from the current path you are drawing, undo your last step, then click the last anchor point with the Pen tool and continue.

6. Press and hold **[Ctrl]** (Win) or ⌘ (Mac) to switch to the Selection tool ▶, then click the artboard to stop drawing the path and to deselect it.

   You need to deselect one path before you can start drawing a new one.
7. Release **[Ctrl]** (Win) or ⌘ (Mac), click **position 1 (start)** on the next path, then click **position 2**.
8. Skip over position 3 and click **position 4**.
9. Using Figure 5 as a guide, position the Pen tool 🖊 anywhere on the segment between points 2 and 4, then click to add a new anchor point.

TIP When the Pen tool is positioned over a selected path, the Add Anchor Point tool 🖊⁺ appears.

10. Click the **Direct Selection tool** ▶, then drag the **new anchor point** to position 3, as shown in Figure 6.

Using the Pen tool, you created two straight paths.

Close a path and align the anchor points

1. Click **View** on the Application bar, then click **pink**.

2. Click the **Pen tool** 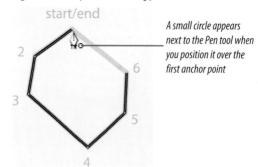, click the **start/end position** at the top of the polygon, then click **positions 2 through 6**.

3. Position the Pen tool, over the first point you created, then click to close the path, as shown in Figure 7.

4. Switch to the **Direct Selection tool**, click **point 3**, press and hold [**Shift**], then click **point 6**.

TIP Use the [Shift] key to select multiple points.

Anchor points that are selected appear as solid blue squares; anchor points that are not selected are white or hollow squares.

5. Click **Object** on the Application bar, point to **Path**, then click **Average**.

6. Click the **Horizontal option button** in the Average dialog box, then click **OK**.

7. The two selected anchor points align on the horizontal axis, as shown in Figure 8.

8. Select both the start/end point and point 4.

9. Use the Average command to align the points on the vertical axis.

10. Select both point 2 and point 5, then use the Average command to align the points on both axes, as shown in Figure 9.

You drew a closed path, then used the Average command to align three sets of points. You aligned the first set on the horizontal axis, the second on the vertical axis. You aligned the third set of points on both axes, which positioned them one on top of the other.

Figure 7 *Close a path at its starting point*

A small circle appears next to the Pen tool when you position it over the first anchor point

Figure 8 *Two points aligned on the horizontal axis*

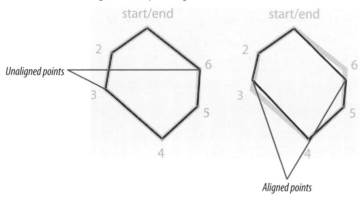

Unaligned points

Aligned points

Figure 9 *Averaging two points on both the horizontal and vertical axes*

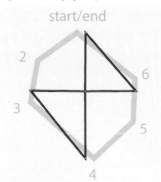

Figure 10 *Cutting points also deletes the segments attached to them*

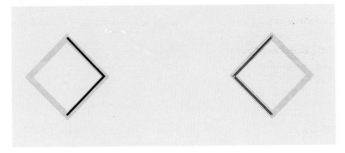

Figure 11 *Join command unites two distant points with a straight segment*

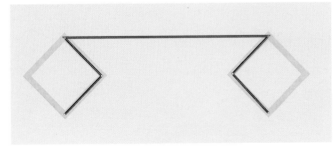

Figure 12 *Joining the two open anchor points on an open path closes the path*

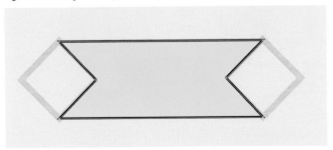

Join anchor points

1. Switch to the mint view of the artboard.
2. Use the Pen tool 🖊 to trace the two diamond shapes.

   TIP Remember to deselect the first diamond path with the Selection tool before you begin tracing the second diamond.

3. Click the **left anchor point** of the first diamond with the Direct Selection tool ▷ , click **Edit** on the Application bar, then click **Cut**.

   Cutting points also deletes the segments attached to them.
4. Cut the right point on the second diamond.

   Your work should resemble Figure 10.
5. Select the top point on each path.
6. Click **Object** on the Application bar, point to **Path**, then click **Join**.

   The points are joined by a straight segment, as shown in Figure 11.

   TIP The shortcut key for Average is [Ctrl][Alt][A] (Win) or [option][command][J] (Mac) and for Join is [Ctrl][J] (Win) or [command][J](Mac).

7. Join the two bottom points.
8. Apply a yellow fill to the object, then save your work.

   Your work should resemble Figure 12.
9. Close the Straight Lines document.

You drew two closed paths. You cut a point from each path, which deleted the points and the segments attached to them, creating two open paths. You used the Join command, which drew a new segment between the two top points and the two bottom points on each path. You then applied a yellow fill to the new object.

Draw CURVED LINES

What You'll Do

In this lesson, you will use the Pen tool to draw and define curved paths, and you will learn techniques to draw lines that abruptly change direction.

Defining Properties of Curved Lines

When you click to create anchor points with the Pen tool, the points are connected by straight segments. You can "draw" a curved path between two anchor points by *clicking and dragging* the Pen tool to create the points instead of just clicking. Anchor points created by clicking and dragging the Pen tool are known as **smooth points**.

When you use the Direct Selection tool to select a point connected to a curved segment, you will expose the point's **direction lines**, as shown in Figure 13. The angle and length of the direction lines

Figure 13 *Direction lines define a curve*

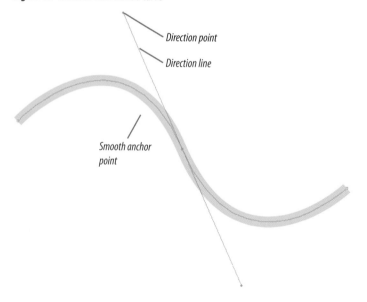

Direction point

Direction line

Smooth anchor point

Drawing and Composing an Illustration

determine the arc of the curved segment. Direction lines are editable. You can click and drag the **direction points**, or handles, at the end of the direction lines to reshape the curve. Direction lines function only to define curves and do not appear when you print your document.

A smooth point always has two direction lines that move together as a unit. The two curved segments attached to the smooth point are both defined by the direction lines. When you manipulate the direction lines on a smooth point, you change the curve of both segments attached to the point, always maintaining a *smooth* transition through the anchor point.

When two paths are joined at a corner point, the two paths can be manipulated independently. A corner point can join two straight segments, one straight segment and one curved segment, or two curved segments. That corner point would have zero, one, or two direction lines, respectively. Figure 14 shows examples of smooth points and corner points.

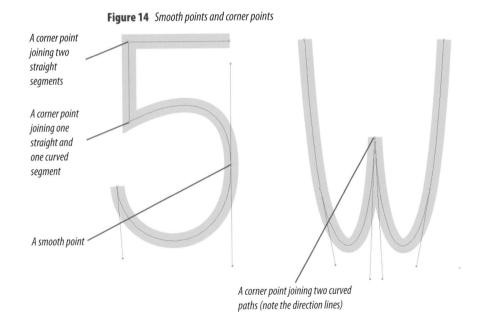

Figure 14 *Smooth points and corner points*

A corner point joining two straight segments

A corner point joining one straight and one curved segment

A smooth point

A corner point joining two curved paths (note the direction lines)

When a corner point joins one or two curved segments, the direction lines are unrelated and are often referred to as "broken." When you manipulate one, the other doesn't move.

Converting Anchor Points

The Convert Anchor Point tool changes corner points to smooth points and smooth points to corner points.

To convert a corner point to a smooth point, you click and drag the Convert Anchor Point tool on the anchor point to *pull out* direction lines. See Figure 15.

The Convert Anchor Point tool works two ways to convert a smooth point to a corner point, and both are very useful when drawing.

When you click directly on a smooth point with the Convert Anchor Point tool, the direction lines disappear. The two attached segments lose whatever curve defined them and become straight segments, as shown in the middle circle in Figure 16.

Figure 15 *Converting a corner point to a smooth point*

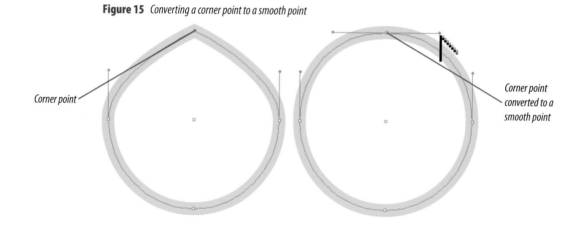

Corner point

Corner point converted to a smooth point

You can also use the Convert Anchor Point tool on one of the two direction lines of a smooth point. The tool "breaks" the direction lines and allows you to move one independently of the other as shown in the third circle in Figure 16. The smooth point is converted to a corner point that now joins two unrelated curved segments.

Once the direction lines are broken, they remain broken. You can manipulate them independently with the Direct Selection tool; you no longer need the Convert Anchor Point tool to do so.

Toggling Between the Pen Tool and the Selection Tools

Drawing points and selecting points go hand in hand so and you will often need to switch back and forth between the Pen tool and one of the selection tools. Clicking from one tool to the other on the Tools panel is unnecessary and will impede your productivity. To master the Pen tool, you must incorporate the keyboard command for "toggling" between the Pen tool and the selection tools. With the Pen tool selected, press [Ctrl] (Win) or [⌘] (Mac), which will switch the Pen tool to the Selection tool or the Direct Selection tool, depending on which tool you used last.

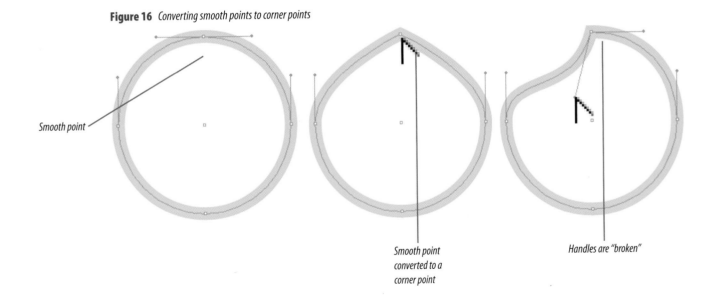

Figure 16 *Converting smooth points to corner points*

Smooth point

Smooth point converted to a corner point

Handles are "broken"

Draw and edit a curved line

1. Open AI 3-2.ai, then save it as **Curved Lines 1**.
2. Click the **Pen tool** ✒, then position it over the first point position on the line.
3. Click and drag upward until the pointer is at the center of the purple star, then release the mouse button.
4. Position the Pen tool ✒ over the second point position.
5. Click and drag down to the red star, then release the mouse button.
6. Using the same method, trace the remainder of the blue lines, as shown in Figure 17.
7. Click the **Direct Selection tool** ▸.
8. Select the second anchor point.
9. Click and drag the **direction handle** of the top direction line to the second purple star, as shown in Figure 18, then release the mouse button.

   The move changes the shape of both segments attached to the anchor point.
10. Select the third anchor point.
11. Drag the **bottom direction handle** to the second red star, as shown in Figure 19, then release the mouse button.
12. Manipulate the direction lines to restore the curves to their appearance in Figure 17.
13. Save your work, then close the Curved Lines 1 document.

You traced a curved line by making smooth points with the Pen tool. You used the Direct Selection tool to manipulate the direction lines of the smooth points and adjust the curves. You then used the direction lines to restore the line to its original curves.

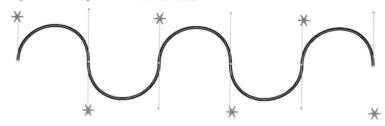

Figure 17 *Smooth points draw continuous curves*

Figure 18 *Moving one direction line changes two curves*

Click the Direct Selection tool on any smooth point to expose its direction lines

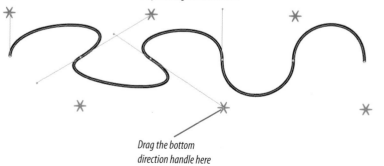

Figure 19 *Round curves are distorted by moving direction lines*

Drag the bottom direction handle here

Figure 20 *Smooth points converted to corner points*

Figure 21 *Smooth points restored from corner points*

Convert anchor points

1. Open AI 3-3.ai, then save it as **Curved Lines 2**.
2. Click **View** on the Application bar, then click **View #1**.
3. Click the **Direct Selection tool** ▸ anywhere on the black line.

   Six anchor points become visible.
4. Click **Object** on the Application bar, point to **Path**, then click **Add Anchor Points**.

   Five anchor points are added that do not change the shape of the line.
5. Click the **Convert Anchor Point tool** ▶, then click **each of the five new anchor points**.

TIP The Convert Anchor Point tool is hidden beneath the Pen tool.

   The smooth points are converted to corner points, as shown in Figure 20.
6. Click **the six original anchor points** with the Convert Anchor Point tool.
7. Position the Convert Anchor Point tool over the sixth anchor point.
8. Click and drag the **anchor point** to the purple star.

   The corner point is converted to a smooth point.
9. Using Figure 21 as a guide, convert the corner points to the left and right of the new curve.

You added five new anchor points to the line, then used the Convert Anchor Point tool to convert all 11 points from smooth to corner points. You then used the Convert Anchor Point tool to convert three corner points to smooth points.

Draw a line with curved and straight segments

1. Click **View** on the Application bar, then click **View #2**.

2. Click the **Pen tool**, position it over the first point position, then click and drag down to the green star.

3. Position the Pen tool over the second point position, then click and drag up to the purple star, as shown in the top section of Figure 22.

4. Click the **second anchor point**.

   The direction line you dragged is deleted, as shown in the lower section of Figure 22.

5. Click the **third point position** to create the third anchor point.

6. Position the Pen tool over the third anchor point, then click and drag a direction line up to the green star.

7. Position the Pen tool over the fourth point position, then click and drag down to the purple star.

8. Click the **fourth anchor point**.

9. Position the Pen tool over the fifth position, then click.

10. While the Pen tool is still positioned over the fifth anchor point, click and drag a direction line down to the green star.

11. Finish tracing the line, then deselect the path.

You traced a line that has three curves joined by two straight segments. You used the technique of clicking the previous smooth point to convert it to a corner point, allowing you to change the direction of the path.

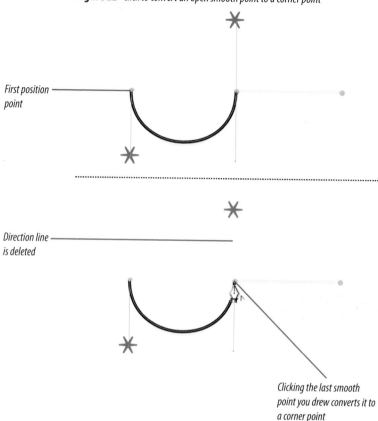

Figure 22 *Click to convert an open smooth point to a corner point*

First position point

Direction line is deleted

Clicking the last smooth point you drew converts it to a corner point

Figure 23 *Use the Convert Anchor Point tool to "break" the direction lines and redirect the path*

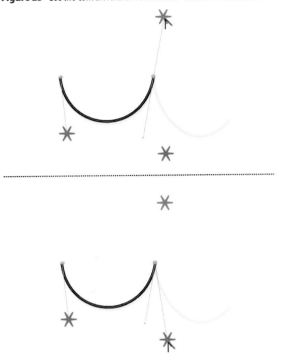

Reverse direction while drawing

1. Click **View** on the Application bar, then click **View #3**.

2. Click the **Pen tool** ✒️, position it over the first point position, then click and drag down to the purple star.

3. Position the Pen tool ✒️ over the second point position, then click and drag up to the red star, as shown in the top section of Figure 23.

4. Press and hold **[Alt]** (Win) or **[option]** (Mac) to switch to the Convert Anchor Point tool ⌐, then click and drag the **direction handle** on the red star down to the second purple star, as shown in the lower section of Figure 23.

   TIP Press [Alt] (Win) or [option] (Mac) to toggle between the Pen and the Convert Anchor Point tools.

5. Release [Alt] (Win) or [option] (Mac), then continue to trace the line using the same method.

   TIP If you switch between the Pen tool and the Convert Anchor Point tool using the Tools panel instead of using [Alt] (Win) or [option] (Mac), you will disconnect from the current path.

6. Save your work, then close the Curved Lines 2 document.

You used the Convert Anchor Point tool to "break" the direction lines of a smooth point, converting it to a corner point in the process. You used the redirected direction line to define the next curve in the sequence.

The Pencil, Smooth, and Path Eraser tools

When drawing paths, be sure to experiment with the Pencil, Smooth, and Path Eraser tools, which are grouped together on the Tools panel. You can draw freehand paths with the Pencil tool and then manipulate them using the Direct Selection tool, the Smooth tool, and the Path Eraser tool. The Smooth tool is used to smooth over line segments that are too bumpy or too sharp. The Path Eraser tool looks and acts just like an eraser found at the end of a traditional pencil; dragging it over a line segment erases that part of the segment from the artboard.

Draw Elements of
AN ILLUSTRATION

What You'll Do

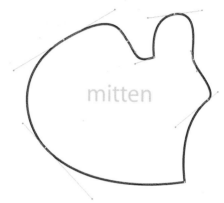

In this lesson, you will draw 14 elements of an illustration. By tracing previously drawn elements, you will develop a sense of where to place anchor points when drawing a real-world illustration.

Starting an Illustration

Getting started with drawing an illustration is often the hardest part. Sometimes the illustration will be an image of a well-known object or a supplied sketch or a picture. At other times, the illustration to be created will exist only in your imagination. In either case, the challenge is the same: How do you translate the concept from its source to the Illustrator artboard?

Drawing from Scratch

Drawing from scratch means that you start with a new Illustrator document and create the illustration, using only the Illustrator tools. This approach is common, especially when the goal is to draw familiar items such as a daisy, fish, or sun.

Illustrator's shape tools (such as the Ellipse tool) combined with the transform tools (such as the Rotate tool) make the program very powerful for creating geometric designs from scratch. The Undo and Redo commands allow you to experiment, and you will often find yourself surprised by the design you end up with!

Typographic illustrations—even complex ones—are often created from scratch.

Many talented illustrators and designers are able to create complex graphics off the cuff. It can be an astounding experience to watch an illustrator start with a blank artboard and, with no reference material, produce sophisticated graphics with attitude, expression, and emotion, as well as unexpected shapes and subtle relationships between objects.

Tracing a Scanned Image

Using the Place command, it is easy to import a scanned image into Illustrator. For complex illustrations, especially those of people or objects with delicate relationships, such as maps or blueprints, many designers find it easier to scan a sketch or a photo and import it into Illustrator as a guide or a point of reference.

Tracing a scanned image is not "cheating." An original drawing is an original drawing, whether it is first created on a computer or on a piece of paper. Rather than being a negative, the ability to use a computer to render a sketch is a fine example of the revolutionary techniques that illustration software has brought to the art of drawing. Figure 24 shows an illustration created from scratch in Illustrator, and Figure 25 shows a scanned sketch that will be the basis for the illustration you will create throughout this chapter.

Figure 24 *An illustration created from scratch*

Figure 25 *Place a scanned sketch in Illustrator, and you can trace it or use it as a visual reference*

Draw a closed path using smooth points

1. Open AI 3-4.ai, then save it as **Snowball Parts**.

2. Click **View** on the Application bar, then click **Arm**.

3. Verify that the fill color is set to [None] and the stroke color is set to Black.

4. Click the **Pen tool** 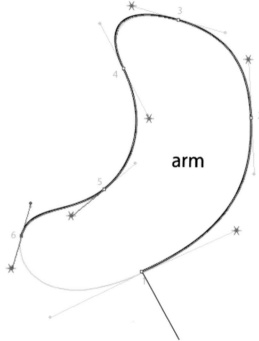, position it over point 1, then click and drag a direction line to the green star on the right side of the 1.

5. Go to position 2, then click and drag a direction line to the next green star.

   TIP Watch the blue preview of the new segment fall into place as you drag the Pen tool. This will help you understand when to stop dragging the direction line.

6. Using the same method, continue to draw points 3 through 6, then compare your screen to Figure 26.

7. Position the Pen tool over point 1.

8. Press and hold **[Alt]** (Win) or **[option]** (Mac), then click and drag to position the ending segment and close the path.

You drew a curved path. To close the path, you used a corner point, which allowed you to position the ending segment without affecting the starting segment.

Figure 26 *Points 1 through 6 are smooth points*

arm

When closing a path, pressing [Alt] (Win) or [option] (Mac) converts the end/start anchor point to a corner point

Drawing and Composing an Illustration

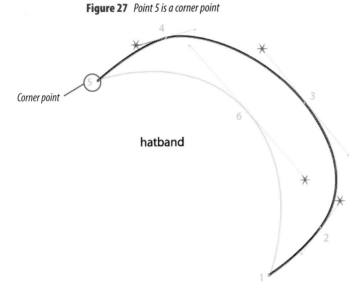

Figure 27 *Point 5 is a corner point*

Corner point

hatband

1. Click **View** on the Application bar, then click **Hatband**.
2. Verify that the fill color is set to [None] and the stroke color is set to Black.
3. Click the **Pen tool**, then click **position 1** to create a corner point.
4. Draw the next two curved segments for positions 2 and 3, using the green stars as guides.
5. Position the Pen tool over position 4, then click and drag to the green star.
6. Click **position 5** to create a corner point, as shown in Figure 27.
7. Position the Pen tool over position 6, then click and drag to the green star.
8. Click **position 1** to close the path with a corner point.
9. Click the **Selection tool**, then deselect the path.

You began a path with a corner point. When it was time to close the path, you simply clicked the starting point. Since the point was created without direction lines, there were no direction lines to contend with when closing the path.

Redirect a path while drawing

1. Click **View** on the Application bar, then click **Nose**.

   The Nose view includes the nose, mouth, eyebrow, and teeth.

2. Click the **Pen tool** 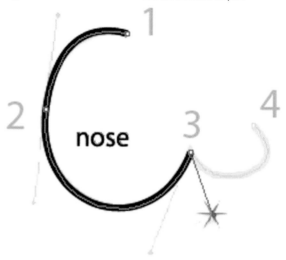, then click **point 1** on the nose to start the path with a corner point.

3. Create smooth points at positions 2 and 3.

   The direction of the nose that you are tracing abruptly changes at point 3.

4. Press and hold [Alt] (Win) or [option] (Mac) to switch to the Convert Anchor Point tool , then move the top direction handle of point 3 down to the red star, as shown in Figure 28.

5. Release [Alt] (Win) or [option] (Mac) to switch back to the Pen tool, click and drag **position 4** to finish drawing the path, click the **Selection tool** , then deselect the path.

   The nose element, as shown in Figure 29, is an open path.

Tracing the nose, you encountered an abrupt change in direction, followed by a curve. You used the Convert Anchor Point tool to redirect the direction lines on point 3, simultaneously converting point 3 from smooth to corner and defining the shape of the curved segment that follows.

Figure 28 *Use the Convert Anchor Point tool to redirect the path*

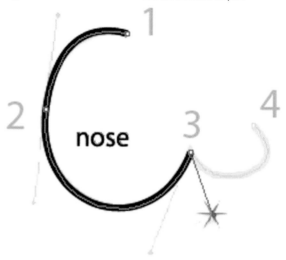

Figure 29 *Nose element is an open path*

Drawing and Composing an Illustration

Figure 30 *Use a scanned sketch as a reference or for tracing*

Place a scanned image

1. Click **View** on the Application bar, then click **Fit All in Window**.

2. Click **File** on the Application bar, then click **Place**.

3. Navigate to the drive and folder where your Data Files are stored.

4. Click **Snowball Sketch.tif**, then click **Place**.

   A scan of the Snowball Sketch illustration is placed in a bounding box at the center of the artboard.

5. Use the Scale tool  to scale the placed file 115%.

   TIP You can apply all of the transform tools to placed files.

6. Click the **Selection tool** , move the placed file into the scratch area, then lock it.

7. Draw the remaining elements of the illustration, referring to the sketch in the scratch area or to Figure 30 for help.

   TIP The mouth, eyebrow, and teeth are located in the Nose view.

8. Save your work after you complete each element.

You placed a file of a scanned sketch to use as a reference guide. You scaled the object, dragged it to the scratch area, locked it, then drew the remaining elements of the illustration.

Apply Attributes
TO OBJECTS

What You'll Do

You will create four new colors on the Color panel and apply each to one of the illustration elements. Using the Eyedropper tool, you will paint the remaining items quickly and easily.

Using the Eyedropper Tool

In Illustrator, **attributes** are formatting that you have applied to an object to affect its appearance. Typographic attributes, for example, would include font, leading, and horizontal scale. Artistic attributes include the fill color, stroke color, and stroke weight.

The Eyedropper tool is handy for applying *all* of an object's attributes to another object. Its icon is particularly apt. The Eyedropper tool "picks up" an object's attributes, such as fill color, stroke color, and stroke weight.

> **QUICK TIP**
> You can think of the Eyedropper tool as taking a sample of an object's attributes.

The Eyedropper tool is particularly useful when you want to apply one object's attributes to another. For example, if you have applied a blue fill with a 3.5 pt orange stroke to an object, you can easily apply those attributes to new or already-existing objects. Simply select the object that you want to format, then click the formatted object with the Eyedropper tool.

This is a simple example, but don't underestimate the power of the Eyedropper tool. As you explore more of Illustrator, you will find that you are able to apply a variety of increasingly complex attributes to objects. The more complex the attributes, the more the Eyedropper tool reveals its usefulness.

You can also use the Eyedropper tool to copy type formatting and effects between text elements. This can be especially useful when designing display type for headlines.

Adding a Fill to an Open Path

You can think of the letter O as an example of a closed path and the letter U as an example of an open path. Although it seems a bit strange, you are able to add a fill to an open path just as you would to a closed path.

The program draws an imaginary straight line between the endpoints of an open path to define where the fill ends. Figure 31 shows an open path in the shape of a U with a red fill. Note where the fill ends. For the most part, avoid applying fills to open paths. Though Illustrator will apply the fill, an open path's primary role is to feature a stroke. Any effect that you can create by filling an open path you can also create with a more effective method by filling a closed path.

Figure 31 *A fill color applied to an open path*

Apply new attributes to closed paths

1. Verify that nothing is selected on the artboard.
2. Open the Color panel, then create a royal blue color on the Color panel.
3. Fill the arm with the royal blue color, then change its stroke weight to 6 pt.

TIP Use the views at the bottom of the View menu to see and select each element with which you need to work. The mouth, eyebrow, and teeth are located in the Nose view.

4. Deselect the arm, then create a deep red color on the Color panel.
5. Fill the hatband with the deep red color, then change its stroke weight to 3 pt.
6. Deselect the hatband, then create a flesh-toned color on the Color panel that is 20% magenta and 56% yellow.
7. Fill the head with the flesh tone; don't change the stroke weight.
8. Fill the pompom with White; don't change the stroke weight.
9. Fill the mouth with Black; don't change the stroke weight.
10. Compare your work with Figure 32.

You applied new attributes to five closed paths by creating three new colors, using them as fills, then changing the stroke weight on two of the objects.

Figure 32 *New attributes applied to five elements*

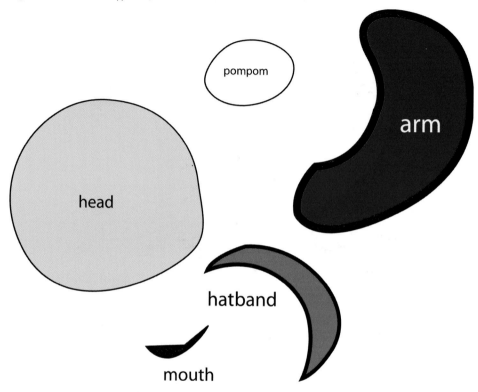

Drawing and Composing an Illustration

Figure 33 *Use the Eyedropper tool to apply the attributes of one object to another with one click*

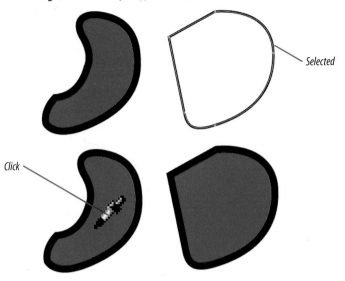

Selected

Click

Figure 34 *All elements ready to be assembled*

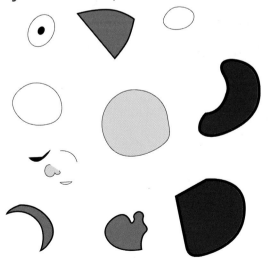

Copy attributes with the Eyedropper tool

1. Select the torso.

2. Click the **Eyedropper tool** 🖊, then click the **blue arm**.

   As shown in Figure 33, the torso takes on the same fill and stroke attributes as the arm.

3. Switch to the Selection tool ➤ , select the hat, click the **Eyedropper tool** 🖊, then click the **hatband**.

4. Using any method you like, fill and stroke the remaining objects using the colors shown in Figure 34.

You applied the attributes of one object to another by first selecting the object to which you wanted to apply the attributes, then clicking the object with the desired attributes with the Eyedropper tool.

Assemble an
ILLUSTRATION

What You'll Do

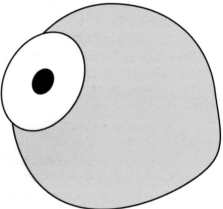

In this lesson, you will arrange the elements that you drew in Lesson 4 to create a composed illustration.

Assembling an Illustration

Illustrator's basic stacking order design is sophisticated enough to compose any illustration. Assembling an illustration with multiple objects will test your fluency with the stacking order commands: Bring to Front, Send to Back, Bring Forward, Send Backward, Paste in Front, Paste in Back, Group, Lock, Unlock All, Hide, and Show All. The sequence in which you draw the elements determines the stacking order (newer elements are in front of older ones), so you'll almost certainly need to adjust the stacking order when assembling the elements. Locking and hiding placed elements will help you to protect the elements when they are positioned correctly.

Figure 35 *Eye positioned on the head*

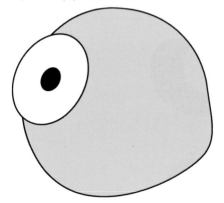

Figure 36 *Second eye is a copy of the first*

Figure 37 *Nose pasted in front of the left eye*

*The nose behind
the left eye*

*The nose in front
of the left eye*

Figure 38 *Eyebrow positioned over the right eye*

Figure 39 *All elements in position*

Assemble the illustration

1. Select and copy all the elements on the artboard.

2. Create a new CMYK Color document that is 9″ × 9″, then save it as **Snowball Assembled**.

3. Paste the copied elements into the Snowball Assembled document.

4. Deselect all objects, select the head, click **Object** on the Application bar, point to **Arrange**, then click **Send to Back**.

5. Group the eye and the iris, then position the eye on the head as shown in Figure 35.

6. Click the **eye**, press **[Alt]** (Win) or **[option]** (Mac), then drag to create a copy of it, as shown in Figure 36.

7. Position the nose on the face, cut the nose, select the left eye, then paste in front.

   The nose is pasted in the same position, but now it is in front of the eye, as shown in Figure 37.

8. Select the teeth, then bring them to the front.

9. Position the teeth over the mouth, then group them.

10. Position the mouth and the teeth on the head, and the eyebrow over the right eye, as shown in Figure 38.

11. Finish assembling the illustration, using Figure 39 as a guide, then save your work.

TIP Use the Object menu and the Arrange menu command to change the stacking order of objects as necessary.

You assembled the illustration, utilizing various commands to change the stacking order of the individual elements.

Stroke Objects for
ARTISTIC EFFECT

What You'll Do

In this lesson, you will experiment with strokes of varying weight and attributes, using options on the Stroke panel. You will then apply pseudo-strokes to all of the objects to create dramatic stroke effects.

Defining Joins and Caps

In addition to applying stroke weights, you use the Stroke panel to define other stroke attributes, including joins and caps, and whether a stroke is solid or dashed. Figure 40 shows the Dashed Line utility and Caps on the Stroke panel.

Caps are applied to the ends of stroked paths. The Stroke panel offers three choices: Butt Cap, Round Cap, and Projecting Cap. Choose Butt Cap for squared ends and Round Cap for rounded ends. Generally, round caps are more appealing to the eye.

The projecting cap applies a squared edge that extends the anchor point at a distance that is one-half the weight of the stroke. With a projecting cap, the weight of the stroke is equal in all directions around the line. The projecting cap is useful when you align two anchor points at a right angle, as shown in Figure 41.

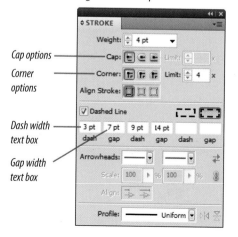

Figure 40 *Stroke panel*

Cap options — Cap options

Corner options — Corner options

Dash width text box

Gap width text box

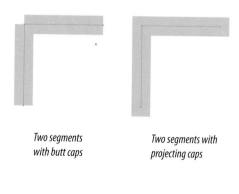

Figure 41 *Projecting caps are useful when segments meet at right angles*

Two segments with butt caps

Two segments with projecting caps

When two stroked paths form a corner point, **joins** define the appearance of the corner. The default is a miter join, which produces stroked lines with pointed corners. The round join produces stroked lines with rounded corners, and the bevel join produces stroked lines with squared corners. The greater the weight of the stroke, the more apparent the join will be, as shown in Figure 42.

Defining the Miter Limit

The miter limit determines when a miter join will be squared off to a beveled edge. The miter is the length of the point from the inside to the outside. The length of the miter is not the same as the stroke weight. When two stroked paths are at an acute angle, the length of the miter will greatly exceed the weight of the stroke, which results in an extreme point that can be very distracting.

QUICK TIP

You can align a stroke to the center, inside, or outside of a path using the Align Stroke buttons on the Stroke panel.

The default miter limit is 4, which means that when the length of the miter reaches 4 times the stroke weight, the program will automatically square it off to a beveled edge. Generally, you will find the default miter limit satisfactory, but remain conscious of it when you draw objects with acute angles, such as stars and triangles. Figure 43 shows the impact of a miter limit on a stroked star with acute angles.

Creating a Dashed Stroke

A dashed stroke is like any other stroked path in Illustrator, except that its stroke has been broken up into a sequence of dashes separated by gaps. The Stroke panel offers you the freedom to customize dashed or dotted lines by entering the lengths of the dashes and the gaps between them in the six dash and gap text boxes. You can create a maximum of three different sizes of dashes separated by three different sizes of gaps. The pattern you establish will be repeated across the length of the stroke.

When creating dashed strokes, remain conscious of the cap choice on the Stroke panel. Butt caps create familiar square dashes,

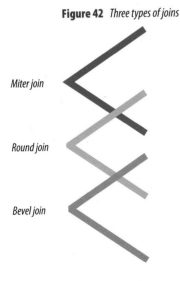

Figure 42 *Three types of joins*

Miter join

Round join

Bevel join

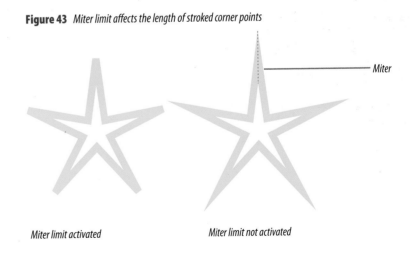

Figure 43 *Miter limit affects the length of stroked corner points*

Miter

Miter limit activated

Miter limit not activated

and round caps create rounded dashes. Creating a dotted line requires round caps. Figure 44 shows two dashed lines using the same pattern but with different caps applied.

Improving the Appearance of a Dashed Stroke

The Stroke panel in Illustrator CS5 offers a new and welcome option for dashed lines. The new options, identified in Figure 44 as Exact Dashes and Adjust Dashes, affect how dashes are distributed along a stroked path or the edge of a stroked object. Figure 45 shows each option. The red rectangle is an example of the Exact Dashes option. The dashes are distributed around the edge of the rectangle with the exact measurements input in the Stroke panel, regardless of the resulting appearance. In this case, the appearance leaves a bit to be desired. All four corners look different and, in the bottom-right corner, two dashes are actually overlapping.

The blue rectangle is an example of the Adjust Dashes option. Though the measurements for the dashed stroke are the same as those input for the red rectangle, here the Adjust Dashes option automatically adjusts the position and gaps of the dash so that the corners all look the same and the overall dashed effect is balanced.

Creating Pseudo-Stroke Effects

Strokes around objects, especially black strokes, often contribute much to an illustration in terms of contrast, dimension, and dramatic effect. A classic technique that designers have used since the early versions of Illustrator is the "pseudo-stroke," or false stroke. Basically, you place a black-filled copy behind an illustration element, then distort the black element with the Direct Selection tool so that it "peeks" out from behind the element in varying degrees.

This technique, as shown in Figure 46, is relatively simple to execute and can be used for dramatic effect in an illustration.

Figure 44 *Caps are an important factor in determining the appearance of a dashed line*

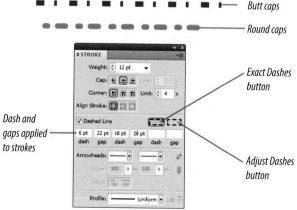

Butt caps

Round caps

Dash and gaps applied to strokes

Exact Dashes button

Adjust Dashes button

Figure 45 *The Exact Dashes and Adjust Dashes options applied to a stroked object*

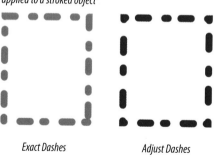

Exact Dashes

Adjust Dashes

Figure 46 *The "pseudo-stroke" effect*

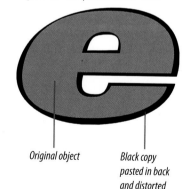

Original object

Black copy pasted in back and distorted

Drawing and Composing an Illustration

Figure 47 *Bevel joins applied to paths*

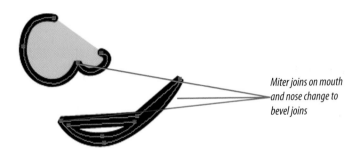

Miter joins on mouth and nose change to bevel joins

Figure 48 *Round joins applied to paths*

Bevel joins on mouth and nose change to round joins

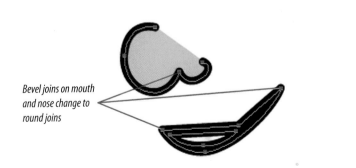

Modify stroke attributes

1. Select the eyebrow, the nose, and the mouth.
2. Click **Select** on the Application bar, then click **Inverse**.

   The selected items are now deselected, and the deselected items are selected.
3. Hide the selected items, then open the Stroke panel.
4. Select all, then change the stroke weight to 3 pt.
5. Click the **Stroke panel options button** ▼≡ , click **Show Options** if options are hidden, then click the **Round Cap button** ⊏ .

   The caps on open paths are rounded.
6. Click the **Bevel Join button** ⌐ .

   The miter joins on the mouth and nose change to a bevel join, as shown in Figure 47.
7. Click the **Round Join button** ⌐ .

   The bevel joins on the mouth and nose change to round joins, as shown in Figure 48.
8. Remove the stroke from the teeth.

   TIP Use the Direct Selection tool to select the teeth, since they are grouped to the mouth.

You hid elements so you could focus on the eyebrow, nose, and mouth. You applied round caps to the open paths and round joins to the corner points.

Create a dashed stroke

1. Show all objects, then select all.
2. Deselect the snowball, then hide the selected items.

   The snowball should be the only element showing.
3. Select the snowball, then change the stroke weight to 4 pt.
4. Click the **Dashed Line check box** on the Stroke panel.
5. Experiment with different dash and gap sizes.
6. Toggle between butt and round caps.

   The dashes change from rectangles to ovals.
7. Enter 1 pt dashes and 4 pt gaps.
8. Click the **Round Cap button** 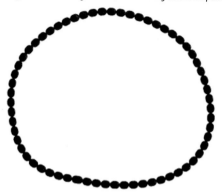, verify that the **NEW** Adjust Dashes option is activated, then compare your snowball to the one shown in Figure 49.
9. Show all of the objects that are currently hidden.

You applied a dashed stroke to the snowball object and noted how a change in caps affected the dashes.

Figure 49 *Creating a dashed stroke using the Stroke panel*

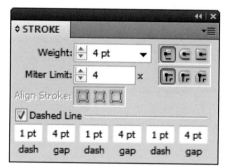

Figure 50 *Pompom with the pseudo-stroke effect*

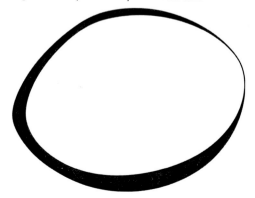

Drawing and Composing an Illustration

Figure 51 *Completed illustration*

Create pseudo-strokes

1. Copy the pompom, then paste in back.

2. Apply a black fill to the copy.

TIP The copy is still selected behind the original white pompom, making it easy to apply the black fill.

3. Click the **white pompom**, then remove the stroke.

4. Lock the white pompom.

5. Using the Direct Selection tool 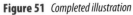, select the bottom anchor point on the black copy.

6. Use the arrow keys to move the anchor point 5 pts down.

   The black copy is increasingly revealed as its size is increased beneath the locked white pompom.

7. Move the left anchor point 4 pts to the left.

8. Move the top anchor point 2 pts up, then deselect.

   Your work should resemble Figure 50.

9. Using the same methods and Figure 51 as a reference, create distorted black copies behind all the remaining elements except the torso, the mouth, and the eyebrow.

10. Save your work, then close Snowball Assembled.

You created black copies behind each element, then distorted them, using the Direct Selection tool and the arrow keys, to create the illusion of uneven black strokes around the object.

Use Live Trace and the
LIVE PAINT BUCKET TOOL

What You'll Do

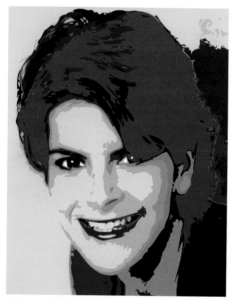

In this lesson, you will use the Live Trace and Live Paint features.

Using Live Trace

Have you ever roughed out a sketch on paper, only to have to recreate it from scratch on your computer? Or, have you ever wished that you could convert a scanned photograph into editable vector graphics to use as the basis of an illustration? With Live Trace, you can have Illustrator trace a graphic for you.

Live Trace offers a number of built-in tracing presets that help you fine-tune your tracing results from the start. Additional presets,

such as Hand Drawn Sketch, Comic Art, and Detailed Illustration, help create even extra special effects.

So what is the "live" in Live Trace, you ask? The live aspects of Live Trace occur in the Tracing Options dialog box, shown in Figure 52. Here, you can click the Preset list arrow to choose which type of preset you want to use to trace the bitmap. (In the figure, Hand Drawn Sketch is the chosen preset.) To see the resulting artwork before you close

Figure 52 *Tracing Options dialog box*

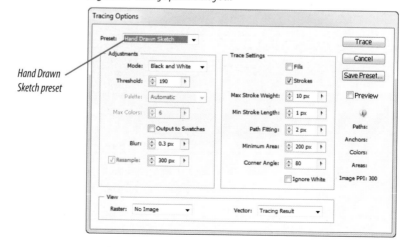

Hand Drawn Sketch preset

Drawing and Composing an Illustration

the dialog box, click the Preview check box. You can also continue to manipulate the graphic by changing the many settings in the Adjustments and Trace Settings sections of the dialog box. Illustrator will continually retrace the graphic to preview the final effect. That's the live part of Live Trace!

Tracing a Line-Art Sketch

Figure 53 shows a magic marker sketch of a dog that has been scanned into Photoshop and placed in Illustrator. Figure 54 shows the artwork after it has been traced using the default Live Trace settings. Not much

difference, you say? Well, that's a good thing, a testament to how accurately Live Trace does its job.

As you were undoubtedly taught years ago, appearances can be deceiving. Though the artwork in Figures 53 and 54 appears similar, they couldn't be more different, because the artwork in Figure 54 is a vector graphic that has been traced from the bitmap graphic shown in Figure 53.

Expanding a Traced Graphic

When a bitmap image is selected in Illustrator, the Live Trace button becomes

available on the Control panel. After Live Trace has been executed, the Expand button becomes available on the Control panel. In order to select and modify the paths and points that make up the new vector graphic, you must first click the Expand button. Once done, the illustration is able to be selected and modified, as shown in Figure 55.

QUICK TIP

Figure 55 shows the artwork in Outline mode so that you can better see the paths and points.

Figure 53 *Bitmap graphic placed in Illustrator*

Figure 54 *Traced graphic*

Figure 55 *Expanded traced graphic in Outline mode*

Tracing a Photograph

You use Live Trace to trace a bitmap photo the same way you trace a sketch. With photographic images, however, the settings in the Tracing Options dialog box can be used to create some really interesting illustration effects.

Figure 56 shows a scanned photograph that has been placed in Illustrator. Clicking the Live Trace button instructs Illustrator to trace the photo using the default Black & White setting. The result is shown in Figure 57.

QUICK TIP

The default Black & White setting is 128 Threshold.

The resulting graphic is not the only result possible—not by a long shot. Rather than use the default setting, you can click the Tracing presets and options list arrow on the Control panel and choose from a variety of styles, such as Comic Art or Technical Drawing. The Tracing presets and options list arrow is also available in the Tracing Options dialog box.

Figure 56 *Scanned photograph placed in Illustrator*

Figure 57 *Photograph traced at default Black & White setting*

Using the Live Paint Feature

When Adobe launched the Live Paint Bucket tool, they called it "revolutionary," and that was not an overstatement. The Live Paint Bucket tool breaks all the fundamental rules of Illustrator, and creates some new ones. For that reason, when you are working with the Live Paint Bucket tool, it's a good idea to think of yourself as working in Live Paint mode, because Illustrator will function differently with this tool than it will with any other.

QUICK TIP

The Live Paint Bucket tool is located behind the Shape Builder tool.

Essentially, the Live Paint Bucket tool is designed to make painting easier and more intuitive. It does this by changing the basic rules of Illustrator objects. In Live Paint mode, the concept of "objects" no longer applies—you can fill and stroke negative spaces. The Live Paint Bucket tool uses two object types called regions and edges. **Regions** and **edges** are comparable to fills and strokes, but they are "live." As shown in Figure 58, where two regions overlap, a third region is created and can be painted with its own color. Where two edges overlap, a third edge is created. It too can be painted its own color.

Adobe likes to say that Live Paint is intuitive—something that looks like it should be able to be filled with its own color can indeed be filled with its own color. As long as you have the Live Paint Bucket tool selected, selected objects can be filled using the new rules of Live Paint mode. Once you leave Live Paint mode, the paint that you have applied to the graphic remains part of the illustration.

Figure 58 *Identifying regions and edges in an illustration*

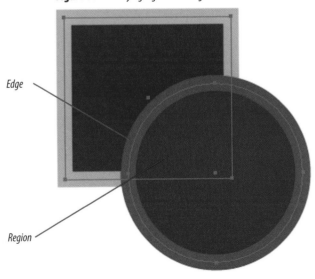

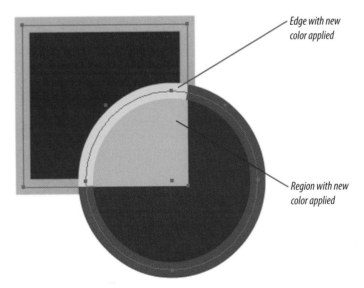

Edge

Region

Edge with new color applied

Region with new color applied

Live Painting Regions

To paint objects with the Live Paint Bucket tool, you must first select the objects you wish to paint. Figure 59 shows three selected rectangles that overlap each other. The selection marks show various shapes created by the overlap. As stated earlier, these overlapping areas or shapes are called regions. To fill the regions, you must first select all the objects that you want to paint. Click the Live Paint Bucket tool, click a color on the Swatches panel, then click a region that you want to fill. As shown

in Figure 60, when you position the Live Paint Bucket tool pointer over a region, that region is highlighted. Click the Live Paint Bucket tool and the region is filled, as shown in Figure 61.

As shown in Figure 62, each region can be filled with new colors. But that's not all that the Live Paint Bucket tool has to offer. The "live" part of Live Paint is that these regions are now part of a **Live Paint group**, and they maintain a dynamic relationship with each other. This means that when any of the objects is moved, the overlapping

area changes shape and fill accordingly. For example, in Figure 63, the tall thin rectangle has been moved to the left. Note how the overlapping regions have been redrawn and how their fills have updated with the move.

> **QUICK TIP**
>
> To select multiple regions in a Live Paint group, click the **Live Paint Selection tool** on the Tools panel, click the first region, press and hold [Shift], then click the remaining regions. The selected regions appear with a gray dotted fill pattern until you click a new color on the Swatches panel and deselect the artwork.

Figure 59 *Three overlapping selected rectangles*

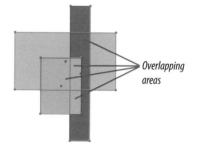

Overlapping areas

Figure 60 *Positioning the Live Paint Bucket tool pointer*

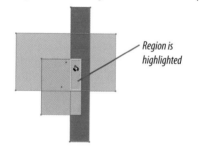

Region is highlighted

Figure 61 *Filling a region with a new color*

Region is filled with new color

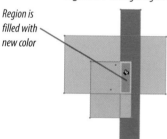

Figure 62 *Filling multiple regions*

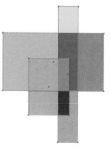

Figure 63 *Moving an object in a Live Paint group*

Rectangle moved to the left

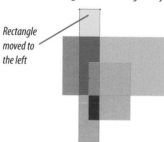

Drawing and Composing an Illustration

Painting Virtual Regions

The intuitive aspect of Live Paint mode goes one step further with virtual regions. Figure 64 shows six Illustrator paths; each path is selected and has a 1-point black stroke and no fill. This simple illustration provides a perfect example of the powers of the Live Paint Bucket tool.

Imagine trying to fill the four center polygons created by the overlapping strokes in "classic"

Illustrator without the Live Paint Bucket tool. This seemingly simple goal would actually be a really tough challenge. You'd need to create four polygons that align perfectly with the shapes created by the overlapping strokes because without the shapes, you'd have nothing to fill. And, because the strokes are so thin, you'd need those polygons to align exactly with the strokes. Finally, if you moved any of the strokes, you'd need to modify the polygons to match the new layout.

With the Live Paint Bucket tool, the regions that are created by the intersection of the paths are able to be filled as though they were objects. Figure 65 shows four regions that have been filled with the Live Paint Bucket tool.

In this case, as in the case of the overlapping rectangles, the dynamic relationship is maintained. Figure 66 shows the paths having been moved, and the filled regions have been redrawn and their fills updated.

Figure 64 *Six paths*

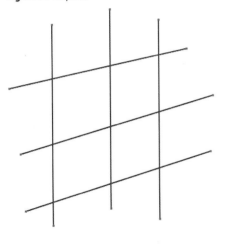

Figure 65 *Four filled regions between paths*

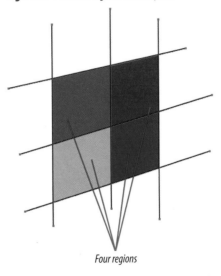

Four regions

Figure 66 *Moving paths in a Live Paint group*

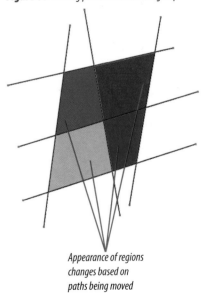

Appearance of regions changes based on paths being moved

Inserting an Object into a Live Paint Group

New objects can be inserted into a Live Paint group. To do so, switch to the Selection tool, then double-click inside any of the regions of the group. As shown in Figure 67, a gray rectangle appears around the group, indicating that you are in insertion mode. Once in **insertion mode**, you can then add an object or objects to the group.

As shown in Figure 68, another tall rectangle has been added to the group. It can now be painted with the Live Paint Bucket tool as part of the Live Paint group. Once you've added all that you want to the Live Paint group, exit insertion mode by double-clicking the Selection tool outside of the Live Paint group.

Figure 67 *Viewing the art in insertion mode*

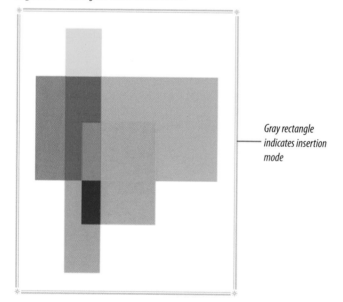

Gray rectangle indicates insertion mode

Figure 68 *Adding an object to the Live Paint group*

New object is added to the Live Paint group

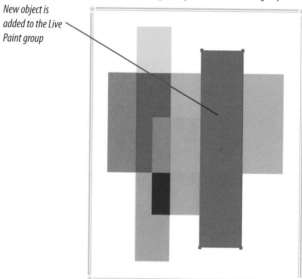

Expanding a Live Paint Group

When you deselect a Live Paint group, the deselected group does not change its appearance. It will print as it appears. You have the option of using the Expand command to release the Live Paint group into its component regions. Simply select the Live Paint group, then click the Expand button on the Control panel. Each region will be converted to an ordinary Illustrator object.

Live Painting Edges

In Live Paint mode, just as regions are akin to fills, edges are akin to strokes. With the Live Paint Bucket tool, you can paint edges as well as regions.

Figure 69 shows two overlapping objects, each with a 6-point stroke. To paint edges (strokes), you must first double-click the Live Paint Bucket tool, then activate the Paint Strokes check box in the Live Paint Bucket Options dialog box, as shown in Figure 70. When activated, the Live Paint Bucket tool will paint either regions or edges, depending on where it's positioned.

When you position the Live Paint Bucket tool over an edge, its icon changes to a paint brush icon. The edge is highlighted and paintable as though it were its own object, as shown in Figure 71.

Figure 69 *Two overlapping rectangles*

Figure 70 *Specifying the Live Paint Bucket tool to paint strokes (edges)*

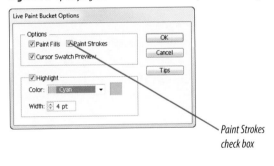

Paint Strokes check box

Figure 71 *Painting edges*

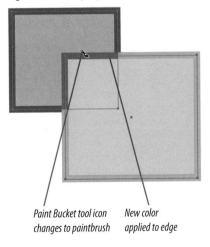

Paint Bucket tool icon changes to paintbrush   *New color applied to edge*

Use Live Trace to trace a sketch

1. Open AI 3-5.ai, then save it as **Live Trace Sketch**.

The file contains a placed marker sketch that was scanned in Photoshop.

2. Click **Window** on the Application bar, then click **Control** if it is not already selected.

3. Click the **Selection tool** , then click the **placed graphic**.

When the placed graphic is selected, the Live Trace button on the Control panel becomes visible.

4. Click the **Live Trace button** on the Control panel.

5. Click the **Expand button** on the Control panel.

As shown in Figure 72, the traced graphic is expanded into vector objects.

6. Deselect all, then using the Direct Selection tool , select and fill the illustration with whatever colors you like.

Figure 73 shows one example.

7. Save your work, then close the Live Trace Sketch document.

You used the default settings of the Live Trace utility to convert a placed sketch into Illustrator objects.

Figure 72 *Expanding the traced graphic*

Figure 73 *One example of the painted illustration*

Drawing and Composing an Illustration

Figure 74 *Photo traced with default Black and White*

Use Live Trace to trace a photo

1. Open AI 3-6.ai, then save it as **Live Trace Photo**.

   The file contains three copies of a placed photo that was scanned in Photoshop.

2. Zoom in on the top photo, click the **Selection tool** , click the **top photo**, then click the **Live Trace button** on the Control panel.

TIP If you do not see the Live Trace button, click the Edit Contents button on the Control panel.

   Using default black and white settings, Live Trace creates the trace shown in Figure 74.

3. Deselect the image, then zoom in on the middle photo.

4. Click the **Selection tool** , click the **middle photo**, click the **Tracing presets and options list arrow** to the right of the Live Trace button, then click **Tracing Options**.

(continued)

5. Click the **Preview check box** to select it if it is not already selected.

6. In the Adjustments section, click the **arrow** to the right of current Threshold value, then drag the **Threshold slider** until the Threshold value reads 200.

   Live Trace redraws the graphic.

7. Drag the **Threshold slider** until the Threshold value reads 160, wait for Live Trace to redraw the graphic, then click **Trace**.

8. Drag the **middle graphic** to the right of the top graphic, then compare the two graphics to Figure 75.

   (continued)

Figure 75 *Comparing a Black and White trace using different threshold values*

Figure 76 *Applying fills to the traced photo*

9. Deselect all, zoom in on the bottom photo, select it, click the **Tracing presets and options list arrow**, then click **Color 6**.

   Color 6 is a tracing preset.

10. Click the **Expand button** on the Control panel, then deselect all.

11. Click the **Direct Selection tool** , then select and fill the objects that make up the illustration.

    Figure 76 shows one example.

12. Save your work, then close the Live Trace Photo.

You used Live Trace to trace a photo three different ways. First, you simply clicked the Live Trace button, which executed the Default preset. Next, you opened the Trace Options dialog box and specified the threshold value for the Black and White trace. Finally, you traced with the Color 6 preset.

Use the Live Paint Bucket tool

1. Open AI 3-7.ai, then save it as **Live Paint Circles**.

2. Open the Swatches panel, fill the top circle with red, fill the left circle with green, then fill the right circle with blue.

3. Select all, double-click the **Live Paint Bucket tool** ◇ to open the Live Paint Bucket Options dialog box, verify that both the Paint Fills and Paint Strokes check boxes are checked, then click **OK**.

4. Click **any of the orange swatches** on the Swatches panel.

   Note that because you are in Live Paint mode, none of the selected objects changes to orange when you click the orange swatch.

5. Position the Live Paint Bucket tool pointer ◇ over the red fill of the red circle, then click.

6. Click **any pink swatch** on the Swatches panel, position the Live Paint Bucket tool pointer ◇ over the area where the orange circle overlaps the blue circle, then click.

   As shown in Figure 77, the region of overlap between the two circles is filled with pink.

   (continued)

Figure 77 *Painting the region that is the overlap between two circles*

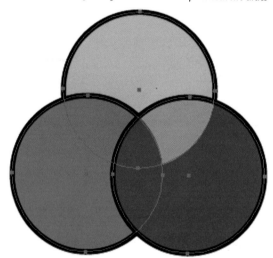

Figure 78 *Viewing seven painted regions*

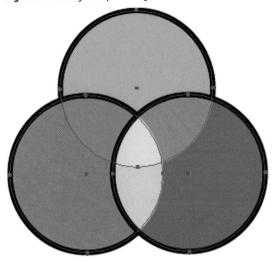

Figure 79 *Viewing 12 painted edges*

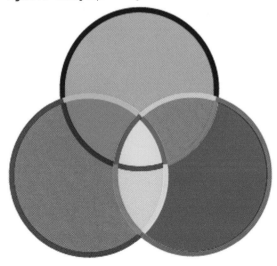

7. Using any colors you like, fill all seven regions so that your artwork resembles Figure 78.

8. Change the Stroke button on the Tools panel to any purple, position the Live Paint Bucket tool pointer over any of the black strokes in the artwork, then click.

   When positioned over a stroke, the Live Paint Bucket tool pointer changes to a paintbrush icon.

9. Using any color you like, change the color of all 12 edges then deselect all so that your artwork resembles Figure 79.

(continued)

10. Click the **Direct Selection tool** then, without pulling them apart, drag the circles in different directions noticing that they stay grouped, as shown in Figure 80.

    The components of the Live Paint group maintain a dynamic relationship.

11. Select all, click **Expand** on the Control panel, deselect all, then pull out all of the regions so that your artwork resembles Figure 81.

    The illustration has been expanded into multiple objects.

12. Save your work, then close the Live Paint Circles document.

You used the Live Paint Bucket tool to fill various regions and edges of three overlapping circles. You then moved various components of the Live Paint group, noting that they maintain a dynamic relationship. Finally, you expanded the Live Paint group, which changed your original circles into multiple objects.

Figure 80 *Exploring the dynamic relationship between regions in a Live Paint group*

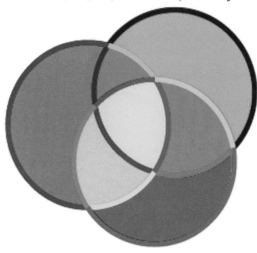

Figure 81 *Dissecting the expanded Live Paint group*

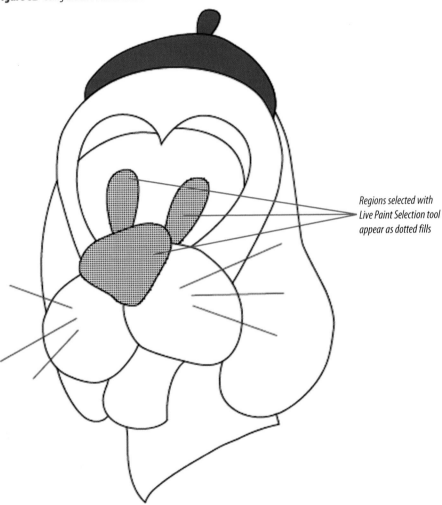

Figure 82 *Using the Live Paint Selection tool*

*Regions selected with
Live Paint Selection tool
appear as dotted fills*

Use the Live Paint Bucket tool to paint an illustration

1. Open AI 3-8.ai, then save it as **Live Paint Dog**.

2. Click the **Selection tool** ⬆ , then click the different colored strokes so that you understand how the illustration has been drawn.

   The illustration has been created with a series of open paths. The only closed path is the nose.

3. Select all, then change the stroke color of all the paths to Black.

4. Click the **Live Paint Bucket tool** 🖌 , then click **a red swatch** on the Swatches panel.

   Note that because you are in Live Paint mode, none of the selected objects changes to red when you click the red swatch.

5. Fill the hat and the knot at the top of the hat with red, then click **Black** on the Swatches panel.

6. Click the **Live Paint Selection tool** 🖌 , click the **nose**, press and hold **[Shift]**, click the **left eye**, then click the **right eye**.

   Your illustration should resemble Figure 82.

   TIP When you select multiple areas with the Live Paint Selection tool, the areas are filled with a dot pattern until you apply a color.

7. Click **Black** on the Swatches panel.

8. Using the same method, select both eyelids, then fill them with a lavender swatch.

   (continued)

9. Click the **Live Paint Bucket** tool , click a **yellow swatch** on the Swatches panel, then paint the illustration so that your illustration resembles Figure 83.

Note the small areas between the whiskers that must be painted yellow.

10. Using the Live Paint Bucket tool , paint the right jowl light brown, paint the left jowl a darker brown, then paint the tongue pink.

11. Click the **Stroke button** on the Tools panel to activate the stroke, then click a **gray swatch** on the Swatches panel.

12. Double-click the **Live Paint Bucket tool** , click the **Paint Stroke check box** in the Live Paint Bucket Options dialog box if it is not already checked, then click **OK**.

(continued)

Figure 83 *Painting the yellow regions*

Drawing and Composing an Illustration

Figure 84 *Viewing the finished artwork*

13. Paint the edges that draw the whiskers.

TIP You will need to click 14 times to paint the six whiskers.

14. Deselect, compare your work to Figure 84, save your work, then close the Live Paint Dog document.

You used the Live Paint Bucket tool to fill regions created by the intersection of a collection of open paths. You also used the tool to paint edges.

Draw straight lines.

1. Open AI 3-9.ai, then save it as **Mighty Montag**.
2. Place Montag Sketch.tif into the Montag document; you will need to navigate to the drive and folder where your Data Files are stored to find it.
3. Position the sketch in the center of the artboard, then lock it.
4. Set the fill color to [None] and the stroke to 1 pt black.
5. Use the Pen tool to create a four-sided polygon for the neck, (*Hint:* Refer to Figure 53 as a guide.)
6. Draw six whiskers.
7. Save your work.

Draw curved lines.

1. Using the Pen tool, draw an oval for the eye.
2. Draw a crescent moon shape for the eyelid.
3. Draw an oval for the iris.
4. Save your work.

Draw elements of an illustration.

1. Trace the left ear.
2. Trace the hat.
3. Trace the nose.
4. Trace the left jowl.
5. Trace the right jowl.
6. Trace the tongue.
7. Trace the right ear.
8. Trace the head.
9. Save your work.

Apply attributes to objects.

1. Unlock the placed sketch and hide it.
2. Fill the hat with a red swatch.
3. Fill the right ear with 9C/18M/62Y.
4. Fill the nose with black.
5. Fill the eye with white.
6. Fill the tongue with salmon.
7. Using Figure 85 as a guide, use the colors on the Swatches panel to finish the illustration.
8. Save your work.

Assemble an illustration.

1. Send the neck to the back of the stacking order, then lock it.
2. Send the head to the back, then lock it.
3. Send the left ear to the back, then lock it.
4. Bring the hat to the front.
5. Bring the right ear to the front.
6. Select the whiskers, group them, then bring them to the front.
7. Select the tongue, then cut it.
8. Select the right jowl, then apply the Paste in Back command.
9. Bring the nose to the front.
10. Select the eye, the eyelid, and the iris, then group them.
11. Drag and drop a copy of the eye group. (*Hint*: Press and hold [Alt] (Win) or [option] (Mac) as you drag the eye group.)
12. Select the right jowl.
13. On the Color panel add 10% K to darken the jowl.
14. Use the Color panel to change the fills on other objects to your liking.
15. Save your work.

Stroke objects for artistic effect.

1. Make the caps on the whiskers round.
2. Change the whiskers' stroke weight to .5 pt.
3. Unlock all.
4. Select the neck and change the joins to round.
5. Apply pseudo-strokes to the illustration. (*Hint:* Copy and paste the elements behind themselves, fill them with black, lock the top objects, then use the Direct Selection tool to select anchor points on the black-filled copies. Use the arrow keys on the keyboard to move the anchor points. The black copies will peek out from behind the elements in front.)
6. Click Object on the Application bar, then click Unlock All.
7. Delete the Montag Sketch file behind your illustration.
8. Save your work, compare your illustration to Figure 85, then close Mighty Montag.

Figure 85 *Completed Skills Review, Part 1*

Use Live Trace and the Live Paint Bucket tool.

1. Open AI 3-10.ai, then save it as **Skills Trace Photo**.
2. Zoom in on the top photo, click the Selection tool, click the top photo, then click the Live Trace button on the Control panel. (*Hint*: If you do not see the Live Trace button, click the Edit Contents button on the Control panel.)
3. Deselect the image, then zoom in on the middle photo.
4. Click the Selection tool, click the middle photo, click the Edit Contents button on the Control panel, click the Tracing presets and options list arrow to the right of the Live Trace button, then click Tracing Options.
5. Click the Preview check box if it is not already checked.
6. In the Adjustments section, click the arrow to the right of the current Threshold value, then drag the Threshold slider until the Threshold value reads 200.
7. Drag the Threshold slider until the Threshold value reads 166, wait for Live Trace to redraw the graphic, then click Trace.
8. Deselect all, zoom in on the bottom photo, select it, click the Edit Contents button, click the Tracing presets and options list arrow, then click Color 6.
9. Click the Expand button on the Control panel, then deselect all.
10. Click the Direct Selection tool, then select and fill the objects that make up the illustration so that your artwork resembles Figure 86.
11. Save your work, then close the file.

Figure 86 *Completed Skills Review, Part 2*

12. Open AI 3-11.ai, then save it as **Live Paint Skills**.
13. Open the Swatches panel, fill the top circle with Orange, fill the left circle with blue, then fill the right circle with purple.
14. Select all, then double-click the Live Paint Bucket tool to open the Live Paint Bucket Options dialog box, verify that both the Paint Fills and Paint Strokes check boxes are checked, then click OK.
15. Click any yellow swatch on the Swatches panel.
16. Position the Live Paint Bucket tool pointer over the orange fill of the orange circle, then click.
17. Click any pink swatch on the Swatches panel, position the Live Paint Bucket tool pointer over the area where the yellow circle overlaps the purple circle, then click.
18. Using any colors you like, fill the remaining five regions with different colors.
19. Click the Stroke button on the Tools panel, click any blue swatch on the Swatches panel, position the Live Paint Bucket tool pointer over any of the black strokes in the artwork, then click.
20. Using any color you like, change the color of all twelve edges then deselect all.
21. Click the Direct Selection tool, then, without pulling them apart, drag the circles in different directions noticing that they stay grouped, as shown in Figure 87.
22. Save your work, then close Live Paint Skills.indd.

Figure 87 *Completed Skills Review, Part 3*

The owner of The Blue Peppermill Restaurant has hired your design firm to take over all of their marketing and advertising, saying they need to expand their efforts. You request all of their existing materials, such as slides, prints, digital files, brochures, and business cards. Upon examination, you realize that they have no vector graphic version of their logo. Deciding that this is an indispensable element for future design and production, you scan in a photo of their signature peppermill, trace it, and apply a blue fill to it.

1. Create a new 6" × 6" CMYK Color document, then save it as **Peppermill**.
2. Place the Peppermill.tif file into the Peppermill Vector document. (*Hint*: The Peppermill.tif file is in the Chapter 3 Data Files folder.)
3. Scale the placed image 150%, then lock it.
4. Set your fill color to [None], and your stroke to 2 pt black.
5. Using the Zoom tool, create a selection box around the round element at the top of the peppermill to zoom in on it.
6. Using the Pen tool, trace the peppermill, adjusting your view as necessary to see various sections of the peppermill as you trace, then fill it with a blue swatch.
7. When you finish tracing, tweak the path if necessary, then save your work.
8. Unlock the placed image and cut it from the document.
9. Save your work, compare your illustration to Figure 88, then close Peppermill.

Figure 88 *Completed Project Builder 1*

You work at a children's library that has recently been remodeled. They've asked you to create a mural theme with interesting shapes of bright colors for the freshly painted walls. You create a sample in Illustrator to present to the staff—a single theme that can be modified to create multiple versions of the artwork.

1. Open AI 3-12.ai, then save it as **Tic Tac Toe**.
2. Select all, then change the stroke colors to black.
3. Click the Live Paint Bucket tool, select a fill color, then click in any of the squares
4. Fill each of the squares with a different color, then deselect all.
5. Click the Direct Selection tool, then change the angles of the black paths.
   Figure 89 shows one possible result.
6. Save your work, then close Tic Tac Toe.

Figure 89 *Completed Project Builder 2*

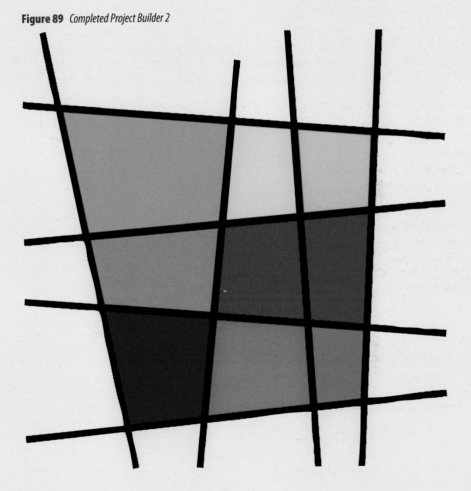

Your design firm is contacted by a company called Stratagem with a request for a proposal. They manufacture molds for plastic products. The terms of the request are as follows: You are to submit a design for the shape of the bottle for a new dishwashing liquid. You are to submit a single image that shows a black line defining the shape. The line art should also include the nozzle. The size of the bottle is immaterial. The design is to be "sophisticated, so as to be in visual harmony with the modern home kitchen." The name of the product is "Sleek."

1. Go to the grocery store and purchase bottles of dishwashing liquid whose shape you find interesting.
2. Use the purchases for ideas and inspiration.
3. Sketch your idea for the bottle's shape on a piece of paper.
4. Scan the sketch and save it as a TIFF file.
5. Create a new Illustrator document, then save it as **Sleek Design**.
6. Place the scan in the document, then lock it.
7. Trace your sketch, using the Pen tool.
8. When you are done tracing, delete the sketch from the document.
9. Tweak the line to define the shape to your specifications.
10. Use the Average dialog box to align points to perfect the shape.
11. Save your work, compare your illustration to Figure 90, then close Sleek Design.

Figure 90 *Completed Design Project*

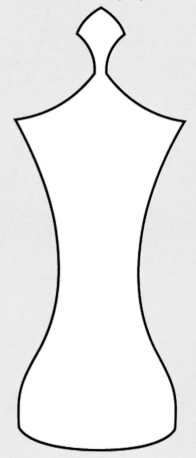

Note to Instructors: The central point of this exercise—a discussion of shapes and their role in the history of mankind—can be had with or without screening *2001: A Space Odyssey*. Should you choose not to show the film, simply omit questions 1 and 2. Rephrase Question 8 so that individuals are instructed to draw any abstract shape from their own imaginations.

The classic sci-fi movie, *2001: A Space Odyssey*, includes a 20-minute "Dawn of Man" sequence that begins millions of years ago with a group of apes, presumably on the African plains. One day, *impossibly*, a tall, black, perfectly rectangular slab appears out of nowhere on the landscape. At first the apes are afraid of it, afraid to touch it. Eventually, they accept its presence.

Later, one ape looks upon a femur bone from a dead animal. With a dawning understanding, he uses the bone as a tool, first to kill for food, and then to kill another ape from an enemy group. Victorious in battle, the ape hurls the bone into the air. The camera follows it up, up, up, and—in one of the most famous cuts in film history—the image switches from the white bone in the sky to the similar shape of a white spaceship floating in space.

1. How do you feel upon first seeing the "monolith" (the black rectangular slab)? Were you frightened? Do you sense that the monolith is good, evil, or neutral?
2. How would you describe the sudden appearance of the straight-edged, right-angled monolith against the landscape. What words describe the shapes of the landscape in contrast to the monolith?
3. Do you think perfect shapes exist in nature, or are they created entirely out of the imagination of human beings?
4. If perfect shapes exist—if they are real—can you name one example? If they are not real, how is it that humankind has proven so many concepts in mathematics that are based on shapes, such as the Pythagorean Theorem?
5. What advancements and achievements of humankind have their basis in peoples' ability to conceive of abstract shapes?
6. Can it be said legitimately that the ability to conceive abstract shapes is an essential factor that distinguishes humankind from all the other species on the planet?
7. Create a new document, then save it as Shape.
8. In Adobe Illustrator, draw any shape that you remember from the opening sequence, except the monolith. Did you render a shape based on the bone?
9. Save your work, compare your results to Figure 91, which is one possible result, then close Shape.

Figure 91 *Completed Portfolio Project*

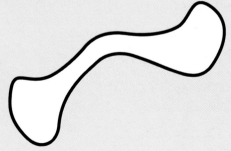

CHAPTER **4** TRANSFORMING AND
DISTORTING OBJECTS

1. Transform objects
2. Offset and outline paths
3. Create compound paths
4. Work with the Pathfinder panel
5. Use the Shape Builder tool
6. Create clipping masks

CHAPTER 4 TRANSFORMING AND
DISTORTING OBJECTS

Putting It All Together

Think about a conventional toolbox. You've got a hammer, nails, a few different types of screwdrivers, screws, nuts, bolts, a wrench, and probably some type of measuring device. That set of tools could be used to build anything from a birdhouse to a dollhouse to a townhouse to the White House.

A carpenter uses tools in conjunction with one another to create something, and that something is defined far less by the tools than by the imagination of the carpenter. But even the most ambitious imagination is tempered by the demands of knowing which tool to use and when.

Illustrator offers a number of sophisticated transform "tools" on the Tools panel, and the metaphor is apt. Each tool provides a

basic function, such as a rotation, scale, reflection, precise move, or precise offset. It is you, the designer, who uses those tools in combination with menu commands and other features to realize your vision. And like the carpenter, your ability to choose the right tool at the right time will affect the outcome of your work.

This is one of the most exciting aspects of working in Illustrator. After you learn the basics, there's no blueprint for building an illustration. It's your skills, your experience, your smarts, and your ingenuity that lead you toward your goal. No other designer will use Illustrator's tools quite the same way you do. People who appreciate digital imagery understand this salient point: Although the tools are the same for everyone, the result is personal. It's *original*.

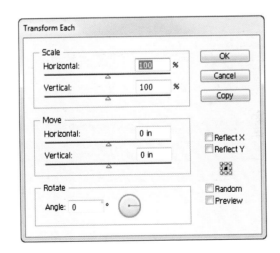

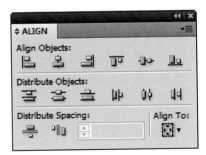

Transform
OBJECTS

What You'll Do

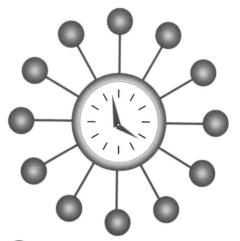

In this lesson, you will explore options for transforming objects with the transform tools.

Defining the Transform Tools

When you change an object's size, shape, or position on the artboard, Illustrator defines that operation as a transformation. Transforming objects is a fundamental operation in Illustrator, one you will perform countless times.

Because transformations are so essential, Illustrator provides a number of methods for doing them. As you gain experience, you will naturally adopt the method that you find most comfortable or logical.

The tools panel contains five transform tools, which are the Rotate, Scale, Reflect, Shear, and Free Transform tools. The Rotate tool rotates an object or a group of objects around a fixed point. The Scale tool enlarges and reduces the size of objects. The Reflect tool "flips" an object across an imagined axis, usually the horizontal or the vertical axis. However, you can define any diagonal as the axis for a reflection. In Figure 1, the illustration has been flipped to create the illusion of a reflection in a mirror.

The Shear tool slants—or skews—an object on an axis that you specify. By definition, the Shear tool distorts an object. Of the five transform tools, you will probably use the Shear tool the least, although it is useful for creating a cast shadow or the illusion of depth.

Finally, the Free Transform tool offers you the ability to perform quick transformations and distort objects in perspective.

Defining the Point of Origin

All transformations are executed in relation to a fixed point. In Illustrator, this point is called the **point of origin**. For each transform tool, the default point of origin is the selected object's center point. However, you can change that point to another point on the object or to a point elsewhere on the artboard. For example, when a majorette twirls a baton, that baton is essentially rotating on its own center. By contrast, the petals of a daisy rotate around a central point that is not positioned on any of the petals themselves, as shown in Figure 2.

There are four basic methods for making transformations with the transform tools. First, select an object, then do one of the following:

■ Click a transform tool, then click and drag anywhere on the artboard. The object will be transformed using its center point as the default point of origin.

■ Double-click the transform tool, which opens the tool's dialog box. Enter the values by which you want to execute the transformation, then click OK. You may also click Copy to create a transformed copy of the selected object. The point of origin for the transformation will be the center point of the selected object.

■ Click a transform tool, then click the artboard. Where you click the artboard defines the point of origin for the transformation. Click and drag anywhere on the artboard, and the selected object will be transformed from the point of origin that you clicked.

■ Click a transform tool, Press [Alt](Win) or [option](Mac), then click the artboard. The tool's dialog box opens, allowing you to enter precise values for the transformation. When you click OK or Copy, the selected object will be transformed from the point of origin that you clicked.

QUICK TIP

If you transform an object from its center point, then select another object and apply the Transform Again command, the point of origin has not been redefined, and the second object will be transformed from the center point of the first object.

Figure 1 *The Reflect tool flips an image horizontally or vertically*

Figure 2 *All transformations are executed from a point of origin*

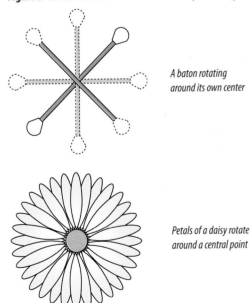

A baton rotating around its own center

Petals of a daisy rotate around a central point

Working with the Transform Again Command

An essential command related to transformations is Transform Again. Whenever you execute a transformation, such as scale or rotate, you can repeat the transformation quickly by using the Transform Again command. This is also true for moving an object. Using the Transform Again command will move an object the same distance and angle entered in the last step. The quickest way to use the Transform Again command is to press [Ctrl][D](Win) or [⌘][D](Mac). To remember this quick key command, think "D for *duplicate*."

A fine example of the usefulness of the Transform Again command is its ability to make transforming in small increments easy.

For example, let's say you have created an object to be used in an illustration, but you haven't decided how large the object should be. Simply scale the object by a small percentage—say 5%—then press the quick key for Transform Again repeatedly until you are happy with the results. The object gradually gets bigger, and you can choose the size that pleases your eye. If you transform again too many times, and the object gets too big, simply undo repeatedly to decrease the object's size in the same small increments.

Using the Transform Each Command

The Transform Each command allows you to transform multiple objects individually, as shown in Figure 3. The Transform Each dialog box offers options to move, scale, rotate, or reflect an object, among others. All of them will affect an object independent of the other selected objects.

Without the Transform Each command, applying a transformation to multiple objects simultaneously will often yield an undesired effect. This happens because the selected objects are transformed as a group in relation to a single point of origin and are repositioned on the artboard.

Using the Free Transform Tool

The Free Transform tool applies an eight-handled bounding box to a selected image. You can move those handles to scale and shear the object. You can click and drag outside the object to rotate the object.

Figure 3 *Multiple objects rotated individually*

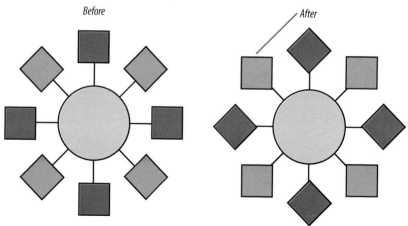

The eight squares are rotated on their own center points

With the Free Transform tool, transformations always use the selected object's center point as the point of origin. In general, the role of the Free Transform tool is to make quick, inexact transformations. However, the tool has a powerful, hidden ability. Moving the handles in conjunction with certain keyboard commands allows you to distort the object or distort the object in perspective, as shown in Figure 4. You start by dragging any handle on the bounding box, then, to make the distortions work, you must apply the following *after* you start dragging a handle: Press and hold [Shift] [Ctrl](Win) or [Shift]⌘ (Mac) to distort the image or press and hold [Shift][Alt] [Ctrl](Win) while dragging to distort in perspective. On a Macintosh, press and hold [Shift][option]⌘ to execute the same transformation.

Using the Transform Panel

The Transform panel displays information about the size, orientation, and location of one or more selected objects. You can type new values directly into the Transform panel to modify selected objects. All values on the panel refer to the bounding boxes of the objects, whether the bounding box is visible or not. You can also identify on the Transform panel the reference point on the bounding box from which the object will be transformed. To reflect an object vertically or horizontally using the Transform panel, click the Transform panel options button, then choose the appropriate menu item, as shown in Figure 5.

Figure 4 *Use the Free Transform tool to distort objects in perspective*

Figure 5 *Transform panel*

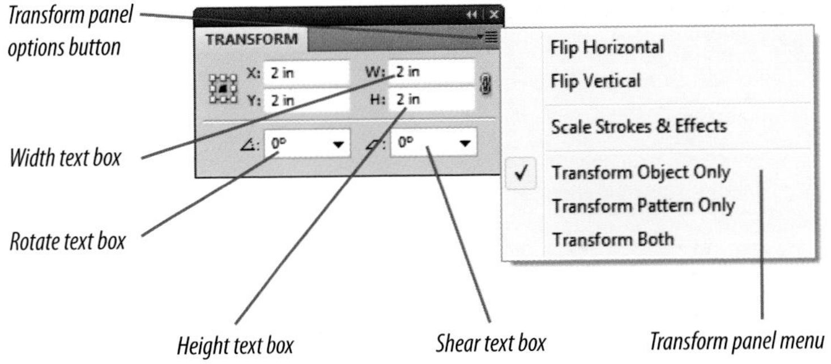

Transform panel options button

Width text box

Rotate text box

Height text box

Shear text box

Transform panel menu

TRANSFORM
X: 2 in   W: 2 in
Y: 2 in   H: 2 in
△: 0°   ⬧: 0°

Flip Horizontal
Flip Vertical
Scale Strokes & Effects
✓ Transform Object Only
Transform Pattern Only
Transform Both

Rotate an object around a defined point

1. Open AI 4-1.ai, then save it as **Mod Clock**.

2. Click the **Selection tool** , click the **brown line**, then click the **Rotate tool** .

3. Press and hold **[Alt]**(Win) or **[option]**(Mac), then click the **bottom anchor point of the line** to set the point of origin for the rotation.

   With a transform tool selected, pressing [Alt] (Win) or [option](Mac) and clicking the artboard defines the point of origin and opens the tool's dialog box.

4. Enter **30** in the Angle text box, then click **Copy**.

5. Press **[Ctrl][D]** (Win) or ⌘ **[D]** (Mac) ten times so that your screen resembles Figure 6.

   [Ctrl][D](Win) or ⌘ [D](Mac) is the quick key for the Transform Again command.

6. Select all 12 lines, group them, send them to the back, then hide them.

7. Select the small orange circle, click **View** on the Application bar, then click **Outline**.

(continued)

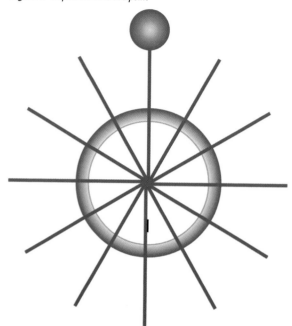

Figure 6 *12 paths rotated at a point*

NEW Understanding X and Y Coordinates

The X and Y coordinates of an object indicate the object's horizontal (X) and vertical (Y) locations on the artboard. These numbers, which appear on the Transform panel and the Control panel, represent the horizontal and vertical distance from the upper-left corner of the artboard. (Note that this is a modified feature in Illustrator CS5; in previous versions, all coordinates were based on the lower-left corner of the artboard.) The current X and Y coordinates also depend on the specified reference point. Nine reference points are listed to the left of the X and Y Value text boxes on the Transform panel. Reference points are those points of a selected object that represent the four corners of the object's bounding box, the horizontal and vertical centers of the bounding box, and the center point of the bounding box.

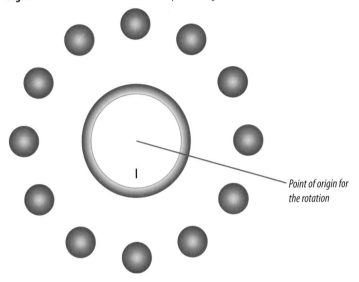

Figure 7 *12 circles rotated around a central point of origin*

Point of origin for
the rotation

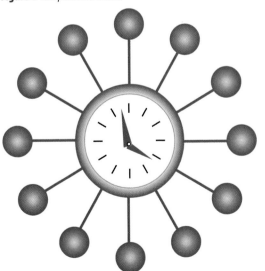

Figure 8 *Completed illustration*

8. Click the **Rotate tool**, press and hold
   [Alt](Win) or **[option]**(Mac), then click the
   center point of the larger circle to set the
   point of origin for the next rotation.

   The small circle will rotate around the center
   point of the larger circle.

TIP Outline mode is especially useful for rotations
   because center points are visible and easy to target
   as points of origin.

9. Enter **30**, click **Copy**, apply the Transform
   Again command ten times, then switch to
   Preview mode.

10. Your screen should resemble Figure 7.

11. Select the small black vertical dash, then
    transform again 11 times.

    The dash is also rotated around the center point
    of the larger circle, since a new point of origin
    has not been set.

12. Unlock the hands in the scratch area, then
    move them onto the clock face.

13. Show all, then deselect all to reveal the 12
    segments, as shown in Figure 8.

14. Save your work, then close the Mod
    Clock document.

*You selected a point on the brown line, then rotated 11 copies
of the object around that point. Second, you defined the point
of origin for a rotation by clicking the center point of the larger
circle, then rotated 11 copies of the smaller circle and the dash
around that point.*

Use the Shear tool

1. Open AI 4-2.ai, then save it as **Shear**.
2. Select all, copy, paste in front, then fill the copy with the swatch named Graphite.
3. Click the **Shear tool** ⬚.

TIP The Shear tool is hidden behind the Scale tool.

4. Press and hold [**Alt**] Win) or [**option**](Mac), then click the **bottom-right anchor** point of the letter R to set the origin point of the shear and open the Shear dialog box.
5. Enter **45** in the Shear Angle text box, verify that the Horizontal option button is checked, then click **OK**.
6. Your screen should resemble Figure 9.
7. Click the **Scale tool** ⬚.
8. Press [**Alt**](Win) or [**option**](Mac), then click any bottom anchor point or segment on the sheared objects to set the point of origin for the scale and open the Scale dialog box.
9. Click the **Non-Uniform option button**, enter **100** in the Horizontal text box, enter **50** in the Vertical text box, then click **OK**.
10. Send the sheared objects to the back.
11. Apply a 1 pt black stroke to the orange letters, deselect, then compare your screen to Figure 10.
12. Save your work, then close the Shear document.

You created a shadow effect using the Shear tool.

Figure 9 *Letterforms sheared on a 45° axis*

The objects are sheared on a 45° angle in relation to a horizontal axis

Figure 10 *Shearing is useful for creating a cast-shadow effect*

The shadow is "cast" from the letters in the foreground

Transforming and Distorting Objects

Figure 11 *Use the Reflect tool for illustrations that demand exact symmetry*

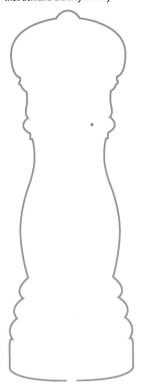

Figure 12 *Selecting two anchor points with the Direct Selection tool*

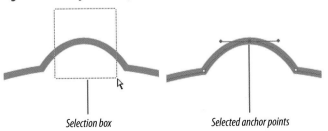

Selection box   Selected anchor points

Use the Reflect tool

1. Open AI 4-3.ai, then save it as **Reflect**.
2. Select all, then zoom in on the top anchor point.
3. Click the **Reflect tool** .

    The Reflect tool is hidden behind the Rotate tool.
4. Press **[Alt]**(Win) or **[option]**(Mac), then click the **top anchor point** to set the point of origin for the reflection.
5. Click the **Vertical option button**, then click Copy.

    A **copy** is positioned, reflected across the axis that you defined, as shown in Figure 11.
6. Deselect all, then click the **Direct Selection tool** .
7. Using Figure 12 as a guide, drag a selection box around the top two anchor points to select them.

    TIP One of the anchor points is directly on top of the other because of the reflected copy.

8. Click **Object** on the Application bar, point to **Path**, click **Average**, click the **Both option button**, then click **OK**.
9. Click **Object** on the Application bar, point to **Path**, click **Join**, then click **OK**.
10. Select the bottom two anchor points, average them on both axes, then join them to close the path.
11. Save your work, then close the Reflect document.

You created a reflected copy of a path, then averaged and joined two pairs of open points.

Use the Free Transform tool to distort in perspective

1. Open AI 4-4.ai, then save it as **Distort in Perspective**.

2. Press **[Ctrl][A]**(Win) or ⌘ **[A]**(Mac), then click the **Free Transform Tool**.

   The Free Transform tool is visible even if selection edges are hidden.

3. Click and begin dragging the **upper-right handle** directly to the right, then, while still dragging, press and hold **[Shift][Ctrl]**(Win) or **[Shift]** ⌘ (Mac) and continue dragging, releasing your mouse when you are halfway to the edge of the artboard.

4. Compare your result to Figure 13.

   The illustration is distorted; the upper-right corner is moved to the right. The other three corners do not move.

5. Click **Edit** on the Application bar, then click **Undo Perspective**.

   The way this command is listed is a bit of a misnomer. You distorted the illustration, but you did not distort in perspective. To be more specific, the command should say "Undo Distort."

   (continued)

Figure 13 *Distorting the illustration*

Shift/Ctrl/Alt

Figure 14 *Distorting the illustration in perspective*

Figure 15 *Illustration distorted in complex perspective*

6. Click and start dragging the **upper-right handle** directly to the right, then, while still dragging, press and hold **[Shift][Ctrl][Alt]** (Win) or **[Shift] [option] ⌘** (Mac) and continue dragging.

7. Release your mouse when you are halfway to the edge of the artboard, then compare your result to Figure 14.

   The illustration is distorted with a different perspective.

8. Click and drag the **upper-left corner** straight down, then while dragging, press and hold **[Shift][Ctrl][Alt]**(Win) or **[Shift][option] ⌘** (Mac) and continue dragging until your illustration resembles Figure 15.

9. Save your work, then close Distort in Perspective.

You used keyboard combinations first to distort the illustration, then to distort it in perspective.

Offset and
OUTLINE PATHS

What You'll Do

In this lesson, you will use the Offset Path command to create concentric squares and the Outline Stroke command to convert a stroked path into a closed path.

Using the Offset Path Command

Simply put, the Offset Path command creates a copy of a selected path set off by a specified distance. The Offset Path command is useful when working with closed paths—making concentric shapes or making many copies of a path at a regular distance from the original.

Figure 16 shows two sets of concentric circles. **Concentric** refers to objects that share the same center point, as the circles in both sets do. The set on the left was made with the Scale tool, applying an 85% scale and

copy to the outer circle, then repeating the transformation ten times. Note that with each successive copy, the distance from the copy to the previous circle decreases. The set on the right was made by offsetting the outside circle -.125", then applying the same offset to each successive copy. Note the different effect.

When you offset a closed path, a positive value creates a larger copy outside the original; a negative value creates a smaller copy inside the original.

Using the Outline Stroke Command

The Outline Stroke command converts a stroked path into a closed path that is the same width as the original stroked path.

This operation is useful if you want to apply a gradient to a stroke. It is also a useful design tool, allowing you to modify the outline of an object more than if it were just a stroke. Also, it is often easier to create an object with a single heavy stroke and then convert it to a closed path than it is to try to draw a closed path directly, as shown with the letter S in Figure 17.

Figure 16 *Two sets of concentric circles*

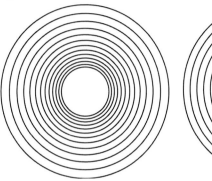 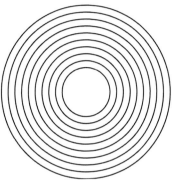

Concentric circles produced by the Scale tool

Concentric circles produced by the Offset Path command

Figure 17 *The Outline Stroke command converts a stroked path to a closed object*

Offset a path

1. Open AI 4-5.ai, then save it as **Squares**.

2. Select the square.

3. Click **Object** on the Application bar, point to **Path**, then click **Offset Path**.

4. Enter **-.125** in the Offset text box, then click **OK**.

   TIP Be sure that your Units preference is set to Inches in the General section of the Units Preferences.

   A negative value reduces the area of a closed path; a positive value increases the area.

5. Apply the Offset Path command with the same value four more times.

   TIP The Transform Again command does not apply to the Offset Path command because it is not one of the transform tools.

6. Deselect all, save your work, compare your screen to Figure 18, then close the Squares document.

   You used the Offset Path command to create concentric squares.

Figure 18 *Concentric squares created with the Offset Path command*

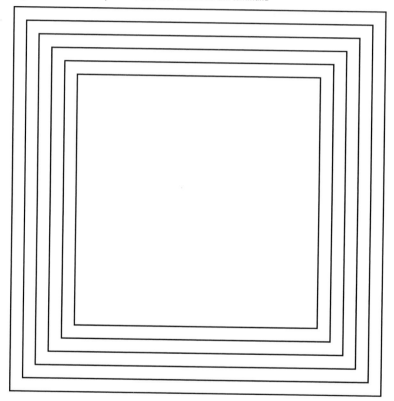

Transforming and Distorting Objects

Figure 19 *The Outline Stroke command converts any stroked path into a closed path*

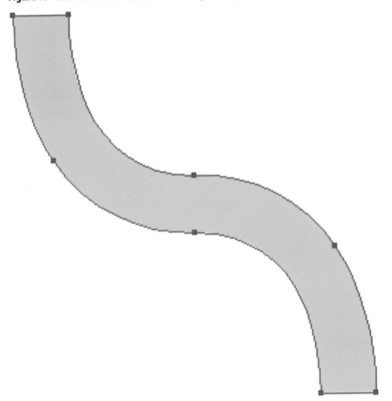

Convert a stroked path to a closed path

1. Open AI 4-6.ai, then save it as **Outlined Stroke**.

2. Select the path, then change the weight to 36 pt.

3. Click **Object** on the Application bar, point to **Path**, then click **Outline Stroke**.

4. The full weight of the stroke is converted to a closed path, as shown in Figure 19.

5. Save your work, then close the Outlined Stroke document.

You applied a heavy weight to a stroked path, then converted the stroke to a closed path, using the Outline Stroke command.

Create Compound
PATHS

What You'll Do

In this lesson, you will explore the role of compound paths for practical use and for artistic effects.

Defining a Compound Path

Practically speaking, you make a compound path to create a "hole" or "holes" in an object. As shown in Figure 20, if you were drawing the letter "D," you would need to create a hole in the outlined shape, through which you could see the background. To do so, select the object in back (in this case, the black outline that defines the letter) and the object in front (the yellow object that defines the hole) and apply the Make Compound Path command. When compounded, a "hole" appears where the two objects overlap.

The overlapping object still exists, however. It is simply *functioning* as a transparent hole in conjunction with the object behind it. If you move the front object independently, as shown in Figure 21, it yields an interesting result. Designers have seized upon this effect and have run with it, creating complex and eye-catching graphics, which Illustrator calls compound shapes.

It is important to understand that when two or more objects are compounded, Illustrator defines them as *one* object. This sounds strange at first, but the concept is as familiar to you as the letter D. You identify the letter D as a single object although it is drawn with two paths—one defining the outside edge, the other defining the inside edge.

Compound paths function as groups. You can select and manipulate an individual element with the Direct Selection tool, but you cannot change its appearance

attributes independently. Compound paths can be released and returned to their original component objects by applying the Release Compound Path command.

Figure 20 *The letter D is an example of a compound path*

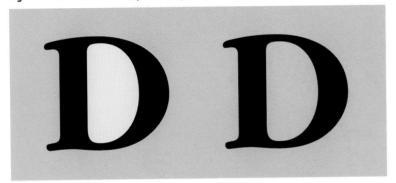

Figure 21 *Manipulating compound paths can yield interesting effects*

Create compound paths

1. Open AI 4-7.ai, then save it as **Simple Compound**.

2. Cut the red circle in the middle of the illustration, then undo the cut.

   The red circle creates the illusion that there's a hole in the life-preserver ring.

3. Select the red background object, then change its fill to the Ocean Blue gradient on the Swatches panel.

   The illusion is lost; the red circle no longer seems to be a hole in the life preserver.

4. Select both the white "life preserver" circle and the red circle in the center.

5. Click **Object** on the Application bar, point to **Compound Path**, then click **Make**.

   As shown in Figure 22, the two circles are compounded, with the top circle functioning as a "hole" in the larger circle behind it.

6. Move the background object left and right, and up and down behind the circles.

   The repositioned background remains visible through the compounded circles.

7. Deselect all, save your work, then close the Simple Compound document.

You selected two concentric circles and made them into one compound path, which allowed you to see through to the gradient behind the circles.

Figure 22 *A compound path creates the effect of a hole where two or more objects overlap*

Transforming and Distorting Objects

Figure 23 *A simple compound path*

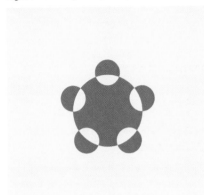

Figure 24 *A more complex compound path*

Each of the five small circles is scaled, using its own center point as the point of origin

Figure 25 *Simple compound paths can yield stunning visual effects*

Create special effects with compound paths

1. Open AI 4-8.ai, then save it as **Compound Path Effects**.

2. Select all.

   The light blue square is locked and does not become part of the selection.

3. Click **Object** on the Application bar, point to **Compound Path**, then click **Make**.

4. Deselect, click the **Direct Selection tool** , then click the **edge** of the large blue circle.

5. Click the **center point** of the circle, then scale the circle 50% so that your work resembles Figure 23.

6. Click **Select** on the Application bar, then click **Inverse**.

7. Click **Object** on the Application bar, point to **Transform**, then click **Transform Each**.

8. Enter **225** in the Horizontal and Vertical text boxes in the Scale section of the Transform Each dialog box, click **OK,** then deselect all.

   Your work should resemble Figure 24.

9. Using the Direct Selection tool , click the **edge of the center circle**, click its center point to select the entire circle, then scale the circle 120%.

10. Apply the Transform Again command twice, then compare your screen to Figure 25.

11. Deselect all, save your work, then close Compound Path Effects.

You made a compound path out of five small circles and one large circle. You then manipulated the size and location of the individual circles to create interesting designs.

Work with the
PATHFINDER PANEL

What You'll Do

In this lesson, you will use shape modes and pathfinders to create compound shapes from simple shapes.

Defining a Compound Shape

Like a compound path, a **compound shape** is two or more paths that are combined in such a way that "holes" appear wherever paths overlap.

The term "compound shape" is used to distinguish a complex compound path from a simple one. Compound shapes generally assume an artistic rather than a practical role. To achieve the effect, compound shapes tend to be composed of multiple objects. You can think of a compound shape as an illustration composed of multiple compound paths.

Understanding Essential Shape Modes and Pathfinders

Shape modes and **pathfinders** are preset operations that help you combine paths in a variety of ways. They are useful operations for creating complex or irregular shapes from basic shapes. In some cases, they are a means to an end in creating an object. In others, the operation they provide will be the end result you want to achieve. Shape modes and pathfinders can be applied to overlapping objects using the Effect menu or the Pathfinder panel.

For the purposes of drawing and creating new objects, the following five shape modes and pathfinders are essential; compare each with Figure 26.

Unite shape mode Converts two or more overlapping objects into a single, merged object.

Minus Front shape mode Where objects overlap, deletes the frontmost object(s) from the backmost object in a selection of overlapped objects.

Intersect shape mode Creates a single, merged object from the area where two or more objects overlap.

Minus Back pathfinder The opposite of Subtract; deletes the backmost object(s) from the frontmost object in a selection of overlapped objects.

Divide pathfinder Divides an object into its component filled faces. Illustrator defines a "face" as an area undivided by a line segment.

Figure 26 *Five essential shape modes and pathfinders*

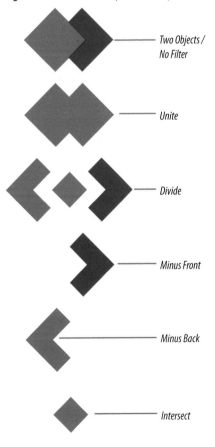

Two Objects /
No Filter

Unite

Divide

Minus Front

Minus Back

Intersect

Using the Pathfinder Panel

The Pathfinder panel contains ten buttons for creating compound shapes, as shown in Figure 27. As you learned earlier, a compound shape is a complex compound path. You can create a compound shape by overlapping two or more objects, then clicking one of the four shape mode buttons in the top row of the Pathfinder panel, or clicking the Pathfinder panel list arrow, then clicking Make Compound Shape. The four shape mode buttons are Unite, Minus Front, Intersect, and Exclude. When you apply a shape mode button, the two overlapping objects are combined into one object with the same formatting as the topmost object in the group before the shape mode button was applied. After applying a shape mode button, the resulting objects in the compound shape can be selected and formatted using the Direct Selection tool. You can also press [Alt](Win) or [option](Mac) when you click a shape mode button. Doing so results in a compound shape whose original objects can be selected and formatted using the Direct Selection tool.

Applying Shape Modes

Figure 28 shows a square overlapped by a circle.

If you apply the Minus Front shape mode button, the resulting object is a compound shape, as shown in Figure 29. Notice the overlapped area is deleted from the square. The circle, too, is deleted, as shown in Figure 29. The result is a simple reshaped object.

If you took the same two overlapping shapes shown in Figure 28, but this time pressed [Alt](Win) or [option](Mac) when

Figure 27 *Pathfinder panel*

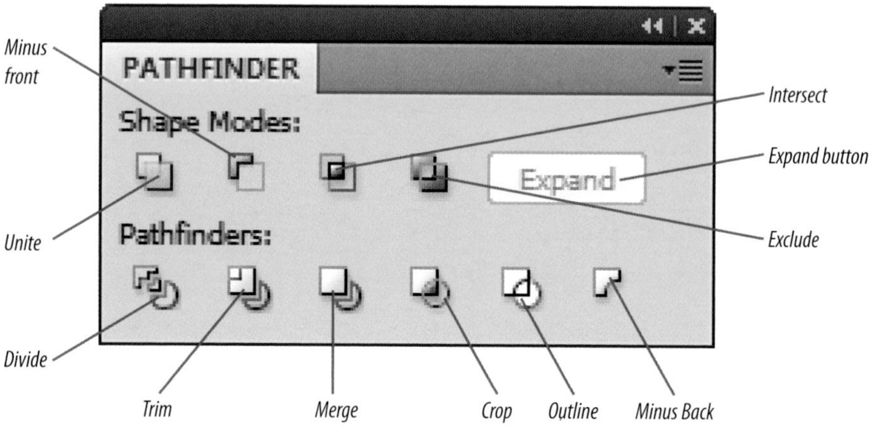

Minus front

Intersect

Expand button

Unite

Exclude

Divide

Trim   Merge   Crop   Outline   Minus Back

Figure 28 *Two overlapping objects*

applying the Subtract shape mode button, the circle would not be deleted but would function as a hole or a "knockout" wherever it overlaps the square, as shown in Figure 30. The relationship is dynamic: You can move the circle independently with the Direct Selection tool to change its effect on the square and the resulting visual effect.

Figure 31 shows a group of objects converted into a compound shape using the Make Compound Shape command on the Pathfinder panel.

Releasing and Expanding Compound Shapes

You can release a compound shape, which separates it back into individual objects.

To release a compound shape, click the Pathfinder panel options button, then click Release Compound Shape. Expanding a compound shape is similar to releasing it, except that it maintains the shape of the compound object. You cannot select the original individual objects. You can expand a compound shape by selecting it, and then clicking the Expand button on the Pathfinder panel.

Figure 29 *Applying the Minus Front shape mode without [Alt] (Win) or [option] (Mac)*

Figure 30 *Applying the Minus Front shape mode with [Alt] (Win) or [option] (Mac)*

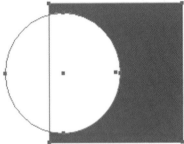

Figure 31 *A compound shape*

Apply the Unite shape mode

1. Open AI 4-9.ai, then save it as **Heart Parts**.
2. Click **Window** on the Application bar, then click **Pathfinder**.
3. Select both circles, then click the **Unite button** 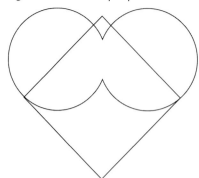 on the Pathfinder panel.

   The two objects are united.
4. Move the diamond shape up so that it overlaps the united circles, as shown in Figure 32.
5. Click the **Delete Anchor Point tool**, then delete the top anchor point of the diamond.
6. Select all, press and hold **[Alt]** (Win) or **[option]** (Mac), click the **Unite button**, then deselect all.

   Your screen should resemble Figure 33.
7. Remove the black stroke, then apply a red fill to the new object.
8. Draw a rectangle that covers the "hole" in the heart, then fill it with black, as shown in Figure 34.
9. Select all, press **[Alt]**(Win) or **[option]**(Mac), then click the **Unite button**.

   The heart turns black.
10. Double-click the **Scale tool**, then apply a non-uniform scale of 90% on the horizontal axis and 100% on the vertical axis.

You created a single heart-shaped object from two circles and a diamond shape using the Unite button.

Figure 32 *A diamond shape in position*

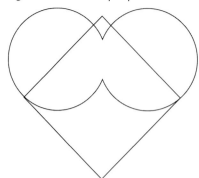

Figure 33 *The diamond shape and the object behind it are united*

Figure 34 *A heart shape created by applying the Unite shape mode to three objects*

Figure 35 *Circle overlaps the square*

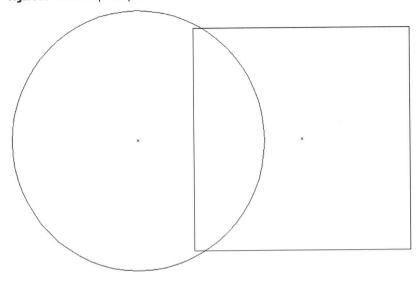

Figure 36 *Right circle is a reflected copy of the left one*

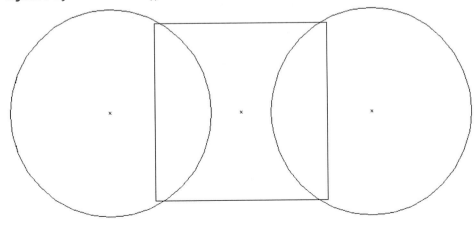

Apply the Minus Back shape mode

1. Rotate the black heart shape 180°, then hide it.
2. Create a square that is 1.5" × 1.5" without a fill color and with a 1 pt black stroke.
3. Create a circle that is 1.75" in width and height.
4. Switch to Outline mode.
5. Move the circle so that it overlaps the square, as shown in Figure 35.
6. Verify that the circle is still selected, click the **Reflect tool** , press **[Alt]**(Win) or **[option]**(Mac), then click the **center point** of the square.
7. Click the **Vertical option button**, click **Copy**, then arrange the three objects so that your work resembles Figure 36.
8. Select all, then click the **Minus Front button** on the Pathfinder panel.

(continued)

9. Switch to Preview mode, then apply a black fill to the new object.

10. Show all, then overlap the new shape with the black heart shape to make a spade shape.

11. Select all, click the **Unite button** 🔲, then deselect.

Your work should resemble Figure 37.

You overlapped a square with two circles, then applied the Minus Front shape mode to delete the overlapped areas from the square. You used the Unite button to unite the new shape with a heart-shaped object to create a spade shape.

Figure 37 *The final shape, with all elements united*

Working with the Align Panel

The Align panel offers a quick and simple solution for aligning selected objects along the axis you specify. Along the vertical axis, you can align selected objects by their rightmost, leftmost, or center point. On the horizontal axis, you can align objects by their topmost point, center point, or bottommost point. You can also use the panel to distribute objects evenly along a horizontal or vertical axis. In contrasting the Align panel with the Average command, think of the Average command as a method for aligning anchor points and the Align panel as a method for aligning entire objects.

When you align and distribute objects, you have the choice of aligning them to a selection, a key object, or the artboard. If you want to align or distribute objects using the artboard, you must first define the artboard area using the Artboard tool on the Tools panel. Click the Align To list arrow on the Align panel, then click Align to Artboard. Resize the artboard as desired. Finally, choose the alignment setting you need on the Align panel.

Figure 38 *Use the Align panel to align objects precisely*

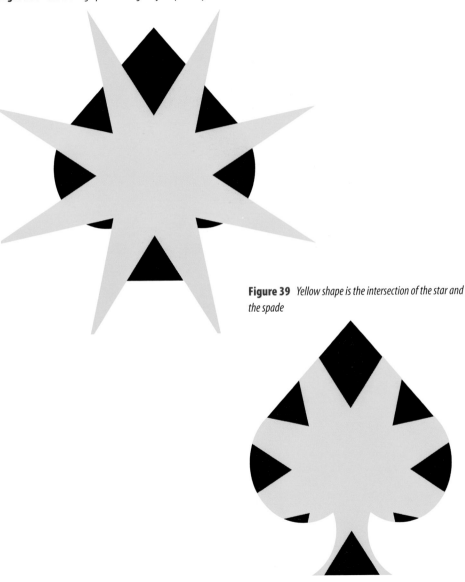

Figure 39 *Yellow shape is the intersection of the star and the spade*

1. Click the **Star tool** ⭐, then click the artboard.

2. Enter **1** in the Radius 1 text box, **3** in the Radius 2 text box, and **8** in the Points text box, then click **OK**.

3. Apply a yellow fill to the star and no stroke.

4. Use the Align panel to align the center points of the two objects so that they resemble Figure 38.

5. Copy the black spade, then paste in front.

   Two black spades are now behind the yellow star; the top one is selected.

6. Press and hold **[Shift]**, then click to add the star to the selection.

7. Click the **Intersect shape mode button** 🔲 on the Pathfinder panel.

   The intersection of the star and the copied spade is now a single closed path. Your work should resemble Figure 39.

   Save your work, then close Heart Parts.

You created a star, then created a copy of the black spade-shaped object. You used the Intersect shape mode button to capture the intersection of the two objects as a new object.

Apply the Divide pathfinder

1. Open AI 4-10.ai, then save it as **Divide**.
2. Select the red line, then double-click the **Rotate tool** 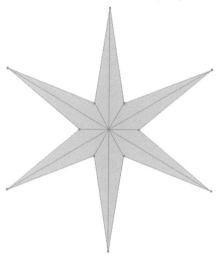.
3. Enter **30** in the Angle text box, then click **Copy**.
4. Repeat the transformation four times.
5. Select all, then click the **Divide button** on the Pathfinder panel.

   The blue star is divided into 12 separate objects, as defined by the red lines, which have been deleted. See Figure 40.
6. Deselect, click the **Direct Selection tool**, select the left half of the top point, press **[Shift]**, then select every other object, for a total of six objects.
7. Apply an orange fill to the selected objects.
8. Select the inverse, then apply a yellow fill so that your work resembles Figure 41.
9. Save your work, then close the Divide document.

You used six lines to define a score pattern, then used those lines and the Divide pathfinder to break the star into 12 separate objects.

Figure 40 *Blue star is divided into 12 objects by the Divide pathfinder*

Figure 41 *Divide pathfinder is useful for adding dimension*

Transforming and Distorting Objects

Figure 42 *An example of the Exclude shape mode*

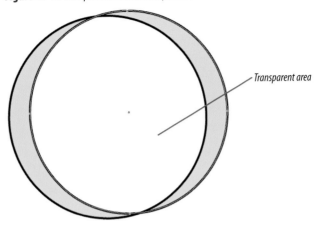

Transparent area

Figure 43 *An example of the Intersect shape mode*

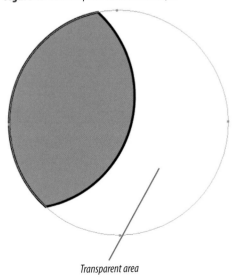

Transparent area

Create compound shapes using the Pathfinder panel

1. Open AI 4-11.ai, then save it as **Compound Shapes**.

2. Click **View** on the Application bar, then click **Yellow**.

3. Select the two yellow circles, press **[Alt]** (Win) or **[option]** (Mac), then click the **Exclude button** on the Pathfinder panel.

   The area that the top object overlaps becomes transparent.

4. Deselect, click the **Direct Selection tool** then move either circle to change the shape and size of the filled areas.

   Figure 42 shows one effect that can be achieved.

5. Select Green from the View menu, select the two green circles, press **[Alt]**(Win) or **[option]**(Mac), then click the **Intersect button** on the Pathfinder panel.

   The area not overlapped by the top circle becomes transparent.

6. Deselect, then use the Direct Selection tool to move either circle to change the shape and size of the filled area.

   Figure 43 shows one effect that can be achieved.

7. Save your work, then close the Compound Shapes document.

You applied shape modes to two pairs of circles, then moved the circles to create different shapes and effects.

Create special effects with compound shapes

1. Open AI 4-12.ai, then save it as **Compound Shape Effects**.

2. Select all, press **[Alt]**(Win) or **[option]**(Mac), then click the **Exclude button** ⊡ on the Pathfinder panel.

   Your work should resemble Figure 44.

3. Deselect all, click the **Direct Selection tool** ⊳, select the three squares, then move them to the right, as shown in Figure 45.

   (continued)

Figure 44 *A compound shape*

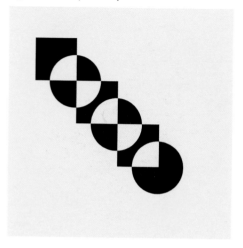

Figure 45 *A compound shape*

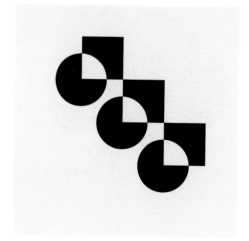

Transforming and Distorting Objects

Figure 46 *A compound shape*

Figure 47 *A compound shape*

4. Drag and drop a copy of the three squares, as shown in Figure 46.

TIP Use [Shift][Alt](Win) or [Shift][option](Mac) to drag and drop a copy at a 45-degree angle or in straight vertical or horizontal lines.

5. Scale each circle 150% using the Transform Each command.

6. Scale the center circle 200%, then bring it to the front of the stacking order.

7. Press **[Alt]**(Win) or **[option]**(Mac), then click the **Intersect button** on the Pathfinder panel.

Figure 47 shows the results of the intersection. Your final illustration may vary slightly.

TIP The topmost object affects all the objects behind it in a compound shape.

8. Save your work, then close Compound Shape Effects.

You made three squares and three circles into a compound shape by excluding overlapping shape areas. You then manipulated the size and location of individual elements to create different effects. Finally, you enlarged a circle, brought it to the front, then changed its mode to Intersect. Only the objects that were overlapped by the circle remained visible.

Use the Shape
BUILDER TOOL

What You'll Do

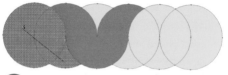

In this lesson, you use the Shape Builder tool to create new shapes from overlapping objects.

NEW The Shape Builder tool, a new feature in Illustrator CS5, is grouped in the Tools panel with the Live Paint Bucket. This makes sense, because the tool functions in a similar manner to the Live Paint Bucket.

The Shape Builder tool is designed to help you create new objects from overlapping objects. Comparing it to the Live Paint Bucket (covered in Chapter 3) can help you understand its role. Where the Live

Paint Bucket fills closed paths created by overlapping objects, the Shape Builder tool creates new closed paths from overlapping objects. From this perspective, you can think of the Shape Builder tool as a combination of the Live Paint Bucket and the Pathfinder tools.

Figure 48 shows eight orange-filled circles overlapping. The Shape Builder tool is selected in the Tools panel, and a pink fill and black stroke has been chosen in the

Figure 48 *Specifying objects to be created with the Shape Builder tool*

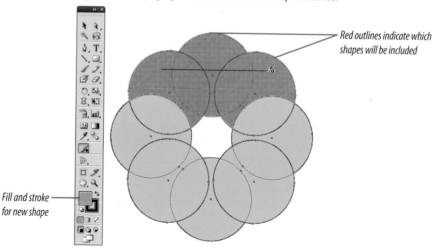

Red outlines indicate which shapes will be included

Fill and stroke for new shape

Tools panel. Closed objects are highlighted when the Shape Builder tool is dragged across them.

In Figure 49, those objects are united into a single object with the pink fill and a black stroke. Note that this is not something you could do with the Unite pathfinder. The Unite pathfinder would have united the three whole circles, but, as shown in this example, the Shape Builder tool created a single object from overlapping components of the circles.

In Figure 50, the Shape Builder tool has been dragged to the negative space in the center so that it will be added to the merged object.

In addition to creating new objects, the Shape Builder tool also deletes closed paths from overlapping objects. To delete an object with the Shape Builder tool, press and hold [Alt](Win) or [option](Mac), then click or drag over the objects you want to delete. Note the minus sign beside the Shape Builder tool icon in Figure 51. Upon release, the objects are deleted, as shown in Figure 52.

Figure 49 *New object created with the Shape Builder tool*

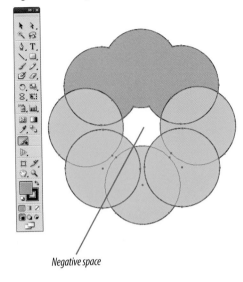

Negative space

Figure 50 *Adding the negative space to the object*

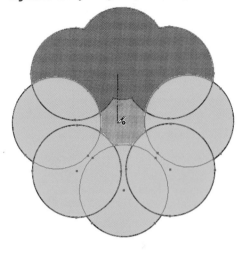

Figure 51 *Specifying objects to be deleted*

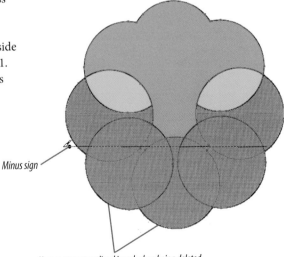

Minus sign

Shapes are not outlined in red when being deleted

Figure 52 *Illustration after deletion*

Create objects with the Shape Builder tool

1. Open AI 4-13.ai, then save it as **Shape Builder**.

2. Select all, then click the **Shape Builder tool**.

3. Set the fill and stroke color to pink and none, respectively.

   Your artboard should resemble Figure 53. Even though the yellow circles are selected, when you set the foreground color to a different color, the circles don't change color.

4. Click and drag to highlight the objects shown in Figure 54.

   When you release your mouse, the objects are united as a single object.

5. Click and drag to highlight the objects shown in Figure 55.

   Because you included the first pink object, the objects are united into a single object, as shown in Figure 56.

6. Save your work.

You dragged with the Shape Builder tool to create a new object.

Figure 53 *Selecting a fill color for the Shape Builder tool*

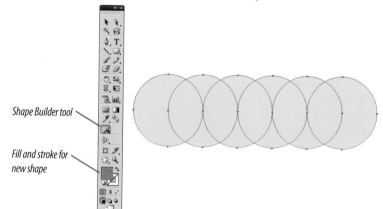

Shape Builder tool

Fill and stroke for new shape

Figure 54 *Highlighting objects to be merged into a new object*

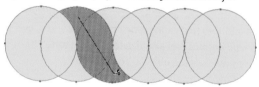

Figure 55 *Adding more objects to the new shape*

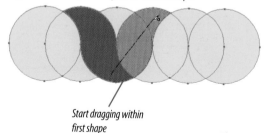

Start dragging within first shape

Figure 56 *The new shape*

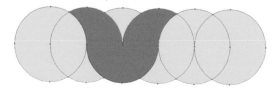

Transforming and Distorting Objects

Figure 57 *Highlighting shapes to be deleted*

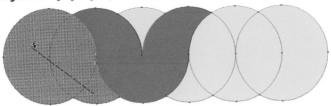

Figure 58 *The final shape*

Delete objects with the Shape Builder tool

1. Verify that the entire illustration is selected.

2. Press and hold **[Alt]**(Win) or **[Option]**(Mac), then drag the Shape Builder tool over the objects shown in Figure 57.

   When you release, the objects are deleted.

3. Press and hold **[Shift][Alt]**(Win) or **[Shift] [Option]**(Mac), then drag the Shape Builder tool over all the yellow objects to the right of the pink shape.

   Adding the Shift key to the combination allows you to drag a selection square to highlight more objects.

4. Press and hold **[Alt]/[Option]**, then click the **last remaining yellow object**.

   Your result should resemble Figure 58.

5. Save your work, then close the file.

You used the Shape Builder tool to delete objects.

Create Clipping
MASKS

What You'll Do

In this lesson, you will explore the role of clipping masks for practical use and for artistic effects.

Defining a Clipping Mask

Clipping masks are used to yield a practical result. And as with compound paths, that practical result can be manipulated to create interesting graphic effects.

Practically speaking, you use a clipping mask as a "window" through which you view some or all of the objects behind the mask in the stacking order. When you select any two or more objects and apply the Make Clipping Mask command, the *top object* becomes the mask and the object behind it becomes "masked." You will be able to see only the parts of the masked object that are visible *through* the mask, as shown in Figure 59. The mask crops the object behind it.

Using Multiple Objects as a Clipping Mask

When you select multiple objects and apply the Make Clipping Mask command, the top object becomes the mask. Since every object has its own position in the stacking order, it stands to reason that there can be only one top object.

If you want to use multiple objects as a mask, you can do so by first making them into a compound path because Illustrator regards compound paths as a single object. Therefore, a compound path containing multiple objects can be used as a single mask.

Creating Masked Effects

Special effects with clipping masks are, quite simply, fun! You can position as many objects as you like behind the mask and position them in such a way that the mask crops them in visually interesting (and eye-popping!) ways. See Figure 60 for an example.

 ## Using the Draw Inside Drawing Mode

The Draw Inside drawing mode does just what its name implies: it allows you to create one object within the perimeter of another object. Drawing one object inside another is essentially the same thing as creating a clipping mask. When you draw an object inside another, the two objects behave the same way any two objects behave in a clipping set. The relationship can be undone with the Clipping Mask/Release command. The big difference between using the Draw Inside drawing mode and making a clipping mask is that the Draw Inside option can involve only two objects.

Figure 59 *Clipping mask crops the object behind it*

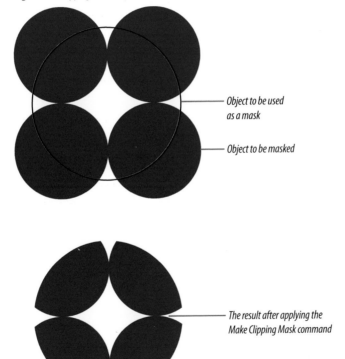

— *Object to be used as a mask*

— *Object to be masked*

— *The result after applying the Make Clipping Mask command*

Figure 60 *Masks can be used for stunning visual effects*

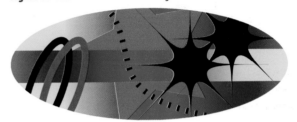

Create a clipping mask

1. Open AI 4-14.ai, then save it as **Simple Masks**.
2. Click **View** on the Application bar, then click **Mask 1**.
3. Move the rectangle so that it overlaps the gold spheres as shown in Figure 61.
4. Apply the Bring to Front command to verify that the rectangle is in front of all the spheres.
5. Select the seven spheres and the rectangle.
6. Click **Object** on the Application bar, point to **Clipping Mask**, then click **Make**.
7. Deselect, then compare your screen to Figure 62.
8. Click **View** on the Application bar, then click **Mask 2**.
9. Select the three circles, then move them over the "gumballs."

   The three circles are a compound path.

10. Select the group of gumballs and the three circles, then apply the Make Clipping Mask command.
11. Deselect, click **Select** on the Application bar, point to **Object**, then click **Clipping Masks**.
12. Apply a 1 pt black stroke to the masks. Your work should resemble Figure 63.
13. Save your work, then close the Simple Masks document.

You used a rectangle as a clipping mask. Then, you used three circles to mask a group of small spheres, and applied a black stroke to the mask.

Figure 61 *Masking objects must be in front of objects to be masked*

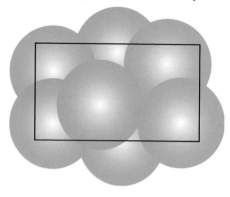

Figure 62 *The rectangle masks the gold spheres*

Figure 63 *A compound path used as a mask*

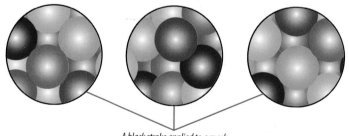

A black stroke applied to a mask

Figure 64 *Lining up the letter g*

Figure 65 *Positioning the magnifying glass*

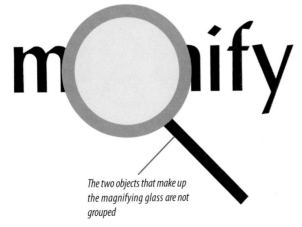

The two objects that make up
the magnifying glass are not
grouped

Apply a fill to a clipping mask

1. Open AI 4-15.ai, then save it as **Magnify**.

2. Move the large text over the small text so that the letters *g* align as shown in Figure 64.

3. Select the smaller text, then hide it.

4. Select the magnifying glass and the handle, then drag them over the letter *g*, as shown in Figure 65.

5. Deselect all, select only the circle and the text, click **Object** on the Application bar, point to **Clipping Mask**, then click **Make**.

   The circle is the masking object.

6. Deselect, click **Select** on the Application bar, point to **Object**, then click **Clipping Masks**.

7. Use the Swatches panel to apply a light blue fill and a gray stroke to the mask.

(continued)

8. Change the weight of the stroke to 8 pt, so that your work resembles Figure 66.

9. Show all, deselect, then compare your screen to Figure 67.

10. Select the mask only, press and hold **[Shift]**, then click the **magnifying glass handle**.

11. Press the **arrow keys** to move the magnifying glass.

    As you move the magnifying glass left and right, it gives the illusion that the magnifying glass is enlarging the text. This would make for an interesting animation in a PDF or on a web page.

12. Save your work, then close the Magnify document.

You used the circle in the illustration as a clipping mask in combination with the large text. You added a fill and a stroke to the mask, creating the illusion that the small text is magnified in the magnifying glass.

Figure 66 *A fill and stroke are applied to a mask*

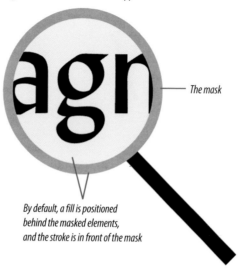

The mask

By default, a fill is positioned behind the masked elements, and the stroke is in front of the mask

Figure 67 *Large text is masked by the magnifying glass*

When a fill is applied to a mask, the fill is positioned behind all the objects that are masked

As the mask moves, different areas of the large text become visible, creating the illusion of a magnifying glass moving over a word

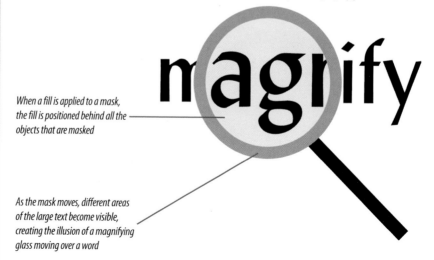

Transforming and Distorting Objects

Figure 68 *Outlined text used as a mask*

MASK

Figure 69 *Curvy object in position to be masked by the letters*

Figure 70 *Object behind the mask is selected*

The rectangle behind
the mask is selected

Use text as a clipping mask

1. Open AI 4-16.ai, then save it as **Mask Effects**.
2. Select the four letters that make the word MASK.

   The word MASK was converted to outlines
   and ungrouped.
3. Make the four letters into a compound path.
4. With the compound path still selected, select the
   rectangle behind it.
5. Apply the Make Clipping Mask command,
   then deselect.
6. Save your work, then compare your text
   to Figure 68.

*You converted outlines to a compound path, then used the
compound path as a mask.*

Use a clipping mask for special effects

1. Position the curvy object with the gradient fill
   over the mask, as shown in Figure 69.
2. Cut the curvy object.
3. Use the **Direct Selection tool** ▸ to select the
   original rectangle behind the mask.

TIP Click slightly above the mask until you see the
   rectangle selected, as shown in Figure 70.

(continued)

4. Paste in front, then deselect so that your screen resembles Figure 71.

The object is pasted in front of the masked rectangle and behind the mask.

5. Click the **Selection tool** , select the purple dotted line, position it over the letter K, then cut the purple dotted line.

6. Select the mask (rectangle) with the Direct Selection tool , click **Edit** on the Application bar, then click **Paste in Front**.

7. Using the same technique, mask the other objects on the artboard in any way that you choose.

When finished, your mask should contain all of the objects, as shown in Figure 72.

TIP Add a stroke to the mask if desired.

8. Save and close Mask Effects.

You created visual effects by pasting objects behind a mask.

 Use the Draw Inside drawing mode

1. Open AI 4-17.ai, save it as **Draw Inside**, click the **Selection Tool** , then select the blue square at the top of the document.

When you select the blue square, by default the Fill and Stroke buttons at the bottom of the tools panel take on the object's colors, which, in this case, are blue and none.

2. Click the **Draw Inside button** at the bottom of the Tools panel, then click the **Ellipse tool**.

Because you must have an object selected to use the Draw Inside drawing mode, the object you draw will always be the same fill and stroke color

(continued)

Figure 71 *Curvy object is masked by the letters*

Figure 72 *Pasting multiple objects behind a mask yields interesting effects*

Figure 73 *Drawing the yellow ellipse inside the blue square*

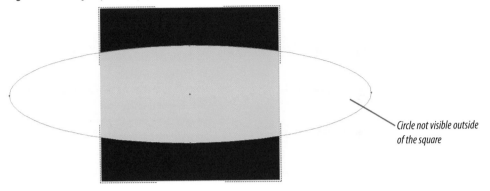

Circle not visible outside of the square

Figure 74 *Drawing the pink ellipse inside the outlines via the Paste command*

as the object you're drawing into. You can make them different colors only after you draw inside.

3. Draw an ellipse of approximately the same size as the pink ellipse already on the artboard, which overlaps the blue square.

4. With the ellipse still selected, change its fill color to yellow.

   Figure 73 shows one example of how the ellipse is drawn within the blue square. Dotted lines around the four corners of the blue square indicate that it is functioning as a mask for the ellipse. As long as you stay in Draw Inside drawing mode, any object you create will be drawn inside the blue square.

5. Click the **Normal drawing mode button**, select the word MASK, click the Type **menu**, then click **Create Outlines**.

6. With the outlines still selected, click the **Object menu**, point to **Compound Path**, click **Make**, then fill them with any green swatch in the Swatches panel.

7. Defined as a compound path, the letter outlines are now a single object into which you can draw.

8. Select the pink ellipse, cut it, select the MASK outlines, then click the **Draw Inside button**.

   Dotted lines appear around the MASK outlines, indicated they can be drawn into.

9. Click the **Edit menu**, click **Paste**, then move the ellipse so that it overlaps the MASK outlines as shown in Figure 74.

10. Save your work, then close Draw Inside.ai.

You used the draw inside drawing mode to create objects within other objects and within outlined text.

Transform objects.

1. Open AI 4-18.ai, then save it as **Transform Skills**.
2. Select "DIVIDE."
3. Scale the text objects non-uniformly: Horizontal = 110% and Vertical = 120%.
4. Rotate the text objects 7°.
5. Shear the text objects 25° on the horizontal axis.
6. Save your work.

Offset and outline paths.

1. Ungroup the text outlines.
2. Using the Offset Path command, offset each letter -.05".
3. Save your work.

Work with the Pathfinder panel.

1. Select all.
2. Apply the Divide pathfinder.

3. Fill the divided elements with different colors, using the Direct Selection tool.
4. Select all, then apply a 2-point white stroke. (*Hint*: Enlarge the view to see the effect better.)
5. Save your work, compare your image to Figure 75, then close the Transform Skills document.

Figure 75 *Completed Skills Review, Part 1*

Create compound paths.

1. Open AI 4-19.ai, then save it as **Compounded**.
2. Select all, press [Alt] (Win) or [option] (Mac), then click the Exclude button on the Pathfinder panel.
3. Deselect, then click the center of the small square with the Direct Selection tool.
4. Rotate a copy of the small square 45°.
5. Save your work, compare your image to Figure 76, then close the Compounded document.

Use the Shape Builder tool.

1. Open AI 4-21.ai, then save it as **Shape Builder Skills**.
2. Select all, then set the fill color on the objects to None so that you can see the shapes being created by the overlapping.
3. Click the Shape Builder tool.
4. Set the fill and stroke color to light blue and none, respectively, then compare your results to Figure 76.

(*Hint*: Even though the circles are selected, when you set the foreground color to a different color with the Shape Builder tool, the circles don't change color.)

5. Click and drag to highlight the objects shown in Figure 77. When you release your mouse, the objects are united as a single object.
6. Change the fill color on the tools panel to a shade of red.

Figure 76 *Completed Skills Review, Part 2*

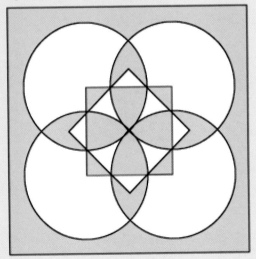

Figure 77 *Highlighting with the Shape Builder tool*

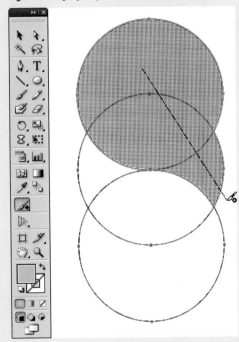

7. Click and drag to highlight the remaining objects shown in Figure 78.

8. Click the Selection tool, then click the artboard to deselect both objects.

9. Click the top blue object, then drag it away from the red object.

10. Save your work, then close Shape Builder Skills.

Create clipping masks.

1. Open AI 4-20.ai, then save it as **Masked Paths**.

2. Position any three of the letters on the right side of the canvas over the artwork on the left.

3. Hide the three letters you didn't choose.

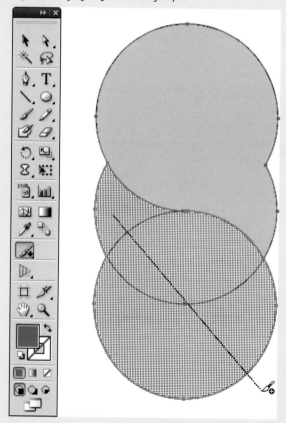

Figure 78 *Highlighting the remaining shapes*

4. Select the three letters over the artwork, click Object on the Application bar, point to Compound Path, then click Make.
5. Select everything on the artboard.
6. Click Object on the Application bar, point to Clipping Mask, then click Make.

7. Deselect all.
8. Click Select on the Application bar, point to Object, then click Clipping Masks.
9. Add a 1.5 pt black stroke to the selection.

10. Compare your results to Figure 79, which shows one potential result.
11. Save your work, then close Masked Paths.ai.

Figure 79 *Completed Skills Review, Part 3*

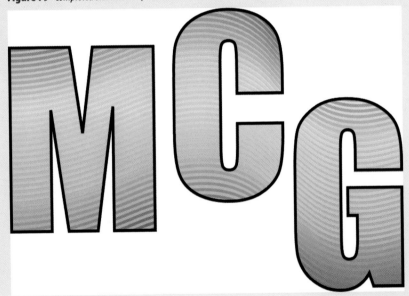

You are entering a contest to design a new stamp. You have decided to use a picture of Mona Lisa, which you have placed in an Illustrator document. You have positioned text over the image. Now, to complete the effect, you want to mimic the perforated edges of a stamp.

1. Open AI 4-22.ai, then save it as **Mona Lisa Stamp**.
2. Select all the circles, then make them into a compound path.
3. Add the rectangle to the selection.
   (*Hint*: The rectangle is behind the circles in the stacking order.)
4. Apply the Minus Front shape mode, then deselect all.
5. Save your work, compare your image to Figure 80, then close Mona Lisa Stamp.

Figure 80 *Completed Project Builder 1*

Transforming and Distorting Objects

You're contracted to design the logo for Wired Gifts, which is an online gift site. Your concept is of a geometric red bow. You feel that your idea will simultaneously convey the concepts of gifts and technology.

1. Open AI 4-23.ai, then save it as **Wired**.
2. Switch to Outline mode.
3. Select the small square, click the Rotate tool, press and hold [Alt](Win) or [option](Mac), then click the center of the large square.
4. Type 15 in the Angle text box, then click Copy.
5. Repeat the transformation 22 times.
6. Delete the large square at the center.
7. Switch to Preview mode.
8. Select all, then fill all the squares with Caribbean Blue. (*Hint*: The color swatches in the Swatches panel in this file have been saved with names.)
9. Apply the Divide pathfinder to the selection.
10. Fill the objects with the Red Bow gradient.
11. Delete the object in the center of the bow. (*Hint*: Use the Direct Selection tool to select the object.)
12. Select all, then remove the black stroke from the objects.
13. Save your work, compare your illustration with Figure 81, then close Wired.

Figure 81 *Completed Project Builder 2*

You're an illustrator for a small town quarterly magazine. You're designing an illustration to accompany an article titled "A Walk Down Main Street." You decide to distort the artwork in perspective to make for a more interesting illustration.

1. Open AI 4-24.ai, then save it as **Main Street Perspective**.
2. Select all of the buildings on the left, then click the Free Transform Tool.
    (*Hint*: The selection marks are hidden, but the Free Transform tool is nevertheless visible. Having selection marks hidden will help you to see the artwork better as you distort it.)
3. Click and begin dragging the upper-right handle straight down.
4. While still dragging, press and hold [Shift][Ctrl] [Alt](Win) or [Shift][Command](Mac) and continue dragging until you like the appearance of the artwork.
5. Release your mouse.
6. Click and drag the middle-left handle to the right to reduce the depth of the distortion.
    Figure 82 shows one possible result.
7. Using the same methodology, distort the buildings on the right in perspective.
    Figure 83 shows one possible solution.
8. Save your work, then close Main Street Perspective.

Figure 82 *Distorting the left of the illustration*

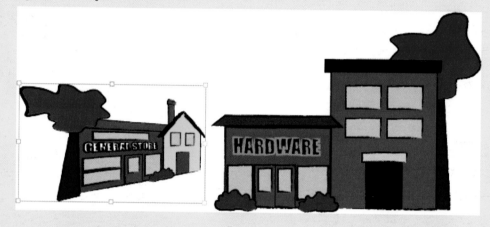

Figure 83 *Completed Design Project*

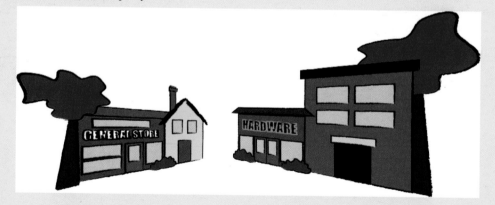

You are the design department manager for a toy company, and your next project is to design a dartboard that will be part of a package of "Safe Games" for kids. The target market is boys and girls ages six to adult. You will design the board but not the darts.

1. Create a new document and name it **Dartboard**.
2. Search the Internet for pictures of dartboards.
3. Research the sport of throwing darts. What are the official dimensions of a dartboard? Is there an official design? Are there official colors?
4. Decide which colors should be used for the board, keeping in mind that the sales department plans to position it as a toy for both girls and boys.
5. Using the skills you learned in this chapter and Figure 84 as a guide, design a dartboard.
6. Save your work, compare your image to Figure 84, then close Dartboard.

Figure 84 *Completed Portfolio Project*

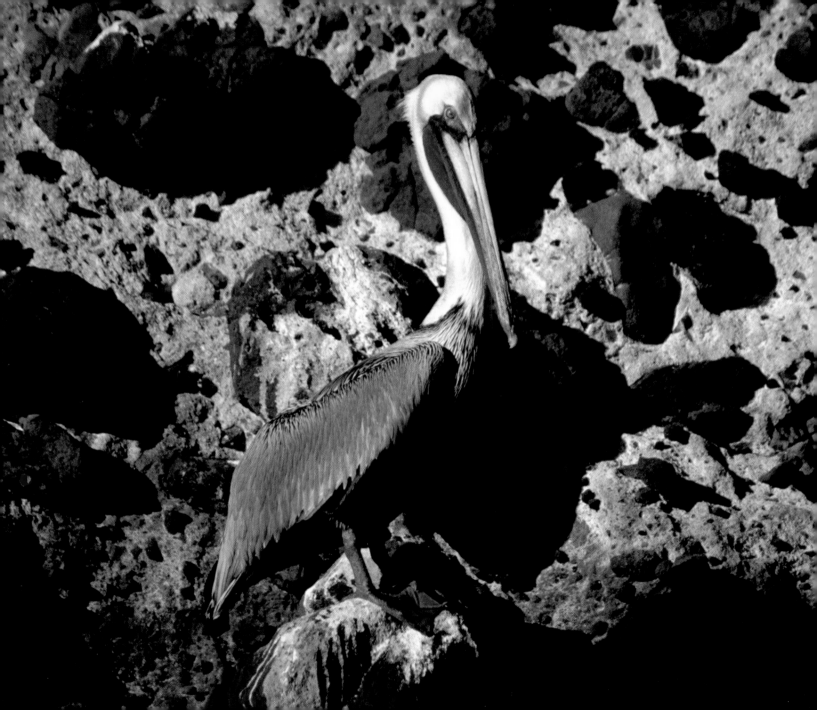

CHAPTER 5 WORKING WITH LAYERS

1. Create and modify layers
2. Manipulate layered artwork
3. Work with layered artwork
4. Create a clipping set

CHAPTER 5 WORKING WITH LAYERS

Designing with Layers

When you're creating complex artwork, keeping track of all the items on the artboard can become a challenge. Small items hide behind larger items and it may become difficult to find, select, and work with them. The Layers panel solves this problem because you can organize your work by placing objects or groups of objects on separate layers. Artwork on layers can be manipulated and modified independently from artwork on other layers. The Layers panel also provides effective options to select, hide, lock, and change the appearance of your work. In addition, layers are an effective solution for storing multiple versions of your work in one file.

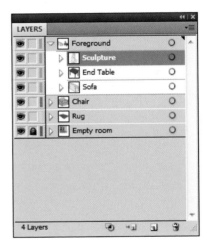

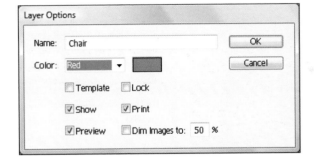

Create and Modify
LAYERS

What You'll Do

 In this lesson, you will create new layers and explore options on the Layers panel for viewing, locking, hiding, and selecting layers and layered artwork.

Creating Layers and Sublayers

Layers are a smart solution for organizing and managing a complex illustration. For example, if you were drawing a map of your home state, you might put all the interstate freeways on one layer, the local freeways on a second layer, secondary roads on a third layer, and all the text elements on a fourth layer.

As the name suggests, the Layers panel consists of a series of layers. By default, every Illustrator document is created with one layer, called Layer 1. As you work, you can create new layers and move objects into them, thereby segregating objects and organizing your work. The first object that is placed on Layer 1 is placed on a sublayer called <Path>. Each additional object placed on the same layer is placed on a separate <Path> sublayer.

Each layer has a **thumbnail**, or a miniature picture, of the objects on that layer, to the left of the layer name. Thumbnails also display the artwork that is positioned on each of the individual sublayers of a layer. You can change the size of the rows on the Layers panel by choosing a new size in the Layer Panel Options dialog box. Click the Layers panel options button, then click Panel Options. Layers and sublayers can also be given descriptive names to help identify their contents.

The stacking order of objects on the artboard corresponds to the hierarchy of layers on the Layers panel. Artwork in the top layer is at the front of the stacking order, while artwork in the bottom layer is in the back. The hierarchy of sublayers corresponds to the stacking order of the objects within a single layer.

Illustrator offers two basic ways to create new layers and sublayers. You can click the New Layer or New Sublayer command on the Layers panel menu, or you can click the Create New Layer or Create New Sublayer button on the Layers panel. Figure 1 shows a simple illustration and its corresponding layers on the Layers panel.

Duplicating Layers

In addition to creating new layers, you can duplicate existing layers by clicking the Duplicate command on the Layers panel menu, or by dragging a layer or sublayer onto the Create New Layer button on the Layers panel. When you duplicate a layer, all of the artwork on the layer is duplicated as well. Note the difference between this and copying and pasting artwork. When you copy and paste artwork, the copied artwork is pasted on the same layer.

Figure 1 *Layers panel*

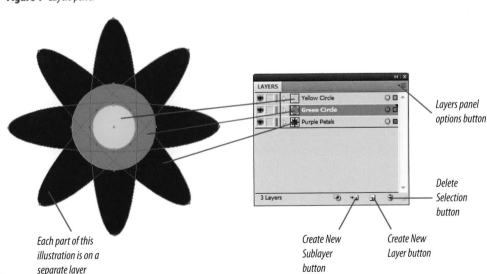

Each part of this illustration is on a separate layer

Layers panel options button

Delete Selection button

Create New Sublayer button

Create New Layer button

Setting Layer Options

The Layer Options dialog box offers a wealth of options for working with layered artwork, many of which are not available to you unless you are working with layers. You can name a layer, and you can also set a selection color for the layer. When an object is selected, its selection marks will be the same color as specified for the layer, making it easy to differentiate layers of artwork on the artboard.

Also in the Layer Options dialog box are options for locking, unlocking, showing, and hiding artwork on the layer. When you lock a layer, all the objects on the layer are locked and protected. When the Show check box is checked, all the artwork that is contained in the layer is displayed on the artboard. When the Show check box is not checked, the artwork is hidden.

The Preview option displays all the artwork on a layer in Preview mode. When the Preview option is not activated, the artwork is displayed in Outline mode. Thus, with layers, some elements on the artboard can be in Preview mode, while others are in Outline mode.

The Print option allows you to choose whether or not to print a layer. This feature is useful for printing different versions of the same illustration. The Dim Images to option reduces the intensity of bitmap images that are placed on the artboard. Dimming a bitmap often makes it easier to trace an image.

Use the Template option when you want to trace the artwork on a layer to create a new illustration. By default, a template layer is locked and cannot be printed.

Buttons on the Layers panel represent ways to lock, unlock, hide, and show artwork on each layer, making it unnecessary to use the Layer Options dialog box to activate these functions. The Toggles Visibility icon (Eye icon) lets you hide and show layers, and the Toggles Lock icon (Lock icon) lets you lock and unlock layers.

Selecting Artwork on Layers and Sublayers

The easiest way to select a layer is to click the layer name or the layer thumbnail. Selecting a layer is referred to as "targeting" a layer. When you select an object on the artboard, its layer is selected (highlighted) on the Layers panel, and the Selected Art icon appears, as shown in Figure 2. Selecting a layer or sublayer on the Layers panel does not select the artwork on that layer.

Changes that you make to layers on the Layers panel affect the artwork on those layers. For example, if you delete a layer, the artwork on the layer will be deleted. The artwork on a layer will be duplicated if the layer is duplicated. Changing a layer's position in the layers hierarchy will move the artwork forward or backward in the stacking order.

Duplicating the artwork on the artboard does not duplicate the layer that the artwork is on. If you delete all the artwork on a layer, you are left with an empty layer. *A layer is never automatically created, copied, or deleted because of something you do to the artwork on the layer.*

The same is *not* true for sublayers. If you delete or copy artwork that is on a sublayer, the *sublayer* is deleted or copied, respectively.

Selecting All Artwork on a Layer

The Select All command makes it easy to select every object on the artboard in one step. At times, however, you will want to select every object on a layer or sublayer, but not every object on the artboard. To select all the artwork on a single layer or sublayer, select the **layer target** to the left of the Selected Art icon, shown in Figure 2. You can also press and hold [Alt](Win) or [option](Mac) and click the layer. All objects on that layer will become selected on the artboard.

Figure 2 *The chair on the artboard and on the Layers panel*

Layer target (click to select all art on layer)

Selected art icon

Selection marks for chair are red, the Chair layer's assigned color

Create a new layer

1. Open AI 5-1.ai, then save it as **Living Room**.

2. Open AI 5-2.ai, then save it as **Showroom**.

   You will work with two documents during this lesson.

3. Click the **Selection tool** 🔖 , select the chair, then copy it.

4. Click the **Living Room.ai document tab** to activate the Living Room document.

   TIP Using the Window menu is another way to switch between open documents.

5. Click the **Layers panel icon** 🗀 in the stack of collapsed icons on the right to open the Layers panel if it is not already open.

   The Layers panel shows two layers. The Empty room layer contains the artwork you see on the artboard. The objects on the Foreground layer are hidden.

6. Click the **Create New Layer button** 🗐 on the Layers panel.

   A new layer named Layer 3 appears above the Foreground layer.

7. Click **Edit** on the Application bar, then click **Paste**.

   The chair artwork is pasted into Layer 3.

8. Position the chair on the artboard as shown in Figure 3.

You created a new layer using the Create New Layer button on the Layers panel, then pasted an object onto that new layer.

Figure 3 *Chair positioned on its own layer*

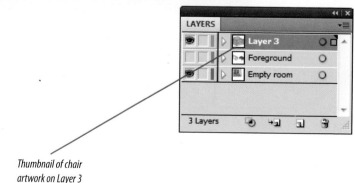

Thumbnail of chair artwork on Layer 3

Figure 4 *Layer Options dialog box*

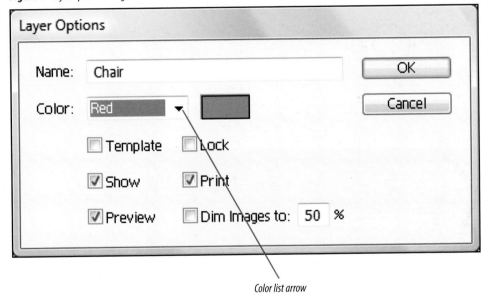

Color list arrow

Name a layer and change a layer's selection color

1. Double-click **Layer 3**.
2. Name the layer **Chair**, then click **OK**.

   The Layers panel reflects the name change.
3. Double-click the **Chair layer**.
4. Click the **Color list arrow**, click **Red**, as shown in Figure 4, then click **OK**.

   Note that the selection marks on the chair are now red, reflecting the new selection color for the Chair layer.
5. Deselect the chair.

You used the Layer Options dialog box to rename Layer 3 and assign it a new selection color.

Select items on a layer and lock a layer

1. Click the **chair** with the Selection tool .

   Note that the Selected Art icon appears when the chair is selected, as shown in Figure 5.

   TIP The Selected Art icon is the same color as its layer.

2. Deselect the chair.

   The Selected Art icon disappears.

3. Press **[Alt]** (Win) or **[option]** (Mac), then click the **Chair layer** on the Layers panel.

   The chair artwork is selected.

4. Click **either of the two mauve walls** in the illustration.

   When an object is selected on the artboard, the layer on which the selected object is placed is highlighted on the Layers panel.

5. Double-click the **Empty room layer**, click the **Lock check box**, then click **OK**.

   The Lock icon 🔒 appears on the Empty room layer, indicating that all the objects on the Empty room layer are locked. See Figure 6.

   You noted the relationship between a selected item and its corresponding layer on the Layers panel. You activated the Selected Art icon and selected the artwork on the Chair layer. You then locked the Empty room layer.

Figure 5 *Selected Art icon identifies the layer of a selected object*

Indicates Selected Art icon

Figure 6 *Lock icon identifies a locked layer*

Lock icon

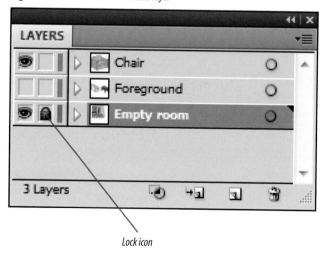

Figure 7 *Foreground layer is locked and hidden*

The absence of the Eye icon indicates this layer is hidden

The Lock icon indicates that this layer is locked

Show and hide layers

1. Double-click the **Foreground layer**.
2. Click the **Color list arrow**, then click **Grass Green**.
3. Click the **Show check box**, then click **OK**.

   The objects on the Foreground layer become visible, and the Eye icon 👁 appears on the Foreground layer.
4. Click the **Eye icon** 👁 on the Foreground layer to hide the objects.
5. Click the **Eye icon** (in its off state) ☐ on the Foreground layer to show the objects.

TIP The Eye and Lock icons appear as empty gray squares in their off state.

6. Click the **Lock icon** (in its off state) ☐ on the Foreground layer.

   The Lock icon 🔒 appears.
7. Click the **Eye icon** 👁 on the Foreground layer to hide the objects.

   Your Layers panel should resemble Figure 7.
8. Save your work.

You used the Eye icon on the Layers panel to toggle between showing and hiding the artwork on two layers. You also locked the Foreground layer.

Manipulate Layered
ARTWORK

What You'll Do

In this lesson, you will learn methods for manipulating layers to change the display of layered artwork. You will change the order of layers on the panel, merge layers, work with sublayers, and move objects between layers.

Changing the Order of Layers and Sublayers

The hierarchy of the layers on the Layers panel determines how objects on the artboard overlap. All the objects on a given layer are behind the objects on the layer above it and in front of the objects on the layer beneath it. Multiple objects within a given layer overlap according to their stacking order and you can reposition them with the standard stacking order commands.

To change the position of a layer or sublayer in the hierarchy, simply drag it up or down on the panel. Small black triangles and a heavy horizontal line identify where the layer will be repositioned, as shown in Figure 8. When you reposition a layer, its sublayers move with it.

Merging Layers

When you have positioned artwork to your liking using multiple layers and sublayers, you will often want to consolidate those layers to simplify the panel. First, you must select the layers that you want to merge. Press [Ctrl](Win) or ⌘ (Mac) to select

multiple layers. Once you have selected the layers that you want to merge, apply the Merge Selected command on the Layers panel menu. When you merge layers, all the artwork from one or more layers moves onto the layer that was last selected before the merge.

Be careful not to confuse merging layers with condensing layers. Condensing layers is simply the process of dragging one layer into another. The repositioned layer becomes a sublayer of the layer into which it was dragged.

Defining Sublayers

Whenever you have one or more objects on a layer, you have sublayers. For example, if you draw a circle and a square on Layer 1, it will automatically have two sublayers—one for the square, one for the circle. The layer is comprised of its sublayers.

As soon as the first object is placed on a layer, a triangle appears to the left of the layer name, indicating that the layer contains sublayers. Click the triangle to expand the layer and see the sublayers, then click it again to collapse the layer and hide the sublayers.

Working with Sublayers

When you place grouped artwork into a layer, a sublayer is automatically created with the name <Group>. A triangle appears on the <Group> sublayer, which, when clicked, exposes the sublayers—one for every object in the group, as shown in Figure 9.

Dragging Objects Between Layers

Sublayers are easy to move between layers; you simply drag and drop a sublayer from one layer to another.

You can move artwork from one layer to another by dragging the Selected Art icon. Select the artwork on the artboard that you want to move; the layer is selected, and the Selected Art icon appears. Drag the button to the destination layer or sublayer, as shown in Figure 10. If you drag the Selected Art icon to a layer, the artwork becomes the top sublayer in the layer. If you drag the Selected Art icon to a sublayer, the artwork is grouped with the object already on the sublayer.

You have two other options for moving objects between layers. You can simply cut

and paste artwork from one layer to another by selecting the object that you want to move, cutting it from the artboard, selecting the layer on which you wish to place it, then pasting. You can also use the Send to Current Layer command. Select the artwork you want to move, click the name of the destination layer to make it the active layer, click Object on the Application bar, point to Arrange, then click Send to Current Layer. Clearly, these two options are more time-consuming; your best method is to simply drag the Selected Art icon.

Figure 8 *Changing the order of layers*

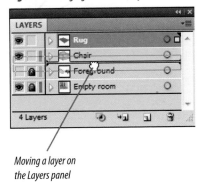

Moving a layer on the Layers panel

Figure 9 *A Group sublayer*

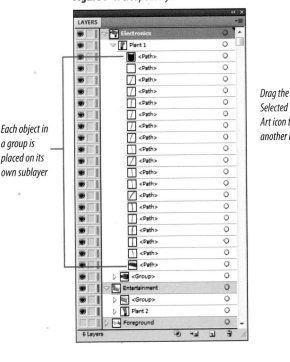

Each object in a group is placed on its own sublayer

Figure 10 *Dragging a sublayer to another layer*

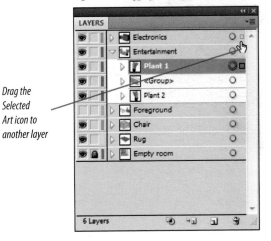

Drag the Selected Art icon to another layer

Change the hierarchy of layers

1. Switch to the Showroom document, copy the rug, then return to the Living Room document.

2. Press **[Ctrl]** (Win) or ⌘ (Mac), then click the **Create New Layer button**  on the Layers panel.

   Pressing [Ctrl] (Win) or ⌘ (Mac) creates a new layer at the top of the layer list.

3. Click **Edit** on the Application bar, then click **Paste**.

   The rug is pasted into the new layer because it is the active, or targeted, layer.

4. Name the new layer **Rug**, set the layer color to yellow, then position the rug artwork with a corner of it hanging slightly off the artboard, as shown in Figure 11.

5. Click and drag the **Rug layer** and position it below the Chair layer until you see a double black line with small triangles beneath the Chair layer, as shown in Figure 12, then release the mouse.

   The rug artwork is now positioned below the chair artwork.

You created a new layer at the top of the Layers panel. You pasted artwork into that layer, then moved the layer below another layer in the hierarchy so that the artwork on the two layers overlapped properly on the artboard.

Figure 11 *The Rug layer is at the top of the layers hierarchy*

Figure 12 *Changing the hierarchy of layers*

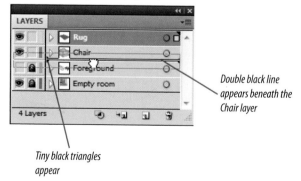

Double black line appears beneath the Chair layer

Tiny black triangles appear

Figure 13 *Sculpture artwork positioned on top of the end table*

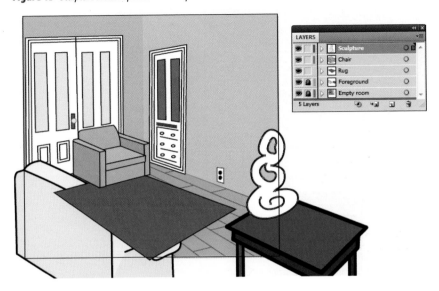

Figure 14 *Foreground and Sculpture layers merged*

Merged layer

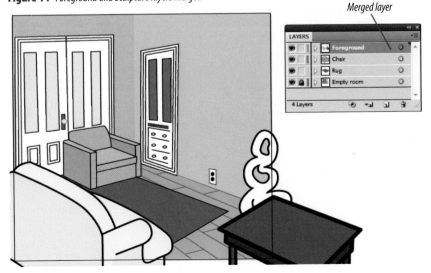

Merge layers

1. Switch to the Showroom document, copy the sculpture, then return to the Living Room document.

2. Press **[Ctrl]** (Win) or ⌘ (Mac), then click the **Create New Layer button** 🔲.

3. Paste the sculpture into the new layer, then name the layer **Sculpture**.

TIP Assign a unique color to this and all other layers you create in this lesson.

4. Show the Foreground layer, then position the sculpture artwork on the brown end table, as shown in Figure 13.

5. Deselect the sculpture, then drag the **Foreground layer** above the Sculpture layer on the Layers panel.

6. Unlock the Foreground layer.

7. Click the **Sculpture layer** to select it, press **[Ctrl]** (Win) or ⌘ (Mac), then click the **Foreground layer**.

   When merging layers, the last layer selected becomes the merged layer.

8. Click the **Layers panel options button**, then click **Merge Selected**.

   The objects from both layers are merged into the Foreground layer; the Sculpture layer is deleted.

TIP Layers must be showing and unlocked in order to be merged.

9. Compare your screen to Figure 14.

   Don't worry that your sculpture is temporarily behind the table.

You merged the Sculpture and the Foreground layers.

Work with sublayers

1. Expand the Foreground layer by clicking the **triangle** ▷ to the left of the layer.

   Three sublayers, all named <Group>, are revealed.

2. Expand the sofa <Group> sublayer by clicking the **triangle** ▷ to the left of it.

   The five paths that compose the sofa are revealed.

3. Select the sofa artwork on the artboard.

   The Selected Art icon appears for each of the selected paths, as shown in Figure 15.

4. Click the **triangle** ▽ to the left of the sofa <Group> sublayer to collapse it, then deselect the sofa.

5. Double-click the **sofa <Group> sublayer**, name it **Sofa**, then click **OK**.

6. Name the sculpture sublayer **Sculpture**, then name the end table sublayer **End Table**.

7. Move the Sculpture sublayer above the End Table sublayer so that your Layers panel resembles Figure 16.

   Notice that the sculpture artwork is on top of the end table.

8. Click the **triangle** ▽ to the left of the Foreground layer to hide the three sublayers.

9. Hide the Foreground layer.

You viewed sublayers in the Foreground layer. You then renamed the three sublayers in the Foreground layer and rearranged the order of the Sculpture and the End Table sublayers.

Figure 15 *Each path in the sofa <Group> sublayer is selected*

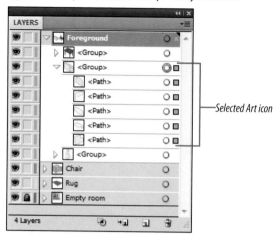

—Selected Art icon

Figure 16 *Sculpture sublayer moved above the End Table sublayer*

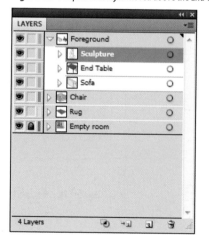

Figure 17 *Cabinet and plant are on the same layer*

Figure 18 *Moving the Plant 2 sublayer*

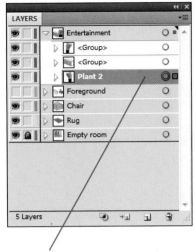

Plant 2 sublayer

Figure 19 *The reflected copy of the plant in position*

The new plant is positioned behind the cabinet

Figure 20 *The reflected copy of the plant, scaled and pruned*

Create new sublayers

1. Switch to the Showroom document, copy the cabinet, then return to the Living Room document.

2. Press **[Ctrl]** (Win) or ⌘ (Mac), then click the **Create New Layer button** ▣.

3. Name the new layer **Entertainment**, select Violet as the layer color, then click **OK**.

4. Paste the cabinet artwork into the new layer.

5. Copy the plant from the Showroom document, then paste the plant artwork into the Entertainment layer.

6. Position the cabinet artwork and the plant artwork as shown in Figure 17.

7. Deselect all, expand the Entertainment layer, then select the plant artwork on the artboard.

8. Double-click the **Reflect tool** ⟁, click the **Vertical option button**, then click **Copy**.

   The reflected copy of the plant is placed on a new sublayer above the original plant sublayer.

9. Rename the new sublayer **Plant 2**.

10. Move the Plant 2 sublayer to the bottom of the Entertainment sublayer hierarchy, as shown in Figure 18.

11. Click the **Selection tool** ▸, then move the new plant artwork into the position shown in Figure 19.

12. Scale the new plant artwork 85%, delete or move some leaves on it so that it's not an obvious copy of the original plant, then compare your screen to Figure 20.

You created and moved new sublayers.

Move objects between layers

1. Switch to the Showroom document, copy the electronics images, then return to the Living Room document.

2. Create a new layer at the top of the hierarchy, name it **Electronics**, choose Magenta as its color, then click **OK**.

3. Paste the electronics on the Electronics layer, then position the electronics artwork on the cabinet.

4. The plant on the right needs to be positioned in front of the electronics for the visual to be realistic.

5. Name the top sublayer in the Entertainment layer **Plant 1**, then select the Plant 1 artwork on the artboard.

   The Selected Art icon appears in the Plant 1 sublayer.

6. Drag the **Selected Art icon** from the Plant 1 sublayer to the Electronics layer, as shown in Figure 21.

   The Plant 1 sublayer moves into the Electronics layer. The Plant 1 sublayer automatically becomes the top sublayer in the Electronics layer.

7. Switch to the Showroom document, copy the Matisse, return to the Living Room document, then create a new layer at the top of the hierarchy, named **Matisse**.

8. Paste the Matisse artwork into the new layer, then position it as shown in Figure 22.

(continued)

Figure 21 *Moving a sublayer from one layer to another*

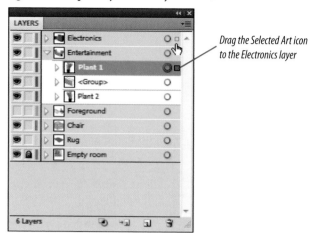

Drag the Selected Art icon to the Electronics layer

Figure 22 *The Matisse in position on its own layer*

Figure 23 *Moving the Matisse layer into the Electronics layer*

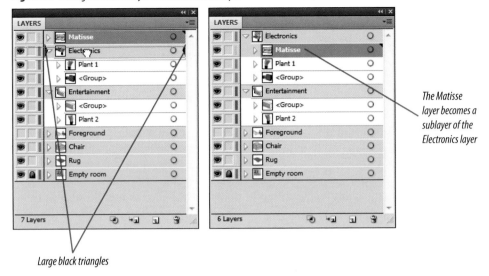

The Matisse layer becomes a sublayer of the Electronics layer

Large black triangles

Figure 24 *The lamp and table in position*

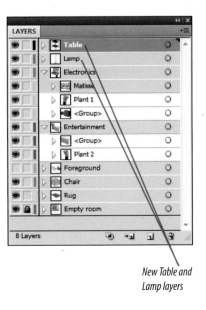

New Table and Lamp layers

9. Drag the **Matisse layer** on top of the Electronics layer.

Two large, black triangles appear on the Electronics layer when the Matisse layer is on top of it, as shown in Figure 23. The Matisse layer is moved into the Electronics layer as the topmost sublayer.

10. Create new layers for the lamp and the table, copy and paste the lamp and table artwork from the Showroom document to the new layers, then position the artwork so that your illustration resembles Figure 24.

11. Save your work.

You created a new layer named Electronics, dragged the Plant 1 sublayer into the Electronics layer by dragging its Selected Art icon to the Electronics layer. You then moved the Matisse layer into the Electronics layer by dragging it on top of the Electronics layer and created new layers for the table and the lamp.

Work with Layered ARTWORK

What You'll Do

In this lesson, you will explore options for managing your work using the Layers panel.

Using the View Buttons on the Layers Panel

The view options available on the Layers panel make working with layers a smart choice for complex illustrations. You can target specific viewing options to each layer in the document. Without layers, your options for viewing your work are limited to the Hide and Show All commands on the Object menu.

The Eye icon makes it easy to change what can be seen on the artboard. Clicking this icon once hides all the artwork on a layer, and the icon disappears. Clicking the empty gray square where the icon was shows all of the artwork on the layer, and the Eye icon reappears. Pressing [Alt](Win) or [option] (Mac) and clicking the Eye icon once shows all layers. Clicking a second time hides all layers except for the layer you clicked.

Pressing [Ctrl](Win) or ⌘ (Mac) and clicking the Eye icon toggles between Outline and Preview modes and all the artwork on the layer will switch between outlined and filled objects. Pressing [Alt] [Ctrl] (Win) or [option] (Mac) and clicking the Eye icon switches all other layers between Outline and Preview modes.

Importing an Adobe Photoshop File with layers

When you use the Open command to import a layered Photoshop file into Illustrator CS5, you have the option to open that file with its layers intact. In the Photoshop Import Options dialog box that appears, click the Convert Layers to Objects option button, then click OK. Display the Illustrator Layers panel and you will see that Illustrator has preserved as much of the Photoshop layer structure as possible.

Locating an Object on the Layers Panel

With complex illustrations, layers and sublayers tend to multiply—so much so that you will often find it easiest to work with collapsed layers, those in which you hide the sublayers. Sometimes it can be difficult to identify an object's layer or sublayer, especially if there are multiple copies of the object in the illustration. The Locate Object command offers a simple solution. Select an object on the artboard, click the Layers panel options button, then click Locate Object. The layers expand, revealing their sublayers, and the selected object's layer or sublayer is selected.

Reversing the Order of Layers

Another option that the Layers panel offers for managing your artwork is the ability to reverse the order of layers. Select the layers whose order you want to reverse. Press [Shift] to select multiple contiguous (those next to each other on the panel) layers. Press [Ctrl] (Win) or ⌘ (Mac) to select multiple noncontiguous layers. Click the Layers panel list arrow, then click Reverse Order.

Making Layers Nonprintable

The ability to choose whether or not to print the artwork on a specific layer is useful, especially during the middle stages of producing an illustration. For example, you could print just the text elements and give them to a copy editor for proofing. You could print just the elements of the illustration that are ready to be shown to the client, holding back the elements that still need work. See Figure 25 for the Print option in the Layer Options dialog box.

Another value of the print option is the ability to print different versions of a document. Let's say you're working on the design of a poster for a client, and you've finalized the artwork but you're still undecided about the typeface for the headline after narrowing down the choices to five typefaces. You could create five layers, one for the headline formatted in each typeface. Then you would print the illustration five times, each with a different headline. This is a smart and simple way to produce comps quickly.

Exporting Illustrator Layers to Photoshop

You can export Illustrator layers to Photoshop. Click File on the Application bar, click Export, then choose Photoshop (PSD) as the file format. When the Photoshop Export Options dialog box opens, verify that the Color Model is set to CMYK and that the Write Layers option button is selected. Click OK to export the layers to a Photoshop document.

Figure 25 *Print Option in the Layer Options Dialog Box*

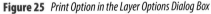

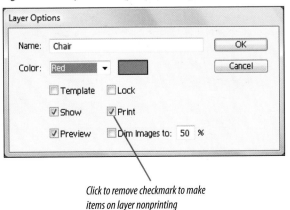

Click to remove checkmark to make items on layer nonprinting

Explore view options on the Layers panel

1. Collapse the Electronics and Entertainment layers, then hide them.

2. Press and hold **[Alt]** (Win) or **[option]** (Mac), then click the **Eye icon** 👁 on the Chair layer.

   All of the layers are displayed.

3. Using the same keyboard commands, click the **Eye icon** 👁 on the Chair layer again.

   All layers, except for the Chair layer, are hidden.

4. Using the same keyboard commands, click the (off state) **Eye icon** ☐ on the Chair layer again so that all of the layers are displayed.

5. Move the Foreground layer to the top of the hierarchy.

6. Press **[Ctrl]**(Win) or ⌘ (Mac), then click the **Eye icon** 👁 on the Chair layer.

   The artwork on the Chair layer switches to Outline mode.

7. Using the same keyboard commands, click the **Eye icon** 👁 on the Chair layer again.

8. Press **[Alt][Ctrl]** (Win) or **[option]** ⌘ (Mac), then click the same **Eye icon** 👁.

   The artwork on every layer, except for the Chair layer, switches to Outline mode, as shown in Figure 26.

9. Using the same keyboard commands, click the **Eye icon** 👁 again.

You learned keyboard commands to explore view options on the Layers panel.

Figure 26 *The Chair layer shown in Preview mode and all other layers shown in Outline mode*

Figure 27 *Duplicating the Lamp layer*

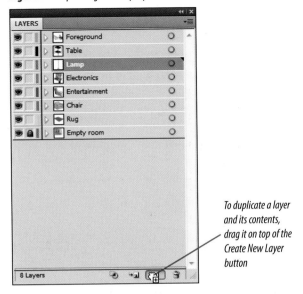

To duplicate a layer
and its contents,
drag it on top of the
Create New Layer
button

Figure 28 *Positioning the second lamp*

Locate, duplicate, and delete layers

1. Select the Plant 2 artwork on the artboard.

2. Click the **Layers panel options button**, then click **Locate Object**.

   The Entertainment layer expands, as does the Plant 2 sublayer.

   TIP The Locate Object command is useful when you are working with collapsed layers or with many layers and sublayers.

3. Collapse the Entertainment layer.

4. Select the Lamp layer, then drag it on top of the Create New Layer button ▣ , as shown in Figure 27.

   The Lamp layer and its contents are duplicated onto a new layer that is created above the original lamp layer. The copied lamp artwork is positioned directly on top of the original lamp artwork.

5. Position the duplicated lamp artwork on the artboard, as shown in Figure 28.

6. Drag the **Lamp copy layer** to the Delete Selection button 👁 on the Layers panel.

You used the Locate Object command to identify a selected object's position on the Layers panel. You duplicated a layer, then deleted it.

Dim placed images

1. Hide all layers, then create a new layer at the top of the hierarchy, named **Photo**.

2. Click **File** on the Application bar, then click **Place**.

3. Navigate to the drive and folder where your Data Files are stored, click **Living Room Original.tif**, then click **Place**.

   The source for the illustration is placed on its own layer.

4. Align the photo with the top-left corner of the artboard, as shown in Figure 29.

5. Double-click the **Photo layer**, click the **Dim Images to check box**, type **50** in the Dim Images to text box, then click **OK**.

   The placed image is less vivid.

TIP Dimming a placed image is useful for tracing.

You created a new layer, placed a photo on the new layer, then used the Layer Options dialog box to dim the photo 50%.

Figure 29 *The source of the illustration, placed on its own layer*

Figure 30 *Using a layer for a message to the printer*

Printer: Use photo for reference if necessary. Thank you!
Call me at 555-1234 if any problems.

1. Create a new layer at the top of the hierarchy, named **Message**.

2. Using any font you like, type a message for the printer, as shown in Figure 30.

3. Convert the message text to outlines. Double-click the **Message layer**, remove the check mark from the Print check box, then click **OK**.

   The Message layer will not print to any output device.

TIP When a layer is set not to print, its name is italicized on the Layers panel.

4. Make the Photo layer nonprintable.

5. Hide the Message and Photo layers.

6. Make all the other layers visible.

7. Save your work.

You created a new layer called Message, typed a message for the printer, then designated the Message and Photo layers as nonprintable. You then displayed all of the layers except for the Message and Photo layers.

Create a
CLIPPING SET

What You'll Do

In this lesson, you will create a clipping mask on a sublayer that will mask the other sublayers in the layer.

Working with Clipping Sets

Adobe uses the terms "clipping mask" and "clipping path" interchangeably. The term **clipping set** is used to distinguish clipping paths used in layers from clipping paths used to mask nonlayered artwork. There's no difference; it's just terminology. Essentially, the term "clipping set" refers to the clipping mask *and* the masked sublayers as a unit.

The following rules apply to clipping sets:

- The clipping mask and the objects to be masked must be in the same layer.
- You cannot use a sublayer as a clipping mask, unless it is a <Group> sublayer. However, the top sublayer in a layer becomes the clipping mask if you first select the layer that the sublayer is in, then create the clipping mask.
- The top object in the clipping set becomes the mask for every object below it in the layer.
- A <Group> sublayer can be a clipping set. The top object in the group will function as the mask.
- Dotted lines between sublayers indicate that they are included in a clipping set.

Flattening Artwork

When you apply the Flatten Artwork command, all visible objects in the artwork are consolidated in a single layer. Before applying the command, select the layer into which you want to consolidate the artwork. If you have a layer that is hidden, you will be asked whether to make the artwork visible so that it can be flattened into the layer or delete the layer and the artwork on it.

Figure 31 *The new <Path> sublayer*

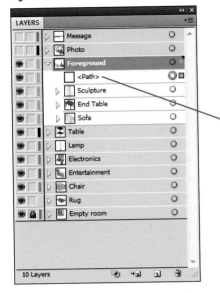

The rectangle is placed on a new sublayer called <Path>, on top of the other sublayers in the Foreground layer

Figure 32 *Clipping path masks only the objects on its own layer*

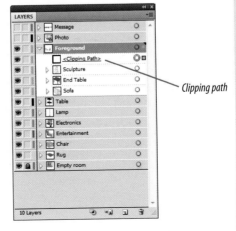

Clipping path

Create clipping sets

1. Select the Foreground layer, click the **Rectangle tool** ▢ , then create a rectangle that is 6.5" wide by 6" tall.

2. Position the rectangle so that it aligns exactly with the edges of the artboard.

3. Apply a black stroke to the rectangle and no fill color.

4. Expand the Foreground layer.

   The rectangle, identified as <Path>, is at the top of the sublayers, as shown in Figure 31.

5. Click the **Make/Release Clipping Mask button** on the Layers panel.

   Any path on the Foreground layer that is positioned off the artboard is masked. The part of the rug that extends beyond the artboard is not masked, because it is not in the same layer as the clipping path. The lamp, too, extends beyond the artboard and is not masked, as shown in Figure 32.

You created a rectangle, then used it as a clipping path to mask the sublayers below it in its layer.

Copy a clipping mask and flatten artwork

1. Click the **Layer target button** ⊙ on the **<Clipping Path> sublayer** to select the artwork.

2. Click **Edit** on the Application bar, click **Copy**, click **Edit** on the Application bar again, then click **Paste in Front**.

   A new sublayer named <Path> is created. The rectangle on the <Clipping Path> sublayer is duplicated on the new <Path> sublayer and can be used to mask other layers.

3. Drag the **Selected Art icon** ☐ on the <Path> sublayer down to the Rug layer, as shown in Figure 33.

4. Expand the Rug layer to see the new <Path> sublayer, select the Rug layer, then click the **Make/Release Clipping Mask button** ⊙.

   Compare your Layers panel to Figure 34. The <Path> sublayer becomes the <Clipping Path> sublayer, and the rectangle on the <Clipping Path> sublayer is used to mask the rug on the artboard.

   (continued)

Figure 33 *Moving the copy of the rectangle to the Rug layer*

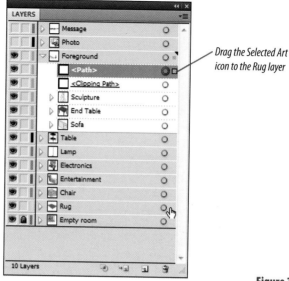

Drag the Selected Art icon to the Rug layer

Figure 34 *Using the duplicate rectangle to mask the rug*

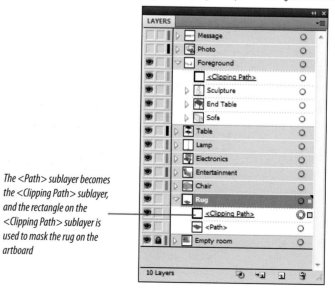

The <Path> sublayer becomes the <Clipping Path> sublayer, and the rectangle on the <Clipping Path> sublayer is used to mask the rug on the artboard

Working with Layers

Figure 35 *Completed illustration*

5. Select the lamp artwork on the artboard, drag the **Selected Art icon** ▭ on the Lamp layer to the Sculpture sublayer of the Foreground layer, then deselect all.

   The lamp artwork moves to the Sculpture sublayer and is therefore masked. Deselect the lamp and your illustration should resemble Figure 35.

TIP When you drag the Selected Art icon from one layer to another, the selected artwork moves to the new layer, but the layer does not move.

6. Select the empty Lamp layer, then click the **Delete Selection button** 🗑 on the Layers panel.

7. Click **File** on the Application bar, then click **Save**.

8. Select the Foreground layer, click the **Layers panel options button**, click **Flatten Artwork**, then click **Yes** when you are asked whether or not you want to discard the hidden art on the hidden layers.

9. Click **File** on the Application bar, click **Save As**, then save the file as **Living Room Flat**.

   Note that we saved the flattened version as a separate file and saved the original Living Room.ai file with all layers intact. Whenever you flatten a layered document, save the flattened version as a copy so that you can preserve your original layered file.

10. Close Showroom.ai and Living Room flat.ai, saving any changes if prompted.

You made a copy of the rectangle, moved the copied rectangle to the Rug layer, then made it into a clipping path to mask the rug artwork. You then moved the lamp artwork into the Sculpture sublayer, which masked the lamp. You deleted the empty Lamp layer and flattened all of the artwork on the Foreground layer.

Create and modify layers.

1. Open AI 5-3.ai, then save it as **Gary**.
2. Create a new layer at the top of the layer hierarchy, named **Text**.
3. Create a new layer at the top of the layer hierarchy, named **Gary Garlic**.
4. Rename Layer 2 **Body Parts**.
5. Save your work.

Manipulate layered artwork.

1. Move the garlic artwork into the Gary Garlic layer.
2. Move the three text groups onto the Text layer.
3. Merge the Background layer with the Box Shapes layer so that the Box Shapes layer is the name of the resulting merged layer. (*Hint*: Click the Background layer, press [Ctrl] (Win) or ⌘ (Mac), click the Box

Shapes layer, click the Layers panel options button, then click Merge Selected.)
4. Move the Body Parts layer to the top of the layer hierarchy.
5. Save your work.

Work with layered artwork.

1. View each layer separately to identify the artwork on each.
2. Using Figure 36 as a guide, assemble Gary Garlic.
3. Merge the Gary Garlic and Body Parts layers so that the resulting merged layer will be named Body Parts.
4. Select all the artwork on the Body Parts layer, then group the artwork.
5. Save your work.

Create a clipping set.

1. Target the Box Shapes layer.
2. Create a rectangle that is 5" wide by 8" in height.
3. Position the rectangle so that it is centered on the artboard.
4. With the rectangle still selected, expand the Box Shapes layer on the Layers panel.
5. Click the Make/Release Clipping Mask button on the Layers panel.
6. Reposition the masked elements (text and box parts) so that your illustration resembles Figure 36.
7. Save your work, then close Gary.

Figure 36 *Completed Skills Review*

You are designing an outdoor sign for Xanadu Haircutters, a salon that recently opened in your town. You are pleased with your concept of using scissors to represent the X in Xanadu, and decide to design the logo with different typefaces so that the client will feel she has some input into the final design.

1. Open AI 5-4.ai, then save it as **Xanadu**.
2. Create a new layer, then move the ANADU headline into that layer.
3. Make four duplicates of the new layer.
4. Change the typeface on four of the layers, for a total of five versions of the logo type.
5. Rename each type layer, using the name of the typeface you chose.
6. Rename Layer 1 **Xanadu Art**.
7. View the Xanadu Art layer five times, each time with one of the typeface layers, so that you can see five versions of the logo.
8. Save your work, compare your illustration with Figure 37, then close Xanadu.

Figure 37 *Completed Project Builder 1*

You are the Creative Director for a Los Angeles design firm that specializes in identity packages for television networks. One of your most important projects this week is delivering the first round of comps for a new cable channel, Milty TV. Your art directors have come up with two concepts—one dark, one light. You decide to bring each to the client with two options for typography, for a total of four comps.

1. Open AI 5-5.ai, then save it as **Milty TV**.
2. Select the four pieces of artwork that comprise the television at the top of the artboard, then group them.

3. Group the four pieces of artwork at the bottom of the artboard, then cut them.
4. Create a new layer, name it **Orange**, then paste the artwork.
5. Position the orange artwork exactly on top of the blue artwork on the artboard so that it is covered.
6. Rename Layer 1 **Blue**, then duplicate the layer and name it **Blue Two**.
7. Duplicate the Orange layer, then name it **Orange Two**.
8. Deselect all, use the Direct Selection tool to select the large M on the Orange Two layer, change its typeface to Cooper Std, then hide the two Orange layers.

(*Hint*: If you do not have Cooper Std as a typeface, choose another one.)

9. Select the Blue Two layer, change the M to Cooper Std, then hide it.
10. View each of the four layers separately. You created two versions of each design.
11. Save your work, compare your Orange Two layer to Figure 38, then close Milty TV.

Figure 38 *Completed Project Builder 2*

You are a freelance designer, working out of your house. The owner of the town's largest plumbing company, Straight Flush, has hired you to redesign his logo. He gives you an Illustrator file with a design created by his son. You study the logo, then decide that it lacks cohesion and focus.

1. Open AI 5-6.ai, then save it as **Straight Flush**.
2. Group the elements of each playing card together.
3. Create four new layers.
4. Move each card to the layer with the corresponding number in the layer name.
5. Select all the layers, click the Layers panel options button, then click Reverse Order.
6. Reposition the cards on each layer so that they are in order, directly behind the ace.
7. Adjust the layout of the cards to your liking to create a new layout for the logo.
8. Save your work, compare your illustration with Figure 39, then close Straight Flush.

Figure 39 *Completed Design Project*

You are a fabric designer for a line of men's clothing. You are asked to supervise a team that will design new patterns for men's ties. Now that you have studied working with layers, how would you approach building a file that shows three patterns for a tie?

1. Open AI 5-7.ai, then save it as **Tie Pattern**.
2. Select various objects to see how the file has been built.
3. Ask yourself how the document would be more practical if it were built with layers.
4. How many masks would be required to show the three patterns?
5. How many layers would be required?
6. Redesign the document with layers so that the three patterns are all in one clipping set with one tie shape functioning as the mask.
7. Save your work, compare your Layers panel with Figure 40, then close Tie Pattern.

Figure 40 *Completed Portfolio Project*

CHAPTER 6 WORKING WITH PATTERNS AND BRUSHES

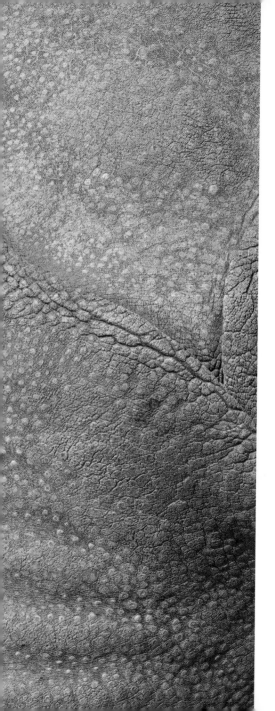

CHAPTER 6 WORKING WITH PATTERNS AND BRUSHES

Working with Patterns and Brushes

Artwork that you create in Illustrator is an end in and of itself; it's the result of your efforts in conceiving an image and rendering it using your skills and talents. However, as you become more familiar with Illustrator, you will also learn to use completed artwork as components of new illustrations.

Using patterns and brushes is a fine example of this working method. You can design artwork and then use it as a pattern to fill and stroke new artwork. This is useful if you are drawing things like flowers in a field, stars in a night sky, or trees on a mountainside.

The powerful options in Illustrator's Brushes panel extend this concept even farther. Using brushes, you can use completed artwork as a stroke, pattern, or freestanding illustration of greater complexity. For example, you could create a custom brush stroke, such as a leaf, and then use the Paintbrush tool to paint with the leaf as a brush stroke. Instead of being limited to filling or stroking an object with leaves, you could paint leaves wherever you wanted on the artboard.

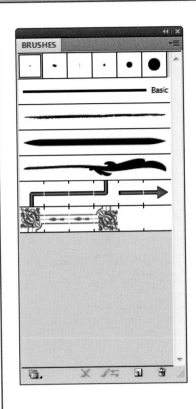

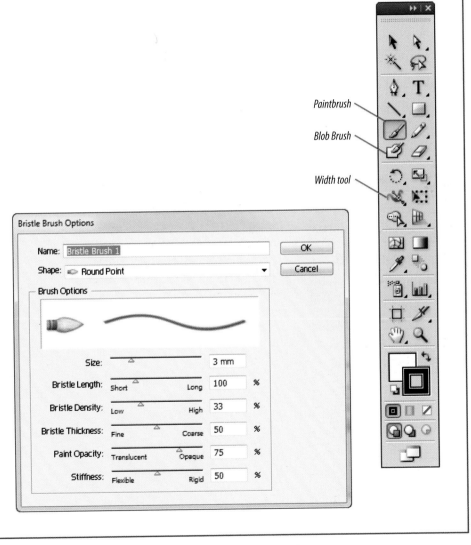

Paintbrush

Blob Brush

Width tool

Use the
MOVE COMMAND

What You'll Do

In this lesson, you will use the Move command to copy an object at precise offsets and create a simple pattern.

Using the Move Command

The word **offset** comes up when you explore the Move command. Quite simply, the term refers to the distance that an object is moved or copied from a starting location to an ending location. In a simple drop shadow, for example, you can describe the effect by saying, "The black copy behind the original has been offset three points to the left and three points down."

The Move command provides the most effective method for moving an object—or a copy of an object—at precise offsets. In the Move dialog box, you enter the horizontal distance and the vertical distance that you want a selected object to move. A positive value moves the object horizontally to the right, and a negative value moves it to the left. On a vertical axis, a positive value moves the object down, and a negative value moves it up. Be sure to make a note of that in Illustrator, down is positive, and up is negative.

An alternate (and seldom used) way to use the Move dialog box is to enter a value for the distance you want the object to move and a value for the angle on which it should move. Entering a distance and an angle is the same as specifying the move in horizontal and vertical values. When you enter values in the Distance and Angle text boxes, the Horizontal and Vertical text boxes update to reflect the move. Conversely, when you enter values in the Horizontal and Vertical text boxes, the Distance and Angle text boxes update to reflect the move. The Move dialog box is shown in Figure 1.

Figure 1 *Move dialog box*

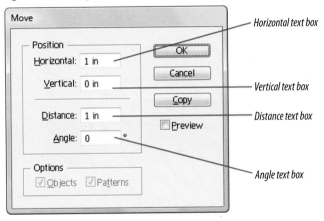

Copy and move objects using the Move dialog box

1. Create a new 4" × 4" document, then save it as **Checkerboard**.

2. Click **Edit** (Win) or **Illustrator** (Mac) on the Application bar, point to **Preferences**, then click **Units**.

3. Verify that the General units of measure are Inches, then click **OK**.

4. Create a 1/2" square, apply a red fill and no stroke, then position it at the upper-left corner of the artboard.

5. Click **Object** on the Application bar, point to **Transform**, then click **Move**.

6. Enter **.5** in the Horizontal text box, press **[Tab]**, enter **0** in the Vertical text box, then press **[Tab]** again.

TIP Values in the Distance and Angle text boxes automatically appear, based on the values entered in the Horizontal and Vertical text boxes.

7. Click **Copy**.

   A copy of the square is positioned immediately to the right of the original.

8. Change the fill on the second square to **black**, select both squares, click **Object** on the Application bar, point to **Transform**, then click **Move**.

9. Enter **1** in the Horizontal text box, then click **Copy**.

10. Click **Object** on the Application bar, point to **Transform**, click **Transform Again**, then repeat this step.

    Your work should resemble Figure 2.

    (continued)

Figure 2 *A simple pattern created using the Move command*

Working with Patterns and Brushes

Figure 3 *A checkerboard created with a single starting square and the Move dialog box*

11. Select all, open the Move dialog box, enter **0** in the Horizontal text box, enter **.5** in the Vertical text box, then click **Copy**.

12. Double-click the **Rotate tool**, enter **180** in the Angle text box, then click **OK**.

13. Select all, open the Move dialog box, enter **1** in the Vertical text box, then click **Copy**.

14. Apply the Transform Again command twice, then save your work.

    Your screen should resemble Figure 3.

15. Close the Checkerboard document.

Starting with a single square, you used the Move command to make multiple copies at precise distances to create a checkerboard pattern.

Create a PATTERN

What You'll Do

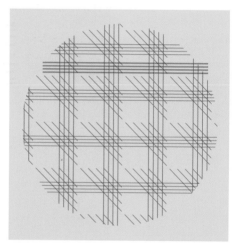

In this lesson, you will create a pattern from a simple illustration, add it to the Swatches panel, name it, and then fill an object with it.

Creating Patterns

In Illustrator you can design patterns to fill objects or stroke objects. You can design patterns that are simple or complex, abstract or specific, and you can save them for future use and applications. The Swatches panel comes preloaded with two patterns, named "Waves" and "Polka Dot," which you can modify.

To create a pattern, you first create artwork for the pattern, then drag that artwork into the Swatches panel, where it is automatically defined as a pattern swatch. You can use paths, compound paths, or text in patterns, but you cannot use gradients, blends, brush strokes, meshes, bitmap images, graphs, masks, or other patterns.

Designing a Pattern

Patterns repeat. A pattern fills an object by repeating the original pattern, a process called **tiling**. The word is used intentionally as a reference to floor tiles. Illustrator creates pattern fills in much the same way that you would use multiple tiles to cover a floor. Think of the pattern as the floor tile and the object to be filled as the floor.

You design fill patterns by designing one tile. For efficiency with previewing and printing, you should create your pattern tiles between a 1/2" and 1" square. When you save it as a pattern and apply it as a fill, the tile will repeat as many times as necessary to fill the object, as shown in Figure 4.

Many times, you will create a pattern that contains no rectangular objects, such as a polka dot or line pattern. In these cases,

Figure 4 *The tile repeats to fill the object*

Working with Patterns and Brushes

you create a **bounding box** to define the perimeter of the pattern tile by positioning an unfilled, unstroked rectangular object at the back of the stacking order of the pattern tile. Illustrator will regard this as the bounding box. All of the objects within the bounding box will be repeated as part of the pattern.

The pattern in Figure 5 is composed of lines only. The square is used as a bounding box. It defines the perimeter of the tile, and the pattern is created by repeating only the elements that fall within the bounding box. Again, a bounding box must have no fill and no stroke, it must be a rectangle or a square, and it must be the backmost object of the pattern tile.

Controlling How a Pattern Fills an Object

The way a pattern fills an object is a tricky concept. The pattern begins from the origin of the ruler, which is, by default, at the bottom-left corner of the artboard.

In other words, by default, the pattern begins at the bottom-left of the artboard, *not* the bottom-left corner of the object.

When you move an object that is filled with a pattern, the pattern changes within the object. If you understand the concept of a clipping mask, the pattern fill is easier to understand. Think of it

this way: The pattern covers the entire artboard and the object that is filled with the pattern functions like a clipping mask—you can see the pattern only through the object.

The best method for controlling how a pattern appears within an object is to align the ruler origin with the bottom-left corner of the object. To do this, display the rulers, then position your cursor at the top-left corner of the window, where the two rulers meet. The cross hairs are the ruler origin. Drag the cross hairs to the bottom-left corner of the filled object, as shown

Figure 5 *Bounding box determines the perimeter of the pattern tile*

Bounding box

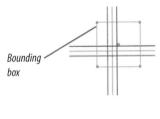

Pattern

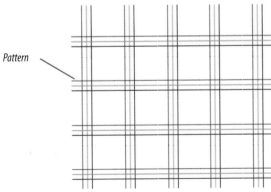

in Figure 6. Because the ruler origin and the bottom-left corner of the square are the same point, the first tile is positioned evenly in the corner. The pattern fills the object left to right, bottom to top.

Transforming Patterns

When an object is filled with a pattern, you can choose to transform only the object, only the pattern, or both the object and the pattern. For example, the Scale tool dialog box, shown in Figure 7, contains options for determining whether or not the transformation will affect a pattern fill.

QUICK TIP

The options that you choose in one transform tool dialog box will be applied to all transform tool dialog boxes.

When you transform a pattern, all subsequent objects that you create will be filled with the transformed pattern. To return a pattern fill to its non-transformed appearance, fill an object with a different swatch, then reapply the pattern swatch.

Figure 6 *Aligning the ruler origin with the bottom-left corner of the filled object*

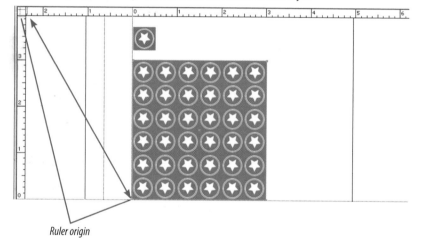

Ruler origin

Figure 7 *Options for patterns in the Scale dialog box*

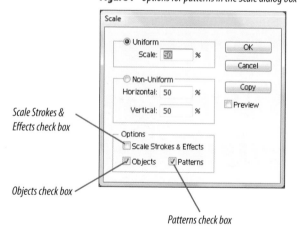

Scale Strokes & Effects check box

Objects check box

Patterns check box

Figure 8 *Artwork to be used as a pattern tile*

Figure 9 *See Artwork applied as a pattern fill*

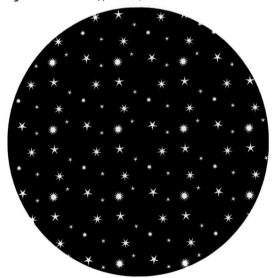

Create a pattern swatch

1. Open AI 6-1.ai, then save it as **Starry Night**.
2. Position the ten stars randomly over the black box.

TIP Enlarge your view of the artboard.

3. Change the fill color of the stars to **White**. Compare your screen to Figure 8.
4. Group the white stars.
5. Select all, then drag the **artwork** into the Swatches panel.

    The Swatches panel automatically identifies and defines the new swatch as a pattern swatch.

6. Deselect the artwork.
7. Double-click the **new swatch** called New Pattern Swatch 1, name it **Starry Night** in the Swatch Options dialog box, then click **OK**.
8. Delete all the artwork on the artboard.
9. Create a circle that is 4" in diameter.
10. Apply the Starry Night swatch to fill the circle.

TIP The Starry Night swatch may have automatically been applied to your circle when you created it because it was still selected on the Swatches panel.

Your screen should resemble Figure 9.

You created a 1"x1" collection of objects, selected all of them, then dragged them into the Swatches panel. You named the new pattern swatch, then applied it as a fill for a circle.

Transform pattern-filled objects

1. Select the circle, then double-click the **Scale tool** 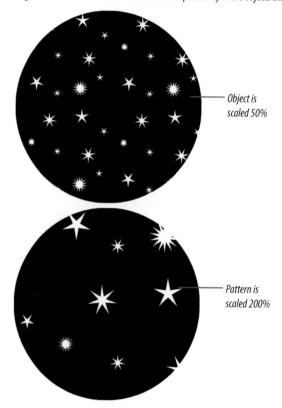.

2. Type **50** in the Scale text box, verify that only the Objects check box is checked in the Options section of the dialog box, then click **OK**.

   The object is scaled 50%; the pattern is not scaled.

3. Drag and drop a copy above the original circle.

4. Double-click the **Scale tool**.

5. Type **200** in the Scale text box, verify that only the Patterns check box is checked, then click **OK**.

   The pattern is scaled 200%; the object is not scaled. Your screen should resemble Figure 10.

6. Save your work, then close the Starry Night document.

You experimented with options for scaling a pattern fill and an object independently using the Scale dialog box.

Figure 10 *Patterns can be transformed independently of the objects that they fill*

Object is scaled 50%

Pattern is scaled 200%

Working with Patterns and Brushes

Figure 11 *Position a bounding box to define a pattern*

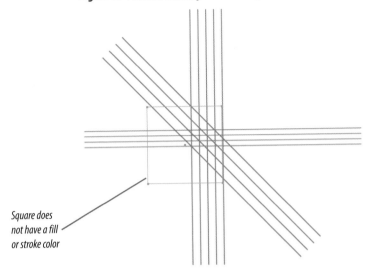

*Square does
not have a fill
or stroke color*

Figure 12 *A yellow square behind a line pattern*

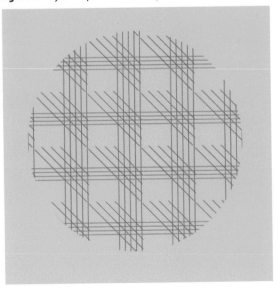

Create a pattern using open paths

1. Open AI 6-2.ai, then save it as **Line Pattern**.

2. Create a 1" square.

3. Position the square over the lines as shown in Figure 11, then remove both the fill and the stroke colors.

   Note that the rightmost purple line is not within the perimeter of the square.

4. Send the square to the back.

TIP If you deselect the square, switch to Outline mode so that you can see the outline of the square to select it, then switch back to Preview mode.

5. Select all, then drag the **objects** into the Swatches panel.

6. Hide the objects on the artboard.

7. Create a 4" circle, then fill it with the new pattern.

8. Create a 5" square, fill it with yellow, remove the stroke color if necessary, send it to the back, then position it behind the circle, as shown in Figure 12.

   The yellow square is visible behind the pattern because the pattern is composed of lines only.

9. Save your work, then close the Line Pattern document.

You placed a 1" square with no fill or stroke behind a group of straight paths. You used all the objects to create a pattern swatch, with the square defining the perimeter of the pattern tile. You filled a circle with the pattern, then positioned a yellow square behind the circle, creating the effect of a circle pattern within a square.

Design
A REPEATING PATTERN

What You'll Do

In this lesson, you will design a visually repetitive pattern. You will then explore options for modifying the pattern after it has been applied as a fill.

Planning Your Tiles

Simple patterns can be tricky to design. Understanding how patterns tile is important for achieving a desired effect. You will often be surprised to find that the tile you design does not create the pattern you had in mind.

In Figure 13, it at first seems logical that the tile on the left could produce the pattern below it. However, it requires the more complex tile on the right to produce what appears to be a "simple" pattern.

Another consideration when designing patterns is whether or not you want the pattern to be apparent. If you were designing a plaid pattern, you would want the pattern to be noticed. However, if you were designing artwork for a field of flowers, you might want the pattern to be subtle, if not invisible. An invisible pattern is difficult to create, especially when it's based on a 1" tile!

In every case, precision is important when creating a pattern. If two objects are meant to align, be certain that they do align; don't rely on just your eye. Use dialog boxes to move and transform objects; don't try to do it by hand.

Modifying Patterns

You modify a pattern by editing the artwork in the pattern tile, then replacing the old pattern on the Swatches panel with the new pattern. When you replace the old pattern, any existing objects on the artboard that were filled with the old pattern will update automatically with the new pattern. Of course, you can always leave the original pattern as is and save the edited pattern as a new swatch. This is often a wise move, because you may want to use that original pattern again sometime.

Figure 13 *Only the top-right tile could create the pattern*

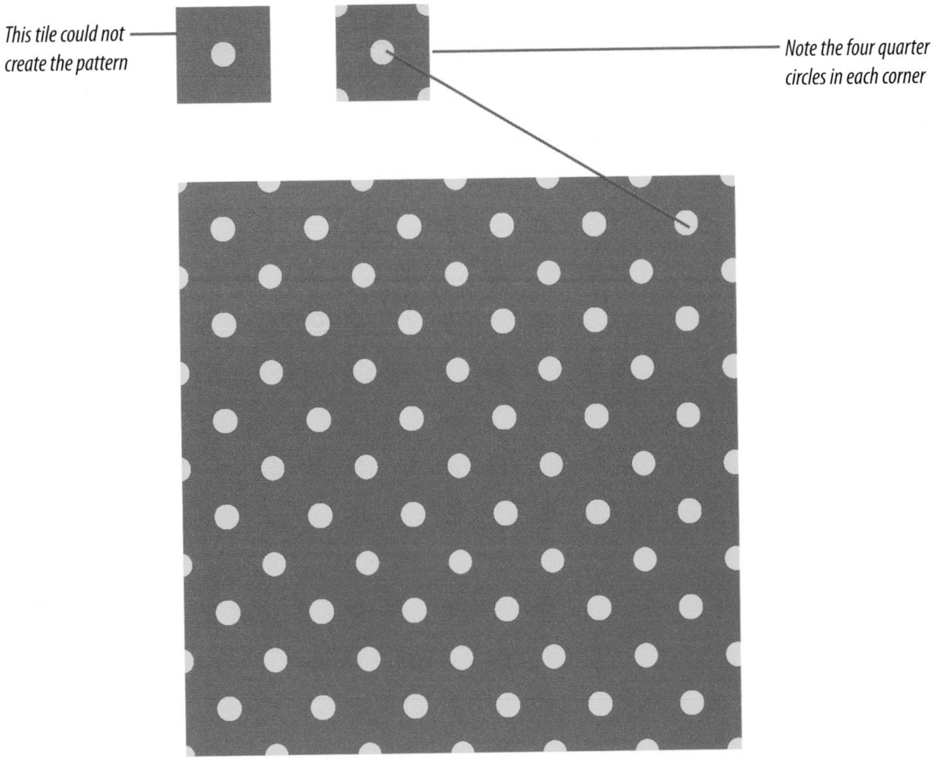

This tile could not create the pattern

Note the four quarter circles in each corner

Create a repeating pattern with precision

1. Open AI 6-3.ai, then save it as **Repeating Pattern**.

2. Select the lavender circle, click **Object** on the Application bar, point to **Transform**, then click **Move**.

3. Enter **1** in the Horizontal text box, enter **0** in the Vertical text box, then click **Copy**.

   A copy of the lavender circle is created at the upper-right corner of the square.

4. Select both lavender circles, open the Move dialog box, enter **0** in the Horizontal text box and **1** in the Vertical text box, then click **Copy**.

   Your screen should resemble Figure 14.

5. Select the blue diamond, then apply the Transform Again command.

   A copy of the blue diamond is created at the bottom edge of the square.

6. Select both blue diamonds, double-click the **Rotate tool** , enter **90** in the Angle text box, then click **Copy**.

   Your work should resemble Figure 15.

7. Select all, then click the **Divide button** on the Pathfinder panel.

(continued)

Figure 14 *Work precisely when designing pattern tiles*

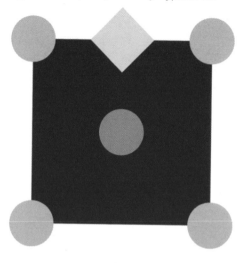

Figure 15 *Use dialog boxes to make transformations when designing pattern tiles*

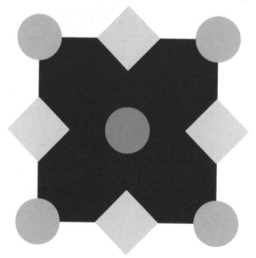

Working with Patterns and Brushes

Figure 16 *Designing pattern tiles can be tricky work*

Figure 17 *A "simple" pattern*

8. Deselect, click the **Direct Selection tool**, click the **artboard**, then delete the areas of the diamonds and circles that are outside the perimeter of the square, so that your design resembles Figure 16.

9. Click the **Selection tool**, select all, drag the **artwork** into the Swatches panel, then name the new pattern **Alpha Shapes**.

10. Delete the artwork on the artboard.

11. Create a 6" × 6" square, fill it with the Alpha Shapes pattern, then center it on the artboard.

12. Compare your screen to Figure 17.

You used the Move command to position multiple objects in a symmetrical pattern over a 1" square. You then used the Divide pathfinder, which allowed you to select and then delete the areas of objects that were positioned outside the square. You dragged the pattern into the Swatches panel. You named the pattern, then created a square with the pattern as its fill.

Modify a pattern

1. Drag the **Alpha Shapes pattern** from the Swatches panel to the scratch area at the upper-right corner of the artboard.

2. Click the **Direct Selection tool** , click the **artboard** to deselect the pattern, then click the **royal blue section** on the pattern.

3. Change the royal blue fill to a purple fill.

4. Switch to the **Selection tool** , then select the entire pattern.

5. Press and hold [**Alt**] (Win) or [**option**] (Mac), then drag the **modified pattern** on top of the Alpha Shapes pattern on the Swatches panel.

6. The Alpha Shapes pattern is replaced on the Swatches panel, and the fill of the square is updated, as shown in Figure 18.

(continued)

Figure 18 *Changing the background color of the pattern*

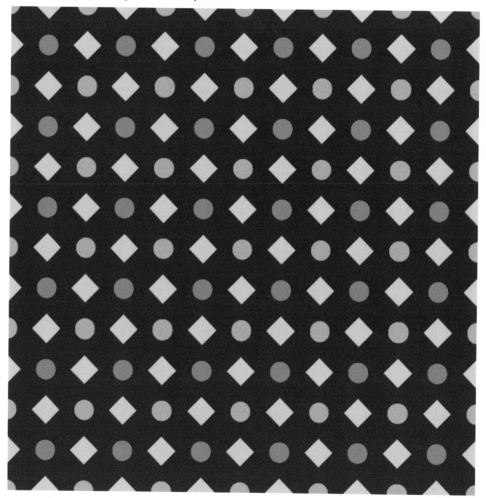

Figure 19 *Updated pattern without the purple background*

7. Using the Direct Selection tool , select all of the pattern pieces in the scratch area, except for the purple section.

8. Press and hold [**Alt**] (Win) or [**option**] (Mac), then drag the **selected objects** on top of the Alpha Shapes swatch on the Swatches panel.

   Your screen should resemble Figure 19.

9. Save and close the Repeating Pattern file.

You dragged the Alpha Shapes pattern swatch out of the Swatches panel and onto the scratch area in order to modify it. You changed a color in the pattern, then replaced the old pattern swatch with the new pattern. The object filled with the original pattern was updated to reflect the changes to the pattern. You modified the pattern again by dragging parts of it to the Swatches panel.

Work with the
BRUSHES PANEL

What You'll Do

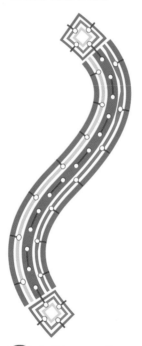

In this lesson, you will create a calligraphic brush, a scatter brush, an art brush, and a pattern brush.

Working with the Brushes Panel

The Brushes panel, shown in Figure 20, houses all of the brush artwork with which you will work in Illustrator. The term **brush** refers to any artwork with which you can paint using the Paintbrush tool or which you can apply to paths.

The Brushes panel comes with standard brushes, but you can use your own Illustrator artwork as a brush. For example, you could create a star shape, then use it as brush artwork. In that case, you'd be able to paint with the star using the Paintbrush tool, or you could apply the star artwork to an open path or a closed object.

Click the Brushes panel options button, then point to Open Brush Library, and you'll see a list of pre-loaded brush libraries. It is worth your time to explore these pre-loaded brushes. Figure 20 shows a number of open brush libraries.

The Brushes panel houses five types of brushes:

Calligraphic brushes apply strokes that resemble those drawn with a calligraphic pen. Figure 21 is an example.

Scatter brushes disperse copies of an object along a path, as shown in Figure 22.

Figure 20 *Brushes panel with pre-loaded brush libraries*

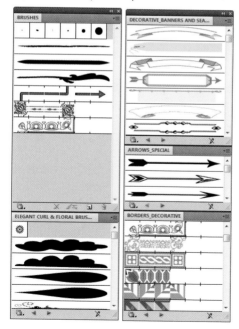

Working with Patterns and Brushes

You can apply artwork—such as an arrow or a feather—to a path with an art brush.

Art brushes stretch an object along the length of a path, as shown in Figure 23.

Bristle brushes create brush strokes with the appearance of a natural brush with hairs and bristles.

Pattern brushes repeat a pattern along a path. Pattern brushes are made with tiles that you create. You can define up to five tiles as components of the pattern: one tile for the side, one for the inner corner, one for the outer corner, and one each for the beginning and ending of the path. Figure 24 shows five tiles and a pattern that was created with them.

You can create any of the five types of brushes. Artwork for brushes must be composed of simple paths, with no gradients, blends, mesh objects, bitmap images, masks, or other brush strokes. Art and pattern brushes cannot include text. You must convert text to outlines before it can be used as artwork for these types of brushes.

Figure 21 *A calligraphic brush applied to a path*

Figure 22 *A scatter brush applied to a path*

Figure 23 *An art brush applied to a path*

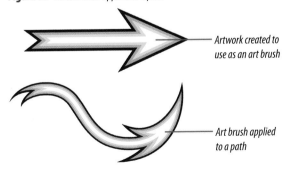

Artwork created to use as an art brush

Art brush applied to a path

Figure 24 *Five tiles used for a pattern brush*

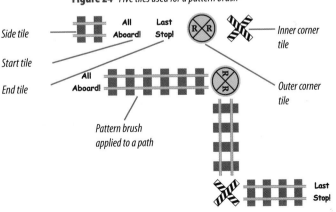

Side tile

Start tile

End tile

Inner corner tile

Outer corner tile

Pattern brush applied to a path

Create a calligraphic brush

1. Open AI 6-4.ai, then save it as **Four Brushes**.
2. Click the **Brushes button** 🖌 to display the Brushes panel.
3. Click the **Brushes panel options button** ▾≡ , then click **New Brush**.
4. Click the **Calligraphic Brush option button** in the New Brush dialog box, then click **OK**.

   The Calligraphic Brush Options dialog box opens, as shown in Figure 25.

5. Type **Twelve Points** in the Name text box, **45** in the Angle text box, and **12** in the Diameter text box, then click **OK**.

   The Twelve Points brush is added to the calligraphy brush section and is selected on the Brushes panel.

6. Click the **Selection tool** ▸ , select the first curved line on the artboard, then click the **Twelve Points brush** on the Brushes panel.
7. Double-click the **Twelve Points brush** on the Brushes panel.

   (continued)

Figure 25 *Calligraphic Brush Options dialog box*

Working with Patterns and Brushes

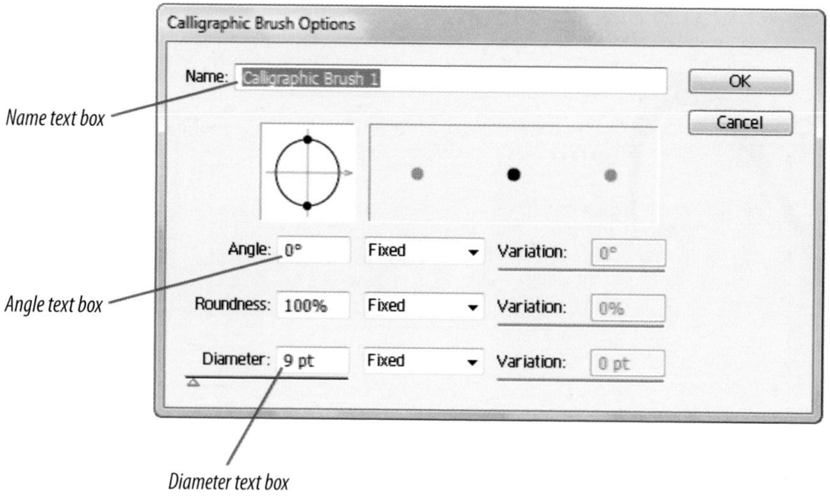

Figure 26 *Applying a calligraphic brush to paths*

8. Click the **Preview check box** in the Calligraphic Brush Options dialog box, change the Roundness to **20%**, then click **OK**.

9. Click **Apply to Strokes** in the Brush Change Alert dialog box.

The curved line updates to reflect the changes.

10. Apply the Twelve Points brush to the circle, then deselect all.

Your screen should resemble Figure 26.

You created and set the parameters for a new calligraphic brush, which you applied to a curved path and to a circle.

Create a scatter brush

1. Select the star target in the lower-right corner of the artboard, click the **Brushes panel options button** 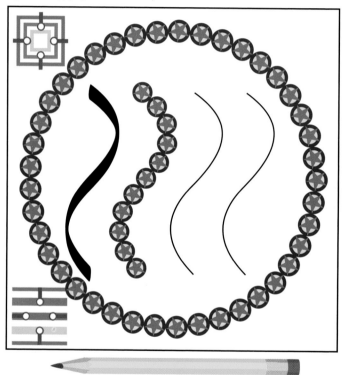, click **New Brush**, click the **Scatter Brush option button**, then click **OK**.

2. Name the brush **Star Target**, type **20** in the Size text box, type **60** in the Spacing text box, then click **OK**.

   The Star Target brush is selected on the Brushes panel.

3. Hide the star target artwork on the artboard.

4. Apply the Star Target brush to the second curved line, then apply it to the circle.

TIP To remove a brush stroke from a path, select the path, then click the Remove Brush Stroke button on the Brushes panel.

5. Double-click the **Star Target brush**, change the spacing to **20%**, click **OK**, then click **Apply to Strokes** in the Brush Change Alert dialog box.

6. Save your work, then compare your screen to Figure 27.

You used a group of simple objects as the artwork for a scatter brush, which you applied to a curved path and to a circle.

Figure 27 *Applying a scatter brush to paths*

Working with Patterns and Brushes

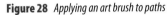

Figure 28 *Applying an art brush to paths*

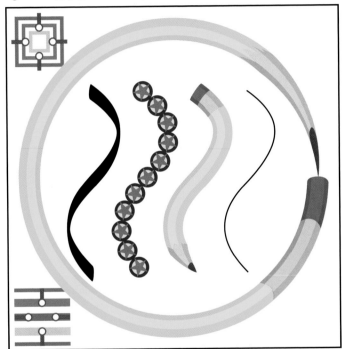

Create an art brush

1. Select the pencil artwork, click the **Brushes panel options button** ▾≣ , click **New Brush**, click the **Art Brush option button**, then click **OK**.

2. Click the **Stroke From Right To Left button** ← in the Art Brush Options dialog box.

   The direction arrow in the preview window updates and points in the same direction as the point of the pencil.

3. Enter **75** in the Width text box, name the brush Pencil, then click **OK**.

   The Pencil brush is selected on the Brushes panel.

4. Hide the pencil artwork on the artboard.

5. Apply the pencil brush to the third curved line, then apply it to the circle.

6. Save your work, then compare your screen to Figure 28.

You used an illustration of a pencil as the art for an art brush. You defined the parameters of the art brush—its direction and its size—then applied the brush to a curved path and to a circle.

Create a pattern brush

1. Verify that your Swatches panel is visible.

2. Select the artwork in the lower-left corner of the artboard, drag it into the Swatches panel, then name it **Green Side**.

3. Hide the artwork used for the Green Side swatch on the artboard.

4. Select the artwork in the top-left corner, drag it into the Swatches panel, then name it **Green Corner**.

5. Hide the artwork used for the Green Corner swatch on the artboard.

6. Click the **Brushes panel options button** ▾☰ , click **New Brush**, click the **Pattern Brush option button**, then click **OK**.

7. Name the new brush **Tomato Worm**.

8. Click the **Side Tile box**, make sure Spacing is set to **0%**, as shown in Figure 29, then click **Green Side** in the list of patterns.

9. Click the **Outer Corner Tile box**, then click **Green Corner** in the list of patterns, as shown in Figure 29.

10. Type **40** in the Scale text box, then click **OK**.

    The Tomato Worm brush is selected on the Brushes panel.

You dragged the two pieces of artwork into the Swatches panel and named them. You created a new pattern brush and then, in the dialog box, defined the first piece of artwork as the side tile of the brush and the second as a corner tile.

Figure 29 *Pattern Brush Options dialog box*

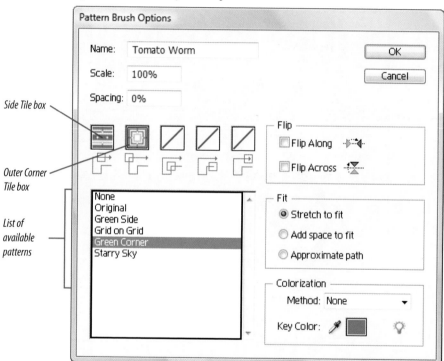

ILLUSTRATOR 6-26

Working with Patterns and Brushes

Figure 30 *Applying the pattern brush to paths*

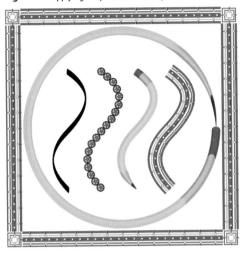

Figure 31 *Modifying the pattern brush*

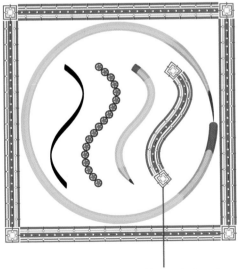

The curved line now begins and
ends with the corner artwork

Modify a pattern brush

1. Apply the Tomato Worm brush to the fourth curved line, then apply it to the square.

   Your screen should resemble Figure 30.

2. Double-click the **Tomato Worm brush** on the Brushes panel.

3. Click the **Start Tile box**, then click **Green Corner** in the list of patterns.

4. Click the **End Tile box**, click **Green Corner** in the list of patterns, click **OK**, then click **Apply to Strokes** in the Brush Change Alert dialog box.

5. The curved line now begins and ends with the corner artwork, as shown in Figure 31.

6. Save your work.

7. Close the Four Brushes document.

You applied the pattern brush to a curved path and to a square. You then modified the brush, adding artwork for a start tile and an end tile.

Work with
SCATTER BRUSHES

What You'll Do

In this lesson, you will work with scatter brushes, enter fixed and random values in the Scatter Brush Options dialog box, and view how those values affect your artwork.

Working with Scatter Brushes

It is easy to underestimate the role of brushes in creating artwork. Many designers identify them as a method for creating really cool strokes and leave it at that. What they are missing is that brushes can themselves be the best option for creating an illustration.

Of the four types of brushes, the scatter brush best illustrates this point. For example, if you were drawing a pearl necklace, a scatter brush would be your smartest choice for creating the illustration, as opposed to dragging and dropping copies of a single pearl illustration along a path, or creating a blend between two pearls.

Why? The reason is that, with the scatter brush, you can manipulate the path endlessly, with precise control of the size, spacing, and rotation of the elements along the path. In addition, you can input a scatter value, which determines how far the objects can be positioned from the path, an option that blending does not offer.

The scatter brush is even more powerful for creating the effect of "randomness." Figure 32 shows a fine example of this effect using a flying beetle as the artwork for the scatter brush. In the Scatter Brush Options dialog box, you can apply a random range for size, spacing, scatter, and rotation and create the effect of a three-dimensional swarm of beetles flying in different directions—some of them closer to you and larger and some of them farther away and smaller.

For each setting in the Brush Options dialog box, you can choose fixed or random values. When you apply random settings to a scatter brush, the positioning of the objects on the path will be different every time you apply the brush.

QUICK TIP

Click the Brush Libraries Menu button on the Brushes panel to display a list of brush libraries. Each brush library opens in a new panel. For example, the Artistic Watercolor brush library includes 12 watercolor brush styles that offer the look and feel of real water color paint strokes.

Figure 32 *A swarm of beetles created with a flying beetle scatter brush*

Modify a scatter brush

1. Open AI 6-5.ai, then save it as **Random Flies**.

2. Select the circle, then apply the Flying Beetle scatter brush.

3. Double-click the **Flying Beetle brush** on the Brushes panel, click the **Preview check box** to add a check mark if necessary, then move the Scatter Brush Options dialog box so that you can see as much of the artboard as possible.

4. Click the **Size list arrow**, then click **Fixed**.

   The beetles become the same size.

TIP Press [Tab] to see changes made to the artwork after you change a value in the dialog box.

5. Type **50** In the Size text box.

   The beetles are 50% the size of the original flying beetle artwork.

6. Click the **Scatter list arrow**, click **Fixed**, then type **0** in the Scatter text box.

   The beetles are positioned on the path.

7. Click the **Spacing list arrow**, click **Fixed**, then type **50** in the Spacing text box.

   The beetles are evenly spaced along the path.

8. Click the **Rotation list arrow**, click **Fixed**, then type **0** in the Rotation text box, as shown in Figure 33.

   The beetles rotate 360° as they move from the beginning to the end of the path.

9. Click the **Rotation relative to list arrow**, then click **Page**.

   The beetles no longer rotate along the path.

(continued)

Figure 33 *Scatter Brush Options dialog box*

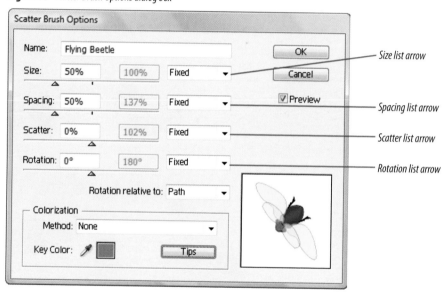

Working with Patterns and Brushes

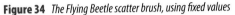

Figure 34 *The Flying Beetle scatter brush, using fixed values*

10. Click the **eyedropper button** in the dialog box, then click the **black leg** of the beetle artwork in the preview window of the dialog box.

    The Key Color box turns black.

11. Click the **Method list arrow**, then click **Tints**.

    The beetles are tinted with the new key color. Your work should resemble Figure 34.

12. Click **OK**, then click **Apply to Strokes** in the Brush Change Alert dialog box.

You explored the parameters that define a scatter brush. You started with scatter brush artwork that was random in size, spacing, scatter, and rotation. By removing the parameters that defined the randomness of the artwork, you gained an understanding of how those parameters created the random effects in the original artwork.

Manipulate random values in a scatter brush

1. Double-click the **Flying Beetle brush** on the Brushes panel.

2. Click the **Size list arrow**, click **Random**, then type **20** in the first Size text box and **100** in the second.

   The beetles will be randomly assigned a size anywhere between 20% and 100% of the original artwork.

3. Click the **Spacing list arrow**, click **Random**, then type **50** in the first Spacing text box and **200** in the second, as shown in Figure 35.

   The beetles are spaced randomly along the path within the set range of values.

4. Click the **Scatter list arrow**, click **Random**, then type **-100** in the first Scatter text box and **100** in the second.

   These values define the distance from each side of the path that the artwork can be positioned. In the case of a circular path, the first value determines how far into the circle the artwork can be positioned, and the second value determines how far outside the circle.

5. Click the **Rotation list arrow**, click **Random**, then type **-180** in the first Rotation text box and **180** in the second.

   The artwork can be rotated to any position within a full 360°.

   (continued)

Figure 35 *Scatter Brush Options dialog box*

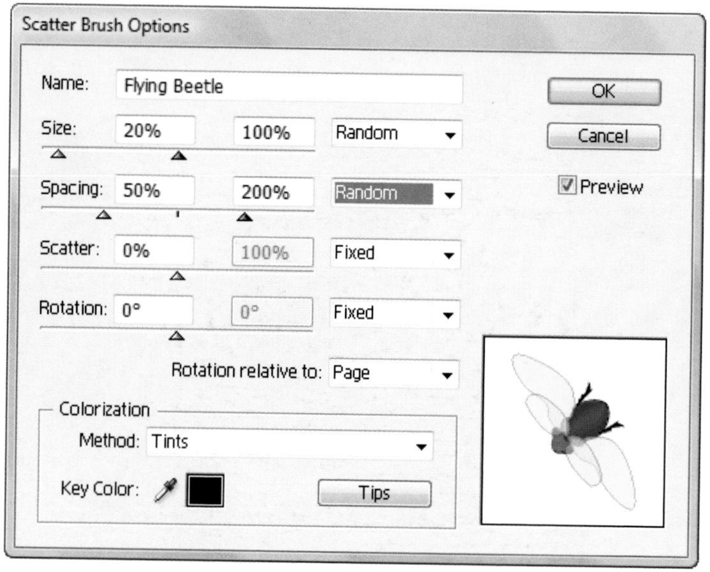

Working with Patterns and Brushes

Figure 36 *Scatter artwork using random values*

6. Click the **Method list arrow**, click **None**, click **OK**, then click **Apply to Strokes**.

   Figure 36 is an example of this brush setting.

7. Click the **Remove Brush Stroke button** ✕ on the Brushes panel, then reapply the Flying Beetle brush.

   The artwork will be different each time you reapply the brush, because the values are determined randomly with each application.

8. Save and close the Random Flies document.

Starting with symmetrical, evenly spaced scatter brush artwork, you manipulated parameters to create artwork that was random in size, spacing, scatter, and rotation values.

Compare the Paintbrush Tool
TO THE BLOB BRUSH TOOL

What You'll Do

In this lesson you will make strokes with the Paintbrush tool and the Blob Brush tool, and then compare and contrast the results.

Working with the Paintbrush Tool

"Drawing" in Illustrator can be accomplished in many different ways. As you saw earlier in the book, one of the main methods of drawing is to use the Pen tool to draw paths. As you saw earlier in this chapter, you can then apply brush strokes to paths. The Paintbrush tool accomplishes both tasks simultaneously. Working with the Paintbrush tool, you choose a brush from the Brushes panel, then simply "paint" on the artboard. The Paintbrush tool creates a path with the selected brush applied as a stroke. As with any path, you can change the brush style applied to the path at any time. You can also set options in the tool's dialog box that determine the smoothness of the stroke or the curve and how far the artwork can stray or scatter from the path you draw.

The main difference between using the Paintbrush tool and the Pen tool to create artwork is largely a measure of control. The Pen tool offers precision; as you draw, you can manipulate handles and anchor points to draw and position the path exactly where you want it to be and exactly how you want it to look. The Paintbrush tool, on the other hand, offers more of a "freehand" approach to drawing. You can use the Paintbrush tool to sketch out a drawing and create artwork that is more spontaneous and "hand-drawn."

Because both tools produce paths, you can manipulate the paths after you've drawn them. That's a big plus. Though you might use the tool to create more spontaneous strokes, you can always go back and manipulate anchor points and paths and perfect any paths that you make with the Paintbrush tool.

Working with Patterns and Brushes

Comparing the Paintbrush Tool with the Blob Brush Tool

The essential difference between the Paintbrush tool and the Blob Brush tool is that the Paintbrush tool creates a stroked path and the Blob Brush tool creates a closed filled object. Figure 37 shows two simple pieces of artwork: the top piece is made with the Paintbrush tool. The bottom piece is made with the Blob Brush tool.

Figure 38 shows the same artwork in Outline mode. Note that the Blob Brush tool created the bottom artwork as a closed, filled object.

Figure 37 *Two brush strokes*

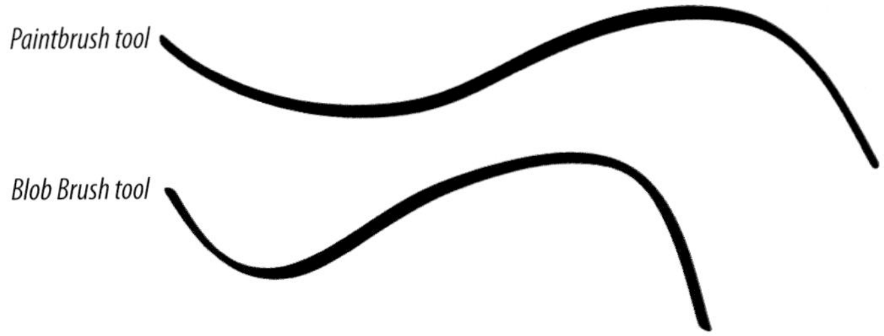

Paintbrush tool

Blob Brush tool

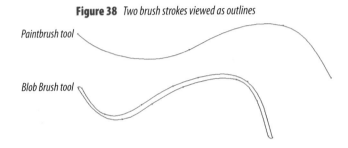

Figure 38 *Two brush strokes viewed as outlines*

Paintbrush tool

Blob Brush tool

Both the Paintbrush tool and the Blob Brush tool paint with color. The Paintbrush tool creates individual, non-connected paths with every stroke of the tool. The Blob Brush tool behaves differently. With the Blob Brush tool, if you overlap one stroke with a second stroke of the same color, the two strokes will be united as one object. Figure 39 shows a horizontal stroke and a vertical stroke created with the Blob Brush tool. Figure 40 shows the artwork in Outline mode, revealed as one closed object.

Figure 39 *An "X" created with the Blob Brush tool*

Figure 40 *The "X" revealed as a single object*

Working with Patterns and Brushes

The Blob Brush tool is sensitive to color. Figure 41 shows a pink stroke crossed by a blue stroke, both created by the Blob Brush tool. Note that they are two separate filled objects. Because the second object was created with a different fill color, the Blob Brush tool does not unite the two objects.

This is an important feature of the Blob Brush tool. Let's say you were using the Blob Brush tool to paint a tree against a sky. You wouldn't want the "tree" to unite with the "sky." You'd want to keep them as separate objects. That's exactly what would happen if you painted the sky blue and the tree green—the Blob Brush tool would create them as two separate objects.

Figure 41 *Two intersecting objects created with the Blob Brush tool*

Use the Paintbrush tool

1. Open AI 6-6.ai, then save it as **Brush and Blob**.

2. Zoom in on the top half of the artboard, then click the **Paintbrush tool** on the Tools panel.

3. Verify that the Fill color is set to **None** and the Stroke color is set to **black**, then click the **45 pt Oval brush** on the Brushes panel.

4. Use the Paintbrush tool to trace the single black dash in the top section.

5. Make two strokes to trace the black "plus" sign.

6. Change the stroke color to **red**, then trace the red component of the X.

7. Change the stroke color to **blue**, then trace the blue component of the X.

8. Switch to Outline mode to see the results of your work.

   As shown in Figure 42, the Paintbrush tool created one open path for each stroke.

9. Switch back to Preview mode, then save your work.

You painted strokes with the Paintbrush tool then switched to Outline mode to reveal that the tool creates simple paths.

Use the Blob Brush tool

1. Zoom in on the bottom half of the artboard, then click the **Blob Brush tool** on the Tools panel.

2. Verify that the Fill color is set to None and the Stroke color is set to black, then verify that the 45 pt Oval brush on the Brushes panel is selected.

(continued)

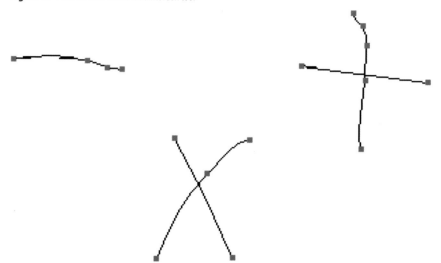

Figure 42 *Paths created with the Paintbrush tool*

Figure 43 *Paths created with the Blob Brush tool*

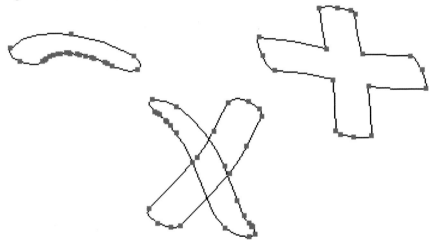

3. Use the Blob Brush tool 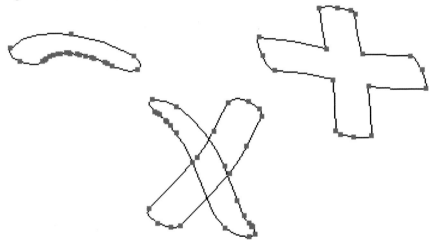 to trace the single black dash in the bottom section.

4. Make two strokes to trace the black "plus" sign.

5. Change the stroke color to **red**, then trace the red component of the X.

6. Change the stroke color to **blue**, then trace the blue component of the X.

7. Click **Object** on the Application bar, then click **Unlock All**.

   The placed image is unlocked and selected.

8. Click **Object** on the Application bar, point to **Hide**, then click **Selection**.

9. Select all, then switch to Outline mode to see the results of your work.

   Your artboard should resemble Figure 43. The Blob brush tool created closed paths with a size the width of the diameter of the brush. Where two brush strokes of the same color overlap, the Blob brush united the two closed paths into a single closed path. Where two different colors overlap, the two closed paths are not united.

10. Switch back to Preview mode, save your work, then close the file.

You painted the same strokes, this time using the Blob Brush tool. Then you switched to Outline mode to compare the results of the Blob Brush tool to that of the Paintbrush tool.

Enhance Artwork with Brushes
AND THE WIDTH TOOL

What You'll Do

In this lesson you will use placed art, art brushes, the Bristle brush and the Width tool to improve the appearance of artwork.

Improving Artwork with Brush Strokes

Figure 44 shows the "Snowball" drawing that you created in Chapter 3. You drew all the objects that make up the illustration and assembled them. It's at this point that many designers hit a wall: What to do next?

The illustration at this point doesn't look great; it looks like a bunch of assembled

Figure 44 *Objects with a simple stroke*

illustrator objects. There's no flare, no nuance, nothing unique.

This is where brushes come in and convert your objects into artwork. In Figure 45, a simple charcoal artbrush has been applied to the same artwork. Notice the dramatic effect it gives the illustration.

Using Placed Art as Brushes

At some point, you might find yourself wanting brush artwork that's even more unique than that which you can create with Illustrator's Brush panel or with Illustrator objects. One technique that designers use is to trace actual pencil, crayon, or marker sketches in Illustrator, then apply the artwork as a brush.

Figure 46 shows a placed bitmap graphic of a simple pencil stroke on paper. That bitmap art can be traced and then saved as a brush.

Figure 45 *Charcoal brush applied to artwork*

Figure 46 *Objects with another stroke*

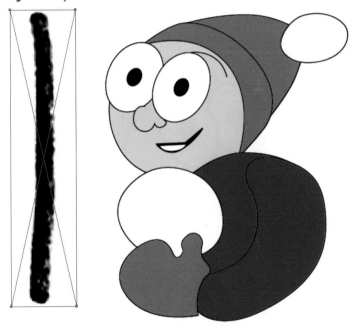

When applied, it creates a unique effect, as shown in Figure 47.

NEW Using the Bristle Brush

If you look at the arc of Adobe Illustrator, from its debut in 1988 to now with CS5, you see that Adobe has endeavored to make Illustrator more and more of a drawing and painting tool. Adobe's challenge has been a tough one:

to somehow devise and develop "computer tools" that mimic traditional art tools such as pens, brushes, crayons, and chalk.

The Bristle brush represents a real step forward toward the goal. The Bristle brush creates a natural brush stroke with the streaks and varying opacities you would find with an actual paint brush, allowing you to mimic the look and feel of traditional

disciplines like watercolor or paint. As with the Paintbrush tool, the Bristle brush creates open paths. When you paint with either brush, if you switch to Outline mode, you'll see a series of path segments. Therefore, colors you apply to those segments while painting with the brushes are applied as strokes. Figure 48 shows an illustration painted with the Bristle brush.

Figure 47 *Artwork "brushed" with the placed art*

Figure 48 *Snowball recreated with the Bristle brush*

To use the Bristle brush, you first create a new brush in the Brushes panel, just as you would an art brush or a scatter brush, and then choose Bristle Brush as the definition. This opens the Bristle Brush Options dialog box, shown in Figure 49. You can choose from different brush shapes, like fan or round, and you can specify the stiffness of the bristles. With the Bristle brush though,

you'll find that the many preferences are best experienced and understood by giving them a try.

To get the most effect out of working with the Bristle brush, use a Wacom or other brand of pen tablet device. Depending on the device and the features available, the pen will incorporate factors like pressure, angle, and rotation. If you use a mouse or non-tablet

device, you can still use the Bristle brush, but it will be like working with a brush fixed at a 45-degree angle.

The key word when working with the Bristle brush is *experiment*. There are no specific sets of steps or specific approaches—you simply need to experiment. And don't forget about the many different brush shapes available to you as shown in Figure 50.

Figure 49 *Bristle Brush Options dialog box*

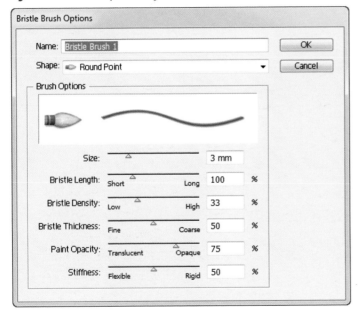

Figure 50 *Brush Shape pull-down menu for Bristle brush*

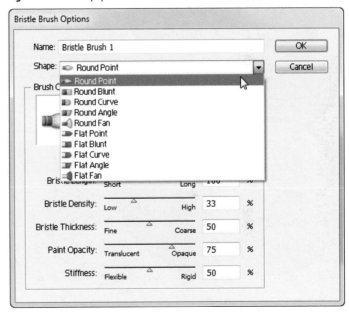

NEW Using the Width Tool

In Chapter 3 of this book, you learned about making "pseudo strokes" by creating black copies behind objects and distorting them to "peek" from behind the front object. Figure 51 shows the Snowball illustration you created in Chapter 3 with pseudo strokes.

The Width tool, new to Illustrator CS5, offers you a method for quickly altering the width of a stroke by clicking and dragging on the stroke itself. In Figure 52, the top image shows a simple stroke and the bottom image shows the same stroke being increased with the Width tool. With the Width tool, you simply position the tool over the stroke,

Figure 51 *Pseudo strokes effect*

Figure 52 *Increasing the width of a stroke with the Width tool*

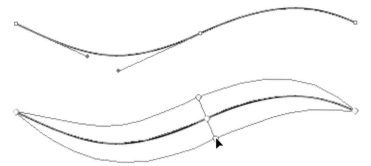

then click and drag to increase the width of the stroke.

What's really great about the Width tool is that you can click and drag any area of a path, not just over an already-existing anchor point. This makes the entire path available for modification. Figure 53 shows the bottom stroke after it has been altered with the Width tool. Note that it is still simply a stroked path.

The Width tool provides a quick way to mimic the pseudo strokes effect. Figure 54 shows the Snowball illustration after being altered with the Width tool. Compare this to the pseudo strokes effect in Figure 51.

Figure 53 *Stroke with an increased width*

Figure 54 *Snowball illustration with altered widths*

Use placed art as a brush

1. Open AI 6-7.ai, then save it as **Flower Brushes**.

2. Evaluate the artwork in terms of shape, color, dimension, and its overall effect.

   The artwork has interesting shapes, and the colors work well together, but overall, the illustration is boring. It looks like what it is: a few Illustrator objects with color fills and a thin black stroke. The illustration is flat—it is not dynamic.

3. Click the **File menu**, then click **Place**.

4. Navigate to where your Data Files are stored, click the file named **Fat Charcoal**, then click **Place**.

   As shown in Figure 55, Fat Charcoal is a digital image of a line drawn with thick charcoal. The line has rough, uneven edges. The image was taken with a smart phone camera, brightened in Photoshop, then saved.

5. Click the **arrow button** next to the Live Trace button on the Control panel to expose the list of tracing presets, then click **Detailed Illustration**.

   The artwork is traced and converted to filled Illustrator objects.

6. Drag the traced artwork into the gray area at the bottom of the Brushes panel

   The New Brush dialog box opens.

7. Click the **Art Brush option button**, then click **OK**.

8. Type **Fat Charcoal** in the Name text box. Click **OK** to close the Art Brush Options dialog box.

   The Fat Charcoal brush appears on the Brushes panel.

9. Delete the placed artwork from the artboard.

(continued)

Figure 55 *Fat Charcoal art placed*

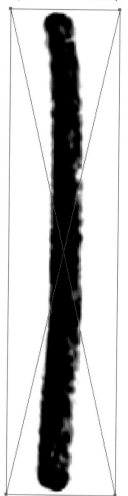

Figure 56 *Artwork with art applied as a brush*

10. Select all of the artwork on the artboard, click **View** on the Application bar, then click **Hide Edges** if necessary.

11. Click the **Fat Charcoal brush thumbnail** on the Brushes panel.

    The Fat Charcoal brush is applied as a stroke to the selected objects. The brush strokes are too wide and need to be reduced.

12. Open the Stroke panel, then reduce the weight of the stroke to **.5 pt**.

    Your artwork should resemble Figure 56.

13. Save your work, then close Flower Brushes.ai.

You placed a graphic of a charcoal streak. You traced it, then created an art brush. You then applied the art brush to the flower artwork.

NEW Use the Width tool

1. Open AI 6-8.ai, then save it as **Flower Width**.
2. Select the vase, then click the **Width tool**.
3. Click and drag to select different areas of the vase path to alter the width.

   Figure 57 shows one possible outcome.
4. Continue clicking and dragging every path in the illustration to create various widths and new shapes.

   Figure 58 shows one example of the finished illustration.
5. Save your work, then close Flower Width.ai.

You altered the width of the stroke on various parts of the vase using the Width tool.

Figure 57 *Applying the Width tool to the vase*

Figure 58 *Illustration modified with the Width tool*

Working with Patterns and Brushes

Figure 59 *Artwork with Bristle brush applied*

Figure 60 *New settings for the Bristle brush*

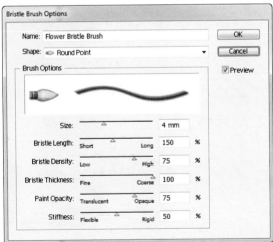

Create, apply, and modify a Bristle brush

1. Open AI 6-9.ai, then save it as **Flower Bristles**.
2. Click the **Brushes panel options button** ▾≣ , then click **New Brush**.
3. Click **Bristle Brush**, then click **OK**.
4. Type **Flower Bristle Brush** in the Name text box, then click **OK** to accept the defaults for the brush.
5. Select all the artwork on the artboard, then change the fill color to **white**.
6. Click the **Flower Bristle Brush** in the Brushes panel, then compare your artwork to Figure 59.
7. Double-click **Flower Bristle Brush** in the Brushes panel.

   The Bristle Brush Options dialog box opens.

   TIP Verify that Preview is checked.

8. Enter the settings shown in Figure 60, click **OK**, then click **Apply to Strokes** if prompted.

   Deselect all, then save your work.

You created a new Bristle brush and applied it to artwork. You then modified the brush with the artwork selected.

NEW Paint with the Bristle brush

1. Verify that the flower artwork is deselected, then open the Layers panel.

2. Click the **Create New Layer button** at the bottom of the Layers panel.

   In this layer, you will paint with the Bristle brush on the empty new layer.

3. Click the **Paintbrush tool** in the Tools panel, then verify that Flower Bristle Brush is selected in the Brushes panel.

4. Set the Stroke color to one of the green swatches in the Swatches panel.

5. Paint the leaves and stems of the flower artwork, setting your stroke color to various shades of green, then compare your results to Figure 61.

   Feel free to set your Paintbrush size and opacity in the Control panel as you like. Your results, obviously, will be unique. You can use the figure as one example of what can be done.

6. Continue painting with various colors to finish the illustration.

   Figure 62 shows one result.

   (continued)

Figure 61 *Starting by painting the green areas of the flower*

Figure 62 *Applying paint to the entire illustration*

Working with Patterns and Brushes

Figure 63 *Painting with a white stroke to add highlights*

Figure 64 *Painting with a black stroke to add detail*

7. Paint with a white stroke to add highlights to the artwork, as shown in Figure 63.

8. Paint with a black stroke to add shadows to the artwork and to strengthen the outlines of the artwork, as shown in Figure 64.

9. Save your work, then close the file.

TIP If you get a dialog box warning you that the document you are currently saving contains multiple Bristle Brush Paths with transparency, click OK.

You painted artwork with the Bristle brush tool.

Use the Move command.

1. Create a new 6" × 6" document, then save it as **Polka Dot Pattern**.
2. Create a 2" square, then fill it with a green fill, and remove any stroke if necessary.
3. Create a .25" circle, then fill it with white.
4. Align the circle and the square by their center points. (*Hint*: Select both the circle and the square, then click the Horizontal Align Center button and the Vertical Align Center button on the Align panel.)
5. Deselect all, select the white circle, click Object on the Application bar, point to Transform, then click Move.
6. Type **-.5** in the Horizontal text box, type **-.5** in the Vertical text box, then click Copy.
7. Keeping the new circle selected, click Object on the Application bar, point to Transform, then click Move.
8. Type **1** in the Horizontal text box, type **0** in the Vertical text box, then click Copy.
9. Select the two new circles, click Object, point to Transform, click Move, type **0** in the Horizontal text box, **1** in the Vertical text box, then click Copy. You moved a copy of them 1 inch below.
10. Fill the center circle with any blue swatch that you like.
11. Save your work.

Create a pattern.

1. Select all the artwork, then drag it into the Swatches panel.
2. Deselect the artwork, then name the new swatch **Green Polka Dot**.
3. Delete the artwork on the artboard.
4. Create a 4" square, then fill it with the Green Polka Dot pattern.

5. Double-click the Scale tool, then scale only the pattern 25%.
6. Save your work.

Design a repeating pattern.

1. Hide the 4" square.
2. Drag the Green Polka Dot pattern swatch from the Swatches panel onto the artboard.
3. Deselect the pattern swatch, draw a diagonal 1 point black line from the bottom-left corner to the top-right corner of the green square.
4. Change the stroke color of the line to a shade of green.
5. Deselect, select the line with the Selection tool, then rotate a copy of the line 90°, making sure the Objects check box in the Rotate dialog box is checked.
6. Click the Direct Selection tool, select the five circles, then cut them.

7. Click the Selection tool, select the two green lines, then paste in front.
8. Select the green square, click Object on the Application bar, point to Path, click Offset Path, type -.5 in the Offset text box, then click OK.
9. Cut the new green square, then paste it in back of the blue circle.
10. Select all the artwork, press and hold [Alt] (Win) or [option] (Mac), then drag the artwork on top of the Green Polka Dot swatch to replace the old pattern with the new one.
11. Delete the artwork from the artboard.
12. Show all, then save your work. Your square should resemble Figure 65.
13. Close Polka Dot Pattern.ai.

Figure 65 *Completed Skills Review, Part 1*

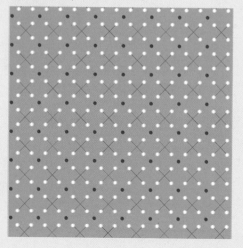

Working with Patterns and Brushes

Work with the Brushes panel.

1. Open AI 6-10.ai, then save it as **Brushes Review**.
2. Select the snowflake artwork on the artboard, click the Brushes panel options button, then click New Brush.
3. Click the Scatter Brush option button, then click OK.
4. Name the new brush **Snowflake**.
5. Set the size to 30%.
6. Set the spacing to 40%, then click OK.
7. Hide the snowflake artwork on the artboard.
8. Create a circle that is 4" in diameter, then apply the Snowflake brush to the circle.
9. Save your work.

Work with scatter brushes.

1. Double-click the Snowflake brush on the Brushes panel.
2. Set all the Scatter and Rotation options to Random.
3. Set the scatter range between 10% and 20%.
4. Set the rotation range between 45° and 25°.
5. Click OK, then click Apply to Strokes if prompted.
6. Save your work, deselect all, compare your screen with Figure 66, then close the Brushes Review document.

Compare the Paintbrush tool to the Blob Brush tool.

1. Open AI 6-11.ai, then save it as **Brush Skills**.
2. Click the Paintbrush tool on the Tools panel.
3. Verify that the Fill color is set to None and the Stroke color is set to red, then verify that the 15 pt Round brush on the Brushes panel is selected.
4. Using the Paintbrush tool, make four strokes to trace the left object.
5. Click the Blob Brush tool on the Tools panel, then make four strokes to trace the right object.

6. Click Object on the Application bar, then click Unlock All.
7. Click Object on the Application bar, point to Hide, then click Selection.
8. Select all, then switch to Outline mode to see the results of your work.
9. Switch back to Preview mode, save your work, then close the file.

Enhance artwork with brushes and the Width tool.

1. Open AI 6-12.ai, then save it as **Dog Width**.

Figure 66 *Completed Skills Review, Part 2*

2. Select the "red beret," then click the Width tool.
3. Click and drag to select different areas of the beret path to alter the width.
4. Continue clicking and dragging every path in the illustration to create various widths and new shapes.
5. Select the six whiskers, then apply the Charcoal brush in the Brushes panel.
   Figure 67 shows one example of the finished illustration.
6. Save your work, then close Dog Width.ai.

Figure 67 *Completed Skills Review, Part 3*

You work in the textile industry as a pattern designer. Your boss asks you to design a pattern for a new line of shower curtains. Her only direction is that the pattern must feature triangles and at least eight colors.

1. Create a new 6" × 6" document, then save it as **New Curtain**.
2. Create a 1" square with a blue fill and no stroke.
3. Copy the square, paste in front, then fill the new square with green.
4. Click Object on the Application bar, point to Path, click Add Anchor Points, then click the Delete Anchor Point tool. (*Hint*: The Delete Anchor Point tool is hidden beneath the Pen tool.)
5. Delete the top-left corner, top-right corner, left side, and right side anchor points, so that the square is converted to a triangle.
6. Use the Move command to create a copy of the two shapes to the right, then two copies below, so that, together, the area of the four tiles is 2" X 2".
7. Change the colors in each tile.
8. Scale the four tiles 15%.
9. Make a new pattern swatch out of the four tiles, name it **Triangle Pattern**, then apply the pattern to a 4" square.
10. Save your work, then compare your pattern to Figure 68.
11. Close the New Curtain document.

Figure 68 *Completed Project Builder 1*

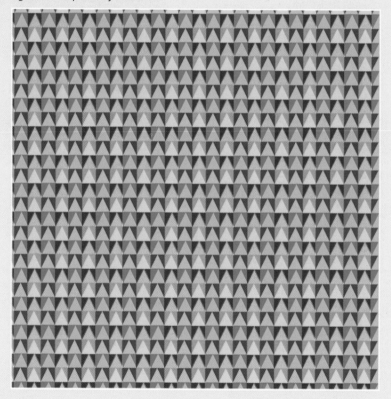

You are a jewelry designer, and you've been hired to create the original design for a new line of necklaces that will be targeted to teenage girls. The necklaces will be made with flat, tinted metals, and you are asked to use bright colors. One catch: Your client tells you that he's "unsure" of what he's looking for and hints that he may make many changes to your design before he's satisfied.

1. Open AI 6-13.ai, then save it as **Jewelry**.
2. Create a new scatter brush with the artwork provided.
3. Name the new brush **Smile**.
4. Set the size to 20%.
5. Set the spacing to 25%.
6. Set the rotation to Random.
7. Set the rotation range from -92° to 92°, make it relative to the page, then click OK.
8. Hide the original artwork.
9. Draw a path resembling the arc of a necklace, then apply the Smile scatter brush to the path.
10. Save your work, then compare your pattern to Figure 69.
11. Close the Jewelry document.

Figure 69 *Completed Project Builder 2*

You own a gallery in Key West called Funky Frames. You are known for designing unusual and festive frames of various sizes. The process of designing the frames is complex, as you use many different kinds of materials. However, they all begin with a brush pattern that you create in Illustrator.

1. Open AI 6-14.ai, then save it as **Funky Frames**.
2. Select the left tile, drag it into the Swatches panel, then name it **Side Tile**.
3. Select the right tile, drag it into the Swatches panel, then name it **Corner Tile**.
4. Hide the artwork on the artboard.
5. Create a new pattern brush.
6. Name the new brush **Funky**.
7. Apply the Side Tile swatch as the side tile and the Corner Tile swatch as the outer corner tile.
8. Set the scale value to 70%, then click OK.
9. Apply the Funky pattern brush as a stroke to a 6" white square.
10. Save your work, then compare your pattern to Figure 70.
11. Close Funky Frames.ai.

Figure 70 *Completed Design Project*

Working with Patterns and Brushes

You have been commissioned to design an original plaid pattern, which will be used to produce kilts for the wedding of a famous singer and her Scottish groom. Your only direction is that it must be an original pattern, and it must have at least three colors.

1. Create a new document, then save it as **Wedding Plaid**.
2. Research the history of plaid patterns and their association with specific groups, families, and organizations.
3. Search the Internet for plaid patterns.
4. Research the Burberry pattern, one of the most famous patterns ever created.
5. Create color swatches to compare and choose colors that work together, then design the pattern.
6. Fill a 6" × 6" square with the new pattern.
7. Save your work, then compare your pattern to Figure 71.
8. Close the Wedding Plaid document.

Figure 71 *Completed Portfolio Project*

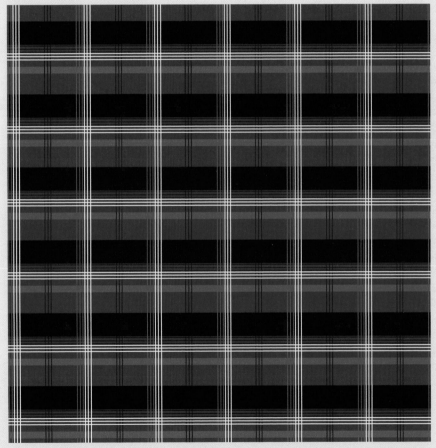

CHAPTER 7

WORKING WITH DISTORTIONS, GRADIENT MESHES, ENVELOPES, AND BLENDS

1. Edit colors and distort objects
2. Work with gradient meshes
3. Work with envelopes
4. Create blends

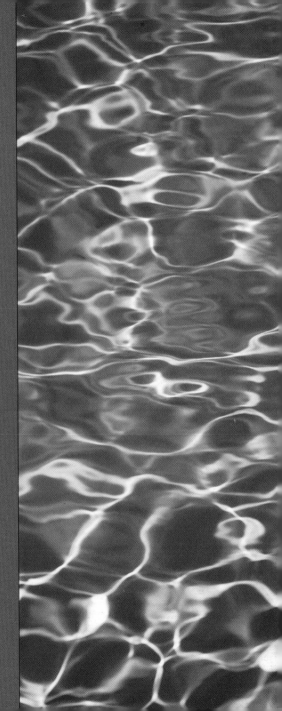

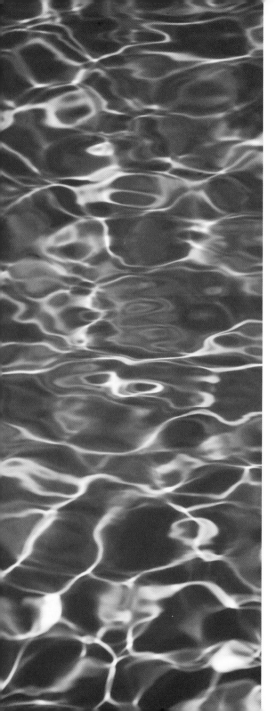

WORKING WITH DISTORTIONS, GRADIENT MESHES, ENVELOPES, AND BLENDS

Illustrator software comes programmed with basic operations, which are mathematical algorithms that create specific effects when applied to objects. These include effects, gradient meshes, envelopes, and blends. There are also color editing commands that affect the color of objects and create color blends between objects. Distort effects twist, pucker, and bloat objects, among other operations. The Create Gradient Mesh command produces a multicolored object on which colors can transition smoothly and flow in different directions. Envelopes are objects that you use to distort other objects. Blends create a series of intermediate objects and colors between two or more selected objects.

When you are working with effects, meshes, envelopes, and blends, you are working at the intermediate level in Illustrator. All are challenging—less in learning how to use them than in activating your imagination for ideas of how to best use them. Of the four, meshes and blends are the broadest in scope, offering powerful options for adding color, shape, depth, and perspective to an illustration.

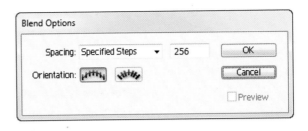

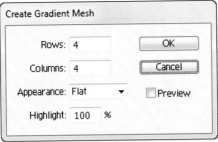

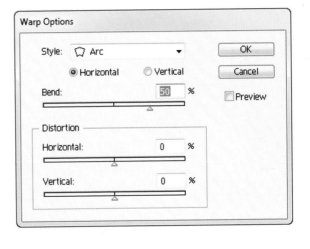

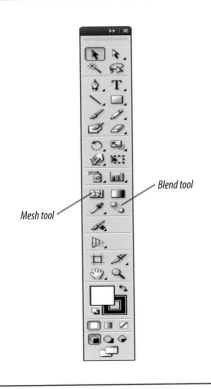

Mesh tool

Blend tool

Edit Colors
AND DISTORT OBJECTS

What You'll Do

In this lesson, you will explore options for manipulating colors and basic shapes with effects.

Introducing Effects

Illustrator provides a number of effects that you can use to alter the shape of an object. These effects provide simple operations that you can use to tweak your illustrations and give them a unique look. Of the many effects that modify shapes, some are essential operations that you will want to have in your skills set.

The Pucker & Bloat effect adjusts the segments between an object's anchor points. With a pucker effect, the segments are moved inward, toward the center of the object, while the anchor points are moved outward, as shown in Figure 1. The bloat effect is achieved by moving the segments outward and the anchor points inward, as shown in Figure 2.

Figure 1 *Pucker effect applied*

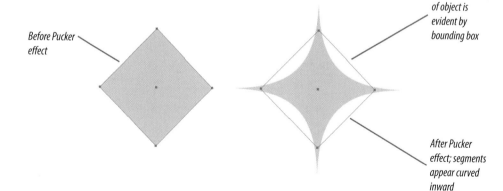

Before Pucker effect

Original shape of object is evident by bounding box

After Pucker effect; segments appear curved inward

Working with Distortions, Gradient Meshes, Envelopes, and Blends

The Twist effect rotates an object more sharply in the center than it does at the edges, creating a whirlpool effect, as shown in Figure 3. With the Twist effect, it's often a good idea to use the Add Anchor Points command to add more anchor points to the object, because it makes the twist effect smoother.

The Pucker & Bloat and Twist exercises in this chapter are intended to familiarize you with these types of transformations, which are useful for designing artwork. In addition, these steps will serve as an introduction to effects.

When you apply the Pucker & Bloat and the Twist commands, they will be applied as effects. Effects change only the appearance of the object. Note how in Figures 1, 2, and 3, that the selected object does not change, even after the effect has been applied. This is evident by the bounding box.

Effects are controlled on the Appearance panel. You will study effects and the Appearance panel in-depth in Chapter 8. In this chapter, focus more on the Pucker & Bloat and Twist effects from a design perspective and how you might use them in your artwork.

Modifying Color with the Edit Colors Command

The Edit Colors commands on the Edit menu are useful for quickly applying color changes to objects. With the Edit Colors commands, the changes are applied directly to the objects; they are not effects.

You can saturate an illustration, which makes colors more intense. Conversely, you can reduce the saturation of an illustration, making its colors duller, with a washed-out appearance. Use the Convert to Grayscale command to completely desaturate an illustration and create the effect of a black-and-white image.

You can also use the Edit Colors commands to make color blends between objects. The Blend Front to Back command creates a color blend through all the objects in the stacking order, using the frontmost object as the starting color and the backmost object as the ending color. This command is useful for adding the effect of color depth to an illustration.

Figure 2 *Bloat effect applied*

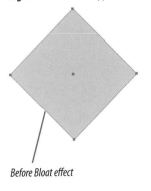

Before Bloat effect

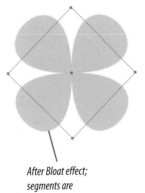

After Bloat effect; segments are moved outward

Figure 3 *Twist effect applied*

Before Twist effect

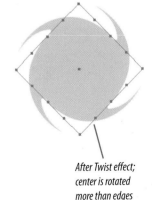

After Twist effect; center is rotated more than edges

Create a front to back blend

1. Open AI 7-1.ai, then save it as **Edit Colors**.

2. Select all, click **Object** on the Application bar, point to **Path**, then click **Outline Stroke**.

3. The strokes are converted to closed paths.

4. Deselect, then fill the smallest object with yellow.

5. Select all, click **Edit** on the Application bar, point to **Edit Colors**, then click **Blend Front to Back**.

6. A color blend is created from the frontmost to the backmost object in the stacking order. Deselect and your work should resemble Figure 4.

TIP The Blend Front to Back command does not work on open paths.

7. Save your work, then close Edit Colors.ai.

You converted stroked paths to outlines, and then used the Blend Front to Back command to create the effect that the objects lighten as they move from left to right.

Figure 4 *Blending colors front to back*

Figure 5 *Illustration with saturated colors*

Working with Distortions, Gradient Meshes, Envelopes, and Blends

Figure 6 *Illustration with the Convert to Grayscale command applied*

Saturate and desaturate an illustration

1. Open AI 7-2.ai, then save it as **Saturation**.
2. Select all, click **View** on the Application bar, then click **Hide Edges**.
3. Click **Edit** on the Application bar, point to **Edit Colors**, then click **Saturate**.
4. Click the **Preview check box**, drag the **Intensity slider** all the way to the right, then click **OK**.
5. Your work should resemble Figure 5.
6. Click **Edit** on the Application bar, point to **Edit Colors**, then click **Convert to Grayscale**.

   Every object is filled with a shade of gray, as shown in Figure 6.
7. Click **View** on the Application bar, then click **Show Edges**.
8. Deselect all by clicking the artboard.
9. Save your work, then close the Saturation document.

You used the Saturate command to intensify the color of an image. You then used the Convert to Grayscale command to remove all chromatic color from the illustration, thereby creating a black and white illustration.

Apply the Pucker & Bloat and Twist effects

1. Open AI 7-3.ai, then save it as **Pucker and Bloat**.

2. Select the large orange square, click **Effect** on the Application bar, point to **Distort & Transform**, then click **Pucker & Bloat**.

3. Type **85** in the text box, then click **OK**.

   TIP A positive value produces a bloat effect; a negative value produces a pucker effect.

4. Select the gray circle, click **Object** on the Application bar, point to **Path**, then click **Add Anchor Points**.

5. Click **Effect** on the Application bar, point to **Distort & Transform**, then click **Pucker & Bloat**.

6. The Pucker & Bloat dialog box opens with the settings last used.

7. Type **-75**, then click **OK**.

   Your work should resemble Figure 7.

   (continued)

Figure 7 *The orange shape is bloated, the gray is puckered*

Working with Distortions, Gradient Meshes, Envelopes, and Blends

Figure 8 *The blue circle with added anchor points and the Bloat and Twist effects applied*

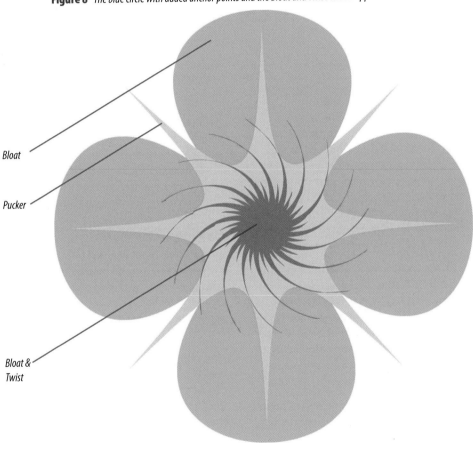

Bloat

Pucker

Bloat &
Twist

8. Select the blue circle, then apply the Add Anchor Points command twice.

9. Open the Pucker & Bloat dialog box, type **180** in the text box, then click **OK**.

10. Click **Effect** on the Application bar, point to **Distort & Transform**, then click **Twist**.

11. Type **90** in the Angle text box, then click **OK**.

12. Deselect and your work should resemble Figure 8.

13. Save your work, then close the Pucker and Bloat document.

You applied the Pucker & Bloat effect in varying degrees to each object, producing three distinctly different effects. You also applied the Twist effect.

Work with GRADIENT MESHES

What You'll Do

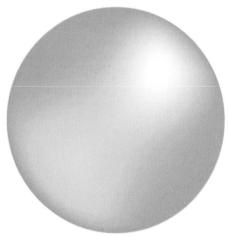

In this lesson, you will create and manipulate a gradient mesh to add dimension to basic shapes.

Working with a Mesh Object

The Mesh tool and the Create Gradient Mesh command can be used to transform a basic object into a mesh object. A mesh object is a single, multicolored object in which colors can flow in different directions, and colors transition gradually from point to point. Meshes exceed the ability of simple radial and linear gradients for applying color blends to objects and are effective for adding contrast and dimension.

When you create a mesh object, multiple mesh lines crisscross the object, joined at their intersections by mesh points. Mesh points are diamond-shaped and work just like anchor points, with the added functionality of taking color assignments. When you assign a color to a mesh point, the color grades outward from the point.

The area between four mesh points is a mesh patch. You can apply color to all four mesh points simultaneously by applying the color to the patch. Work with this method to apply broad color changes to the object.

Mesh points can be added, deleted, and moved along the mesh line without altering the shape of the mesh.

Anchor points are also part of the mesh, and they function as they do on simple paths. Just as with simple paths, you can manipulate the anchor points' direction lines to alter the shape of the mesh. Figure 9 shows an example of a mesh object.

Creating a Mesh Object

You can create a mesh object from any path. You cannot create a mesh object from compound paths or text objects. You can create a mesh object with the Mesh tool or by applying the Create Gradient Mesh command.

Generally, you'll be happiest creating a mesh object using the Create Gradient Mesh command, which creates a mesh object with regularly spaced mesh lines and mesh points. The Create Gradient Mesh dialog box is shown in Figure 10. The Mesh tool adds a mesh point and its intersecting mesh lines where you click. The tool is most effective when you want to add a particular mesh point, such as a highlight, to an existing mesh.

The Create Gradient Mesh command is always the best choice when converting complex objects.

Once a mesh object has been created, it cannot be converted back into a simple path. Keep in mind that complex mesh objects are a memory drain and may affect your computer's performance. Also, it's better to create a few simple mesh objects than a single complex one.

 Adding Transparency to a Gradient Mesh

With Illustrator CS5, you can apply opacity settings to any mesh point on a gradient mesh. Reducing the opacity allows you to make any mesh point or patch on a gradient mesh increasingly transparent, thus adding the option to create even more complex visual effects.

To affect opacity, select one or more points on the mesh, then drag the Opacity slider in Transparency panel, Control panel or the Appearance panel. The ability to reduce the opacity on a single point or patch on the gradient mesh offers the powerful option of applying transparency effects to specific areas of the mesh without affecting other areas.

Figure 9 *Elements of a mesh object*

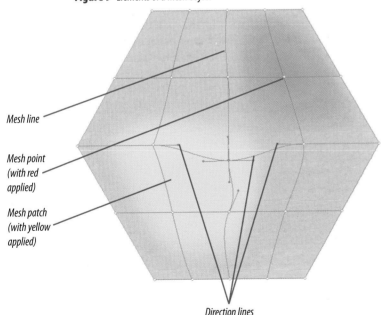

Mesh line

Mesh point (with red applied)

Mesh patch (with yellow applied)

Direction lines

Figure 10 *Create Gradient Mesh dialog box*

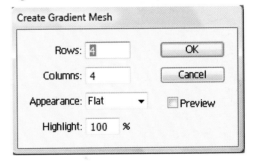

Create a gradient mesh

1. Open AI 7-4.ai, then save it as **Circle Mesh**.

2. Verify that the Layers panel is visible.

3. Select the circle, click **Object** on the Application bar, then click **Create Gradient Mesh**.

4. Type **2** in the Rows text box and **2** in the Columns text box, then click **OK**.

5. Deselect, then click the **edge of the circle** with the Direct Selection tool ▷.

6. Select the **center mesh point**, then click a **yellow swatch** on the Swatches panel.

7. Move the center mesh point to the green X, as shown in Figure 11.

8. Move the direction lines at the top, bottom, left, and right of the circle's edge, as shown in Figure 12.

(continued)

Figure 11 *Mesh points can be moved, just like anchor points*

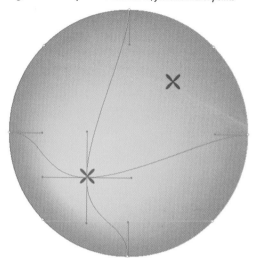

Figure 12 *The shape of the mesh is manipulated by direction lines*

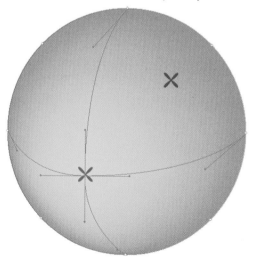

Working with Distortions, Gradient Meshes, Envelopes, and Blends

Figure 13 *Gradient meshes add dimension to an object*

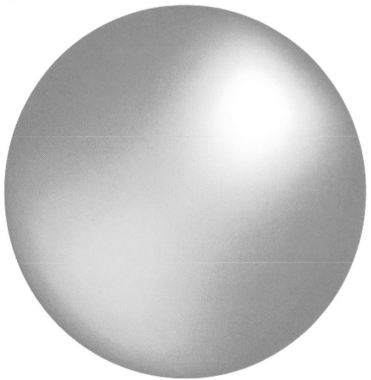

9. Click the **Mesh tool** 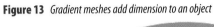 , then click the **blue X**.

   A new mesh point is added to the mesh, and, by default, the same yellow fill has been applied to it.

   TIP Press [Shift] while you click the Mesh tool to add a mesh point without applying the current fill color.

10. Click the **white swatch** on the Swatches panel to change the color of the mesh point to white.

11. Hide Layer 2 on the Layers panel, deselect all, then compare your artwork to Figure 13.

12. Save your work, then close the Circle Mesh document.

You applied a gradient mesh to a circle with the Create Gradient Mesh command, changed the color of a mesh point, then moved the mesh point. You then used the Mesh tool to expand the mesh. You changed the color of the new mesh point to white to add a highlight to the sphere.

Manipulate a gradient mesh

1. Open AI 7-5.ai, then save it as **Heart Mesh**.
2. Select the heart, click **Object** on the Application bar, then click **Create Gradient Mesh**.
3. Type **4** in the Rows text box and **4** in the Columns text box, then click **OK**.
4. Deselect, then click the **edge of the heart** with the Direct Selection tool ☐.
5. Click the **mesh point in the upper-left section of the heart**, as shown in Figure 14, then change the mesh point color to 10% black, using the Color panel.
6. The new color gradates out from the mesh point.
7. Click the **Mesh tool** ☐.
8. Press and hold **[Shift]**, then drag the mesh point along the mesh path to the left, as shown in Figure 15.
9. Repeat Steps 5-8 for the mesh point in the upper-right section of the heart, then deselect so that your work resembles Figure 16.

(continued)

Figure 14 *Selecting a mesh point*

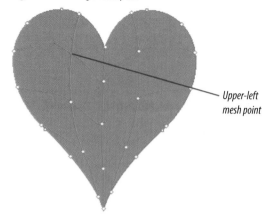

Upper-left
mesh point

Figure 15 *Mesh points can be moved without changing the shape of the mesh*

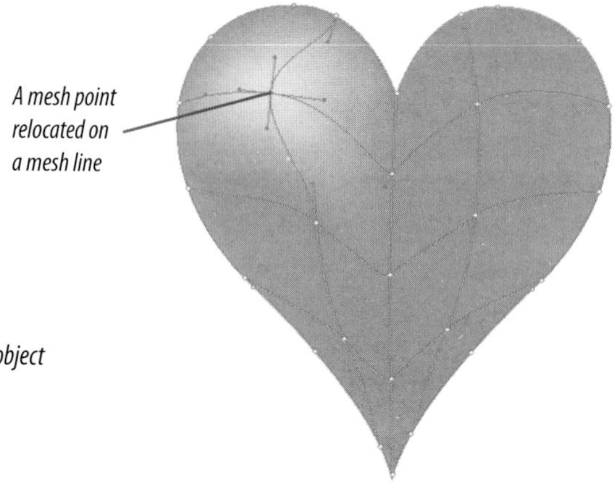

A mesh point
relocated on
a mesh line

Figure 16 *The mesh reconfigured on both sides of the object*

Figure 17 *Selecting mesh points*

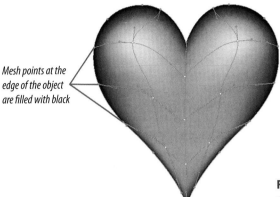

Mesh points at the edge of the object are filled with black

Figure 18 *Mesh points are like anchor points with the added functionality of accepting color assignments*

Three interior mesh points, darkened

Figure 19 *Meshes allow you to manipulate gradients precisely*

10. Click the **Direct Selection tool** , press and hold **[Shift]**, then select the 20 mesh points and anchor points all around the edge of the heart.

TIP Mesh points appear as diamonds and have the same properties as anchor points, with the added capability of accepting color.

11. Apply a black fill to the selected mesh points.

12. The selected anchor points are unaffected. Your work should resemble Figure 17.

13. Deselect, select the three interior mesh points in the lower third of the heart as shown in Figure 18, then apply a 60% black fill so that your work resembles Figure 18.

14. Select the mesh point at the center of the heart between the two 10% black highlights.

15. Apply a 60% black fill, deselect, then compare your work to Figure 19.

16. Save your work, then close the Heart Mesh document.

You applied a gradient mesh to a heart shape, then created highlights by changing the color of two mesh points. Next, you relocated the highlight mesh points without changing the shape of the mesh lines. You then darkened the color of other mesh points to add contrast and dimension to the artwork.

Work with ENVELOPES

What You'll Do

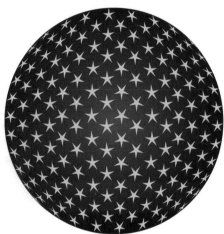

In this lesson, you will create envelope distortions using a top object, a mesh, and a warp.

Understanding Envelopes

Envelopes are objects that are used to distort other selected objects; the distorted objects take on the shape of the envelope object.

Imagine that you have purchased a basketball as a gift, and you want to wrap it with paper that has a polka-dot pattern. If these were objects in Illustrator, the basketball would be the envelope object, and the sheet of wrapping paper would be the object to be distorted. Figure 20 is a good example of what an envelope distortion looks like.

You can make envelopes with objects that you create, or you can use a preset warp shape or a mesh object as an envelope. You can use envelopes with compound paths, text objects, meshes, and blends. Using envelopes, you can add a lot of life to otherwise dull text. For example, you can create wavy text by applying the Wave or the Flag style in the Warp Options dialog box. Powerful effects can be achieved by applying envelopes to linear gradient fills or pattern fills.

Figure 20 *An envelope created using a top object*

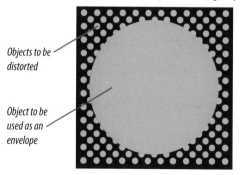

Objects to be distorted

Object to be used as an envelope

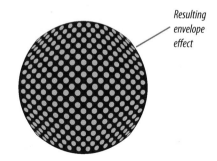

Resulting envelope effect

Creating Envelopes with Top Objects, Meshes, and Warps

You create an envelope by using the Envelope Distort command on the Object menu. The Envelope Distort command offers you three options for creating an envelope, which are Make with Warp, Make with Mesh, and Make with Top Object. The top object is the topmost selected object. Warps are simply 15 premade shapes to use as your top object. Warps are especially useful when you don't want to draw your own top object. The envelope in Figure 21 was created using the Flag warp. Meshes are the same as gradient meshes made with the Mesh tool. Creating an envelope with a mesh allows you to apply a mesh to multiple objects, which is not the case when you create a mesh using the Create Gradient Mesh command or the Mesh tool. The envelope in Figure 22 was created using a mesh.

Applying Envelopes to Gradient and Pattern Fills

Envelopes can be used to distort objects that have linear gradient fills or pattern fills, but you must first activate the option to do so. In the Envelope Options dialog box, you can check the Distort Linear Gradients or Distort Pattern Fills check box to apply an envelope to either of the fills. Figure 23 shows the options in the Envelope Options dialog box.

Figure 21 *An envelope created using a warp*

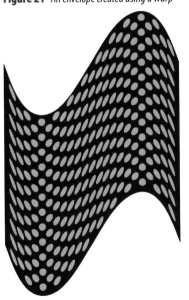

Figure 22 *An envelope created using a mesh*

Figure 23 *Envelope Options dialog box*

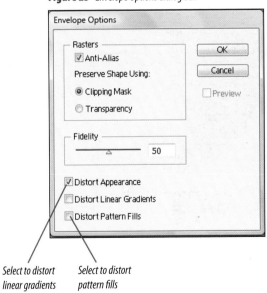

Select to distort linear gradients

Select to distort pattern fills

Create an envelope distortion with a top object

1. Open AI 7-6.ai, then save it as **Envelope Top Object**.

2. Copy the **yellow circle**, paste in front, then hide the copy.

3. Select all, click **Object** on the Application bar, point to **Envelope Distort**, then click **Make with Top Object**.

   Your work should resemble Figure 24.

4. Show all, then fill the yellow circle with the Purple Berry gradient on the Swatches panel.

5. Send the circle to the back, so that your work resembles Figure 25.

6. Save your work, then close the Envelope Top Object document.

You used a circle as the top object in an envelope distortion. Because you cannot apply a fill to the circle after it's been used to make the envelope, you filled a copy of the circle with a gradient, then positioned it behind the distorted objects to achieve the effect.

Figure 24 *A round envelope distorting a flat star pattern*

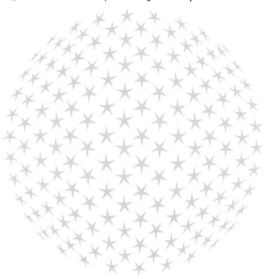

Figure 25 *A radial blend enhancing the effect of an envelope distortion*

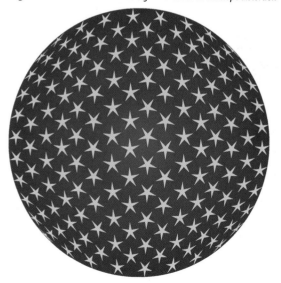

Working with Distortions, Gradient Meshes, Envelopes, and Blends

Figure 26 *Select all of the mesh points in the second and fourth columns*

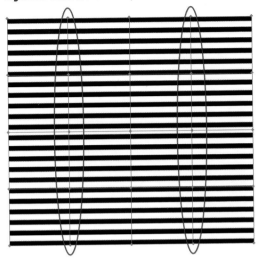

Figure 27 *An envelope distortion created using a mesh*

Create an envelope distortion with a mesh

1. Open AI 7-7.ai, then save it as **Envelope Mesh**.
2. Select all, click **Object** on the Application bar, point to **Envelope Distort**, then click **Make with Mesh**.
3. Type **4** in the Rows text box and **4** in the Columns text box, then click **OK**.

   There are five mesh points on each horizontal line.
4. Deselect, then select the second and fourth columns of mesh points, top to bottom, using the Direct Selection tool ▸ , as shown in Figure 26.
5. Press and hold **[Shift]**, press **[↑]** two times, then release **[Shift]**.

   Pressing an arrow key in conjunction with [Shift] moves a selected item ten keyboard increments.

   TIP The keyboard increment value can be adjusted in the General Preferences dialog box.

6. Select the middle column of mesh points.
7. Press and hold **[Shift]**, press **[↓]** two times, deselect, then compare your screen to Figure 27.
8. Save your work, then close the Envelope Mesh document.

You applied an envelope distortion with a mesh to a series of rectangles, then moved the mesh points to create a wave effect.

Create an envelope distortion with a warp effect

1. Open AI 7-8.ai, then save it as **Envelope Warp**.
2. Select all, click **Object** on the Application bar, point to **Envelope Distort**, then click **Make with Warp**.
3. Click the **Style list arrow**, click **Fish**, then click **OK**.

   Your screen should resemble Figure 28.
4. Undo the distort, then make Layer 2 visible.
5. Select all.

(continued)

Figure 28 *An envelope distortion created using a warp*

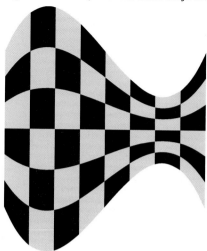

Figure 29 *Warp tools panel*

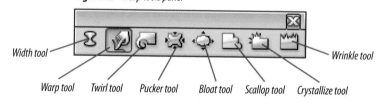

Width tool — Warp tool — Twirl tool — Pucker tool — Bloat tool — Scallop tool — Crystallize tool — Wrinkle tool

Using the Warp Tools

The Warp tool, found on the Tools panel, applies a "warp effect" to objects on the artboard. Simply drag the Warp tool over an object and watch it change before your eyes. Objects do not have to be selected before you apply the tool. To adjust the Warp tool settings before you use it, double-click the Warp tool to open the Warp Tool Options dialog box. Hiding behind the Warp tool are six more tools offering you interesting ways to distort your text and graphics. As shown in Figure 29, these tools include Twirl, Pucker, Bloat, Scallop, Crystallize, and Wrinkle. Like the Warp tool, each has its own Options dialog box. Residing with the warp tools is the Width tool. The Width tool is used to modify the width of stroked paths and is covered in depth in Chapter 6.

Working with Distortions, Gradient Meshes, Envelopes, and Blends

Figure 30 *An envelope distortion using a premade shape*

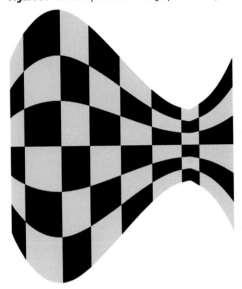

6. Click **Object** on the Application bar, point to **Envelope Distort**, then click **Make with Top Object**.

   As shown in Figure 30, you get the same result as you did using the fish-style warp. The reason for this is that using the Envelope Distort feature with a warp is the same as using the feature with a top object. The difference is that warps are premade shapes rather than ones you have made on your own.

7. Save your work, then close the Envelope Warp document.

You applied an envelope distortion with a Fish warp effect. You then used an object in the shape of the Fish warp as the top object in a new envelope, with the same result as in the first distortion. Through this comparison, you got a better sense of how Illustrator creates warp effects with envelopes.

Printing Color Blends and Gradient Meshes

Print and prepress professionals have long known that some output devices have trouble printing color blends. The most common problem is banding, an effect in which the transitions of the gradient are visibly harsh rather than smooth. This problem was especially common on early PostScript devices. In addition, gradient meshes (which are a newer feature in Illustrator) may print incorrectly, even on PostScript Level 3 printers. If you are having trouble outputting either color blends or meshes, you can print them as bitmaps instead of vectors. To do so, display the Flattener Preview panel, click Refresh on the panel, then save the preset with a descriptive name by clicking the Flattener Preview panel options button, then clicking the Save Transparency Flattener Preset. When you are ready to print your document, click File on the Application bar, click Print, click Advanced in the box on the left side of the Print dialog box, select the Print as Bitmap check box, choose your named preset from the Preset list arrow, then click Print. Anyone who has experience with printing bitmaps knows that the quality can vary greatly. Use this option only if you are having problems, then decide if the output is acceptable. If not, you may need to go to a professional prepress department to output the file.

Create
BLENDS

 In this lesson, you will use blends to manipulate shapes and colors for various effects.

Defining a Blend

A blend is a series of intermediate objects and colors between two or more selected objects. If the selected objects differ in fill color, for example, the intermediate objects will be filled with intermediate colors. Therefore, in a blend, both shapes and colors are "blended." Figure 31 is an example of a blend using shapes and colors.

Blends are created with either the Blend tool or the Make Blend command. You can make blends between two open paths, such as two different lines. You can make blends between two closed paths, such as a square and a star. You can blend between objects filled with gradients. You can even blend between blends, as shown in Figure 32.

Figure 31 *In a blend, both shapes and colors are blended*

Working with Distortions, Gradient Meshes, Envelopes, and Blends

Specifying the Number of Steps in a Blend

The fewer the number of steps in a blend, the more distinct each intermediary object will be. At a greater number of steps, the intermediate objects become indistinguishable from one another, and the blend creates the illusion of being continuous or "smooth."

In the Blend Options dialog box, select from the following options for specifying the number of steps within a blend.

- **Specified Steps** Enter a value that determines the number of steps between the start and the end of the blend.
- **Specified Distance** Enter a value to determine the distance between the steps in the blend. The distance is measured

from the edge of one object to the corresponding edge on the next object.

- **Smooth Color** Illustrator determines the number of steps for the blend, calculated to provide the minimum number of steps for a smooth color transition. This is the default option, which poses a bit of a problem in that the minimum number of steps will not always give you the effect you desire, as shown in Figure 33.

Figure 32 *A blend between blends*

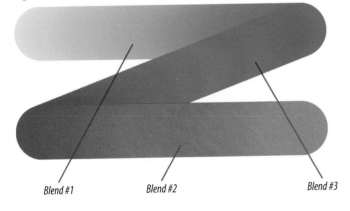

Blend #1   Blend #2   Blend #3

Figure 33 *Sometimes the Smooth Color option doesn't produce the blend effect you desire*

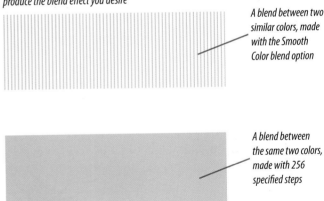

A blend between two similar colors, made with the Smooth Color blend option

A blend between the same two colors, made with 256 specified steps

Manipulating Blends

Once a blend is created, you can change its appearance by making changes to one or more of the original objects. For example, using the Direct Selection tool, you can select one of the original objects, then change its fill color, stroke color, or stroke weight. Illustrator will automatically update the appearance of the steps to reflect newly added attributes, thus changing the appearance of the entire blend. You can also change a blend by transforming one or more of the original objects, for example by scaling, rotating, or moving them.

You can affect the appearance of a blend by manipulating its spine. When a blend is created, a path is drawn between the starting and ending objects. Illustrator refers to this path as the spine, but it can be manipulated like a path. For example, you can add anchor points to the spine with the Pen tool, then move them with the Direct Selection tool. The blend is updated when you alter the spine. Figure 34 shows how a blend's spine can be manipulated.

One of the most stunning manipulations of a blend happens when you replace its spine. Draw any path with the Pen tool, then select it along with any blend. Apply the Replace Spine command, and the blend replaces its spine with the new path!

Figure 34 *Manipulating the blend's spine changes the arc of the blend*

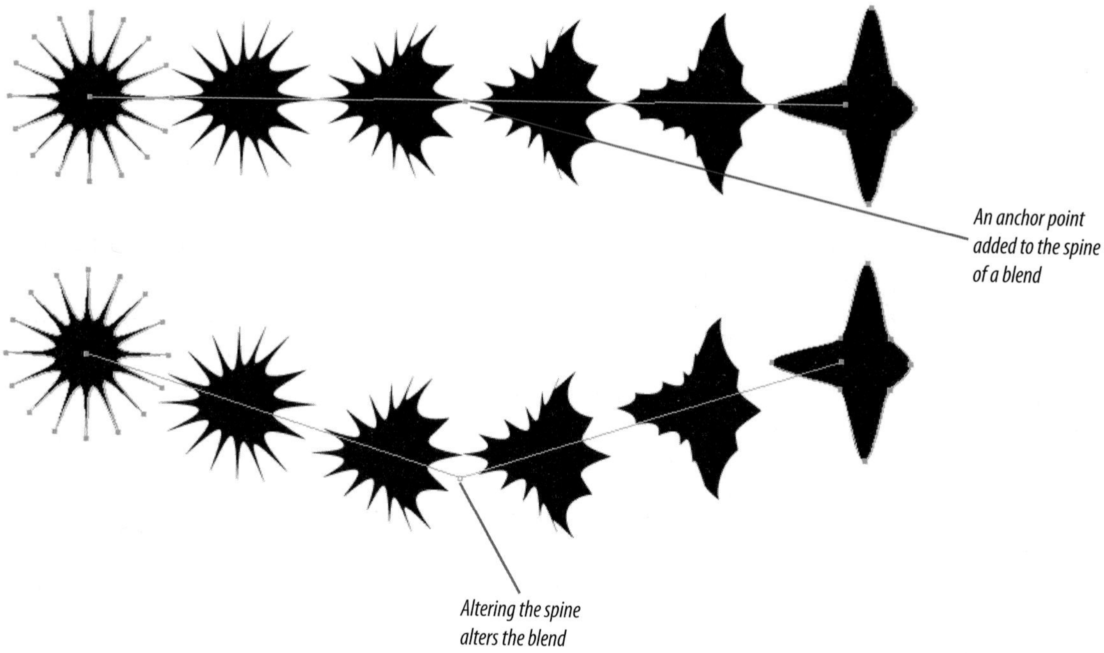

An anchor point added to the spine of a blend

Altering the spine alters the blend

Working with Distortions, Gradient Meshes, Envelopes, and Blends

Figure 35 *The red and blue objects blended with five steps*

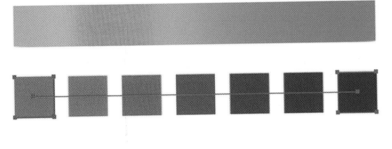

Create blends between shapes

1. Open AI 7-9.ai, then save it as **Blend Tutorial**.
2. Click the **Blend tool** , click **anywhere on the orange square**, then click **anywhere on the green square**.

   TIP You can click the Blend tool on two or more unselected objects to blend them.

3. Click the **Selection tool** , select the red and blue squares, then double-click the **Blend tool** .
4. Click the **Spacing list arrow**, click **Specified Steps**, type **5** in the Spacing text box, then click **OK**.
5. Click **Object** on the Application bar, point to **Blend**, then click **Make**.
6. Five intermediary squares are created, as shown in Figure 35.
7. Switch to the Selection tool , then deselect the blend.
8. Click the **Blend tool** , then click from left to right on each of the three purple shapes.
9. Keeping the purple blend selected, click **Object** on the Application bar, point to **Blend**, then click **Blend Options**.

   TIP You can also access the Blend Options dialog box by double-clicking the Blend tool.

   (continued)

Recording Steps as a Reusable Action

An action is a series of steps and commands that you record and which are stored in the Actions panel. Once recorded, those steps are available to you to use over and over again on other objects or files. For example, let's say your work often calls for you to flatten a file, convert it to CMYK, then save it as an Illustrator EPS. You can record those steps as an action. Then, in the future, rather than step through every time, simply execute the action in the Actions panel, and the process will happen automatically. You can even "batch process" an action on multiple files all at once. The Actions panel functions like a tape recorder. Simply click New Action in the Actions panel menu then click the Record button at the bottom of the panel. The Actions panel records the steps you are making. Once you are done, click the Stop Playing/Recording button. All the steps will be listed in the panel under the name you give to the action. Even after you close the file or quit Illustrator, the action remains and will be available when you start the program again.

10. Click the **Spacing list arrow**, click **Specified Steps**, type **2** in the Steps text box, then click **OK**.

The intermediary steps are reduced to two.

11. Deselect the purple blend.

12. Select the Heart view on the View menu.

13. Double-click the **Blend tool** , change the Specified Steps to **256**, then click **OK**.

14. Click the **heart**, click the **small pink circle in the center of the heart**, then deselect.

15. The 256 intermediary steps blend the heart to the circle in both color and shape. Your screen should resemble Figure 36.

16. Save your work, then close the Blended Shapes document.

You used the Blend tool to create a smooth blend and evenly distributed shapes between two sets of squares. You created a blend between differing shapes, then used the Blend Options dialog box to change the number of steps in the blend. You also used a smooth blend to add dimension to the heart.

Figure 36 *Blends are effective for adding dimension to objects*

Working with Distortions, Gradient Meshes, Envelopes, and Blends

Figure 37 *A blend between two open paths*

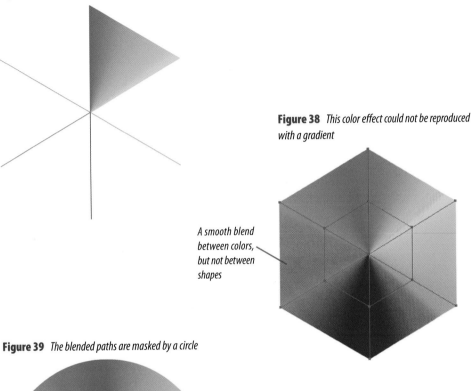

Figure 38 *This color effect could not be reproduced with a gradient*

A smooth blend
between colors,
but not between
shapes

Figure 39 *The blended paths are masked by a circle*

The use of 256 specified
steps improves the
appearance of the blend

Create a clockwise color blend

1. Open AI 7-10.ai, then save it as **Clockwise Blend**.

2. Double-click the **Blend tool** ▣, click the **Spacing list arrow**, click **Specified Steps**, type **256** in the Spacing text box, then click **OK**.

3. Click the **top of the green line**, then click the **top of the yellow line** to create a blend, as shown in Figure 37.

TIP The Blend tool pointer turns black when it is successfully positioned over an anchor point.

4. Click the **remaining five lines**, ending with the green line, to make five more blends, so that your work resembles Figure 38.

5. Draw a circle over the blend that does not exceed the perimeter of the blend.

6. Select all, click **Object** on the Application bar, point to **Clipping Mask**, then click **Make**.

7. Click the **Selection tool** ▶, deselect, then compare your image to Figure 39.

8. Save your work, then close the Clockwise Blend document.

You created blends among six lines. You specified the number of steps between each pair of paths to be 256, which resulted in a visually uninterrupted blend. You then masked the blend with a circle.

Edit blends

1. Open AI 7-11.ai, then save it as **Blends on a Path**.

2. Click the **blended objects** with the Selection tool ▸ .

3. Click **Object** on the Application bar, point to **Blend**, then click **Reverse Front to Back**.

4. The stacking order of the blended objects is reversed.

5. Click **Object** on the Application bar, point to **Blend**, then click **Reverse Spine**.

6. The order of the objects on the path is reversed.

7. Select all.

8. Click **Object** on the Application bar, point to **Blend**, click **Replace Spine**, then deselect.

9. The curved path becomes the new spine for the blend, as shown in Figure 40.

10. Save your work, then close the Blends on a Path document.

You reversed the stacking order of a blend, then reversed its spine. You then replaced the spine with a curved path to create a 3-D effect.

Figure 40 *Blends can be applied to paths*

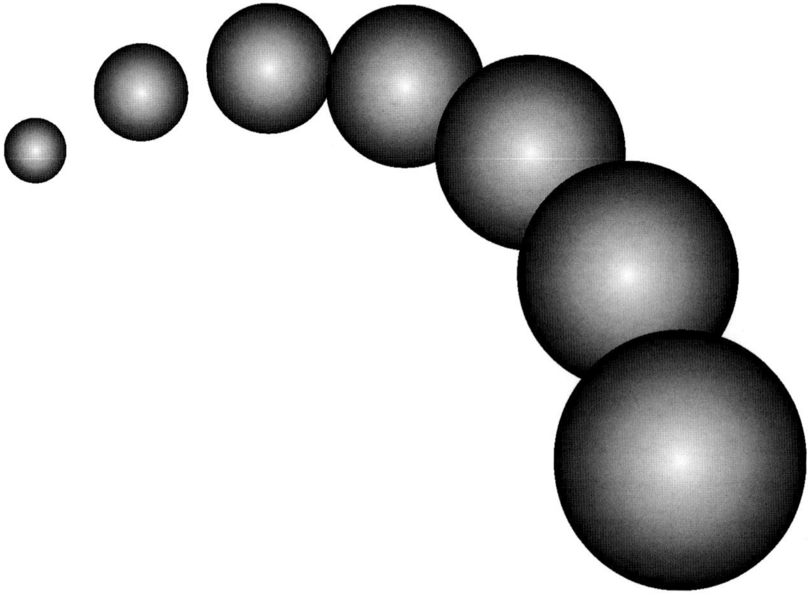

Figure 41 *A simple blend between open paths*

Figure 42 *Chrome letters created with a blend and a mask*

Create color effects with blends

1. Open AI 7-12.ai, then save it as **Chrome**.
2. Double-click the **Blend tool** ⬚ , then set the number of specified steps to 256.
3. Switch to Outline mode, click the **Selection tool** ▶ , then select the five paths at the bottom of the artboard.

   Two of the paths are stroked with white and cannot be seen in Preview mode.
4. Switch to Preview mode, click the **Blend tool** ⬚ , then, starting from the bottom of the artboard, create a blend between each pair of paths, so that your work resembles Figure 41.
5. Position the text in front of the blend.
6. Keeping the text selected, click **Object** on the Application bar, point to **Compound Path**, then click **Make**.
7. Select all, click **Object** on the Application bar, point to **Clipping Mask**, then click **Make**.
8. Deselect all, click **Select** on the Application bar, point to **Object**, then click **Clipping Mask**.
9. Apply a 2-point black stroke to the mask.
10. Deselect, save your work, compare your screen to Figure 42, then close the Chrome document.

You selected five paths with the Blend tool, created a blend between each pair of paths, positioned text in front of the blend, then made a compound path. You selected all, made a Clipping Mask, then applied a 2-point black stroke to the mask.

Edit colors and distort objects.

1. Create a new 6" × 6" CMYK Color document, then save it as **Distort Skills**.
2. Create a 4" circle with a yellow fill and no stroke.
3. Apply the Add Anchor Points command.
4. Apply the Bloat effect at 35%.
5. Apply the Twist effect at 50°.
6. Use the Scale Tool Options dialog box to make a 50% copy of the object.
7. Apply the Transform Again command twice.
8. With the top object still selected, fill it with a dark shade of blue.
9. Select all, then use the Edit Colors command to blend the objects from front to back.
10. Save your work, deselect, compare your illustration with Figure 43, then close the document.

Work with gradient meshes.

1. Open AI 7-13.ai, then save it as **Mesh Skills**.
2. Select the yellow hexagon.
3. Apply the Create Gradient Mesh command with 4 rows and 4 columns.
4. Click the Direct Selection tool, deselect the hexagon, then click the edge of it.
5. Select the top row of mesh points, then click orange on the Swatches panel. (*Hint*: Click and drag the Direct Selection tool on the artboard to create a selection box that includes the top row of mesh points.)
6. Select the middle row of mesh points, then click red on the Swatches panel.
7. Select the four mesh patches at the bottom of the hexagon, then click a shade of orange on the Swatches panel. (*Hint*: Select each mesh patch one at a time.)
8. Select the five mesh points at the bottom of the hexagon, then click a shade of red on the Swatches panel.
9. Save your work, deselect, then compare your mesh object with Figure 44.
10. Close the Mesh Skills document.

Figure 43 *Completed Skills Review, Part I*

Figure 44 *Completed Skills Review, Part II*

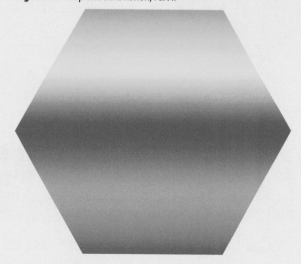

Working with Distortions, Gradient Meshes, Envelopes, and Blends

Work with envelopes.

1. Open AI 7-14.ai, then save it as **Envelope Skills**.
2. Click Object on the Application bar, point to Envelope Distort, then click Envelope Options.
3. Verify that there is a check mark in the Distort Pattern Fills check box and in the Distort Appearance check box, then click OK.
4. Position a triangle in front of the square with the pattern fill. (*Hint*: Click the Polygon tool, click the artboard, type 3 in the Sides text box, then click OK.)
5. Scale the triangle so that it covers most of the square behind it.
6. Select all, click Object on the Application bar, point to Envelope Distort, then click Make with Top Object.
7. Enlarge the size of the illustration if you like.
8. Save your work, deselect, compare your illustration to Figure 45, then close the Envelope Skills document.

Create blends.

1. Open AI 7-15.ai, then save it as **Star**.
2. Create a 15% copy of the star.
3. Fill the copy with White.
4. Double-click the Blend tool, then set the Specified Steps value to 256.
5. Blend the two stars.
6. Save your work, deselect, then compare your illustration to Figure 46.
7. Close the Star document.

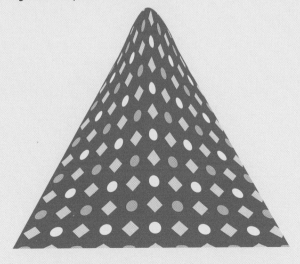

Figure 45 *Completed Skills Review, Part III*

Figure 46 *Completed Skills Review, Part IV*

The owner of Tidal Wave Publishing hires your design firm to redesign their logo. She shows you her original logo, which is a meticulous line drawing of a wave. She explains that the line drawing has been their logo for more than 25 years, and she feels that it's time for something "more contemporary." She cautions you that she doesn't want anything that feels "too artificial" or looks like "cookie-cutter computer graphics."

1. Create a new 6" × 6" document, then save it as **Tidal Wave**.
2. Create an ellipse that is 2.5" wide and 2.25" tall, then fill it with any color and no stroke.
3. Apply the Add Anchor Points command three times.
4. Apply the Pucker & Bloat effect at -80%.
5. Apply the Twist effect at 200°.
6. Deselect, save your work, see illustration Figure 47 for one possible solution, then close the Tidal Wave document.

Figure 47 *Completed Project Builder 1*

Working with Distortions, Gradient Meshes, Envelopes, and Blends

Miltie Berger, a famous journalist from Los Angeles, commissions your design firm to create a logo for her new column, which will be titled "Poison Pen." She explains that it will be a gossip column that will "skewer" all the big names in Hollywood. Refer to Figure 48 as you perform the steps.

1. Open AI 7-16.ai, then save it as **Poison Pen**.
2. Double-click the Blend tool, set the number of specified steps to 40, then click anywhere on the two white objects on the right side of the artboard to blend them. (*Hint*: They do not need to be selected first.)
3. Deselect, then click the Direct Selection tool.
4. Select only the bottom object of the blend, then change its fill color to Black and its stroke color to White. (*Hint*: Refer to this new object as the "feather" blend.)
5. Click the Selection tool, select the very narrow white curved stroke at the center of the artboard, copy it, paste in front, then hide the copy.
6. Select the white stroke again, click Object on the Application bar, point to Path, then click Outline Stroke.

7. Deselect all, double-click the Blend tool, change the number of steps to 256, then blend the white outlined stroke with the pointy black quill shape that is behind it.
8. Lock the new blend, then show all. The hidden white stroke appears and is selected.

9. Click the Selection tool, press and hold [Shift], then click the "feather" blend to add it to the selection.
10. Click Object on the Application bar, point to Blend, then click Replace Spine.
11. Save your work, compare your illustration with Figure 48, then close the Poison Pen document.

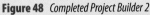 **Figure 48** *Completed Project Builder 2*

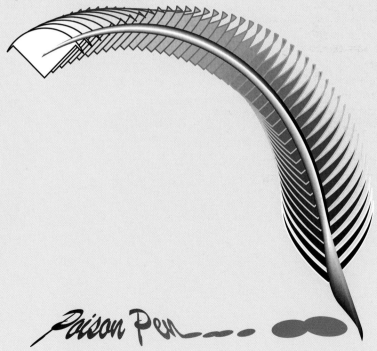

You create graphics for a video game company. Your assignment for the morning is to create an illustration for a steel cup that will be used to store magical objects in a game.

1. Open AI 7-17.ai, then save it as **Steel Cup**.
2. Select the gray object, then apply the Create Gradient Mesh command using 7 rows and 3 columns.
3. Deselect, then click the edge of the mesh object with the Direct Selection tool.
4. Press and hold [Shift], then select the four mesh points shown in Figure 49.

5. Click the Color panel options button, then click Grayscale if necessary.
6. Make sure the Fill button is active on the Tools panel, then drag the K slider on the Color panel to 15% to lighten the selected mesh points.
7. Select the top right mesh patch and darken it, using the Color panel.
8. Select the mesh points along the left edge and the bottom edge of the "steel cup," then click Black.

9. Lock the gradient mesh object.
10. Click the edge of the black object with the Direct Selection tool, then select the five horizontal mesh points in the second row from the top.
11. Fill the mesh points with White.
12. Deselect, then unlock all.
13. Save your work, compare your steel cup with Figure 50, then close the Steel Cup document.

Figure 49 *Click the mesh points indicated by the red ellipse*

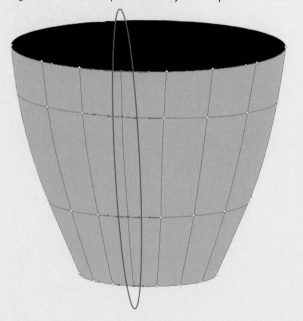

Figure 50 *Completed Design Project*

Working with Distortions, Gradient Meshes, Envelopes, and Blends

You own a small design firm in the Caribbean, and you have just been contracted to do a major project for the island of Bellucia, a new nation in the West Indies. Having recently gained independence, Bellucia wants you to consult with their new government on the design of their flag. After the first meeting, you begin working on a composite illustration. Your only direction from the government group is that the flag must be composed of abstract shapes, with no elements such as words, stars, and symbols.

1. Create a new 6" × 6" CMYK Color document, then save it as Bellucia Flag.
2. Search the Internet and collect pictures of as many flags from Caribbean nations as you can find.
3. Experiment with different width-to-height ratios in determining the shape of the banner.
4. Garner fabric samples from local merchants and textile designers.
5. Sketch a design, then recreate the design in Illustrator with an envelope distort so that the flag appears to be waving.
6. Save your work, see Figure 51 for one possible solution, then close the document.

Figure 51 *Completed Portfolio Project*

CHAPTER 8

RECOLORING ARTWORK AND WORKING WITH TRANSPARENCY, EFFECTS, AND GRAPHIC STYLES

1. Use the Transparency panel and the Color Picker
2. Recolor artwork
3. Apply effects to objects
4. Use the Appearance panel
5. Work with graphic styles
6. Use opacity masks

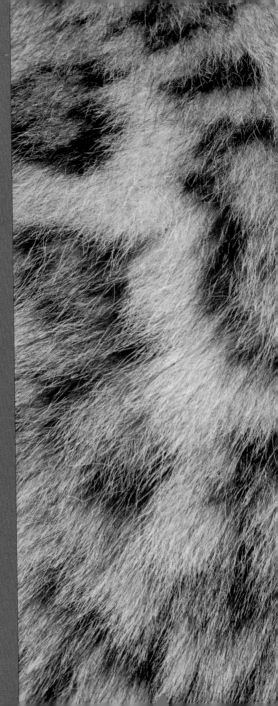

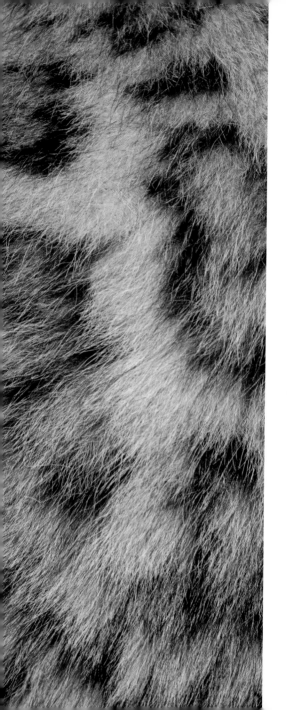

CHAPTER 8
RECOLORING ARTWORK AND WORKING WITH TRANSPARENCY, EFFECTS, AND GRAPHIC STYLES

From the get-go, Adobe Illustrator has been a sophisticated software package. However, if you could compare the first version of Illustrator to the current CS5 version, you would be amazed at how much Illustrator has evolved over the years and the many upgrades added into this powerhouse application, especially in the areas of color and special effects.

In this chapter, we'll explore four advanced features that you can use to produce effects that would have been unimaginable in the early days of Illustrator.

The first of these effects is the transparency of an object. The Transparency panel allows you to control the **opacity** of an object, which is the degree to which you can "see through" it. You can modify the opacity of specific areas of an object using opacity masks. An opacity mask is useful for fading objects and fading type. The Transparency panel also includes a list of **blending modes**. Blending modes are fun, preset filters that control how colors blend when two objects overlap.

The Recolor Artwork feature is another powerful set of effects that allows you to manipulate color dynamically and access the Color Guide panel, which contains color groups, or, sets of swatches based on various established color models. You can use the color groups to help you choose colors that work well together or even just browse them for color inspiration. In the Recolor Artwork dialog box, you can manipulate the color of selected artwork dynamically by dragging various sliders and controls. It is a gigantic step forward and truly takes Illustrator to a whole new level of color control.

Other advanced features you can use to enhance your graphics include Effects and Graphic styles. **Effects** are appearance attributes accessed through the Effect menu. **Graphic styles** are named sets of appearance attributes that are stored on the Graphic Styles panel.

Effects are versatile in that they are properties you apply to an object that affect the look of an object but not its underlying structure. You can easily remove these appearance attributes and return the object to its original state. Graphic styles provide an easy way to apply a set of appearance attributes consistently to a variety of objects.

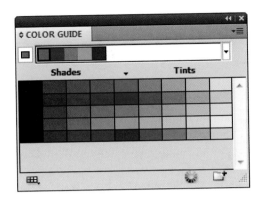

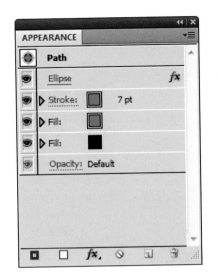

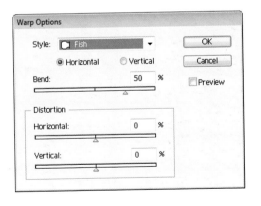

Use the Transparency Panel
AND THE COLOR PICKER

What You'll Do

In this lesson, you will use the Transparency panel to change the opacity and blending modes of objects, and you will use the Color Picker to specify a new fill color.

Understanding Opacity

The term opacity is a derivative of the word "opaque," which describes an object that is neither transparent nor translucent but, rather, impenetrable. Simply put—you cannot see through it. By default, objects in Illustrator are created with 100% opacity; they are opaque. Whenever one object overlaps another on the artboard, the top object hides all or part of the object behind it. If you were drawing a face behind a veil, clouds in a blue sky, or fish in a tinted goldfish bowl, having the ability to change the opacity of objects is critical to creating the illustration. Figure 1 shows an example of opacity.

Working with the Transparency Panel

The Transparency panel allows you to control the degree to which an object is transparent. You can change the opacity amount by dragging the Opacity slider in

Figure 1 *Reducing opacity causes objects to appear translucent*

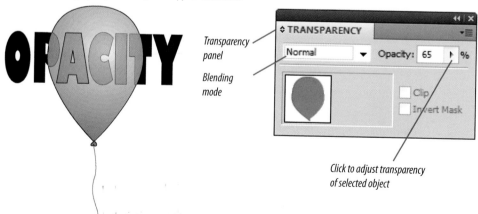

Transparency panel

Blending mode

Click to adjust transparency of selected object

the panel. The Opacity slider works with percentages, with 100% being completely opaque and 0% being completely transparent, or invisible.

Working with Blending Modes

Blending modes are preset filters in the Transparency panel that vary the way the colors of objects blend with the colors of underlying objects when they overlap. You cannot determine the amount or intensity of a blending mode, but only choose whether or not to apply one. Thus, you will find yourself working with blending modes by trial and error, but it's fun experimenting with them. Apply a blending mode and if you like it, keep it. If not, try another.

Of all the blending modes, the most essential is Multiply. The Multiply blending mode makes the top object transparent and blends the colors of the overlapped and overlapping objects in an effect that is similar to overlapping magic markers. Objects that overlap black become black, objects that overlap white retain their original color, and, as with magic markers, objects with color darken when they overlap other colors.

Imagine you are drawing a puddle of pink lemonade spilled on a black, white, and yellow tiled floor. You would use the Multiply blending mode on the object you draw to represent the lemonade, as shown in Figure 2. The color of the lemonade would not change where it overlapped the white tiles, because multiplying a color

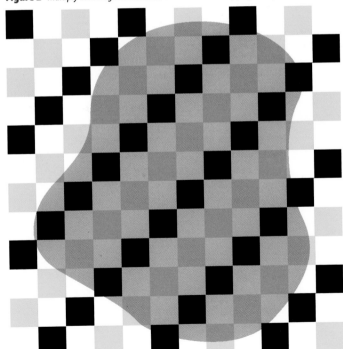

Figure 2 *Multiply blending mode mimics the effect of overlapping transparent ink, like a magic marker*

with white produces no change in the color. The lemonade would appear black where it overlapped the black tiles, because any color multiplied with black produces a black result. Where the pink lemonade overlapped the yellow tiles, the area would appear as a dark orange.

Because the Multiply blending mode reproduces real-world color situations, it is important for you to identify it as an essential component of your skills set. Don't forget that it's there!

Working with the Color Picker

You use the Color Picker to specify new colors to be used as fills, strokes, or parts of effects, such as drop shadows. The easiest way to access the Color Picker is to double-click the Fill or Stroke button on the Tools panel.

In addition to allowing you to choose a new color, the Color Picker offers a valuable opportunity for studying the most fundamental color model, HSB, or Hue, Saturation, and Brightness.

The **hue** is the color itself. Blue, red, orange, and green are all hues. The Color Picker identifies hues based on the concept of a color wheel. Because there are 360 degrees to a circle, the hues on the color wheel are numbered 0–360. This is why you see a small degree symbol beside the H (hue) text box in the Color Picker dialog box. The color wheel is represented in the Color Picker by the vertical color slider. Move the triangles along the color slider and watch the number in the H (hue) text box change to identify the corresponding hue on the color slider.

Does this mean that only 360 colors can be specified in the Color Picker? No, because each hue is modified by its saturation and brightness value.

Saturation refers to the intensity of the hue. A comparison of the colors of a tomato and a cranberry would be a fine illustration of different saturation values. Both have hues that fall within a "red" range. However, the tomato's red is far more intense, or saturated. In the Color Picker, 100% is the highest degree of saturation. A saturation value

of 0% means that there is no hue, only a shade of gray. A black-and-white photo, for example, has no saturation value.

The reds of the tomato and cranberry also differ in brightness. The tricky thing about understanding the brightness component of a color is that the term "brightness" is so common that it's difficult to know how it applies specifically to colors. A good example is a room with no windows filled with furniture and artwork. If you flood the room with light, all of the colors of the objects in the room will appear at their most vivid. If you have only a single, dim light source (like a flickering candle), the colors will appear less vivid, and many hues will be indistinguishable from others. If there were no light source whatsoever, no colors would appear, because in the absence of light there is no color.

In the Color Picker, 100% is the highest degree of brightness. A brightness of 0% is always black, regardless of the hue or saturation value specified. Thus, 100% saturation and 100% brightness produce a "pure" hue. Any lesser amount of saturation or brightness is a degradation of the hue.

The Color Picker, shown in Figure 3, is made up of a large color field. The color field represents the current hue and all of its variations of saturation and brightness. By dragging the circle around in the color field, you can sample different saturation and brightness values of the selected hue. Saturation values lie on the horizontal axis;

as you move the circle left to right, the saturation of the color increases from 0% to 100%. Note that the colors along the left edge of the color field are only shades of gray. This is because the colors along the left edge have 0% saturation.

Brightness values lie on the vertical axis. All the colors at the bottom of the field are black (0% brightness). The color's brightness increases as you move up. Thus, the pure hue

(100% saturation and 100% brightness) is at the top-right corner of the field.

For a hands-on example of these essential color concepts, you can drag the circle cursor around the color field. As the sampled color changes, you'll see that the H (hue) number remains constant while the S (saturation) and B (brightness) numbers change. You can change the hue by dragging the triangles along the color slider.

Figure 3 *Color Picker dialog box*

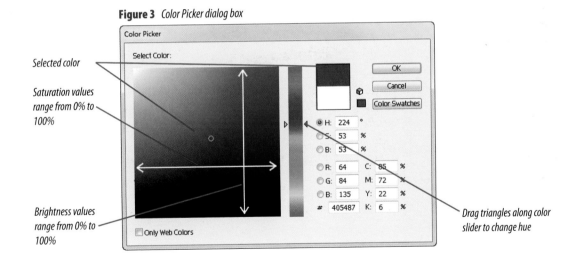

Selected color

Saturation values range from 0% to 100%

Brightness values range from 0% to 100%

Drag triangles along color slider to change hue

Change the opacity and blending mode of objects

1. Open AI 8-1.ai, then save it as **Transparency**.
2. Click **Window** on the Application bar, then click **Transparency**.
3. Select both the yellow circle and the letter T.

   The selection appears on the Transparency panel.
4. Click the **Opacity list arrow**, then drag the **Opacity slider** to **50**.
5. Select the cyan and magenta circles, click the **Opacity list arrow**, then drag the **Opacity slider** to **20** so that your screen resembles Figure 4.
6. Select the T and the three circles, then change the opacity to **100%**.
7. Click the **Blending Mode list arrow**, click **Multiply**, then deselect all so that your screen resembles Figure 5.
8. Save your work, then close the Transparency document.

You changed the opacity of objects and applied the Multiply blending mode to overlapping objects.

Figure 4 *The three circles and the T at reduced opacity*

Figure 5 *The Multiply blending mode effect on overlapping objects*

Recoloring Artwork and Working with Transparency, Effects, and Graphic Styles

Figure 6 *Small circle indicates the saturation and brightness values of the selected hue*

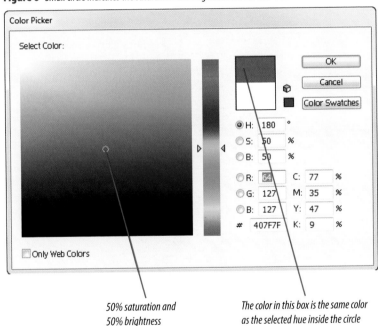

50% saturation and
50% brightness

The color in this box is the same color
as the selected hue inside the circle

Use the Color Picker

1. Open AI 8-2.ai, then save it as **Limeade**.

2. Click **File** on the Application bar, point to **Document Color Mode**, then verify that RGB Color is checked.

3. Double-click the **Fill button** on the Tools panel to open the Color Picker.

4. Type **180** in the H text box.

5. Type **50** in the S text box, then press [**Tab**].

   The circle in the color field moves to 50% of the width of the color field, and the values in the CMYK and RGB text boxes are updated to reflect the change.

6. Type **50** in the B text box, then press [**Tab**].

   The color circle moves down to 50% of the height of the color field, as shown in Figure 6.

7. Type **40** in the R text box, type **255** in the G text box, type **0** in the B text box, then click **OK**.

8. Add the new color to the Swatches panel, name it **Lime Green**, then save and close the Limeade document.

You used the Color Picker to select a new fill color. You entered specific values for hue, saturation, and brightness, and entered specific values for red, green, and blue. You then added the new color to the Swatches panel.

Recolor
ARTWORK

What You'll Do

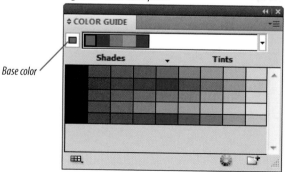

In this lesson, you will manipulate color with color groups and the Recolor Artwork dialog box.

Recoloring Artwork

To put it simply, the Recolor Artwork dialog box is a giant step for color management in Adobe Illustrator. Why is it so revolutionary? Because it puts to rest the select objects/fill objects paradigm that has been the sole color management procedure since Illustrator 88.

The Recolor Artwork feature uses the Color Guide panel and the Recolor Artwork dialog box as an interface for unprecedented dynamic color manipulation for an entire illustration. Rather than fill objects with various colors, you can now drag sliders and watch the colors in your illustration change as you drag.

Recoloring artwork starts with the Color Guide panel, shown in Figure 7. The Color Guide uses harmony rules, which are based on color models with complementary colors, to help you select colors for your illustration that work well together.

Note the base color in Figure 7. Whenever you click a swatch on the Swatches panel or a color on the Color panel, that color automatically becomes the base color for the current harmony rules in the Color Guide.

Figure 7 *Color Guide panel*

Base color

Recoloring Artwork and Working with Transparency, Effects, and Graphic Styles

Figure 8 shows some of the harmony rules available for the red base color.

When you select an object on the artboard then choose a harmony rule in the Color Guide, the selected object does not change color. Instead, the Color Guide loads a group of swatches, called variations, based on the harmony rule. These swatches all work well together and can be used to color your illustration.

Figure 9 shows the Color Guide panel with a harmony rule named Analogous 2. Note the variations available. In addition, you can modify any set of variations on the Color Guide panel menu, such as Tints/Shades, Warm/Cool, and Vivid/Muted, as shown in Figure 10. Figure 11 also shows the Analogous 2 harmony rule with the same base color, but the Show Warm/Cool option is selected so the variations you see are different.

Figure 8 *Harmony rules available for the red base color*

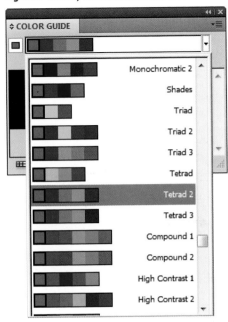

Figure 9 *Analogous 2 harmony rule and available variations*

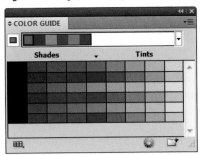

Figure 10 *Color Guide panel menu*

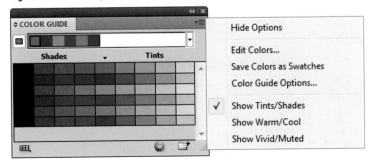

Figure 11 *Variations modified by the Show Warm/Cool option*

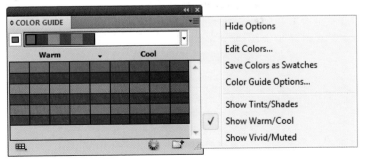

Assigning Color in the Recolor Artwork Dialog Box

You can access the Recolor Artwork dialog box by clicking the Edit or Apply Colors button on the Color Guide panel. If you do so with art selected, any changes you make in the Recolor Artwork dialog box will affect the selected art.

The Recolor Artwork dialog box functions based on two modes, which are Assign and Edit. Both have essentially the same

effect, but they use different methods to manipulate color. Figure 12 shows the dialog box in Assign mode. When working in Assign mode, you choose a harmony rule, and that harmony rule alters the colors of the selected artwork.

In Figure 12, a harmony rule named Compound 2 has been loaded. The Current Colors column shows that the selected artwork contains 8 colors, including six chromatic colors plus black and white.

The New column shows each of the six colors from the Compound 2 harmony rule. It's important to understand that each of the six new colors has been randomly assigned to one of the six current colors. (By default, black and white are not affected.) You can, at any time, reassign the new colors from the harmony rule to different current colors simply by dragging and dropping them. Figure 13 shows the same set of original colors and the harmony rule. Compare this to

Figure 12 *Recolor Artwork dialog box in Assign mode*

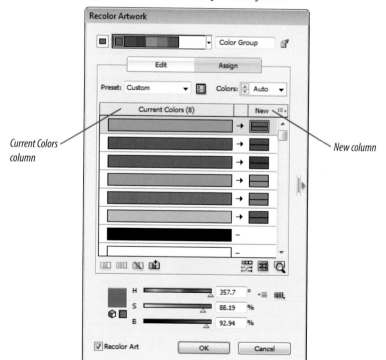

Current Colors column

New column

Figure 13 *Reassigning colors from the chosen harmony rule*

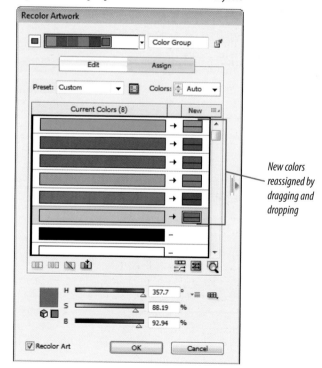

New colors reassigned by dragging and dropping

Recoloring Artwork and Working with Transparency, Effects, and Graphic Styles

Figure 12 to see how the new colors have been reassigned. For example, red is now assigned to the light tan original current color, which means that any object in the illustration filled with the light tan color will now be red.

Your options for manipulating color in the Recolor Artwork dialog box are virtually unlimited, and that means that you are not limited to using only the colors in the harmony rule that you selected. Click any of the new colors in the new column, and you can manipulate the sliders at the bottom of the dialog box to change that color to any color you choose. As you drag the sliders, you will see the color in the illustration change dynamically. Figure 14 shows that the red color in the New column has been changed to lime green.

QUICK TIP

Click the arrow button beside the sliders to change the mode that the sliders use to specify color. For example, you can specify color in RGB mode.

Editing Color in the Recolor Artwork Dialog Box

As we said in the previous section, Edit and Assign modes in the Recolor Artwork dialog box essentially provide the same options for manipulating color but use different methods. However, whenever you see the Recolor Artwork dialog box demonstrated, it's Edit mode that gets all the attention, because it's so much more visually interesting and makes it so much easier to understand what's going on than Assign mode.

Figure 15 shows the Recolor Artwork dialog box in Edit Mode. The top illustration of the cat is the original, and the bottom is the selected art being manipulated. (When the Recolor Artwork dialog box is open, selection marks are automatically hidden for selected artwork on the artboard.)

The six circles in the dialog box represent the six colors for the loaded harmony rule, and each corresponds to one of the six chromatic colors in the original artwork. The circles are called color tools, and the color tool with the heavy border is the base color for the loaded harmony rule.

The big difference between Edit mode and Assign mode is that Edit mode does not show you a list of your current colors. Instead, when in Edit mode, the illustration on the artboard is your only reference to your current colors and how they're being affected.

In Edit mode, you adjust color by moving the color tools to different positions on the color wheel, and the corresponding colors

Figure 14 *Modifying a new color*

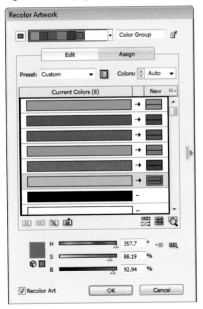

Figure 15 *Recolor Artwork dialog box in Edit mode*

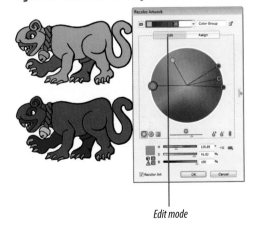

Edit mode

in the artwork are affected. In Figure 16, the base color circle has been repositioned. By default, when you move the base color tool, the other tools move with it. Note the effect on the illustration.

If you click the Unlink harmony colors button, you can move the color tools independently of one another. In addition, you can select any of the color tools, then modify that color with the color sliders at the bottom of the dialog box. In Figure 17, the color tools have been unlinked and repositioned independently. The brightness of each color tool has been increased with the Adjusts brightness slider immediately below the color wheel.

Reducing an Illustration's Colors in the Recolor Artwork Dialog Box

In most cases, when you select artwork and then choose a harmony rule in the Recolor Artwork dialog box, the harmony rule will not have the same number of colors as the number of colors in the selected artwork. When the harmony rule contains fewer colors than what is selected in the artwork, the color in the artwork must be reduced to whatever is available in the harmony rule. This is achieved with tints. For example, if you have six objects with six different colors selected, and you choose a harmony rule that contains only three colors, each of the three colors in the harmony rule creates a second tint version of itself to assign to the three additional colors.

In Figure 18, the six current colors have been reduced to a harmony rule that contains only three colors. Where two colors are reduced to one color on the harmony rule, one becomes a tint of the other. Thus, the illustration at the bottom is painted with only three colors, which are red, yellow, and blue, but the light red, light yellow, and light blue tints effectively maintain the illustration's six-color appearance.

Figure 16 *Repositioning the base color tool*

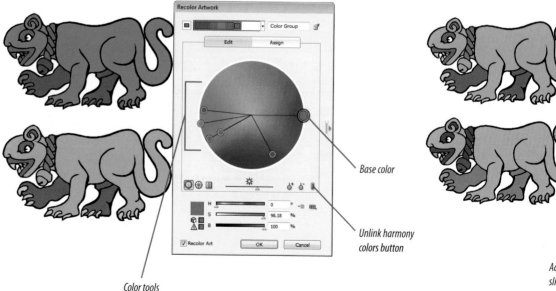

Base color

Unlink harmony
colors button

Color tools

Figure 17 *Repositioning the color tools independently of one another*

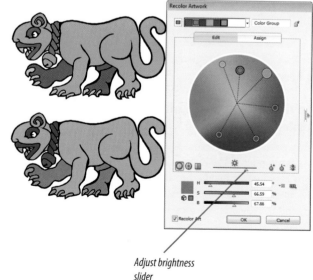

Adjust brightness
slider

Reducing Artwork to a Two-Color Job

Reducing the color results of multi-colored artwork to a two-color job is probably the most practical feature offered in the Recolor Artwork dialog box. For example, it is common for designers to create "two-color jobs," which, in most cases, include black and a spot, or Pantone, color. If the designer is working with artwork that has already been filled with multiple colors, the Recolor Artwork dialog box can convert those colors quickly to various shades of a spot color that you choose.

Figure 19 shows five current colors all reduced to a single color in the Assign mode. In addition, the red new color has been specified as PANTONE 185, and the black colors in the original are, by default, unaffected. Thus, if this illustration were to be color separated, it would separate into black and six tints of PANTONE 185.

Using Isolation Mode

In addition to locking and unlocking or hiding and showing objects and layers, Isolation Mode is a feature that helps you select groups of objects with ease. When you use Isolation Mode, the selected group appears in full color, while all the remaining objects on the art board are dimmed and unselectable. This allows you to access the isolated group without any of the other objects getting in the way.

To work in Isolation Mode, select any grouped objects on the artboard. The Isolate selected group button appears on the Control panel. You can click the button to enter Isolation Mode, or you can simply double-click the grouped objects. When in Isolation Mode, the button changes to Exit Isolation Mode. Click it to return to the normal view of the art board.

When you are in Isolation Mode, the Layers panel displays only the artwork in the isolated sublayer or group. You cannot access any other layers. When you exit Isolation Mode, the other layers and groups reappear on the Layers panel.

Figure 18 *Reducing six colors to a three-color harmony rule*

Figure 19 *Reducing six colors to six tints of one spot color*

Explore the Color Guide panel

1. Open AI 8-3.indd, then save it as **El Gato**.

2. Click the **Magenta swatch** on the Swatches panel.

3. Open the Color Guide panel.

TIP Like all panels, the Color Guide panel is listed on the Window menu.

4. Click the **Harmony Rules list arrow**.

    As shown in Figure 20, the Color Guide panel contains a long list of harmony rules, all of which are sets of color swatches grouped together based on various established color models.

5. Note that the first color—the leftmost swatch—in all of the harmony rules is the Magenta swatch that you clicked on the Swatches panel.

    Whenever you click a swatch on the Swatches panel, that swatch automatically becomes the base color on the Color Guide panel. All of the harmony rules in the current list use the Magenta swatch as the basis for their individual color groupings.

6. Click **Analogous** from the Harmony Rules list so that your Color Guide panel resembles Figure 21.

    The rows of swatches in the lower section of the Color Guide panel are referred to as the variation grid. The center column in the variation grid, as shown in Figure 21, contains the same colors from the Analogous harmony rule. The swatches to the left and right of this column are darker and lighter shades, all based on the same Analogous harmony rule.

    (continued)

Figure 20   *A list of harmony rules in the Color Guide panel*

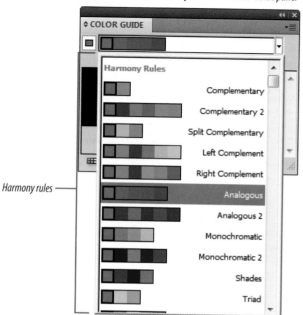

Harmony rules ——

Figure 21   *Color Guide panel showing the Analogous harmony rule for the Magenta swatch*

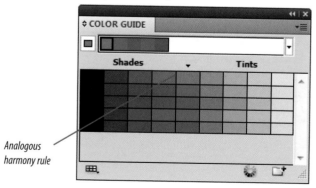

Analogous
harmony rule

Recoloring Artwork and Working with Transparency, Effects, and Graphic Styles

Figure 22 *Lion illustration painted with swatches from the Analogous harmony rule*

Figure 23 *Base color indicated on the Color Guide panel*

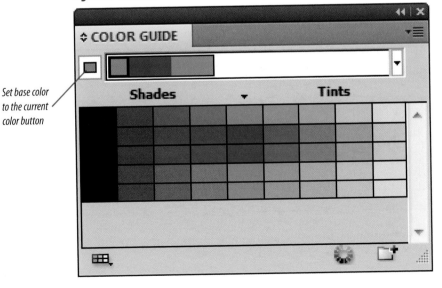

Set base color to the current color button

TIP If the colors on your Color Guide panel differ from the figure, click the Color Guide list arrow then verify that Show Tints/Shades is checked.

7. Apply various swatches from this variation grid to the various parts of the illustration of the lion.

   Figure 22 shows one example.

8. Click **File** on the Application bar, then click **Revert** to remove the colors that you applied to the illustration.

You explored the Color Guide panel, viewing various harmony rules. You then chose the Analogous harmony rule and applied swatches from that collection to the illustration. You then reverted the file to its original state.

Set a base color and save a color group

1. Verify that the Color Guide panel is showing, verify in the Tools panel that the foreground color is active and in front of the stroke color, then click the **Pure Cyan swatch** on the Swatches panel.

2. The Pure Cyan swatch becomes the base color, as indicated by the Set base color to the current color button shown in Figure 23. All the harmony rules are updated to reflect that change.

TIP Whenever you click a swatch on the Swatches panel or click a color on the Color panel, that color automatically becomes the base color in the Color Guide.

3. Click the **Selection tool** , then click the **orange square** above the illustration.

   The harmony rules on the Color Guide panel do not change. However, the orange from the selected item now appears in the Set base color to the current color button on the Color Guide panel.

   (continued)

4. On the Color Guide panel, click the **Set base color to the current color button**, then click the **Harmony Rules list arrow**.

5. As shown in Figure 24, the Color Guide panel and all the harmony rules update, with the orange from the selected item now functioning as the new base color.

6. Click the **Harmony Rules list arrow** again if the list is not still displayed, then click **Analogous 2**.

7. Click the **Save color group to Swatch panel button** ⬚⁺ on the Color Guide panel, then go to the Swatches panel to see the color group.

   Figure 25 shows the color group on the Swatches panel.

8. Use the color group on the Swatches panel to paint the illustration as shown in Figure 26.

9. Save your work, then close El Gato.

You clicked a swatch on the Swatches panel, noting that it automatically became the base color on the Color Guide panel. You then selected an object on the artboard and set it as the base color. You chose a harmony rule and then applied those colors to the illustration.

Use Isolation Mode to examine groups in an illustration

1. Open AI 8-4.indd, then save it as **Mayan Warrior**.

2. Verify that the Control panel is visible.

   The illustration features five colors plus black and white.

3. Click the **Selection tool** ▶, then **click one of the turquoise blue "jewels."**

   All of the jewels are selected because they are grouped.

   (continued)

Figure 24 *Color Guide panel with the new base color*

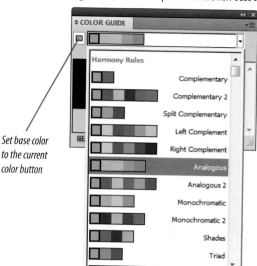

Set base color to the current color button

Figure 25 *Color group on the Swatches panel*

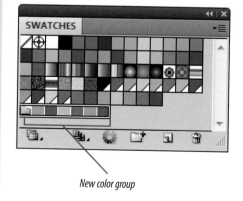

New color group

Figure 26 *Illustration painted with swatches from the new color group*

Recoloring Artwork and Working with Transparency, Effects, and Graphic Styles

Figure 27 *Illustration in Isolation Mode*

4. Click the **Isolate Selected Object button** ▣ on the Control panel.

   As shown in Figure 27, the selected group remains visible, but the selection marks disappear. All of the other non-selected objects in the illustration are dimmed. Note that the jewels are the only objects in the illustration painted blue.

5. Click **any of the dimmed objects** in the illustration.

   In Isolation Mode, dimmed objects cannot be selected.

6. Click **any one of the blue jewels**.

   Only one jewel is selected. In Isolation Mode, grouped objects are selected individually— even with the Selection tool.

7. Click the **Exit Isolation Mode button** ▣ on the Control panel.

8. Click **Edit** (Win) or **Illustrator** (Mac) on the Application bar, point to **Preferences**, then click **General**.

9. Verify that the Double Click To Isolate check box is checked, then click **OK**.

10. Double-click the **headdress**.

    Double-clicking isolates the group in Isolation Mode. The headdress and the eyelid are painted dark brown.

11. Click the **Exit Isolation Mode button** ▣ on the Control panel, then double-click the **gold wristband**.

    Gold is the third color you have viewed in Isolation Mode.

    (continued)

12. Click the **Exit Isolation Mode button** ⊡ on the Control panel, then double-click the **gray belt**.

   Gray is the fourth color you have viewed in Isolation Mode.

13. Click the **Exit Isolation Mode button** ⊡ on the Control panel, then double-click the **face**.

   The group is shown in Isolation Mode. Tan is the fifth color you have viewed in Isolation Mode.

14. Click the **Exit Isolation Mode button** ⊡ on the Control panel.

You used the Isolation Mode feature to view five groups in an illustration.

Assign colors with the Recolor Artwork dialog box

1. Click the **tan face object**, then click the **Set base color to the current color button** ▣ on the Color Guide panel.

2. Select all, click the **Edit or Apply Colors button** 🔘 on the Color Guide panel, click the **Edit button** at the top of the Recolor Artwork dialog box, then compare your screen to Figure 28.

   Note that the selection marks on the art are automatically hidden. Note, too, that because you had art selected when you clicked the Edit or Apply Colors button, the Recolor Art check box is automatically checked.

TIP Depending on the last settings you chose, the dialog box may show different colors from what you see in the figure.

3. Click the **Assign button** so that the Recolor Artwork dialog box is in Assign mode.

(continued)

Figure 28 *Recolor Artwork dialog box*

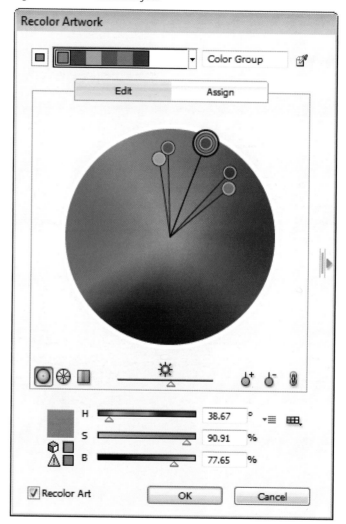

Figure 29 *Pentagram harmony rule applied to the artwork*

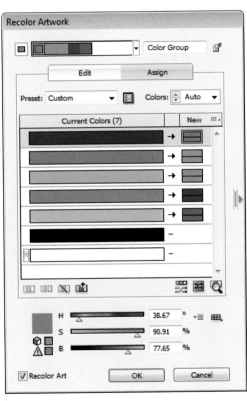

4. Click the **Harmony Rules list arrow**, then experiment with different harmony rules, noting how each affects the art.

5. Click the **Pentagram harmony rule** from the list, then compare your art and your Recolor Artwork dialog box to Figure 29.

   Like the illustration itself, the Pentagram harmony rule has five colors. In the Recolor Artwork dialog box, the list of colors on the left, which includes five colors plus black and white, represents the original colors used in the illustration. The smaller color squares to the right represent the new colors assigned with the Pentagram harmony rule. Because we chose a five-color harmony rule, the relationship between the original and the new colors is 1 to 1. For example, the turquoise used to paint the jewelry has now been changed to navy blue, and the original gray on the belt and the paddle have now changed to red.

6. Click and drag the **red color box** in the New column up and release it on top of the purple color box.

   The swap is reflected in the art—the jewels are now red, and the belt and paddle are now purple.

7. Double-click the **green color box** in the New column.

   The Color Picker opens.

8. Type **237**, **184**, and **107** in the R, G, and B text boxes, respectively, then click **OK**.

   The dialog box and the artwork are updated with the change.

   (continued)

9. Click the **purple color box** one time to select it, drag the **hue slider** at the bottom of the dialog box to 29° then compare your artwork and your Recolor Artwork dialog box to Figure 30.

10. Click the **New Color Group button** ⊡ at the top of the dialog box.

TIP You may need to expand the dialog box to see the New Color Group button.

The new color group is saved. Note that this saved group is not the Pentagram harmony rule that you first selected. The saved group is the Pentagram harmony rule with all of the edits that you made to it.

11. Click **OK**, deselect, then save your work.

You used the Assign mode of the Recolor Artwork dialog box to assign a harmony rule to an illustration, then you modified the new colors in the Recolor Artwork document to control how they affected the artwork.

Edit colors with the Recolor Artwork dialog box

1. Select all, then click the **Edit or Apply Colors button** ⬚ on the Color Guide panel.

2. Verify that the Assign button is active, click the **Harmony Rules list arrow**, then click **Pentagram**.

This is the same harmony rule that you applied in the previous lesson. Note that the color in the artwork is updated.

(continued)

Figure 30 *Illustration with new colors assigned in the Recolor Artwork dialog box*

Recoloring Artwork and Working with Transparency, Effects, and Graphic Styles

Figure 31 *Recolor Artwork dialog box in Edit mode*

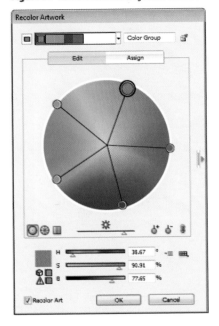

Figure 32 *Positioning the base color tool*

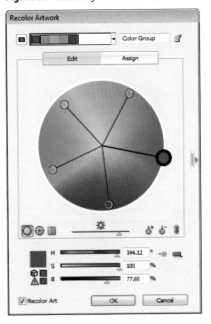

Figure 33 *The result of moving the base color*

3. Click the **Edit button**, then look at Figure 31.

   In Edit mode, the Recolor Artwork dialog box shows you harmony rules in relation to a color wheel. In Figure 31, note how the Pentagram harmony rule has five points on the color wheel, all of them equidistant from one another, just like a pentagram. Each of the five points corresponds to a color in the illustration. The color tool with the heavy circle is the base color of the active harmony rule.

4. Click and drag the **base color tool** to the position shown in Figure 32.

   All of the colors in the illustration change dynamically with the movements in the dialog box. When you move the base color tool, the other color tools move with it, thus maintaining the original relationship established by the Pentagram harmony rule. The illustration in Figure 33 shows the result of the move; by definition, the new colors are all in mathematical harmony with one another, despite the change.

5. Click and drag the **base color tool** halfway to the center of the color wheel.

   All the color tools move with the base color tool. The color in the illustration is desaturated, because in a color wheel, colors with the highest saturation are at the outside of the wheel.

   (continued)

6. Click and drag the **Brightness slider** to **50**, then compare your dialog box and illustration to Figure 34.

7. Click and drag the **Brightness slider** to **100**.

8. Drag the **base color tool** back to the outside of the color wheel.

9. With the base color tool still selected, type **0**, **100**, and **100** in the H, S, and B dialog boxes, respectively.

10. Experiment with various hues by dragging the **H slider** to various locations.

    Dragging the Hue slider with the base color tool selected is the same as dragging the base color tool by hand—all of the color tools move with the base color tool and the relationships are maintained.

11. Drag the **H slider** back to **0**, then click the **Unlink harmony colors button** 🔗 .

    The solid lines connecting the color tools become dotted, representing that the colors are no longer linked.

12. Click the **top (gold) color tool**, drag it to the location shown in Figure 35, then note the effect on the illustration.

    Only the "skin" group is affected, because the color tool you moved represents that group in the illustration.

13. Drag the **B slider** to **80%**.

    Only the "skin" group is affected.

14. Click the **Display segmented color wheel button** ⚙ , then drag the **green "headdress" color tool** to the location shown in Figure 36.

    (continued)

Figure 34 *Adjusting the brightness*

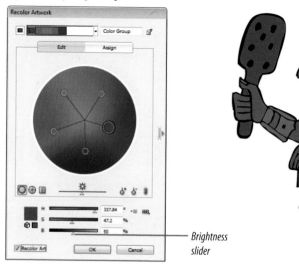

Brightness slider

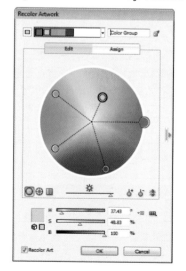

Figure 35 *New location of the gold color tool*

Figure 36 *New location of the green color tool*

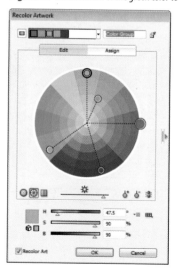

Recoloring Artwork and Working with Transparency, Effects, and Graphic Styles

Figure 37 *New location of the red and navy blue color tools*

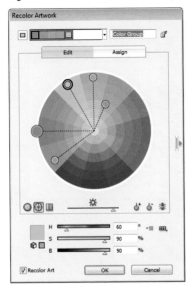

Figure 38 *Result of adjusting the hue of the green color tool*

Figure 39 *Viewing the Test harmony rule*

Figure 40 *New location of dark green*

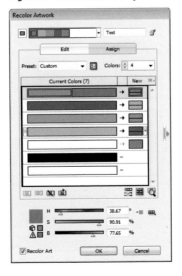

15. Drag the **red base color tool** to the same location on the opposite side of the color wheel, then drag the **navy blue color tool** to the bright yellow segment, as shown in Figure 37.

16. Click the **Link harmony colors button** ⚙, click the **green color tool** to select it, type **72** in the Hue slider text box, press **[Tab]**, then compare your illustration to Figure 38.

17. Click the **Show color group storage button** ▷ if necessary, to expose the right side of the dialog box, then click the **New Color Group button** ⊡.

18. Click **OK**, save your work, then close the file.

You edited the colors in the illustration using the Recolor Artwork dialog box.

Reduce colors in the Recolor Artwork dialog box

1. Open AI 8-5.ai, then save it as **2-Color Job**.

2. Select all, click the **Edit or Apply Colors button** 🎨 on the Color Guide panel, then click the **Assign button**.

3. Click **Test** in the Color Groups section, then compare your dialog box to Figure 39.

   The five original colors in the illustration correspond to each of the five colors in the Test harmony rule.

TIP This step is not necessary for reducing colors—you did this only so that your illustration and dialog box are working with the same colors shown in Figure 39.

4. Click the **Hide color group storage button** ◁.

5. Click and drag the **fifth color** in the list, which is dark green, on top of the first color in the list so that your dialog box resembles Figure 40.

(continued)

6. Click and drag the **remaining three colors** up to the top of the list so that your dialog box resembles Figure 41.

7. Compare your illustration to Figure 42.

   All five original colors in the illustration have been replaced by tints of the base color of the Test harmony group. The black border lines and white eye remain untouched.

8. Click the **Limits the color group to colors in a swatch library button** ▦ , point to **Color Books**, then click **Pantone solid coated**.

   Colors in the color group can now be only those found in the Pantone solid coated swatch library.

9. Double-click the **tan color box** in the New column to the right of the five combined colors, click **Pantone Blue 072 C**, then click **OK**.

10. Click **OK** to close the Recolor Artwork dialog box, save changes when prompted, then compare your illustration to Figure 43.

    The five colors in the illustration are now all tints of Pantone Blue 072 C. However, the tints are all very similar, making it difficult to distinguish various objects in the illustration.

    (continued)

Figure 41 *Result of dragging the remaining three colors*

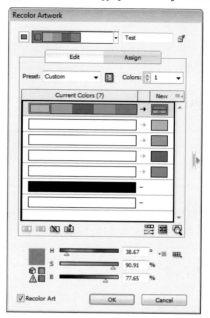

Figure 42 *Illustration with tints of the base color*

Figure 43 *Illustration with tints of Pantone Blue 072 C*

Recoloring Artwork and Working with Transparency, Effects, and Graphic Styles

Figure 44 *Final illustration*

11. Click the **Color button** to display the Color panel.

12. Deselect all, click the **Selection tool**, click the **face** (skin group), then note that the group is filled with an 80% tint of **Pantone** Blue 072 C.

13. Drag the **slider** to **10%**.

14. Using this method, use the Color panel to distinguish the various objects in the illustration with tints of Pantone Blue 072 C.

    Figure 44 shows one outcome.

TIP Feel free to use the Direct Selection tool and colorize objects in groups with different tints.

15. Save your work, then close 2-Color Job.

    This illustration will color separate into Black and Pantone Blue 072 C.

You reduced the number of colors in the illustration using the Recolor Artwork dialog box.

Apply Effects
TO OBJECTS

What You'll Do

In this lesson, you will work with a series of effects found on the Effect menu.

Working with Effects

The commands listed on the Effect menu can be applied to objects to alter their appearance without altering the object itself. You can apply effects, such as distort, transform, outline, and offset, without changing the original size, anchor points, and shape of the object. The object in Figure 45 is a simple square with a number of effects applied to it, creating the appearance of a complex illustration.

So what is the point of working with effects? The best answer is that working with effects offers you the ability to change your mind and change your work at any point, because each effect can be easily removed from an object without disturbing other effects that may be applied to it.

Many effect dialog boxes include a color box that, when clicked, opens up the Color Picker dialog box, which you can simply call, the Color Picker. Of all the ways to choose colors in Illustrator, using the Color Picker is the most sophisticated. In this dialog box, you can specify colors numerically as CMYK, RGB, HSB, or hexadecimal (a numbering system based on 16). You can also access the Color Picker by double-clicking the Fill or Stroke buttons on the Tools panel.

When you work with effects, all of your actions are recorded and listed on the Appearance panel. You can, at any time, select an effect on the panel and modify its settings or delete it.

The Appearance panel also provides a useful record of what you've done to create an illustration.

Figure 45 *One square with multiple effects applied*

Apply a Bloat effect

1. Open the Limeade document that you started working on in Lesson 1.

2. Click **Window** on the Application bar, then click **Appearance**.

3. Click the **Selection tool** ▶ , then click **each letter object in LIMEADE** so that they are all selected.

   The Appearance panel displays a new entry called Mixed Objects, meaning that mixed objects are selected. The A and the D are compound paths, while the remaining letters are regular closed paths.

4. Click **Effect** on the Application bar, point to **Distort & Transform** in the Illustrator Effects section, then click **Pucker & Bloat**.

5. Type **11** in the text box, then click **OK**.

   The Pucker & Bloat item is listed on the Appearance panel.

6. Compare your image to Figure 46.

   The selection marks represent those of the letters before the Bloat effect was applied, reflecting the fact that the original objects have not actually been changed by the effect.

You applied a Bloat effect to letter objects. You noted that the effect was listed on the Appearance panel and that the selection marks of the object did not change as a result of the applied effect.

Figure 46 *Pucker & Bloat effect applied to letter objects*

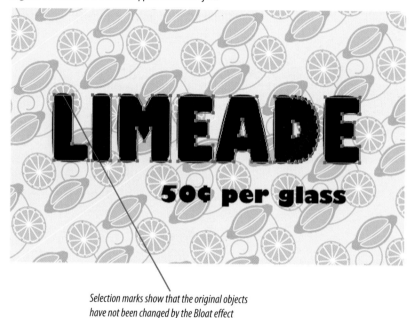

Selection marks show that the original objects have not been changed by the Bloat effect

Recoloring Artwork and Working with Transparency, Effects, and Graphic Styles

Figure 47 *Inner Glow effect affects the black stroke*

Figure 48 *Inflate Warp effect*

Apply an Inner Glow and a Warp effect

1. Fill the LIMEADE letter objects with Lime Green.
2. Click **Effect** on the Application bar, point to **Stylize** in the Illustrator Effects section, then click **Inner Glow**.
3. Verify that Mode is set to Screen, that Opacity is set to **75%**, that the Edge option button is selected, then type **.15** in the Blur text box.

TIP If your dialog box does not show inches, type .15 in in the Blur text box.

4. Click the **color box** next to the Mode list arrow to open the Color Picker.
5. Type **10** in the C text box, **0** in the M text box, **100** in the Y text box, and **0** in the K text box, then click **OK**.
6. Click **OK** again to close the Inner Glow dialog box.
7. Click the **Stroke button** on the Tools panel, click **Black** on the Swatches panel, then on the Stroke panel, click the **Weight list arrow**, then click **3 pt** so that your work resembles Figure 47.

   The stroke does not appear black because the Inner Glow effect is altering its appearance.
8. Click **Effect** on the Application bar, point to **Warp** in the Illustrator Effects section, then click **Inflate**.
9. Type **30** in the Bend text box.
10. Type **-30** in the Horizontal text box, click **OK**, then hide the selection marks.

    Your work should resemble Figure 48.

You applied the Inner Glow effect to the letter objects, increased the Blur value, then specified the color of the glow, using the Color Picker. You applied a 3-pt Black stroke, creating an interesting effect in conjunction with the Inner Glow effect. You then applied the Inflate Warp effect.

Lesson 3   Apply Effects to Objects

Apply a Drop Shadow effect

1. Show the selection marks of the LIMEADE letter objects.

2. Click **Effect** on the Application bar, point to **Stylize** in the Illustrator Effects section, then click **Drop Shadow**.

3. Click the **Mode list arrow**, then click **Normal**.

4. Click the **Opacity list arrow**, then drag the **Opacity slider** to **100**.

5. Verify that the X and Y Offset text boxes are both set to **0.1 in** and that Blur is set to **0.07 in**.

6. Click the **Color option button**, then click the **color box** to open the Color Picker.

7. Type **240** in the H text box, type **100** in the S and B text boxes, then click **OK**.

   The new color appears in the color box in the Drop Shadow dialog box.

8. Click **OK** to close the Drop Shadow dialog box.

   The Drop Shadow effect is listed on the Appearance panel.

9. Compare your screen to Figure 49.

You applied the Drop Shadow effect, using the Normal blending mode. You also accessed the Color Picker from within the Drop Shadow dialog box to determine the color of the shadow.

Figure 49 *Drop Shadow effect with a Normal blending mode*

Normal blending mode produces an opaque drop shadow

Figure 50 *Grain effect, isolated on its own layer*

Figure 51 *Grain effect, multiplied at 25% opacity*

Apply a Grain effect

1. Verify that the LIMEADE letter objects are still selected, copy them, then paste in front.

2. Verify that the Layers panel is displayed, create a new layer, then move the selected art to the new layer.

   TIP Move the selected art by dragging the Indicates Selected Art button on Layer 1 to the new layer.

3. Click **Effect** on the Application bar, point to **Texture** in the Photoshop Effects section, then click **Grain**.

4. Verify that the Grain Type is set to **Regular**, type **71** in the Intensity text box, type **61** in the Contrast text box, then click **OK**.

5. Click the **Eye Icon** 👁 on Layer 1 to hide Layer 1 so that you can see the results of the effect on Layer 2, as shown in Figure 50, then click the **empty box where the Eye Icon** 👁 **is hidden** to show the layer.

   Note that the drop shadow areas were included when the Grain effect was applied.

6. Click the **Opacity list arrow** on the Transparency panel, then drag the **Opacity slider** to **25**.

   TIP When you change the opacity of a layer, all objects on the layer are affected.

7. Click the **Blending Mode list arrow**, then click **Multiply**.

8. Deselect, save your work, then compare your screen to Figure 51.

You viewed LIMEADE on a new layer to view the Grain effect independently. You changed the opacity of the copied letters, then changed the blending mode to Multiply, allowing the original letters to be seen through the effect.

Use the
APPEARANCE PANEL

What You'll Do

In this lesson, you will explore the role of the Appearance panel in controlling the appearance attributes of objects.

Working with the Appearance Panel

The Appearance panel does far more than simply list appearance attributes. It is the gateway for controlling and manipulating all of the appearance attributes of your artwork. The Appearance panel, as shown in Figure 52, shows the fills, strokes, and effects that you have applied to your artwork and offers you the ability to manipulate those attributes.

When you select an object on the artboard, the Appearance panel lists the associated attributes. Fills and strokes are listed according to their stacking order (front to back), and effects are listed in the order in which they are applied. You can double-click an effect on the Appearance panel to open the effect's dialog box, which will show the settings you used to apply the effect. This is an extremely valuable function of the panel. Imagine opening an illustration after six months and trying to remember how you built it! The Appearance panel provides a trail.

When you have applied a set of effects to an object, and you then draw a new object, you can use the Appearance panel to decide whether or not the new object is created with

the effects with which you've been working. Click the Appearance panel options button and note the New Art Has Basic Appearance menu item. By default it will be checked and active. When it's active, any new object you create will have a "basic appearance," which means it will be a normal Illustrator object, with a simple fill and stroke but with no effects pre-applied.

To remove all appearances from an object, including the fill and stroke, click the Clear Appearance button on the Appearance panel.

If you remove the check mark next to the New Art Has Basic Appearance menu item, any new objects you create will "inherit" the effects you've applied to previous objects.

If you want to remove all effects from a selected object, simply click the Appearance panel options button, then click Reduce to Basic Appearance. The object will only retain the current fill and stroke on the Tools panel.

Duplicating Items on the Appearance Panel

A strange operation that you can execute with the Appearance panel is the application of multiple fills (and strokes) to a single object. Simply select the Fill attribute on the Appearance panel, then click the Duplicate Selected Item button on the panel. You can also duplicate an attribute by clicking the Appearance panel options button, then clicking Duplicate Item.

The Appearance panel is the only place where you can duplicate a fill. One would likely ask, "Why would I need two fills anyway?" The answer is that you don't need two fills. The Appearance panel

uses the second fill as a means to create a new object as part of the illustration. The second fill can be distorted and transformed and made to appear as an additional object, as shown in Figure 53. In this figure, the black circle is the original fill, and the yellow and pink objects are duplicate fills. Note that the distortion (Pucker) and transformation (Rotate) of the duplicate fills are effects. Thus, this is a single object despite its appearance.

Changing the Order of Appearance Attributes

You can change the order of attributes on the Appearance panel simply by dragging them up or down. The hierarchy of attributes directly affects the appearance of the object. For example, if you dragged the yellow fill attribute on the Appearance panel above the pink fill attribute, the illustration would appear as shown in Figure 54.

Figure 52 *Appearance panel*

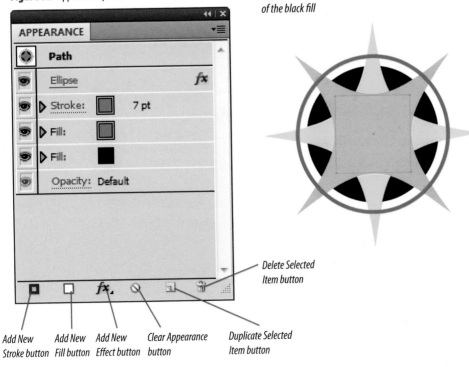

Add New Stroke button   Add New Fill button   Add New Effect button   Clear Appearance button   Duplicate Selected Item button   Delete Selected Item button

Figure 53 *Pink and yellow attributes are copies of the black fill*

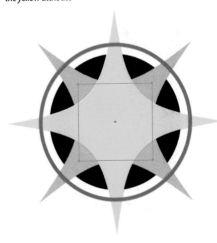

Figure 54 *The pink attribute is moved behind the yellow attribute*

Modify effects

1. Hide Layer 2.

2. Select the LIMEADE letter objects on Layer 1, then click **Drop Shadow** on the Appearance panel.

3. Click the **Mode list arrow**, then click **Multiply**.

4. Type **.15** in the X Offset text box, then click **OK**.

   Your work should resemble Figure 55.

5. Click the **Inner Glow layer** (not the underlined name) on the Appearance panel, click the **Appearance panel options button** ▼≣, then click **Duplicate Item**.

   The Inner Glow effect is doubled.

6. Deselect, then compare your work to Figure 56.

You opened the effect's dialog box, which listed the parameters of the effect as you previously applied it. You changed the blending mode of the effect to Multiply and changed the horizontal offset of the drop shadow. On the Appearance panel, you duplicated the Inner Glow effect.

Figure 55 *Drop Shadow effect with a Multiply blending mode*

Multiply blending mode produces
transparent drop shadow

Figure 56 *Inner Glow effect is intensified when duplicated on the Appearance panel*

Recoloring Artwork and Working with Transparency, Effects, and Graphic Styles

Figure 57 *Line inherits the current attributes on the Appearance panel*

Figure 58 *Stroke panel settings*

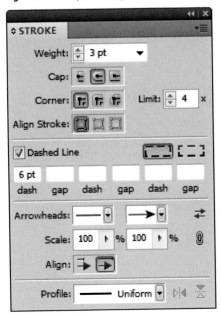

Remove effects from new art

1. Click the **Appearance panel options button** ▼≡, then click the New Art Has Basic Appearance menu item in order to remove the check mark.

   TIP If the check mark is already removed, do not select the menu item.

   TIP New Art Has Basic Appearance is a setting that is checked and active by default. When it is active, any new art you create has a basic appearance, with no effects applied.

2. Change the fill to [None] and the stroke to Black on the Tools panel.

3. Click the **Line Segment tool** ╲, click and drag starting to the left of the number 5, then release the mouse button directly below the L, so that your work resembles Figure 57.

   Because New Art Has Basic Appearance is not checked on the Appearance panel, the line automatically inherits the effects on the Appearance panel.

4. Click the **Appearance panel options button** ▼≡, then click **Reduce to Basic Appearance**.

   The effects are removed from the new line.

5. Using the Stroke panel, click the **Round Cap button** ⊂, then set the weight to **3 pts**.

6. Click the **Dashed Line check box**, type **6** in the first dash text box, then press [**Enter**] (Win) or [**return**] (Mac).

7. Click the **Right Arrowhead menu** in the Stroke panel, click **Arrow 2,** then deselect all.

   TIP If your arrowhead is pointing in the wrong direction, click the Swap start and end arrowheads button. Your stroke panel should resemble Figure 58.

   (continued)

8. Click the **Appearance panel options button** , then click **New Art Has Basic Appearance** to add a check mark if necessary.

   When the New Art Has Basic Appearance option is active, newly created art will not inherit the current attributes.

9. Click the **Rectangle tool**, draw a rectangle around the lime wallpaper background, then remove the dashes so that the stroke is solid.

   The rectangle does not inherit any effects.

10. Show Layer 2, then deselect so that your screen resembles Figure 59.

11. Save your work, then close the Limeade document.

You created a simple line, noting that it automatically inherited the effects on the Appearance panel, then you removed the effects. You added the Add Arrowheads effect. You then chose the New Art Has Basic Appearance button on the Appearance panel, and, when you drew a rectangle, noted that it did not inherit any effects.

Figure 59 *Black rectangle has a basic appearance*

Recoloring Artwork and Working with Transparency, Effects, and Graphic Styles

Figure 60 *Appearance panel*

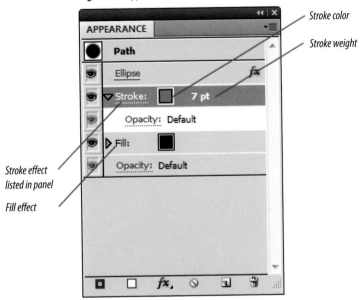

Stroke color

Stroke weight

Stroke effect
listed in panel

Fill effect

Figure 61 *Outer circle is created with the Offset Path effect*

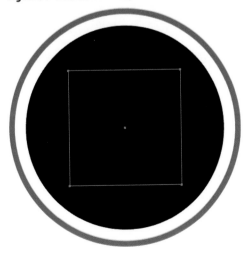

Create a complex appearance from a single object

1. Create a new 6" x 6" document, then save it as **Triple Fill**.

2. Create a 2" square with a black fill and no stroke.

3. Click **Effect** on the Application bar, point to **Convert to Shape**, then click **Ellipse**.

4. Verify that the Relative option button is selected, type **.25** in the Extra Width text box, type **.25** in the Extra Height text box, then click **OK**.

   The square appears as a larger circle.

5. Click the **Stroke layer** (not the underlined name) on the Appearance panel, then use the options that appear beside the item to set the color to **CMYK Green** and the weight to **7 pt**.

   TIP You will need to expand the Stroke item on the panel to see any effects applied to the stroke.

6. Compare your Appearance panel with Figure 60.

7. Click **Effect** on the Application bar, point to **Path** in the Illustrator Effects section, click **Offset Path**, type **.25** in the Offset text box, then click **OK**.

   Your screen should resemble Figure 61.

8. Click the **Fill layer** on the Appearance panel, then click the **Duplicate Selected Item button** on the Appearance panel.

9. Click the **color swatch list arrow** beside the new Fill item, then click **CMYK Green**.

   (continued)

10. Click **Effect** on the Application bar, point to **Distort & Transform** in the Illustrator Effects section, click **Pucker & Bloat**, type **-65** in the text box, then click **OK**.

The green fill is distorted above the original black fill, as shown in Figure 62.

11. Click the **Green Fill layer** on the Appearance panel so that it's highlighted, then click the **Duplicate Selected Item button** 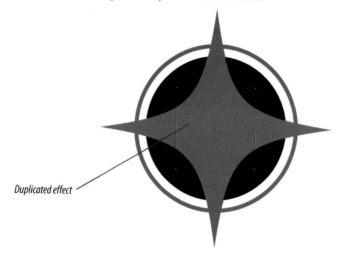 on the Appearance panel.

12. Click the **middle Fill item**, click **Effect** on the Application bar, point to **Distort & Transform**, click **Transform**, type **45** in the Angle text box, then click **OK**.

(continued)

Figure 62 *Duplicated fill effect is distorted*

Duplicated effect

Figure 63 *Rotation on the third fill is an effect*

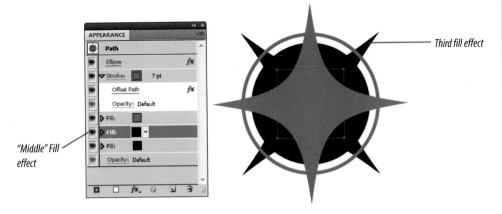

Third fill effect

"Middle" Fill effect

13. Click the **color swatch list arrow** beside the middle Fill item, then change it to black so that your work resembles Figure 63.

14. Drag the **middle Fill item** above the top Fill item, then deselect so that your work resembles Figure 64.

    Note that the illustration is a single object—the one single square you created with many effects applied.

15. Save and close the Triple Fill document.

You applied a number of effects to a simple square, creating the appearance of multiple objects. You also changed the appearance of the illustration by changing the order of the items on the Appearance panel.

Figure 64 *Changing the order of effects changes appearance*

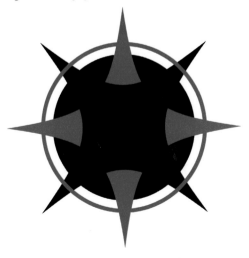

Work with
GRAPHIC STYLES

What You'll Do

In this lesson, you will create and apply graphic styles.

Creating and Applying Graphic Styles

Graphic styles are named sets of appearance attributes that are accessed on the Graphic Styles panel. To create a new style, select the artwork whose attributes you want to save as a style, then do one of the following:

- Click the New Graphic Style button on the Graphic Styles panel.
- Drag a selected object from the artboard into the Graphic Styles panel.
- Drag a thumbnail from the Appearance panel into the Graphic Styles panel.

A graphic style can include fills, strokes, effects, patterns, opacity settings, blending modes, and gradients. However, you can only create a graphic style from a single set of attributes. In other words, you can create the graphic style from one object and its attributes. The Graphic Styles panel is shown in Figure 65.

When you apply a graphic style to an object, the new graphic style overrides any graphic style that you previously applied to the object. When you apply a graphic style to a group or a layer, all objects in the group or on the layer take on the graphic style's attributes. Graphic styles are associated with the layers to which they are applied. If you move an object from a layer that has a graphic style applied to it, the object will lose the graphic style attributes.

Merging Graphic Styles

You can also create new graphic styles by merging two or more graphic styles on the Graphic Styles panel. [Ctrl]-click (Win) or ⌘- click (Mac) to select all the graphic styles that you want to merge, click the Graphic Styles panel options button, then click Merge Graphic Styles. The new graphic style will contain all of the attributes of the selected graphic styles and will be added to the Graphic Styles panel as a new graphic style.

Figure 65 *Graphic Styles panel*

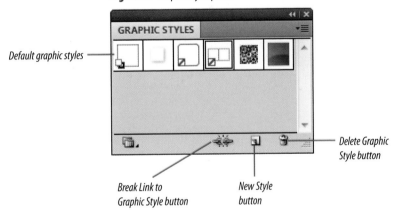

Default graphic styles

Break Link to Graphic Style button

New Style button

Delete Graphic Style button

Create a new graphic style

1. Open AI 8-6.ai, then save it as **Dolphin Blue**.

2. Create a rectangle that is 1" wide and 2" tall.

3. Fill the rectangle with the Blue Radial swatch and remove any stroke.

4. Click the **Gradient tool** , then drag the **Gradient tool pointer** from just below the top-left corner to the bottom-right corner of the rectangle.

   Try to make your fill resemble Figure 66.

5. Click **Effect** on the Application bar, point to **Stylize** in the Illustrator Effects section, click **Round Corners**, type **.15** in the Radius text box, then click **OK**.

6. Click **Effect** on the Application bar, point to **Stylize** in the Illustrator Effects section, then click **Outer Glow**.

7. Verify that the Mode is set to **Multiply** and that the Opacity is set to **75%**, change the color to **black** in the Color Picker if necessary, type **.1** in the Blur text box, then click **OK**, so that your work resembles Figure 67.

8. Verify that the Graphic Styles and Appearance panels are visible.

9. Select all, then drag the **thumbnail** next to Path on the Appearance panel to the Graphic Styles panel, as shown in Figure 68.

10. Double-click the **new swatch** on the Graphic Styles panel, then name it **Dolphin Blue**.

You created an illustration with the Round Corners and Outer Glow effects, then saved the appearance attributes as a new graphic style on the Graphic Styles panel.

Figure 66 *Applying the gradient to the rectangle*

Figure 67 *An Outer Glow effect added to the rectangle*

Figure 68 *Creating a new graphic style*

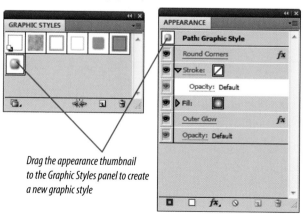

Drag the appearance thumbnail
to the Graphic Styles panel to create
a new graphic style

Recoloring Artwork and Working with Transparency, Effects, and Graphic Styles

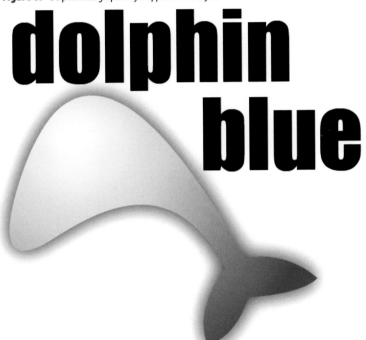

Figure 69 *Dolphin Blue graphic style applied to an object*

dolphin blue

Apply a graphic style to an object

1. Cut the rectangle from the artboard.
2. Click **Object** on the Application bar, then click **Show All**.

   A dolphin object and the words Dolphin blue appear.
3. Deselect all, select the dolphin artwork, click **Dolphin Blue** on the Graphic Styles panel, then deselect.

   Your work should resemble Figure 69.

You applied a graphic style to a simple object.

Apply a graphic style to text

1. Click the **Graphic Styles panel options button** ⯆☰, then remove the check mark to the left of the Override Character Color command if necessary.

2. Select the text, then click **Dolphin Blue** on the Graphic Styles panel.

   The text takes on all the attributes of the graphic style except the fill color, which remains black.

3. Undo your last step.

4. Click the **Graphic Styles panel options button** ⯆☰, click **Override Character Color** to select it, then apply the Dolphin Blue graphic style to the Dolphin blue text.

   Your work should resemble Figure 70.

5. Undo your last step, click **Type** on the Application bar, then click **Create Outlines** to convert the text to outlines.

6. Click **Object** on the Application bar, then click **Ungroup**.

7. Apply the Dolphin Blue graphic style to the objects so that your work resembles Figure 71.

   Because each of the letterforms has been ungrouped, the style fills each letterform individually.

8. Compare the text fills in Figure 71 to those in Figure 70.

You explored three ways of applying a graphic style to text and text outlines for different effects.

Figure 70 *Dolphin Blue graphic style applied to text*

Figure 71 *Dolphin Blue graphic style applied to each object*

Recoloring Artwork and Working with Transparency, Effects, and Graphic Styles

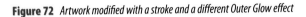
Figure 72 *Artwork modified with a stroke and a different Outer Glow effect*

Modify a graphic style

1. Select all, then apply a 1.5-pt. green stroke to the dolphin and the letters.

2. Click the **underlined Outer Glow effect** on the Appearance panel.

   The Outer Glow dialog box opens.

3. Click the **color box** in the Outer Glow dialog box to open the Color Picker.

4. Type **48** in the H (hue) text box, **100** in the S (saturation) text box, and **100** in the B (brightness) text box, then click **OK**.

5. Set the Mode to **Normal**.

6. Click **OK** again to close the Outer Glow dialog box, then deselect all.

   Your work should resemble Figure 72.

7. Press and hold [**Alt**] (Win) or [**option**] (Mac), then drag the **Mixed Objects thumbnail** from the Appearance panel directly on top of the Dolphin Blue graphic style on the Graphic Styles panel.

   The Dolphin Blue graphic style is updated to include the green stroke and the orange outer glow.

8. Save your work, then close Dolphin Blue.

You modified the Dolphin Blue graphic style by changing the settings on the Appearance panel, then replacing the old graphic style with the new appearance attributes.

Use Opacity
MASKS

What You'll Do

I DON'T WANT TO
FADE AWAY

 In this lesson, you will use an opacity mask to fade type in different directions.

Using Opacity Masks

You use an **opacity mask** and a **masking object** to alter the transparency of artwork in specific areas that you choose. The opacity mask is applied in the Transparency panel. The masking object is an object you create that defines which areas are transparent and the degree to which they are transparent. Where the opacity mask is white, the artwork is fully visible. Where the opacity mask is black, the artwork is fully transparent, or invisible. Shades of gray in the mask result in varying degrees of transparency in the artwork, with lighter grays resulting in more visible artwork and darker grays resulting in less visible artwork.

You can use any colored object or even a placed bitmap image as the masking object. Note, however, that masks only function in terms of grayscale, or black and white. If you use a color object as a masking object, Illustrator will use the grayscale equivalents of the colors in the masking object to determine the opacity levels.

You create and manipulate an opacity mask in the Transparency panel. Select artwork on the artboard, click the Transparency panel

options button, then click Make Opacity Mask. As shown in Figure 73, when you do, by default, a black layer mask will be added, and the artwork will be invisible.

> **QUICK TIP**
>
> When working with complex artwork, as in Figure 73, group the artwork before applying the opacity mask.

The Clip option on the Transparency panel automatically fills unused areas of the opacity mask with black. Thus, when you first create an opacity mask, the entire mask is filled with black. It's a good idea to uncheck the Clip option and start working with a white mask, as shown in Figure 74.

You work with opacity masks by adding objects to the mask that affect the transparency of the related artwork. When you click the mask, a black frame appears around the mask, indicating that the mask is targeted. With the mask targeted, any objects you create are created in the mask. Figure 75 shows a mask targeted in the Transparency panel. Inside the mask are two objects: a black rectangle and a dark gray rectangle.

Figure 73 *A black mask causing artwork to be completely hidden*

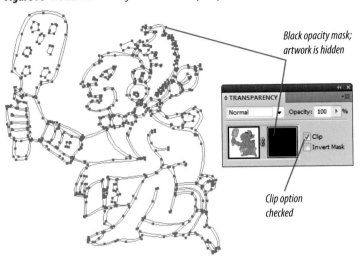

Black opacity mask;
artwork is hidden

Clip option
checked

Figure 74 *A white mask causing artwork to be completely visible*

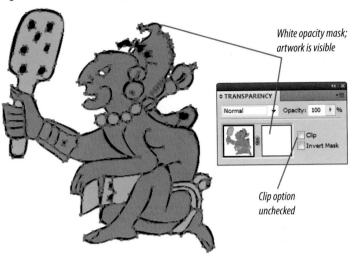

White opacity mask;
artwork is visible

Clip option
unchecked

Figure 75 *Black and gray objects in a mask affecting artwork differently*

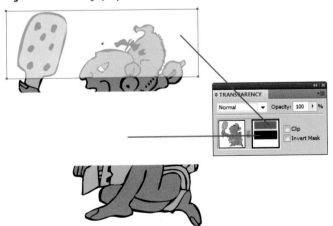

The artwork is completely hidden where the black rectangle is positioned in the mask. The artwork has a reduced opacity where the dark gray rectangle is positioned.

When working with opacity masks, you can create very complex visual effects with transparency. However, you might find the practical uses of opacity masks to be just as appealing. In Figure 76, the mask has been filled with a white to black gradient, top to bottom. Note the effect on the artwork.

Editing a Masking Object

Once you've added an opacity mask to an object and added a masking object to the opacity mask, you can edit a masking object at any time to change the transparency of the mask. When you click the opacity mask (right thumbnail) on the Transparency panel, you can then select the masking object and modify its attributes, such as shape and color. You can think of clicking the opacity mask in the Transparency panel as entering mask-editing mode because, once you have clicked it, everything you do will be done to the masking object. When you click the artwork (left thumbnail) on the Transparency panel, anything you do will affect the artwork itself. You can think of clicking the artwork thumbnail as exiting mask-editing mode.

You will often want to see the masking object as you are working. [Alt]-click (Win) or [option]-click (Mac) the opacity mask thumbnail to view the mask and the masking object.

If you want to hide and show the mask, press and hold [Shift] and click the opacity mask thumbnail. When the opacity mask is deactivated, a red x appears over the mask thumbnail in the Transparency panel.

When you add an opacity mask to selected artwork, the artwork and the masking object are linked by default. This means that if you move the artwork, the artwork and the masking object move together and the relationship is maintained. This relationship is represented by the link icon in the Transparency panel between the artwork and opacity mask thumbnails. Click to remove the link, and then you can move the artwork and the masking object(s) independently of one another.

To remove an opacity mask, select the masked artwork, then click Release Opacity Mask in the Transparency panel menu. Removing the opacity mask does not delete the masking object. The masking object reappears on top of the objects that were masked.

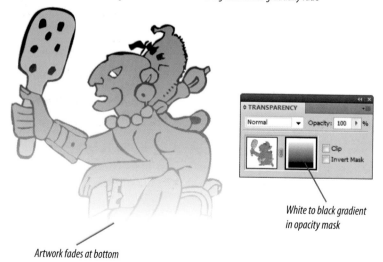

Figure 76 *A white to black gradient in the mask causing artwork to gradually fade*

White to black gradient in opacity mask

Artwork fades at bottom

Figure 77 *Applying an opacity mask*

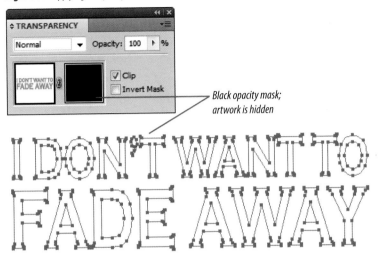

Black opacity mask;
artwork is hidden

Figure 78 *"Masking" the text with a black rectangle in the opacity mask*

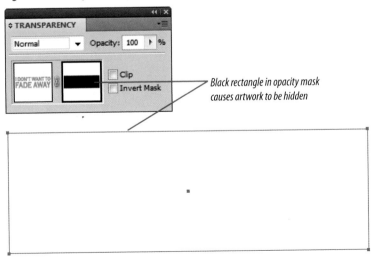

Black rectangle in opacity mask
causes artwork to be hidden

Change the opacity and blending mode of objects

1. Open AI 8-7.ai, then save it as **Simple Opacity Mask**.
2. Verify that the Transparency panel is visible.
3. Select all, click **Object** on the Application bar, then click **Group**.

TIP   When working with multiple objects, it's a smart idea to group them before applying an opacity mask.

4. Click the **Transparency panel options button** ▾≡ , then click **Make Opacity Mask**.

   As shown in Figure 77, a black opacity mask thumbnail appears in the Transparency panel to the right of the artwork thumbnail. The artwork remains selected, but it is invisible because the opacity mask is black.

5. Click the **Clip check box** on the Transparency panel to uncheck it.

   The mask fill changes to white, and the text becomes visible again. When you create an opacity mask, you can think of it as being empty because there are no masking objects in the mask. The Clip option automatically fills all empty areas of a mask—areas where there are no masking objects—with black.

6. In the Transparency panel, click the **opacity mask thumbnail**.

   The text is deselected. When you click the opacity mask thumbnail, a black border appears around the thumbnail, indicating that you are in edit-mask mode. Anything you do will affect the mask.

7. Set the Foreground color on the Tools panel to **black**, then set the stroke color to **none**.

8. Draw a rectangle around the text, then compare your result to Figure 78.

(continued)

You added a black rectangle to the opacity mask, a rectangle that overlapped the text. Thus, the text is no longer visible. The rectangle remains selected, so you can continue to modify it.

9. Click the **white to black linear gradient swatch** in the Swatches panel, then compare your result to Figure 79.

The fill on the rectangle changes to a white to black gradient, from left to right. Thus, the text is 100% visible at the left and gradually fades to 100% hidden on the right.

10. Save your work.

You created an opacity mask, then added a masking object. You applied a linear gradient to the masking object to create a fade effect on the text artwork.

Edit masked artwork and a masking object

1. In the Transparency panel, click the **artwork thumbnail**.

A black border appears on the artwork thumbnail, which is the left thumbnail. The masking object, which is the rectangle, is deselected and the artwork is selected.

2. Click **any red swatch in the Swatches panel** to change the fill color of the artwork.

3. Click the **opacity mask thumbnail**.

The rectangle is automatically selected.

4. Press and hold **[Alt]**(Win) or **[Option]**(Mac), then click the opacity mask.

As shown in Figure 80, the view changes to that of the opacity mask and the masking object.

(continued)

Figure 79 *Fading the text with a linear gradient in the opacity mask*

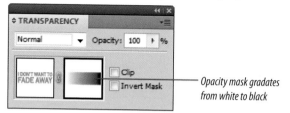

Opacity mask gradates from white to black

Artwork gradates from visible to invisible

Figure 80 *Viewing the opacity mask and the masking object*

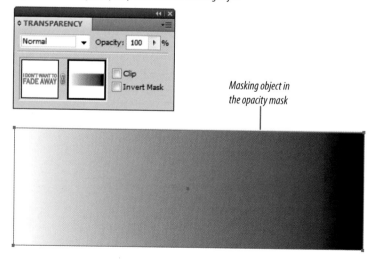

Masking object in the opacity mask

Figure 81 *Modifying the gradient in the masking object*

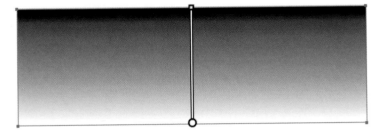

Figure 82 *Results of inverting the mask*

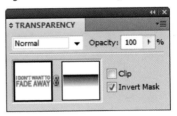

5. Click the **Gradient tool**, then click and drag from the bottom to the top of the rectangle.

    Your screen should resemble Figure 81.

6. In the Transparency panel, click the **artwork thumbnail**.

7. Click the **View menu**, then click **Hide Edges**.

8. Click the **Invert Mask** option on the Transparency panel, then compare your artwork to Figure 82.

    The Invert Mask option inverts the functionality of the mask. Black areas become visible, and white areas become masked. Thus the white to black gradient, which runs bottom to top in the opacity mask, results in the artwork moving from less visible on the bottom to more visible on the top.

9. Press and hold **[Shift]**, then click the opacity mask.

    A red X appears on the mask, and the mask is deactivated

10. Press and hold **[Shift]**, then click the **opacity mask** again.

    The mask is reactivated.

11. Save your work, then close Simple Opacity Mask.

You modified the color of masked artwork. You modified the gradient fill in a masking object. You used the Invert Mask option to see its affect on masked artwork.

Use the Transparency panel and the Color Picker.

1. Open AI 8-8.ai, then save it as **Channel Z**.
2. Double-click the Fill button on the Tools panel to open the Color Picker, create a color using the following values: hue = 59, saturation = 34, and brightness = 74, then drag the new color to the Swatches panel.
3. Select the square on the artboard, show the Gradient panel if necessary, click the black color stop on the gradient slider, press [Alt] (Win) or [option] (Mac), then click the new color swatch on the Swatches panel.
4. Change the opacity of the square to 60%.
5. Save your work.

Apply effects to objects.

1. On the Appearance panel, duplicate the Fill item.
2. Click the new Fill layer gain to activate it, click Effect on the Application bar, point to Texture, click Grain, click the Grain Type list arrow, then click Regular.
3. Type **70** for the Intensity and **60** for the Contrast, then click OK.
4. Click the underlined Stroke item on the Appearance panel, then change its weight to 1 pt and its color to orange. (*Hint*: Use any orange swatch.)
5. Click Effect on the Application bar, point to Path, click Offset Path, type **.1** in the Offset text box, then click OK.
6. Save your work.

Use the Appearance panel.

1. Click the top Fill layer on the Appearance panel.
2. Click Effect on the Application bar, point to the first Stylize command, click Round Corners, type **.5** in the Radius text box, then click OK.

3. On the Transparency panel, change the blending mode to Multiply.
4. Select the bottom Fill layer, then apply the Grain effect using the same settings that you previously used.
5. Expand the top Fill item if necessary, click the word Grain to open the Grain dialog box, then change the Intensity to 100.
6. Duplicate the top Fill item, then change the Color attribute of the middle Fill item to the original Orange Black gradient on the Swatches panel.
7. On the top Fill item, drag the *fx* icon next to the Round Corners item to the trashcan icon on the bottom of the Appearance panel to remove the effect from the top item.
8. Collapse the three Fill items on the Appearance panel.
9. Save your work.

Work with graphic styles.

1. Show the Graphic Styles panel if necessary.
2. Drag the Path thumbnail from the Appearance panel to the Graphic Styles panel.

3. Name the new graphic style **Noise**.
4. Cut the artwork from the artboard.
5. Click Object on the Application bar, click Show All, then change the fill on the text to None.
6. Verify that Override Character Color is checked on the Graphic Styles panel menu.
7. Apply the Noise style to the text.
8. Expand the Stroke item on the Appearance panel, then change its color to Black and its weight to 1.5 pt.
9. Double-click the Offset Path item, then change the offset to .15.
10. Delete the Round Corners effect from the middle Fill item.
11. Update the Noise graphic style with the new attributes by pressing [Alt] (Win) or [option] (Mac) as you drag the thumbnail on the Appearance panel on top of the Noise style on the Graphic Styles panel.
12. Save your work, compare your screen to Figure 83, then close Channel Z.

Figure 83 *Completed Skills Review, Part 1*

Recoloring Artwork and Working with Transparency, Effects, and Graphic Styles

Recolor artwork.

1. Open AI 8-9.ai, then save it as **Jaguar**.
2. Double-click the orange nose to see the orange group in Isolation Mode.
3. Click the Exit Isolated Group button on the Control panel.
4. Click the Eyedropper tool, sample the orange color from the nose, then click the Set base color to the current color button on the Color Guide panel.
5. Select all, then click the Edit or Apply Colors button on the Color Guide panel.
6. Click the Assign button if necessary to open the Recolor Artwork dialog box.
7. Click the Harmony Rules list arrow, then choose the Pentagram harmony rule from the list.
8. Click and drag the red color box in the New column up and release it on top of the color box at the top of the column.
9. Double-click the green color box in the New column, type **237**, **184**, **107** in the R, G, & B text boxes respectively, then click OK.
10. Click the navy blue color box in the New column one time to select it, then drag the hue slider at the bottom of the dialog box to 133°.
11. Click OK, deselect, save your work, then compare your illustration to Figure 84.

Figure 84 *Completed Skills Review, Part 2*

Use opacity masks.

1. Open AI 8-10.ai, then save it as **Opacity Mask Skills**.
2. Verify that the Transparency panel is visible.
3. Select all, click Object on the Application bar, then click Group.
4. Click the Transparency panel options button, then click Make Opacity Mask.
5. Click to uncheck the Clip option on the Transparency panel.
   (*Hint*: Verify that Invert Mask is not checked.)
6. Click the Edit menu, then click Copy.
7. In the Transparency panel, click the opacity mask thumbnail.
8. Click the Edit menu, then click Paste in Front.
9. Click the black swatch in the Swatches panel to change the fill of the masking object to black. The text on the artboard is completely hidden.
10. Click the white to black linear gradient swatch in the Swatches panel, then compare your result to Figure 85.

Figure 85 *Applying a gradient to the opacity mask*

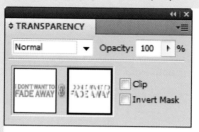

11. In the Transparency panel, click the artwork thumbnail.
12. Click the CMYK Magenta swatch in the Swatches panel to change the fill color of the artwork.
13. Click the opacity mask thumbnail.
14. Press and hold [Alt](Win) or [Option](Mac), then click the opacity mask.
15. Click the Gradient tool, then click and drag from the bottom to the top of the text outlines.
16. In the Transparency panel, click the artwork thumbnail.
17. Click the View menu, then click Hide Edges.
18. Click the Invert Mask option on the Transparency panel, then compare your artwork to Figure 86.
19. Press and hold [Shift], then click the opacity mask thumbnail.
20. Press and hold [Shift], then click the opacity mask thumbnail again.
    (*Hint*: This is an alternative method to the same exercise you did in Lesson 6. The one problem with this method is that, because the artwork and the mask are perfectly aligned, a faint line appears around the edges of the text. In other words, because the mask doesn't extend the artwork, the edges of the artwork aren't fully masked, and the text therefore doesn't fully fade away.)
21. Save your work, then close Opacity Mask Skills.

Figure 86 *Completed Skills Review, Part 3*

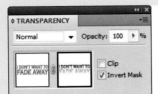

The local VFW has contracted you to design their monthly newsletter. You are happy because it means a regular monthly payment. However, since their budget is modest, you want to streamline your work as much as possible. One design element of the newsletter that is used every month is a red and blue frame positioned around pictures. You decide to create this as a graphic style in Illustrator.

1. Open AI 8-11.ai, then save it as **Frame**.
2. Show the Brushes panel, then apply the 10 pt Round brush to the square.
3. Click Effect on the Application bar, point to Stylize, then click Feather.
4. Accept the default settings in the Feather Radius text box, then click OK.
5. On the Appearance panel, duplicate the stroke, then change the duplicate stroke color to blue.
6. Click Effect on the Application bar, point to Path, click Offset Path.
7. Type **.18** in the Offset text box, then click OK.
8. Save the appearance attributes as a new graphic style on the Graphic Styles panel.
9. Name the new graphic style **Picture Frame**.
10. Save your work, compare your screen to Figure 87, then close the Frame document.

Figure 87 *Completed Project Builder 1*

You are a designer and have just finished a color illustration for a client who calls to tell you that the project is being changed. Because of budgetary constraints, it's going to be reduced from a four-color to a two-color job. The client tells you to use black ink plus any red PANTONE color that you think will work best.

1. Open AI 8-12.ai, then save it as **2 Color Jaguar**.
2. Select all, click the Edit or Apply Colors button on the Color Guide panel, then click the Assign button.
3. Click the Harmony Rules list arrow, then choose the Pentagram harmony rule from the list.
4. Click and drag the fifth color in the Current Colors list, which is red, on top of the first color in the list.
5. Click and drag the remaining three colors up to the top of the list (don't move the black and white colors).
6. Click the Limits the color group to colors in a swatch library button, point to Color Books, then click PANTONE solid coated.
7. Double-click the color box in the New column to the right of the five combined colors, click PANTONE 200 C, then click OK.
8. Click OK to close the Recolor Artwork dialog box, save changes when prompted, then compare your illustration to Figure 88.
9. Save your work, then close 2 Color Jaguar.

Figure 88 *Completed Project Builder 2*

Recoloring Artwork and Working with Transparency, Effects, and Graphic Styles

Burr Marina contacts your design firm for a consultation. They ask you to update their logo, which they've been using for a number of years. They tell you that the logo can't really change because the look is already established. You tell them that you can add some texture to provide some visual interest without dramatically changing the logo.

1. Open AI 8-13.ai, then save it as **Burr Marina**.
2. Verify that both the Transparency and Layers panels are visible.
3. Click the Selection tool, click the royal blue shape, then copy it.
4. On the Layers panel, make the Swirls layer visible, then click the layer to target it.
5. Click the target on the Swirls layer to select the artwork on that layer.
6. On the Transparency panel, click the panel options button, then click Make Opacity Mask.
7. Click the opacity mask so that a black border appears around the mask.
8. Paste in place, then note that the object remains selected.
9. Click the white to black linear gradient swatch on the Swatches panel.
10. Click the artwork thumbnail, click the Blending Mode list arrow on the Transparency panel, then click Multiply.
11. Save your work, compare your screen to Figure 89, the close the file.

Figure 89 *Completed Design Project*

Your client wants you to redo the two-color mask you made for her because she doesn't like red. She says you can choose any other color you think looks good. You decide, for practice, to make the two-color mask from one of the original four-color graphics you created for her. You'll use black and a PANTONE color of your choice.

1. Open AI 8-14.ai, then save it as **2 Color Mask**.
2. Select all, then open the Recolor Artwork dialog box.
3. Reduce all the colors (except black and white) to a single color.
4. Change the single color to any PANTONE color of your choice.
5. Modify the color areas of the image to your liking and refer to Figure 90 for one possible outcome.
6. Save your work, then close 2 Color Mask.

Figure 90 *Completed Portfolio Project*

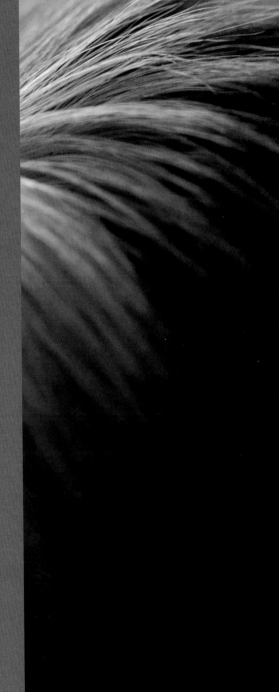

CHAPTER 9

CREATING AND
DESIGNING GRAPHS

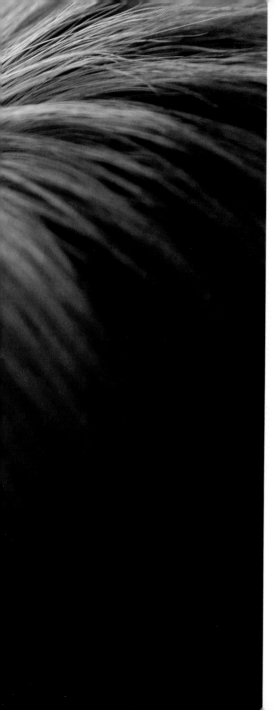

CREATING AND
DESIGNING GRAPHS

When you think of graphs, you may think of those standard, premade, click-a-button graphs that you can make with any presentation or financial software package. As a designer, you'll be excited by the graphs you can create with Illustrator tools. You can enter the data directly into Illustrator and have all of its design and drawing power at your fingertips.

For the right project, visually interesting and smartly designed graphs are a powerful tool for conveying information. Rather than using "canned" graphs from business software, think instead of using Illustrator graphs as an opportunity for expressing data artistically. Since people naturally pay more attention to a well-designed graph than to blocks of text, using graphs in a presentation will help you to make your points more persuasively. And using Illustrator graphs will help make your presentations one-of-a-kind.

Group Selection tool

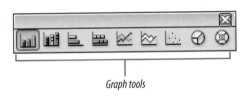

Graph tools

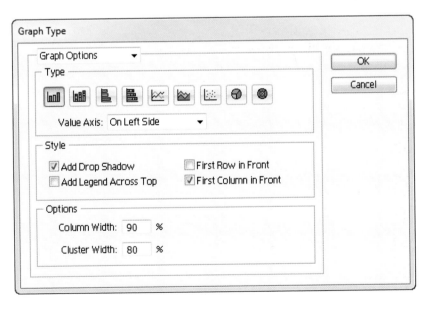

Create
A GRAPH

What You'll Do

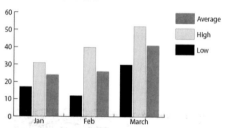

In this lesson, you will enter data and create a column graph.

Defining a Graph

A graph is a diagram of data that shows relationships among a set of numbers. A set of data can be represented by a graphic element, such as a bar, line, or point. Different types of graphs are used to emphasize different aspects of the data. The right type of graph can help you simplify complex data and communicate a message more effectively.

Illustrator offers nine types of graphs:

- Column
- Stacked column
- Bar
- Stacked bar
- Line
- Area
- Scatter
- Pie
- Radar

Illustrator creates the graph you specify and allows you to modify the graph objects to create unique artwork. You can also easily convert one type of graph into another type and create custom designs that you can then apply to the graph.

Creating a Graph

Before you create a graph, it is important to understand how data is plotted in Illustrator's Graph Data window. The first column (vertical axis) of the Graph Data window is reserved for category labels, while the first row (horizontal axis) is reserved for legend labels. See Figure 1.

Category labels describe non-numeric data, such as the months of the year, the days of the week, or a group of salespersons' names.

Legend labels describe numeric data that may change, such as weekly sales totals, payroll amounts, or daily temperatures; they appear in a box next to the graph, called the legend.

The legend, like a map legend, contains the legend labels and small boxes filled with colors that represent the columns on the graph.

Figure 1 *Entering category labels and legend labels*

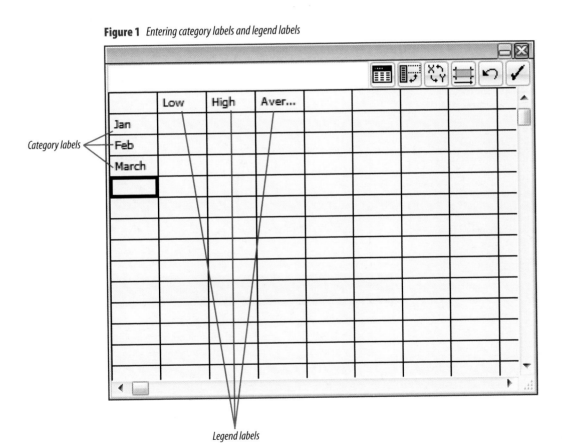

Category labels

Legend labels

Create a column graph

1. Open AI 9-1.ai, then save it as **Graph**.

2. Verify that you are using inches as your General unit of measure by checking your Units Preferences.

3. Click the **Column Graph tool** 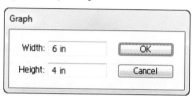, then click the **center of the artboard**.

4. Type **6** in the Width text box and **4** in the Height text box, as shown in Figure 2, then click **OK**.

   The Graph Data window appears in front of the graph and consists of rows and columns. The intersection of a row and a column is called a **cell**. The first cell, which is selected, contains the number 1.00 as sample data to create a temporary structure for the graph. The appearance of the graph will change after you enter data.

5. Press [**Delete**], then press [**Tab**] to eliminate the 1.00 from the first cell and select the next cell in the first row.

   You must always remove the number 1.00 from the first cell before entering new data.

6. Type **Low**, press [**Tab**], type **High**, press [**Tab**], then type **Average**.

   You have entered three legend labels.

   (continued)

Figure 2 *Graph dialog box*

Changing the Number of Decimal Points in Graph Data

Numbers in the Graph Data window are initially displayed with two decimals. For example, if you type the number 86, it appears as 86.00. To modify the number of decimals in any or all cells in the Graph Data window, click the cell(s) that you want to change, then click the Cell style button in the Graph Data window. The Cell Style dialog box opens. Increase or decrease the number in the Number of decimals text box to change the decimal place (set it to 0 if you do not want any decimal place), then click OK. You can also increase or decrease the column width in the Cell Style dialog box by changing the value in the Column width text box.

Figure 3 Graph Data window

Legend labels

Category labels

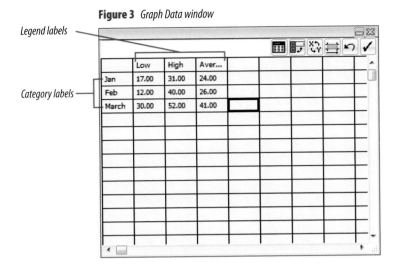

Figure 4 Column graph

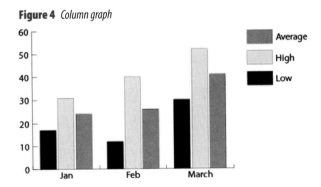

7. Click the **second cell** in the first column, type **Jan**, press [**Enter**] (Win) or [**return**] (Mac), type **Feb**, press [**Enter**] (Win) or [**return**] (Mac), type **March**, then press [**Enter**] (Win) or [**return**] (Mac).

   You have entered three category labels. Compare the positions of your labels with those shown in Figure 3.

TIP Category labels are listed vertically and legend labels are listed horizontally in the Graph Data window. If you enter your labels incorrectly, you can click the Transpose row/column button in the Graph Data window to switch them.

8. Enter the remaining data shown on the artboard, using [Tab] and [Enter] (Win) or [Tab] and [return] (Mac), and the four arrow keys on your keyboard to move between cells.

TIP Often you will want to create labels that consist of numbers, such as a ZIP code or the year. Since these labels are meant to describe categories, they must be set in quotes ("2010") so that Illustrator will not mistake them for data that should be plotted.

9. Close the Graph Data window, saving the changes you made, then reposition the graph on the artboard if it is not centered.

10. Deselect, save your work, then compare your graph to Figure 4.

You defined the size of the graph, then entered three legend labels, three category labels, and numbers in the Graph Data window.

Edit a Graph Using the
GRAPH DATA WINDOW

What You'll Do

In this lesson, you will change the data that is the basis of the column graph, then update the graph to reflect the new data.

Editing Data and Graphs

A project that calls for a graph often calls for edits to the graph. Fortunately, it is easy to make changes to the data that defines the graph and just as easy to update the graph. For every graph in Illustrator, the data you used to plot it is stored in the Graph Data window. This data is editable. If you make changes, you can preview them by clicking the Apply button in the Graph Data window.

When you create text and data in another program that you want to use in an Illustrator graph, the document must be saved as a text-only file with commas separating each number from the next. If you are importing an Excel worksheet, it must be saved as a tab-delimited text file for Illustrator to support it. To import data from Word or Excel, you must have the Graph Data window open and selected. Click the Import data button. You will then be prompted to open the file you wish to import.

Figure 5 *Changing data in the Graph Data window*

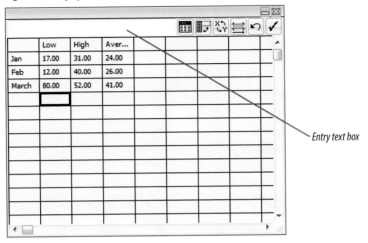

Entry text box

Figure 6 *Viewing the new graph*

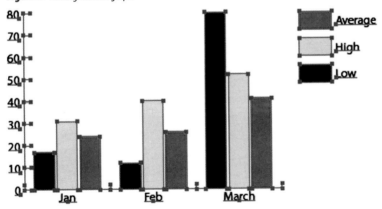

1. Click **View** on the Application bar, then click **Hide Print Tiling** if it is not already activated.

2. Click the **Selection tool** ▶, then select and delete the text at the top of the artboard.

3. Click the **graph**, click **Object** on the Application bar, point to **Graph**, then click **Data**.

TIP The separate objects that make up the graph are automatically grouped when the graph is created.

4. Click the **cell that contains the number 30.00**, type **80**, press [**Enter**] (Win) or [**return**] (Mac), then compare your screen to Figure 5.

   When you click a cell, the number in the cell becomes highlighted in the Entry text box of the Graph Data window, allowing you to change it to a new number.

5. Click the **Apply button** ✓ in the Graph Data window, then compare your graph to Figure 6.

6. Change the number 80.00 to **34**, click the **cell that contains the number 41.00**, type **43**, then press [**Enter**](Win) or [**return**](Mac).

7. Close the Graph Data window, then save changes when prompted.

TIP To remove data from cells in the Graph Data window, select the cells from which you want to delete the data, click Edit on the Application bar, then click Clear.

You edited the graph's data in the Graph Data window, then clicked the Apply button to view the changes to the graph.

Use the Group
SELECTION TOOL

What You'll Do

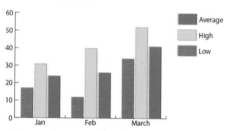

In this lesson, you will use the Group Selection tool to select different areas of the graph for modification.

Using the Group Selection Tool

Graphs are grouped objects, consisting of many individual groups grouped together. Each set of colored columns represents an individual group within the larger group. For example, all of the black columns in Figure 7 represent the low temperatures for each month. The gray columns are the average-temperature group, and the light gray columns are the high-temperature group.

The Group Selection tool allows you to select entire groups within the larger group for the purpose of editing them with the Illustrator tools and menu commands.

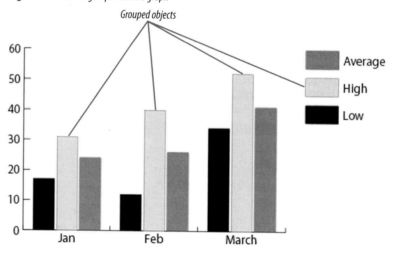

Figure 7 *Individual groups within a graph*

Creating and Designing Graphs

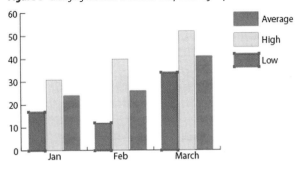

Figure 8 *Changing the color of the low-temperature group to red*

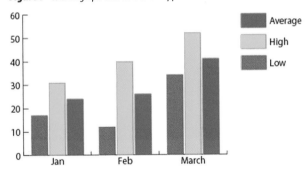

Figure 9 *Column graph with new colors applied*

1. Click the **artboard** to deselect the graph.

2. Click the **Group Selection tool** ▸⁺.

TIP The Group Selection tool is hidden beneath the Direct Selection tool.

3. Click the **first black column** above the Jan label, then click it again.

   The first click selects the first black column, and the second click selects the two remaining black columns.

4. Click the **first black column** a third time to select the low-temperature legend box.

   If you click too many times, you will eventually select the entire graph instead of an individual group. In that case, deselect and try again.

5. Change the fill color of the selected columns to red, as shown in Figure 8.

6. Click the **first light gray column** above the Jan label, click it again, click it a third time, then change the fill color of the high-temperature columns and legend box to yellow.

7. Select the gray columns and legend box, change the fill color to green, then deselect all.

   Your graph should resemble Figure 9.

8. Save your work.

TIP The text labels, value axis labels, and legend labels are also individual groups within the larger graph group. Click twice to select them, then change their font, size, or color as desired.

You used the Group Selection tool to select groups within the graph, then changed the colors of the columns and the legend boxes.

Use the Graph
TYPE DIALOG BOX

What You'll Do

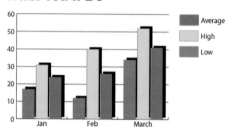

In this lesson, you will modify the graph using the Graph Type dialog box.

Using the Graph Type Dialog Box

The Graph Type dialog box provides a variety of ways to change the look of your graph. For example, you can add a drop shadow behind the columns in a graph or change the appearance of the tick marks.

Tick marks are short lines that extend out from the value axis, which is the vertical line to the left of the graph. Tick marks help viewers interpret the meaning of column height by indicating incremental values on the value axis. You can also move the value axis from the left side of the graph to the right side, or display it on both sides.

Values on the value axis can be changed, and symbols such as $, %, and ° can be added to the numbers for clarification.

DESIGNTIP

Choosing a Chart Type

Keep in mind the following guidelines when choosing a chart type:

- Pie or column charts are typically used to show quantitative data as a percentage of the whole.
- Line or bar charts are used to compare trends or changes over time.
- Area charts emphasize volume and are used to show a total quantity rather than to emphasize a portion of the data.
- Scatter or radial charts show a correlation among variables.

Figure 10 *Graph Type dialog box*

Graph Options menu →

Graph types →

Add Drop Shadow →

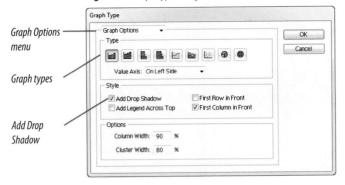

Figure 11 *Choosing options for the value axis*

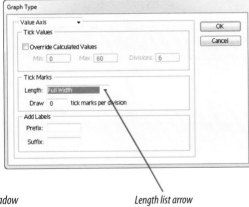

Length list arrow

Figure 12 *Graph with full-width tick marks and a drop shadow*

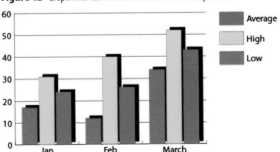

Lesson 4   Use the Graph Type Dialog Box

Use the Graph Type dialog box

1. Click the **Selection tool** , then click the **graph**.

   The entire graph must be selected to make changes in the Graph Type dialog box.

2. Click **Object** on the Application bar, point to **Graph**, then click **Type**.

3. Click the **Add Drop Shadow check box**, as shown in Figure 10.

4. Click the **Graph Options list arrow**, then click **Value Axis**.

   All of the options in this window now refer to the value axis, which is the vertical line located to the left of the columns on the graph.

5. Click the **Length list arrow** in the Tick Marks section of the window, click **Full Width**, compare your Graph Type dialog box to Figure 11, then click **OK**.

6. Deselect the graph, save your work, then compare your graph to Figure 12.

TIP The Graph Type dialog box does not provide an option for displaying the number or value that each column in the graph represents. For example, it will not display the number 32 on top of a column that represents 32°. If you want to display the actual values of the data on the chart, you must add those labels manually, using the Type tool.

You used the Graph Type dialog box to add a drop shadow to the graph and to extend the tick marks to run the full width of the graph.

Create a COMBINATION GRAPH

What You'll Do

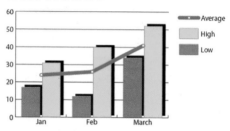

In this lesson, you will create a combination graph to show one set of data as compared to other data.

Defining a Combination Graph

A **combination graph** is a graph that uses two graph styles to plot numeric data. This type of graph is useful if you want to emphasize one set of numbers in comparison to others. For example, if you needed to create a column graph showing how much more paper than glass, plastic, or aluminum is recycled in a major city over a one-year period, you could plot the paper recycling data as a line graph, leaving the other recycling categories as columns. Your audience would be able to compare how much more paper is recycled than the other three products by looking at the line in relationship to the columns on the graph.

Figure 13 *Graph Type dialog box*

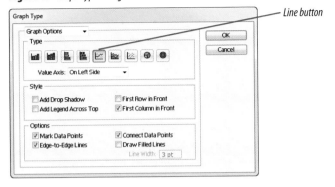

Line button

Figure 14 *Selecting the line graph*

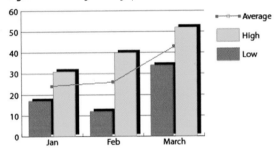

Figure 15 *Formatting the line graph*

Markers

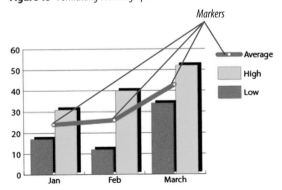

Lesson 5   Create a Combination Graph

Create a combination graph

1. Click the **Group Selection tool** ▶⁺, then select all four items of the Average (green) group.

2. Click **Object** on the Application bar, point to **Graph**, then click **Type**.

3. Click the **Line button** ☒, then click the **Add Drop Shadow check box** to remove the check mark.

4. Click the **Edge-to-Edge Lines check box**, make sure that there are check marks in the Mark Data Points and Connect Data Points check boxes, as shown in Figure 13, then click **OK**.

   The four green columns are replaced by four small square markers.

5. Click the **artboard** to deselect the graph.

6. Click the **Group Selection tool** ▶⁺, then click the **first line segment connecting the markers** three times to select the entire line and the corresponding information in the legend, as shown in Figure 14.

7. Click **Object** on the Application bar, point to **Arrange**, then click **Bring to Front**.

8. Change the stroke weight to 10 pt, the fill color of the line to [None], the stroke color of the line to green, and the cap to a round cap.

9. Deselect, select the four gray markers using the Group Selection tool ▶⁺, change their fill color to White, then deselect again.

10. Save your work, compare your graph to Figure 15, then close the Graph document.

You created a combination graph.

Create a Custom
GRAPH DESIGN

What You'll Do

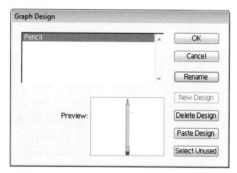

In this lesson, you will define artwork for a custom graph.

Creating a Custom Graph Design

This is where Illustrator really shines as a design tool for graphs. A **custom graph design** is a picture of something used to replace traditional columns, bars, or markers in Illustrator graphs. For example, when reporting on financial news, newspapers such as *USA Today* often print graphs made with custom designs of coins or dollars instead of columns and bars.

Only vector-based objects can be used for custom graph designs, however. You cannot use bitmaps, objects created with the Paintbrush tool, or objects filled with gradients.

Illustrator contains predefined column and marker designs as well as graph designs. These files are located in Adobe Illustrator CS5/Cool Extras/Sample Files. To use these designs, first open one of the sample files, create a new document and then create a new graph. Select the graph, click Object on the Application bar, point to Graph, then click Column. All of the column designs will appear in the Graph Column dialog box.

DESIGNTIP

Using Supplied Custom Graph Designs

Illustrator comes with two documents full of custom designs that you can apply to graphs. These designs include flags, cats, hammers, diamonds, dollar signs, stars, and men and women. In addition, three-dimensional objects such as cylinders, hexagons, cubes, arrows, and pyramids are available. It's a good idea to open these files just to see what's there. Navigate to the folder that holds your Adobe Illustrator CS5 application, then look for the folder called Cool Extras. In there, you'll find sample graphs and the custom designs.

Figure 16 *Creating a custom graph design*

Part A

Two guides

Part B

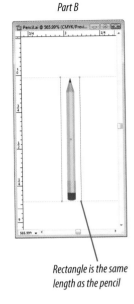

Rectangle is the same
length as the pencil

Part C

Rectangle is behind
the pencil and both
are selected

Figure 17 *Graph Design dialog box*

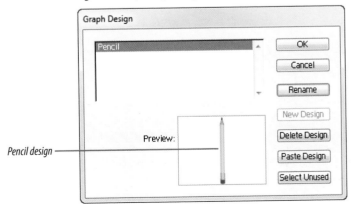

Pencil design

Create a custom graph design

1. Open AI 9-2.ai, then save it as **Pencil**.
2. Click **View** on the Application bar, then click **Pencil**.
3. Click the **Selection tool**, drag a selection marquee around the entire pencil to select all of it, then group it.
4. Show the rulers if they are hidden, then align two guides with the top and bottom of the pencil, as shown in Part A of Figure 16.
5. Deselect the pencil if it is still selected, then change the fill and stroke colors to [None] on the Tools panel.
6. Click the **Rectangle tool**, then create a rectangle around the pencil that snaps to the top and bottom guides, as shown in Part B of Figure 16.

   The height of the rectangle should exactly match the height of the custom design, to ensure that data values are represented correctly on the graph.
7. While the rectangle is still selected, click **Object** on the Application bar, point to **Arrange**, then click **Send to Back**.

   The rectangle must be behind the illustration.
8. Select both the rectangle and the pencil, as shown in Part C of Figure 16, click **Object** on the Application bar, point to **Graph**, then click **Design**.
9. Click **New Design**, click **Rename**, name the design **Pencil**, then click **OK**.

   The pencil design appears in the Graph Design dialog box, as shown in Figure 17.
10. Click **OK** to close the Graph Design dialog box, then save your work.

You created a custom design for graphs using the Graph Design dialog box.

Apply a Custom
DESIGN TO A GRAPH

What You'll Do

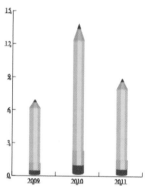

In this lesson, you will apply the pencil custom design to a graph.

Applying a Custom Design to a Graph

Custom designs are typically applied to column graphs and line graphs. Illustrator provides four options for displaying custom designs on a graph: uniformly scaled, vertically scaled, repeating, and sliding.

Uniformly scaled designs are resized vertically and horizontally, whereas vertically scaled designs are resized only vertically. Figure 18 shows an example of a uniformly scaled design, and Figure 19 shows an example of a vertically scaled design. Repeating designs assign a value to the custom design and repeat the design as many times as necessary. For example, if the pencil is assigned a value of 1 school, 3 pencils would represent 3 schools. Sliding-scale designs allow you to define a point on the custom design from which the design will stretch, so that everything below that point remains uniform.

Creating and Designing Graphs

Figure 18 *A uniformly scaled custom design*

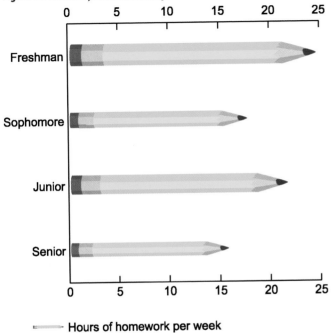

Hours of homework per week

Figure 19 *A vertically scaled custom design*

Hours of homework per week

Lesson 7   Apply a Custom Design to a Graph

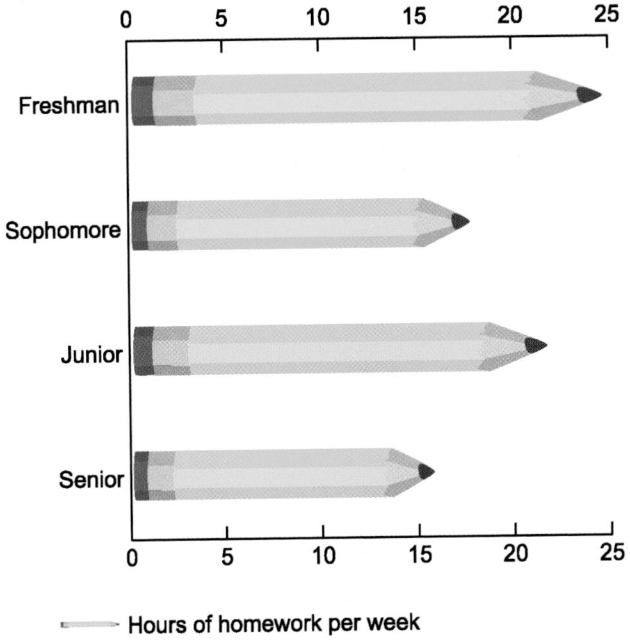

Apply a custom graph design

1. Click **View** on the Application bar, then click **Fit Artboard in Window**.

2. Click the **graph** with the **Selection tool** ▶ .

3. Click **Object** on the Application bar, point to **Graph**, then click **Column**.

   The Graph Column dialog box shows a list of custom designs you can apply to your graph.

4. Click **Pencil**, then verify that Vertically Scaled is selected for the Column Type and that the Rotate Legend Design check box is not checked, as shown in Figure 20.

   (continued)

Figure 20 *Graph Column dialog box*

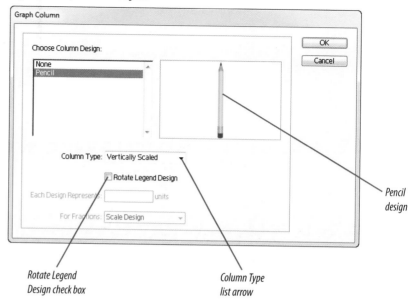

Rotate Legend Design check box

Pencil design

Column Type list arrow

Using the Glyph and OpenType Panels to Obtain Special Characters

OpenType is a type of font formatting. OpenType fonts often come with alternative characters. For example, when the letter f is followed by the letter i, an OpenType font might offer you a ligature character that is one character of the f and i combined. Click Window on the Application bar, point to Type, then click OpenType to specify your preferences for applying alternate characters in OpenType fonts. For example, you can specify that you want to use standard ligatures for a given font, or you could choose to use dingbat characters to make checkboxes or radio buttons. Note that the OpenType panel works hand-in-hand with the Glyphs panel. You can view all the characters in any given font using the Glyphs panel.

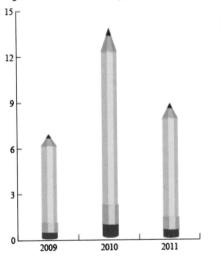

Figure 21 *Pencil custom design applied to the graph*

students with full scholarships

5. Click **OK**, click the **artboard** to deselect the graph, then compare your work to Figure 21.

   The three columns on the graph are replaced with pencils that are each a different length, indicating how many scholarships were given out. Note, however, that the erasers and the points on the pencils are all inconsistent.

6. Save your work.

TIP To remove a custom design from a graph, select the graph, then click None in the Graph Column dialog box.

You selected a custom design in the Graph Design dialog box, you selected Vertically Scaled for the column type, and then you applied the custom design to a graph. The artwork is scaled vertically to represent the graph data.

Create and Apply a
SLIDING-SCALE DESIGN

What You'll Do

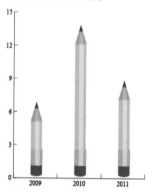

In this lesson, you will define the area on the pencil design that will be affected by a sliding-scale design. Then you will apply a sliding-scale design to the existing graph.

Creating a Sliding-Scale Design and Applying It to a Graph

When you apply a vertically scaled design style to a column graph, the entire design stretches to accommodate the value assigned to it. This expansion may present a problem if the custom design needs to maintain an aspect ratio. For example, a custom logo design might become unreadable if it is stretched too far. For this reason, a vertically scaled design can sometimes be unsatisfactory.

The answer to the problem is the sliding-scale design, which allows you to define a point on the custom design from which the graph will stretch. Thus a portion of the design can be specified to remain at its original size and not stretch. Figure 22 shows an example of a sliding-scale design. Note how only the handles lengthen in the graph, while the "shovels" at the bottom are not scaled.

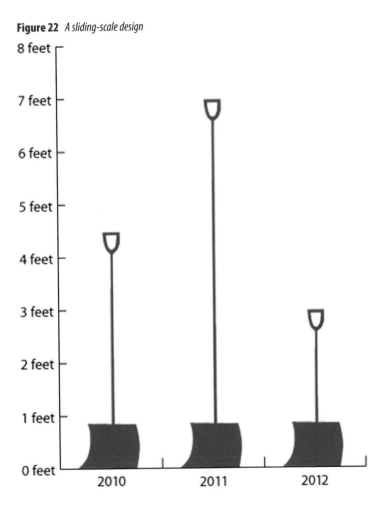

Figure 22 *A sliding-scale design*

Create and apply a sliding-scale design

1. Return to the Pencil view, click **View** on the Application bar, point to **Guides**, click **Clear Guides**, then set the stroke color to Black on the Tools panel.

2. Using the **Line Segment tool** ╲, draw a black line across the pencil, as shown in Figure 23, Part A.

3. Click the **Selection tool** ▶, select the entire line, click **View** on the Application bar, point to **Guides**, then click **Make Guides**.

   The black line turns into a guide, as shown in Figure 23, Part B.

4. Click **View** on the Application bar, point to **Guides**, then verify that Lock Guides is not checked.

5. Select the pencil, the rectangle, and the guide, so that all three objects are selected, as shown in Figure 23, Part C.

TIP Drag a selection marquee around the pencil to make sure you select the rectangle too, or switch to Outline view to see the outline of the rectangle. Because the rectangle has no fill or stroke, it is "invisible" in Preview.

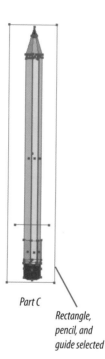

Figure 23 *Creating a sliding-scale design*

Part A — *Short, straight, black line*

Part B — *Line converted to a guide*

Part C — *Rectangle, pencil, and guide selected*

Figure 24 *Graph Column dialog box*

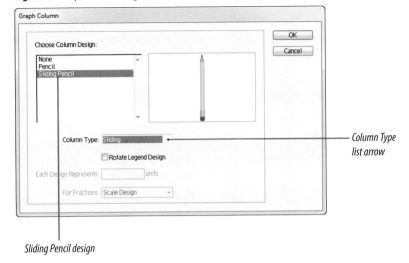

Column Type list arrow

Sliding Pencil design

6. Click **Object** on the Application bar, point to **Graph**, then click **Design**.

7. Click **New Design**, click **Rename**, name the design **Sliding Pencil**, click **OK**, then click **OK** again to close the Graph Design dialog box.

8. Hide the guides, fit the artboard in the window, then select the graph.

9. Click **Object** on the Application bar, point to **Graph**, click **Column**, click **Sliding Pencil**, click **Sliding** from the Column Type list, as shown in Figure 24, then click **OK**.

10. Deselect, then save your work.

    Notice that the metal and the eraser tip of the three pencils and the pencil points remain unscaled and identical despite the varying lengths, as shown in Figure 25.

11. Close the Pencil document.

You created a guide on top of the pencil design to identify the area of the artwork that will not be scaled in the graph. You then saved the new artwork as a new sliding-scale design.

Figure 25 *Completed graph*

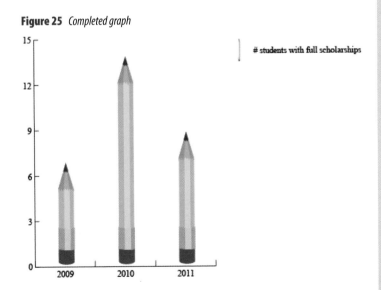

students with full scholarships

Create a graph.

1. Open AI 9-3.ai, then save it as **Nice Weather**.
2. Click the Column Graph tool, then click the artboard.
3. Type **6** in the Width text box, type **4** in the Height text box, then click OK.
4. Delete the number 1.00 from the first cell in the Graph Data window.
5. Press [Tab] to select the next cell in the first row.
6. Type **Rain**, press [Tab], type **Sun**, press [Tab], type **Clouds**, then press [Tab].
7. Click the second cell in the first column, type **June**, press [Enter] (Win) or [return] (Mac), type **July**, press [Enter] (Win) or [return] (Mac), type **August**, then press [Enter] (Win) or [return] (Mac).
8. Enter the rest of the data that is supplied in the upper-left corner of the artboard to fill in the cells underneath Rain, Sun, and Clouds.
9. Close the Graph Data window, saving your changes to it.
10. Move the graph onto the artboard if it is not fully on it.

Edit a graph using the Graph Data window.

1. Delete the text at the top of the artboard.
2. Click the graph to select it.
3. Click Object on the Application bar, point to Graph, then click Data.
4. Click the cell that contains the number 7 and change it to 8.
5. Click the cell that contains the number 20 and change it to 19.
6. Drag the Graph Data window down slightly to view the artboard, then click the Apply button in the Graph Data window.
7. Close the Graph Data window.
8. Save your work.

Use the Group Selection tool.

1. Deselect the graph, then click the Group Selection tool.
2. Click the first black column above the June label, click a second time, then click a third time to select the Rain group.

3. Change the fill color of the selected columns to green.
4. Change the fill color of the Sun group to yellow.
5. Change the fill color of the Clouds group to a shade of blue.
6. Save your work.

Use the Graph Type dialog box.

1. Click the Selection tool, then click the graph.
2. Click Object on the Application bar, point to Graph, then click Type.
3. Click the Add Drop Shadow check box if it is not already selected to add a drop shadow.
4. Click the Graph Options list arrow, then click Value Axis.
5. Click the Length list arrow in the Tick Marks section of the window, and click Full Width if it is not already selected.
6. Click OK.
7. Save your work.

Creating and Designing Graphs

Create a combination graph.

1. Deselect the graph, then, using the Group Selection tool, select the entire Sun group.
2. Click Object on the Application bar, point to Graph, then click Type.
3. Click the Line button.
4. Click the Add Drop Shadow check box to deselect the option.
5. Click the Edge-to-Edge Lines check box.
6. Verify that both the Mark Data Points and Connect Data Points check boxes are checked, then click OK.
7. Click the artboard to deselect the graph.
8. Using the Group Selection tool, select the line that connects the markers and the small corresponding line in the legend.
9. Change the stroke weight of the line to 10 pt.
10. Remove the fill color from the line, then change the stroke color of the line to yellow.
11. Save your work, compare your graph to Figure 26, then close the Nice Weather document.

Create a custom graph design.

1. Open AI 9-4.ai, then save it as **Flower Graph**.
2. Click View on the Application bar, then click Flower.
3. Click View on the Application bar, then click Show Rulers if they are not already showing.
4. Drag two guides from the horizontal ruler. Position one at the very top of the flower and the other at the bottom of the stem.
5. Lock the guides, then set the fill and stroke colors to [None] on the Tools panel.

6. Create a rectangle that is slightly wider than the width of the flower and that snaps to the top and bottom of the guides.
7. Send the rectangle to the back. (*Hint*: If you deselect the rectangle and cannot see it, switch to Outline view, repeat Step 7, then switch back to Preview view.)
8. Select the flower and the rectangle.
9. Click Object on the Application bar, point to Graph, then click Design.
10. Click New Design, click Rename, name the design **Flower**, click OK, then click OK again.
11. Delete the flower artwork at the top of the document window, then hide the guides.

Apply a custom design to a graph.

1. Click View on the Application bar, then click Graph.
2. Select the graph with the Selection tool.
3. Click Object on the Application bar, point to Graph, then click Column.
4. Click Flower, then make sure that Vertically Scaled is chosen for the Column Type.
5. Click the Rotate Legend Design check box to remove the check mark, then click OK.
6. Click the artboard to deselect the graph.
7. Save your work, then compare your graph to Figure 27.

Figure 26 *Completed Skills Review, Part 1*

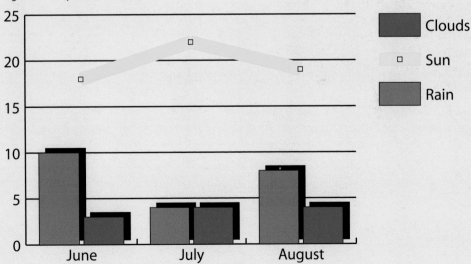

Create and apply a sliding-scale design.

1. Click the graph with the Selection tool.
2. Click Object on the Application bar, point to Graph, then click Column.
3. Click the Column Type list arrow, then click Repeating.

4. Type **10** in the units text box next to "Each Design Represents."
5. Verify that there is not a check mark in the Rotate Legend Design check box.

6. Click the For Fractions list arrow, then click Chop Design.
7. Click OK, then save your work.
8. Deselect the graph, compare your graph to Figure 28, then close the Flower Graph document.

Figure 27 *Completed Skills Review, Part 2*

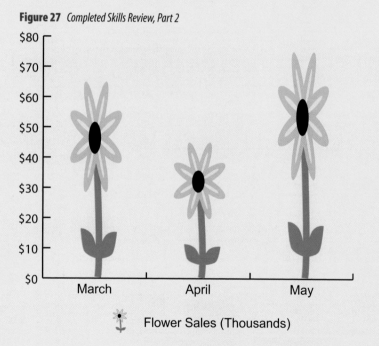

Figure 28 *Completed Skills Review, Part 3*

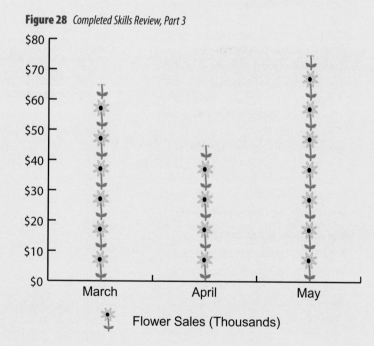

Your apartment is heated and cooled electrically, and your monthly bills vary month to month. You decide to create a graph to get an idea of which months are most costly.

1. Open AI 9-5.ai, then save it as **Electrical Expenses**.
2. Create a 6" wide by 4" tall column graph.
3. Delete 1.00 from the first cell, then press [Tab].
4. Type **Monthly Electrical Expenses**. (*Hint*: Don't worry if the title is not in full view.)
5. Enter the data as shown in Figure 29.
6. Close the Graph Data window, saving your changes to the data.
7. Change the fill color of the graph columns and legend box to the Jade swatch.
8. Place a drop shadow behind the columns.
9. Click Object on the Application bar, point to Graph, click Type, click the Graph Options list arrow, click Value Axis, type **$** in the Prefix text box, then click OK.
10. Click Object on the Application bar, point to Graph, click Type, click the Graph Options list arrow, click Value Axis, click the Length list arrow under Tick Marks, click Full Width, then click OK.
11. Compare your graph to Figure 30, save your work, then close the Electrical Expenses document.

Figure 29 *Project Builder 1 data*

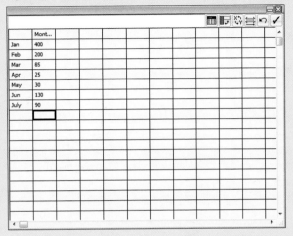

Figure 30 *Completed Project Builder 1*

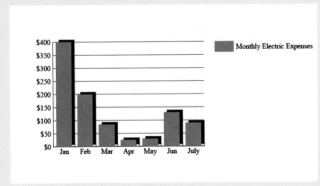

You own an independent market research consulting business that specializes in the television industry. You have recently conducted a survey of 1000 people who describe their television-watching habits as "regularly watch television." The question they were asked was, "What is your favorite TV program?" Your research assistants have tabulated the data and supplied the breakdown to you as a column graph in an Illustrator file. You note that the words under the columns are running into each other, and you decide the graph would work better as a pie chart.

1. Open AI 9-6.ai, then save it as **Television**.
2. Create a 6" wide by 4" tall column graph.
3. Delete 1.00 from the first cell, then press [Tab].
4. Type **What is your favorite TV program?**
5. Using the information at the top of the artboard, enter the rest of the data.
6. Close the Graph Data window, saving your changes to the data.
7. Verify that the graph is selected, click Object on the Application bar, point to Graph, then click Type.
8. Click the Pie button, remove the check mark in the Add Drop Shadow check box, if necessary, then click OK.
9. Click Object on the Application bar, point to Graph, then click Data.
10. Click the Transpose row/column button in the Graph Data window. (*Hint*: The Transpose row/column button is the second button in the Graph Data window.)
11. Close the Graph Data window, save changes, then delete the information at the top of the artboard.
12. Choose colors that you like for each section of the pie graph and the corresponding legend box.
13. Save your work, compare your graph to Figure 31, then close the Television document.

Creating and Designing Graphs

Figure 31 *Completed Project Builder 2*

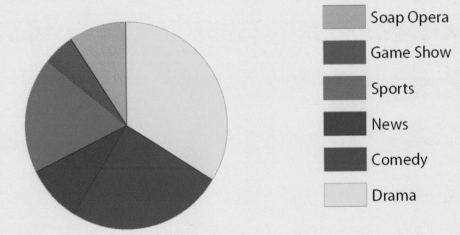

What is your favorite TV program?

Soap Opera

Game Show

Sports

News

Comedy

Drama

You are a freelance designer, and you are hired by a small market research company that specializes in television. They are submitting an annual report to one of their network clients. The report contains a number of pie charts. They want you to design a look that is more eye-catching.

1. Open AI 9-7.ai, then save it as **Designer Pie**.
2. Click the Group Selection tool, then click the largest wedge two times. (*Hint*: The largest wedge and the Drama legend box are selected.)
3. Change the fill of the two objects to any red.
4. Moving clockwise, fill the remaining wedges and legend boxes with any of the orange, yellow, green, blue, and violet swatches, respectively.
5. Deselect all, click the Direct Selection tool, drag a marquee to select the pie chart only, then scale the chart 150%.
6. Deselect, click the Type tool, type **34%** on top of the red wedge, change the font size to 27 pt, then set the fill color to White.
7. Moving clockwise, type the following percentage values on the remaining wedges: **25**, **9**, **18**, **5**, and **9**. (*Hint*: Change the fill color of the values on top of the yellow and orange wedges to Black.)
8. Using the Direct Selection tool, move each word from the legend over its corresponding wedge. (*Hint*: The words "Game Show" and "Soap Opera" must be positioned outside of their corresponding wedge because they are too long.)

9. Change the fill color of Sports and Drama to White.
10. Hide the legend boxes, then reposition the What is your favorite TV program? text, and any other objects if necessary.
11. Select only the wedges of the graph, using the Direct Selection tool.

12. Click Effect on the Application bar, point to Stylize, click Round Corners, type **.139**, then click OK.
13. Apply a 2-point Black stroke to the pie wedges.
14. Save your work, compare your graph to Figure 32, then close Designer Pie.

Figure 32 *Completed Design Project*

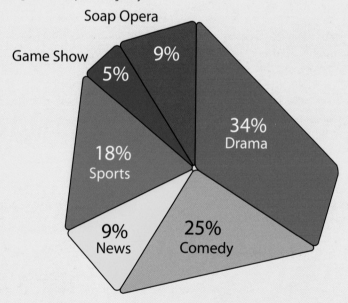

What is your favorite TV program?

Creating and Designing Graphs

You are the chief designer of an in-house design group in a large department store. The head of the Digital Department has asked you to help with a presentation that shows how computers, scanners, and printers have been selling in comparison to one another over the last four weeks. Specifically, she wants you to create a graph that emphasizes how many more scanners she sells each week than computers or printers. You have gathered the weekly sales data from each of the three departments and collected it in the table below. You are now ready to start work on your graph.

	Computers	Printers	Scanners
Week One	11	13	55
Week Two	12	15	40
Week Three	14	6	61
Week Four	9	11	35

1. Draw a simple bar graph on scrap paper, showing the sales relationships among the three products.
2. Think about what would be the best type of graph to convey the data.
3. Decide the colors and fonts that you will use in the graph.
4. Create a new CMYK Color document, then save it as **Sales**.
5. Create a column graph that is 4" wide by 4" high.
6. Enter the data from the table above in the Graph Data window.
7. Close the Graph Data window, saving changes to it.
8. Select the Scanners group using the Group Selection tool, then apply the line graph type to it.
9. Change the color and thickness of the line graph so that it is easy to see.
10. Format the rest of the graph (labels, Printers group, and Computers group) if desired.
11. Save your work, compare your graph to Figure 33, then close the Sales document.

Figure 33 *Completed Portfolio Project*

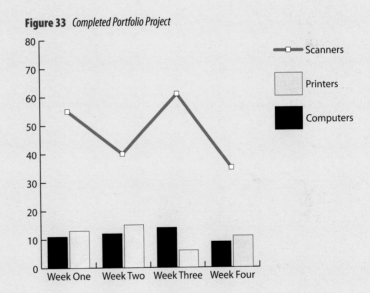

CHAPTER 10 CREATING 3D OBJECTS

1. Extrude objects
2. Revolve objects
3. Manipulate surface shading and lighting
4. Map artwork to 3D objects
5. Work with a perspective grid

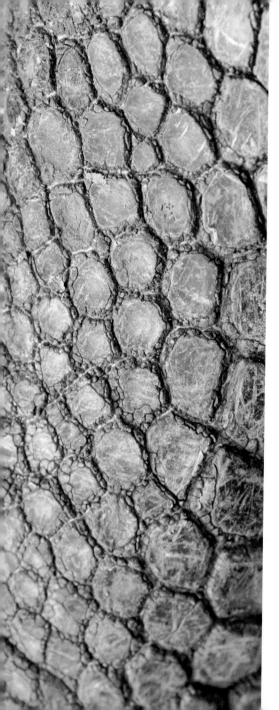

CREATING
3D OBJECTS

Creating 3D objects is one of the more exciting features in Illustrator CS5. With unprecedented ease, you can transform a simple two-dimensional (2D) object into an eye-popping three-dimensional (3D) graphic. You can extrude 2D objects to give them depth, and you can add interesting details by applying a bevel edge. You can revolve 2D objects around an axis to create stunning 3D graphics, complete with surface shading and highlights. You have a number of options for manipulating that surface shading. Apply diffuse shading for subtle highlights or apply plastic shading to make the object reflect light as though its surface were shiny. You can even add and delete light sources to dramatically change the way a 3D graphic is lit. If that's not enough, once you've designed the 3D object, you can "map" 2D graphics, making them appear to "wrap around" the 3D object. Very cool!

You'll also enjoy working with the perspective grid, new to Illustrator CS5. The perspective grid offers you a number of powerful options for drawing and creating objects in perfect perspective.

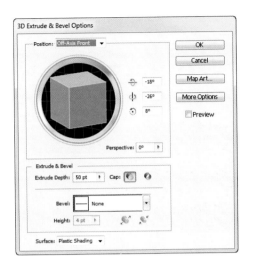

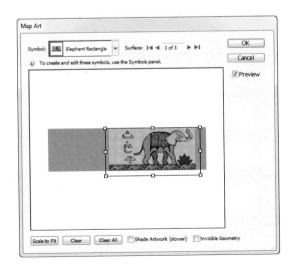

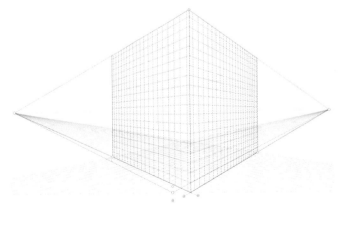

Extrude
OBJECTS

What You'll Do

In this lesson, you will use the 3D Extrude & Bevel effect to extrude objects.

Extruding Objects

Illustrator's **Extrude & Bevel** effect makes two-dimensional objects three-dimensional. A two-dimensional object has two axes, which are the X axis representing the width and the Y axis representing the height. When you **extrude** an object, you add depth to an object by extending it on its Z axis, as shown in Figure 1. An object's Z axis is always perpendicular to the object's front surface.

Figure 2 shows four 2D objects before and after being extruded. Note the changes to each object's fill color on the front surface and the light and dark shadings on the other surfaces. These shadings create the 3D effect and are applied automatically when the Extrude & Bevel effect is applied.

QUICK TIP

3D effects may produce fills with flaws. These are usually screen aberrations that are an issue with your monitor and don't show when you print the document.

You determine the degree of extrusion by changing the Extrude Depth value in the 3D Extrude & Bevel Options dialog box,

Figure 1 *Identifying the Z-axis on an extruded object*

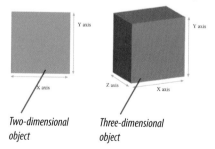

Two-dimensional object

Three-dimensional object

Figure 2 *Four objects before and after being extruded*

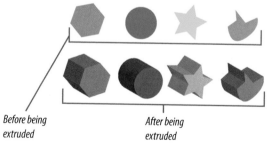

Before being extruded

After being extruded

Creating 3D Objects

shown in Figure 3. Extrusion depth is measured in points. The greater the value, the more the object is extended on its Z axis, as shown in Figure 4.

Use the Cap buttons in the 3D Extrude & Bevel Options dialog box to make extruded objects appear solid or hollow. The Turn cap on for solid appearance (Solid cap) button is the default setting. It produces an object in which the front and back faces (surfaces) are solid, as shown in Figure 5. The Turn cap off for hollow appearance (Hollow cap) button

Figure 3 *3D Extrude & Bevel Options dialog box*

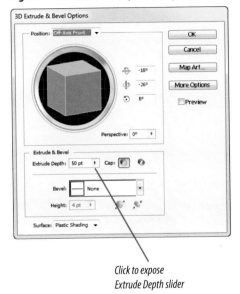

Click to expose
Extrude Depth slider

Figure 4 *Two objects extruded to different depths*

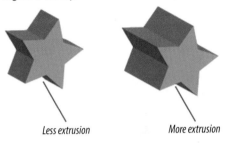

Less extrusion   *More extrusion*

Figure 5 *Activating the Solid cap button*

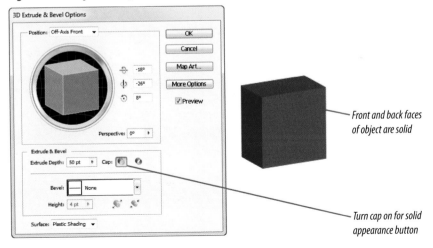

Front and back faces
of object are solid

Turn cap on for solid
appearance button

makes the front and back faces invisible, producing an object that appears hollow, as shown in Figure 6.

Rotating 3D Objects

The 3D Extrude & Bevel Options dialog box offers controls for rotating extruded objects.

You can rotate the object manually by dragging the rotation cube, shown in Figure 7. The three text boxes to the right of the cube represent the selected object's X, Y, and Z axes. When you rotate the cube, the values in these text boxes update to reflect the changes you make. You may also enter values in these text boxes to rotate the selected object at specific angles.

Once an object has been extruded, you can use the rotation cube to view any surface of the object, such as the front, back, left, or right. The surface shading will update whenever you rotate an object.

Figure 6 *Activating the Hollow cap button*

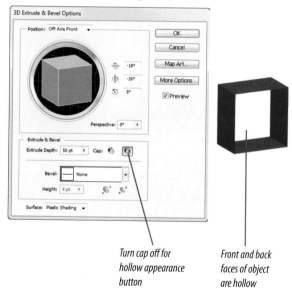

Turn cap off for hollow appearance button

Front and back faces of object are hollow

Figure 7 *Options for rotating 3D objects*

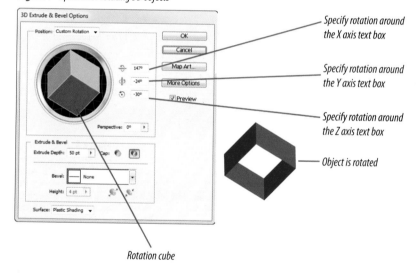

Specify rotation around the X axis text box

Specify rotation around the Y axis text box

Specify rotation around the Z axis text box

Object is rotated

Rotation cube

Creating 3D Objects

Extruding Compound Paths

Applying the Extrude & Bevel effect to a compound path can yield results that are visually interesting. Figure 8 shows a simple compound path, which, in this case, is a circle with a square "knocked out" from its center, positioned in front of a light blue square. Figure 9 shows the same object after being extruded. Generally speaking, the more surfaces that an object has, the more interesting the 3D effect will be. Figure 10 shows a complex compound path, and Figure 11 shows the results of applying the Extrude & Bevel effect.

Figure 8 *Simple compound path*

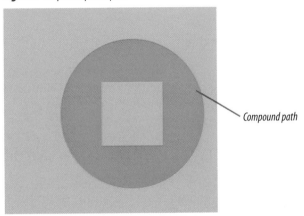

Compound path

Figure 9 *Simple compound path, extruded*

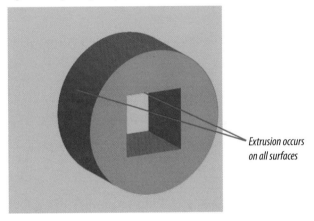

Extrusion occurs on all surfaces

Figure 10 *Complex compound path*

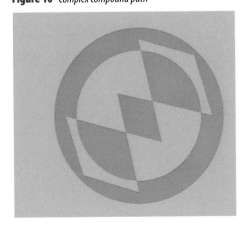

Figure 11 *Complex compound path, extruded*

Applying a Bevel Edge to an Extruded Object

A **bevel** is the angle that one surface makes with another when they are not at right angles. Figure 12 shows an example of an object with a bevel edge.

The Bevel menu, shown in Figure 13, offers ten pre-defined bevel shapes that you can apply to the edges of extruded objects. The width of the bevel edge is controlled by the Height slider. Figure 14 shows six objects, each with a different bevel shape applied to its edge. Each bevel has a width of 4 points.

Figure 12 *Identifying a bevel edge*

Figure 14 *Six objects with bevel shapes applied to edges*

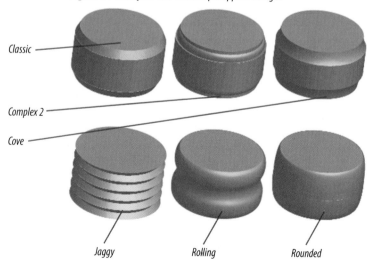

Classic

Complex 2

Cove

Jaggy

Rolling

Rounded

Figure 13 *Viewing the Bevel menu*

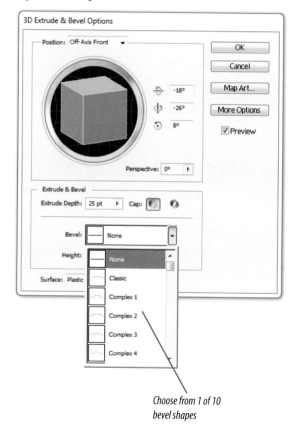

Choose from 1 of 10 bevel shapes

Creating 3D Objects

As shown in Figure 15, text can be extruded without first having to convert it to outlines. Once extruded, you can add a bevel edge to text. Figure 16 shows the same text with the Rounded bevel shape.

Because many letters are complex shapes, applying a bevel to extruded text often causes problems. Simply put, the shapes are too intricate to be rendered with a bevel edge. In Figure 16, the two Ts and the E handle the bevel edge quite well, but you can see that the X is becoming disfigured. In Figure 17, the Classic bevel shape has been applied, but it isn't rendered properly.

Whenever Illustrator is having difficulty rendering an object with a bevel edge, a warning appears in the 3D Extrude & Bevel Options dialog box, as shown in Figure 18. When problems do occur, sometimes there is no solution. Your best bet, however, is to reduce the width of the bevel.

Figure 15 *Extruding text*

Figure 16 *Extruded text with the Rounded bevel shape applied*

The "X" is becoming disfigured

Figure 17 *Identifying problems with a bevel edge*

The "X" isn't rendered properly

Figure 18 *Warning regarding a bevel edge*

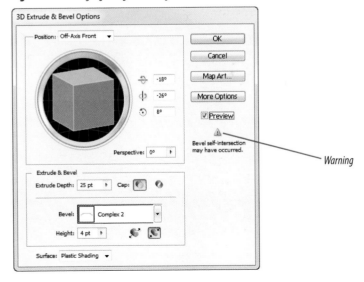

Warning

Figure 19 shows the same text with the same Classic bevel shape shown in Figure 17, but in this figure, the bevel width has been reduced from four points to three points. The dialog box continues to warn that there may be problems with the bevel edge. Though that may be the case, the problems are less obvious.

When you apply a bevel shape to an object's edge, you can decide how the bevel will be applied to the object using the Bevel Extent In and Bevel Extent Out buttons in the 3D Extrude & Bevel Options dialog box. The Bevel Extent In button produces a bevel edge that carves away from the edge of the existing object. The Bevel Extent Out button adds the bevel edge to the object. Figure 20 shows the Bevel Extent Out and Bevel Extent In buttons. Generally speaking, the Bevel Extent In option is the better choice, because it stays within the already-established boundaries of the object.

Figure 19 *Reducing the width of a bevel edge*

*The "X" is rendered
fairly well*

Figure 20 *Bevel Extent Out and Bevel Extent In buttons*

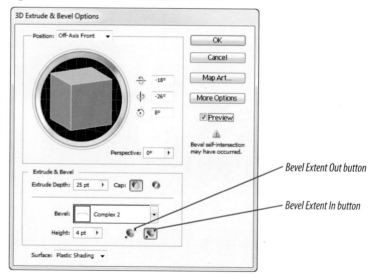

Bevel Extent Out button

Bevel Extent In button

Creating 3D Objects

Figure 21 *Applying the 3D Extrude & Bevel effect*

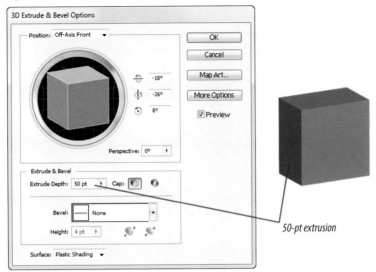

50-pt extrusion

Figure 22 *Viewing the effect on the Appearance panel*

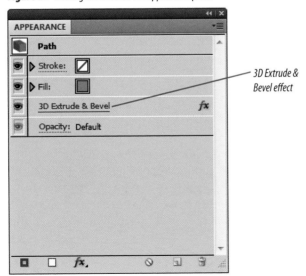

3D Extrude &
Bevel effect

Extrude an object

1. Open AI 10-1.ai, then save it as **Extrude Objects**.
2. Click **View** on the Application bar, then click **Blue Square**.
3. Click the **Selection tool** ▶, select the blue square, click **View** on the Application bar, then click **Hide Edges**.
4. Click **Effect** on the Application bar, point to **3D**, then click **Extrude & Bevel**.
5. Position the 3D Extrude & Bevel Options dialog box so that you can see the blue square, then click the **Preview check box**.

   As shown in Figure 21, the blue square is extruded 50 points on the Z axis.
6. Click the **Extrude Depth list arrow**, drag the **slider** to 96 pt, then click **OK**.
7. Click the **Appearance icon** ◉ in the stack of collapsed panels to display the Appearance panel.

TIP If you do not see the Appearance icon in the stack of collapsed panels, click Window on the Application bar, then click Appearance to display the Appearance panel.

As shown in Figure 22, the Appearance panel lists the 3D Extrude & Bevel effect applied to the object.

(continued)

8. Click **3D Extrude & Bevel** on the Appearance panel to open the dialog box, then click the **Preview check box**.

9. Click the **Hollow cap button** 📄.

   The object's front and back "capping faces" become transparent, making the object appear hollow.

10. Click **OK**, then compare your work to Figure 23.

You applied the 3D Extrude & Bevel effect to a selected object, increased the depth of the extrusion, then changed the cap so that the 3D object would appear hollow.

Extrude and rotate an object

1. Click **View** on the Application bar, then click **Orange Star**.

2. Hide edges for this object and objects in all remaining lessons in this chapter.

3. Click the **star**, click **Effect** on the Application bar, point to **3D**, then click **Extrude & Bevel**. Click the **Preview check box**, then change the Extrude Depth value to 60 pt.

4. Position your cursor over the top-front edge of the rotation cube so that a rotate cursor appears, as shown in Figure 24.

(continued)

Figure 23 *Viewing the extrusion with hollow caps*

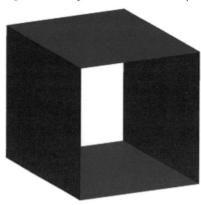

Figure 24 *Manipulating the rotation cube manually*

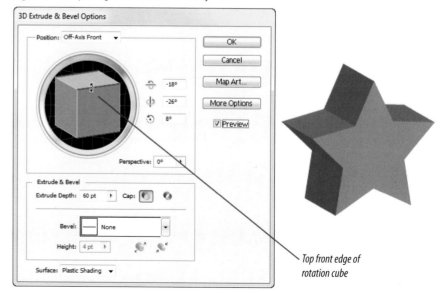

Top front edge of rotation cube

Figure 25 *Entering rotation values*

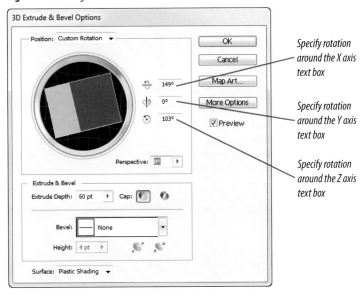

Specify rotation around the X axis text box

Specify rotation around the Y axis text box

Specify rotation around the Z axis text box

Figure 26 *Viewing the rotated star*

5. Click and drag to rotate the cube, noting that the value in the Specify rotation around the X axis text box is the only value that changes as you drag.

6. Experiment with different rotations by dragging the rotation cube from all sides and note the changes to the orange star object on the page.

7. Double-click the **Specify rotation around the X axis text box**, as shown in Figure 25, to select its contents, type **149**, making sure you have deleted the negative sign that was there, then press **[Tab]**.

8. Type **0** in the Specify rotation around the Y axis text box, press **[Tab]**, type **103** in the Specify rotation around the Z axis text box, press **[Tab]**, then compare your dialog box to Figure 25.

9. Click **OK**, then compare your work to Figure 26.

You applied the 3D Extrude & Bevel effect to a star-shaped object, then manipulated the rotation cube to rotate the object.

Extrude a compound path

1. Click **View** on the Application bar, then click **Target**.

2. Select all three circles, click **Object** on the Application bar, point to **Compound Path**, then click **Make**.

3. Click **Effect** on the Application bar, point to **3D**, then click **Extrude & Bevel**.

4. Click the **Preview check box**, then change the Extrude Depth value to 100 pt.

5. Experiment with different rotations by dragging the rotation cube from all sides.

6. Double-click the **Specify rotation around the X axis text box**, make sure the negative sign is also selected, type **28**, then press **[Tab]**.

7. Type **-26** in the Specify rotation around the Y axis text box, press **[Tab]**, type **8** in the Specify rotation around the Z axis text box, then press **[Tab]**.

8. Click **OK**, then compare your work to Figure 27.

You created a compound path, applied the 3D Extrude & Bevel effect, then rotated the graphic, all the time noting the visual effect created by applying the effect to a compound path.

Figure 27 *Viewing the 3D Extrude & Bevel effect applied to a compound path*

Figure 28 *Text outlines with the Classic bevel shape applied*

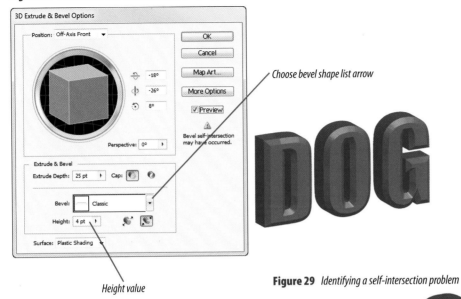

Choose bevel shape list arrow

Height value

Figure 29 *Identifying a self-intersection problem*

problem

Figure 30 *Viewing the Complex 2 bevel*

1. Click **View** on the Application bar, then click **DOG**.

   The text has been converted to outlines and made into a compound path.

2. Click the **Selection tool** , click any letter of the text, click **Effect** on the Application bar, point to **3D**, then click **Extrude & Bevel**.

3. Click the **Preview check box**, then change the Extrude Depth value to 25 pt.

4. Click the **Choose bevel shape list arrow**, click **Classic**, verify that the Height value is set to 4 pt, then compare your screen to Figure 28.

5. Note that the Bevel Extent In button is pressed, click the **Bevel Extent Out button** , then note the change to the graphic, as shown in Figure 29.

6. Note the warning in the dialog box that says Bevel self-intersection may have occurred, and note the problem with the graphic circled in the figure.

7. Click the **Bevel Extent In button** , click the **Choose bevel shape list arrow**, then click **Complex 2**.

   Your graphic should resemble Figure 30.

8. Click **OK**, save your work, then close Extrude Objects.

You applied two bevel shapes to extruded text outlines. You also experimented with the Bevel Extent In and Bevel Extent Out buttons.

Revolve OBJECTS

What You'll Do

In this lesson, you will use the 3D effect to revolve objects.

Revolving Objects

Revolving is another method that Illustrator provides for applying a 3D effect to a 2D object. Imagine taking a large, hard cover book and opening it so much that its front and back covers touch. The pages would fan out from one cover to the other, all of them with their inside edges adhering to the spine of the book. This example is similar to what happens when the Revolve effect is applied to an object.

Revolving an object "sweeps" a path in a circular direction around the Y axis. Figure 31 shows a familiar shape—the letter E—before and after the Revolve effect is applied. The blue selection marks show the original path, and the left edge of that path is the Y axis around which the path was revolved. The surface shading is applied automatically with the effect.

Figure 31 *The letter E before and after being revolved*

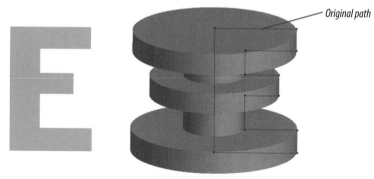

Original path

Creating 3D Objects

By default, an object is revolved around a vertical axis that represents its leftmost point. An example of this is shown in

Figure 32. The 3D Revolve Options dialog box, shown in Figure 33, also offers the option to revolve the object from its right

edge. Revolving the object from its right edge yields an entirely different result, as shown in Figure 34.

Figure 32 *Revolving an object around its left edge*

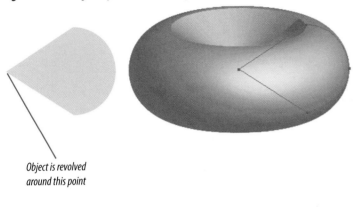

Object is revolved
around this point

Figure 33 *Choosing the edge for the revolution*

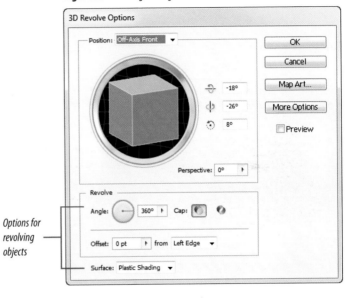

Options for
revolving
objects

Figure 34 *Revolving an object around its right edge*

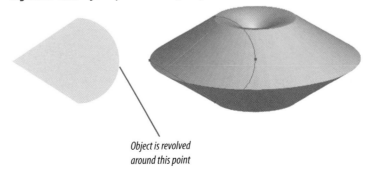

Object is revolved
around this point

Because a revolution occurs around a vertical axis, in most cases, the starting path will depict half of the object you want to revolve. This is more easily explained with examples. Figure 35 shows the original path and the result of applying the Revolve effect to that path. Note how the original path is a two-dimensional half of the revolved three-dimensional object.

Once revolved, an object can be rotated by manipulating the rotation cube in the 3D Revolve Options dialog box. This feature is extremely powerful with a revolved graphic. You can use the rotation cube to present all surfaces of the graphic. Figure 36 shows four sides of the bottle graphic, all of them created by manipulating the rotation cube.

Figure 35 *Identifying the path used to produce the revolved 3D graphic*

Figure 36 *A revolved graphic rotated four ways*

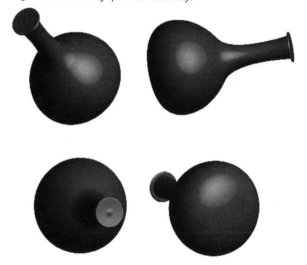

Creating 3D Objects

Revolving Multiple Objects

You can apply the Revolve effect to multiple paths simultaneously, and you can revolve open or closed paths. As shown in Figure 37, when you select multiple paths and apply the Revolve effect, each path is revolved around its own axis. For this reason, it is often best to align the left edges of multiple paths on the same Y axis, as shown in Figure 38.

As the figure shows, aligning separate paths on the same Y axis can be useful when revolving. However, unwanted results can occur when rotating those paths, even when they are aligned on the same Y axis. Figure 39 shows the same two paths being rotated. Note that because they are separate paths, they rotate separately, each on its own axis. This problem can be resolved by grouping the paths.

Figure 37 *Multiple paths revolved on their own axis*

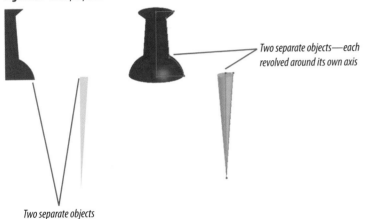

Two separate objects—each revolved around its own axis

Two separate objects

Figure 38 *Multiple paths aligned, then revolved*

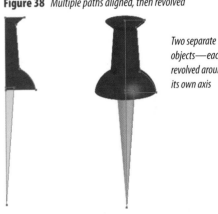

Two separate objects aligned on their left edges

Two separate objects—each revolved around its own axis

Figure 39 *Multiple paths rotated on their own axis*

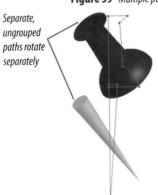

Separate, ungrouped paths rotate separately

Revolving Grouped Objects

When grouped, multiple paths are revolved around a single axis. This can yield unexpected results. In Figure 40, the two paths (left) are grouped, but they don't share the same Y axis. When revolved, both paths revolve around the leftmost axis.

When multiple paths are grouped and revolved, they will also rotate together. Figure 41 shows four versions of two grouped and revolved paths after they have been rotated in the 3D Revolve Options dialog box. In every case, the two paths rotate together because they are grouped. Compare this to Figure 39, in which the two ungrouped paths rotated separately, each on their own axes.

Figure 40 *Two grouped paths revolved around a single Y-axis*

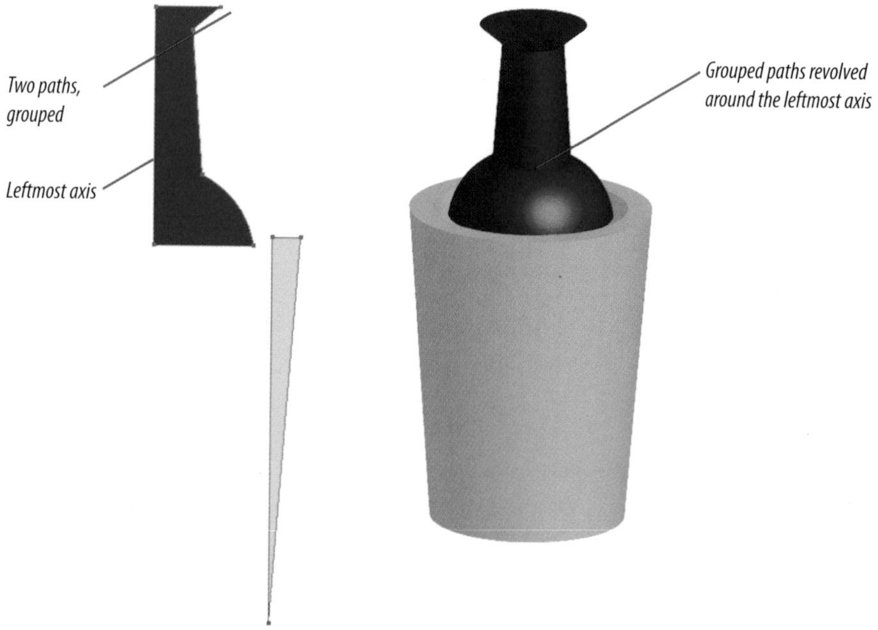

Two paths, grouped

Leftmost axis

Grouped paths revolved around the leftmost axis

Figure 41 *Four grouped paths after being revolved and rotated*

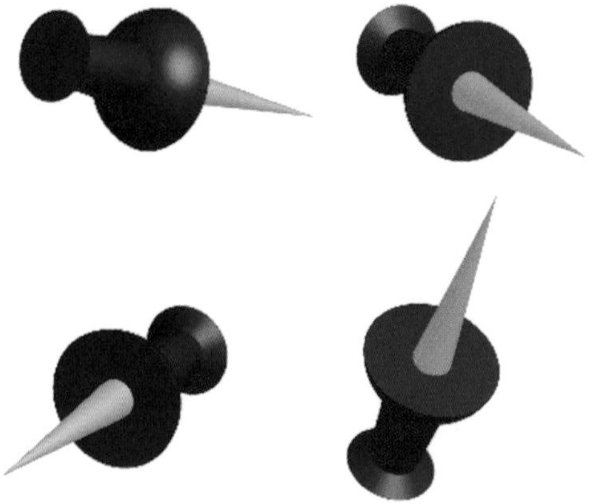

Creating 3D Objects

Applying an Offset to a Revolved Object

By default, an object is revolved around a vertical axis that represents its leftmost point. Figure 42 illustrates this point. Increasing the Offset value in the 3D Revolve Options dialog box, as shown in Figure 43, increases how far from the Y axis the object is revolved. Figure 44 shows the same revolved object shown in Figure 42 with a 90-point offset value. The path revolves around the same Y axis, but it does so at a distance of 90 points. Figure 45, in which the object has been rotated, shows the offset more clearly. Try to visualize that the object is a series of half circles rotated around a single vertical axis—90 points from that vertical axis.

Figure 42 *Object revolved around its leftmost point*

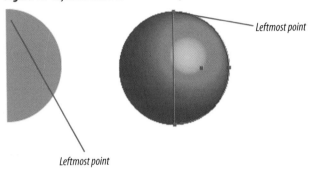

Leftmost point

Leftmost point

Figure 43 *Offset slider in the 3D Revolve Options dialog box*

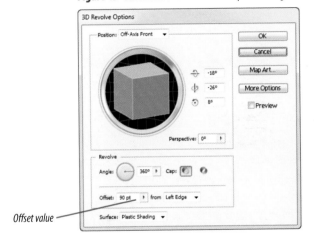

Offset value

Figure 44 *Object revolved with a 90-point offset from its Y-axis*

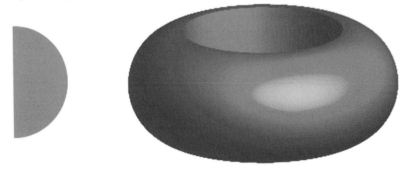

Figure 45 *Rotated object shows 90-point offset more clearly*

Revolve an object

1. Open AI 10-2.ai, then save it as **Green Bottle**.

2. Click the **Selection tool** ▸ , click the **green object**, click **View** on the Application bar, then click **Hide Edges**.

3. Click **Effect** on the Application bar, point to **3D**, click **Revolve**, then click the **Preview check box**.

   As shown in Figure 46, the object is revolved on its axis and appears as a bottle. Highlights and shadows are applied automatically.

4. Click **OK**, save your work, then close Green Bottle.

You revolved a simple object to produce a three-dimensional graphic.

Revolve multiple objects

1. Open AI 10-3.ai, then save it as **Revolve Objects**.

2. Select the second row of blue objects, click **Effect** on the Application bar, point to **3D**, then click **Revolve**.

3. Click the **Preview check box**.

   Each object revolves on its own axis.

4. Click **OK**, then compare your work to Figure 47.

   The graphic on the left has a hard edge because the original object was a rectangle. The round edge of the original object on the right produced a 3D graphic that also has a round edge.

5. Select the second row of red objects, click **Effect** on the Application bar, point to **3D**, then click **Revolve**.

   (continued)

Figure 46 *Revolving an object*

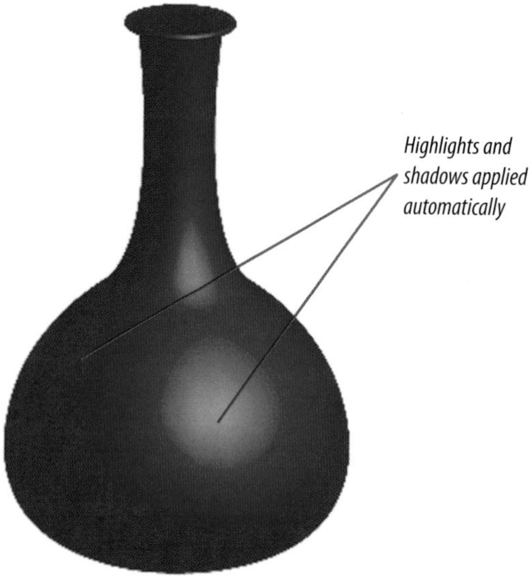

Highlights and shadows applied automatically

Figure 47 *Revolving multiple objects*

Figure 48 *Revolving three objects*

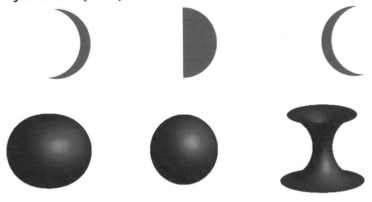

Figure 49 *Rotating a revolved object*

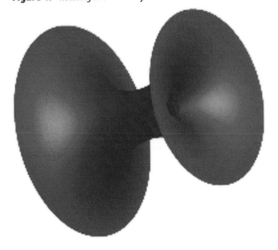

6. Click **OK**, deselect all, then compare your work to Figure 48.

   The first two graphics produced spheres when revolved, but only the middle graphic is a perfect sphere. The two crescent shapes, because they face in opposite directions, produce two drastically different results when revolved.

7. Select the rightmost red object, click **3D Revolve** on the Appearance panel, manipulate the rotation cube to rotate the graphic any way that you like, then click **OK**.

   Figure 49 shows one possible result.

8. Save your work, then close Revolve Objects.

You selected multiple objects, applied the 3D Revolve effect, then noted that each object revolved on its own axis. You compared the results with the original objects, then rotated one of the revolved objects.

Revolve grouped objects

1. Open AI 10-4.ai, then save it as **Push Pins**.
2. Click **View** on the Application bar, click **Green Pin**, then select the two objects in the Green Pin view.

TIP The two objects in Green Pin view are not grouped.

3. Click **Effect** on the Application bar, point to **3D**, then click **Revolve**.
4. Click the **Preview check box**, then note the effect on the objects on the page.
5. Manipulate the rotation cube in any direction.

   As shown in Figure 50, the two objects are each rotated on their own axis and the illustration is no longer realistic.

TIP Because your rotation will differ, your results will differ from the figure.

6. Click **OK**, click **View** on the Application bar, click **Red Pin**, click one of the objects in the Red Pin view.

TIP The two objects are grouped.

7. Click **Effect** on the Application bar, point to **3D**, click **Revolve**, then click the **Preview check box**.

   As shown in Figure 51, because the two objects are grouped, they are both revolved around the same axis.

(continued)

Figure 50 *Rotating revolved objects that are not grouped*

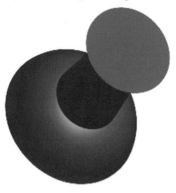

Figure 51 *Two grouped objects revolved around the same axis*

Creating 3D Objects

Figure 52 *Two grouped objects revolved around the same axis*

Figure 53 *Rotating revolved objects that are grouped*

8. Click **OK**, click **View** on the Application bar, click **Blue Pin**, select the two objects, click **Object** on the Application bar, then click **Group**.

9. Click **Effect** on the Application bar, point to **3D**, click **Revolve**, then click the **Preview check box**.

   As shown in Figure 52, the two grouped objects are revolved around the same axis. Because they both share the same axis (their left edge) the illustration is realistic.

TIP The selection edges are showing in the figure so that you can see the left edge that both graphics share.

10. Manipulate the rotation cube in any direction that you like.

    Figure 53 shows one possible result.

11. Click **OK**, save your work, then close Push Pins.

You explored the results of revolving grouped and ungrouped objects. With the green pin, you noted that ungrouped objects cannot be rotated together. With the red pin, you noted that grouped objects are revolved around the same axis. With the blue pin, you noted that grouped objects can be rotated together.

Offset a revolved object

1. Open AI 10-5.ai, then save it as **Desk Lamp**.

2. Select the silver object, click **Effect** on the Application bar, point to **3D**, click **Revolve**, then click **OK**.

3. Select the gold diagonal line, click **Effect** on the Application bar, point to **3D**, click **Revolve**, then click the **Preview check box**.

   As shown in Figure 54, the object's leftmost point is the axis around which it is revolved.

   (continued)

Figure 54 *Revolving an object around its leftmost point*

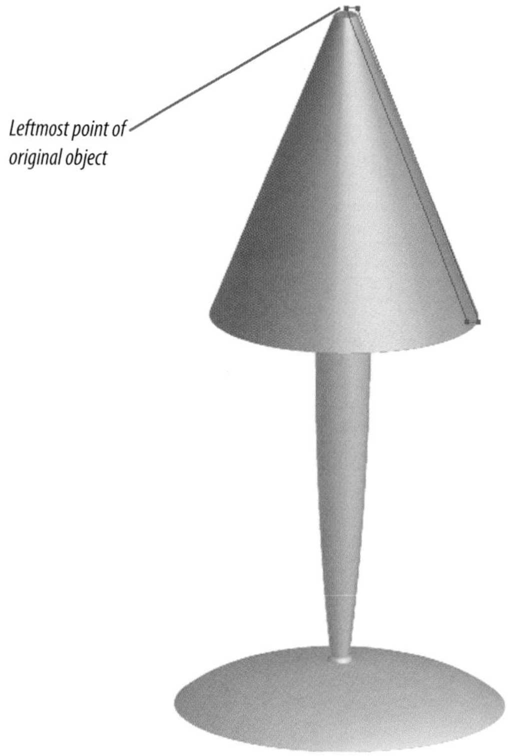

Leftmost point of
original object

4. Double-click the **value in the Offset text box**, type **50**, press **[Tab]**, then compare your work to Figure 55.

   The object is revolved at a radius that is 50 points from its axis.

5. Click **OK**, save your work, then close Desk Lamp.

You used an increased offset value to manipulate how an object is revolved in relation to its axis.

Figure 55 *Revolving an object with a 50-pt offset from its axis*

50-pt offset from leftmost point

Manipulate Surface
SHADING AND LIGHTING

What You'll Do

In this lesson, you will familiarize yourself with the controls that allow you to manipulate the highlight effects of a 3D object.

Applying Surface Shading

When the Extrude & Bevel effect or the Revolve effect is applied to an object, surface shading and lighting are applied automatically. However, you can manipulate these effects.

Surface shading controls how the object's surface appears. When an object is revolved, four surface shadings are available:

Wireframe, No Shading, Diffuse Shading, and Plastic Shading. Examples of all four are shown in Figure 56.

Plastic shading is the default surface shade. With plastic shading, the object reflects light as though it were made of a shiny plastic material. Distinct highlight areas appear on the surface of an object.

Diffuse shading offers a surface that reflects light in a soft, diffuse pattern. With Diffuse Shading, no distinct highlights appear on the surface of the object.

The Wireframe option makes all surfaces transparent and shows the object's geometry. The No Shading option, as its name suggests, applies no new shading to the object. Its surface is identical to that of the 2D object.

Manipulating Lighting Controls

When you choose Diffuse Shading or Plastic Shading, a number of lighting controls are available for you to manipulate the lighting effects that are applied to the object automatically.

Lighting Intensity controls the strength of the light on the object. The range for lighting intensity is 0-100, with 100 being the default.

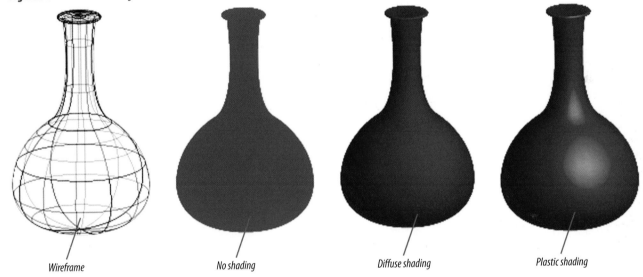

Figure 56 *Four surface shading choices*

Wireframe   *No shading*   *Diffuse shading*   *Plastic shading*

Ambient Light determines how the object is lit globally. The range for Ambient Light is 0-100. Any changes that you make with the Ambient Light slider affect the brightness of the object uniformly, though the effect is much more pronounced in the shadow areas than in the highlights. Decreasing the ambient light noticeably makes the shadow areas darker, which increases the overall contrast of the object, from shadow to highlight. Figure 57 shows two objects, one with 60% ambient light and one with 20% ambient light.

Highlight Intensity controls how intense a highlight appears. The more intense the highlight, the more white it appears. Figure 58 shows two objects, one with 100% highlight intensity and one with 60% highlight intensity. Note that at 100%, the highlight is too white and "glaring." At 60%, the highlight is a good mixture of white and the object's color.

Highlight Size controls how large the highlights appear on the object.

Blend Steps controls how smoothly the shading appears on the object's surface and is most visible in the transition from the

Figure 57 *Comparing ambient lighting*

60% ambient lighting

20% ambient lighting

Figure 58 *Comparing highlight intensity*

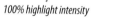

100% highlight intensity

60% highlight intensity

highlight areas to the diffusely lit areas. The range for blend steps is 1-256, with higher numbers producing more paths and therefore smoother transitions. If your computer can handle it, use 256 blend steps, but be aware that the higher the number, the more computer memory will be required to render the object.

Manipulating Light Sources

In addition to manipulating lighting controls, you can manipulate the light itself. When you choose Diffuse Shading or Plastic Shading as the surface shading, a default light source, shown in Figure 59, is applied. You can drag the light source to a new location to light the object from a different

angle, as shown in Figure 60. This can be effective for manipulating the overall lighting of the object.

In addition to relocating the default light source, you can add additional light sources by clicking the New Light button. By default, the new light source appears at the center of the lighting key, but you can

Figure 59 *Viewing default light source settings*

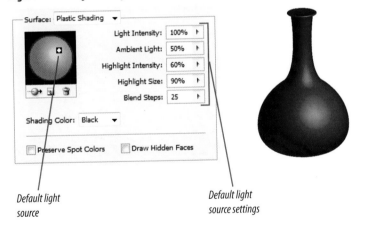

Default light source

Default light source settings

Figure 60 *Relocating a light source*

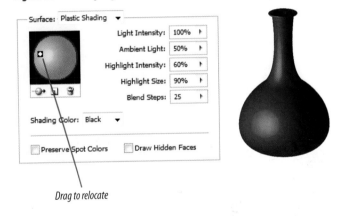

Drag to relocate

relocate it as well, as shown in Figure 61. You can apply different light intensity values to individual light sources. It is often a good idea for one light source to be more dominant than the other(s).

To delete a light source, select it and then click the Delete Light button. The Move selected light to back of object button moves the light source to the back of the object. This is most effective when there's a background object that allows the back light to be more apparent. In Figure 62, the second light has been moved behind the object; the highlights on the right side of the object are from the back light.

Figure 61 *Relocating a second light source*

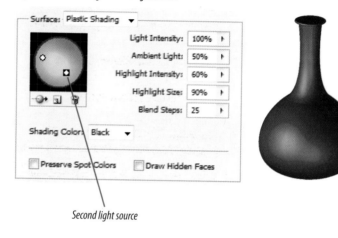

Second light source

Figure 62 *Using a light source as a back light*

Back light source

Move selected
light to back of
object button

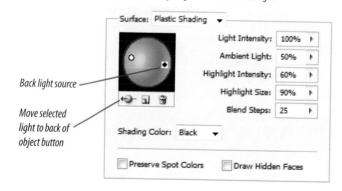

Highlight from back light source

Creating 3D Objects

Figure 63 *Viewing the object with the Plastic Shading surface applied*

1. Open AI 10-6.ai, then save it as **Surface Lighting**.
2. Click the **object** to select it, then click **3D Revolve** on the Appearance panel.
3. Click the **Preview check box**, then note the subtle lighting effects on the object.

   The Diffuse Shading surface type is applied to the object.
4. Click the **Surface list arrow**, then click **No Shading**.
5. Click the **Surface list arrow**, then click **Wireframe**.
6. Click the **Surface list arrow**, click **Plastic Shading**, then compare your artwork to Figure 63.

You examined four types of surface shadings as applied to a revolved object.

Manipulate lighting controls

1. Click **More Options** in the dialog box.

2. Click the **Ambient Light list arrow**, then drag the **slider** to 20.

3. Click the **Highlight Intensity list arrow**, then drag the **slider** to 75.

4. Click the **Highlight Size list arrow**, then drag the **slider** to 75.

5. Click the **Light Intensity list arrow**, drag the **slider** to 50, note the change in the object, then drag the **slider** to 100.

6. Click the **Blend Steps list arrow**, then drag the **slider** to 128.

7. Click **OK**, then compare your artwork to Figure 64.

You manipulated five surface shading controls, noting their effect on a 3D object.

Manipulate light sources

1. Verify that the green object is selected, click **3D Revolve** on the Appearance panel, then click the **Preview check box**.

2. Drag the **light** to the top center of the sphere, as shown in Figure 65.

3. Click the **New Light button** to add a second light.

TIP By default, a new light is positioned at the center of the sphere.

(continued)

Figure 64 *Manipulating surface shading on a 3D object*

Figure 65 *Relocating a light*

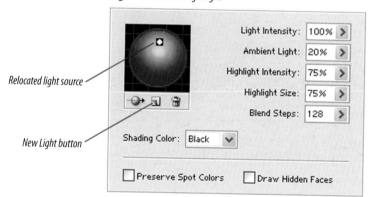

Relocated light source

New Light button

Figure 66 *Relocating the new light*

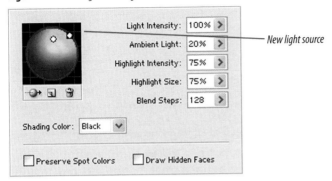

New light source

Figure 67 *Relocating the third light*

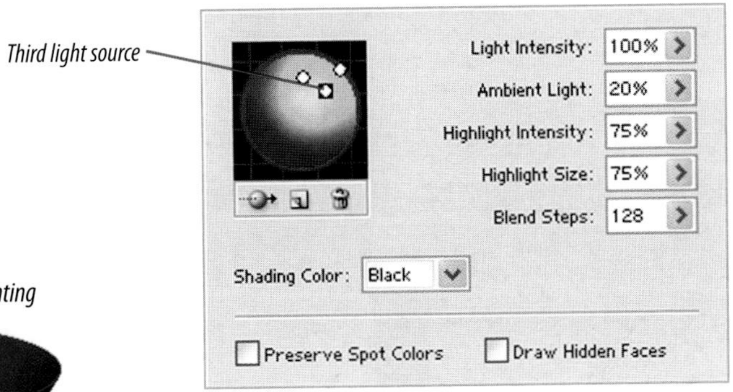

Third light source

Figure 68 *The object with different lighting*

4. Drag the **new light** to the top-right corner of the sphere, as shown in Figure 66.

5. Click the **New Light button** to add a third light, then move it to the location shown in Figure 67.

6. Click **OK**, compare your work to Figure 68, then compare Figure 68 to Figure 64 to see the results of adding the two lights.

7. Save your work, then close Surface Lighting.

You added and positioned lights to modify the lighting effects applied to the 3D object.

Map Artwork
TO 3D OBJECTS

What You'll Do

In this lesson, you will map 2D artwork to a 3D object.

Mapping Artwork

Once you have created a three-dimensional object, you can "map" two-dimensional artwork to the three-dimensional object. A good example of this concept is a soup can and a soup label. The two dimensional soup label is designed and printed. It is then wrapped around the three-dimensional soup can.

The process of mapping a 2D object to a 3D object first includes converting the 2D object to a symbol. Figure 69 shows a revolved 3D object and 2D artwork that will be mapped to it.

Figure 69 *Viewing 3D object and 2D artwork to be mapped*

2D Illustrator
artwork

3D object

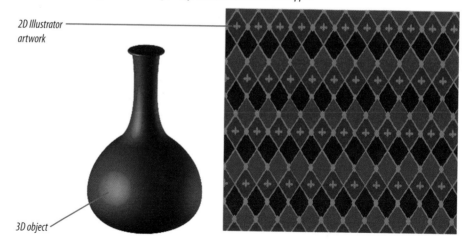

Creating 3D Objects

To map the artwork, you first select the 3D object, then click Map Art in the 3D Revolve Options dialog box. In the Map Art dialog box, shown in Figure 70, you must first choose to which surface you intend to map the art. When you click the surface buttons, the active surface is shown in red wireframe on the 3D object. In this example, we are mapping the wrapping paper to surface 1 of 4, which is shown in Figure 71.

The grid pattern represents the *complete* surface of surface 1 of 4. Understand that this means not only the front surface that you see, but the entire surface, all the way around. For this exercise, we're interested in mapping the wrapping paper to the front surface that we can see. That area is defined by the curved lines, identified in Figure 71.

Figure 70 *Map Art dialog box*

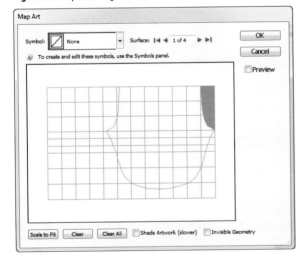

Figure 71 *Identifying the surface to be mapped*

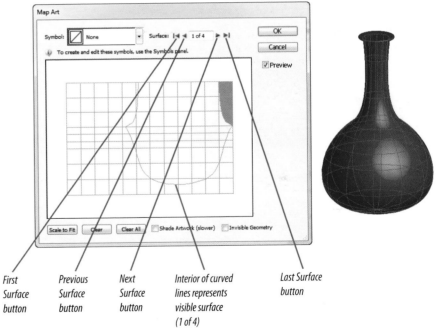

First Surface button

Previous Surface button

Next Surface button

Interior of curved lines represents visible surface (1 of 4)

Last Surface button

Artwork that you want to map to an object must first be converted into a symbol in the Symbols panel. Drag the artwork into the Symbols panel and the Symbol Options dialog box opens, allowing you to name the symbol and identify it as a graphic. Symbols are covered extensively in Chapter 12.

Once you have chosen the surface, you then choose the symbol to be mapped by clicking the Symbol list arrow in the Map Art dialog box and selecting the appropriate symbol. When you do so, the symbol artwork is centered on the grid. In this example, the symbol is named Wrapping Paper.

For this exercise, we drag the artwork so that it completely covers the curved lines that represent the front face, as shown in Figure 72.

Once the artwork is mapped, it reshapes itself to the three-dimensional object, as shown in Figure 73.

Figure 72 *Positioning the symbol artwork*

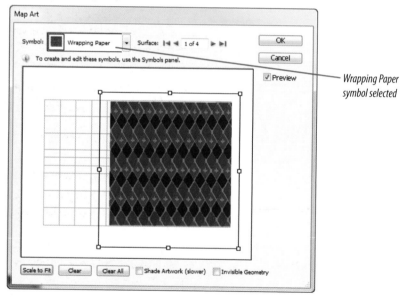

Wrapping Paper symbol selected

Figure 73 *Viewing the mapped art*

Figure 74 *Creating the "tea can" and "lid"*

Prepare a document for mapped artwork

1. Open AI 10-7.ai, then save it as **Tea Can**.

2. Select all, click **Effect** on the Application bar, point to **3D**, click **Revolve**, then click **OK**.

   Your artwork should resemble Figure 74.

3. Open AI 10-8.ai, select all, click **Edit** on the Application bar, click **Copy**, close the document, then return to Tea Can.ai.

4. Click the **Symbols button** ♣ to display the Symbols panel, click **Edit** on the Application bar, click **Paste**, then drag the pasted artwork into the Symbols panel.

   The Symbol Options dialog box opens.

5. Name the new symbol **Elephant Rectangle**, click the **Type list arrow**, click **Graphic**, then click **OK**.

   The artwork is added as a symbol in the Symbols panel.

6. Delete the pasted artwork from the artboard.

7. Open AI 10-9.ai, select all, copy the artwork, close the document, return to Tea Can.ai, then paste the artwork.

8. Drag the pasted artwork into the Symbols panel, name it **Elephant Circle**, click the **Type list arrow**, click **Graphic,** then click **OK**.

9. Delete the pasted artwork from the artboard.

You used the 3D Revolve effect to create the artwork to which the 2D artwork will be mapped. You then created two symbols, one for each part of the 2D artwork.

Map rectangular artwork

1. Click the **Selection tool**, click the **silver object**, then press ↑ eight times so that the silver artwork is fully "under" the purple lid.

2. Click **3D Revolve** on the Appearance panel to open the 3D Revolve Options dialog box, click the **Preview check box**, then click **Map Art**.

3. Note that the Surface text box reads 1 of 3 and that a red line indicates that surface on the object, as shown in Figure 75.

4. Click the **Next Surface button** two times, so that the Surface text box reads 3 of 3.

   The light gray areas of the layout grid represent the visible area of the silver object at this viewing angle.

5. Click the **Symbol list arrow**, then click **Elephant Rectangle**.

6. Drag the **top-left and bottom-right resizing handles** on the symbol's bounding box so that the artwork fits into the light gray areas of the layout grid, as shown in Figure 76.

7. Drag the **bottom-middle resizing handle** up slightly so that the silver "can" will show beneath the "elephant label."

8. Click the **Shade Artwork (slower) check box**.

9. Click **OK**, click **More Options** if they are not already showing, change the Ambient Light setting to 65%, change the Highlight Intensity setting to 80%, change the number of blend steps to 128, then move the light to the location shown in Figure 77.

(continued)

Figure 75 *Viewing surface 1 of 3 in the Map Art dialog box*

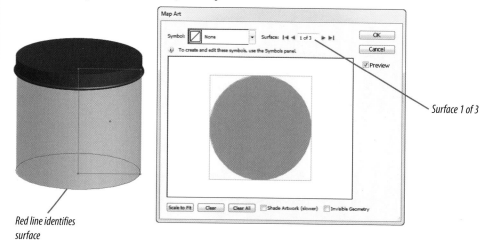

Surface 1 of 3

Red line identifies surface

Figure 76 *Resizing the artwork to the visible area*

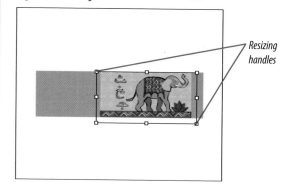

Resizing handles

Figure 77 *Adjusting surface shading and lighting*

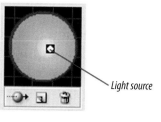

Light source

Figure 78 *Viewing the mapped art*

10. Click **OK**, deselect all, then compare your work to Figure 78.

In the Map Art dialog box, you selected the symbol that you wanted to map and the surface to which you wanted to map it. You resized the symbol artwork so that it fit onto the surface properly, then you activated the shading option to make the artwork appear more realistic as a label. You modified surface shading settings and lighting to improve the appearance of the artwork.

Map round artwork

1. Click the **purple "cover" object**, click **3D Revolve** on the Appearance panel, click the **Preview check box**, then click **Map Art**.

2. Click the **Next Surface button** once, so that the Surface text box reads 2 of 5.

3. Click the **Symbol list arrow**, then click **Elephant Circle**.

4. Point to the **upper-right resizing handle** until a rotate cursor appears, then drag to rotate the graphic to the position shown in Figure 79.

5. Click **OK** to close the Map Art dialog box, click **OK** again, deselect all, then compare your artwork to Figure 80.

You mapped a circular piece of 2D artwork to an oval 3D object.

Figure 79 *Rotating the mapped art*

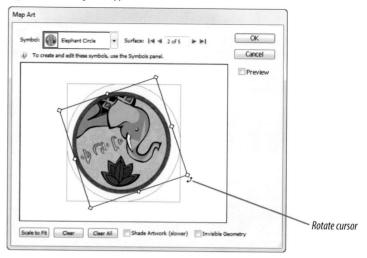

Rotate cursor

Figure 80 *Viewing the mapped art*

Figure 81 *Positioning the artwork*

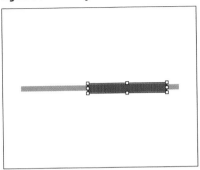

Figure 82 *Relocating the light*

Figure 83 *Viewing the finished artwork*

Map texture artwork

1. Open AI 10-10.ai, select all, copy the artwork, close the document, then return to Tea Can.ai.

2. Verify that the Symbols panel is visible, click **Edit** on the Application bar, click **Paste**, then drag the pasted artwork into the Symbols panel.

3. Name the new symbol **Cover Texture**, click the **Type list arrow**, click **Graphic**, then click **OK**.

4. Delete the pasted artwork from the artboard.

5. Click the **purple "cover" object**, click **3D Revolve (Mapped)** on the Appearance panel, click the **Preview check box**, then click **Map Art**.

6. Click the **Next Surface button** until the Surface text box reads 5 of 5.

7. Click the **Symbol list arrow**, then click **Cover Texture**.

8. Position the symbol artwork so that it covers the entire light gray area, as shown in Figure 81.

9. Click **OK** to close the Map Art window, then drag the light to the location shown in Figure 82.

10. Click **OK**, deselect all, then compare your work to Figure 83.

11. Save your work, then close Tea Can.

You mapped artwork to the front face of a 3D object to add texture.

Work with
A PERSPECTIVE GRID

What You'll Do

In this lesson, you will use the perspective grid and the Perspective Selection tool to draw objects in perspective.

Working with the Perspective Grid

Illustrator CS5 features a powerful **perspective grid** feature that you can use to draw and create objects in perspective. Like guides, the default perspective grid is listed in the View menu, where you can choose to hide or show it. But the perspective grid is more than just a visual guide; it's a drawing tool. When you're working with the perspective grid, it's like you're working in "perspective mode." The grid allows you to draw, copy and transform objects in perspective. It even adjusts the shape of the object to keep it in perspective as you move it around the artboard.

Illustrator CS5 features three types of grids: 1-Point Perspective, 2-Point Perspective, and 3-Point Perspective, as shown in Figure 84. The term "point" refers to vanishing points. So, for example, a 2-Point Perspective grid has two vanishing points. Of the three types of grids, 2-Point Perspective is most applicable for most types of Illustrator artwork and is therefore the default grid.

You access the Perspective Grid by selecting to show it in the View menu or by clicking the Perspective Grid tool in the Tools panel. When you do, the default 2-Point Perspective grid appears, as shown in Figure 85. You can resize and reshape the grid by clicking and dragging the handles, known as widgets. When you've resized and reshaped the grid to your liking, you can save the modified grid as a **Perspective Grid Preset**. When you do, the saved grid is available in the View menu for future uses. You can also edit the preset after saving it by clicking the Edit menu, then clicking Perspective Grid Presets.

Figure 86 shows a modified perspective grid. Note the change in shape, size, color, and opacity. Many users like to use a reduced opacity for the grid, making it a bit easier to see the artwork as you draw on the grid.

Creating 3D Objects

NEW Drawing in Perspective

When you click the Perspective Grid tool and the grid becomes visible, the Basic shape tools, such as the Rectangle, Ellipse, and Star tools function differently, allowing you to draw objects in perspective.

When drawing in perspective, you should first specify on which perspective plane you want to draw by clicking one of the faces on the Plane Switching Widget that appears with the perspective grid.

Figure 84 *1, 2, & 3-Point perspective grids*

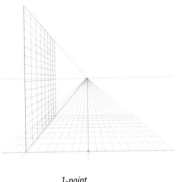

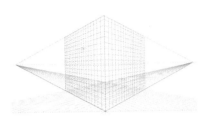

1-point perspective grid

2-point perspective grid

3-point perspective grid

Figure 85 *Default 2-Point perspective grid*

Figure 86 *Modified grid*

Perspective Grid tool

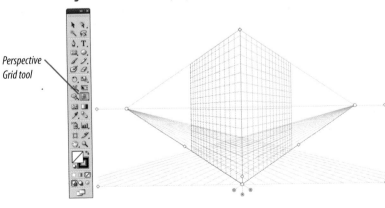

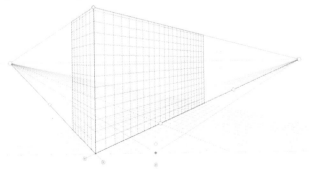

Figure 87 shows three views of the widget for a 2-Point perspective grid. Figure 88 shows a rectangle drawn in perspective on the left plane. Figure 89 shows a rectangle drawn on the right plane.

You can also use the number keys on your keypad to specify the plane on which you want to draw. For example, you can type 1 to draw on the left plane, 2 to draw on the bottom plane, and 3 to draw on the right plane. Refer to Figure 87.

Figure 87 *Plane Switching Widget in three modes*

1   *2*   *3*

Figure 88 *Drawing on the left plane*

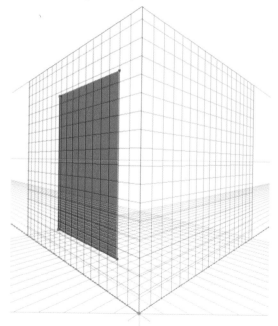

Figure 89 *Drawing on the right plane*

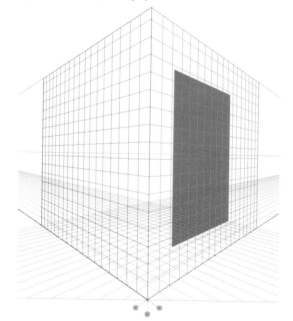

Using the Perspective Selection Tool

Once you've drawn objects in perspective, the Perspective Selection tool allows you to move and modify the objects in perspective. Let us not mince words here—this is a really cool tool! When you click and drag an object with the Perspective Selection tool, it moves in perspective. Figure 90 shows an ellipse in perspective on the left plane. Figure 91 shows three copies of the ellipse dragged and dropped with the Perspective Selection tool. Note how they automatically reduce in perspective as they move toward the left vanishing point.

You can also use the Perspective Selection tool to move an object or multiple objects between different planes on the grid.

While dragging an object, type the number of the plane to which you want to move it. For example, let's say you have an object on the left plane. If you drag it with the Perspective Selection tool, press the number 3 on your keypad while dragging, and the object will be redrawn in perspective on the right plane.

Figure 90 *Ellipse in perspective on the left plane*

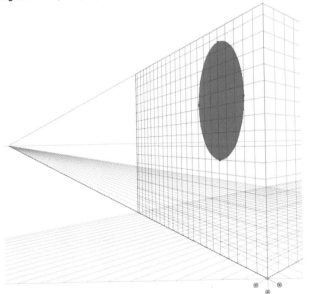

Figure 91 *Three copies of the ellipse dragged and dropped with the Perspective Selection tool*

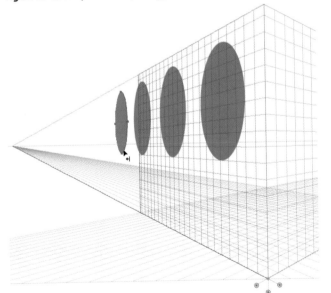

Incorporating Text Into a Perspective Grid

When working with the perspective grid, the shape tools will draw in perspective, but any text you create will be created in the normal fashion, not in perspective.

You can use the Perspective Selection tool to bring "flat" text and objects onto the perspective grid.

Figure 92 shows selected text on the artboard. (The selection marks are hidden). Note that the right plane is highlighted in the Plane Switching Widget. In Figure 93, the text has been clicked and dragged with the Perspective Selection tool and is now in perspective on the right plane.

Figure 92 *"Flat" text*

Right plane (3) selected

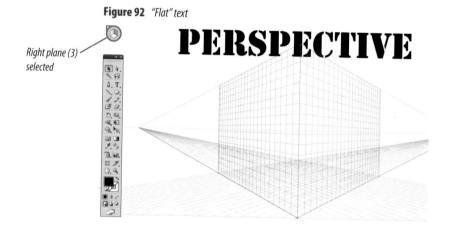

Figure 93 *Text put into perspective with the Perspective Selection tool*

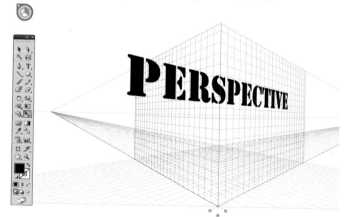

Creating 3D Objects

This technique is also useful when putting complex artwork into perspective. Figure 94 shows an illustration composed of multiple objects. The illustration is grouped. In Figure 95, the artwork is in perspective on the left plane.

When bringing flat objects onto the perspective grid in this manner, you might ask yourself how this is any different—or any better—than using the Free Transform tool to distort in perspective. The answer is in the specifics. The artwork in Figure 95 has been distorted to the specific perspective grid of the left plane. If you were to add additional objects to the illustration, such as a headline or rules, you could be sure that the perspective effect on all the objects would be correct because they'd be exactly the same.

Figure 94 *Complex "flat" artwork*

Left plane (1) selected

Figure 95 *Artwork put into perspective with the Perspective Selection tool*

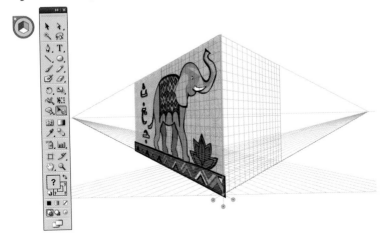

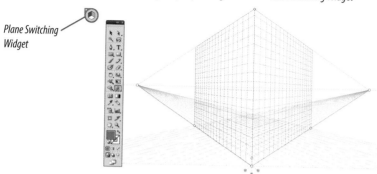 NEW Draw on a perspective grid

1. Open AI 10-11.ai, then save it as **Basic Planes**.
2. On the Tools panel, set the fill color to none, set the stroke color to black, then set the stroke weight to 3 pts.
3. Click **View** the Application bar, point to **Perspective Grid**, point to **Two Point Perspective**, then click **[2P-Normal View]**.
4. Click the **Perspective Grid tool** 🔲 .

   As shown in Figure 96, when you click the Perspective Grid tool, the default perspective grid appears on the page, along with the Plane Switching Widget. The default perspective grid is a two point perspective grid, blue on the left, orange on the right, with both planes being equal size.

   TIP The Perspective Grid tool might be hidden behind the Perspective Selection tool.

5. On your keypad, press **1, 2,** and **3** repeatedly and note that it toggles between three planes on the Plane Switching Widget.
6. Press **1** on the keypad.
7. Click the **Rectangle tool**, position it near the top-center of the perspective grid, then click and drag to create a rectangle that resembles Figure 97.

   The Rectangle tool draws an object on the same plane that is active in the Plane Switching Widget.

8. Press **3** on your keypad, then position the cursor over the same starting point at the top-center of the grid.

   The anchor point on the first rectangle you drew enlarges automatically so that the next rectangle you draw will align to it.

9. Click and drag to draw a second rectangle similar to that in Figure 98.

(continued)

Figure 96 *Viewing the perspective grid and the Plane Switching Widget*

Plane Switching Widget

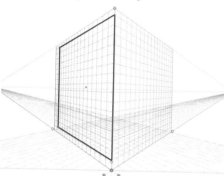

Figure 97 *Drawing the first rectangle*

Figure 98 *Drawing the second rectangle*

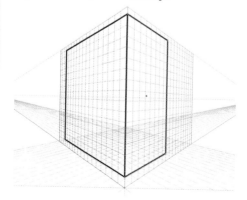

Figure 99 *Drawing the third rectangle*

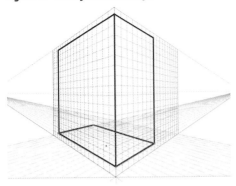

Figure 100 *Drawing two more rectangles*

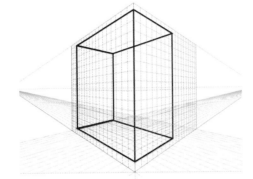

Figure 101 *Viewing the illustration without the grid*

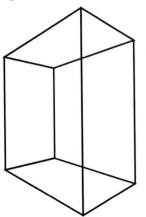

The rectangle is drawn on active plane in the widget.

10. Press **2** on your keypad, position your cursor over the bottom center intersection of the two rectangles, then draw a third rectangle as shown in Figure 99.

TIP Pressing 4 on your keypad is the "no plane" option for the Plane Switching Widget, allowing you to draw objects without perspective.

11. Using the same methodology, draw two more rectangles so that your screen resembles Figure 100.

12. Click **View** on the Application bar, point to **Perspective Grid**, then click **Hide Grid**.

13. Switch to Outline mode, tweak the objects so that they align exactly, switch back to Preview mode, then compare your illustration to Figure 101.

14. Save your work, then close the file.

You used the perspective grid to draw multiple rectangles in perspective on different planes.

Modify and save a perspective grid

1. Open AI 10-12.ai, save it as **Receding Rectangles**, then verify that guides are showing.

   The artboard has a single rectangular guide.

2. Click the **Perspective Grid tool** 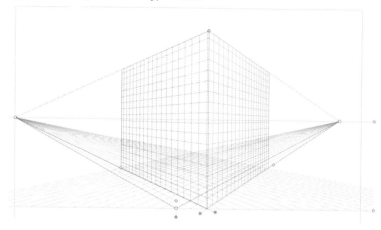.

3. Drag the **left vanishing point handle** left to the guide, as shown in Figure 102.

   The perspective grid changes shape as you drag.

4. Drag the **right vanishing point handle** right, to the guide.

5. Drag the **top diamond handle** up to the guide.

   Your perspective grid should resemble Figure 103.

6. Click **View** on the Application bar, point to **Guides**, then click **Hide Guides**.

   The rectangular guide is hidden, but the perspective grid remains visible.

7. Click **View** on the Application bar, point to **Perspective Grid**, then click **Save Grid as Preset**.

8. Change the name to **Receding Rectangles**.

   The values in the Save Grid As Preset dialog box reflect the specifics of the grid as it was created by default and as you modified it. You can continue to modify the grid within this dialog box.

9. Click the **Left Grid list arrow**, choose **Brick Red**, click the **Right Grid list arrow**, then choose **Dark Blue**.

   Your dialog box should resemble Figure 104.

10. Click **OK**.

    The perspective grid does not change.

    (continued)

Figure 102 *Moving the left vanishing point handle*

Figure 103 *Moving right and top handles*

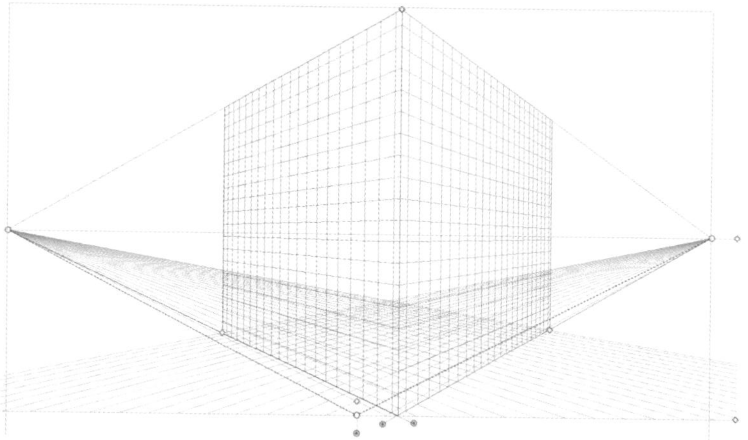

Figure 104 *Save Grid As Preset dialog box*

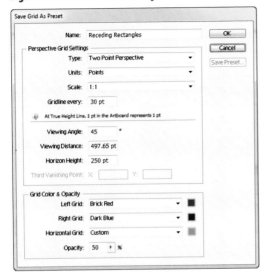

Figure 105 *"Receding Rectangles" perspective grid*

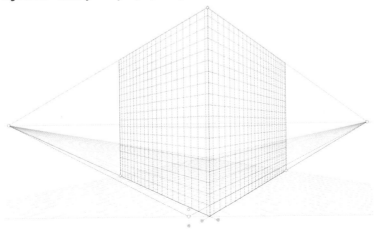

11. Click **View** on the Application bar, point
    to **Perspective Grid**, point to **Two Point
    Perspective**, then click **Receding Rectangles**.

    As shown in Figure 105, the perspective grid
    you edited, named, and saved is loaded.

12. Click **View** on the Application bar, point
    to **Perspective Grid**, point to **Two Point
    Perspective**, then click **[2P-Normal View]**.

    The default Two Point Perspective grid is
    loaded. The Receding Rectangles perspective
    grid preset can be further edited.

13. Click **Edit** on the Application bar, then click
    Perspective Grid Presets.

    The Perspective Grid Presets dialog box opens.

14. In the (top) Presets window, click
    Receding Rectangles, then click the **Edit
    button** on the right.

15. Reduce the Opacity setting to 30, click **OK** to
    close the dialog box, then click **OK** again to
    close the Perspective Grid Presets dialog box.

16. Click **View** on the Application bar, point
    to **Perspective Grid**, point to **Two Point
    Perspective**, then click **Receding Rectangles**.

    The Receding Rectangles grid is reloaded and
    appears to have faded, reflecting the reduction
    in opacity.

17. Save your work.

*You modified the size and shape of the default two point
perspective grid. You saved it as a preset, named it, and changed
its colors. You loaded it to make it the active perspective grid on
the artboard. You loaded the default two point perspective grid,
then edited the Receding Rectangles preset, reducing its opacity.*

NEW Use the Perspective Selection tool

1. On the Tools panel, set the fill color to black and the stroke color to none.

2. Press **1** on your keypad, click the **Rectangle tool**, then draw a rectangle as shown in Figure 106.

3. Click the **Perspective Selection tool** , then click and drag the **rectangle** around the artboard.

   The rectangle remains in perspective anywhere you drag it. It enlarges as you drag to the right and reduces as you move it left and closer to the vanishing point.

4. "Drop" the rectangle anywhere, then undo the move so that the rectangle is returned to its original position.

5. Press and hold **[Shift][Alt]** (Win) or **[Shift] [Option]**(Mac), then drag and drop a copy of the rectangle to the left, as shown in Figure 107.

(continued)

Figure 106 *Creating a rectangle*

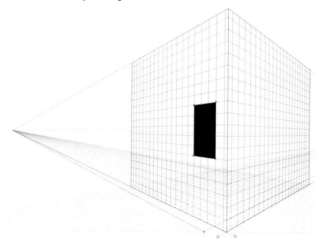

Figure 107 *Duplicating the rectangle*

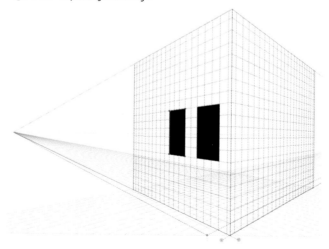

Creating 3D Objects

Figure 108 *Repeating the transformation in perspective*

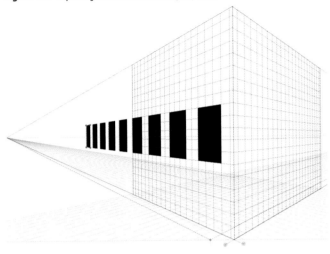

Figure 109 *Creating the top copy of rectangles*

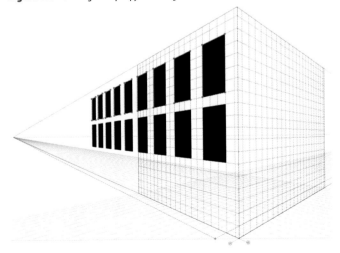

6. Press **[Ctrl][D]**(Win) or ⌘ **[D]**(Mac) seven times to repeat the transformation as shown in Figure 108.

7. Select all, then drag and drop **a copy of the rectangles** above them, as shown in Figure 109.

   The copies are in perspective on the same plane as the original and recede toward the vanishing point.

   (continued)

8. Drag and drop a **copy of the rectangles** below the original row, as shown in Figure 110.

9. Click and drag the **rectangles** toward the right of the artboard, then, while still dragging, press **3** on your keypad once, but do not release the mouse button.

When you press 3, the rectangles' perspective changes to that of the right plane.

10. Continue dragging, then press and hold **[Alt]** (Win) or **[Option]**(Mac).

(continued)

Figure 110 *Creating the bottom copy of rectangles*

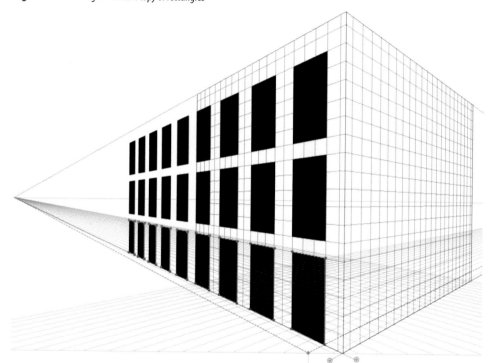

Creating 3D Objects

11. Position the copied rectangles as shown in Figure 111.

12. Save your work, then close **Receding Rectangles**.

You used the Perspective Selection tool to move objects in perspective, to drag and drop copies of objects in perspective, and to copy objects from one plane to another.

Figure 111 *Moving a copy of rectangles onto the right plane*

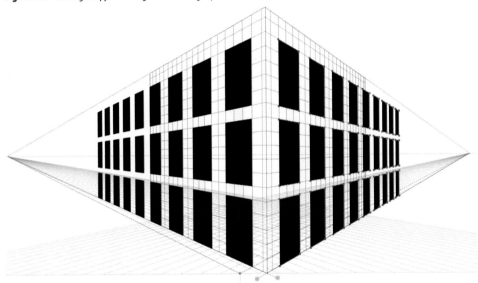

Add text and composed artwork to a perspective grid

1. Open AI 10-13.ai, save it as **Perspective Text**, then verify that guides are showing.

   The artboard has a single rectangular guide.

2. Click the **Perspective Grid tool** ▦ .

3. Drag the **left vanishing point handle** left to the guide.

4. Drag the **right vanishing point handle** right to the guide.

5. Click **View** on the Application bar, point to **Guides**, then click **Hide Guides**.

6. Click **View** on the Application bar, point to **Perspective Grid**, point to **Two Point Perspective**, then click **[2P-Normal View]**.

7. Click **Object** on the Application bar, then click **Show All**.

8. Move the red illustration onto the grid, click the **Free Transform tool**, then scale the artwork and position it so that your artboard resembles Figure 112.

TIP The figures in this chapter show the artwork with selection marks hidden.

9. Press **1** on your keypad.

10. Click the **Perspective Selection tool** ▸⊙ , then drag over the artwork and position it as shown in Figure 113.

(continued)

Figure 112 *Scaling and positioning the artwork to be distorted in perspective*

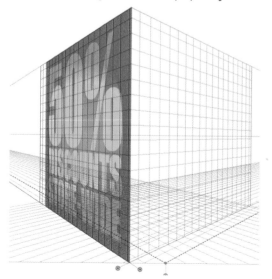

Figure 113 *Positioning the artwork on the perspective grid*

Creating 3D Objects

Figure 114 *The completed illustration*

11. Press **3** on your keypad.
12. Using the same methodology, position the blue artwork in perspective on the right plane so that your artwork resembles Figure 114.
13. Save your work and close the file.

You used the Perspective Selection tool to position flat artwork and text in perspective on the perspective grid.

Extrude objects.

1. Open AI 10-14.ai, then save it as **Extrude & Bevel Skills**.
2. Click the Selection tool, select the blue octagon, click View on the Application bar, then click Hide Edges.
3. Click Effect on the Application bar, point to 3D, click Extrude & Bevel, then click the Preview check box.
4. Click the Extrude Depth list arrow, then increase the depth to 75 pt.
5. Click the Hollow cap button, then click OK.
6. Select the orange letter H, click Effect on the Application bar, point to 3D, then click Extrude & Bevel.
7. Click the Preview check box, then change the Extrude Depth value to 60 pt.
8. Double-click the Specify rotation around the X axis text box to select its contents, type **17**, then press [Tab].
9. Type **-17** in the Specify rotation around the Y axis text box, press [Tab], type **-31** in the Specify rotation around the Z axis text box, then click OK.
10. Select the green octagon and the two objects inside it, click Object on the Application bar, point to Compound Path, then click Make.
11. Click Effect on the Application bar, point to 3D, then click Extrude & Bevel.
12. Click the Preview check box, then experiment with different rotations by clicking and dragging the rotation cube from all sides.
13. Double-click the Specify rotation around the X axis text box, type **26**, then press [Tab].
14. Type **-9** in the Specify rotation around the Y axis text box, press [Tab], then type **5** in the Specify rotation around the Z axis text box.

15. Click OK.
16. Select the hollow blue octagon at the top of the artboard, then click 3D Extrude & Bevel on the Appearance panel.
17. Click the Preview check box, then click the Solid cap button.
18. Click the Bevel list arrow, click Complex 3, then drag the Height slider to 6.
19. Click the Bevel Extent Out button, click OK, then compare your work to Figure 115.
20. Save your work, then close Extrude & Bevel Skills.

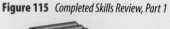

Figure 115 *Completed Skills Review, Part 1*

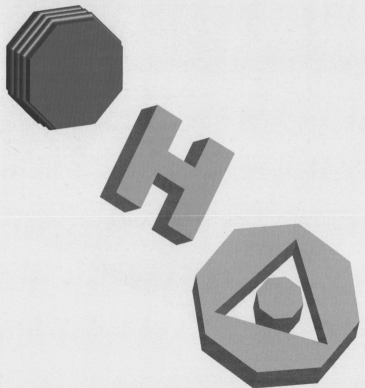

Revolve objects.

1. Open AI 10-15.ai, then save it as **Gold Urn**.
2. Click the Selection tool, select all, click View on the Application bar, then click Hide Edges if it is not already selected.
3. Click the Horizontal Align Left button on the Align panel.
4. Click Effect on the Application bar, point to 3D, click Revolve, then click the Preview check box.
5. Manipulate the rotation cube in any direction, note that the three objects all rotate on their own axes, then click Cancel.
6. Click Object on the Application bar, then click Group.
7. Click Effect on the Application bar, point to 3D, click Revolve, then click the Preview check box.
8. Manipulate the rotation cube in any direction.
9. Click Cancel.
10. Click Effect on the Application bar, point to 3D, click Revolve, then click the Preview check box.
11. Click the Offset list arrow, change the offset value to 48, then click OK.

Manipulate surface shading and lighting.

1. Click 3D Revolve on the Appearance panel.
2. Click the Preview check box, click the Surface list arrow, then click No Shading.
3. Click the Surface list arrow, then click Diffuse Shading.
4. Click the Surface list arrow, then click Plastic Shading.
5. Click More Options if they are not already displayed, click the Ambient Light list arrow, then drag the slider to 45.
6. Drag the light to the top center of the sphere.
7. Click the New Light button to add a second light.
8. Drag the Light Intensity slider to 30.

Map artwork to 3D objects.

1. Drag the Offset slider to 0, then click Map Art.
2. Click the Next Surface button until the Surface text box reads 5 of 13.
3. Click the Symbol list arrow, then click Wrapping Paper.
4. Click OK.
5. Click OK, then compare your work to Figure 116.
6. Save your work, then close Gold Urn.

Figure 116 *Completed Skills Review, Part 2*

Work with a perspective grid.

1. Open AI 10-16.ai, save it as **Receding Circles**, then verify that guides are showing.
2. Click the Perspective Grid tool.
3. Drag the left vanishing point handle left to the guide.
4. Drag the right vanishing point handle right to the guide.
5. Drag the top diamond handle up to the guide.
6. Click View on the Application bar, point to Guides, then click Hide Guides.
7. Click View on the Application bar, point to Perspective Grid, then click Save Grid as Preset.
8. Change the name to **Receding Circles**.
9. Click the Left Grid list arrow, choose Grass Green, click the Right Grid list arrow, then choose Dark Blue.
10. Click OK.
11. Click View on the Application bar, point to Perspective Grid, point to Two Point Perspective, then click Receding Circles.
12. Click Edit on the Application bar, then click Perspective Grid Presets.
13. In the (top) Presets window, click Receding Circles, then click the Edit button on the right.
14. Increase the Opacity setting to 100, click OK to close the dialog box, then click OK again to close the Perspective Grid Presets dialog box.

15. Click View on the Application bar, point to Perspective Grid, point to Two Point Perspective, then click Receding Circles.
16. On the Tools panel, set the fill color to black and the stroke color to none.

17. Press 1 on your keypad, click the Ellipse tool, press and hold [Shift] then draw an ellipse as shown in Figure 117.

Figure 117 *Positioning the first ellipse*

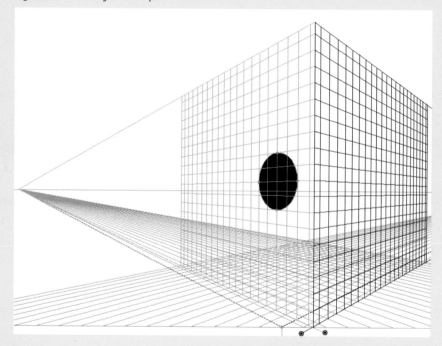

18. Press and hold Shift-Alt (Win) or Shift-Option (Mac), then drag and drop a copy of the ellipse to the left.
19. Enter [Ctrl][D](Win) or [⌘][D](Mac) seven times to repeat the transformation.
20. Select all, then drag and drop a copy above them.

21. Drag and drop a copy below the original row.
22. Click and drag the ellipses toward the right of the artboard and, while still dragging, press the number 3 on your keypad once.

23. Continue dragging, then press and hold [Alt](Win) or [Option](Mac).
24. Position the copied ellipses as shown in Figure 118.
25. Save your work, the close Receding Circles.

Figure 118 *Completed Skills Review, Part 3*

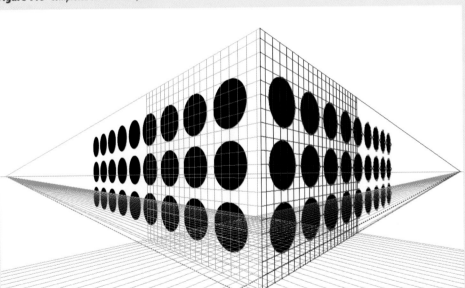

You are a freelance illustrator, and you have been hired to draw an old-fashioned lava lamp to be part of a montage. To begin work on the illustration, you decide to draw three paths, then use the 3D Revolve effect.

1. Open AI 10-17.ai, then save it as **Lava**.
2. Click the Selection tool, then drag the three path segments so that they are aligned with the blue guide.
3. Hide the guides.
4. Select all, click Effect on the Application bar, point to 3D, then click Revolve.
5. Click the Preview check box, note the results, then click Cancel.
6. Group the three paths, apply the Revolve effect again, then click the Preview check box.
7. Click More Options if necessary, apply Plastic Shading as the surface shading, then drag the Ambient Light slider to 45.
8. Click OK, deselect all, then compare your work to Figure 119.
9. Save your work, then close Lava.

Figure 119 *Completed Project Builder 1*

You are a designer for a game company, and you are designing the packaging for a chess game. You decide to use basic shapes and the 3D Revolve effect to create a graphic for the cover art.

1. Open AI 10-18.ai, then save it as **Chess**.
2. Click the Selection tool, then align each shape with the black rules.

3. Hide the Assembled layer, then verify that the Pawn Parts layer is targeted.
4. Select all on the Pawn Parts layer, then hide edges.
5. Click Effect on the Application bar, point to 3D, then click Revolve.
6. Click the Preview check box, note the results, then click Cancel.
7. Click the Horizontal Align Left button on the Align panel.

8. Press and hold [Alt] (Win) or [option] (Mac), then click the Unite button on the Pathfinder panel.
9. Click Effect on the Application bar, point to 3D, click Revolve, then click the Preview check box.
10. Select the contents of the Specify rotation around the X axis text box, type **-57**, then click OK.
11. Click the White Pawn swatch on the Swatches panel, then compare your work to Figure 120.
12. Save your work, then close the Chess document.

Figure 120 *Completed Project Builder 2*

You are a designer for a T-shirt company. Presently, your assignment is to develop shirts that feature peoples' names in 3D. To come up with a design, you experiment using your own name.

1. Create a new 8" × 8" document, then save it as **T-Shirt**.
2. Type your first name in a bold font at a large point size. (*Hint*: The typeface used in Figure 121 is Franklin Gothic Heavy, 134 point. Try to use the same or a similar typeface at the same point size in your work.)
3. Change the fill color to something other than black.
4. Click Effect on the Application bar, point to 3D, then click Extrude & Bevel.
5. Click the Preview check box, then change the Extrude Depth value to 115 pt.

6. Double-click the Specify rotation around the X axis text box to select its contents, type **–8**, then press [Tab].
7. Type **0** in the Specify rotation around the Y axis text box, press [Tab], type **0** in the Specify rotation around the Z axis text box, press [Tab], then press [Tab].
8. Slowly drag the Perspective slider to 95°.

9. Click the More Options button if necessary to expand the dialog box, then position the light source to your liking.
10. Click OK, then compare your result to Figure 121. (*Hint*: Illustrator sometimes has trouble displaying 3D effects correctly. If you do not get good results, try again.)
11. Save your work, then close the file.

Figure 121 *Sample completed Design Project*

This portfolio project is designed to challenge your ability to visualize simple paths and how they will appear when the 3D Revolve effect is applied. You will look at nine graphics, all of which are simple paths to which the 3D Revolve effect has been applied. Use a piece of paper and a pencil and try to draw the simple path that is the basis for each graphic. Note that for each 3D graphic, no rotation or offset has been applied—each is the result of simply applying the 3D Revolve effect to a simple path. Note also that two of the simple paths are open paths, and the other seven are all closed paths.

1. Refer to Figure 122.
2. Look at Graphic #1, and try to visualize what it would look like if the 3D Revolve effect were removed.
3. Using a pencil and paper, draw the original path that was used to create the graphic.
4. Do the same for the remaining eight graphics.
5. Open AI 10-19.ai, then save it as **Mystery Shapes**.
6. Select each graphic, then delete the 3D Revolve effect from the Appearance panel.
7. Compare your pencil drawings to the graphics in the file.
8. Save Mystery Graphics, then close the file.

Figure 122 *Reference for Portfolio Project*

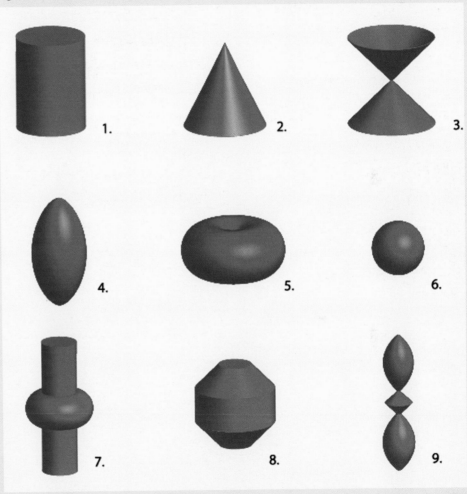

CHAPTER 11

PREPARING A DOCUMENT FOR
PREPRESS AND PRINTING

1. Explore color theory and resolution issues
2. Work in CMYK mode
3. Specify spot colors
4. Create crop marks
5. Create bleeds
6. Save a file as a PDF

CHAPTER 11

PREPARING A DOCUMENT FOR
PREPRESS AND PRINTING

Illustrator is so widely praised for its excellence as a drawing tool, it's easy to forget that the application is also a top-notch page layout solution. Illustrator CS5 is a powerhouse print production utility, a state-of-the-art interface with the world of professional prepress and printing. Everything that you need to produce an output-ready document is there—crop marks, trim marks, reliable process tints, the full PANTONE library of non-process inks—all backed by a sophisticated color separations utility. If you are new to the world of prepress and printing, Illustrator CS5 makes for an excellent training ground, with straightforward, easy-to-use panels and dialog boxes. If you are experienced, you will admire how Illustrator seamlessly transitions from design and drawing to layout and output, thoughtfully and thoroughly encompassing the gamut of a printer's needs, demands, and wishes.

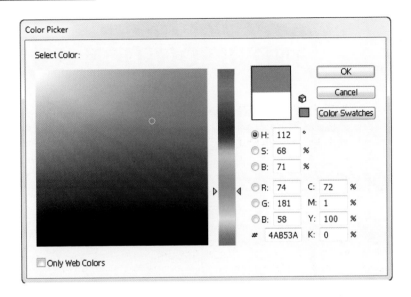

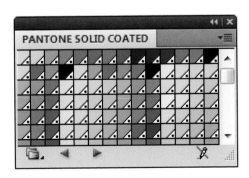

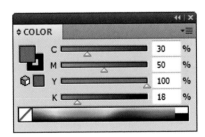

Explore Color Theory
AND RESOLUTION ISSUES

What You'll Do

▶ *In this lesson, you will learn basic color theory to gain an understanding of the role of CMYK ink in offset printing.*

Exploring Basic Color Theory

All of the natural light in our world comes from the sun. The sun delivers light to us in waves. The entirety of the sun's light—the electromagnetic spectrum—contains an infinite number of light waves, some which are at high frequencies, some which are at low frequencies—many of which will sound familiar to you. X-rays, gamma rays, and ultraviolet rays are all components of the electromagnetic spectrum.

The light waves that we see in our world are only a subset of the electromagnetic spectrum. Scientists refer to this subset— this range of wavelengths—as visible light. Because this light appears to us as colorless (as opposed to, say, the red world of the planet Mars), we refer to visible light as "white light."

From your school days, you may remember using a prism to bend light waves to reveal what you probably referred to as a rainbow. It is through this bending, or "breaking down" of white light, that we see color. The rainbow with which we are all so familiar is called the visible spectrum, and it is composed of seven distinct colors: red, orange, yellow, green, blue, indigo, and violet. Though the colors are distinct, the color range of the visible spectrum is infinite. For example, there's no definable place in the spectrum where orange light ends and yellow light begins.

Colors in the visible spectrum can themselves be broken down. For example, because red light and green light, when combined, produce yellow light, yellow light

can, conversely, be broken down, or reduced, to those component colors.

Red, green, and blue light (RGB) are the additive primary colors of light, as shown in Figure 1. The term "primary" refers to the fact that red, green, and blue light cannot themselves be broken down or reduced. The term additive refers to the fact that these same colors combine to produce other colors. For example, red and blue light, when

combined, produce violet hues. As primary colors, red, green, and blue light are the irreducible component colors of white light. Therefore, it logically follows that when red, green, and blue light are combined equally, they produce white light.

Finally, you'll note that nowhere in this paradigm is the color black. That is because, in the natural world, there is no such color as black. True black is the absence of all light.

Figure 1 *Red, green, and blue are the additive primary colors of light*

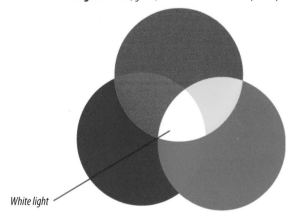

White light

Understanding Subtractive Primary Colors

Three things can happen when light strikes an object: the light can be reflected, absorbed, or transmitted, as shown in Figure 2.

Reflection occurs when light strikes an object and "bounces" off the object. Any object that reflects all of the light that strikes it appears as pure white.

Absorption occurs when light strikes an object and is not reflected, but instead is absorbed by the object. Any object that absorbs all of the light that strikes it appears as pure black.

Transmission occurs when light strikes an object and passes through the object. Any object that transmits all of the light that strikes it becomes invisible.

There are no truly invisible objects in our world (only some gasses are invisible). Nor are there any purely white or purely black objects. Instead, depending on the physical properties of the object, varying amounts of light are reflected, absorbed, and transmitted.

If an object absorbs some light, it logically follows that not all the white light that strikes the object will be reflected. Put another way, red, green, and blue light will not be reflected in full and equal amounts. What we perceive as the object's color is based on the percentages of the red, green, and blue light that are reflected and the color that that combination of light produces.

An object appears as cyan if it absorbs all of the red light that strikes it and also reflects or transmits all of the green and all of the blue light. An object that absorbs all of the green light that strikes it and also reflects or transmits all of the red and all of the blue light appears as magenta. An object that absorbs all of the blue light that strikes it and also reflects, or transmits, all of the red and all of the green light appears as yellow, as shown in Figure 3.

Cyan, magenta, and yellow are called **subtractive primary colors**. The term subtractive refers to the fact that each is produced by removing or subtracting one of the additive primary colors, and overlapping all three pigments would absorb all colors.

> **QUICK TIP**
>
> You may be thinking back to your school days and remembering that red, blue, and yellow are primary colors. They are the primary colors for mixing opaque (nontransmissive) paint, but that is entirely extraneous to the concepts covered in this chapter.

Figure 2 *Visual representations of reflection, absorption, and transmission*

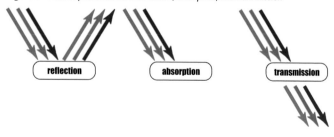

Figure 3 *Printers often refer to cyan as "minus red," magenta as "minus green," and yellow as "minus blue"*

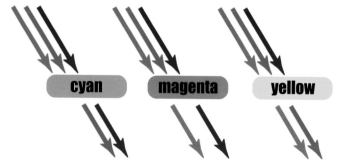

Understanding the Theory of Four-Color Process Printing

Color printing uses the three subtractive primary colors (plus black) to produce a color image or tint. To understand this, read the two points below carefully:

- The standard color for paper is white. The paper appears as white because it is manufactured to reflect RGB light in equal amounts.
- Cyan, magenta, and yellow inks are transparent—they are manufactured so that light passes through them. For example, cyan ink is manufactured to absorb red light and transmit green and blue light.

Here is the key to the whole theory: The color that you see when you look at a printed page is not reflected off the inks; it is light reflected off the paper. The light that is reflected off the paper is that which has not been absorbed (or subtracted) by the inks. Figure 4 demonstrates this concept.

If all of this color theory talk is making your head spin, don't worry about it. Working in Illustrator and producing a printed project does not require that you have these theories in your head. As you become more experienced with the printing process (and if you generally like this kind of stuff), these concepts will make more sense. Until then, remember the two essential points of this discussion: The offset printing process uses transparent CMYK inks; the color you see on a printed page is reflected off the paper, not the inks.

Understanding CMYK Inks

CMYK inks are called process inks. Process inks are manufactured by people, so they're not perfect. For example, no cyan ink can be manufactured so that it absorbs 100% of the red light that strikes it. Some is reflected and some is transmitted, as shown in Figure 5. Perfect magenta and yellow inks cannot be manufactured either. In addition, an ink's ability to transmit light is not perfect. That same cyan ink should, if it were a true cyan, transmit both blue and green light. Manufactured cyan inks actually absorb a small percentage of blue and green light.

Figure 4 *The color of the printed image is reflected off the paper, not the inks*

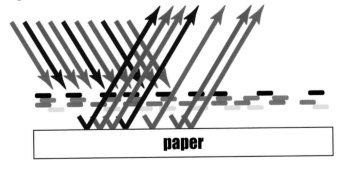

Figure 5 *Cyan ink in theory vs. reality*

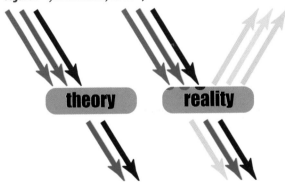

These imperfections become crucial when you try to use cyan, magenta, and yellow (CMY) to print dark areas of an image. In theory, if you overlapped all three inks, the area would appear black because each would absorb an additive primary, and no light would be reflected off the paper, as shown in Figure 6.

Because, in reality, the inks are unable to achieve 100% absorption and some light gets through and is reflected off the paper, CMY inks are unable to produce satisfactory shadows and dark areas of an image, as shown in Figure 7.

Figure 6 *If "perfect" inks were overlapped, no light would be reflected; the area of the overlap would appear black*

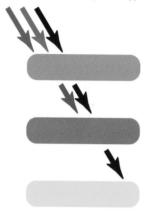

Figure 7 *In reality, CMY inks are insufficient to produce black areas*

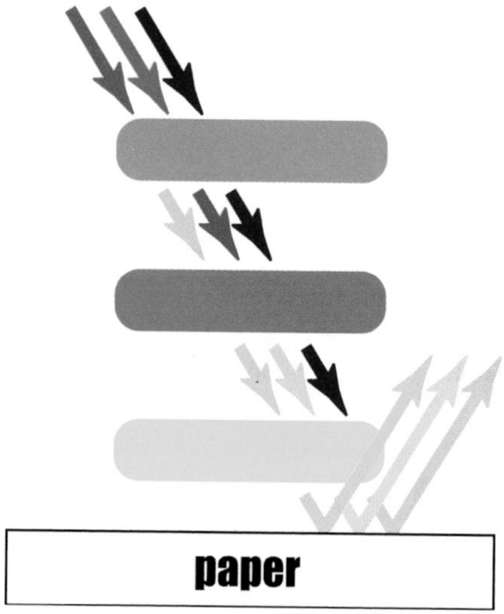

Creating a Rich Black

For many designers, black is the most powerful "color" on the panel. No other color can provide such contrast. Black can be used to trigger emotions. Black is neutral, but it's never silent. Use black ink (K) for text and lines and small areas of your artwork. When you have designed artwork with large black areas, keep in mind that black ink alone may not be enough to produce a dramatic black effect. To produce deep blacks, printers create a process tint that is 100% K plus 50% C. The cyan ink overlapped with the black produces a dark, rich black, which is why printers refer to this tint as a "rich black." Keep this idea in mind when you are working with black, but remember also that rich blacks are never used for text or lines.

Preparing a Document for Prepress and Printing

To compensate, black ink is used to produce deep shadows and fine detail. Printers refer to black ink as "K." They do not refer to it as "B" because "B" could be confused with blue, and blue could be confused with cyan. Also, printers have long referred to black as the "key" for aligning (registering) the four colors. Thus, the K in CMYK, though not a subtractive primary, is nevertheless essential to the subtractive printing process, as shown in Figure 8.

Rasterizing a Vector Graphic

Illustrator is a vector-based drawing program; the graphics you create are called vector graphics. Vector graphics have no pixels, thus they have no resolution. Graphics professionals refer to vector graphics as being **resolution independent**. This means that when you place an illustrator graphic into a layout, you can use it at any size—tiny or enormous—without concern for quality. An illustrator graphic will print with the same level of quality at any size.

Note, however, that Illustrator is not exclusively vector-oriented, nor are Illustrator graphics limited to vectors. If your illustration is very complex, you may wish to convert a vector graphic into a bitmap graphic by a process called **rasterization**, which converts it to a simple bitmap image. Sometimes output devices have trouble with complex vector graphics and effects, such as gradient meshes and transparent objects. If you rasterize the vector graphic, you will see immediately if the effects translated properly.

If so, the artwork is ready to print, as a simple, standard bitmap image.

Understanding Bitmap Graphics

A bitmap images is comprised of a rectangular grid of colored squares called **pixels**. Because pixels (a contraction of "picture elements") can render subtle gradations of tone, they are the most common medium for continuous tone images—what you perceive as a photograph on your computer.

All scanned images are composed of pixels. All "digital images" are composed of pixels. And all rasterized Illustrator images are composed of pixels. Figure 9 shows an example of a bitmap image. The enlarged section shows you the pixels that compose the image.

Figure 8 *The image on the left was printed with only CMY inks; black ink adds contrast and depth to the image on the right*

Figure 9 *Bitmap graphic*

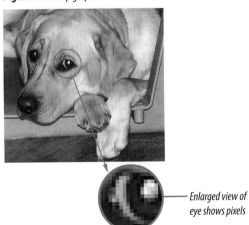

Enlarged view of eye shows pixels

Understanding Bitmap Image Resolution

The number of pixels in a given inch is referred to as the image's **resolution**. To be effective, pixels must be small enough to create an image with the illusion of continuous tone. The standard resolution for images for the web is 72 pixels per inch (ppi). For images that will be professionally printed, the standard resolution is 300 pixels per inch (ppi).

The term **effective resolution** refers to the resolution of a placed image based on its size in the layout. The important thing to remember about bitmap images in relation to printing is that the size of the image has a direct effect on the image's resolution.

Think about it—if you rasterize an image you create in Illustrator, converting it from a vector graphic to a bitmap graphic, and then, increase its size, the pixels that make up the image are spread out over a larger area. Thus, the effective resolution of the image goes down because there are now fewer pixels per inch. This decrease in resolution will have a negative impact on the quality of an image when it is printed.

Let's use a clear example to illustrate this. Let's say you have a bitmap image that it is 1" × 1" at 300 ppi. (300 ppi is the resolution of the image.) The image contains a total of 90,000 pixels (300x300=90,000).

Now, let's say you place the image into a 2" × 2" frame in a layout application, like InDesign, and enlarge the image 200% to fill the frame. Those same 90,000 pixels are spread out to fill a 2" × 2" frame. Thus, the effective resolution is 150 (ppi)—too low for professional printing. Figure 10 illustrates this example.

Enlarging a bitmap graphic beyond 10% results in a loss of quality, even if you do it in a program like Photoshop. That's because interpolated data is only duplicated data—inferior to the original data that you get from a scan or a digital image that you download from your digital camera.

In a nutshell, you should try your best to create bitmap graphics at both the size and resolution that they will be used at the final output stage. When rasterizing a vector graphic for output, whether for high-resolution printing or to appear on the

Figure 10 *Illustration of effective resolution*

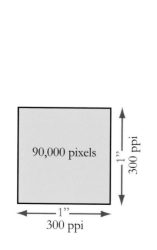

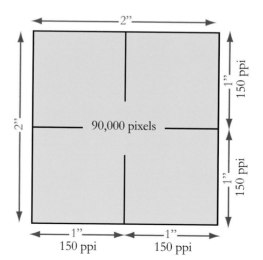

Internet, you must determine the resolution (the number of pixels per inch) that the resulting bitmap will contain. You can input the desired resolution for the resulting bitmap file in the Document Raster Effects Settings dialog box, which you can open by clicking Document Raster Effects Settings on the Effect menu.

Remember, nothing in this discussion applies to basic vector graphics, graphics you create in Illustrator. Vector graphics are resolution independent. You can feel free to enlarge and reduce vector graphics to your heart's content.

Misused Resolution Terminology

The misuse of the terms "resolution" and "DPI" by designers, printers, and even software programmers has resulted in some confusion over this concept. In general, when the term "resolution" is used, it is in reference to the number of pixels per inch in a bitmap image, or PPI. Unfortunately, many people use the term DPI instead of PPI; PPI is the only correct term for the resolution of a bitmap image. DPI stands for "dots per inch," which is the resolution of an output device. Dots are dots, and pixels are pixels; they are mutually exclusive.

The resolution of your laser printer is probably 600 dpi or 1200 dpi, which is a satisfactory number of printing device dots to print text and lines that appear to be smooth. For bitmap images and blends, a minimum resolution of 2400 dpi is required for the output device to produce the smooth transitions of tone.

Add to this confusion a third type of resolution—the resolution of a printed document. Lines per inch, LPI, or "line screen" is the number of lines of halftone dots (ink dots) in a printed image (professionally printed, not output from a desktop printer). Many printers refer to this resolution as, you guessed it, DPI. Lines are lines, and dots are dots. LPI is the correct term for the resolution of a printed image. Standard line screens for color printing are 133 LPI and 150 LPI.

Standard Resolutions for Rasterized Images

A fluency with resolution terminology will help you in Illustrator when you want to rasterize a vector graphic (convert it to a bitmap image). When doing so, you must determine the resolution of the resulting bitmap image, or the PPI. The PPI for a bitmap graphic that will be used on the Internet is 72 ppi. The PPI for a bitmap graphic that will be printed is twice the LPI and is usually 300 ppi for a high-resolution graphic.

Printing Transparent Artwork

Whenever you have a document with transparent objects (objects with blending modes applied or whose opacity is set to less than 100%), you can check the transparency preferences before printing the file. When you print or save artwork that contains transparency, Illustrator performs a process called flattening. When flattening, Illustrator identifies transparent artwork, then isolates the areas that are overlapped by the transparent object by dividing the areas into components. Illustrator then analyzes those components to determine if they can be output with vector data or if they must be rasterized (converted to pixels). The flattening process works very well in most cases. However, if you are unsatisfied with the appearance of the high-resolution output, you may want to step in and rasterize the artwork yourself. Before outputting the file, you can use Illustrator's Overprint Preview mode (found on the View menu), which approximates how transparency and blending will appear in color-separated output.

Work in CMYK MODE

What You'll Do

 In this lesson, you will use Illustrator's Color Picker, Color panel, and print options in CMYK Color mode.

Understanding Color Gamut

RGB, CMYK, and HSB are all known as **color models**. Color models are essentially mathematical algorithms that computers use to calculate and manage the color you see on your monitor. The **color mode** determines the color model used to display and print Illustrator documents. Illustrator offers two color modes for documents: RGB and CMYK.

As we've discussed, offset color printing is based on the CMYK color model. All light-emitting devices, such as your television or your monitor, produce color based on the RGB color model. If you flick a drop of water at your television screen, you will be able to see that the image is composed of very small red, green, and blue pixels. The full range of color that you perceive when you watch TV is the result of the additive properties of light; the red, green, and blue light are combining to produce the image.

Color gamut refers to the range of colors that can be printed or displayed by a given color model. A good monitor, based on the RGB color model, can produce a color gamut of more than 16 million colors. However, the spectrum of colors that can be viewed by the human eye is wider than any man-made method for reproducing color.

Setting Up Color Management

Illustrator's Color Settings dialog box simplifies the goal of setting up a color-managed workflow by bringing most of the standard color management controls to a single place. Click Edit on the Application bar, then click Color Settings to open the Color Settings dialog box. You can choose predefined RGB or CMYK configurations designed to help you achieve color consistency in a production workflow.

The CMYK color model is substantially smaller than the RGB color model. Therefore, when you are creating computer graphics, remember that some colors that you can see on your monitor cannot be reproduced by the CMYK printing process.

Illustrator addresses this reality in different ways. For example, if you are working in RGB mode and choosing colors in the Color Picker or the Color panel, Illustrator

will warn you if you have chosen a color that is "out-of-gamut"—that is, a color that cannot be printed. Also, if you have created an image in RGB mode and you convert to CMYK mode, Illustrator will automatically replace the out-of-gamut colors applied to images with their closest CMYK counterparts.

As shown in Figure 11, the colors in RGB that are out-of-gamut for the CMYK color

model are the brightest, most saturated, and most vibrant hues.

Don't despair. As you have certainly noted from looking at art books, posters, and even some high-quality magazines, the CMYK color model can be used to reproduce stunning color images. (*Note*: Because this book is a printed product and therefore based on the CMYK color model, we are unable to show you examples of out-of-gamut colors.)

Figure 11 *CMYK color model is unable to reproduce the brightest and most saturated hues that you can see on your screen*

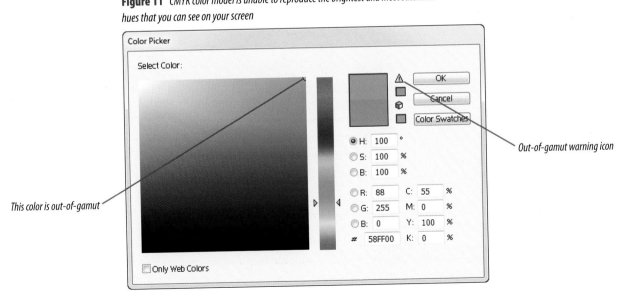

This color is out-of-gamut

Out-of-gamut warning icon

Specifying CMYK Tints

Tints are, quite simply, colors that you print by mixing varying percentages of CMYK inks. The lighter colors are produced with smaller percentages of ink, and darker colors are produced with higher percentages. You can purchase process tint books that show you, with a high degree of fidelity, a large number of the color combinations available in the CMYK gamut.

In Illustrator, you specify CMYK tints by entering percentages in the Color Picker and the Color panel, as shown in Figure 12. If this idea is setting off alarms in your head… good for you! All the color produced by your monitor is based on the RGB color model so you cannot "see" the CMYK color model (or real CMYK tints, for that matter) on your monitor.

In the early days of desktop publishing, this contradiction generated enormous fear in the hearts of print professionals and created an entire cottage industry of color calibration hardware and software. Despite the dire warnings, however, color calibration problems turned out to be a phantom menace. Simply put, the majority of print work produced is not so color-critical that variation in color is a problem (if the variation is even noticed).

Practically speaking, you must accept that the colors in your illustration on-screen will never be an exact match to the printed version. However, the numbers that you enter when specifying percentages of CMYK are exactly the percentages that will be output when the illustration goes to the printer. Therefore, if you must have a specific tint, find the color in a process tint book, and enter the percentages as specified. Then, don't worry about how the tint looks on your screen. If it looks close, that's great. If not, it doesn't matter. The printer is contractually responsible to be able to reproduce the tint that you specified.

Figure 12 *Specifying a process tint on the Color panel*

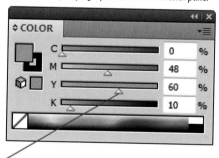

Dragging sliders on the Color panel is referred to as "specifying" or "mixing" a color

Preparing a Document for Prepress and Printing

Tabbing Through the Color Panel

The easiest way to mix process tints on the Color panel is to start out by double-clicking the C text box to select the current value, then enter the percentage of cyan that you want for the new tint. Press [Tab] to advance to the next text box, enter the new percentage, and so on. After you have entered the percentage in the B (black) text box, be sure to press [Tab] again. If you want to reverse direction, press and hold [Shift] while tabbing.

When working in Illustrator, you have the option to specify a fill or a stroke to overprint. However, in most cases, only separation devices support overprinting. When you print to a composite, or when your artwork contains overprinted objects that interact with transparent objects, you need to choose what to do with the objects you have set to overprint. You can choose to simulate the overprint or to discard the overprint altogether. Choose File on the Application bar, then click Print. Select Advanced on the left side of the Print dialog box. Select Simulate or Discard from the Overprints list arrow.

Using Creative Suite Color Settings

If you use other programs in the Adobe Creative Suite, such as InDesign and Photoshop, you'll be glad to know that there is a way to ensure that color settings can be synchronized across each CS5 program. Before you start your work on a new document or even an old one, you should synchronize your color settings. Adobe Bridge is the tool for this job. Simply open Bridge from your current application by clicking File on the Application bar, then clicking Browse in Bridge. In Bridge, click Edit on the Application bar, then click Creative Suite Color Settings.

To see all of the color settings, click the Show Expanded List Of Color Setting Files check box. Once you choose a color setting, click Apply. You can also install a custom settings file, such as a file you received from a printer or service bureau. To choose a custom settings file, click the Show Saved Color Settings Files button, then navigate to its location on your hard drive.

Specify process tints in the Color Picker

1. Open AI 11-1.ai, then save it as **Oahu**.

2. Select the placed image, then hide it.

3. Double-click the **Fill button** ☐ or **Stroke button** ◼ on the Tools panel to open the Color Picker, then type **189** for the hue, **100** for the saturation, and **100** for the brightness.

   The out-of-gamut warning icon appears, as shown in Figure 13.

4. Click the **blue square** under the out-of-gamut warning icon.

   The closest process color is specified as the new fill color.

5. Click **OK** to close the Color Picker dialog box.

6. Add the new color to the Swatches panel, then name it **Maverick**.

You chose a color in the Color Picker that was out-of-gamut for CMYK. You chose the process match that the out-of-gamut warning offered as a new fill color, then added it to the Swatches panel.

Figure 13 *Out-of-gamut warning in the Color Picker*

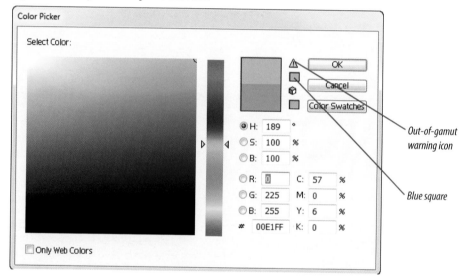

Out-of-gamut
warning icon

Blue square

Figure 14 *Applying process tints to the artwork*

Mix process tints on the Color panel

1. Click **Window** on the Application bar, then click **Color** to show the Color panel if the panel is not already showing.

2. Click the **Color panel options button** [icon], then click **CMYK** if it is not already selected.

3. Using the sliders on the panel, mix a process tint that is 5C/70M/100Y, then press [**Enter**] (Win) or [**return**] (Mac).

   In standard notation for process tints, zero is not specified. As there is no black in this tint, the K percentage is not noted.

TIP You will not see the new color on the Color panel if the cursor is still flashing in the text box in which you last entered a new value. Pressing [Tab] advances your cursor to the next text box.

4. Add the new color to the Swatches panel, then name it **Living**.

5. Mix a new process tint that is 5C/40M/5Y.

6. Add the new color to the Swatches panel, then name it **Amazing**.

7. Mix a new process tint that is 30M/100Y.

8. Add the new color to the Swatches panel, then name it **Twist**.

9. Apply the four new tints that you have added to the Swatches panel to the artwork, as shown in Figure 14.

10. Save your work.

You mixed three different process tints on the Color panel, saved them on the Swatches panel, then applied the four tints you created so far in this chapter to the artwork.

Specify SPOT COLORS

What You'll Do

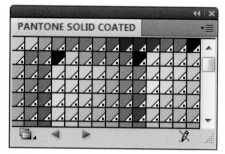

In this lesson, you will create and apply spot colors.

Understanding Spot Colors

Though printing is based on the four process colors CMYK, it is not limited to them.

Imagine that you are an art director designing the masthead for the cover of a new magazine. You have decided that the masthead will be an electric blue, vivid and eye-catching. If you were working with process tints only, you would have a problem. First, you would find that the almost-neon blue that you want to achieve is not within the CMYK gamut and can't be printed. Even if it could, you would have an even bigger problem with consistency issues. You want that blue to be the same blue on every issue of the magazine, month after month. But process tints will vary on press. As the cover is printed, the blue color in the masthead will shift in tone, sometimes sharply.

Designers and printers use non-process inks to solve this problem. Non-process inks

are special premixed inks that are printed separately from process inks. The color gamut of non-process inks available far exceeds that of CMYK. Non-process inks also offer consistent color throughout a print run.

The print world refers to non-process inks by a number of names:

Spot color refers to the fact that non-process inks print on the "spots" of the paper where the process inks do not print.

Fifth color refers to the fact that the non-process ink is often printed in addition to the four process inks. Note, however, that non-process inks are not necessarily the "fifth" color. For example, many "two-color" projects call for black plus one non-process ink.

PANTONE color refers to "Pantone" as a manufacturer of non-process inks.

PMS color is an acronym for PANTONE Matching System.

Preparing a Document for Prepress and Printing

Loading Spot Colors

In Illustrator, you use the Swatch Libraries menu item to select from a range of color systems (or libraries), including PANTONE, which is the standard library for non-process inks. When you import the PANTONE library, it appears as a separate panel, as shown in Figure 15.

QUICKTIP

To access the PANTONE color library in Illustrator, click Window on the Application bar, point to Swatch Libraries, then point to Color Books.

Outputting Documents with Spot Colors

All spot colors in the PANTONE library have a process match, which is of course a misnomer: if the process tint matched the spot color, there would be no need for the spot color in the first place. Some process tints—especially in the yellow hues—can come close to matching a spot color. Others—especially deep greens and blues—don't even come close.

When a four-color document is printed on a printing press, each of the four colors is printed separately: first yellow, then magenta, then cyan, then black. When an Illustrator document is output for printing, the document must be output as separations. Separations isolate each of the four process colors on its own "plate."

When a color document is printed with four colors and a spot color, the spot color requires its own plate on the printing press so that the non-process ink can be laid down separately from the process inks.

In Illustrator, all spot colors that you use in a document will automatically be converted to their process match when separated, unless you deselect the Convert to Process option in the Separation Setup dialog box, which you access through the Print dialog box. See Figure 16.

Figure 15 *PANTONE solid coated library appears as a separate panel*

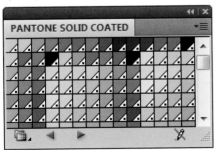

Figure 16 *Spot colors are converted to their process match when separated*

Import and apply spot colors

1. Click **Window** on the Application bar, point to **Swatch Libraries**, point to **Color Books**, then click **PANTONE solid coated**.

A new panel appears with small sample colors of each color in the library, as shown in Figure 17.

TIP You can purchase PANTONE swatch books from the Pantone web site at *www.pantone.com*.

2. Click in the **Find text box** in the PANTONE solid coated panel.

TIP If the Find text box is not available, click the PANTONE solid coated panel options button, then click Show Find Field.

3. Type **663** in the Find text box.

Color number 663 C is selected on the PANTONE solid coated panel.

TIP To display the number for each PANTONE color, click the PANTONE solid coated panel options button, click List View, then click Small or Large View.

4. Click the **OAHU letters**, then click the **PANTONE 663 C color swatch**.

The PANTONE 663 C color swatch is added to the standard Swatches panel.

(continued)

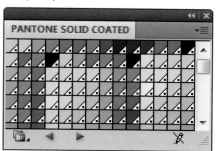

Figure 17 *PANTONE solid coated panel library appears as a separate panel*

Using the Separations Preview Panel

You can use the Separations Preview panel, located in the Window menu, to preview how your CMYK color layouts will color separate and overprint. The panel also allows you to preview spot colors in your document.

You can think of using the Separations Preview panel as a quality check before sending your job out to a printer or other vendor. Using the panel, you can identify which areas will print as rich black or process black (K) ink mixed with color inks for increased opacity and richer color. You can preview how blending, transparency, and overprinting will appear in a final document.

Note that the Separations Preview panel will work in Document CMYK mode only. Note, too, that the panel will not preview complex professional printing procedures such as trapping, emulsion options, printer's marks, and halftone screens and resolution. For these considerations, you should consult your printer.

Figure 18 *Spot color applied to the artwork*

5. Double-click the **PANTONE 663 C swatch** on the standard Swatches panel.

6. Click the **Color Mode list arrow**, then click **CMYK**.

7. Note that Spot Color is listed as the Color Type in the Swatch Options dialog box, then note the CMYK values.

   The CMYK values represent the values you would use to create the closest possible match of PANTONE 663 C with process inks.

8. Click **Cancel** to close the Swatch Options dialog box.

9. Change the fill of the red frame to PANTONE 663 C.

10. Show all, then send the placed image to the back.

    Your work should resemble Figure 18.

11. Save your work, then close the Oahu document.

You displayed the PANTONE solid coated library of swatches. You then applied a spot color to artwork.

Create
CROP MARKS

What You'll Do

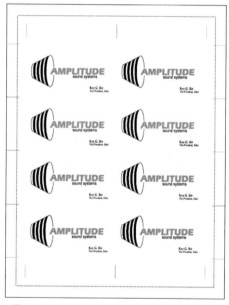

In this lesson, you will set up documents to print with crop marks.

Creating Crop Marks

The **trim size** of a document refers to the size of the finished document. By default, Illustrator crops the artwork at the size of the artboard, which you specify when you create the document. The document size is the trim size. **Crop marks** are short, thin lines that you can use to define areas of the page that you want be trimmed after the document is printed. Figure 19 shows crop marks around a graphic. When the trim size and the document size (the size of the artboard) are the same, you don't need to create your own crop marks.

You can create custom-sized crop marks on the artboard by drawing a rectangle that is precisely the same size as the document's trim size. Then, keeping the rectangle selected, click Effect on the Application bar, then click Crop Marks in the Illustrator Effects section of the menu. Crop marks will be added, representing the same size as the selected rectangle.

Illustrator CS5 adds crop marks as effects. Like all effects, crop marks are listed on the Appearance panel.

Editing Crop Marks

Once you've created crop marks, you cannot directly select them to edit them. Because they are added as effects, you must first expand the appearance to select and edit the crop marks. Click Object on the Application bar, then click Expand Appearance.

Creating Multiple Crop Marks for Multiple Objects

You can select multiple objects of different sizes on a page and create crop marks for each of those objects. The method is the same as for a single object: select the objects, click Effect on the Application bar, then click Crop Marks.

This situation often occurs when you "gang up" artwork on a page. For example, when printing business cards, printers use a standard sized 8.5" × 11" sheet of paper. Printing a single business card on that size paper would be a waste, so printers position multiple copies of the card on one sheet. Each of those copies must be trimmed, as shown in Figure 20.

When you apply the Crop Marks effect to multiple objects, you will often find that the effect creates redundant and/or overlapping crop marks. Simply expand the appearance and remove the crop marks you don't need.

Creating Templates

Templates are used to save time in creating documents like business cards that require common settings such as size, layout, design elements, and crop marks. To create a template, open a new or existing document. Set up the document the way you want it, add artwork or other elements, delete any existing swatches, styles, brushes, or symbols that you don't want to retain. Click File on the Application bar, then click Save as Template.

Figure 19 *Crop marks define the trim size of the artwork*

Figure 20 *Multiple crop marks define marks for multiple cuts*

Create crop marks

1. Open AI 11-2.ai, then save it as **Crop Marks**.
2. Click **View** on the Application bar, then click **Business Card**.
3. Select the 2" × 3.5" rectangle.

   2" × 3.5" is the standard size for business cards.

   TIP Switch to Outline mode if you have trouble selecting the rectangle.

4. Click **Effect** on the Application bar, then click **Crop Marks**.

   The rectangle remains; crop marks appear that define the trim size as that of the rectangle. Your screen should resemble Figure 21.

   TIP Switch back to Preview mode, if necessary, to see the crop marks.

5. Save your work, then close the Crop Marks document.

You selected a rectangle, then you applied the Crop Marks effect.

Figure 21 *Applying crop marks*

Using the Flattener Preview Panel

When you overlap objects, Illustrator allows you to create transparency effects, as though you are seeing one object through another. For example, if you overlap a blue circle with a yellow circle with a transparency effect, the overlapped area will appear green.

When you are viewing transparency effects on your monitor, everything looks great. It's when you print a document that unexpected colors can result from transparency effects.

If your document or artwork contains transparency, it usually needs to undergo a process called flattening before being output. To understand flattening, it helps to think of overlapping areas as separate shapes with their own fills. To use the above example, think of the green overlapped area not as a section of the blue object overlapped by the yellow object, but as a separate object with a green fill. That's how Illustrator—through flattening—manages overlapped areas with transparency effects. Flattening divides the artwork into vector-based areas and rasterized areas.

Click the Refresh button to get a preview of artwork affected by flattening on the Flattener Preview panel. You can use this preview to verify that your output artwork will output the way you expect.

Figure 22 *Applying crop marks*

Figure 23 *Delete crop marks that lie on trim lines*

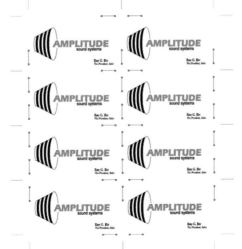

Use the Create Crop Marks effect

1. Open AI 11-3.ai, then save it as **Multiple Crop Marks**.

2. Select all.

   The artwork is locked. Only the eight rectangles that represent each business card are selected.

3. Click **Effect** on the Application bar, click **Crop Marks**, then deselect.

   As shown in Figure 22, crop marks appear for each rectangle.

4. Note that Crop Marks is listed on the Appearance panel.

5. Select all, click **Object** on the Application bar, then click **Expand Appearance**.

   The rectangles are deleted. All of the crop marks become selectable.

6. Use the Direct Selection tool to select the crop marks shown in Figure 23.

   All of these crop marks are redundant; they all define the same cuts that are defined by the crops outside of the artwork.

7. Delete the selected crops.

8. Save your work, then close the file.

You applied crop marks to eight objects, expanded the appearance of the effect, then deleted the redundant crop marks.

Create **BLEEDS**

What You'll Do

In this lesson, you will modify artwork to accommodate bleeds.

Creating Bleeds and Safety Guides

Artwork that extends to the trim is referred to as a "bleed" element, or simply a bleed. Based on printer lingo, this means that to print correctly, the ink must bleed off the page.

Imagine that you have designed a business card that shows white lettering against a black background. You have used the Crop Marks effect so that the marks define the "live area" as 2" × 3.5". When the cards are trimmed, if the cutter is off by the slightest amount, 1/10 of an inch, for example, your black business card will have a white line on one edge.

To accommodate variations in trimming, a printer will ask you to "build a bleed." What he or she is asking you to do is to extend bleed artwork so that it exceeds the cropped area by a minimum of .125". This is something you do manually to the artwork on the artboard. Artwork can bleed off any one or all four sides of the trim. Two of the most straightforward ways of doing this are to create a bleed object with the Offset Path command or to extend the existing artwork off the artboard using the Move command for precision. Figure 24 shows an example of using bleeds.

Preparing a Document for Prepress and Printing

In Illustrator CS5, you can specify a bleed amount in the New Document dialog box when you create the document. If you don't know the bleed size you're planning to use, or if you've already created the document and now want to apply a bleed (which will often be the case), you can specify the bleed setting in the Document Setup dialog box.

When you input a bleed amount in these dialog boxes, it doesn't actually *create* bleeds in the document. However, the information for the bleed amount is saved with the file.

In addition to bleeds, as a designer you should be conscious of your safety margin. All elements that aren't designed to bleed should be kept a minimum of .125" from the trim edge. This practice is known as maintaining safety or type safety. As with bleeds, safety guides anticipate variations in the trim cut and are designed to keep artwork from being accidentally trimmed off the page.

Figure 24 *Bleeds extend the crop marks to accommodate variations when trimming*

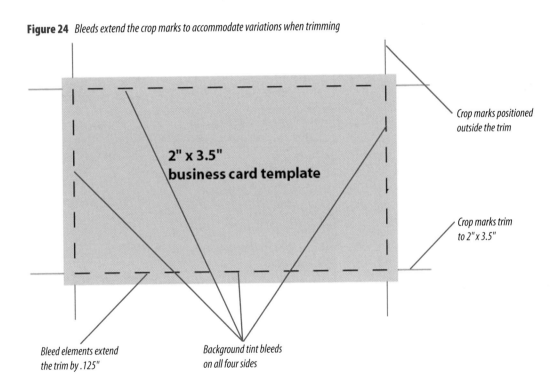

2" x 3.5"
business card template

*Crop marks positioned
outside the trim*

*Crop marks trim
to 2" x 3.5"*

*Bleed elements extend
the trim by .125"*

*Background tint bleeds
on all four sides*

Create a bleed using the Offset Path command

1. Open AI 11-4.ai, then save it as **Oahu Bleed**.
2. Click **File** on the Application bar, then click **Document Setup**.
3. Enter **.125** in all four Bleed text boxes, then click **OK**.

   Red guides appear around the artboard indicating the bleed area.
4. Select the frame of the artwork that is filled with PANTONE 663 C.
5. Click **Object** on the Application bar, point to **Path**, then click **Offset Path**.
6. Type **.125** in the Offset text box, then click **OK**.

   The Offset Path command creates a new object, in this case, a bleed object that extends the artboard .125" on all sides. Your artwork should resemble Figure 25.
7. Verify that the new bleed object is still selected, then send it to the back.
8. Save your work, but don't close the Oahu Bleed document.

You used the Offset Path command to extend the edges of a bleed object .125".

Figure 25 *A bleed object created with the Offset Path command*

.125" bleed

Figure 26 *Three sides of the blue rectangle must bleed*

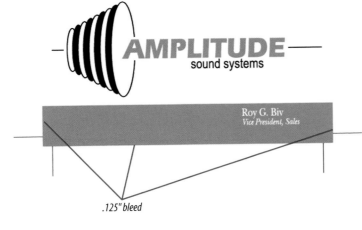

.125" bleed

Figure 27 *The rule must also bleed*

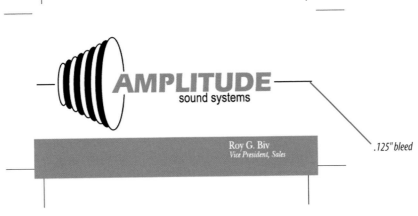

.125" bleed

Create a bleed using the Move command

1. Open AI 11-5.ai, then save it as **Three Sided Bleed**.
2. Click **View** on the Application bar, then click **Business Card**.
3. Select the black-stroked rectangle, click **Effect** on the Application bar, then click **Crop Marks**.
4. Click **Object** on the Application bar, click **Expand Appearance**, then use the Direct Selection tool to delete the black rectangle.
5. Click the **bottom edge of the blue rectangle**.
6. Click **Object** on the Application bar, point to **Transform**, click **Move**, type **0** in the Horizontal text box, type **.125** in the Vertical text box, then click **OK**.
7. Select the left edge of the blue rectangle with the Direct Selection tool, then move it -.125" to the left.
8. Select the right edge of the blue rectangle with the Direct Selection tool, then move it .125" to the right.

   The blue rectangle bleeds on all three sides, as shown in Figure 26.
9. Select only the left anchor point of the black line, then move the point -.125" horizontally.
10. Select only the right anchor point of the black line, then move the point .125" horizontally, so that your work resembles Figure 27.
11. Save your work, then close the Three Sided Bleed document.

You extended individual lines and anchor points outside the crop marks as bleeds.

Save a File
AS A PDF

What You'll Do

In this lesson, you will save an Illustrator file as a PDF for both print and email.

Saving a PDF for Print and for Email

PDF (portable document format) is one of the most common export formats for emailing documents and printing high-res output. The key to the relationship between Illustrator and PDF is that, as a PDF, the Illustrator document is complete and self-contained. Issues with placed graphics and fonts become non-issues. The PDF file includes all imported graphics and fonts. The recipient of the file does not need to have the document fonts loaded to view the file correctly.

The self-contained nature of PDFs, and the issues that it solves, makes PDF the format of choice for both professional printing and for emailing documents. In advertising and design agencies, it's standard procedure to export an InDesign document as a PDF to email to the client for approval. For professional printing, it's becoming more and more the case that, rather than asking for an InDesign document packaged with all the supporting graphics and fonts, printers just ask for a single "high-res" PDF. If you're using Illustrator as your layout software, the PDF format offers the same options.

When a layout includes placed graphics, especially high-resolution, large-file-size Photoshop images, how you save the PDF affects how the document is compressed to reduce the resulting file size.

When emailing a layout as a PDF, you will save the document with compression utilities activated to reduce the file size for email. These compression utilities will compress the file size of placed images. Figure 28 shows the PDF dialog box with compression utilities activated.

When sending a layout to a printer for professional printing, you won't want the placed graphics to be compressed. In this case, you'll export the PDF with compression utilities turned off. The resulting PDF will likely be too large to email, but it will remain high quality for printing.

Creating a PDF Preset

PDF settings are not only used for conserving file size. The PDF format offers a number of useful options. You can choose whether or not the resulting PDF shows crop marks and printer marks, for example, or you can choose whether the filename and the date and time of the creation of the PDF is listed at the top. You also specify whether the resulting file will be in the CMYK or RGB color space.

Most users rely on pre-defined presets in the PDF dialog box. Most predefined presets are shared across Adobe Creative Suite components, including InDesign, Illustrator, Photoshop, and Acrobat. However, you can always create and save your own unique settings as new presets.

Figure 28 *PDF dialog box*

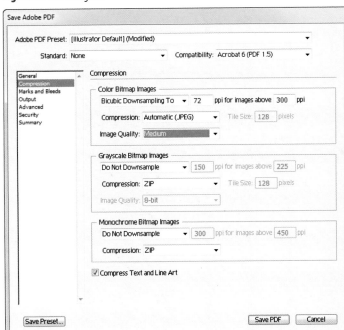

Save a compressed PDF for email

If you do not have Adobe Acrobat on your computer you will be able to step through most of this exercise but will not be able to save your PDF at the end.

1. Return to the Oahu Bleed.ai document, click **File** on the Application bar, then click **Save A Copy**.

2. In the Save A Copy dialog box, name the file **Oahu for Email**.

3. Click the **Save as type list arrow** (Win) or the **Format list arrow** (Mac), click **Adobe PDF**, then click **Save**.

4. In the Save Adobe PDF dialog box, enter the General settings as shown in Figure 29.

   These are default settings for saving a PDF for general use.

5. Click **Compression** in the box on the left side of the dialog box, then enter the settings shown in Figure 30.

   The settings indicate that for both color and grayscale images, the Illustrator will use JPEG compression with High image quality to reduce the file size. The settings also indicate that Illustrator will use Bicubic Downsampling (standard pixel interpolation) to reduce to 72 pixels per inch any color or grayscale graphics that are over 72 pixels per inch. Downsampling refers to reducing the resolution of a bitmap image. Thus, a 300 pixel per inch PSD graphic in the layout will be reduced to a 72 pixel per inch JPEG with High quality in the PDF.

   (continued)

Figure 29 *General settings for the PDF*

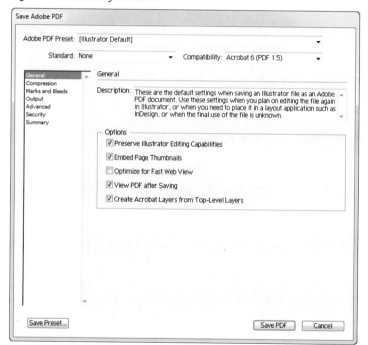

Figure 30 *Compression settings for the PDF*

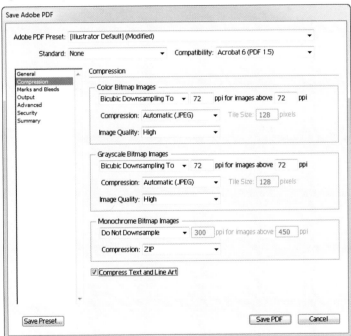

6. Click **Marks and Bleeds** in the box on the left side of the dialog box and verify that nothing is checked.

Note that the word (Modified) now appears after [Illustrator Default] in the Adobe PDF Preset box at the top of the dialog box. This indicates that the Illustrator Default preset has been modified because you changed the compression settings.

7. Click the **Save Preset button** in the lower-left corner, type **Use For Email** in the Save Preset dialog box, then click **OK**.

These new settings are now saved and will be available in the Preset list for any future PDFs that you want to email.

8. Click **Save PDF**.

The PDF will open in Acrobat for you to view. The exported PDF file size is less than 5MB. If you do not have Adobe Acrobat installed on your computer, you will receive an error message and will not be able to save the PDF you created.

You exported the Oahu Bleed document as an Adobe PDF file with a file size small enough to email. You entered settings for JPEG compression and for reducing the resolution of placed images. You then saved a preset for the settings you entered.

Export an uncompressed PDF

If you do not have Adobe Acrobat on your computer you will be able to step through most of this exercise but will not be able to save your PDF at the end.

1. Return to the Oahu Bleed.ai document, click **File** on the Application bar, then click **Save a Copy**.

2. In the Save a Copy dialog box, name the file **Oahu for Hi-Res Print**.

3. Click the **Save as type list arrow** (Win) or the **Format list arrow** (Mac), click **Adobe PDF**, then click **Save**.

4. In the Save Adobe PDF dialog box, enter the same General settings shown in Figure 29.

5. Click **Compression** on the left side of the dialog box, then enter the settings shown in Figure 31.

   The settings indicate that no compression or downsampling will be applied to any of the images in the layout. Thus, if this document were built for professional printing, with high resolution images, the images would not be affected.

6. Click **Marks and Bleeds** in the box on the left side of the dialog box, then enter the settings shown in Figure 32.

   Printer's marks include crop marks and color bars. Note that Use Document Bleed Settings is checked. The bleed you created in Illustrator will be represented in the final PDF.

   (continued)

Figure 31 *Compression and Downsampling deactivated*

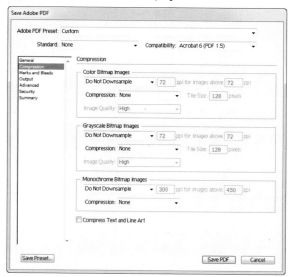

Figure 32 *Marks and Bleeds*

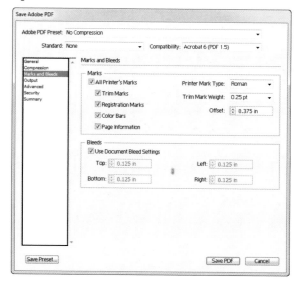

Preparing a Document for Prepress and Printing

Figure 33 *Exported PDF with no compression and with printer's marks and bleed and slug*

7. Note that the word Custom now appears beside High Quality Print at the top of the dialog box.

8. Click the **Save Preset button** in the lower-left corner, type **No Compression** in the Save Preset As dialog box, then click **OK**.

   These new settings are now saved and will be available in the Preset list for any future PDFs that you want to export with no compression.

9. Click **Save PDF**.

   The PDF will open in Acrobat as shown in Figure 33. The OAHU image has not been affected in any way since being placed in Illustrator. If you do not have Adobe Acrobat installed on your computer, you will get an error message and your PDF will not be created.

10. Save your work, then close all open files.

You exported the Oahu Bleed document as an Adobe PDF file with no compression.

Explore color theory and resolution issues.

1. List the seven distinct colors of the visible spectrum.
2. What are the three additive primary colors?
3. What are the three subtractive primary colors?
4. When red, green, and blue light are combined equally, what color light do they produce?
5. Explain the term "subtractive" in terms of the subtractive primary colors.
6. Explain the term "transmission" in terms of light striking an object.
7. Which additive primary color would be 100% absorbed by a perfect cyan ink?
8. Which additive primary color would be 100% absorbed by a perfect magenta ink?
9. Which additive primary color would be 100% absorbed by a perfect yellow ink?
10. What is the fourth color in the four-color printing process, and why is it necessary?
11. What is the difference between a vector graphic and a bitmap graphic?
12. What does effective resolution mean?
13. Why are Illustrator graphics called resolution independent?

Work in CMYK mode.

1. Open AI 11-6.ai, then save it as **Sleep Center**.
2. Using the Color panel, create a new process tint that is 55M/75Y.
3. Save the process tint on the Swatches panel as **text color**.
4. Fill the words THE SLEEP CENTER with the text color swatch.
5. Deselect the text, then save your work.

Specify spot colors.

1. Click Window on the Application bar, point to Swatch Libraries, point to Color Books, then click PANTONE solid coated.
2. Select the object with the gradient on the artboard.
3. Select the black color stop on the gradient slider on the Gradient panel.
4. Press [Alt] (Win) or [option] (Mac), then click a purple swatch in the PANTONE solid coated panel.
5. Save your work.

Create crop marks.

1. Click Effect on the Application bar, then click Crop Marks.
2. Click Object on the Application bar, then click Expand Appearance.
3. Save your work.

Create bleeds.

1. Deselect, then click the left edge of the rectangle with the Direct Selection tool.
2. Click Object on the Application bar, point to Transform, then click Move.
3. Type **-.125** in the Horizontal text box, type **0** in the Vertical text box, then click OK.
4. Select the top edge of the rectangle.
5. Open the Move dialog box, type **0** in the Horizontal text box, type **.125** in the Vertical text box, then click OK.
6. Select the right edge of the rectangle.
7. Open the Move dialog box, type **.125** in the Horizontal text box, type **0** in the Vertical text box, then click OK.
8. Save your work, then compare your illustration to Figure 34.

Save a file as a PDF.

1. Click File on the Application bar, then click Save a Copy.
2. In the Save a Copy dialog box, name the file **Sleep Center for Email**.
3. Click the Save as type list arrow (Win) or the Format list arrow (Mac), click Adobe PDF, then click Save.
4. In the Save Adobe PDF dialog box, enter the same General settings shown in Figure 29.

5. Click Compression on the left side of the dialog box, then enter the settings shown in Figure 31. Because this illustration has no placed bitmap graphics, its file size is already low enough to email without a problem. You could also load the No Compression preset if you have already completed Lesson 6 in this chapter.

6. Click Marks and Bleeds in the box on the left side of the dialog box and verify that nothing is checked.
7. Click Save PDF.
   The PDF will open in Acrobat for you to view. If you do not have Acrobat, you will receive a warning message and will not be able to save the file as a PDF.
8. Save changes, then close Sleep Center.ai.

Figure 34 *Completed Skills Review*

You work in the computer department at a small print shop. Your boss brings you an Illustrator file for a business card for USAchefs, an Internet company that works with the top chefs and restaurants in the city. Your boss asks you to create a print proof, which she will show to the customer. She asks you to create it with a rich black, add crops, and build a bleed, then says, with a wink, "But not necessarily in that order." You realize that she's challenging you to figure out the right order in which to get all three processes accomplished.

1. Open AI 11-7.ai, then save it as **USAchefs**.
2. Select the black rectangle, click Effect on the Application bar, then click Crop Marks.
3. Click Object on the Application bar, then click Expand Appearance.
4. Use the Offset Path command to offset the black rectangle path .125" on all four sides.
5. Keeping the rectangle selected, increase the cyan portion of its fill color 50% to create a rich black.
6. Save your work, then compare your illustration to Figure 35.
7. Close the document.

Figure 35 *Completed Project Builder 1*

You own a design firm in a small town. A new client delivers his logo to you on disk, telling you that it has two colors: PANTONE 255 and 70% PANTONE 5767. He tells you, "It's all set to go." You know that this client knows only enough to be dangerous. You open his file and, sure enough, you note immediately that all of the tints are process tints. You must change the fills and strokes to the proper PANTONE colors. Because this is a complex logo, and because you know that your client's knowledge of Illustrator is limited, you are aware that you must be very careful not to miss any elements.

1. Open AI 11-8.ai, then save it as **City Square**.
2. Apply the Show All command, just to avoid any potential surprises.
3. Delete the green letters.
4. Display the PANTONE solid coated panel, and verify that the Find field is showing.
   If the panel isn't displaying the Find field, open it using the Panel options menu.
5. Select the letter C in the center of the logo.
6. Click Select on the Application bar, point to Same, then click Fill Color.
7. Apply PANTONE 255 C to the fill, then hide the selection (*Hint*: If the Find Field text box does not work, you'll have to scroll around to find the correct swatch.)
8. Select the top white rectangle.
9. Click Select on the Application bar, point to Same, then click Stroke Color.
10. Apply PANTONE 255 C to the stroke, then hide the selection.
11. Click the green square in the center, then change the black stroke to PANTONE 255 C.
12. Click Select on the Application bar, point to Same, then click Fill Color.
13. Apply PANTONE 5767 C to the fill.
14. Display the Color panel if necessary, then drag the slider to 80%.
15. Hide the selection.
16. Select all and note that all the remaining items have a white fill.
17. Show all, save your work, then compare your illustration with Figure 36.
18. Close the City Square document.

Figure 36 *Completed Project Builder 2*

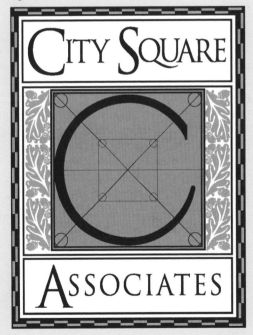

You are the assistant art director for OAHU magazine. The art director tells you that, at the last minute, the editor in chief has changed the cover photo. You place the new photo in the Illustrator file and realize immediately that the colors that worked so well with the previous photo no longer work with this new photo.

1. Open AI 11-9.ai, then save it as **Oahu 2**.
2. Choose a new PANTONE color for the title and the frame.
3. Mix a new process tint, then apply it to the word "living."
4. Mix three new process tints, then apply them to the three subheads.
5. Save your work. See Figure 37, for one possible solution, then close Oahu 2.

Figure 37 *Completed Design Project*

Preparing a Document for Prepress and Printing

You are the head of the film output department for a small printer. You receive an Illustrator file for the business card for USAchefs. The file is complete with a rich black, crop marks, and bleeds. With so many years' experience, you know how best to lay out and print standard-sized business cards for maximum cost-effectiveness. However, you have a group of six new workers whom you hired for the third shift, and you realize that the issues involved with preparing this job would make for a great lesson.

1. Open AI 11-10.ai, then save it as **Chef Output**. (*Hint*: The single card is 2" wide by 3.5" tall. The document is 8.5" by 11.")
2. What would be the most cost-efficient layout for the card on an 8.5" × 11" sheet? How many cards can be positioned on the sheet while still keeping a minimum .25" margin from the edge of the sheet?
3. Once you have calculated the number of cards that can fit on the page, calculate the size of the total area (without bleeds) covered by the artwork.
4. Use the Move dialog box to position 12 cards (4 across, 3 down) centered on the 8.5" × 11" page.
5. Select just the black rectangles, copy them, paste in front, then bring them to the front.
6. Open the Pathfinder panel, then click the Unite button. (*Hint*: The 12 rectangles are united as one rectangle.)
7. Hide the new rectangle.
8. Select just the black rectangles again, click Effect on the Application bar, then click Crop Marks.

9. Click Object on the Application bar, then click Expand Appearance.
10. Deselect, then use the Direct Selection tool to move the outside crop marks onto the 8.5" × 11" document. (*Hint*: Move the crops close to the black rectangles, but don't let them touch.)
11. Select the black rectangles, then hide them.
12. Delete all the redundant interior crop marks so that your document resembles Figure 38.
13. Reveal the hidden objects, then deselect.

14. Select the large black rectangle, click Object on the Application bar, point to path, then click Offset path.
15. Type **.125** in the Offset text box, then click OK.
16. Click Object on the Application bar, point to Arrange, then click Send to Back.
17. Deselect all, click the center of the large black triangle to select it, then delete it.
18. Compare your results to Figure 39, save your work, then close the file.

Figure 38 *Interior crop marks deleted*

Figure 39 *Completed Portfolio Project*

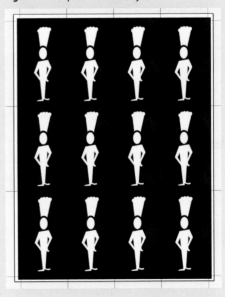

CHAPTER 12

DRAWING WITH SYMBOLS

1. Create symbols
2. Place symbol instances
3. Modify symbols and symbol instances
4. Create symbol instance sets
5. Modify symbol instance sets

DRAWING
WITH SYMBOLS

In Illustrator, the file size of a document is largely determined by the number and complexity of objects in the document. The greater the number of objects in the document, the greater the file size. A large number of objects with gradients, blends, and effects greatly increases the file size. When you are creating graphics for the internet, file size becomes a serious concern.

Symbols are one solution for creating complex files while maintaining a relatively low file size. **Symbols** are graphic objects that you create and store on the Symbols panel.

Imagine that you were drawing a field of flowers, and you have drawn a pink, a blue, and a yellow flower. Each flower has a radial gradient in its center and color blends to add dimension to the petals and green leaves. Now imagine that you must drag and drop 200 copies of each to create your field of flowers!

Along with a cramp in your hand, you would have an unusually large Illustrator file.

With the three flowers defined as symbols, you can create 200 symbol instances of each flower symbol quickly and easily. The key is that you haven't actually added the complex artwork multiple times, because the instances don't really exist as artwork. **Symbol instances** are merely a reference to the original artwork that is the symbol, and the instances function only to show the positioning of the symbol artwork on the artboard. Think of it this way: Symbol instances are merely virtual representations of a symbol.

Symbolism tools allow you to edit large numbers of symbol instances quickly and effectively. Whenever you are using the same artwork multiple times in a document, consider using symbols to save time and disk space.

Symbols panel

SYMBOLS

Symbolism tools

Create
SYMBOLS

What You'll Do

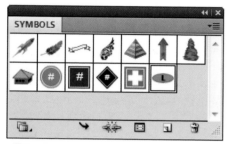

 In this lesson, you will create symbols from Illustrator artwork and save them on the Symbols panel.

Creating Symbols

You can create symbols from any Illustrator artwork, including text, compound paths, and grouped paths. Symbols may also include blends, effects, brush strokes, gradients, and even other symbols.

The Symbols panel, shown in Figure 1, is a great place to store artwork that you plan to use again. When you use symbol artwork, you can modify the symbol instance on the artboard, without affecting its original appearance on the panel. In this way, you can think of the Symbols panel as a database of your original art.

Figure 1 *Symbols panel*

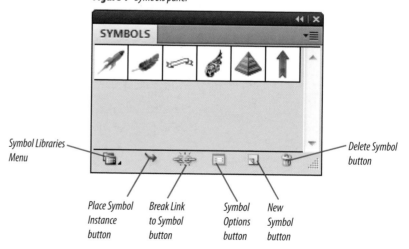

Symbol Libraries Menu

Place Symbol Instance button

Break Link to Symbol button

Symbol Options button

New Symbol button

Delete Symbol button

Figure 2 *Symbol Options dialog box*

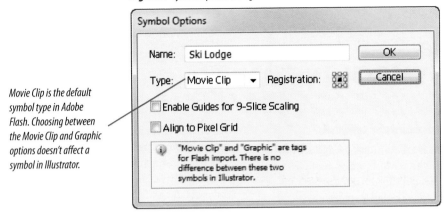

Movie Clip is the default symbol type in Adobe Flash. Choosing between the Movie Clip and Graphic options doesn't affect a symbol in Illustrator.

Figure 3 *Symbols panel with new symbols added*

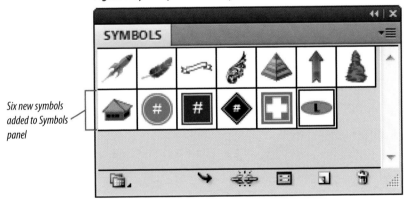

Six new symbols added to Symbols panel

Create symbols

1. Open AI 12-1.ai, then save it as **Trail Map**.
2. Click the **Symbols panel icon** 🍀 in the dock of collapsed panels to open the Symbols panel.

TIP If you do not see the Symbols panel icon there, open the Symbols panel using the Window menu.

3. Select the brown house picture in the scratch area on the artboard.
4. Click the **Symbols panel options button** ▼≡, then click **New Symbol**. The Symbol Options dialog box opens.
5. Type **Ski Lodge** in the Name text box, note the default Movie Clip type option, then compare your Symbol Options dialog box to Figure 2.
6. Click **OK** to add ski lodge symbol to Symbol panel.
7. Select the green circle icon in the scratch area, then drag it into the Symbols panel. The Symbol Options dialog box opens.
8. Type **Novice** in the Name text box, then click **OK**. Throughout this chapter, all symbols that you create should be Movie Clip types because that is standard notation for Flash exports.
9. Add the blue square icon to the Symbols panel, then name it **Intermediate**.
10. Add the black diamond icon to the Symbols panel, then name it **Expert**.
11. Add the red square icon to the Symbols panel, then name it **First Aid**.
12. Add the yellow oval icon to the Symbols panel, then name it **Chairlift**. Your Symbols panel should resemble Figure 3.
13. Delete the Ski Lodge, Novice, Intermediate, Expert, First Aid, and Chairlift icons on the artboard, then save your work.

You created new symbols by using the Symbols panel menu and by dragging and dropping.

Place
SYMBOL INSTANCES

What You'll Do

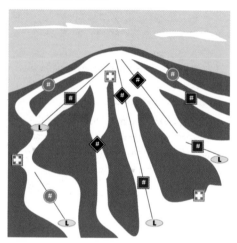

In this lesson, you will place symbol instances on the artboard.

Placing Instances of Symbols

If a symbol is artwork stored on the Symbols panel, then the artwork, when put to use in the document, is called a symbol instance. You can place a **symbol instance** on the artboard by first selecting the symbol on the Symbols panel, then dragging it to the artboard, or by selecting it, then clicking the Place Symbol Instance button on the Symbols panel, as shown in Figure 4. You can also use the Place Symbol Instance command on the Symbols panel menu.

Symbol instances are "linked" to their corresponding symbols on the panel. This relationship introduces powerful functionality when you work with symbol instances. Imagine an illustration showing a field with hundreds of flowers, all of them yellow. If the flowers were all symbol instances, you could change the single symbol to pink, and all the yellow instances would update immediately.

Figure 4 *Placing a symbol instance*

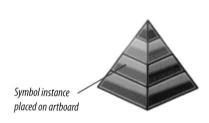

Symbol instance
placed on artboard

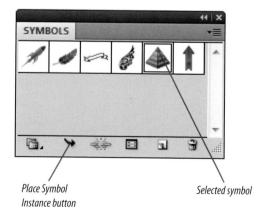

Place Symbol
Instance button

Selected symbol

Drawing with Symbols

Figure 5 *Positioning symbol instances*

Figure 6 *Positioning copies of the Chairlift symbol instance*

Place instances of a symbol

1. Click the **Novice symbol** on the Symbols panel.
2. Click the **Symbols panel options button** , then click **Place Symbol Instance**.

   A single Novice symbol instance appears on the artboard.
3. Drag the **Novice symbol instance** to the location shown in Figure 5.
4. Click the **Intermediate symbol** on the Symbols panel, then drag it to the artboard above the Novice symbol instance.
5. Drag a **symbol instance** of the Expert, First Aid, and Chairlift symbols onto the artboard, then position them as shown in Figure 5.
6. Click the **Chairlift symbol instance** on the artboard, press and hold **[Alt]** (Win) or **[option]** (Mac), then drag and drop three copies as shown in Figure 6.

(continued)

7. Copy and reposition the Novice, Intermediate, Expert, and First Aid symbol instances so that your screen resembles Figure 7.

Dragging and dropping copies is the easiest way to duplicate the symbol instances.

8. Save your work.

You placed symbol instances of five symbols on the artboard. You then duplicated the symbol instances and positioned them on the artboard.

Figure 7 *Positioning the Novice, Intermediate, Expert, and First Aid symbol instances*

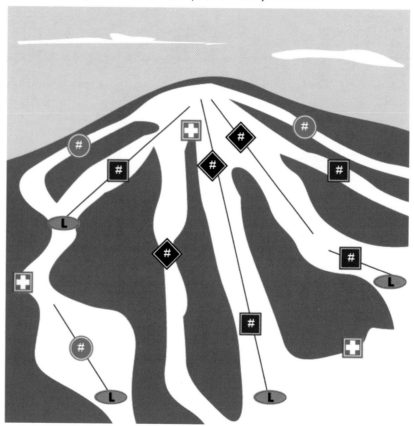

Figure 8 *Editing a symbol in Isolation mode*

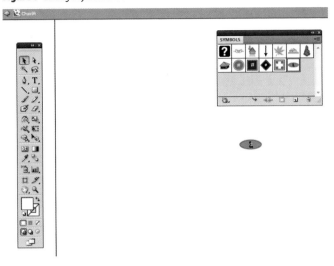

Figure 9 *Chairlift symbol instances updated*

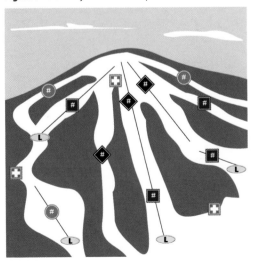

Edit a symbol

1. Double-click the **Chairlift symbol** on the Symbols panel.

   As shown in Figure 8, when you double-click a symbol in the Symbols panel, Illustrator switches to Isolation mode and the symbol is isolated on a blank artboard.

2. Click the **Direct Selection tool**, then select the orange fill background of the symbol.

3. Change the fill color to Yellow.

4. Press **[Esc]** to exit Isolation mode.

5. Compare your screen to Figure 9.

   All instances of the Chairlift symbol instance are updated with the yellow fill.

6. Save your work.

You modified a symbol in the Symbols panel, noting that all instances on the artboard automatically update.

Modify Symbols
AND SYMBOL INSTANCES

What You'll Do

In this lesson, you will modify both symbol instances and the symbols themselves.

Modifying Symbol Instances

When working with symbol instances, approach them as you would any other Illustrator artwork. You can transform symbol instances by using commands on the Object menu or by using any of the transform tools. You can cut, copy, and drag and drop copies of symbol instances. You can perform any operation from the Transparency, Appearance, and Graphic Styles panels. For example, you can reduce the opacity of a symbol instance and you can apply effects, such as a drop shadow or a distortion.

Symbols are most often composed of multiple objects, such as you would expect to find in a drawing of a butterfly or a flower, for example. When you select a symbol instance on the artboard, its selection marks show only a simple bounding box, as shown in Figure 10; the individual elements of the artwork are not selected.

You can, however, select the individual components of a symbol instance by using the Expand command on the Object menu. The bounding box disappears, and the individual elements of the artwork are available to be selected (and modified), as shown in Figure 11.

Redefining Symbols

Once you have modified a symbol instance, you can use the modified artwork to redefine the associated symbol on the panel by replacing the original symbol. When you do so, all existing symbol instances are updated and reflect the changes to the symbol.

If you don't want a particular symbol instance to be updated, you can select the instance and break the link to the symbol.

The symbol instance will no longer be associated with the symbol.

You can also modify a symbol instance on the artboard and use it to create a new symbol without affecting the original symbol on which it is based. Thus, the Symbols panel is useful for storing subtle or dramatic variations of artwork. For example, if you are drawing a landscape that features a wind farm, you can draw a single windmill, save it as a symbol,

rotate the blades on the original artwork, then save a new symbol, and so forth.

QUICK TIP

Symbols, ideal for web graphics, can be output as Scalable Vector Graphics (SVG) or Flash files (SWF). To output your symbol artwork as SVG, click File on the Application bar, click Save As, then click SVG from the Save as type list arrow. To output your symbol artwork as Flash, click File on the Application bar, click Export, then click Flash (SWF) from the Save as type list arrow. Both formats offer an Options dialog box for you to make further specifications about your final product.

Figure 10 *When you select a symbol instance, the individual elements of the artwork are not selected*

Figure 11 *The Expand command allows you to select the individual elements of the artwork*

Edit symbol instances

1. Using the Selection tool ![Selection tool], select the green Novice symbol instance in the lower-left corner of the artboard.

   A bounding box identifies the selection. The elements of the artwork cannot be selected individually.

2. Click **Object** on the Application bar, then click **Expand**.

TIP If you receive a message saying, "You are about to edit the Symbol definition. Any edits to the symbol will be applied to all its instances. Do you want to continue?" click OK.

3. In the Expand dialog box, verify that the Object check box is checked and the Fill check box is not checked, then click **OK**.

   The elements of the symbol instance are selected individually.

4. Deselect the symbol instance, click the **Type tool** ![Type tool], highlight the # sign in the symbol instance, then type **1**.

   Your screen should resemble Figure 12.

TIP If you receive a message stating that the text was created in a previous version of Illustrator, click OK.

5. Using the same method, expand the Novice, Intermediate, and Expert symbol instances, then change their numbers to those shown in Figure 13.

6. Select every symbol instance and each of the blue chair lift lines on the artboard, then hide them.

7. Save your work.

You used the Expand command to allow you to select individual elements of a symbol instance and edit those elements.

Figure 12 *Editing a symbol instance*

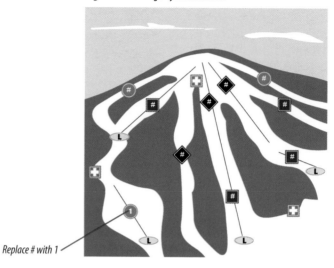

Replace # with 1

Figure 13 *Adding numbers to symbol instances*

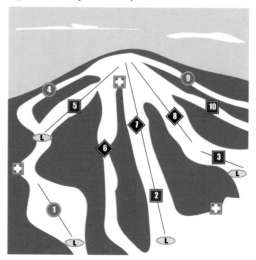

Figure 14 *Positioning four symbol instances of the Ski Lodge symbol*

Figure 15 *Updated instances of the Ski Lodge symbol*

This ski lodge graphic not updated because no longer linked to the Ski Lodge symbol

Edit a symbol

1. Position four symbol instances of the Ski Lodge symbol, as shown in Figure 14.
2. Select the bottom-right Ski Lodge symbol instance, then click the **Break Link to Symbol button** on the Symbols panel.
3. Select the top Ski Lodge symbol instance, then click the **Break Link to Symbol button**.
4. Scale the top ski lodge artwork 50%.
5. Press and hold [**Alt**] (Win) or [**option**] (Mac), then drag the **scaled artwork** on top of the Ski Lodge symbol on the Symbols panel.

    The three symbol instances of the Ski Lodge symbol are updated, as shown in Figure 15. The bottom ski lodge artwork does not change.
6. Click the **Sequoia symbol**, then place one instance of the symbol in the scratch area.
7. Click the **Break Link to Symbol button**.
8. Reduce the artwork 50%.
9. Press and hold [**Alt**] (Win) or [option] (Mac), then drag the **edited tree artwork** on top of the Sequoia symbol on the Symbols panel.
10. Delete the Sequoia symbol instance in the scratch area.

You edited symbols by modifying instances, then replacing the original symbols with the edited artwork. You protected a symbol instance from modification by breaking its link.

Transform symbol instances

1. Select the six green objects within the snow area of the artboard, change their fill color to a light gray, then position an instance of the Sequoia symbol so that your screen resembles Figure 16.

   TIP Use the Color panel to mix a new light gray color if necessary.

2. Drag and drop nine copies of the Sequoia symbol instance on the artboard, so that your screen resembles Figure 17.

3. Verify that the Sequoia symbol is still selected on the Symbols panel, click the **Symbols panel options button** ▾≡ , then click **Select All Instances**.

   All instances of the Sequoia symbol are selected on the artboard.

   (continued)

Figure 16 *Positioning the Sequoia symbol instance*

Figure 17 *Positioning nine copies of the Sequoia symbol instance*

4. Scale the symbol instances 75%.

5. Drag and drop 14 copies of the newly scaled Sequoia symbol instance to the opposite side of the artboard, as shown in Figure 18.

TIP Press [Alt](Win) or [option](Mac) while dragging to create copies.

6. Save your work.

You positioned one instance of a symbol on the artboard, then copied it nine times. You used the Select All Instances command to select the ten instances of the symbol quickly, scaled them 75%, then positioned 14 copies of the scaled symbol instance.

Figure 18 *Positioning 14 copies of the Sequoia symbol instance*

Create Symbol
INSTANCE SETS

What You'll Do

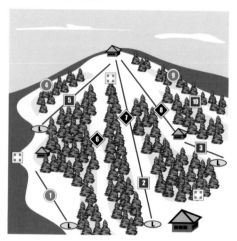

In this lesson, you will use the Symbol Sprayer tool to create sets of symbol instances and mixed symbol instance sets.

Creating a Symbol Instance Set

Instead of creating symbol instances one at a time using the Symbols panel, you can use the Symbol Sprayer tool to create multiple symbol instances quickly. Imagine that you have a symbol of a star and you want to draw a night sky filled with stars. The Symbol Sprayer tool would be a good choice for applying the star symbol multiple times.

Symbol instances created with the Symbol Sprayer tool are called **symbol instance sets**. Incorporate the term "set" into your work with symbols to differentiate the multiple symbol instances created with the Symbol Sprayer tool from individual instances of a symbol that you create using the Symbols panel.

To create a symbol instance set, click the symbol that you want to use on the Symbols panel, then drag the Symbol Sprayer tool where you want the symbols to appear on the artboard.

Working with Symbol Instance Sets

When you create a symbol instance set with the Symbol Sprayer tool, the entire set of symbols is identified within a bounding box, as shown in Figure 19. If the set is selected and you begin dragging the Symbol Sprayer tool again, the new symbol instances will be added to the selected set—even if the new symbol instances are outside of the existing set's bounding box. (The bounding box will expand to encompass the new symbol instances.)

You can also create mixed symbol instance sets. Mixed symbol instance sets include symbol instances based on more than one symbol. To create a mixed symbol instance set, create your first set of symbol instances, click a different symbol on the Symbols panel, then drag the Symbol Sprayer tool where you want the new symbols to appear on the artboard.

The new symbol instances will be added to the existing set, as shown in Figure 20.

Even though a symbol instance set, by definition, appears as multiple objects, it is best to think of it as a single object. A symbol instance set can be modified and transformed (as a whole). Figure 21 shows a symbol instance set that has been reflected using the Reflect tool.

Figure 19 *A symbol instance set created with the Symbol Sprayer tool*

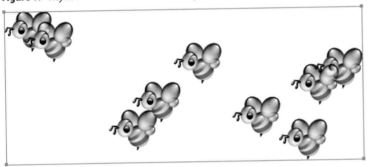

Figure 20 *A mixed symbol instance set*

Figure 21 *A symbol instance set transformed with the Reflect tool*

Setting Options for the Symbol Sprayer Tool

The Symbol Sprayer tool has many options to help you control the dispersion of symbol instances. You can access these options in the Symbolism Tools Options dialog box by double-clicking the Symbol Sprayer tool on the Tools panel.

The Diameter setting determines the brush size of the tool. Use a larger brush size to disperse symbol instances over a greater area of the artboard. Note that the brush size does not determine the size of the symbol instances themselves.

The Intensity setting determines the number of instances of the symbol that will be sprayed. The higher the intensity setting, the greater the number of symbol instances that will be dispersed in a given amount of time.

The Symbol Set Density setting determines how closely the symbol instances will be positioned to each other. The higher the density setting, the more closely packed the instances will appear. Figure 22 shows a symbol instance set with a high symbol set density, and Figure 23 shows a symbol instance set with a low symbol set density.

Figure 22 *A symbol instance set with a high symbol set density*

Figure 23 *A symbol instance set with a low symbol set density*

Expanding a Symbol Set

Despite the many options available with the Symbol Sprayer tool, it is often difficult to position multiple symbols exactly where you want them. For this reason alone, it is best to think of the Symbol Sprayer tool as a means to quickly disperse symbol instances but not as a tool to position symbols precisely.

Once you have created a symbol instance set that contains roughly the number of symbol instances with which you want to work and have positioned them roughly where you want them to be on the artboard, you can then apply the Expand command to release the set into individual symbol instances. Figure 24 shows a symbol instance set expanded into individual symbol instances.

The power of this operation cannot be overstated. Once expanded, all the symbol instances of the set are available to you to be transformed, repositioned, duplicated, or deleted. Expand the individual symbol instances to be able to select their component parts.

Figure 24 *A symbol instance set expanded into individual symbol instances*

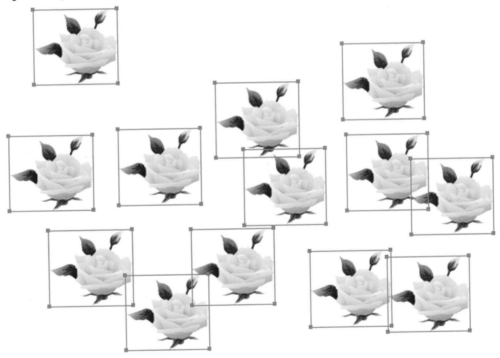

Use the Symbol Sprayer tool

1. Click the **Sequoia symbol** on the Symbols panel if it is not already selected.

2. Double-click the **Symbol Sprayer tool** on the Tools panel.

3. Type **.5** in the Diameter text box, type **3** in the Intensity text box, type **5** in the Symbol Set Density text box, then click **OK**.

4. Click and drag the **Symbol Sprayer tool** to spray instances of the Sequoia symbol over the gray areas so that your artboard resembles Figure 25.

TIP   Don't try to create all the instances in one move. Click and drag the Symbol Sprayer tool multiple times in short bursts. Your results will vary from the figure.

5. Press and hold [**Alt**] (Win) or [**option**] (Mac), then click the **Symbol Sprayer tool** over symbol instances that you do not want to include to remove them.

6. With the entire set still selected as a unit, click **Object** on the Application bar, click **Expand**, verify that only the Object check box is checked, then click **OK**.

7. Deselect, then using the Direct Selection tool , move the individual Sequoia symbol instances so that your work resembles Figure 26.

   You may also copy and/or delete instances as necessary.

(continued)

Figure 25   *Instances of the Sequoia symbol created with the Symbol Sprayer tool*

Figure 26   *Moving and deleting symbol instances from the set*

8. Click **Object** on the Application bar, click **Show All**, then, while the hidden objects are still selected, bring them to the front, then deselect.

Your screen should resemble Figure 27.

9. Save your work, then close Trail Map.

You defined the diameter, the intensity, and the symbol set density for the Symbol Sprayer tool. You then used the Symbol Sprayer tool to create a set of Sequoia symbols.

Figure 27 *The majority of the trail map artwork is created with symbol instances*

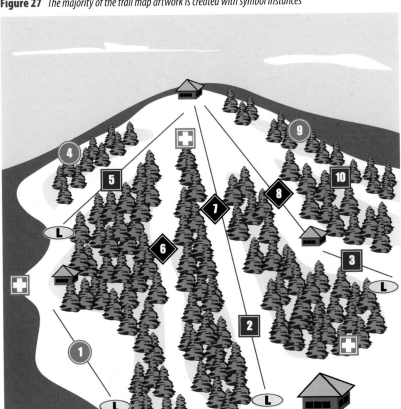

Create a mixed symbol instance set

1. Open AI 12-2.ai, then save it as **Fish Tank**.
2. Click the **Red Stone symbol** on the Symbols panel.
3. Double-click the **Symbol Sprayer tool** .
4. Type **1** in the Diameter text box, type **8** in the Intensity text box, type **5** in the Symbol Set Density text box, then click **OK**.
5. Click and drag the **Symbol Sprayer tool** over the "sand," as shown in Figure 28.
6. Click the **Purple Stone symbol**, then drag the **Symbol Sprayer tool** over the "sand," as shown in Figure 29.

   The Purple Stone symbols are added to the set, creating a mixed symbol instance set.

   (continued)

Figure 28 *Spraying instances of the Red Stone symbol*

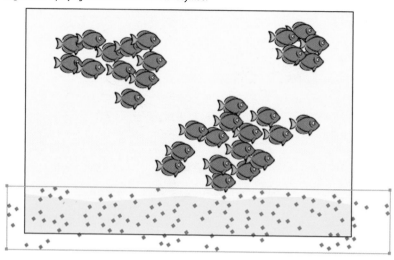

Figure 29 *Spraying instances of the Purple Stone symbol*

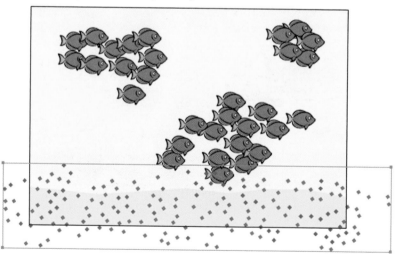

Drawing with Symbols

Figure 30 *Spraying instances of the Green Stone, Orange Stone, and Tan Stone symbols*

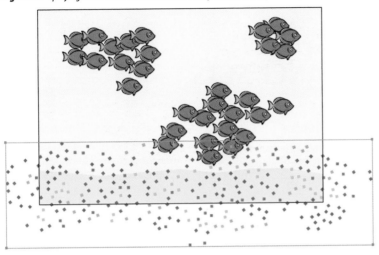

Figure 31 *Masking the mixed symbol instance set*

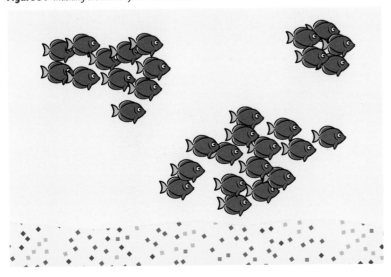

7. Add the Green Stone, Orange Stone, and Tan Stone symbols to the set, so that your screen resembles Figure 30.

8. Select the sand object, copy it, paste in front, then bring the copy to the front.

9. Press and hold [**Shift**], then click the **mixed symbol instance set** so that the sand and the set of rocks are selected.

10. Click **Object** on the Application bar, point to **Clipping Mask**, click **Make**, deselect, then save your work.

   The sand acts as a mask to hide the rocks that extend beyond the sand object, as shown in Figure 31.

You used five different symbols and the Symbol Sprayer tool to create a mixed set of symbol instances.

Modify Symbol
INSTANCE SETS

What You'll Do

 In this lesson, you will use various symbolism tools to modify symbol instance sets.

Using Symbolism Tools

Illustrator offers eight symbolism tools that you can use to modify symbol instances or sets of symbol instances. You will most often use the symbolism tools to affect symbol instances within a set, since individual symbol instances are easy to select and modify directly with transform tools and menu commands. Table 1 lists each symbolism tool and its function. Figure 32 shows an illustration of a symbol instance set with each tool applied to the set.

When you apply symbolism tools to mixed symbol instance sets, each corresponding

TABLE 1: SYMBOLISM TOOLS	
Symbolism tool	**Function**
Symbol Sprayer tool	Places symbol instances on the artboard
Symbol Shifter tool	Moves symbol instances and/or changes their stacking order in the set
Symbol Scruncher tool	Pulls symbol instances together or apart
Symbol Sizer tool	Increases or decreases the size of symbol instances
Symbol Spinner tool	Rotates symbol instances
Symbol Stainer tool	Changes the color of symbol instances gradually to the current fill color on the Tools panel
Symbol Screener tool	Increases or decreases the transparency of symbol instances
Symbol Styler tool	Applies the selected style on the Styles panel to symbol instances

symbol must be selected on the Symbols panel in order for each type of symbol instance to be modified by the tool. For example, imagine you have created a mixed symbol instance set of four types of flowers, such as daisies, tulips, roses, and lilies, and only the daisy symbol is selected on the Symbols panel. If you apply a symbolism tool to the mixed symbol instance set, only the instances of the daisy symbol will be modified.

When working with symbolism tools, it is also important that you set realistic goals. The symbolism tools are particularly useful if you have created a symbol set that is intended to appear random. For example, if you use symbol instances to render multiple stars in the night sky, the symbolism tools will be an excellent choice for modifying their orientation on the artboard. However, if your goal is to position symbol instances precisely in your artwork, you should expand the symbol set and use the selection tools and transform tools to modify each instance directly.

Figure 32 *Applying the symbolism tools*

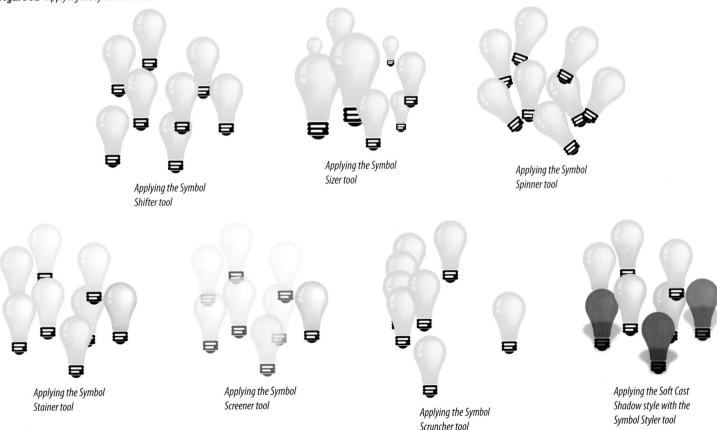

Applying the Symbol Shifter tool

Applying the Symbol Sizer tool

Applying the Symbol Spinner tool

Applying the Symbol Stainer tool

Applying the Symbol Screener tool

Applying the Symbol Scruncher tool

Applying the Soft Cast Shadow style with the Symbol Styler tool

Use the Symbol Stainer tool

1. Click **Object** on the Application bar, then click **Unlock All**.

2. Deselect, then select the set of fish symbol instances.

3. Change the fill color on the Tools panel to green.

4. Click the **Symbol Stainer tool** .

   The Symbol Stainer tool is hidden beneath the Symbol Sprayer tool.

   TIP Press and hold the current Symbol tool until you see all of the Symbol tools, then click the Tearoff tab at the end of the row of tools to create a floating panel of all of the symbolism tools.

5. Click and drag the **Symbol Stainer tool** over the 11 fish symbol instances in the upper-left region of the artboard so that your work resembles Figure 33.

   TIP Using the Symbol Stainer tool results in increased file size and may tax your computer's performance.

(continued)

Figure 33 *Applying the Symbol Stainer tool with a green fill*

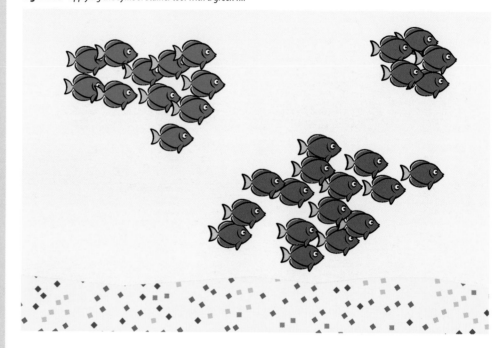

Figure 34 *Applying the Symbol Stainer tool with a yellow fill*

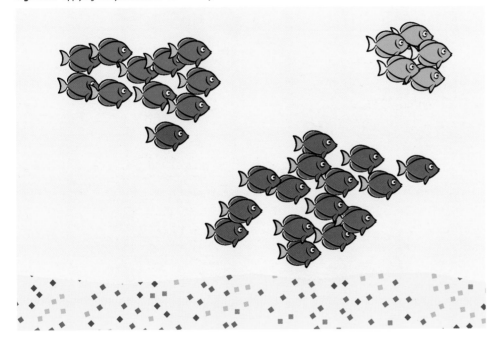

6. Position the Symbol Stainer tool ![icon] over the **bottommost fish symbol instance** in the same group.

7. Press and hold [**Alt**] (Win) or [**option**] (Mac), then press and hold the mouse button for approximately two seconds.

   Pressing [Alt] (Win) or [option] (Mac) while using the Symbol Stainer tool gradually removes color applied by the Symbol Stainer tool. The symbol instance that you clicked returns to its original blue color. The surrounding symbol instances are not affected as directly; their color changes toward the original blue color, but remains somewhat green. Your results may vary.

8. Change the fill color on the Tools panel to yellow.

9. Drag the **Symbol Stainer tool** over the five fish symbol instances in the upper-right region of the artboard, so that your work resembles Figure 34.

You used the Symbol Stainer tool to modify the color of symbol instances within a set.

Use the Symbol Shifter tool

1. Double-click the **Symbol Shifter tool** to open the Symbolism Tools Options dialog box.

   The Symbol Shifter tool is hidden beneath the current symbolism tool if you did not tear off the Symbolism Tools panel.

2. Type **.25** in the Diameter text box, then click **OK**.

3. Position the Symbol Shifter tool over **any of the green fish**, press and hold [**Shift**], then click the **fish instance**.

   The symbol instance is brought to the front of the set.

   TIP It's usually a good idea to enter a small diameter setting when you want to affect the stacking order of instances in a set. A larger brush will affect the stacking order of surrounding instances.

4. Press and hold [**Shift**][**Alt**] (Win) or [**Shift**][**option**] (Mac), then click a **green fish**.

   The symbol instance is sent to the back. Figure 35 shows an example of the green fish instances after the stacking order has been affected by the Symbol Shifter tool. Compare your choices and results.

5. Change the diameter setting of the Symbol Shifter tool to 2.5.

6. Click and drag the **Symbol Shifter tool** over the yellow fish until they no longer touch each other, as shown in Figure 36.

   Your results may vary.

You used the Symbol Shifter tool to change the stacking order of instances within the symbol set and to move symbol instances within the set.

Figure 35 *Using the Symbol Shifter tool to change the stacking order of instances in a set*

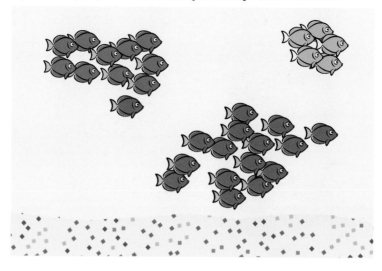

Figure 36 *Using the Symbol Shifter tool to reposition instances within the set*

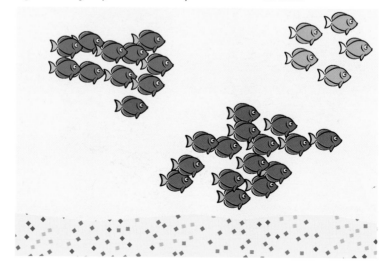

Figure 37 *Using the Symbol Spinner tool on the green fish*

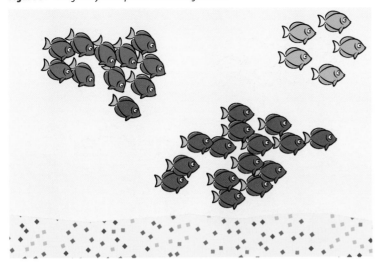

Figure 38 *Using the Symbol Spinner tool on the yellow fish*

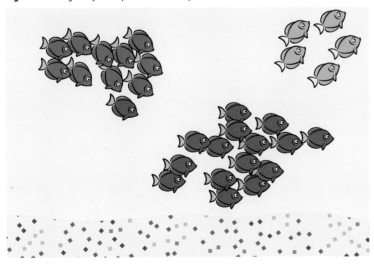

Use the Symbol Spinner tool

1. Double-click the **Symbol Spinner tool** ⟳ .
2. Type **2.6** in the Diameter text box, type **10** in the Intensity text box, then click **OK**.
3. Position the Symbol Spinner tool over the **center of the green fish group**.
4. Click and drag slightly to the right, so that the fish rotate, as shown in Figure 37.

   Your results may vary.

   TIP The blue arrows that appear when you click and drag the Symbol Spinner tool are not always reliable predictors of the final rotation of the symbol instances. The diameter and intensity settings and the location of the tool in regard to the instances all affect the impact of the rotation.

5. Position the Symbol Spinner tool over the **center of the yellow fish group**.
6. Click and drag slightly to the upper-left so that the yellow fish rotate, as shown in Figure 38.

   Your results may vary.

You used the Symbol Spinner tool to rotate symbol instances within the set.

Use the Symbol Sizer tool

1. Double-click the **Symbol Sizer tool** .

2. Type **2** in the Diameter text box, type **8** in the Intensity text box, then click **OK**.

3. Position the Symbol Sizer tool over the **center of the green fish group**.

4. Press and hold the mouse button for approximately two seconds so that your work resembles Figure 39.

   Your results may vary.

5. Position the Symbol Sizer tool over the **center of the blue fish group**.

   (continued)

Figure 39 *Using the Symbol Sizer tool to enlarge symbol instances*

6. Press and hold [**Alt**] (Win) or [**option**] (Mac), then press and hold the mouse button for approximately three seconds.

7. Deselect all, then save your work.

Your screen should resemble Figure 40. Your results may vary.

8. Close the Fish Tank document.

You used the Symbol Sizer tool to change the size of symbol instances within the set.

Figure 40 *Using the Symbol Sizer tool to reduce symbol instances*

Create symbols.

1. Open AI 12-3.ai, then save it as **Winter Ball Fun**.
2. Show the Brushes panel, then drag the Radiant Star brush onto the artboard.
3. Verify that the Symbols panel is displayed, then drag the Radiant Star artwork into the Symbols panel.
4. Name the new symbol **Snowflake**.
5. Delete the Radiant Star artwork from the artboard.

Place symbol instances.

1. Click the Snowflake symbol on the Symbols panel.
2. Click the Place Symbol Instance button on the Symbols panel.
3. Position the symbol instance between the words ball and December.

Modify symbols and symbol instances.

1. Scale the Snowflake symbol instance 35%, then reposition the Snowflake symbol instance if necessary.
2. Click Effect on the Application bar, point to Distort & Transform, click Pucker & Bloat, type **50** in the text box, then click OK.
3. Change the opacity of the symbol instance to 75%.
4. Click the Break Link to Symbol button on the Symbols panel.
5. Press [Alt] (Win) or [option] (Mac), then drag the modified snowflake artwork directly on top of the Snowflake symbol on the Symbols panel.

Create symbol instance sets.

1. Double-click the Symbol Sprayer tool.
2. Type **1** for the Diameter, **2** for the Intensity, and **1** for the Symbol Set Density in the Symbolism Tools Options dialog box.
3. Spray approximately 25 symbol instances of the Snowflake symbol evenly over the artboard.

Modify symbol instance sets.

1. Use the Symbol Sizer tool to enlarge and reduce symbol instances.
2. Expand the symbol set.
3. Move or delete symbols to your liking.
4. Save your work, then see Figure 41 for one possible solution.
5. Close Winter Ball Fun.

Figure 41 *Completed Skills Review*

Drawing with Symbols

You work in the design department of a major Internet portal site. As part of the promotion of this year's Hooray for Hollywood Awards, your site will link to the Awards' site. You are asked to create a banner that says "click here to meet the stars" against a starry sky.

1. Open AI 12-4.ai, then save it as **Hollywood Stars**.
2. Double-click the Symbol Sprayer tool.

3. Type **2** for the Diameter, **1** for the Intensity, and **10** for the Symbol Set Density.
4. Click the 5 Point Star symbol on the Symbols panel, then drag the Symbol Sprayer tool across the gradient-filled rectangle.
5. Repeat Step 4, using the 8 Point Star symbol on the Symbols panel.
6. Expand the symbol set.

7. Use the Symbol Shifter tool to move symbol instances that overlap each other.
8. Use the Symbol Sizer tool to enlarge and reduce symbol instances to add depth and variety.
9. Show all to reveal the semitransparent text.
10. Save your work, compare your illustration to Figure 42, then close the Hollywood Stars document.

Figure 42 *Completed Project Builder 1*

You work at a busy design firm. Your boss emails you an Illustrator file. He tells you that the file contains a symbol of the American flag that he saved some months ago. He wants you to update the existing symbol on the Symbols panel so that the flag is scaled 25% and the opacity of the flag is 50%. He also wants the new symbol to show the flag waving.

1. Open AI 12-5.ai, then save it as **American Flag Symbol**.
2. Show the Symbols panel if necessary, then place an instance of the American Flag symbol on the artboard.
3. Break the link between the symbol instance and the symbol.
4. Click Object on the Application bar, point to Envelope Distort, then click Make with Warp.
5. Click the Style list arrow, then click Flag.
6. Type **-35** for the Bend value, then click OK.
7. Scale the artwork 25%.
8. In the Transparency panel, change the opacity of the artwork to 50%.
9. Replace the original American Flag symbol with the modified artwork, then remove the flag artwork from the artboard.
10. Save your work, then compare your Symbols panel with Figure 43.
11. Close the American Flag Symbol document.

Figure 43 *Completed Project Builder 2*

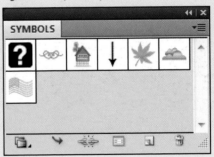

The nice lady who works at your town's Chamber of Commerce has created a poster for this year's Memorial Day parade and asks you if you could jazz it up. Since your firm is very busy, your improvements must be quick and simple. You email a file containing a symbol of the American flag to an employee with instructions for updating the symbol. He emails the file back to you with the updated symbol, and you paste the parade text into the file.

1. Open AI 12-6.ai, then save it as **Memorial Day Parade**.
2. Fill the black rectangle with orange, then hide it.
3. Select all the elements on the artboard, then hide them.
4. Place an instance of the American Flag symbol in the lower-left corner of the artboard.
5. Create a pattern out of the American Flag symbol instances that covers the entire artboard, referring to Figure 44 for ideas.
6. Select all the symbol instances, group them, then send them to the back.
7. Show all, then deselect all.
8. Select the orange rectangle and the symbol instances, then make a clipping mask.
9. Apply a 10% cyan fill and a 3-point Black stroke to the clipping mask.
10. Save your work, compare your screen to Figure 44, then close Memorial Day Parade.

Figure 44 *Completed Design Project*

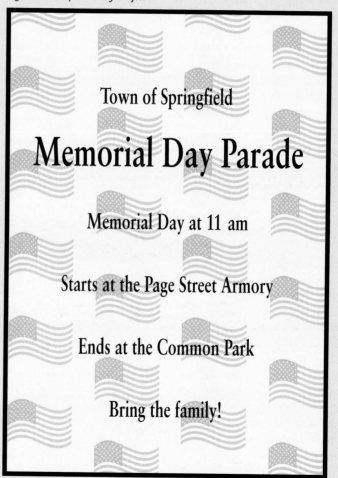

You own a design firm in Silicon Valley that specializes in solutions for web sites. You are approached by a representative of Black Swan Technologies, a global company noted for engineering breakthrough devices in the medical field. The representative tells you that he wants you to redesign the splash page of their Web site to convey the fact that they work with all sectors of the medical industry. The company's motto is, "We Are Everywhere."

1. Open AI 12-7.ai, then save it as **Black Swan**.
2. Think about ways to design the Black Swan Technologies logo.
3. Do you think that parts of the logo suggest a bat more than a bird?
4. How do you think that the concept "We Are Everywhere" can be incorporated visually into the splash page?
5. Discuss how reproducing the logo as a symbol presents possibilities for a splash page design based on the phrase "We Are Everywhere."
6. Create a new symbol using the swan artwork by modifying the artwork using any Illustrator tools or features that you want before adding the new symbol to the Symbols panel.
7. Use the swan symbol and the symbolism tools to create a new splash page for Black Swan Technologies.
8. Save your work, then compare your results with Figure 45.
9. Close the Black Swan document.

Figure 45 *Sample Portfolio Project*

black swan technologies

CHAPTER 13

PREPARING GRAPHICS
FOR THE WEB

CHAPTER 13

PREPARING GRAPHICS FOR THE WEB

It's funny to think that, when Illustrator debuted in the late 80s, there was only one type of output for an Illustrator file—print. No Internet, no cell phones, no iPods, no iPads—it was either a working file on your computer, or it was on paper.

So much has, of course, changed since then, and the web has had an impact on all design and layout programs, Illustrator included. It's had its impact on Adobe as well. Who could have foreseen that Dreamweaver would become an Adobe product?

Fortunately for Illustrator lovers who don't necessarily want to design in Dreamweaver or Flash, Adobe has endowed Illustrator with the tools necessary to convert a layout into slices and to optimize those slices for download. Additionally, you can export any of your Illustrator artwork as an SWF or SVG graphic for the web.

With the success of Dreamweaver and Flash as industry standards for web page and web graphic creation, it's unlikely that you'll see Illustrator used exclusively to create a website. Nevertheless, it's good to know that you still can use Illustrator to create web pages and that Illustrator is fully conversant with Dreamweaver and Flash.

Create SLICES

What You'll Do

In this lesson, you will create slices using guides. You will also combine slices.

Understanding Web Graphics

When you create graphics for the web, you will need to pay attention to different considerations than you would when designing graphics for print. The web is an entirely different medium, and you need to become familiar with, if not fluent in, many issues.

Color is an essential consideration when producing web graphics. Since a computer's monitor functions as a light source, it produces color based on the additive model, in which the color is created by combining light. Thus, graphics that you create must be saved in RGB mode.

For the designer, this is great news: The RGB color gamut is much larger than the CMYK color gamut. When designing for the web, you can use the brightest, most saturated colors. However, the colors you see on your artboard aren't necessarily the colors that will appear in your web browser. Color choices, file formats, and the degree of compression all affect the appearance of color.

Resolution is another essential consideration when using bitmap graphics on the web. You'll want to remember when creating your Illustrator file that 72 pixels per inch (PPI) is the standard resolution for bitmap graphics on the web.

When choosing the correct file format for your web graphics, you also need to consider file size and display characteristics. Two standard compression file formats for bitmap graphics—JPEG and GIF—both reduce file size significantly, but through dramatically different processes. Knowing which to choose, and then choosing the degree to which each compresses the file, requires understanding and experience.

Understanding Sliced Artwork

If you were to use Illustrator to create artwork for a web page or for an entire web site, you would want to consider making the artwork into slices to reduce file size for faster download and to segregate different types of page elements, such as HTML text, bitmap graphics, and Illustrator symbols.

When you create slices in Illustrator, you literally divide the artwork into areas to be output as individual and, therefore, smaller files. Imagine a 100-piece puzzle whose

Preparing Graphics for the Web

pieces are all rectangular. Imagine that the entire puzzle, when put together, weighs exactly one pound. It would stand to reason that each of the 100 pieces weighs far less than one pound. Imagine each slice as a piece of the puzzle, smaller in area and, more importantly, smaller in file size. The only difference is, when a puzzle is completed, the lines between the pieces are visible; with artwork, the "lines" between the slices are invisible when viewed in a web browser.

Using slices to segregate page elements, such as HTML text and bitmap images, allows you to output them differently. For example, if you create a slice that contains a bitmap image and another that contains HTML text,

you can output the bitmap slice as a JPEG file and the text slice as an HTML file.

Creating Slices with the Make Slice Command and the Slice Tool

The Make Slice command creates a slice with dimensions that match those of the bounding box of the object. This command also creates a slice that captures text with its basic formatting characteristics. With the Make Slice command, the object is the slice, and vice versa. If you move or modify the object, the slice automatically adjusts to encompass the new artwork.

The Slice tool allows you to draw a rectangular slice anywhere on the artboard.

Slices that you create with the Slice tool are independent of the underlying artwork. In other words, if you move the artwork, the slice does not move with the artwork.

Whether you use the Make Slice command or the Slice tool to create slices, Illustrator generates automatic slices that cover the remainder of the artboard. Illustrator does this to create a complete HTML table, in case the document is saved as a web page.

In Figure 1, slice 3 was drawn with the Slice tool. Slices 1, 2, and 4 were generated automatically.

Figure 1 *Slice 3 was created with the Slice tool; slices 1, 2, and 4 were generated automatically*

Put quite simply, automatic slices are cumbersome, tricky, and hard to manage. Every time you add or edit slices, Illustrator must regenerate automatic slices; thus, the slice pattern on the artboard continues to change.

Creating Slices from Guides

You can use standard ruler guides to define how you want artwork to be divided into slices. Figure 2 shows three guides that were positioned so as to isolate the graphic of the dog.

By definition, guides extend across and beyond the artboard. Therefore, when you use guides to define areas to be sliced, the length of the guide can get in the way. For example, the two vertical guides in Figure 2 extend up beyond the dog area into the headline.

Figure 2 *Guides isolate the dog graphic into its own area*

Horizontal guide   Two vertical guides

Thus, the headline is unnecessarily divided into three sections.

This problem can sometimes seem extreme. Figure 3 shows two additional horizontal guides positioned on the artwork to isolate each of the three photos and their corresponding text on the right. Each will be used as a link that will take the viewer to a different page. Therefore, it is necessary to create a slice for each link. Note, however, that the horizontal guides extend across the dog area, dividing that artwork into three parts.

When you apply the Create from Guides command, Illustrator generates slices for

Figure 3 *Two additional horizontal guides divide the dog graphic into three sections*

each area defined by a guide, as shown in Figure 4. 12 slices are not necessary to save this artwork for the web. For example, slices 04, 07, and 10, if combined, could be saved as a very small file. Also, one might want to try to save the dog graphic as one file. Breaking the dog artwork into three slices runs the risk that each slice might vary slightly in color because of the file format and the compression that is applied.

Figure 4 *The Create from Guides command generates only slices—not automatic slices*

Note, however, that each slice…is a slice! The Create from Guides command generates only slices—no automatic slices. Each slice can be selected with the Slice Selection tool.

Therefore, slices can be easily combined, as shown in Figure 5.

Of the three main ways that Illustrator offers for making slices, using guides and then combining excess slices is the simplest, most straightforward, and hassle-free method.

Figure 5 *Slices can be combined easily*

Make slices

1. Open AI 13-1.ai, then save it as **SDS**.
2. Close all panels except for the Tools panel.
3. Change the style of the guides to **Dots** and the color of the guides to **Yellow**.

TIP If you are using Macintosh OS 10, your preference settings are on the Illustrator menu.

4. Show the rulers, then position a guide on all four sides of the photo, as shown in Figure 6.
5. Position a vertical guide to the left of the three text buttons, then position another guide to the right of the three text buttons.
6. Position a horizontal guide above the large purple text at the bottom, as shown in Figure 7.
7. Position a horizontal guide above and below the "purchase show tickets" button, as shown in Figure 8.
8. Verify that your guides are unlocked.
9. Click **Object** on the Application bar, point to **Slice**, then click **Create from Guides**.

   30 slices are generated, as shown in Figure 9.

TIP The View menu has commands to hide and show slices.

You positioned guides, then used them to create slices.

Figure 6 *Positioning guides on all four sides of the photo*

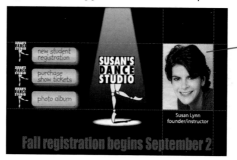

Position guides on all four sides of this photo

Figure 7 *Positioning a guide above the text*

Horizontal guide above text

Figure 8 *Positioning guides above and below the "purchase show tickets" button*

Purchase show tickets button

Figure 9 *30 slices generated from guides*

Preparing Graphics for the Web

Figure 10 *Slices 06, 11, and 16 selected*

Slices 06,
11, and 16

Figure 11 *Three slices combined into one*

Newly combined slice ———

Figure 12 *After combining slices, 14 slices remain*

Combine slices

1. Click the **Selection tool** ▸ , then click **anywhere in the scratch area** to deselect the slices.

2. Click the **Slice Selection tool** ⌖ .

TIP The Slice Selection tool is hidden beneath the Slice tool.

3. Using [Shift], select slices 06, 11, and 16 as shown in Figure 10.

TIP The easiest way to select a slice is to click the slice number.

4. Click **Object** on the Application bar, point to **Slice**, then click **Combine Slices**.

   The three slices are combined into one slice; all of the slices are renumbered, as shown in Figure 11.

5. Hide the guides.

6. Using the same method, combine the four slices that contain all of the purple "Fall registration text."

7. Combine the six black slices on the right-hand margin.

8. Combine the three slices that contain the photo.

9. Combine the five slices that contain the logo in the spotlight, so that your slices correspond to Figure 12.

10. Save your work.

You combined slices to create single slices for specific areas of the artwork.

Specify Slice Type
AND SLICE OPTIONS

What You'll Do

In this lesson, you will specify slices as Image or No Image, and you will add URL links to image slices.

Specifying Slice Type

A slice's type and the options assigned to it determine how the artwork contained in the slice will function on a web page. A slice must be selected in order for you to assign a type and apply options to it. The Slice Options dialog box allows you to specify one of three categories for a slice's type. Basically, a slice's type defines its content.

The Image type is used when you want the content of a slice to become a linked image file on a web page.

The No Image type is used when you want the area to contain text or a solid color. You enter the text or the color information directly into the Slice Options dialog box. You cannot view No Image slice content in Illustrator; you must use a web browser to preview it.

Choosing between Image and No Image is not always as straightforward as it would at first seem. Consider slice 2 in Figure 13, for example. It contains no artwork, and certainly would not function as a link. However, it does contain a background color—the same background color that is shared by all of the slices.

If you were to define the slice type of slice 2 as No Image, it would by default have no background color. If you saved the file for the web, the content of slice 2 would appear white on the web page. You could try applying a background color in the Slice Options dialog box and specifying the color to have the same RGB values as the background color in the Image slices. This solution may work well. However, you also have the option of specifying slice 2's type as Image—a single color image with no links. In this case, slice 2 would be output using the same file format as the other slices, logically a safer bet for color consistency.

The third type of slice is HTML Text, which you use if you want to capture Illustrator text and its basic formatting. You can only create this type of slice using the Make Slice command.

Generally, you will use Illustrator to create display text intended to be used as a design element, such as a headline. Rather than saving display text as text for the web, it is a smart decision to simply save a version of your artwork with display text converted to outlines and defined as an image. With this method, you know for certain that your text will appear exactly as you designed it, with no risk of its being modified by or being in conflict with a browser's preset preferences.

Setting Options for Image Content Slices

When you specify a slice as an Image slice, you have the following options in the Slice Options dialog box:

Name By default, the slice name is used as the file name when you save the web page. By default, the slice is named with the slice number. It is a good idea to rename an important slice with a name that is more descriptive of its content.

URL Specify a URL to make the slice a hotspot on the web page.

Target If you've specified a URL, the target specifies the frame that you want the link

to target. You can enter the name of a target frame, or you can use one of the standard targets in the pop-up menu. If you are unfamiliar with frames, note that _parent and _blank are the most common. _blank means that a new browser window will be opened, or "spawned," to show the linked page. _parent, the more standard of the two, means that the current window will change to show the linked page.

Figure 13 *Slice 2 could be specified as an Image or a No Image type*

Message The information you type in the Message text box is what will appear in the status bar of a browser window when you position your cursor over the corresponding image slice. Messages usually convey information about the current image or that to which it links.

Alt Think of Alt as an "alternative" to an image. Alternative text is for sight impaired web surfers. They will hear the alt text rather than see the image.

Background If you are saving a bitmap image with a transparent background, you can specify a color for the background behind the transparent areas.

Setting Options for No Image Content Slices

In the Slice Options dialog box, you can set the following options:

Text In the Text Displayed in Cell text box, you can enter text that will appear in the slice. You can format the text using standard HTML tags. Be careful not to enter more text than can fit in the slice. If you do, the overflow will extend into neighboring slices. Because you cannot view the text in Illustrator, you will need to save the file for the web and open it in a browser to view your work.

Alignment Use the Horizontal and Vertical list arrows to specify the horizontal and vertical alignment of the text.

Background Choose a background color for the slice.

Viewing and Modifying Document Metadata Information

Metadata contains basic information about a file, such as the author's name, the file's resolution, copyright information, the color space, and keywords that have been "tagged" to the file. You can use metadata to streamline your workflow and organize your files. The File Info dialog box in Illustrator is command central for viewing and modifying metadata. The File Info dialog box displays camera data, file properties, an edit history, copyright, and author information. It also displays custom metadata panels. You can add new metadata information for a file directly in the File Info dialog box. To access the dialog box, click File Info on the File menu.

Specify the type of slice

1. Click the **Slice Selection tool** 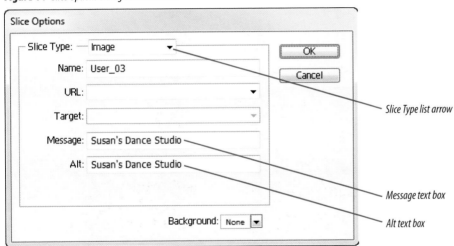, then click **slice 03**.
2. Click **Object** on the Application bar, point to **Slice**, then click **Slice Options**.
3. Click the **Slice Type list arrow**, then click **Image**.
4. Type **Susan's Dance Studio** in both the Message and Alt text boxes, as shown in Figure 14.
5. Click **OK** to close the Slice Options dialog box.
6. Click **File** on the Application bar, then click **Save** to update your slice numbers.
7. Click **slice 14**, click **Object** on the Application bar, point to **Slice**, click **Slice Options**, specify it as an Image slice, type **Fall registration** in the Message and Alt text boxes, click **OK**, then save.

TIP Each time you make changes to a slice or combine slices, the slice numbering is thrown off. Saving your work reapplies the correct slice numbers to the slices.

8. Select slice 01, define it as No Image, click the **Background list arrow**, click **Black**, click **OK**, then save.

   The black background will be coded in HTML. If you wanted to use the underlying black object as the black background, you would specify the slice type as an image, just as you did the logo.

9. Repeat Step 8 to specify slices 02, 04, 05, 11, and 12 as No Image slices with a black background, one at a time.

TIP You cannot apply Slice Options to multiple slices simultaneously.

10. Save your work.

You used the Slice Options dialog box to specify slices as Image slices and No Image slices.

Figure 14 *Slice Options dialog box for slice 03*

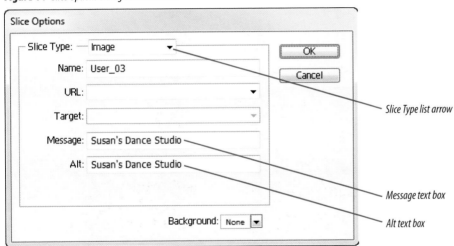

Set options for image content slices

1. Click the **Slice Selection tool** if it is not already active, click **slice 13**, click **Object** on the Application bar, point to **Slice**, then click **Slice Options**.

2. Click the **Slice Type list arrow**, then click **Image**.

3. Type **http://www.sds.com/bio/index.html** in the URL text box, as shown in Figure 15.

   In a web browser, clicking slice 13 will link to an HTML biography page.

4. Click the **Target list arrow**, then click _parent.

   In a web browser, clicking slice 13 will change the current window to the HTML biography page.

5. Type **Susan Lynn bio** in the Message and Alt text boxes, as shown in Figure 15, click **OK**, then save.

6. Click **slice 08**, open the Slice Options dialog box, repeat Steps 2–5 so that slice 08 contains the same slice information as slice 13, then save.

7. Click **slice 06**, open the Slice Options dialog box, verify that the Slice Type is set to Image, click **OK**, then save.

8. Click **slice 07**, open the Slice Options dialog box, type the information shown in Figure 16, click **OK**, then save.

(continued)

Figure 15 *Slice Options dialog box for slice 13*

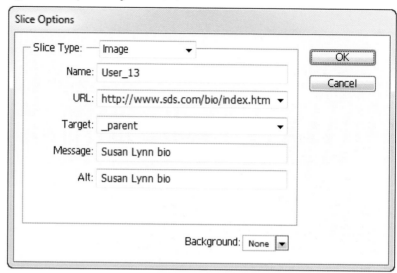

Figure 16 *Slice Options dialog box for slice 07*

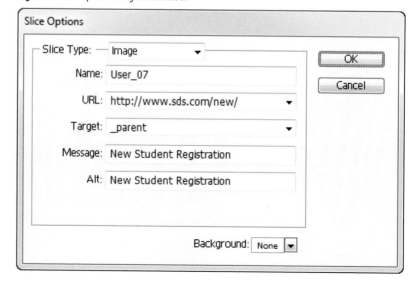

Figure 17 *Slice Options dialog box for slice 09*

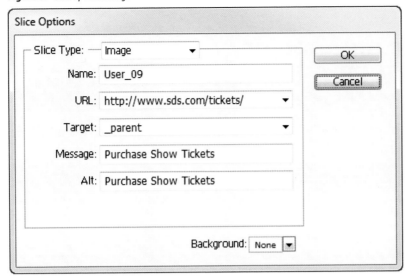

Figure 18 *Slice Options dialog box for slice 10*

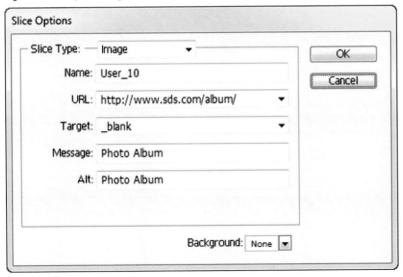

9. Specify the slice options for slice 09 as shown in Figure 17, then save.

10. Specify the slice options for slice 10 as shown in Figure 18, then save.

   Because the target for slice 10 is _blank, slice 10, when clicked, will open a new browser window for the photo album page.

11. Save your work.

You used the Slice Options dialog box to specify URLs to which the image slices will link when clicked in a browser application.

Use the Save for
WEB & DEVICES DIALOG BOX

What You'll Do

 In this lesson, you will optimize slices for the web, using the Save for Web & Devices dialog box.

Optimizing Artwork for the Web and Other Devices

Most artwork, even when sliced, requires optimization. **Optimization** is a process by which the file size is reduced through standard color compression algorithms.

Illustrator CS5 offers a number of optimization features to save artwork in different web graphics file formats. Your choice of a file format will have the greatest effect on the optimization method that is performed on the artwork.

The Save for Web & Devices dialog box presents many options for previewing images. The tabs at the top of the image area define the display options. The Original display presents the artwork with no optimization. The Optimized display presents the artwork with the current optimization setting applied. The 2-Up display presents two versions of the artwork—the original and the optimized version—side by side, and the 4-Up display presents the original beside three optimized versions.

Optimizing with the GIF File Format

GIF is a standard file format for compressing images with flat color, which makes it an excellent choice for many types of artwork generated in Illustrator. GIFs provide effective compression for the right type of artwork, especially line art and logos. GIFs maintain excellent quality with crisp detail. In many cases, the compression has no noticeable effect on the image.

GIF compression works by lowering the number of colors in the file. The trick with GIFs is to lower the number of available colors as much as possible without adversely affecting the appearance of the image. Generally, if the number of colors is too low, problems with the image are obvious, as shown in Figure 19.

Optimizing with the JPEG File Format

JPEG is a standard file format for compressing continuous-tone images, gradients, and blends. JPEG compression relies on "lossy" algorithms—"lossy" refers to a loss of data. In the JPEG format, data is selectively discarded.

You choose the level of compression in the JPEG format by specifying the JPEG's quality setting. The higher the quality setting, the more detail is preserved. Of course, the more detail preserved, the less the file size is reduced.

When JPEG compression is too severe for an image, the problems with the image are obvious and unappealing, as shown in Figure 20.

JPEG has emerged as one of the most used, if not the most used, file formats on the Internet. As a result, many designers ignore GIFs in favor of JPEGs, though many times GIFs would be the better choice.

Using Device Central

With the omnipresence of iPods and cell phones—and now iPads, it seems only natural that Illustrator CS5 would incorporate utilities for exporting graphics to various handheld and other devices. But if you think back to even just five years ago—who would have ever thought of exporting an Illustrator graphic to a phone!

Device Central is a mini application that interfaces all the applications in the Creative Suite. Design Central is equipped with presets for output to a large number of handheld devices, and that output can include basic graphics, video files, and even HTML. With Device Central, creative professionals and developers can preview how different types of files, such as Photoshop, Illustrator, and Flash files, will appear on a handheld device.

But Device Central goes beyond just previewing. With Device Central, you can scale and position graphics in a visual rendering of various cell phone designs. And you can rely on Design Central's size presets to be sure that your graphic is sized correctly and will appear exactly as it's previewed.

Device Central supports a long list of file formats including SWF, JPG, JPEG, PNG, GIF, WBM, MOV, 3GP, M4V, MPG, MPEG, AVI, HTM, HTML, XHTML, CHTML, URL, and WEBLOC. You can access Device Central in the File menu.

Figure 19 *A GIF file with too few colors available to render the image adequately*

Figure 20 *Problems with JPEGs are obvious and unappealing*

Optimize a slice as a JPEG

1. Click **File** on the Application bar, then click **Save for Web & Devices**.

2. Click the **Optimized tab** if it is not active.

   The Optimized view shows you the artwork with the current optimization settings applied.

3. In the Save for Web & Devices dialog box, click the **Slice Select tool** ✎, click **slice 03**, click the **Preset list arrow** in the options on the right side of the dialog box, then click **JPEG High**.

   The selected slice is updated.

4. Click the **4-Up tab** at the top of the dialog box.

   The image area is divided into four views of the artwork. The upper-right window is selected.

5. Click the **Hand tool** 🖐 in the Save for Web & Devices dialog box, then drag the upper-right window as needed so that all of slice 03 is visible, as shown in Figure 21.

   TIP Use the Zoom tool to zoom in or out if necessary.

6. Compare the file size of the original to the other three.

7. Compare the download times and quality settings, as listed in the upper-right and bottom windows.

8. Examine the three images.

   The quality of the lower-right image is unsatisfactory. Distracting pixels are visible at the edges of the logo and on the legs.

9. Click the **lower-left window**, click the **Quality list arrow**, then drag the **slider** to 40.

10. Keep the Save for Web & Devices dialog box open.

You used the 4-Up view of the Save for Web & Devices dialog box to compare three optimized JPEG files, each with different settings.

Figure 21 *Save for Web & Devices dialog box*

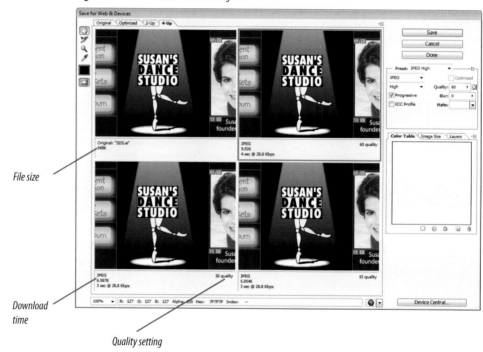

File size

Download time

Quality setting

Figure 22 *Slice 14, optimized as a GIF using 8 colors*

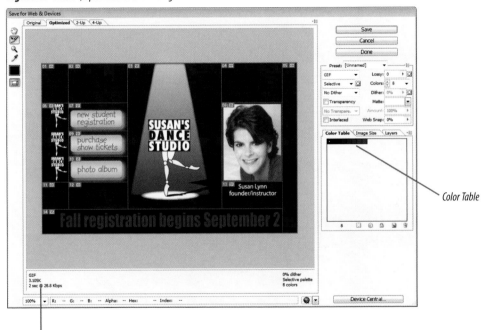

Color Table

Change in file size

Optimize slices as GIFs

1. Click the **Optimized tab**.

2. Click the **Slice Select tool** , click **slice 06**, press and hold [**Shift**], then click **slice 13** to add it to the selection.

3. Click the **Preset list arrow**, then click **GIF 32 Dithered**.

4. Remove the check mark from the Transparency check box.

5. Deselect, click **slice 06** only, then click the **Color Table tab** in the options in the right side of the dialog box.

   The Color Table shows the 32 total colors that are used to represent the artwork.

6. Click **slice 14**, click the **Preset list arrow**, then click **GIF 32 No Dither**.

   Note the change to the swatches in the Color Table. Though the setting is for 32 colors, only 17 colors are required to reproduce the artwork.

7. Note the change in file size in the lower-left corner.

8. Click the **Colors list arrow**, then click **8**.

   Note the change in the Color Table and the change in file size, as shown in Figure 22. Note also the high quality of the artwork with only eight colors.

9. Remove the check mark from the Transparency check box.

10. Keep the Save for Web & Devices dialog box open.

You optimized a slice as a GIF. You lowered the number of colors available to draw the image, noting the changes in image quality and file size.

Compare and contrast JPEG and GIF formats

1. Click the **Slice Select tool** 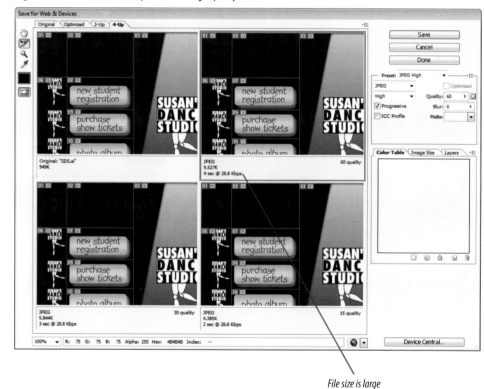 if it is not still active, click **slice 07**, press and hold [**Shift**], then click slices **09** and **10** to add them to the selection.

2. Click the **Preset list arrow**, click **JPEG High**, then click the **4-Up tab**.

3. Compare the quality of the three JPEGs to the original.

   The High quality JPEG in the upper-right window is the only version with acceptable quality. Note that the file size is over 9K, as shown in Figure 23.

   TIP Your file size may slightly differ.

4. Click the **Optimized tab**.

5. Click the **Preset list arrow**, click **GIF 128 No Dither**, then remove the check mark from the Transparency check box.

6. Click the **4-Up tab**, then use the Hand tool to move the image to see as much of the three buttons as possible.

7. Click the **lower-left window**, then note that its Selective palette is 64 colors, one-half that of the image in the upper-right window.

8. Click the **Colors list arrow**, then click **32**.

   The Selective palette of the image in the lower-left corner is reduced by half, yet the quality remains acceptable.

   (continued)

Figure 23 *Slices 07, 09, and 10 optimized as a high-quality JPEG*

File size is large

Figure 24 *Slices 07, 09, and 10 optimized as a GIF*

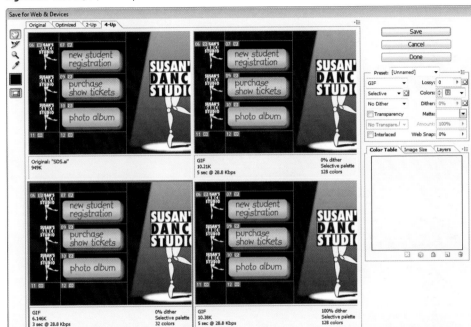

9. Click the **Colors list arrow**, then click **16**.

   The reduced palette does not contain enough colors to represent the buttons' drop shadows smoothly.

10. Click the **Colors list arrow**, then click **32**.

    The file size is around 6 kilobytes—2/3 that of the acceptable JPEG—and the quality is almost indistinguishable from the original, as shown in Figure 24.

11. Keep the Save for Web & Devices dialog box open.

You experimented with optimizing a slice as both a JPEG and a GIF, comparing file size and image quality. You found that the GIF format optimized the slice with higher quality at a lower file size than the JPEG format.

Create photo effects with a GIF

1. Click the **Optimized tab**.

2. Click the **Slice Select tool**  if it is not active, then click **slice 08**.

3. Click the **Preset list arrow**, then click **GIF 32 Dithered**.

4. Click the **Color Table tab** if it is not active.

   The Color Table shows the 32 total colors that are used to present the photo in slice 08.

5. Click the **Colors list arrow**, then click **16**.

   The number of colors in the Color Table is reduced.

6. Click the **Colors list arrow**, click **8**, then note the effect on the photo and the file size shown in the lower-left corner of the dialog box.

7. Click the **Colors list arrow**, click **4**, click the **Dither list arrow**, then drag the **slider** to 10%.

8. Click the **Specify the dither algorithm list arrow**, then click **Noise** so that the photo resembles Figure 25.

9. Keep the Save for Web & Devices dialog box open.

You specified an Image slice as a GIF, then lowered the number of colors available to reproduce the image, noting the effect on the image. You then added noise as the type of dither algorithm to create a special effect.

Figure 25 *An effect created by optimizing a photo as a GIF*

Figure 26 *Web page shown in a browser window*

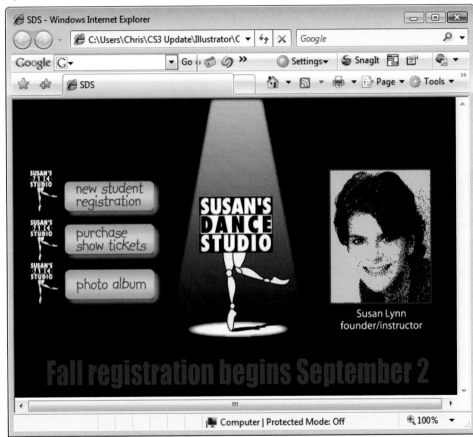

1. Click the **Save button** in the upper-right corner of the dialog box, name the file **SDS.html**, then click **Save**.

2. Launch your web browser, such as Safari or Internet Explorer.

TIP If you do not have access to a web browser, proceed to the next lesson.

3. Open SDS.html in your web browser application.

4. Point to different images and note the messages that you entered in the Slice Options dialog box, in the status bar of the browser window.

TIP If you do not see messages in the status bar, your browser may be set to block specific content.

Your screen should resemble Figure 26.

5. Close (Win) or Quit (Mac) your browser, then save and close the SDS document.

You saved the file with the optimization settings that you specified in the Save for Web & Devices dialog box. You then viewed the HTML file in a web browser application.

Create an
IMAGE MAP

What You'll Do

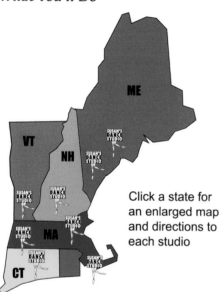

Click a state for
an enlarged map
and directions to
each studio

*In this lesson, you will change the colors in an illustration
to web safe colors and create polygonal image maps with
URLs attached to them for use on web page.*

Working with Web Safe Colors

Given all of the variables that might affect
color display on the Internet, such as
different monitors with different settings,
different web browsers with different
settings, as well as many other conditions,
you can never be certain that the colors you
specify in your document will appear the
same way when viewed as a web page. You
can't even be certain that they'll be consistent
from computer to computer. To alleviate this
problem to some degree, Illustrator offers
a Web Safe RGB mode on the Color panel
and a Web swatch library. The Web swatch
library contains predefined colors that
are coded so as to be recognized by most
computer displays, and by the common web
browser applications. When color is critical,
it is best to think of the web safe gamut as a
safe bet for achieving reasonable consistency,
understanding that a guarantee is a bit too
much to expect.

Understanding Image Maps

Image maps allow you to define an area of an
illustration as a link. In a web browser, when
a user clicks the area of the image defined as
a link, the web browser loads the linked file.

Image maps differ from slices in that artwork and links in image maps are stored in a single file. Another main difference is that slices are always rectangular, while image maps enable you to create links from polygons and odd-shaped objects, as shown in Figure 27.

Image maps are quite simple to make in Illustrator. The Attributes panel contains an Image list arrow, which allows you to choose a shape for your image map. You can then enter the URL for the link. The resulting image map is not visible in Illustrator or the browser. The area that the user clicks on the image map is also known as a **hotspot**.

Figure 27 *Image maps enable you to define odd-shaped areas of an image as links to a URL*

Choose web safe colors

1. Open AI 13-2.ai, then save it as **New England Map**.

2. Show the Color panel.

3. Click the **Color panel options button** ▾≣, then click **Web Safe RGB**.

4. Verify that the Fill button is in front of the Stroke button on the Tools panel, click the **Selection tool** ▸, then click the **state of Maine**.

   The Color panel, as shown in Figure 28, shows the current fill color, the Out of Web Color Warning button, and the In Web Color button. The In Web Color button shows the closest possible web safe color to the green fill.

5. Click the **In Web Color button** ▦ on the Color panel.

   The object's fill color changes to a web safe color.

6. Click the **state of New Hampshire**, then click the **In Web Color button** ▢ on the Color panel.

7. Using the same method, change the fill color of the state of Vermont to a web safe color.

You used the In Web Color button on the Color panel to change objects' fills to web safe colors.

Figure 28 *Color panel in Web Safe RGB mode*

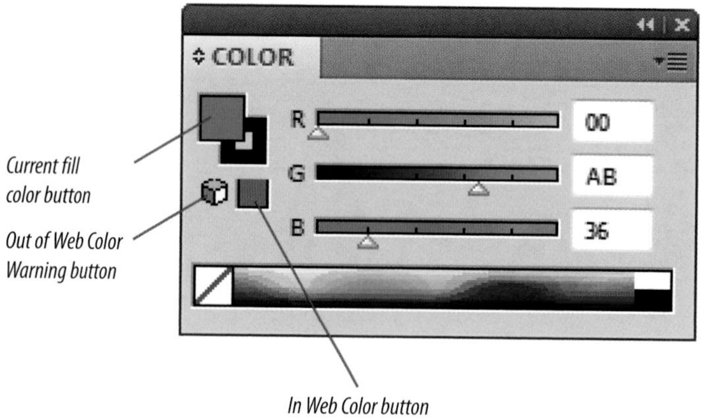

Current fill color button

Out of Web Color Warning button

In Web Color button

Figure 29 *The image map artwork, optimized as a GIF*

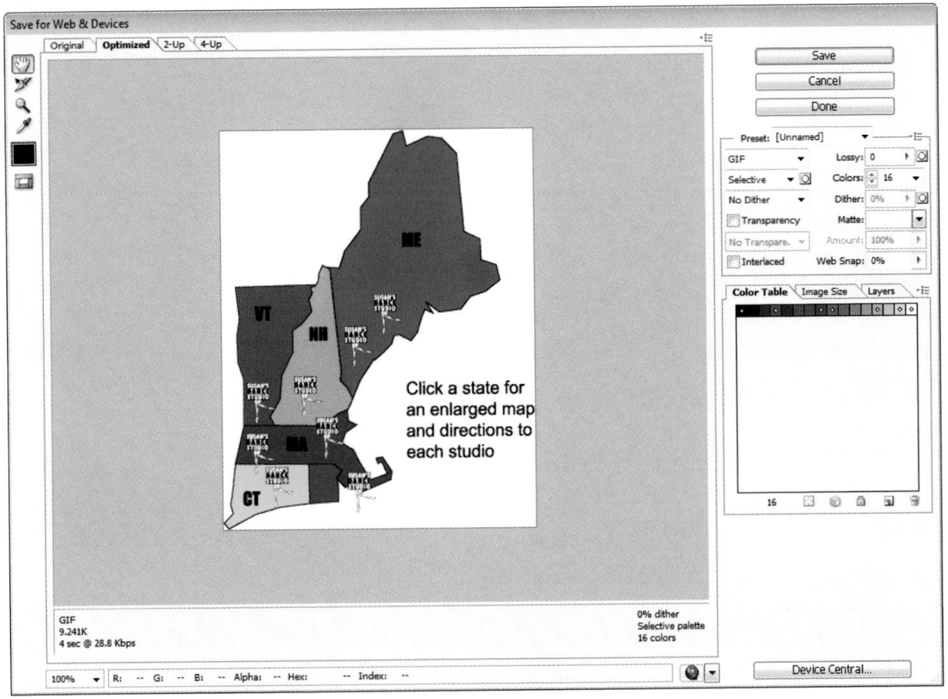

Create hotspots

1. Select the state of Maine, click **Window** on the Application bar, then click **Attributes**.

2. Click the **Image Map list arrow** on the Attributes panel, then click **Polygon**.

   An invisible hotspot that closely follows the outline of the selected object is created.

3. Type **http://www.sds.com/map/me** in the URL text box.

4. Select the state of New Hampshire, click the **Image Map list arrow**, then click **Polygon**.

5. Type **http://www.sds.com/map/nh** in the URL text box.

6. Add polygon hotspots using the following URLs to Vermont, Massachusetts, and Connecticut: **http://www.sds.com/map/vt**, **http://www.sds.com/map/ma**, and **http://www.sds.com/map/ct**.

7. Click **File** on the Application bar, click **Save for Web & Devices**, then click the **Optimized tab** if it is not already active.

8. Click the **Preset list arrow**, then click **GIF 32 No Dither**.

9. Click the **Colors list arrow**, then click **16**.

10. Remove the check mark from the Transparency check box. Your screen should resemble Figure 29.

11. Click the **Save button** in the Save for Web & Devices dialog box, accept the current file name, then click **Save**.

12. Save and close New England Map.

You created five polygonal image maps with corresponding URLs. You then used the Save for Web & Devices dialog box to specify the artwork as a GIF file.

Export Illustrator GRAPHICS FOR THE WEB

What You'll Do

In this lesson, you will export Illustrator graphics and animations for the web.

Exporting to SWF

SWF is an acronym for Shockwave Flash, though it's also been known offhand as "small web format." For Illustrator graphics, SWF will be your export format of choice. With SWF, you can export your file to be placed and used in Adobe Flash, or the file can be opened directly by web browser software like Internet Explorer or Firefox. You could also upload your SWF as content on your web site.

When you export to SWF, the SWF Options dialog box opens, as shown in Figure 30. The choice you make in the Export As menu will determine how Illustrator layers are exported to Flash.

- Choose AI File to SWF File to export the Illustrator file as a single SWF file. In other words, as a single flattened file.
- Choose AI Layers to SWF Frames to export the artwork on each layer to a separate SWF frame, thus creating an animated SWF.
- The Version option in the dialog box allows you to choose to which version of Flash you want to export, from oldest to most current.

- The Preset option allows you to choose from settings that you have saved previously. Imagine that you are exporting multiple graphics, all with the same settings. You don't want to have to load those settings each time. Instead, save a preset. You create new presets by setting the options that you want and then choosing Save Settings from the panel menu.
- The Curve Quality option allows you to specify how well the curved paths in the Illustrator file are rendered. A higher number produces a better curve but results in a larger file size. However, most vector graphic file sizes are tiny, so using the highest setting won't be a problem.
- Frame Rate Specifies the rate at which the animation will play in a Flash viewer. This option is available only for AI Layers to SWF Frames.
- The Loop plays an animation continuously, rather than just one time. This option is available only for AI Layers to SWF Frames.
- Preserve Appearance converts strokes into stroke-shaped fills and flattens any blending modes and transparency.

It's a good idea to activate this option to be sure of no unexpected content shifts or color shifts in the exported file.

- Preserve Editability is the opposite of Preserve Appearance. Use this option if you want to edit strokes or transparent color relationships in Adobe Flash.

Using Illustrator as an Animation Tool

You might be surprised (and excited) to learn that you can export Illustrator graphics as animations for the web or in Flash.

Animation is a big part of most web sites and interactive presentations. Animation can be an obvious component, like an illustration of a race car moving across the screen. But animation can also be subtle. In many web sites, for example, a button will shift slightly when you click it with your mouse, or an image will appear small and enlarge gradually when the page is refreshed.

Adobe Flash offers many controls for creating and specifying animations as part of its web page authoring environment. Because Flash is a vector-based design tool that offers many controls for designing and creating buttons, graphics and layouts, you might be surprised by how much it resembles Illustrator. Nevertheless, some designers are more comfortable designing in Illustrator and prefer it to Flash. This can especially be the case with animations, which often involve complex graphics. That's where the ability to design in Illustrator and export an animated SWF to Flash really comes into play.

Figure 30 *SWF Options dialog box*

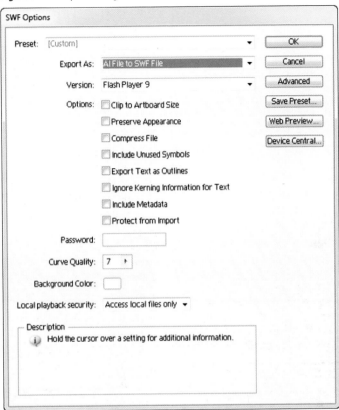

Creating Artwork Using Variables

Variable libraries enable designers and developers to coordinate their work through an XML file. The developer can use the XML file to link variables and data sets to a database and write a script to render the final artwork. To import variables into Illustrator from an XML file, choose Load Variable Library from the Variables panel menu. To export variables from Illustrator to an XML file, choose Save Variable Library from the Variables panel menu.

Illustrator's Blend tool is itself something of an animation tool. When you create an animation, such as a 6-step animation between a circle and a square as shown in Figure 31, you can think of those six objects as each being part of an animation that transitions the original circle into a square. The Blend tool creates the "in between" objects.

Illustrator allows you to export a blend as an animation. To export any illustrator artwork—blend or no blend—as an animation, you must choose AI Layers to SWF Frames in the Export As dialog box, as shown in Figure 32. This terminology can be a bit misleading when exporting blends as animations, because usually your blended artwork will not contain any layers. Nevertheless, you need to choose this option in the Export dialog box.

When you choose AI Layers to SWF Frames, the Advanced SWF Options dialog box offers controls for animations. As shown in Figure 33, you can specify the frame rate and whether or not the animation will loop.

If the artwork you're exporting is a blend, be sure to check Animate Blends. When you do, Illustrator will export each object in the blend as its own frame in the animation. You can choose between the Sequence and Build options. Choosing "Sequence" means that each subsequent frame will contain the next object in the blend. Choosing "Build" means that each subsequent frame will add the next object in the blend, with each frame

"building." In other words, the first frame will contain the first object, the second frame will contain the first and second objects, the third frame will contain the first, second and third objects, and so on. With blended artwork, generally speaking, you'll want to choose the Sequence option.

Note that the Advanced SWF Options dialog box allows you to choose the layer order for the animation. This can be a bit confusing with blends, because blended artwork is on a single layer. When exported as an animation though, Illustrator must regard it as each object being on a separate layer. Remember that in the Layers panel, each new layer is created above the existing layers. Therefore, if the blend in Figure 31 were exported as an animation, the red circle would be on the bottom most layer, and the blue square would be on the top, because the blend was created left to right, starting with the circle. If you chose the default Bottom Up for the Layer Order, the animation would play starting with the circle and ending with the square.

Figure 31 *6-step blend*

Figure 32 *AI Layers to SWF Frames option in SWF Options dialog box*

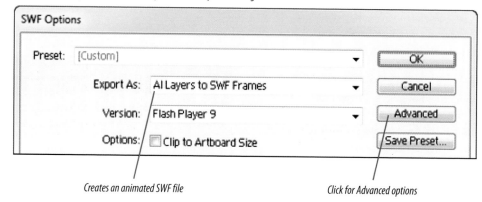

Creates an animated SWF file   *Click for Advanced options*

Exporting Non-Blend Artwork as an Animation

Illustrations that you create in Illustrator without blends can also be exported as animations. To do so, you must first put the components of the artwork on separate layers.

Figure 34 shows a type of Illustrator artwork that can be exported successfully as an animation. You could start with the larger square animating down to the smaller square, creating the illusion that the squares are collapsing into themselves. To export the illustration as an animation, you'd need to place each square on its own layer in the order that you want the animation to proceed.

Rather than do this by hand, you can use the Release to Layers command in the Layers Panel. This will move each object onto an individual layer, from bottom to top, in the order they were created. You always have the option of reordering the layers by hand if you want to manipulate that order.

Figure 33 *Animation controls in the SWF Options dialog box*

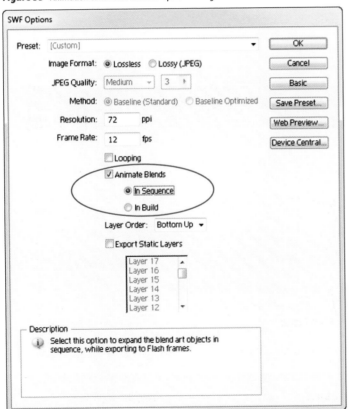

Figure 34 *Non-blend artwork*

Export artwork as an SWF file

1. Open AI 13-3.ai, then save it as **SWF Export**.

2. Click **File** on the Application bar, then click **Export**.

   The Export dialog box opens.

3. Navigate to the folder in which you save your solutions files.

4. Choose **Flash (*.SWF)** as the file format.

5. Click **Save** (Win) or **Export** (Mac).

   The SWF Options dialog box opens.

6. Apply the settings shown in Figure 35.

   For the Version option, choose the version of the Flash Player that you have installed. If you don't know, use the default Flash Player 9.

7. Click **OK**.

   (continued)

Figure 35 *SWF Options dialog box*

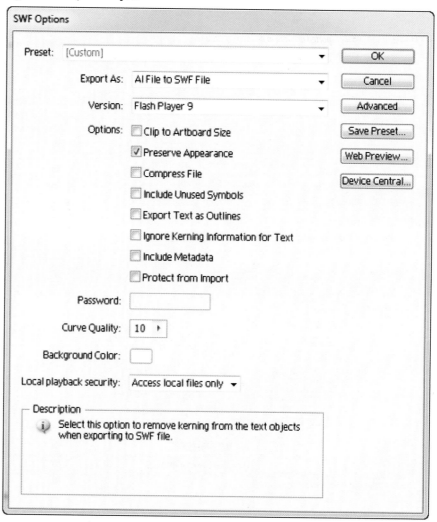

Figure 36 *Viewing exported artwork in an Internet browser*

The file is now available to be used in Adobe Flash as part of a Flash presentation.

8. Launch Internet Explorer or Firefox, then navigate to where you exported the SWF file.

9. Open the SWF Export.swf file.

   As shown in Figure 36, the file opens in the browser software.

10. Return to the Illustrator file, save your work, then close the file.

You exported Illustrator artwork as an SWF file. You opened the file in your Internet browser.

Export a blend as an animated SWF file

1. Open AI 13-4.ai, then save it as **Animated Blend**.

2. Click the **Selection tool** 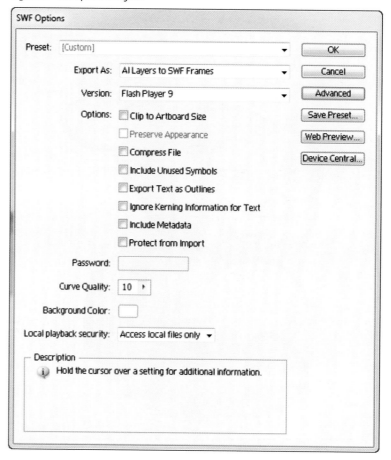, then select the artwork on the artboard.

   The artwork is a simple 12-step blend between a circle and a star created with the Blend tool. The spine of the blend has been altered so that it curves.

3. Click **File** on the Application bar, then click **Export**.

4. Navigate to the folder in which you save your solutions files.

5. Choose **Flash (*.SWF)** as the file format.

6. Click **Save** (Win) or **Export** (Mac).

   The SWF Options dialog box opens.

7. Specify the settings shown in Figure 37.

   Note that the Export As option is specified as AI Layers to SWF Frames. The file will be exported as an animated SWF, with each object in the blend a different frame in the animation.

   (continued)

Figure 37 *SWF Options dialog box*

Figure 38 *Animation settings in the Advanced section*

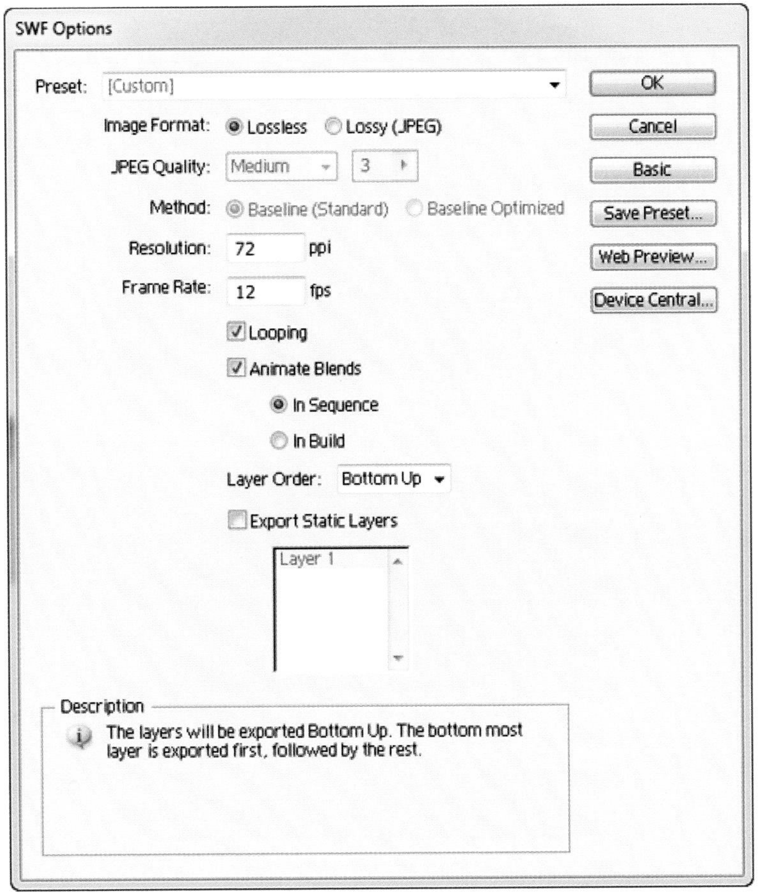

8. Click the **Advanced** button, then specify the settings shown in Figure 38.

   Note the Frame Rate is set to 12 frames per second. Animate Blends is checked and will be animated in sequence, meaning each object in the blend will appear in sequence. Note, too, that the animation has been set to Loop, which means it will play continuously.

9. Click **OK**.

   The file is now available to be used in Adobe Flash as part of a Flash presentation.

10. Launch Internet Explorer or Firefox, then navigate to where you exported the SWF file.

11. Open the Animated Blend.swf file.

    The animation will play in the browser window.

TIP You may need to temporarily disable security measures installed with your browser software that might inhibit your ability to play the animation.

12. Return to the Illustrator file, save your work, then close the file.

You exported Illustrator artwork as an animated SWF file. You opened the file in your Internet browser.

Export non-blend artwork as an animated SWF file

1. Open AI 13-5.ai, then save it as **Animated Flower**.

   The artwork started with the single red "petal" at the top. It was rotated counter-clockwise to create the additional petals one at a time.

2. Select all the artwork on the artboard.

3. Open the Layers panel menu, then click **Release to Layers (Build)**.

   As shown in Figure 39, each object is moved to its own layer. The layers are created in sequence, from bottom to top, in the order that objects were created. The first object created—the top red petal—is the bottommost layer. The next layer up is the red petal plus the orange petal. With each subsequent layer, from bottom up, a new petal is added. Thus the illustration "builds" from bottom up.

   (continued)

Figure 39 *Each object is moved to its own layer*

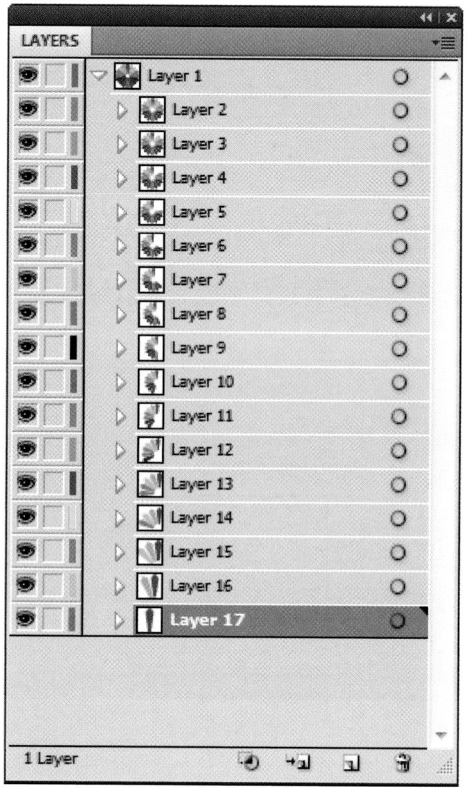

Figure 40 *SWF Options dialog box*

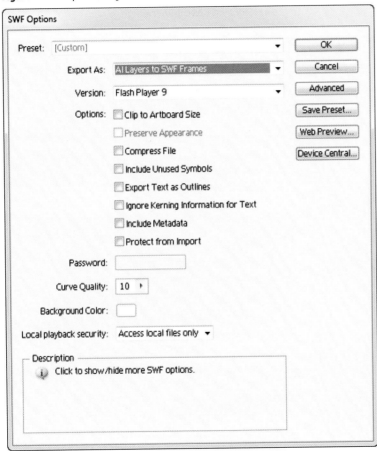

4. Click **File** on the Application bar, then click **Export**.

5. Choose **Flash (*.SWF)** as the file format.

6. Click **Save** (Win) or **Export** (Mac).

   The SWF Options dialog box opens.

7. Specify the settings shown in Figure 40.

TIP You may have to click the Basic button if the Advanced options are showing.

(continued)

8. Click the **Advanced** button if the Advanced options are not already showing, then specify the settings shown in Figure 41.

Note that Animate Blends is not checked—this is not blended artwork. The Layer Order option is set to Bottom Up.

9. Click **OK**, then open the SWF file in your web browser.

The illustration "builds" in a counter-clockwise animation. Each subsequent frame adds another petal to the illustration until the entire flower is complete.

10. Return to the Illustrator file, then save your work.

(continued)

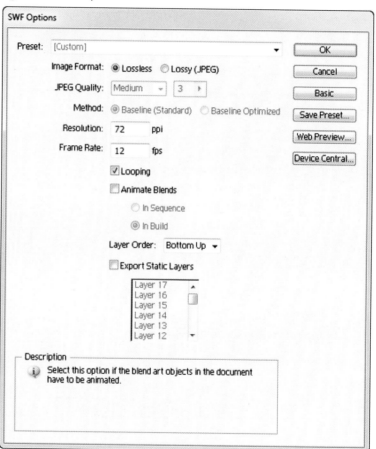

Figure 41 *Advanced options*

Figure 42 *Selecting multiple layers*

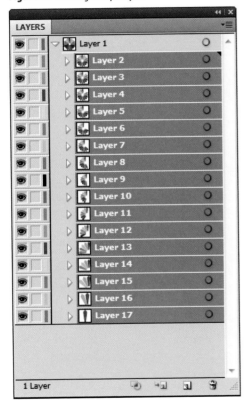

Figure 43 *Selecting copied layers*

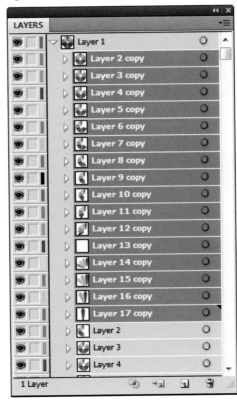

11. In the Layers panel, select all the layers except Layer 1, as shown in Figure 42.

12. Open the Layers panel menu, then click **Duplicate Selection**.

    New duplicate layers are created. They all have the word "copy" in their names. No layers are selected in the panel.

13. Select all the layers with the word "copy" in their name, as shown in Figure 43.

14. Open the Layers panel menu, then click **Reverse Order**.

15. Export the file with the same name and the same settings.

    When asked, overwrite the previous export.

16. Open the exported .SWF file in your web browser.

    The illustration builds counter-clockwise, reverses, then petals disappear clockwise.

17. Return to the Illustrator file, save your work, then close the file.

You used the Release to Layers command to position every object in an illustration onto separate layers. You then exported the layers as animation frames.

Create slices.

1. Open AI 13-6.ai, then save it as **Hana**.
2. Show rulers, then place a horizontal guide just above the five photos. (*Hint*: Change your guides to a darker color.)
3. Place a horizontal guide just below the five photos, above the blue text.
4. Place a vertical guide between each photo and the next, for a total of four vertical guides.
5. Verify that your guides are unlocked.
6. Click Object on the Application bar, point to Slice, then click Create from Guides.
7. Deselect all.
8. Click the Slice Selection tool.
9. Select slices 01 and 02, click Object on the Application bar, point to Slice, click Combine Slices, then save.
10. Combine slices 02, 03, and 04, then save.
11. Combine slices 08 and 09, then save.
12. Combine slices 10 and 11, then save.
13. Save your work.

Specify slice type and slice options.

1. Select slice 01, click Object on the Application bar, point to Slice, then click Slice Options.
2. Define slice 01 as an Image slice, click OK, then save.
3. Select slice 02, click Object on the Application bar, point to Slice, then click Slice Options.
4. Define slice 02 as a No Image slice, click the Background list arrow, click White, click OK, then save.
5. Select slice 08, define slice 08 as a No Image slice, click the Background list arrow, click White, click OK, then save.

6. Select slice 09, click Object on the Application bar, point to Slice, then click Slice Options.
7. Define slice 09 as an Image slice, click OK, then save.
8. Select slice 03, define it as an Image slice, then type **http://www.hana.com/photo1** in the URL text box.
9. Click the Target list arrow, then click _blank.
10. Type **Explore by car** in the Message and Alt text boxes, then click OK.
11. Save your work.

Use the Save for Web & Devices dialog box.

1. Click File on the Application bar, then click Save for Web & Devices.
2. Click the Slice Select tool if it is not already active, click slice 01, click the Preset list arrow in the right side of the dialog box, click GIF 32 Dithered, then remove the check mark from the Transparency check box.
3. Click slice 09, click the Preset list arrow, click GIF 32 Dithered, remove the check mark from the Transparency check box, click the Colors list arrow, then click 8.
4. Click slice 03, click the Preset list arrow, then click JPEG High.
5. Click the 4-Up tab, click the Hand tool, then drag the Hand tool over the selected window until slice 03 is visible in all four windows.
6. Compare the quality and file sizes of the three optimized images.
7. Click Done.

Create an image map.

1. Click Window on the Application bar, then click Attributes if it is not already checked.
2. Click the Selection tool, then click the purple diamond in slice 01.
3. Click the Image list arrow on the Attributes panel, then click Polygon.
4. Type **http://www.hana.com/car** in the URL text box on the Attributes panel.
5. Click the gold diamond.
6. Click the Image list arrow on the Attributes panel, then click Polygon.
7. Type **http://www.hana.com/horse** in the URL text box.
8. Click the green diamond.
9. Click the Image list arrow on the Attributes panel, then click Polygon.
10. Type **http://www.hana.com/foot** in the URL text box.
11. Click the blue diamond.
12. Click the Image list arrow on the Attributes panel, then click Polygon.
13. Type **http://www.hana.com/bike** in the URL text box.
14. Save your work, then compare your window to Figure 44.
15. Close the Hana document.

Export Illustrator graphics for the web.

1. Open AI 13-7.ai, then save it as **Dog Export**.
2. Click File on the Application bar, then click Export. The Export dialog box opens.
3. Navigate to the folder in which you save your solutions files.
4. Choose Flash (*.SWF) as the file type.
5. Click Save (Win) or Export (Mac). The SWF Options dialog box opens.
6. Apply the settings shown in Figure 45.
7. Click OK.
8. Launch your Internet browser software, then navigate to where you exported the SWF file.
9. Open the Dog Export.swf file.
10. Return to the Illustrator file, save your work, then close the file.

Figure 44 *Completed Skills Review, Part 1*

Figure 45 *SWF Options dialog box*

SWF Options

Preset: [Custom]

Export As: AI File to SWF File

Version: Flash Player 9

Options: ☐ Clip to Artboard Size
☐ Preserve Appearance
☐ Compress File
☐ Include Unused Symbols
☐ Export Text as Outlines
☐ Ignore Kerning Information for Text
☐ Include Metadata
☐ Protect from Import

Password:

Curve Quality: 10

Background Color:

Local playback security: Access local files only

OK
Cancel
Advanced
Save Preset...
Web Preview...
Device Central...

Description
ⓘ Hold the cursor over a setting for additional information.

You work in the online department of OAHU magazine as an art manager. Every month, when the magazine hits the newsstands, you update the magazine's website with the new online issue. The top page always features this month's cover of the magazine, reduced 50% to fit on the page. The print department sends you an Illustrator file. Your job is to prepare the file to be used on the web. You dislike this month's cover choice, which is a dark, busy, and out-of-focus image, and note that the subheads must remain bright when they are converted to web safe colors.

1. Open AI 13-8.ai, then save it as **Oahu Online**.
2. Click File on the Application bar, point to Document Color Mode, then click RGB Color.
3. Click Window on the Application bar, then click Color if it is not checked.
4. Click the Color panel options button, then click Web Safe RGB.
5. Select the word OAHU, which is grouped with the magazine cover frame.
6. Click the In Web Color button on the Color panel.
7. Select the word "living."
8. Click the In Web Color button on the Color panel.
9. Change the colors for the three subheads (TWIST & SHOUT, A-MAZE-ING, and MAVERICK) to web safe colors.
10. Save your work, then compare your document to Figure 46.
11. Close the Oahu Online document.

Figure 46 *Completed Project Builder 1*

You work in the online department of OAHU magazine as a webmaster. Every month, you receive the color-corrected version of this month's cover, which you position on the top page of the website. The cover is one of your favorite features of the OAHU magazine web site because users can click the three featured cover stories and go immediately to the online article. You create the slices and specify the slice options.

1. Open AI 13-9.ai, then save it as **Oahu Magazine**.
2. Show the rulers if they are not displayed, then place a vertical guide between the A and H in OAHU.
3. Place a horizontal guide beneath the word living.
4. Place a horizontal guide above the word A-MAZE-ING.
5. Place a horizontal guide above the word MAVERICK.
6. Use the guides to make slices.
7. Combine slices 5 and 7, then save.
8. Define the options for slice 5 as follows:
   Slice Type: Image
   URL: **http://www.oahu.com/twist**
   Target: _blank
9. Save your work.
10. Define the options for slice 7 as follows:
    Slice Type: Image
    URL: **http://www.oahu.com/amazeing**
    Target: _blank
11. Save your work.

12. Define the options for slice 8 as follows:
    Slice Type: Image
    URL: **http://www.oahu.com/maverick**
    Target: _top
13. Save your work.
14. Define slices 1, 2, 3, and 4 as Image slices.
15. Save your work, compare your document to Figure 47, then close the file.

Figure 47 *Completed Project Builder 2*

You work in the online department of OAHU magazine as an art director. Every month, you personally optimize the cover image for the website. You feel strongly that the process of compressing a cover image demands a critical eye to maintain image quality. You note that you'll be able to optimize the image substantially, because the photo is so busy and out-of-focus that it will be hard to see any flaws created by compression. Your goal is to compress each slice to approximately 8K or less, while maintaining acceptable quality.

1. Open AI 13-10.ai, then save it as **Oahu Cover**.
2. Click File on the Application bar, then click Save for Web & Devices.
3. Click the Optimized tab if it is not active.
4. Select all seven slices.
5. Click the Preset list arrow, then click JPEG High.
6. Click the 4-Up tab.
7. Note that the quality of the JPEG with the quality setting of 30 is unacceptable, then click the Optimized tab.
8. Note the file size and download time of the total image.
9. Deselect by clicking outside the magazine cover, then select each slice, noting the file size of each one in the lower-left corner of the window.
10. Select all of the slices.
11. Click the Preset list arrow, then click GIF 64 Dithered; note the file size.

12. Click the Preset list arrow, then click GIF 32 Dithered, as shown in Figure 48.
13. Note any changes in quality.

14. Deselect all, then select each slice, noting the file size of each one.
15. Click Done, then close the Oahu Cover document.

Figure 48 *Completed Design Project*

You're a freelance designer, and it's your first day working for a web design company. They ask you to produce an animation for a web site they're building. You don't work in Flash, so you decide to design the animation in Illustrator and export it as a Flash animation.

1. Open AI 13-11.ai, then save it as **Animated Squares**.
2. Select the square, click Object on the Application bar, point to Path, then click Offset Path.
3. In the Offset textbox, type -.25 in, then click OK.
4. Repeat Step 3 eight times.
   Your artwork should resemble Figure 49.
5. Select all the artwork on the artboard.
6. Open the Layers panel menu, then click Release to Layers (Sequence).
7. In the Layers panel, select Layer 2 through Layer 11.
8. Open the Layers panel menu, then click Duplicate Selection.
9. Select all the layers with the word "copy" in their name.
10. Open the Layers panel menu, then click Reverse Order.
11. Export the file as an animated SWF that loops.
12. Open the animated SWF file in your web browser.
13. Return to the Illustrator file, save your work, then close the file.

Figure 49 *Artwork to be animated*

To access the online content for this book, take the following steps:

1. Open your browser and go to http://www.cengagebrain.com
2. Type the author, title, or ISBN of this book in the Search window. (The ISBN is listed on the back cover.)

3. Click the book title in the list of search results.
4. When the book's main page is displayed, click the Access Now button.
5. Click Student Resources in the left navigation pane to access the PDF files you'll need.

You can download and print the PDF files for your reference, or read them in Acrobat Reader.

ACE CERTIFICATION GRID FOR ADOBE ILLUSTRATOR CS5

Topic Area	Objectives	Chapter(s)
1.0 Working with Illustrator documents	1.1 Create a document with multiple artboards, defining its options with a New Document Profile	1 (p. 62-63, 68-69)
	1.2 Create a new artboard in a document (options include the Artboard tool and Artboard Options)	1 (p. 64-66, 69-71)
	1.3 Given a scenario, manage objects on a single artboard or the entire work area (options include views, rulers, select, and pasting objects)	1 (p. 63, 68-69)
	1.4 Given a scenario, modify and use multiple artboards (options include move, duplicate, rearrange, renumber, resize, re-orient, and re-name artboards)	1 (p. 64-67, 69-72)
	1.5 Manage multiple open documents (including arranging windows, using tabbed windows, and using n-up view)	1 (p. 17-18, 20, 22-23)
	1.6 Control the working environment with Application Frame, Application Bar, workspace, and Panels states	1 (p. 4-15, 19-21), additional material online
	1.7 Given a scenario, choose a preview mode to visualize the document	1 (p. 17, 22-23)
	1.8 Given a scenario, choose the proper settings in the Preferences dialog box	1 (p. 17, 20-21, 27-28)
	1.9 Customize keyboard shortcuts with the Keyboard Shortcuts dialog box	1 (p. 19), additional material online
	1.10 Given a scenario, create Guides, Grids, and use Smart Guides	1 (p. 15-16, 20-22, 34-35)
	1.11 Build a document structure based on layers (options include moving and copying objects to layers)	5 (p. 4-29)
	1.12 View and modify document metadata information	13 (p. 14), additional material online
	1.13 Given a scenario, save a document with the best format and options (options include various "Save…" and Export commands, choosing artboards, and file formats)	11 (p. 30-35) 13 Lessons 3 & 5, additional material online

ACE CERTIFICATION GRID FOR ADOBE ILLUSTRATOR CS5

Topic Area	Objectives	Chapter(s)
2.0 Drawing and transforming objects	2.1 Control object size and other options using the Control bar	4 (p. 4-13), additional material online
	2.2 Create and modify a vector object using the Pen tool and Bezier controls	3 (p. 4-23), additional material online
	2.3 Given a scenario, customize the visual appearance of strokes (options include the Stroke panel and the Width tool)	1 (p. 40-43) 3 (p. 30-35) 6 (p. 44-45, 48, 53)
	2.4 Given a scenario, modify vector paths and anchor points using the appropriate tool	1 (p. 54-55, 57-58, 61) 3 (p. 4-22)
	2.5 Use Isolation Mode to edit objects, groups, symbols, or layers8	8 (p.15, 18-20)
	2.6 Given a scenario, create either a clipping mask or layer-level clipping set to hide parts of objects	4 (p. 38-45) 5 (p. 26-29)
	2.7 Given a scenario, use a mix of open/closed paths, compound paths, and compound shapes (options include Pathfinder operations)	4 (p. 18-33)
	2.8 Align or distribute objects precisely on an artboard	1 (p. 15-16, 20-22, 34-35) 4 (p. 28)
	2.9 Select and control the stacking order of two or more objects	1 (p. 56, 59-60)
	2.10 Modify an object with one or more transformation tools	4 (p. 4-13), additional material online
	2.11 Create and apply a pattern swatch	6 (p. 8-19)
	2.12 Record steps as a reusable Action	7 (p. 25)
3.0 Managing color and transparency	3.1 Given a scenario, set up Color Management settings and proof color on screen	11 (p. 12), additional material online
	3.2 Given a scenario, create or load swatches, organize them, and apply them to objects	2 (p. 18-27), additional material online
	3.3 Apply transparency options to objects (options include opacity, color mode, and opacity masks)	8 (p. 4-9) 8 (p. 48-53)
	3.4 Given a scenario, recolor and fine-tune artwork in a document	8 (p. 10-27)
	3.5 Explore color combinations using the Color Guide panel	8 (p. 10-27)
	3.6 Given a scenario, use the appropriate tools to create a smooth color mix (options include Blend, Gradient, and Gradient Mesh)	2 (p. 28-33) 7 (p. 10-15) 7 (p. 22-29)

ACE CERTIFICATION GRID FOR ADOBE ILLUSTRATOR CS5

Topic Area	Objectives	Chapter(s)
4.0 Using type	4.1 Given a scenario, create the appropriate text object (options include point type, area text, and text on a path)	2 (p. 6-17)
	4.2 Format type using character and paragraph attributes	2 (p. 6-10)
	4.3 Create and apply character and paragraph styles to text	2 (p. 13)
	4.4 Use the Glyph and OpenType panels to obtain special characters	2 (p. 9) 9 (p. 20)
	4.5 Format a story (options include threading text frames and text wrap)	2 (p. 26), additional material online
	4.6 Locate or replace fonts inside a document	2 (p. 15), additional material online
	4.7 Given a scenario, customize language dictionaries	2 (p. 14), additional material online
	4.8 Given a scenario, adjust and apply hyphenation	2 (p. 5)
5.0 Controlling effects, appearances, and graphic styles	5.1 Manage fills, strokes, transparency, or effects in the Appearance panel (options include adding, editing, and viewing)	8 (p. 34-41)
	5.2 Given a scenario, apply the appropriate Live Effect to an object	8 (p. 28-41), additional material online
	5.3 Given a scenario, save and apply graphic styles to objects	8 (p. 42-47)
	5.4 Use the Eyedropper tool to copy attributes between elements	3 (p. 24-27)
6.0 Building graphic objects	6.1 Create and format a graph (options include entering data, controlling type options, and design)	9 Entire chapter
	6.2 Given a scenario, create and use the appropriate brush options	6 (p. 20-51)
	6.3 Create and use a symbol (options include placing it onto the artboard, editing it, and manipulating it with Symbolism tools)	12 Entire chapter
	6.4 Build a complex shape (option include Live Paint, Shape Builder and Pathfinder)	3 (p. 36-43) 3 (p. 48-53) 4 (p. 22-31) 4 (p. 34-37)
	6.5 Apply and edit an object distortion envelope	7 (p. 16-21), additional material online
	6.6 Given a scenario, use the Eraser tool, Blob Brush, or Bristle Brush (including editing the tool options)	6 (p. 34-39) (p. 42-43) (p. 49-51), additional material online
	6.7 Given a scenario, define and use a perspective grid	10 Entire Lesson 5
	6.8 Given a scenario, draw and move one or more objects in perspective	10 Entire Lesson 5

CERTIFICATION GRID
(CONTINUED)

ACE CERTIFICATION GRID FOR ADOBE ILLUSTRATOR CS5		
Topic Area	**Objectives**	**Chapter(s)**
7.0 Working with images	7.1 Import images into your document	3 (p. 23), additional material online
	7.2 Manage assets with the Links panel	3 (p. 45)
	7.3 Convert an image into a vector object using Live Trace	3 (p. 36-38) 3 (p. 44-47)
8.0 Preparing graphics for web or screen display	8.1 Given a scenario, choose the appropriate settings to save illustrator artwork for web or mobile devices	13 (p. 18-25) (p. 30-41), additional material online
	8.2 Prepare your document for Flash authoring (options include Symbols, Flash Text, SWF format)	13 (p. 30-41), additional material online
	8.3 Given a scenario, prepare web graphics choosing the proper settings (options include pixel alignment, slices, anti-aliasing)	13 (p. 4-17), additional material online
	8.4 Given a scenario, save document to either SWF or FGX format	13 (p. 30-41), additional material online
9.0 Preparing document for print	9.1 Analyze the content of a document with the Document Info panel	1 (p. 12), additional material online
	9.2 Use the Flattener Preview to preview and create custom settings to control the transparency flattening process.	11 (p. 24)
	9.3 Preview and analyze onscreen color separations	11 (p. 20)
	9.4 Given a scenario, choose the right PDF presets or customize options	11 (p. 30-35)
	9.5 Given a scenario, choose the correct print options and create custom print presets	11 (p. 4-35)

ADOBE ILLUSTRATOR CS5			
Chapter	Data File Supplied	Student Creates File	Used in
Chapter 1	AI 1-1.ai		L1-L2
	AI 1-2.ai		L2-L3
	AI 1-3.ai		L3
		Basic Shapes	L4-L7
	AI 1-4.ai		L8
		Winning Business Collateral	L9
	AI 1-5.ai		Skills Review
	AI 1-6.ai		Skills Review
	AI 1-7.ai		Skills Review
	AI 1-8.ai		Skills Review
	AI 1-9.ai		Project Builder 1
		Iris Vision Design	Project Builder 2
	AI 1-10.ai		Design Project
	AI 1-11.ai		Portfolio Project
Chapter 2	AI 2-1.ai		L1-L6
	AI 2-2.ai		L2
	AI 2-3.ai		Skills Review
		Desert Oasis	Project Builder 1
	AI 2-4.ai		Project Builder 2
		Vanish	Design Project
		Firehouse Chili	Portfolio Project

DATA FILES LIST

(CONTINUED)

ADOBE ILLUSTRATOR CS5			
Chapter	**Data File Supplied**	**Student Creates File**	**Used in**
Chapter 3	AI 3-1.ai		L1
	AI 3-2.ai		L2
	AI 3-3.ai		L2
	AI 3-4.ai		L3-L4
		Snowball Assembled	L5-L6
	AI 3-5.ai AI 3-6.ai AI 3-7.ai AI 3-8.ai		L7
	AI 3-9.ai AI 3-10.ai AI 3-11.ai		Skills Review
		Peppermill	Project Builder 1
	AI 3-12.ai		Project Builder 2
		Sleek Design	Design Project
		Shape	Portfolio Project

ADOBE ILLUSTRATOR CS5			
Chapter	**Data File Supplied**	**Student Creates File**	**Used in**
Chapter 4	AI 4-1.ai AI 4-2.ai AI 4-3.ai AI 4-4.ai		L1
	AI 4-5.ai AI 4-6.ai		L2
	AI 4-7.ai AI 4-8.ai		L3
	AI 4-9 .ai AI 4-10 .ai AI 4-11 .ai AI 4-12.ai		L4
	AI 4-13.ai		L5
	AI 4-14.ai AI 4-15.ai AI 4-16.ai AI 4-17.ai		L6
	AI 4-18.ai AI 4-19.ai AI 4-20.ai AI 4-21.ai		Skills Review
	AI 4-22.ai		Project Builder 1
	AI 4-23.ai		Project Builder 2
	AI 4-24.ai		Design Project
		Dartboard	Portfolio Project

ADOBE ILLUSTRATOR CS5			
Chapter	**Data File Supplied**	**Student Creates File**	**Used in**
Chapter 5	AI 5-1.ai AI 5-2.ai		L1-L4
	AI 5-3.ai		Skills Review
	AI 5-4.ai		Project Builder 1
	AI 5-5.ai		Project Builder 2
	AI 5-6.ai		Design Project
	AI 5-7.ai		Portfolio Project
Chapter 6		Checkerboard	L1
	AI 6-1.ai AI 6-2.ai		L2
	AI 6-3.ai		L3
	AI 6-4.ai		L4
	AI 6-5.ai		L5
	AI 6-6.ai		L6
	AI 6-7.ai AI 6-8.ai AI 6-9.ai		L7
	AI 6-10.ai AI 6-11.ai AI 6-12.ai	Polka Dot Pattern	Skills Review
		New Curtain	Project Builder 1
	AI 6-13.ai		Project Builder 2
	AI 6-14.ai		Design Project
		Wedding Plaid	Portfolio Project

ADOBE ILLUSTRATOR CS5			
Chapter	**Data File Supplied**	**Student Creates File**	**Used in**
Chapter 7	AI 7-1.ai AI 7-2.ai AI 7-3.ai		L1
	AI 7-4.ai AI 7-5.ai		L2
	AI 7-6.ai AI 7-7.ai AI 7-8.ai		L3
	AI 7-9.ai AI 7-10.ai AI 7-11.ai AI 7-12.ai		L4
		Distort Skills	Skills Review
	AI 7-13.ai AI 7-14.ai AI 7-15.ai		
		Tidal Wave	Project Builder 1
	AI 7-16.ai		Project Builder 2
	AI 7-17.ai		Design Project
		Bellucia Flag	Portfolio Project

DATA FILES LIST

(CONTINUED)

ADOBE ILLUSTRATOR CS5			
Chapter	**Data File Supplied**	**Student Creates File**	**Used in**
Chapter 8	AI 8-1.ai AI 8-2.ai		L1
	AI 8-3.ai AI 8-4.ai AI 8-5.ai		L2
	Limeade.ai**		L3–L4
		Triple Fill	L4
	AI 8-6.ai		L5
	AI 8-7.ai		L6
	AI 8-8.ai AI 8-9.ai AI 8-10.ai		Skills Review
	AI 8-11.ai		Project Builder 1
	AI 8-12.ai		Project Builder 2
	AI 8-13.ai		Design Project
	AI 8-14.ai		Portfolio Project

** Students open Limeade.ai which they created in Lesson 1 and continue to work on it in Lesson 3 and Lesson 4.

ADOBE ILLUSTRATOR CS5			
Chapter	Data File Supplied	Student Creates File	Used in
Chapter 9	AI 9-1.ai		L1-L5
	AI 9-2.ai		L6-L8
	AI 9-3.ai AI 9-4.ai		Skills Review
	AI 9-5.ai		Project Builder 1
	AI 9-6.ai		Project Builder 2
	AI 9-7.ai		Design Project
		Sales	Portfolio Project
Chapter 10	AI 10-1.ai		L1
	AI 10-2.ai AI 10-3.ai AI 10-4.ai AI 10-5.ai		L2
	AI 10-6.ai		L3
	AI 10-7.ai AI 10-8.ai AI 10-9.ai AI 10-10.ai		L4
	AI 10-11.ai AI 10-12.ai AI 10-13.ai		L5
	AI 10-14.ai AI 10-15.ai AI 10-16.ai		Skills Review
	AI 10-17.ai		Project Builder 1
	AI 10-18.ai		Project Builder 2
		T-Shirt	Design Project
	AI 10-19.ai		Portfolio Project

Data Files List

DATA FILES LIST
(CONTINUED)

ADOBE ILLUSTRATOR CS5			
Chapter	**Data File Supplied**	**Student Creates File**	**Used in**
Chapter 11	AI 11-1.ai		L2-L4
	AI 11-2.ai AI 11-3.ai		L4
	AI 11-4.ai AI 11-5.ai		L5
	AI 11-6.ai		Skills Review
	AI 11-7.ai		Project Builder 1
	AI 11-8.ai		Project Builder 2
	AI 11-9.ai		Design Project
	AI 11-10.ai		Portfolio Project
Chapter 12	AI 12-1.ai		L1-L4
	AI 12-2.ai		L4-L5
	AI 12-3.ai		Skills Review
	AI 12-4.ai		Project Builder 1
	AI 12-5.ai		Project Builder 2
	AI 12-6.ai		Design Project
	AI 12-7.ai		Portfolio Project

ADOBE ILLUSTRATOR CS5			
Chapter	**Data File Supplied**	**Student Creates File**	**Used in**
Chapter 13	AI 13-1.ai		L1-L3
	AI 13-2.ai		L4
	AI 13-3.ai		L5
	AI 13-4.ai		
	AI 13-5.ai		
	AI 13-6.ai		Skills Review
	AI 13-7.ai		
	AI 13-8.ai		Project Builder 1
	AI 13-9.ai		Project Builder 2
	AI 13-10.ai		Design Project
	AI 13-11.ai		Portfolio Project

Chapter	**Support Files Supplied**
Chapter 1	Winning Logo.ai
Chapter 3	Snowball Sketch.tif, Skills Photo Trace.psd, Peppermill.tif, Montag Sketch.tif, Dog Sketch.psd BW photo.tif
Chapter 4	Mona Lisa.psd
Chapter 5	Living Room Original.tif
Chapter 6	Brushes.tif, Fat Charcoal.psd
Chapter 13	AI13-4.swf, animated blend.swf, animatedblend.ai

GLOSSARY

A

Absorption
Occurs when light strikes an object and is absorbed by the object.

Additive primary colors
Refers to the fact that Red, Green, and Blue light cannot be broken down themselves but can be combined to produce other colors.

Adobe Bridge
A sophisticated, stand-alone file browser, tightly integrated with the CS5 applications. The main role of Bridge is to help you locate, browse and organize files—also called "assets"—more easily.

Ambient light
Determines how an object is lit globally.

Area text
Text that you create inside an object.

Art brushes
A brush style that stretches an object along the length of a path.

Artboard tool
Gateway to working with multiple artboards.

Attributes
Formatting which has been applied to an object that affects its appearance.

B

Bevel
The angle that one surface makes with another when they are not at right angles.

Bevel join
Produces stroked lines with squared corners.

Bitmap images
Graphics created using a grid of colored squares called pixels.

Bleed
Artwork that extends to the trim and must extend the trim size by .125" to allow for variations when trimmed.

Blend
A series of intermediate objects and colors between two or more selected objects.

Blend Steps
Controls how smoothly shading appears on an object's surface and is most visible in the transition from the highlight areas to the diffusely lit areas.

Blending modes
Preset filters that control how colors blend when two objects overlap.

Bridge
See Adobe Bridge.

Brightness
The degree of lightness of a color.

Bristle Brush
Brush style that mimics traditional media like watercolors.

Butt caps
Squared ends of a stroked path.

C

Calligraphic brushes
Brush style that applies strokes that resemble those drawn with a calligraphic pen.

Caps
The ends of stroked paths.

Clipping mask
An object whose area crops objects behind it in the stacking order.

Clipping set
Term used to distinguish clipping paths used in layers from clipping paths used to mask non-layered artwork.

CMYK
Cyan, Magenta, Yellow, and Black; four inks essential to professional printing.

Color gamut
Refers to the range of colors that can be printed or displayed within a given color model.

Color mode
Illustrator setting determining the color model of a document: RGB or CMYK.

Color model
A system used to represent or reproduce color.

Color Picker
A sophisticated dialog box for specifying colors in Illustrator.

Color tools
Circle icons in the Live Color dialog box which represent the colors for the loaded harmony rule.

Combination graph
A graph that uses two graph styles to plot numeric data; useful for emphasizing one set of data in comparison to others.

Compound path
Two or more paths that define a single object. When overlapped, the overlapped area becomes a negative space.

Compound shape
A term used to distinguish a complex compound path from a simple one. Compound shapes generally assume an artistic rather than a practical role.

Corner point
An anchor point joining two straight segments, one straight segment, and one curved segment, or two curved segments.

Crop marks
Short, thin lines that define where artwork is trimmed after it is printed.

Custom graph design
Artwork used to replace traditional columns, bars, or markers in Illustrator graphs.

———————— D ————————

Direction lines
Emanating from an anchor point, they determine the arc of a curved segment.

'Drag & drop' a copy
Pressing [Alt](Win) or [option](Mac) when moving an object; creates a copy of the object.

Drawing mode
Functionality option in which you can draw behind or inside of existing objects.

———————— E ————————

Edge
Similar to a stroke, an edge is a new shape or area created by the overlap of Illustrator objects when the Live Paint Bucket tool is applied. Edges appear as strokes but can be filled with color using the Live Paint Bucket tool.

Effect
A type of appearance attribute which alters an object's appearance without altering the object itself.

Envelopes
Objects that are used to distort other objects into the shape of the envelope object.

Extrude
To add depth to an object by extending it on its Z axis. An object's Z axis is always perpendicular to the object's front surface.

Extrude & Bevel effect
A 3D effect that applies a three-dimensional effect to two-dimensional objects.

———————— F ————————

Flatten Artwork
Consolidating all layers in a document into a single layer.

———————— G ————————

GIF
A standard file format for compressing images by lowering the number of colors available to the file.

Gradient / Gradient Fill
A graduated blend between two or more colors used to fill an object or multiple objects.

Graph
A diagram of data that shows relationships among a set of numbers.

Graph type
A dialog box that provides a variety of ways to change the look of an Illustrator graph.

Graphic Styles
Named sets of appearance attributes.

———————— H ————————

Harmony Rule
Sets of complimentary colors in the Color Guide, which work well together and help you choose colors for your illustration.

Highlight Intensity
Controls how intense a highlight appears.

Highlight Size
Controls how large the highlights appear on an object.

Hue
The name of a color, or its identity on a standard color wheel.

———————— I ————————

Image map
A graphic with areas defined as links for the Internet.

Imageable area
The area inside the dotted line on the artboard which represents the portion of the page that a standard printer can print.

Insertion mode
The drawing mode in Illustrator that allows you to add a new object to a live paint group. A gray rectangle surrounding a live paint group indicates Insertion mode is active.

Isolation mode
A work mode in Illustrator in which a selected group appears in full color, while all the remaining objects on the artboard are dimmed and non-selectable.

─────────── **J** ───────────

Joins
Define the appearance of the corner where two paths meet.

JPEG
A standard file format for compressing continuous tone images, gradients, and blends.

─────────── **K** ───────────

Kerning
Increasing or decreasing the horizontal space between any two text characters.

Keyboard increment
The distance that a single press of an arrow key moves a selected item; editable as a preference.

─────────── **L** ───────────

Layers
A solution for organizing and managing a complex illustration by segregating artwork.

Lighting Intensity
Controls the strength of the light on the object. The range for lighting intensity is 0-100, with 100 being the default.

Linear gradient
A gradient which can fill an object from left to right, top to bottom, or on any angle.

Live paint group
A live paint group is created when the Live Paint Bucket tool is applied to selected objects. All of the resulting regions and edges are part of the live paint group and share a dynamic relationship.

─────────── **M** ───────────

Menu bar
At the top of the Illustrator window; a bar which includes all of the Illustrator menus.

Mesh lines
Paths that crisscross a mesh object, joined at their intersections by mesh points.

Mesh object
A single, multicolored object in which colors can flow in different directions and transition gradually from point to point.

Mesh patch
The area between four mesh points.

Mesh points
Diamond-shaped points that function like anchor points to which you can assign color.

Miter join
Produces stroked lines with pointed corners.

Miter limit
Determines when a Miter join will be squared off to a beveled edge.

Multiply
An essential blending mode in which the colors of overlapping objects create an effect that is similar to overlapping magic markers.

─────────── **N** ───────────

Non-process Inks
Special pre-mixed inks that are printed separately from process inks.

─────────── **O** ───────────

Offset
(noun) The distance that an object is moved from a starting location to a subsequent location.

Offset path
A command that creates a copy of a selected path repositioned at a specified distance.

Opacity
The degree to which an object is transparent.

Opacity Mask
Function that allows selective control of where an object is transparent.

Optimization
A process by which a file's size is reduced through standard color compression algorithms.

Outline stroke
A command that converts a stroked path into a closed path that is the same width as the original stroked path.

Outlined text
A command that changes text in a document to standard vector graphics.

─────────── **P** ───────────

Panels
Windows containing features for modifying and manipulating Illustrator objects.

PANTONE
The standard library of non-process inks.

Pathfinders
Preset operations that combine paths in a variety of ways; useful for creating complex or irregular shapes from basic shapes.

Pattern brushes
A brush style that repeats a pattern along a path.

Pattern fill
Multiple objects used as a fill for an object; the object is filled by repeating the artwork.

Perspective Grid
Grid and functionality that allows you to draw and copy objects in a fixed perspective.

PDF
Acronym for Portable Document Format. As a PDF, an original Illustrator file is complete and self-contained. Useful for emailing Illustrator artwork to others who don't have Illustrator installed.

Pica
12 points, or 1/6 of an inch.

Pixel
Picture element. Small, single-colored squares which compose a bitmap image.

Point
1/72 of an inch.

Point of origin
The point from which an object is transformed; by default, the center point of an object, unless another point is specified.

Point text
Text that you create by clicking the artboard.

Process tints
Colors that can be printed by mixing varying percentages of CMYK inks.

Projecting cap
Produces a squared edge that extends the anchor point of a stroked path by a distance that is 1/2 the weight of the stroke.

—————————— R ——————————

Radial gradient
A gradient which fills an object as a series of concentric circles.

Recolor Artwork
An Illustrator utility that offers you the ability to affect color in an entire illustration dynamically—rather than fill objects with various colors individually.

Reflection
Occurs when light strikes an object and 'bounces' off the object.

Region
Similar to a fill, a region is a new shape or area created by the overlap of Illustrator objects. Regions are created when the Live Paint Bucket tool is applied.

Resolution
The number of pixels in a given inch of a bitmap graphic.

Resolution-independent
Refers to a graphic which can be scaled with no impact on image quality.

Revolve
Another method that Illustrator CS5 provides for applying a 3D effect to a 2D object by "sweeping" a path in a circular direction around the Y axis of the object.

RGB
Red, Green and Blue; the additive primary colors of light.

Rich black
A process tint that is 100% Black plus 50% Cyan; used to print deep, dark black areas of a printed page.

Round cap
Produces a stroked path with rounded ends.

Round join
Produces stroked lines with rounded corners.

—————————— S ——————————

Saturation
The intensity of a hue.

Scatter brush
A brush style which disperses copies of an object along a path.

Scratch area
The area outside the artboard where objects may be stored for future use; objects on the scratch area will not print.

Shape Builder tool
Complex tool that allows you to unite multiple objects as a single object.

Slice
Divided artwork to be output as individual and, therefore, smaller files.

Smart guides
Non-printing words that appear on the artboard and identify visible or invisible objects, page boundaries, intersections, anchor points, etc.

Smooth points
Anchor points created by clicking and dragging the Pen tool; the path continues uninterrupted through the anchor point.

Snap to point
Automatically aligns points when they get close together.

Stacking order
The hierarchy of objects on the artboard, from frontmost to backmost.

Status bar
A utility on the artboard that contains a list arrow menu from which you can choose a status line with information about the current tool, the date and time, the amount of free memory, or the number of undo operations.

Subtractive Primary Colors
Cyan, Magenta and Yellow; the term subtractive refers to the concept that each is produced by removing or subtracting one of the additive primary colors and that overlapping all three pigments would absorb all colors.

SWF
Acronym for Shockwave Flash. File format that supports vector graphics for the web.

Symbol instance
A single usage of a symbol.

Symbol instance set
Symbol instances created with the Symbol Sprayer tool.

─────────── **T** ───────────

Tick marks
Short lines that extend out from the value axis of a graph and aid viewers in interpreting the meaning of column height by indicating incremental values on the value axis.

Tile
Artwork, usually square, used repeatedly in a pattern fill.

Tiling
The process of repeating a tile as a fill for a pattern.

Title bar
At the top of the Illustrator window; contains the name of the document, magnification level, and color mode.

Tools panel
A panel containing Illustrator tools for creating, selecting, and manipulating objects in Illustrator.

Tracking
The process of inserting or removing uniform spaces between text characters to affect the width of selected words or entire blocks of text.

Transmission
Occurs when light strikes an object and passes through the object.

Trim marks
Like crop marks, define where a printed image should be trimmed; used to create multiple marks for multiple objects on a page that are to be trimmed.

Trim size
The size to which artwork or a document is to be cut.

Tweaking
Making small, specific improvements to artwork or typography.

Type area select
An Illustrator preference which allows the user to select text simply by clicking anywhere in the text.

─────────── **V** ───────────

Variation
A group of swatches loaded by the Color Guide panel when you select an object on the artboard and then choose a harmony rule.

Vector graphics
Resolution-independent graphics created with lines, curves, and fills.

Visible light
Light waves that are visible to the human eye.

─────────── **W** ───────────

White light
Refers to the concept that natural light on Earth appears to people as not having any dominant hue.

Workspace
The positioning of panels on the artboard/computer monitor; Illustrator CS5 includes preset workspaces targeted for specific types of work, such as typography and painting.

─────────── **Z** ───────────

Zoom text box
A utility in the lower-left corner of the Illustrator window that displays the current magnification level.

ART CREDITS

ILLUSTRATOR ART CREDITS	
Chapter	**Art credit for opening pages**
Chapter 1	© Ronald Van Der Beed | Dreamstime.com ©Smellme | Dreamstime.com
Chapter 2	©iStockphoto.com/Malsbury Enterprises Ltd ©Anke Van Wyk | Dreamstime.com
Chapter 3	©Naluphoto | Dreamstime.com ©Aaron Bunker | Shutterstock Images
Chapter 4	©Nilanjan Bhattacharya | Dreamstime.com ©Clearviewstock | Dreamstime.com
Chapter 5	©Bruce Turner | Dreamstime.com ©123RF LIMITED \cbpix
Chapter 6	©Neal Cooper | Dreamstime.com ©iStockphoto.com/ETIEN
Chapter 7	©Richard Carey | Dreamstime.com ©iStockphoto.com/Alex Bramwell
Chapter 8	©Chris Lorenz | Dreamstime.com ©Vladimir Sazonov | Shutterstock Images
Chapter 9	©Gkuna | Dreamstime.com © Tony Emmett | Shutterstock Images
Chapter 10	©Morten Elm | Dreamstime.com ©Michael Zysman | Dreamstime.com
Chapter 11	©iStockphoto.com/Nico Smit Photography ©iStockphoto.com/Freder
Chapter 12	©iStockphoto.com/Malsbury Enterprises Ltd ©iStockphoto.com/charcoal design
Chapter 13	©Jemini Joseph | Dreamstime.com © Janice Mccafferty | Dreamstime.com
Data Files/Glossary/Index	©Christian Bech | Dreamstime.com ©iStockphoto.com/ThaiEagle